Classics

From the Renaissance to the nineteenth century, Latin and Greek were compulsory subjects in almost all European universities, and most early modern scholars published their research and conducted international correspondence in Latin. Latin had continued in use in Western Europe long after the fall of the Roman empire as the lingua franca of the educated classes and of law, diplomacy, religion and university teaching. The flight of Greek scholars to the West after the fall of Constantinople in 1453 gave impetus to the study of ancient Greek literature and the Greek New Testament. Eventually, just as nineteenth-century reforms of university curricula were beginning to erode this ascendancy, developments in textual criticism and linguistic analysis, and new ways of studying ancient societies, especially archaeology, led to renewed enthusiasm for the Classics. This collection offers works of criticism, interpretation and synthesis by the outstanding scholars of the nineteenth century.

The Golden Bough: The Third Edition

This work by Sir James Frazer (1854–1941) is widely considered to be one of the most important early texts in the fields of psychology and anthropology. At the same time, by applying modern methods of comparative ethnography to the classical world, and revealing the superstition and irrationality beneath the surface of the classical culture which had for so long been a model for Western civilisation, it was extremely controversial. Frazer was greatly influenced by E.B. Tylor's *Primitive Culture* (also reissued in this series), and by the work of the biblical scholar William Robertson Smith, to whom the first edition is dedicated. The twelve-volume third edition, reissued here, was greatly revised and enlarged, and published between 1911 and 1915; the two-volume first edition (1890) is also available in this series. Volume 9 (1913) considers the role of the scapegoat in maintaining the stability of the community.

Cambridge University Press has long been a pioneer in the reissuing of out-of-print titles from its own backlist, producing digital reprints of books that are still sought after by scholars and students but could not be reprinted economically using traditional technology. The Cambridge Library Collection extends this activity to a wider range of books which are still of importance to researchers and professionals, either for the source material they contain, or as landmarks in the history of their academic discipline.

Drawing from the world-renowned collections in the Cambridge University Library and other partner libraries, and guided by the advice of experts in each subject area, Cambridge University Press is using state-of-the-art scanning machines in its own Printing House to capture the content of each book selected for inclusion. The files are processed to give a consistently clear, crisp image, and the books finished to the high quality standard for which the Press is recognised around the world. The latest print-on-demand technology ensures that the books will remain available indefinitely, and that orders for single or multiple copies can quickly be supplied.

The Cambridge Library Collection brings back to life books of enduring scholarly value (including out-of-copyright works originally issued by other publishers) across a wide range of disciplines in the humanities and social sciences and in science and technology.

The Golden Bough
The Third Edition

VOLUME 9:
THE SCAPEGOAT

J.G. FRAZER

CAMBRIDGE
UNIVERSITY PRESS

CAMBRIDGE UNIVERSITY PRESS

Cambridge, New York, Melbourne, Madrid, Cape Town,
Singapore, São Paolo, Delhi, Mexico City

Published in the United States of America by Cambridge University Press, New York

www.cambridge.org
Information on this title: www.cambridge.org/9781108047388

© in this compilation Cambridge University Press 2012

This edition first published 1913
This digitally printed version 2012

ISBN 978-1-108-04738-8 Paperback

THE GOLDEN BOUGH

A STUDY IN MAGIC AND RELIGION

THIRD EDITION

PART VI

THE SCAPEGOAT

MACMILLAN AND CO., Limited
LONDON · BOMBAY · CALCUTTA
MELBOURNE

THE MACMILLAN COMPANY
NEW YORK · BOSTON · CHICAGO
DALLAS · SAN FRANCISCO

THE MACMILLAN CO. OF CANADA, Ltd.
TORONTO

THE SCAPEGOAT

BY

J. G. FRAZER, D.C.L., LL.D., Litt.D.

FELLOW OF TRINITY COLLEGE, CAMBRIDGE
PROFESSOR OF SOCIAL ANTHROPOLOGY IN THE UNIVERSITY OF LIVERPOOL

MACMILLAN AND CO., LIMITED
ST. MARTIN'S STREET, LONDON

1913

COPYRIGHT

PREFACE

WITH *The Scapegoat* our general discussion of the theory and practice of the Dying God is brought to a conclusion. The aspect of the subject with which we are here chiefly concerned is the use of the Dying God as a scapegoat to free his worshippers from the troubles of all sorts with which life on earth is beset. I have sought to trace this curious usage to its origin, to decompose the idea of the Divine Scapegoat into the elements out of which it appears to be compounded. If I am right, the idea resolves itself into a simple confusion between the material and the immaterial, between the real possibility of transferring a physical load to other shoulders and the supposed possibility of transferring our bodily and mental ailments to another who will bear them for us. When we survey the history of this pathetic fallacy from its crude inception in savagery to its full development in the speculative theology of civilized nations, we cannot but wonder at the singular power which the human mind possesses of transmuting the leaden dross of superstition into a glittering semblance of gold. Certainly in nothing is this alchemy of thought more conspicuous than in the process which has refined the base and foolish custom of the scapegoat into the sublime conception of a God who dies to take away the sins of the world.

Along with the discussion of the Scapegoat I have included in this volume an account of the remarkable religious ritual of the Aztecs, in which the theory of the

Dying God found its most systematic and most tragic expression. There is nothing, so far as I am aware, to shew that the men and women, who in Mexico died cruel deaths in the character of gods and goddesses, were regarded as scapegoats by their worshippers and executioners ; the intention of slaying them seems rather to have been to reinforce by a river of human blood the tide of life which might else grow stagnant and stale in the veins of the deities. Hence the Aztec ritual, which prescribed the slaughter, the roasting alive, and the flaying of men and women in order that the gods might remain for ever young and strong, conforms to the general theory of deicide which I have offered in this work. On that theory death is a portal through which gods and men alike must pass to escape the decrepitude of age and to attain the vigour of eternal youth. The conception may be said to culminate in the Brahmanical doctrine that in the daily sacrifice the body of the Creator is broken anew for the salvation of the world.

J. G. FRAZER.

CAMBRIDGE,
21st June, 1913.

CONTENTS

vii

CHAPTER IV.—PUBLIC SCAPEGOATS   Pp. 170-223

Chapter V.—On Scapegoats in General

Pp. 224-228

The immediate and the mediate expulsions of evil identical in intention, 224; annual expulsion of evil generally coincides with a change of season, 224 *sq.*; annual expulsion of evil preceded or followed by a period of general license, 225 *sq.*; remarkable use of a divine animal or man as a scapegoat, 226 *sq.*; why a dying god should serve as a scapegoat, 227; the use of a divinity as a scapegoat explains an ambiguity in the "Carrying out of Death," 227 *sq.*

Chapter VI.—Human Scapegoats in Classical Antiquity . . . Pp. 229-274

Chapter VIII.—The Saturnalia and Kindred Festivals . . . Pp. 306-411

CHAPTER I

THE TRANSFERENCE OF EVIL

§ 1. *The Transference to Inanimate Objects*

IN the preceding parts of this work we have traced the practice of killing a god among peoples in the hunting, pastoral, and agricultural stages of society; and I have attempted to explain the motives which led men to adopt so curious a custom. One aspect of the custom still remains to be noticed. The accumulated misfortunes and sins of the whole people are sometimes laid upon the dying god, who is supposed to bear them away for ever, leaving the people innocent and happy. The notion that we can transfer our guilt and sufferings to some other being who will bear them for us is familiar to the savage mind. It arises from a very obvious confusion between the physical and the mental, between the material and the immaterial. Because it is possible to shift a load of wood, stones, or what not, from our own back to the back of another, the savage fancies that it is equally possible to shift the burden of his pains and sorrows to another, who will suffer them in his stead. Upon this idea he acts, and the result is an endless number of very unamiable devices for palming off upon some one else the trouble which a man shrinks from bearing himself. In short, the principle of vicarious suffering is commonly understood and practised by races who stand on a low level of social and intellectual culture. In the following pages I shall illustrate the theory and the practice as they are found among savages in all their naked simplicity, undisguised by the refinements of metaphysics and the subtleties of theology.

The devices to which the cunning and selfish savage resorts for the sake of easing himself at the expense of his neighbour are manifold ; only a few typical examples out of a multitude can be cited. At the outset it is to be observed that the evil of which a man seeks to rid himself need not be transferred to a person ; it may equally well be transferred to an animal or a thing, though in the last case the thing is often only a vehicle to convey the trouble to the first person who touches it. In some of the East Indian islands they think that epilepsy can be cured by striking the patient on the face with the leaves of certain trees and then throwing them away. The disease is believed to have passed into the leaves, and to have been thrown away with them.[1] In the Warramunga and Tjingilli tribes of Central Australia men who suffered from headache have often been seen wearing women's head-rings. " This was connected with the belief that the pain in the head would pass into the rings, and that then it could be thrown away with them into the bush, and so got rid of effectually. The natives have a very firm belief in the efficacy of this treatment. In the same way when a man suffers from internal pain, usually brought on by overeating, his wife's head-rings are placed on his stomach ; the evil magic which is causing all the trouble passes into them, and they are then thrown away into the bushes, where the magic is supposed to leave them. After a time they are searched for by the woman, who brings them back, and again wears them in the ordinary way." [2] Among the Sihanaka of Madagascar, when a man is very sick, his relatives are sometimes bidden by the diviner to cast out the evil by means of a variety of things, such as a stick of a particular sort of tree, a rag, a pinch of earth from an ant's nest, a little money, or what not. Whatever they may be, they are brought to the patient's house and held by a man near the door, while an exorcist stands

[1] J. G. F. Riedel, *De sluik- en kroesharige rassen tusschen Selebes en Papua* (The Hague, 1886), pp. 266 *sq.*, 305, 357 *sq.* ; compare *id.*, pp. 141, 340.

[2] Baldwin Spencer and F. J. Gillen, *The Northern Tribes of Central Australia* (London, 1904), p. 474.

in the house and pronounces the formula necessary for casting out the disease. When he has done, the things are thrown away in a southward direction, and all the people in the house, including the sick man, if he has strength enough, shake their loose robes and spit towards the door in order to expedite the departure of the malady.[1] When an Atkhan of the Aleutian Islands had committed a grave sin and desired to unburden himself of his guilt, he proceeded as follows. Having chosen a time when the sun was clear and unclouded, he picked up certain weeds and carried them about his person. Then he laid them down, and calling the sun to witness, cast his sins upon them, after which, having eased his heart of all that weighed upon it, he threw the weeds into the fire, and fancied that thus he cleansed himself of his guilt.[2] In Vedic times a younger brother who married before his elder brother was thought to have sinned in so doing, but there was a ceremony by which he could purge himself of his sin. Fetters of reed-grass were laid on him in token of his guilt, and when they had been washed and sprinkled they were flung into a foaming torrent, which swept them away, while the evil was bidden to vanish with the foam of the stream.[3] The Matse negroes of Togoland think that the river Awo has power to carry away the sorrows of mankind. So when one of their friends has died, and their hearts are heavy, they go to the river with leaves of the raphia palm tied round their necks and drums in their hands. Standing on the bank they beat the drums and cast the leaves into the stream. As the leaves float away out of sight to the sound of the rippling water and the roll of the drums, they fancy that their sorrow too is lifted from them.[4] Similarly, the ancient Greeks imagined that the pangs of love might be healed by bathing in the river Selemnus.[5] The Indians of Peru sought to purify themselves from their sins by plunging their heads

Evils swept away by rivers.

[1] J. Pearse, " Customs connected with Death and Burial among the Sihanaka," *The Antananarivo Annual and Madagascar Magazine*, vol. ii., *Reprint of the Second four Numbers* (Antananarivo, 1896), pp. 146 *sq.*

[2] Ivan Petroff, *Report on the Population, Industries, and Resources of Alaska*, p. 158.

[3] H. Oldenberg, *Die Religion des Veda* (Berlin, 1894), p. 322.

[4] J. Spieth, *Die Ewe-Stämme* (Berlin, 1906), p. 800.

[5] Pausanias, vii. 23. 3.

in a river; they said that the river washed their sins away.[1]

An Arab cure for melancholy or madness caused by love is to put a dish of water on the sufferer's head, drop melted lead into it, and then bury the lead in an open field; thus the mischief that was in the man goes away.[2] Amongst the Miotse of China, when the eldest son of the house attains the age of seven years, a ceremony called "driving away the devil" takes place. The father makes a kite of straw and lets it fly away in the desert, bearing away all evil with it.[3] When an Indian of Santiago Tepehuacan is ill, he will sometimes attempt to rid himself of the malady by baking thrice seven cakes; of these he places seven in the top of the highest pine-tree of the forest, seven he lays at the foot of the tree, and seven he casts into a well, with the water of which he then washes himself. By this means he transfers the sickness to the water of the well and so is made whole.[4] The Baganda believed that plague was caused by the god Kaumpuli, who resided in a deep hole in his temple. To prevent him from escaping and devastating the country, they battened him down in the hole by covering the top with plantain-stems and piling wild-cat-skins over them; there was nothing like wild-cat-skins to keep him down, so hundreds of wild cats were hunted and killed every year to supply the necessary skins. However, sometimes in spite of these precautions the god contrived to escape, and then the people died. When a garden or house was plague-stricken, the priests purified it by transferring the disease to a plantain-tree and then carrying away the tree to a piece of waste land. The way in which they effected the transference of the disease was this. They first made a number of little shields and spears out of plantain fibre and reeds and placed them at intervals along the path leading from the garden to the main road. A young plantain-tree, about

[1] P. J. de Arriaga, *Extirpacion de la Idolatria del Piru* (Lima, 1621), p. 29.

[2] This I learned from my friend W. Robertson Smith, who mentioned as his authority David of Antioch, *Tazyin*, in the story "Orwa."

[3] R. Andree, *Ethnographische Paral-* *lele und Vergleiche* (Stuttgart, 1878), pp. 29 *sq.*

[4] "Lettre du curé de Santiago Tepehuacan à son évêque sur les mœurs et coutumes des Indiens soumis à ses soins," *Bulletin de la Société de Géographie* (Paris), Deuxième Série, ii. (1834) p. 182.

to bear fruit, was then cut down, the stem was laid in the path leading to one of the plague-stricken huts, and it was speared with not less than twenty reed spears, which were left sticking in it, while some of the plantain-fibre shields were also fastened to it. This tree was then carried down the path to the waste land and left there. It went by the name of the Scapegoat (*kyonzire*). To make quite sure that the plague, after being thus deposited in the wilderness, should not return by the way it went, the priests raised an arch, covered with barkcloth, over the path at the point where it diverged from the main road. This arch was thought to interpose an insurmountable barrier to the return of the plague.[1]

Dyak priestesses expel ill-luck from a house by hewing and slashing the air in every corner of it with wooden swords, which they afterwards wash in the river, to let the ill-luck float away down stream. Sometimes they sweep misfortune out of the house with brooms made of the leaves of certain plants and sprinkled with rice-water and blood. Having swept it clean out of every room and into a toy-house made of bamboo, they set the little house with its load of bad luck adrift on the river. The current carries it away out to sea, where it shifts its baleful cargo to a certain kettle-shaped ship, which floats in mid-ocean and receives in its capacious hold all the ills that flesh is heir to. Well would it be with mankind if the evils remained for ever tossing far away on the billows ; but, alas, they are dispersed from the ship to the four winds, and settle again, and yet again, on the weary Dyak world. On Dyak rivers you may see many of the miniature houses, laden with manifold misfortunes, bobbing up and down on the current, or sticking fast in the thickets that line the banks.[2]

These examples illustrate the purely beneficent side of the transference of evil ; they shew how men seek to alleviate human sufferings by diverting them to material objects, which are then thrown away or otherwise disposed of so as to render them innocuous. Often, however, the

Marginal notes: Dyak transference of evil to things.

Marginal note: Evils transferred to other persons through the medium of things.

[1] Rev. J. Roscoe, *The Baganda* (London, 1911), pp. 309 *sq.*

[2] C. Hupe, "Korte Verhandeling over de Godsdienst, Zeden enz. der Dajakkers," *Tijdschrift voor Neêrlands Indië*, 1846, dl. iii. pp. 149 *sq.* ; F. Grabowsky, "Die Theogonie der Dajaken auf Borneo," *Internationales Archiv für Ethnographie*, v. (1892) p. 131.

transference of evil to a material object is only a step towards foisting it upon a living person. This is the maleficent side of such transferences. It is exemplified in the following cases. To cure toothache some of the Australian blacks apply a heated spear-thrower to the cheek. The spear-thrower is then cast away, and the toothache goes with it in the shape of a black stone called *karriitch.* Stones of this kind are found in old mounds and sandhills. They are carefully collected and thrown in the direction of enemies in order to give them toothache.[1] In Mirzapur a mode of transferring disease is to fill a pot with flowers and rice and bury it in a pathway covered up with a flat stone. Whoever touches this is supposed to contract the disease. The practice is called *chalauwa,* or "passing on" the malady. This sort of thing goes on daily in Upper India. Often while walking of a morning in the bazaar you will see a little pile of earth adorned with flowers in the middle of the road. Such a pile usually contains some scabs or scales from the body of a smallpox patient, which are placed there in the hope that some one may touch them, and by catching the disease may relieve the sufferer.[2] The Bahima, a pastoral people of the Uganda Protectorate, often suffer from deepseated abscesses : "their cure for this is to transfer the disease to some other person by obtaining herbs from the medicine-man, rubbing them over the place where the swelling is, and burying them in the road where people continually pass ; the first person who steps over these buried herbs contracts the disease, and the original patient recovers."[3] The practice of the Wagogo of German East Africa is similar. When a man is ill, the native doctor will take him to a cross-road, where he prepares his medicines, uttering at the same time the incantations which are necessary to give the drugs their medical virtue. Part of the dose is then administered to the patient, and part is buried under a pot turned upside down at the cross-road. It is hoped that somebody will step over the pot, and catching

[1] J. Dawson, *Australian Aborigines* (Melbourne, Sydney, and Adelaide, 1881), p. 59.

[2] W. Crooke, *Popular Religion and Folk-lore of Northern India* (West-minster, 1896), i. 164 *sq.*

[3] Rev. J. Roscoe, "The Bahima, a Cow Tribe of Enkole," *Journal of the Royal Anthropological Institute,* xxxvii. (1907) p. 103.

the disease, which lurks in the pot, will thereby relieve the original sufferer.   A variation of this cure is to plaster some of the medicine, or a little of the patient's blood, on a wooden peg and to drive the peg into a tree ; any one who passes the tree and is so imprudent as to draw out the peg, will carry away with it the disease.[1]

Sometimes in case of sickness the malady is transferred to an effigy as a preliminary to passing it on to a human being.   Thus among the Baganda the medicine-man would sometimes make a model of his patient in clay ; then a relative of the sick man would rub the image over the sufferer's body and either bury it in the road or hide it in the grass by the wayside.   The first person who stepped over the image or passed by it would catch the disease. Sometimes the effigy was made out of a plantain-flower tied up so as to look like a person ; it was used in the same way as the clay figure.   But the use of images for this maleficent purpose was a capital crime ; any person caught in the act of burying one of them in the public road would surely have been put to death.[2]   Among the Sena-speaking people to the north of the Zambesi, when any one is ill, the doctor makes a little pig of straw to which he transfers the sickness. The little pig is then set on the ground where two paths meet, and any passer-by who chances to kick it over is sure to absorb the illness and to draw it away from the patient.[3] Among the Korkus, a forest tribe of the Central Provinces in India, when a person wishes to transfer his sickness to another, he contrives to obtain the loin-cloth of his intended victim and paints two figures on it in lamp black, one upright and the other upside down.   As soon as the owner of the loin-cloth puts it on, he falls a victim to the ailment which afflicted the artist who drew the figures.[4]   Every nine years a Mongol celebrates a memorial festival of his birth for the purpose of ensuring the continuance of his life and welfare.   At this solemn ceremony two lambskins, one

Evils transferred to images.

Mongol transference of evil to things.

[1] Rev. J. Cole, "Notes on the Wagogo of German East Africa," *Journal of the Anthropological Institute*, xxxiii. (1902) p. 313.

[2] Rev. J. Roscoe, *The Baganda* (London, 1911), pp. 343 *sq.*

[3] Dudley Kidd, *The Essential Kafir* (London, 1904), p. 146.

[4] *Central Provinces, Ethnographic Survey*, iii., *Draft Articles on Forest Tribes* (Allahabad, 1907), p. 63.

black and the other white, are spread on the floor of the hut, which is further covered with a felt carpet, and on the carpet are made nine little ridges of earth brought from nine mountains, the bottom of a river, and a sepulchral mound. The owner of the hut, for whose benefit the rite is performed, next seats himself on the black lambskin, and opposite him is set an effigy of himself made of dough by a lama. The priest then throws a black stone at the effigy, praying that the black arrow of death may pierce it, after which he throws a white stone at the master of the hut, praying that the bright beam of life may endow him with wondrous strength. After that the Mongol gets up, steps over one of the ridges of earth and says, " I have overcome a mishap, I have escaped a death." This ceremony he performs nine times, stepping over all the ridges, one after the other. Then he sits down on the white lambskin, and the lama takes the dough effigy, swings it thrice round the man whom it represents, spits on it thrice, and hands it to attendants who carry it away into the steppe. A little holy water sprinkled over the Mongol now completes his protection against perils and dangers.[1] This last is a case of the beneficent transference of evil ; for in it no attempt seems to be made to shift the burden of misfortune to anybody else.

§ 2. *The Transference to Stones and Sticks*

Fatigue transferred to stones, sticks, or leaves.

In the western district of the island of Timor, when men or women are making long and tiring journeys, they fan themselves with leafy branches, which they afterwards throw away on particular spots where their forefathers did the same before them. The fatigue which they felt is thus supposed to have passed into the leaves and to be left behind. Others use stones instead of leaves.[2] Similarly in the Babar Archipelago tired people will strike themselves with stones, believing that they thus transfer to the stones the weariness which they felt in their own bodies. They then throw away the stones in places which are

---

[1] M. v. Beguelin, " Religiöse Volksbräuche der Mongolen," *Globus*, lvii. (1890) pp. 209 *sq.*

[2] J. G. F. Riedel, " Die Landschaft Dawan oder West-Timor," *Deutsche geographische Blätter*, x. 231.

specially set apart for the purpose.[1] A like belief and practice in many distant parts of the world have given rise to those cairns or heaps of sticks and leaves which travellers often observe beside the path, and to which every passing native adds his contribution in the shape of a stone, or stick, or leaf. Thus in the Solomon and Banks' Islands the natives are wont to throw sticks, stones, or leaves upon a heap at a place of steep descent, or where a difficult path begins, saying, " There goes my fatigue." The act is not a religious rite, for the thing thrown on the heap is not an offering to spiritual powers, and the words which accompany the act are not a prayer. It is nothing but a magical ceremony for getting rid of fatigue, which the simple savage fancies he can embody in a stick, leaf, or stone, and so cast it from him.[2]

An early Spanish missionary to Nicaragua, observing that along the paths there were heaps of stones on which the Indians as they passed threw grass, asked them why they did so. " Because we think," was the answer, " that thereby we are kept from weariness and hunger, or at least that we suffer less from them." [3]   When the Peruvian Indians were climbing steep mountains and felt weary, they used to halt by the way at certain points where there were heaps of stones, which they called *apachitas*.   On these heaps the weary men would place other stones, and they said that when they did so, their weariness left them.[4]   In the passes of the eastern Andes, on the borders of Argentina and Bolivia, " large cairns are constantly found, and every Puna Indian, on passing, adds a stone and a coca leaf, so that neither he nor his beast of burden may tire on the way." [5]

Heaps of stones or sticks among the American Indians.

---

[1] J. G. F. Riedel, *De sluik- en kroesharige rassen tusschen Selebes en Papua* (The Hague, 1886), p. 340.

[2] R. H. Codrington, D.D., *The Melanesians* (Oxford, 1891), p. 186.

[3] G. F. de Oviedo, *Histoire du Nicaragua* (Paris, 1840), pp. 42 *sq.* (Ternaux-Compans, *Voyages, Relations et Mémoires originaux, pour servir à l'Histoire de la Découverte de l'Amérique*).

[4] P. J. de Arriaga, *Extirpacion de*

la Idolatria del Piru (Lima, 1621), pp. 37, 130. As to the custom compare J. J. von Tschudi, *Peru* (St. Gallen, 1846), ii. 77 *sq.* ; H. A. Weddell, *Voyage dans le Nord de la Bolivia et dans les parties voisines du Pérou* (Paris and London, 1853), pp. 74 *sq.* These latter writers interpret the stones as offerings.

[5] Baron E. Nordenskiöld, "Travels on the Boundaries of Bolivia and Argentina," *The Geographical Journal,* xxi. (1903) p. 518.

In the country of the Tarahumares and Tepehuanes in Mexico heaps of stones and sticks may be observed on high points, where the track leads over a ridge between two or more valleys. "Every Indian who passes such a pile adds a stone or a stick to it in order to gain strength for his journey. Among the Tarahumares only the old men observe this custom. Whenever the Tepehuanes carry a corpse, they rest it for some fifteen minutes on such a heap by the wayside that the deceased may not be fatigued but strong enough to finish his long journey to the land of the dead. One of my Huichol companions stopped on reaching this pile, pulled up some grass from the ground and picked up a stone as big as his fist. Holding both together he spat on the grass and on the stone and then rubbed them quickly over his knees. He also made a couple of passes with them over his chest and shoulders, exclaiming '*Kenestíquai*!' (May I not get tired!) and then put the grass on the heap and the stone on top of the grass."[1] In Guatemala also piles of stones may be seen at the partings of ways and on the tops of cliffs and mountains. Every passing Indian used to gather a handful of grass, rub his legs with it, spit on it, and deposit it with a small stone on the pile, firmly persuaded that by so doing he would restore their flagging vigour to his weary limbs.[2] Here the rubbing of the limbs with the grass, like the Babar custom of striking the body with a stone, was doubtless a mode of extracting the fatigue from them as a preliminary to throwing it away.

Heaps of stones or sticks among the natives of Africa.

Similarly on the plateau between Lakes Tanganyika and Nyassa the native carriers, before they ascend a steep hill with their loads, will pick up a stone, spit on it, rub the calves of their legs with it, and then deposit it on one of those small piles of stones which are commonly to be found at such spots in this part of Africa. A recent English traveller, who noticed the custom, was informed that the carriers practise it " to

[1] C. Lumholtz, *Unknown Mexico* (London, 1903), ii. 282.

[2] Brasseur de Bourbourg, *Histoire des Nations civilisées du Mexique et de l'Amérique - Centrale* (Paris, 1857–1859), ii. 564 ; compare iii. 486. Indians of Guatemala, when they cross a pass for the first time, still commonly add a stone to the cairn which marks the spot. See C. Sapper, "Die Gebräuche und religiösen Anschauungen der Kekchi - Indianer," *Internationales Archiv für Ethnographie*, viii. (1895) p. 197.

make their legs light," [1] in other words, to extract the fatigue from them. On the banks of the Kei river in Southern Africa another English traveller noticed some heaps of stones. On enquiring what they meant, he was told by his guides that when a Caffre felt weary he had but to add a stone to the heap to regain fresh vigour.[2] In some parts of South Africa, particularly on the Zambesi, piles of sticks take the place of cairns. "Sometimes the natives will rub their leg with a stick, and throw the stick on the heap, 'to get rid of fatigue,' they avow. Others say that throwing a stone on the heap gives one fresh vigour for the journey." [3]

From other accounts of the Caffre custom we learn that these cairns are generally on the sides or tops of mountains, and that before a native deposits his stone on the pile he spits on it.[4] The practice of spitting on the stone which the weary wayfarer lays on the pile is probably a mode of transferring his fatigue the more effectually to the material vehicle which is to rid him of it. We have seen that the practice prevails among the Indians of Guatemala and the natives of the Tanganyika plateau, and it appears to be observed also under similar circumstances in Corea, where the cairns are to be found especially on the tops of passes.[5] From the primitive point of view nothing can be more

The heaps of stones or sticks generally on the tops of mountains or passes.

---

[1] F. F. R. Boileau, "The Nyasa-Tanganyika Plateau," *The Geographical Journal*, xiii. (1899) p. 589. In the same region Mr. L. Decle observed many trees or rocks on which were placed little heaps of stones or bits of wood, to which in passing each of his men added a fresh stone or bit of wood or a tuft of grass. "This," says Mr. L. Decle, "is a tribute to the spirits, the general precaution to ensure a safe return" (*Three Years in Savage Africa*, London, 1898, p. 289). A similar practice prevails among the Wanyamwezi (*ibid.* p. 345). Compare J. A. Grant, *A Walk across Africa* (Edinburgh and London, 1864), pp. 133 *sq.*
[2] Cowper Rose, *Four Years in Southern Africa* (London, 1829), p. 147.
[3] Dudley Kidd, *The Essential Kafir* (London, 1904), p. 264.

[4] S. Kay, *Travels and Researches in Caffraria* (London, 1833), pp. 211 *sq.*; Rev. H. Callaway, *Religious System of the Amazulu*, i. 66 ; D. Leslie, *Among the Zulus and Amatongas* (Edinburgh, 1875), pp. 146 *sq.* Compare H. Lichtenstein, *Reisen im südlichen Africa* (Berlin, 1811–1812), i. 411.
[5] W. Gowland, "Dolmens and other Antiquities of Corea," *Journal of the Anthropological Institute*, xxiv. (1895) pp. 328 *sq.* ; Mrs. Bishop, *Korea and her Neighbours* (London, 1898), i. 147, ii. 223. Both writers speak as if the practice were to spit on the cairn rather than on the particular stone which the traveller adds to it ; indeed, Mrs. Bishop omits to notice the custom of adding to the cairns. Mr. Gowland says that almost every traveller carries up at least one stone from the valley and lays it on the pile.

natural than that the cairns or the heaps of sticks and leaves to which the tired traveller adds his contribution should stand at the top of passes and, in general, on the highest points of the road. The wayfarer who has toiled, with aching limbs and throbbing temples, up a long and steep ascent, is aware of a sudden alleviation as soon as he has reached the summit ; he feels as if a weight had been lifted from him, and to the savage, with his concrete mode of thought, it seems natural and easy to cast the weight from him in the shape of a stone or stick, or a bunch of leaves or of grass. Hence it is that the piles which represent the accumulated weariness of many foot-sore and heavy-laden travellers are to be seen wherever the road runs highest in the lofty regions of Bolivia, Tibet, Bhootan, and Burma,[1] in the passes of the Andes and the Himalayas, as well as in Corea, Caffraria, Guatemala, and Melanesia.

Fatigue let out with the blood. While the mountaineer Indians of South America imagine that they can rid themselves of their fatigue in the shape of a stick or a stone, other or the same aborigines of that continent believe that they can let it out with their blood. A French explorer, who had seen much of the South American Indians, tells us that " they explain everything that they experience by attributing it to sorcery, to the influence of maleficent beings. Thus an Indian on the march, when he feels weary, never fails to ascribe his weariness to the evil spirit ; and if he has no diviner at hand, he wounds himself in the knees, the shoulders, and on the arms in order to let out the evil with the blood. That is why many Indians, especially the Aucas [Araucanians], have always their arms covered with scars. This custom, differently applied, is almost general in America ; for I

---

[1] D. Forbes, "On the Aymara Indians of Peru and Bolivia," *Journal of the Ethnological Society of London*, ii. (1870) pp. 237 *sq.*; G. C. Musters, "Notes on Bolivia," *Journal of the Royal Geographical Society*, xlvii. (1877) p. 211 ; T. T. Cooper, *Travels of a Pioneer of Commerce* (London, 1871), p. 275 ; J. A. H. Louis, *The Gates of Thibet, a Bird's Eye View of Independent Sikkhim, British Bhootan,* and the Dooars (Calcutta, 1894), pp. 111 *sq.* ; A. Bastian, *Die Völker des östlichen Asien*, ii. (Leipsic, 1866) p. 483. So among the Mrus of Aracan, every man who crosses a hill, on reaching the crest, plucks a fresh young shoot of grass and lays it on a pile of withered deposits of former travellers (T. H. Lewin, *Wild Races of South-Eastern India*, London, 1870, pp. 232 *sq.*).

found it up to the foot of the Andes, in Bolivia, among the Chiriguana and Yuracares nations." [1]

But it is not mere bodily fatigue which the savage fancies he can rid himself of by the simple expedient of throwing a stick or a stone. Unable clearly to distinguish the immaterial from the material, the abstract from the concrete, he is assailed by vague terrors, he feels himself exposed to some ill-defined danger on the scene of any great crime or great misfortune. The place to him seems haunted ground. The thronging memories that crowd upon his mind, if they are not mistaken by him for goblins and phantoms, oppress his fancy with a leaden weight. His impulse is to flee from the dreadful spot, to shake off the burden that seems to cling to him like a nightmare. This, in his simple sensuous way, he thinks he can do by casting something at the horrid place and hurrying by. For will not the contagion of misfortune, the horror that clutched at his heart-strings, be diverted from himself into the thing? will it not gather up in itself all the evil influences that threatened him, and so leave him to pursue his journey in safety and peace? Some such train of thought, if these gropings and fumblings of a mind in darkness deserve the name of thought, seems to explain the custom, observed by wayfarers in many lands, of throwing sticks or stones on places where something horrible has happened or evil deeds have been done. When Sir Francis Younghusband was travelling across the great desert of Gobi his caravan descended, towards dusk on a June evening, into a long depression between the hills, which was notorious as a haunt of robbers. His guide, with a terror-stricken face, told how not long before nine men out of a single caravan had been murdered, and the rest left in a pitiable state to continue their journey on foot across the awful desert. A horseman, too, had just been seen riding towards the hills. "We had accordingly to keep a sharp look-out, and when we reached the foot of the hills, halted, and, taking the loads off the camels, wrapped ourselves up in our sheepskins and watched through the long hours of the night. Day broke at last, and then we silently advanced and entered the hills.

Piles of stones or sticks on the scene of crimes.

---

[1] A. d'Orbigny, *Voyage dans l'Amérique Méridionale*, ii. (Paris and Strasburg, 1839–1843) pp. 92 *sq.*

Very weird and fantastic in their rugged outline were they, and here and there a cairn of stones marked where some caravan had been attacked, and as we passed these each man threw one more stone on the heap."[1] In the Norwegian district of Tellemarken a cairn is piled up wherever anything fearful has happened, and every passer-by must throw another stone on it, or some evil will befall him.[2] In Sweden and the Esthonian island of Oesel the same custom is practised on scenes of clandestine or illicit love, with the strange addition in Oesel that when a man has lost his cattle he will go to such a spot, and, while he flings a stick or stone on it, will say, " I bring thee wood. Let me soon find my lost cattle."[3] Far from these northern lands, the Dyaks of Batang Lupar keep up an observance of the same sort in the forests of Borneo. Beside their paths may be seen heaps of sticks or stones which are called "lying heaps." Each heap is in memory of some man who told a stupendous lie or disgracefully failed in carrying out an engagement, and everybody who passes adds a stick or stone to the pile, saying as he does so, "For So-and-so's lying heap."[4] The Dyaks think it a sacred duty to add to every such "liar's mound " (*tugong bula*) which they pass ; they imagine that the omission of the duty would draw down on them a supernatural punishment. Hence, however pressed a Dyak may be for time, he will always stop to throw on the pile some branches or twigs.[5] The person to start such a heap is one of the men who has suffered by a malicious lie. He takes a stick, throws it down on some spot where people are constantly passing, and says, "Let any one who does not add to this liar's heap suffer from pains in the head." Others then do likewise, and every passer-by throws a stick on the spot lest he should suffer pains. In this way the heap often grows to a large size, and the liar by whose name it is known is greatly ashamed.[6]

The Liar's Heap.

---

[1] (Sir) F. E. Younghusband, " A Journey across Central Asia," *Proceedings of the Royal Geographical Society*, x. (1888) p. 494.

[2] F. Liebrecht, *Zur Volkskunde* (Heilbronn, 1879), pp. 274 *sq.*

[3] F. Liebrecht, *Zur Volkskunde*, p. 274 ; J. B. Holzmayer, " Osiliana," *Verhandlungen der gelehrten Estnischen Gesellschaft zu Dorpat*, vii. (1872) p. 73.

[4] Spenser St. John, *Life in the Forests of the Far East*[2] (London, 1863), i. 88.

[5] E. H. Gomes, *Seventeen Years among the Sea Dyaks of Borneo* (London, 1911), pp. 66 *sq.*

[6] Ch. Hose and W. McDougall,

But it is on scenes of murder and sudden death that this Heaps of stones, sticks, or leaves on scenes of murder. rude method of averting evil is most commonly practised. The custom that every passer-by must cast a stone or stick on the spot where some one has come to a violent end, whether by murder or otherwise, has been observed in practically the same form in such many and diverse parts of the world as Ireland, France, Spain, Sweden, Germany, Bohemia, Lesbos, Morocco, Armenia, Palestine, Arabia, India, North America, Venezuela, Bolivia, Celebes, and New Zealand.[1] In Fiji, for example, it was the practice for every passer-by to throw a leaf on the spot where a man had been clubbed to death ; " this was considered as an offering of respect to him, and, if not performed, they have a notion they will soon be killed themselves." [2] Sometimes the scene of the murder or death may Heaps of stones or sticks on graves. also be the grave of the victim, but it need not always be so, and in Europe, where the dead are buried in consecrated ground, the two places would seldom coincide. However, the custom of throwing stones or sticks on a grave has undoubtedly been observed by passers-by in many parts

The Pagan Tribes of Borneo (London, 1912), i. 123.

[1] A. C. Haddon, "A Batch of Irish Folk-lore," *Folk-lore*, iv. (1893) pp. 357, 360; Laisnel de la Salle, *Croyances et Légendes du Centre de la France* (Paris, 1875), ii. 75, 77 ; J. Brand, *Popular Antiquities*, ii. 309; Hylten-Cavallius, quoted by F. Liebrecht, *Zur Volkskunde*, p. 274 ; K. Haupt, *Sagenbuch der Lausitz* (Leipsic, 1862-1863), ii. 65 ; K. Müllenhoff, *Sagen, Märchen und Lieder der Herzogthümer Schleswig, Holstein und Lauenburg* (Kiel, 1845), p. 125; A. Kuhn, *Märkische Sagen und Märchen* (Berlin, 1843), p. 113 ; A. Kuhn und W. Schwartz, *Norddeutsche Sagen, Märchen ~ und Gebräuche* (Leipsic, 1848), p. 85 ; A. Treichel, "Reisighäufung und Steinhäufung an Mordstellen," *Am Ur-Quelle*, vi. (1896) p. 220 ; Georgeakis et Pineau, *Folk-lore de Lesbos*, p. 323 ; A. Leared, *Morocco and the Moors* (London, 1876), pp. 105 *sq.* ; E. Doutté, "Figuig," *La Géographie, Bulletin de la Société de Géographie* (Paris), vii. (1903) p. 197 ; *id.*, *Magie et Religion dans l'Afrique du Nord* (Algiers, 1908), pp. 424 *sq.* ; A. von Haxthausen, *Transkaukasia* (Leipsic, 1856), i. 222 ; C. T. Wilson, *Peasant Life in the Holy Land* (London, 1906), p. 285 ; W. Crooke, *Popular Religion and Folk-lore of Northern India* (Westminster, 1896), i. 267 *sq.* ; J. Bricknell, *The Natural History of North Carolina* (Dublin, 1737), p. 380; J. Adair, *History of the American Indians* (London, 1775), p. 184 ; K. Martin, *Bericht über eine Reise nach Nederlandsch West-Indien*, Erster Theil (Leyden, 1887), p. 166; G. C. Musters, "Notes on Bolivia," *Journal of the Royal Geographical Society*, xlvii. (1877) p. 211; B. F. Matthes, *Einige Eigenthümlichkeiten in den Festen und Gewohnheiten der Makassaren und Büginesen*, p. 25 (separate reprint from *Travaux de la 6e Session du Congrès International des Orientalistes à Leide*, vol. ii.) ; R. A. Cruise, *Journal of a Ten Months' Residence in New Zealand* (London, 1823), p. 186.

[2] Ch. Wilkes, *Narrative of the United States Exploring Expedition*, New Edition (New York, 1851), iii. 50.

of the world, and that, too, even when the graves are not those of persons who have come to a violent end. Thus we are told that the people of Unalashka, one of the Aleutian Islands, bury their dead on the summits of hills and raise a little hillock over the grave. "In a walk into the country, one of the natives, who attended me, pointed out several of these receptacles of the dead. There was one of them, by the side of the road leading from the harbour to the village, over which was raised a heap of stones. It was observed, that every one who passed it, added one to it."[1] The Roumanians of Transylvania think that a dying man should have a burning candle in his hand, and that any one who dies without a light has no right to the ordinary funeral ceremonies. The body of such an unfortunate is not laid in holy ground, but is buried wherever it may be found. His grave is marked only by a heap of dry branches, to which each passer-by is expected to add a handful of twigs or a thorny bough.[2] The Hottentot god or hero Heitsi-eibib died several times and came to life again. When the Hottentots pass one of his numerous graves they throw a stone, a bush, or a fresh branch on it for good luck.[3] Near the former mission-station of Blydeuitzigt in Cape Colony there was a spot called Devil's Neck where, in the opinion of the Bushmen, the devil was interred. To hinder his resurrection stones were piled in heaps about the place. When a Bushman, travelling in the company of a missionary, came in sight of the spot he seized a stone and hurled it at the grave, remarking that if he did not do so his neck would be twisted round so that he would have to look backwards for the term of his natural life.[4] Stones are cast by passers-by on the graves of murderers in some parts of Senegambia.[5]

[1] Captain James Cook, *Voyages* (London, 1809), vi. 479.

[2] E. Gerard, *The Land beyond the Forest* (Edinburgh and London, 1888), i. 311, 318.

[3] H. Lichtenstein, *Reisen im Süd-lichen Africa* (Berlin, 1811–1812), i. 349 *sq.* ; Sir James E. Alexander, *Expedition of Discovery into the Interior of Africa* (London, 1838), i. 166 ; C. J. Andersson, *Lake Ngami*, Second Edition (London, 1856), p. 327 ; W. H. I.

Bleek, *Reynard the Fox in South Africa* (London, 1864), p. 76 ; Th. Hahn, *Tsuni-‖Goam, the Supreme Being of the Khoi-Khoi* (London, 1881), p. 56. Compare *The Dying God*, p. 3.

[4] Th. Hahn, "Die Buschmänner," *Globus*, xviii. 141.

[5] Th. Waitz, *Anthropologie der Naturvölker*, ii. (Leipsic, 1860) p. 195, referring to Raffenel, *Nouveau Voyage dans le pays des nègres* (Paris, 1856), i. 93 *sq.*

In Syria deceased robbers are not buried like honest folk, but left to rot where they lie ; and a pile of stones is raised over the mouldering corpse. Every one who passes such a pile must fling a stone at it, on pain of incurring God's malison.[1] Between sixty and seventy years ago an Englishman was travelling from Sidon to Tyre with a couple of Musalmans. When he drew near Tyre his companions picked up some small stones, armed him in the same fashion, and requested him to be so kind as to follow their example. Soon afterwards they came in sight of a conical heap of pebbles and stones standing in the road, at which the two Musalmans hurled stones and curses with great vehemence and remarkable volubility. When they had discharged this pious duty to their satisfaction, they explained that the missiles and maledictions were directed at a celebrated robber and murderer, who had been knocked on the head and buried there some half a century before.[2]

In these latter cases it may perhaps be thought that the sticks and stones serve no other purpose than to keep off the angry and dangerous ghost who might be supposed to haunt either the place of death or the grave. This interpretation seems certainly to apply to some cases of the custom. For example, in Pomerania and West Prussia the ghosts of suicides are much feared. Such persons are buried, not in the churchyard, but at the place where they took their lives, and every passer-by must cast a stone or a stick on the spot, or the ghost of the suicide will haunt him by night and give him no rest. Hence the piles of sticks or stones accumulated on the graves of these poor wretches sometimes attain a considerable size.[3] Similarly the Baganda of Central Africa used to stand in great fear of the ghosts of

Stones and sticks hurled as missiles at dangerous ghosts and demons.

[1] Eijūb Abēla, " Beiträge zur Kenntniss abergläubischer Gebräuche in Syrien," *Zeitschrift des Deutschen Palaestina-Vereins*, vii. (1884) p. 102.
[2] Note by G. P. Badger, on *The Travels of Ludovico di Varthema*, translated by J. W. Jones (Hakluyt Society, 1863), p. 45. For more evidence of the custom in Syria see W. M. Thomson, *The Land and the Book* (London, 1859), p. 490 ; F. Sessions, "Some

Syrian Folklore Notes," *Folk-lore*, ix. (1898) p. 15 ; A. Jaussen, *Coutumes des Arabes au pays de Moab* (Paris, 1908), p. 336.
[3] A. Treichel, "Reisig- und Steinhäufung bei Ermordeten oder Selbstmördern," *Verhandlungen der Berliner Gesellschaft für Anthropologie, Ethnologie und Urgeschichte, 1888*, p. (569) (bound up with *Zeitschrift für Ethnologie*, xx. 1888).

suicides and they took many precautions to disarm or even destroy these dangerous spirits. For this purpose the bodies of suicides were removed to waste land or cross-roads and burned there, together with the wood of the house in which the deed had been done or of the tree on which the person had hanged himself. By these means they imagined that they destroyed the ghost so that he could not come and lure others to follow his bad example. Lest, however, the ghost should survive the destruction of his body by fire, the Baganda, in passing any place where a suicide had been burnt, always threw grass or sticks on the spot to prevent the ghost from catching them. And they did the same, for the same reason, whenever they passed the places on waste ground where persons accused of witchcraft and found guilty by the poison ordeal had been burnt to death. Baganda women had a special reason for dreading all graves which were believed to be haunted by dangerous ghosts ; for, imagining that they could conceive children without intercourse with the other sex, they feared to be impregnated by the entrance into them of the ghosts of suicides and other unfortunate or uncanny people, such as persons with a light complexion, twins, and particularly all who had the mishap to be born feet foremost. For that reason Baganda women were at pains, whenever they passed the graves of any such persons, to throw sticks or grass upon them ; " for by so doing they thought that they could prevent the ghost of the dead from entering into them, and being reborn." Hence the mounds which accumulated over these graves became in course of time large enough to deflect the path and to attract the attention of travellers. It was not merely matrons who thus took care not to become mothers unaware ; the same fears were entertained and the same precautions were adopted by all women, whether old or young, whether married or single ; since they thought that there was no woman, whatever her age or condition, who might not be impregnated by the entrance into her of a spirit.[1] In these

---

[1] Rev. J. Roscoe, *The Baganda* (London, 1911), pp. 20 *sq.*, '46 *sq.*, 124 *sq.*, 126 *sq.*, 289 *sq.* Stones are not mentioned among the missiles hurled at ghosts, probably because stones are scarce in Uganda. See J. Roscoe, *op. cit.* p. 5.

cases, therefore, the throwing of sticks or grass at graves is a purely defensive measure; the missiles are intended to ward off the assaults of dangerous ghosts. Similarly we are told that in Madagascar solitary graves by the wayside have a sinister reputation, and that passers-by, without looking back, will throw stones or clods at them "to prevent the evil spirits from following them."[1] The Maraves of South Africa, like the Baganda, used to burn witches alive and to throw stones on the places of execution whenever they passed them, so that in time regular cairns gradually rose on these spots.[2] No doubt with these Maraves, as with the Baganda, the motive for throwing missiles at such places is to protect themselves against the ghosts. A protective motive is also assigned for a similar custom observed in Chota Nagpur, a region of India which is the home of many primitive tribes. There heaps of stones or of leaves and branches may often be seen beside the path; they are supposed to mark the places where people have been killed by wild beasts, and the natives think that any passer-by who failed to add a stone or a stick to the pile would himself be seized and devoured by a wild animal.[3] Here, though the ghost is not explicitly mentioned, we may perhaps suppose that out of spite he is instrumental in causing others to perish by the same untimely death by which he was himself carried off. The Kayans of Borneo imagine that they can put evil spirits to flight by hurling sticks or stones at them; so on a journey they will let fly volleys of such missiles at the rocks and dens where demons are known to reside.[4] Hence, whenever the throwing of stones at a grave is regarded as an insult to the dead, we may suppose that the missiles are intended to hit and hurt the ghost. Thus Euripides represents the murderer Aegisthus as leaping on the tomb of his victim Agamemnon and pelting it with stones;[5] and Propertius invites all lovers to discharge

---

[1] Father Finaz, S.J., in *Les Missions Catholiques*, vii. (1875) p. 328.

[2] "Der Muata Cazembe und die Völkerstämme der Maraves, Chevas, Muembas, Lundas, und andere von Süd- Afrika," *Zeitschrift für allgemeine Erdkunde*, vi. (1856) p. 287.

[3] *Journal of the Asiatic Society of Bengal*, lxxii. Part iii. (Calcutta, 1904) p. 87.

[4] A. W. Nieuwenhuis, *In Centraal Borneo* (Leyden, 1900), i. 146.

[5] Euripides, *Electra*, 327 *sq.*

stones and curses at the dishonoured grave of an old bawd.[1]

But if this theory seems adequately to account for some cases of the custom with which we are concerned, it apparently fails to explain others. The view that the sticks and stones hurled at certain places are weapons turned against dangerous or malignant spirits is plausible in cases where such spirits are believed to be in the neighbourhood ; but in cases where no such spirits are thought to be lurking, we must, it would seem, cast about for some other explanation. For example, we have seen that it has been customary to throw sticks or stones on spots which have been defiled by deeds of moral turpitude without any shedding of blood, and again on spots where weary travellers stop to rest. It is difficult to suppose that in these latter cases the evil deeds or the sensations of fatigue are conceived in the concrete shape of demons whom it is necessary to repel by missiles, though many South American Indians, as we saw, do attribute fatigue to a demon. Still more difficult is it to apply the purely defensive theory to cases where beneficent spirits are imagined to be hovering somewhere near, and where the throwing of the stones or sticks is apparently regarded by those who practise it as a token of respect rather than of hostility. Thus amongst the Masai, when any one dies away from the kraal, his body is left lying on the spot where he died, and all persons present throw bunches of grass or leaves on the corpse. Afterwards every passer-by casts a stone or a handful of grass on the place, and the more the dead man was respected, the longer is the usage observed.[2] It is especially the graves of Masai medicine-men that are honoured in this way.[3] In the forest near Avestad, in Sweden, the traveller, Clarke, observed " several heaps made with sticks and stones ; upon which the natives, as they pass, cast either a stone, or a little earth, or the bough of a tree ; deeming it an uncharitable act to omit this tribute, in their journeys to and fro. As this custom appeared closely allied to the pious practice in the Highlands of Scotland, of

[1] Propertius, v. 5. 77 *sq.*

[2] M. Merker, *Die Masai* (Berlin, 1904), p. 193.

[3] A. C. Hollis, *The Masai* (Oxford, 1905), pp. 305 *sq.*

casting a stone upon the cairn of a deceased person, we, of course, concluded these heaps were places of sepulture." They were said to be the graves of a band of robbers, who had plundered merchants on their passage through the forest, but had afterwards been killed and buried where they fell.[1] However, in all these cases the practice of throwing stones on the grave, though interpreted as a mark of respect and charity, may really be based on the fear of the ghosts, so that the motive for observing the custom may be merely that of self-defence against a dangerous spirit. Yet this explanation can hardly apply to certain other cases. Thus in Syria it is a common practice with pious Moslems, when they first come in sight of a very sacred place, such as Hebron or the tomb of Moses, to make a little heap of stones or to add a stone to a heap which has been already made. Hence every here and there the traveller passes a whole series of such heaps by the side of the track.[2] In Northern Africa the usage is similar. Cairns are commonly erected on spots from which the devout pilgrim first discerns the shrine of a saint afar off; hence they are generally to be seen on the top of passes. For example, in Morocco, at the point of the road from Casablanca to Azemmour, where you first come in sight of the white city of the saint gleaming in the distance, there rises an enormous cairn of stones shaped like a pyramid several hundreds of feet high, and beyond it on both sides of the road there is a sort of avalanche of stones, either standing singly or arranged in little pyramids. Every pious Mohammedan whose eyes are gladdened by the blessed sight of the sacred town adds his stone to one of the piles or builds a little pile for himself.[3]

Cairns raised in honour of Moslem saints.

Such a custom can hardly be explained as a precaution adopted against a dangerous influence supposed to emanate from the saint and to communicate itself even to people at a distance. On the contrary, it points rather to a desire of communion with the holy man than to a wish to keep

Stones as channels of communication with saints, living or dead.

[1] E. D. Clarke, *Travels in various Countries of Europe and Asia*, vi. (London, 1823) p. 165.
[2] W. H. D. Rouse, "Notes from Syria," *Folk-lore*, vi. (1895) p. 173. Compare F. Sessions, "Some Syrian Folklore Notes, gathered on Mount Lebanon," *Folk-lore*, ix. (1898) p. 15.
[3] E. Doutté, *Magie et Religion dans l'Afrique du Nord* (Algiers, 1908), pp. 420-422.

him at bay. The mode of communion adopted, however strange it may seem to us, is apparently quite in harmony with the methods by which good Mohammedans in Northern Africa attempt to appropriate to themselves the blessed influence (*baraka*) which is supposed to radiate on all sides from the person of a living saint. " It is impossible to imagine," we are told, " the extremity to which the belief in the blessed influence of saints is carried in North Africa. To form an exact idea of it you must see a great saint in the midst of the faithful. ' The people fling themselves down on his path to kiss the skirt of his robe, to kiss his stirrup if he is on horseback, to kiss even his footprint if he is on foot. Those who are too far from him to be able to touch his hand touch him with their staff, or fling a stone at him which they have marked previously so as to be able to find it afterwards and to embrace it devoutly.'"[1] Thus through the channel of the stone or the stick, which has been in bodily contact with the living saint, his blessed influence flows to the devotee who has wielded the stick or hurled the stone. In like manner we may perhaps suppose that the man who adds a stone to a cairn in honour of a dead saint hopes to benefit by the saintly effluence which distils in a mysterious fashion through the stone to him.[2]

---

[1] E. Doutté, *Magie et Religion dans l'Afrique du Nord*, p. 440, quoting De Ségonzac, *Voyage au Maroc*, p. 82.

[2] I follow the exposition of E. Doutté, whose account of the sanctity or magical influence (*baraka*) ascribed to the persons of living Mohammedan saints (marabouts) is very instructive. See his *Magie et Religion dans l'Afrique du Nord*, pp. 438 *sqq.* Mr. E. S. Hartland had previously explained the custom of throwing stones and sticks on cairns as acts of ceremonial union with the spirit who is supposed to reside in the cairn. See his *Legend of Perseus*, ii. (London, 1895) p. 128. While this theory offers a plausible explanation of some cases of the custom, I do not think that it will cover them all. M. René Dussaud argues that the stones deposited at shrines of holy men are simply material embodiments of the prayers which at the same time the suppliants address to the saints; and he holds that the practice of depositing stones at such places rests on a principle entirely different from that of throwing stones for the purpose of repelling evil spirits. See René Dussaud, " La matérialisation de la prière en Orient," *Bulletins et Mémoires de la Société d'Anthropologie de Paris*, V. Série, vii. (1906) pp. 213-220. If I am right, the fundamental idea in these customs is neither that the stones or sticks are offerings presented to good spirits nor that they are missiles hurled at bad ones, but that they embody the evil, whether disease, misfortune, fear, horror, or what not, of which the person attempts to rid himself by transferring it to a material vehicle. But I am far from confident that this explanation applies to all cases. In particular it is difficult to reconcile it with the custom, described in the text, of throw-

When we survey the many different cases in which
passing travellers are accustomed to add stones or sticks
to existing piles, it seems difficult, if not impossible, to
explain them all on one principle; different and even
opposite motives appear, at least at first sight, to have
operated in different cases to produce customs superficially
alike. Sometimes the motive for throwing the stone is to
ward off a dangerous spirit; sometimes it is to cast away an
evil; sometimes it is to acquire a good. Yet, perhaps, if we
could trace them back to their origin in the mind of primitive man, we might find that they all resolve themselves
more or less exactly into the principle of the transference of
evil. For to rid ourselves of an evil and to acquire a good
are often merely opposite sides of one and the same operation; for example, a convalescent regains health in exactly
the same proportion as he shakes off his malady. And
though the practice of throwing stones at dangerous spirits,
especially at mischievous and malignant ghosts of the dead,
appears to spring from a different motive, yet it may be
questioned whether the difference is really as great to the
savage as it seems to us. To primitive man the idea of
spiritual and ghostly powers is still more indefinite than it is
to his civilized brother: it fills him with a vague uneasiness
and alarm; and this sentiment of dread and horror he, in
accordance with his habitual modes of thought, conceives in
a concrete form as something material which either surrounds
and oppresses him like a fog, or has entered into and taken
temporary possession of his body. In either case he imagines
that he can rid himself of the uncanny thing by stripping it
from his skin or wrenching it out of his body and transferring
it to some material substance, whether a stick, a stone, or
what not, which he can cast from him, and so, being eased

The rite
of throwing
sticks or
stones is
perhaps
best ex-
plained as
a mode of
purifica-
tion, the
evil being
thought
to be
embodied
in the
missile
which is
thrown
away.

---

ing a marked stone at a holy man and
then recovering it. Are we to suppose
that the stone carries away the evil to
the good man and brings back his
blessing instead? The idea is perhaps
too subtle and far-fetched.

The word *baraka*, which in North
Africa describes the powerful and in
general beneficent, yet dangerous, influence which emanates from holy per-

sons and things, is no doubt identical with the Hebrew *bĕrakhah* (בְּרָכָה)
"blessing." The importance which the
ancient Hebrews ascribed to the blessing or the curse of a holy man is
familiar to us from many passages in
the Old Testament. See, for example,
Genesis xxvii., xlviii. 8 *sqq.*; Deuteronomy xxvii. 11 *sqq.*, xxviii. 1 *sqq.*

of his burden, can hasten away from the dreadful spot with a lighter heart. Thus the throwing of the sticks or stones would be a form of ceremonial purification, which among primitive peoples is commonly conceived as a sort of physical rather than moral purgation, a mode of sweeping or scouring away the morbid matter by which the polluted person is supposed to be infected. This notion perhaps explains the rite of stone-throwing observed by pilgrims at Mecca; on the day of sacrifice every pilgrim has to cast seven stones on a cairn, and the rite is repeated thrice on the three following days. The traditional explanation of the custom is that Mohammed here drove away the devil with a shower of stones;[1] but the original idea may perhaps have been that the pilgrims cleanse themselves by transferring their ceremonial impurity to the stones which they fling on the heap.

This interpretation of stone-throwing agrees with ancient Greek and Indian tradition and custom.

The theory that the throwing of stones is practised in certain circumstances as a mode of purification tallies very well with the tradition as to the origin of those cairns which were to be seen by wayside images of Hermes in ancient Greece, and to which every passer-by added a stone. It was said that when Hermes was tried by the gods for the murder of Argus all the gods flung stones at him as a means of freeing themselves from the pollution contracted by bloodshed; the stones thus thrown made a great heap, and the custom of rearing such heaps at wayside images of Hermes continued ever afterwards.[2] Similarly Plato recommended that if any man had murdered his father or mother, his brother or sister, his son or daughter, he should be put to death, and that his body should be cast forth naked at a cross-road outside of the city. There the

---

[1] E. Doutté, *Magie et Religion dans l'Afrique du Nord* (Algiers, 1908), pp. 430 *sq.*; J. Wellhausen, *Reste arabischen Heidentums*[2] (Berlin, 1897), p. 111. The explanation given in the text is regarded as probable by Professor M. J. de Goeje (*Internationales Archiv für Ethnographie*, xvi. (1904) p. 42.

[2] *Etymologicum Magnum*, *s.v.* 'Ερμαῖον, pp. 375 *sq.*; Eustathius on Homer, *Odyssey*, xvi. 471. ,As to the heaps of stones see Cornutus, *Theologiae Graecae Compendium*, 16; Babrius, *Fabulae*, xlviii. 1 *sq.*; Suidas, *s.v.* 'Ερμαῖον; Scholiast on Nicander, *Ther.* 150; M. P. Nilsson, *Griechische Feste* (Leipsic, 1906), pp. 388 *sqq.* The method of execution by stoning may perhaps have been resorted to in order to avoid the pollution which would be entailed by contact with the guilty and dying man.

magistrates should assemble on behalf of the city, each carrying in his hand a stone, which he was to cast at the head of the corpse by way of purifying the city from the pollution it had contracted by the crime. After that the corpse was to be carried away and flung outside the boundaries.[1] In these cases it would seem that the pollution incurred by the vicinity of a murderer is thought to be gathered up in the stones as a material vehicle and to be thrown away with them. A sacrificial custom of the Brahmans, prescribed in one of their sacred books, is susceptible of a like interpretation. At a certain stage of the ritual the sacrificer is directed to put a stone into a waterpot and to throw it away in a south-westerly direction, because that is the region of Nirriti, the goddess of Evil or Destruction. With the stone and the pitcher he is supposed to cast away his pain and evil ; and he can transfer the pain to another by saying, as he throws away the stone and the pitcher, " Let thy pain enter him whom we hate," or " Let thy pain enter so-and-so," naming his enemy ; but in order to ensure the transference of the pain to his enemy he must take care that the stone or the pitcher is broken.[2]

This mode of interpreting the custom of throwing sticks and stones on piles appears preferable to the one which has generally found favour with European travellers and writers. Imperfectly acquainted for the most part with the notions which underlie primitive magic, but very familiar with the religious conception of a deity who requires sacrifice of his worshippers, they are apt to interpret the missiles in question as cheap and easy offerings presented by pious but frugal worshippers to ghosts or spirits whose favour they desire to win.[3] Whether a likely mode of conciliating a

The throwing of sticks or stones on piles is sometimes explained as a sacrifice.

[1] Plato, *Laws*, ix. 12, p. 873 A-C λίθον ἕκαστος φέρων ἐπὶ τὴν κεφαλὴν τοῦ νεκροῦ βάλλων ἀφοσιούτω τὴν πόλιν ὅλην.
[2] *Satapatha Brahmana*, ix. I. 2. 9-12, Part iv. p. 171 of J. Eggeling's translation (*Sacred Books of the East*, vol. xliii., Oxford, 1897). As to Nirriti, the Goddess of Destruction, see H. Oldenberg, *Die Religion des Veda* (Berlin, 1894), pp. 323, 351, 354, 489 note [3].
[3] See, for example, O. Baumann,

Durch Massailand zur Nilquelle (Berlin, 1894), p. 214 ; G. M. Dawson, " Notes on the Shuswap People of British Columbia," *Transactions of the Royal Society of Canada*, ix. (1891) section ii. p. 38 ; F. Liebrecht, *Zur Volkskunde* (Heilbronn, 1879), pp. 267 *sq.*, 273 *sq.*, 276, 278 *sq.* ; R. Andree, *Ethnographische Parallelen und Vergleiche* (Stuttgart, 1878), p. 48 ; Catat, in *Le Tour du Monde*, lxv. (1893), p. 40. Some of these writers have made ghost or spirit is to throw sticks and stones at him is a question about which opinions might perhaps differ. It is difficult to speak with confidence about the tastes of spiritual beings, but as a rule they bear a remarkable likeness to those of mere ordinary mortals, and it may be said without fear of contradiction that few of the latter would be gratified by being set up as a common target to be aimed at with sticks and stones by everybody who passed within range.[1] Yet it is quite possible that a ceremony, which at first was purely magical, may in time have a religious gloss or interpretation put on it even by those who practise it; and this seems in fact to have sometimes happened to the particular custom under consideration. Certainly some people accompany the

Certainly the throwing of stones is sometimes accompanied by sacrifices.

throwing of the stone on the pile with the presentation of useful articles, which can hardly serve any other purpose than that of propitiating some local spirits. Thus travellers in Sikhim and Bhootan offer flour and wine, as well as stones, at the cairns; and they also burn incense and recite incantations or prayers,[2] or they tear strips from their garments, tie them to twigs or stones, and then lay them on the cairn, calling out to the spirit of the mountain, "Pray accept our offering! The spirits are victorious! The devils are defeated!"[3] Indians of Guatemala offered, according to their means, a little cotton, salt, cacao, or chili.[4] They now burn copal and sometimes dance on the tops of the passes where the cairns are to be seen, but perhaps these devotions may be paid to the crosses which at the present day are generally set up in such situations.[5] The Indian of Bolivia will

---

a special study of the practices in question. See F. Liebrecht, "Die geworfenen Steine," *Zur Volkskunde*, pp. 267-284; R. Andree, "Steinhaufen," *Ethnographische Parallelen und Vergleiche*, pp. 46-58; E. S. Hartland, *The Legend of Perseus*, ii. (London, 1895) pp. 204 *sqq.*; E. Doutté, *Magie et Religion dans l'Afrique du Nord* (Algiers, 1908), pp. 419 *sqq.* With the views of the last of these writers I am in general agreement.

[1] However, at the waterfall of Kriml, in the Tyrol, it is customary for every passer-by to throw a stone into the water; and this attention is said to

put the water-spirits in high good humour; for they follow the wayfarer who has complied with the custom and guard him from all the perils of the dangerous path. See F. Panzer, *Beitrag zur deutschen Mythologie* (Munich, 1848-1855), ii. 236 *sq.*

[2] J. A. H. Louis, *The Gates of Thibet*, Second Edition (Calcutta, 1894), pp. 111 *sq.*

[3] L. A. Waddell, *Among the Himalayas* (Westminster, 1899), pp. 115, 188.

[4] Brasseur de Bourbourg, *Histoire des nations civilisées du Mexique et de l'Amérique-Centrale*, ii. 564.

[5] C. Sapper, "Die Gebräuche und

squirt out the juice of his coca-quid, or throw the quid itself on the cairn, to which he adds a stone; occasionally he goes so far as to stick feathers or a leathern sandal or two on the pile. In passing the cairns he will sometimes pull a hair or two out of his eyebrows or eyelashes and puff them away towards the sun.[1] Peruvian Indians used similarly to make cheap offerings of chewed coca or maize, old shoes, and so forth, on the cairns.[2] In Sweden and Corea a little money is sometimes thrown on a cairn instead of a stick or stone.[3] The shrine of the Jungle Mother in Northern India is usually a pile of stones and branches to which every passer-by contributes. When she is displeased, she lets a tiger or leopard kill her negligent votary. She is the great goddess of the herdsmen and other dwellers in the forest, and they vow to her a cock and a goat, or a young pig, if she saves them and their cattle from beasts of prey.[4] In the jungles of Mirzapur the cairn which marks the spot where a man has been killed by a tiger, and to which each passer-by contributes a stone, is commonly in charge of a Baiga or aboriginal priest, who offers upon it a cock, a pig, or some spirits, and occasionally lights a little lamp at the shrine.[5] Amongst the Baganda members of the Bean clan worshipped the spirit of the river Nakiza. "There was no temple, but they had two large heaps of sticks and grass, one on either side of the river by the ford; to these heaps the members went, when they wished to make an offering to

Heaps of sticks at the fords of rivers in Africa.

religiösen Anschauungen der Kekchí-Indianer," *Internationales Archiv für Ethnographie*, viii. (1895) pp. 197 *sq.*

[1] D. Forbes, "On the Aymara Indians of Bolivia and Peru," *Journal of the Ethnological Society of London*, ii. (1870) pp. 237 *sq.*; G. C. Musters, "Notes on Bolivia," *Journal of the Royal Geographical Society*, xlvii. (1877) p. 211; Baron E. Nordenskiöld, "Travels on the Boundaries of Bolivia and Argentina," *The Geographical Journal*, xxi. (1903) p. 518.

[2] P. J. de Arriaga, *Extirpacion de la Idolatria del Piru* (Lima, 1621), pp. 37, 130.

[3] F. Liebrecht, *Zur Volkskunde*, p. 274; Brett, "Dans la Corée Septentrionale," *Les Missions Catholiques*,

xxxi. (1899) p. 237.

[4] W. Crooke, *Popular Religion and Folk-lore of Northern India* (Westminster, 1896), i. 115. "In some parts of Bilaspore there may be seen heaps of stones, which are known as *kuriyā*, from the word *kurhonā*, meaning to heap or pile-up. Just how and why the practice was started cannot explain; but to this day every one who passes a *kuriyā* will take up a stone and throw it on the pile. This, they say, has been done as long as they can remember" (E. M. Gordon, *Indian Folk Tales*, London, 1908, p. 14).

[5] W. Crooke, *Popular Religion and Folk-lore of Northern India* (Westminster, 1896), i. 267 *sq.*

the spirit, or to seek his assistance. The offerings were usually goats, beer, barkcloth, and fowls. When people crossed the river they threw a little grass or some sticks on to the heap before crossing, and again a little more on to the second heap after crossing ; this was their offering to the spirit for a safe crossing." [1] There is a ford on the Calabar river in West Africa which has an ill repute, for the stream is broad, the current rapid, and there are crocodiles in the deep places. Beside the ford is a large oval-shaped stone which the Ekoi regard as an altar of Nimm, a powerful goddess, who dwells in the depth of the river Kwa and manifests herself in the likeness now of a crocodile and now of a snake. In order to ensure a safe passage through the river it is customary to pluck a leaf, rub it on the forehead over the pineal gland, and throw it on a heap of leaves in front of the stone. As he rubs the leaf on his forehead, the person who is about to plunge into the river prays, " May I be free from danger ! May I go through the water to the other side ! May I see no evil ! " And when he throws the leaf on the heap he prays again, saying, " I am coming across the river, may the crocodile lay down his head ! " [2] Here the leaves appear to be a propitiatory offering presented to the dread goddess in the hope that she will suffer her worshipper to pass the ford unmolested. At another but smaller stream, called the River of Good Fortune, the Ekoi similarly rub leaves on their foreheads, praying for luck, and throw them on a heap before they pass through the water. They think that he who complies with this custom will have good luck throughout the year. Again, when the Ekoi kill a chameleon on the road, they do not throw the body away in the forest, but lay it by the wayside, and all who pass by pluck a few leaves and drop them on the dead animal, saying, " Look ! Here is your mat." In this way heaps of leaves accumulate over the carcases of chameleons. The custom is intended to appease the shade of the chameleon, who, if he were not pacified, would go to the Earth-god Obassi Nsi and pray for vengeance on the race of those who

---

[1] Rev. J. Roscoe, *The Baganda* (London, 1911), p. 163.

[2] P. Amaury Talbot, *In the Shadow of the Bush* (London, 1912), p. 242. As to the goddess Nimm, see *id.*, pp. 2 *sq.*

had caused his death.[1]   The Washamba of German East Africa believe that certain stony and dangerous places in the paths are the abodes of spirits; hence at any such spot a traveller who would have a prosperous journey must dance a little and deposit a few small stones.[2]   The dance and the stones are presumably intended to soften the heart of the spirits and induce them to look favourably on the dancer. In Papa Westray, one of the Orkney Islands, there is a ruined chapel called St. Tredwels, "at the door of which there is a heap of stones; which was the superstition of the common people, who have such a veneration for this chapel above any other, that they never fail, at their coming to it, to throw a stone as an offering before the door: and this they reckon an indispensable duty enjoined by their ancestors." [3]

Prayers, too, as we have seen, are sometimes offered at these piles.   In Laos heaps of stones may be seen beside the path, on which the passenger will deposit a pebble, a branch, or a leaf, while he beseeches the Lord of the Diamond to bestow on him good luck and long life.[4]   In the Himalayan districts of the North-Western Provinces of India heaps of stones and sticks are often to be seen on hills or at cross-roads.   They are formed by the contributions of passing travellers, each of whom in adding his stone or stick to the pile prays, saying, "Thou goddess whose home is on the ridge, eater of wood and stone, preserve me." [5]   Tibetan travellers mutter a prayer at the cairns on the tops of passes to which they add a few stones gathered by them on the ascent.[6]   A native of South-Eastern Africa who places a small stone on a cairn is wont to say as he does so, "Cairn, grant me strength and prosperity." [7]   In the same circumstances the Hottentot

The throwing of stones and sticks is sometimes accompanied by prayers.

----

[1] P. Amaury Talbot, *op. cit.* p. 91.

[2] A. Karasek, "Beiträge zur Kenntniss der Waschambaa," *Baessler-Archiv,* i. (1911) p. 194.

[3] M. Martin, "A Description of the Western Islands of Scotland," in John Pinkerton's *Voyages and Travels* (London, 1808–1814), iii. 691.

[4] E. Aymonier, *Notes sur le Laos* (Saigon, 1885), p. 198.

[5] E. T. Atkinson, *The Himalayan Districts of the North-Western Pro-*

vinces of India, ii. (Allahabad, 1884) p. 832.

[6] T. T. Cooper, *Travels of a Pioneer of Commerce* (London, 1871), p. 275. Compare W. W. Rockhill, *The Land of the Lamas* (London, 1891), pp. 126 *sq.*

[7] Rev. J. Macdonald, "Manners, Customs, Superstitions, and Religions of South African Tribes," *Journal of the Anthropological Institute,* xx. (1891) p. 126.

prays for plenty of cattle,[1] and the Caffre that his journey may be prosperous, that he may have strength to accomplish it, and that he may obtain an abundant supply of food by the way.[2] It is said that sick Bushmen used to go on pilgrimage to the cairn called the Devil's Neck, and pray to the spirit of the place to heal them, while they rubbed the sick part of their body and cried, "Woe! woe!" On special occasions, too, they resorted thither and implored the spirit's help.[3] Such customs seem to indicate the gradual transformation of an old magical ceremony into a religious rite with its characteristic features of prayer and sacrifice. Yet behind these later accretions, as we may perhaps regard them, it seems possible in many, if not in all, cases to discern the nucleus to which they have attached themselves, the original idea which they tend to conceal and in time to transmute. That idea is the transference of evil from man to a material substance which he can cast from him like an outworn garment.

Gradual transformation of an old magical ceremony into a religious rite.

---

[1] Sir James E. Alexander, *Expedition of Discovery into the Interior of Africa* (London, 1838), i. 166.

[2] S. Kay, *Travels and Researches in Caffraria* (London, 1833), pp. 211 *sq.* When the Bishop of Capetown once passed a heap of stones on the top of a mountain in the Amapondo country he was told that "it was customary for every traveller to add one to the heap that it might have a favourable influence on his journey, and enable him to arrive at some kraal while the pot is yet boiling" (J. Shooter, *The Kaffirs of Natal*, London, 1857, p. 217). Here there is no mention of a prayer. Similarly a Basuto on a journey, when he fears that the friend with whom he is going to stay may have eaten up all the food before his guest's arrival, places a stone on a cairn to avert the danger (E. Casalis, *The Basutos*, London, 1861, p. 272). The reason alleged for the practice in these cases is perhaps equivalent to the one assigned by the Melanesians and others; by ridding the traveller of his fatigue it enables him to journey faster and so to reach his destination before supper is over. But sometimes a travelling Mowenda will place a stone, not on a cairn, but in the fork of a tree, saying, "May the sun not set before I reach my destination." See Rev. E. Gottschling, "The Bawenda," *Journal of the Anthropological Institute*, xxxv. (1905) p. 381. This last custom is a charm to prevent the sun from setting. See *The Magic Art and the Evolution of Kings*, i. 318. In Senegal the custom of throwing stones on cairns by the wayside is said to be observed "in order to ensure a speedy and prosperous return." See Dr. Bellamy, "Notes ethnographiques recueillies dans le Haut-Sénégal," *Revue d'Ethnographie*, v. (1886) p. 83. In the Fan country of West Africa the custom of adding a leafy branch to a heap of such branches in the forest was explained by a native, who said that it was done to prevent the trees and branches from falling on the traveller's head, and their roots from wounding his feet. See Father Trilles, "Mille lieues dans l'inconnu," *Les Missions Catholiques*, xxxiv. (1902) p. 142.

[3] Th. Hahn, "Die Buschmänner," *Globus*, xviii. 141. As to the cairn in question, see above, p. 16.

§ 3. The Transference to Animals

Animals are often employed as a vehicle for carrying away or transferring the evil. A Guinea negro who happens to be unwell will sometimes tie a live chicken round his neck, so that it lies on his breast. When the bird flaps its wings or cheeps the man thinks it a good sign, supposing the chicken to be afflicted with the very pain from which he hopes soon to be released, or which he would otherwise have to endure.[1] When a Moor has a headache he will sometimes take a lamb or a goat and beat it till it falls down, believing that the headache will thus be transferred to the animal.[2] In Morocco most wealthy Moors keep a wild boar in their stables, in order that the jinn and evil spirits may be diverted from the horses and enter into the boar.[3] In some parts of Algeria people think that typhoid fever can be cured by taking a tortoise, putting it on its back in the road, and covering it over with a pot. The patient recovers, but whoever upsets the pot catches the fever. In Tlemcen a pregnant woman is protected against jinn by means of a black fowl which is kept in the house from the seventh month of her pregnancy till her delivery. Finally, the oldest woman in the house releases the fowl in the Jews' quarter ; the bird is supposed to carry the jinn away with it.[4] Amongst the Caffres of South Africa, when other remedies have failed, " natives sometimes adopt the custom of taking a goat into the presence of a sick man, and confess the sins of the kraal over the animal. Sometimes a few drops of blood from the sick man are allowed to fall on the head of the goat, which is turned out into an uninhabited part of the veldt. The sickness is supposed to be transferred to the animal, and to become lost in the desert." [5] After an illness a Bechuana king seated himself upon an ox which lay stretched on the

Evils transferred to animals in Africa.

---

[1] J. Smith, *Trade and Travels in the Gulph of Guinea* (London, 1851), p. 77.

[2] O. Dapper, *Description de l'Afrique* (Amsterdam, 1686), p. 117.

[3] A. Leared, *Morocco and the Moors* (London, 1876), p. 301. Compare E. Doutté, *Magie et Religion dans l'Afrique du Nord* (Algiers, 1908), p. 454.

[4] E. Doutté, *op. cit.* pp. 454 *sq.*

[5] Dudley Kidd, *The Essential Kafir* (London, 1904), p. 261.

ground. The native doctor next poured water on the king's head till it ran down over his body. Then the head of the ox was held in a vessel of water till the animal expired; whereupon the doctor declared, and the people believed, that the ox died of the king's disease, which had been transferred from him to it.[1] The Baganda of Central Africa also attempted to transfer illness from a person to an animal. " The medicine-man would take the animal, pass some herbs over the sick man, tie these to the animal, and then drive it away to some waste land, where he would kill it, taking the meat as his perquisite. The sick man would be expected to recover." [2] The Akikuyu of East Africa think that a man can transfer the guilt of incest by means of " an ignoble ceremony " to a goat, which is then killed ; this saves the life of the culprit, who otherwise must die.[3] When disease breaks out among the cattle of the Bahima, a pastoral people of Central Africa, the priest " collects herbs and other remedies to attract the disease from the cattle. An animal is chosen from the herd in the evening, which is to be the scapegoat for the herd ; the herbs, etc., are tied round its neck, with certain fetiches to ensure the illness leaving the other animals ; the cow is driven round the outside of the kraal several times, and afterwards placed inside with the herd for the night. Early the following morning the animal is taken out and again driven round the kraal ; the priest then kills it in the gateway, and some of the blood is sprinkled over the people belonging to the kraal, and also over the herd. The people next file out, each one jumping over the carcase of the cow, and all the animals are driven over it in the same way. The disease is thus transferred to the scapegoat and the herd is saved. All the fetiches and herbs, which were upon the scapegoat, are fastened upon the door-posts and lintel of the kraal to prevent the disease from entering again." [4]

When the cattle of the Huzuls, a pastoral people of the

[1] Rev. John Campbell, *Travels in South Africa* (London, 1822), ii. 207 sq.

[2] Rev. J. Roscoe, *The Baganda* (London, 1911), pp. 342 sq.

[3] P. Cayzac, " La religion des Kikuyu," *Anthropos*, v. (1910) p. 311.

[4] Rev. J. Roscoe, " The Bahima, a Cow Tribe of Enkole," *Journal of the Royal Anthropological Institute*, xxxvii. (1907) p. 111.

Carpathians, are sick and the owner attributes the sickness to witchcraft, he throws glowing coals into a vessel of water and then pours the water on a black dog; thus the sickness passes into the dog and the cattle are made whole.[1] In Arabia, when the plague is raging, the people will sometimes lead a camel through all the quarters of the town in order that the animal may take the pestilence on itself. Then they strangle it in a sacred place and imagine that they have rid themselves of the camel and of the plague at one blow.[2] In Annam, when sickness is caused by the presence of a demon in the body of the sufferer, a skilful exorcist will decoy the unwary devil into a fowl and then, quick as thought, decapitate the bird and throw it out of the door. But lest the fiend should survive this severe operation, cabalistic figures are posted on the outside of the door, which preclude him from entering the premises and assaulting the patient afresh.[3] It is said that when smallpox is raging the savages of Formosa will drive the demon of disease into a sow, then cut off the animal's ears and burn them or it, believing that in this way they rid themselves of the plague.[4] When a Kabyle child is pining for jealousy of a younger brother or sister, the parents imagine that they can cure it as follows. They take fifteen grains of wheat, wrap them up in a packet, and leave the packet all night under the head of the jealous child. Then in the morning they throw the grains into an ant - hill, saying, "Salutation to you, oh beautiful beings clad in black ; salutation to you who dig the earth so well without the aid of any hoe by the help of God and the angels! May each of you take his share of the jealousy attached to these grains ! "[5]

Amongst the Malagasy the vehicle for carrying away evils is called a *faditra*. "The faditra is anything selected by the sikidy [divining board] for the purpose of taking

Marginal notes: Evils transferred to animals in various parts of the world. Vehicles for the transference of evils in Madagascar.

[1] Dr. R. F. Kaindl, "Zauberglaube bei den Huzulen," *Globus*, lxxvi. (1899) p. 254.

[2] J. Goldziher, *Muhammedanische Studien* (Halle a. S., 1888–1890), i. 34.

[3] E. Diguet, *Les Annamites* (Paris, 1906), pp. 283 *sq.*

[4] W. Müller, "Über die Wildenstämme der Insel Formosa," *Zeitschrift für Ethnologie*, xlii. (1910) p. 237. The writer's use of the pronoun (*sie*) is ambiguous.

[5] Father E. Amat, in *Annales de la Propagation de la Foi*, lxx. (1898) pp. 266 *sq.*

away any hurtful evils or diseases that might prove injurious to an individual's happiness, peace, or prosperity. The faditra may be either ashes, cut money, a sheep, a pumpkin, or anything else the sikidy may choose to direct. After the particular article is appointed, the priest counts upon it all the evils that may prove injurious to the person for whom it is made, and which he then charges the faditra to take away for ever. If the faditra be ashes, it is blown, to be carried away by the wind. If it be cut money, it is thrown to the bottom of deep water, or where it can never be found. If it be a sheep, it is carried away to a distance on the shoulders of a man, who runs with all his might, mumbling as he goes, as if in the greatest rage against the faditra, for the evils it is bearing away. If it be a pumpkin, it is carried on the shoulders to a little distance, and there dashed upon the ground with every appearance of fury and indignation."[1] A Malagasy was informed by a diviner that he was doomed to a bloody death, but that possibly he might avert his fate by performing a certain rite. Carrying a small vessel full of blood upon his head, he was to mount upon the back of a bullock ; while thus mounted, he was to spill the blood upon the bullock's head, and then send the animal away into the wilderness, whence it might never return.[2]

Extraction of klepto-mania by spiders and crabs.
Among the Toradjas of Central Celebes a chief's daughter, who suffered from kleptomania, was healed by a wise woman, who placed a bag containing spiders and crabs on the patient's hands. The physician calculated that the prehensile claws of these creatures, so suggestive of a thief's hands in the act of closing on his prey, would lay hold of the vicious pro-pensity in the young woman's mind and extract it as neatly as a pair of forceps nips out a thorn from the flesh.[3] The Battas of Sumatra have a ceremony which they call

[1] Rev. W. Ellis, *History of Mada-gascar* (London, N.D.), i. 422 *sq.* ; compare *id.*, pp. 232, 435, 436 *sq.* ; Rev. J. Sibree, *The Great African Island* (London, 1880), pp. 303 *sq.* As to divination by the *sikidy*, see J. Sibree, "Divination among the Malagasy," *Folk-lore*, iii. (1892) pp. 193-226.
[2] W. Ellis, *op. cit.* i. 374 ; J. Sibree,

The Great African Island, p. 304 ; J. Cameron, in *Antananarivo Annual and Madagascar Magazine, Reprint of the First Four Numbers* (Antananarivo, 1885), p. 263.

[3] N. Adriani en Alb. C. Kruijt, *De Bare'e-sprekende Toradja's van Midden-Celebes*, i. (Batavia, 1912) p. 399.

"making the curse to fly away." When a woman is child- Evils
less, a sacrifice is offered to the gods of three grasshoppers, transferred to birds,
representing a head of cattle, a buffalo, and a horse. Then which fly
a swallow is set free, with a prayer that the curse may fall away with them.
upon the bird and fly away with it.[1] " The entrance into a
house of an animal which does not generally seek to share
the abode of man is regarded by the Malays as ominous of
misfortune. If a wild bird flies into a house, it must be
carefully caught and smeared with oil, and must then be
released in the open air, a formula being recited in which it
is bidden to fly away with all the ill-luck and misfortunes
(*sial jambalang*) of the occupier."[2] In antiquity Greek
women seem to have done the same with swallows which
they caught in the house : they poured oil on them and let
them fly away, apparently for the purpose of removing ill-
luck from the household.[3] The Huzuls of the Carpathians
imagine that they can transfer freckles to the first swallow
they see in spring by washing their face in flowing water and
saying, " Swallow, swallow, take my freckles, and give me
rosy cheeks."[4] At the cleansing of a leper and of a house
suspected of being tainted with leprosy among the Hebrews
the priest used to let a living bird fly away into the open
field,[5] no doubt in order to carry away the leprosy with it.
Similarly among the ancient Arabs a widow was expected
to live secluded in a small tent for a year after her husband's
death ; then a bird or a sheep was brought to her, she made
the creature touch her person, and let it go. It was believed
that the bird or the sheep would not live long thereafter ;
doubtless it was supposed to suffer from the unclean-

[1] W. Ködding, "Die Batakschen Götter," *Allgemeine Missions - Zeitschrift*, xii. (1885) p. 478 ; Dr. R. Römer, " Bijdrage tot de Geneeskunst der Karo-Batak's," *Tijdschrift voor Indische Taal- Land- en Volkenkunde*, l. (1908) p. 223.
[2] W. E. Maxwell, "The Folklore of the Malays," *Journal of the Straits Branch of the Royal Asiatic Society*, No. 7 (June, 1881), p. 27 ; W. W. Skeat, *Malay Magic* (London, 1900), pp. 534 *sq.*
[3] Dio Chrysostom, *Orat.* liii. vol. ii. pp. 164 *sq.* ed. L. Dindorf (Leipsic,

1857). Compare Plato, *Republic*, iii. 9, p. 398 A, who ironically proposes to dismiss poets from his ideal state in the same manner. These passages of Plato and Dio Chrysostom were pointed out to me by my friend Professor Henry Jackson. There was a Greek saying, attributed to Pythagoras, that swallows should not be allowed to enter a house (Plutarch, *Quaest. Conviv.* viii. 7, 1).

[4] Dr. R. F. Kaindl, "Zauberglaube bei den Huzulen," *Globus*, lxxvi. (1899) pp. 255 *sq.*
[5] Leviticus xiv. 7, 53.

ness or taint of death which the widow had transferred to it.[1]

Evils transferred to animals in India. Among the Majhwar, a Dravidian race of South Mirzapur, if a man has died of a contagious disease, such as cholera, the village priest walks in front of the funeral procession with a chicken in his hands, which he lets loose in the direction of some other village as a scapegoat to carry the infection away. None but another very experienced priest would afterwards dare to touch or eat such a chicken.[2] Among the Badagas of the Neilgherry Hills in Southern India, when a death has taken place, the sins of the deceased are laid upon a buffalo calf. For this purpose the people gather round the corpse and carry it outside of the village. There an elder of the tribe, standing at the head of the corpse, recites or chants a long list of sins such as any Badaga may commit, and the people repeat the last words of each line after him. The confession of sins is thrice repeated. " By a conventional mode of expression, the sum total of sins a man may do is said to be thirteen hundred. Admitting that the deceased has committed them all, the performer cries aloud, ' Stay not their flight to God's pure feet.' As he closes, the whole assembly chants aloud ' Stay not their flight.' Again the performer enters into details, and cries, ' He killed the crawling snake. It is a sin.' In a moment the last word is caught up, and all the people cry ' It is a sin.' As they shout, the performer lays his hand upon the calf. The sin is transferred to the calf. Thus the whole catalogue is gone through in this impressive way. But this is not enough. As the last shout ' Let all be well ' dies away, the performer gives place to another, and again confession is made, and all the people shout ' It is a sin.' A third time it is done. Then, still in solemn silence, the calf is let loose. Like the Jewish scapegoat, it may never be used for secular work." At a Badaga funeral witnessed by the Rev. A. C. Clayton the buffalo calf was led thrice round the bier, and the dead man's hand was laid on its head.

---

[1] J. Wellhausen, *Reste arabischen Heidentumes* (Berlin, 1887), p. 156; W. Robertson Smith, *Religion of the Semites*, New Edition (London, 1894),

pp. 422, 428.

[2] W. Crooke, *Tribes and Castes of the North-Western Provinces and Oudh* (Calcutta, 1896), iii. 434.

"By this act, the calf was supposed to receive all the sins of the deceased. It was then driven away to a great distance, that it might contaminate no one, and it was said that it would never be sold, but looked on as a dedicated sacred animal."[1] "The idea of this ceremony is, that the sins of the deceased enter the calf, or that the task of his absolution is laid on it. They say that the calf very soon disappears, and that it is never after heard of."[2] Some of the Todas of the Neilgherry Hills in like manner let loose a calf as a funeral ceremony ; the intention may be to transfer the sins of the deceased to the animal. Perhaps the Todas have borrowed the ceremony from the Badagas.[3] In Kumaon, a district of North-Western India, the custom of letting loose a bullock as a scapegoat at a funeral is occasionally observed. A bell is hung on the bullock's neck, and bells are tied to its feet, and the animal is told that it is to be let go in order to save the spirit of the deceased from the torments of hell. Sometimes the bullock's right quarter is branded with a trident and the left with a discus.[4] Perhaps the original intention of such customs was to banish the contagion of death by means of the animal, which carried it away and so ensured the life of the survivors. The idea of sin is not primitive.

[1] E. Thurston, *Castes and Tribes of Southern India* (Madras, 1909), i. 113-117 ; *id.*, *Ethnographic Notes in Southern India* (Madras, 1906), pp. 192-196 ; Captain H. Harkness, *Description of a Singular Aboriginal Race inhabiting the Summit of the Neilgherry Hills* (London, 1832), p. 133 ; F. Metz, *The Tribes inhabiting the Neilgherry Hills*, Second Edition (Mangalore, 1864), p. 78 ; Jagor, "Ueber die Badagas im Nilgiri-Gebirge," *Verhandlungen der Berliner Gesellschaft für Anthropologie* (1876), pp. 196 *sq.* At the Badaga funerals witnessed by Mr. E. Thurston "no calf was brought near the corpse, and the celebrants of the rites were satisfied with the mere mention by name of a calf, which is male or female according to the sex of the deceased."

[2] H. Harkness, *l.c.*

[3] J. W. Breeks, *An Account of the Primitive Tribes and Monuments of the Nīlagiris* (London, 1873), pp. 23 *sq.*; W. H. R. Rivers, *The Todas* (London, 1906), pp. 376 *sq.*

[4] E. T. Atkinson, *The Himalayan Districts of the North-Western Provinces of India*, ii. (Allahabad, 1884) pp. 927 *sq.* In other parts of North-Western India on the eleventh day after a death a bull calf is let loose with a trident branded on its shoulder or quarter "to become a pest." See (Sir) Denzil C. J. Ibbetson, *Report on the Revision of Settlement of the Panipat Tahsil and Karnal Parganah of the Karnal District* (Allahabad, 1883), p. 137. In Behar, a district of Bengal, a bullock is also let loose on the eleventh day of mourning for a near relative. See G. A. Grierson, *Bihār Peasant Life* (Calcutta, 1885), p. 409.

§ 4. The Transference to Men

Evils transferred to human beings in India and elsewhere.

Again, men sometimes play the part of scapegoat by diverting to themselves the evils that threaten others. An ancient Hindoo ritual describes how the pangs of thirst may be transferred from a sick man to another. The operator seats the pair on branches, back to back, the sufferer with his face to the east, and the whole man with his face to the west. Then he stirs some gruel in a vessel placed on the patient's head and hands the stir-about to the other man to drink. In this way he transfers the pangs of thirst from the thirsty soul to the other, who obligingly receives them in his stead.[1] There is a painful Telugu remedy for a fever: it is to embrace a bald-headed Brahman widow at the earliest streak of dawn. By doing so you get rid of the fever, and no doubt (though this is not expressly affirmed) you at the same time transfer it to the bald-headed widow.[2] When a Cinghalese is dangerously ill, and the physicians can do nothing, a devil-dancer is called in, who by making offerings to the devils, and dancing in the masks appropriate to them, conjures these demons of disease, one after the other, out of the sick man's body and into his own. Having thus successfully extracted the cause of the malady, the artful dancer lies down on a bier, and shamming death, is carried to an open place outside the village. Here, being left to himself, he soon comes to life again, and hastens back to claim his reward.[3] In 1590 a Scotch witch of the name of Agnes Sampson was convicted of curing a certain Robert Kers of a disease "laid upon him by a westland warlock when he was at Dumfries, whilk sickness she took upon herself, and kept the same with great groaning and torment till the morn, at whilk time there was a great din heard in the house." The noise was made by the witch in her efforts to shift the disease, by means of clothes, from herself to a cat or dog. Unfortunately

---

[1] W. Caland, *Altindisches Zauberritual* (Amsterdam, 1900), p. 83; *Hymns of the Atharva-Veda*, translated by Maurice Bloomfield (Oxford, 1897), pp. 308 *sq.* (*Sacred Books of the East*, vol. xlii.).

[2] M. N. Venketswami, "Telugu Superstitions," *The Indian Antiquary*, xxiv. (1895) p. 359.

[3] A. Grünwedel, "Sinhalesische Masken," *Internationales Archiv für Ethnographie*, vi. (1893) pp. 85 *sq.*

the attempt partly miscarried. The disease missed the animal and hit Alexander Douglas of Dalkeith, who dwined and died of it, while the original patient, Robert Kers, was made whole.[1] The Dyaks believe that certain men possess in themselves the power of neutralizing bad omens. So, when evil omens have alarmed a farmer for the safety of his crops, he takes a small portion of his farm produce to one of these wise men, who eats it raw for a small consideration, "and thereby appropriates to himself the evil omen, which in him becomes innocuous, and thus delivers the other from the ban of the *pemali* or taboo."[2]

"In one part of New Zealand an expiation for sin was felt to be necessary; a service was performed over an individual, by which all the sins of the tribe were supposed to be transferred to him, a fern stalk was previously tied to his person, with which he jumped into the river, and there unbinding, allowed it to float away to the sea, bearing their sins with it."[3] In great emergencies the sins of the Rajah of Manipur used to be transferred to somebody else, usually to a criminal, who earned his pardon by his vicarious sufferings. To effect the transference the Rajah and his wife, clad in fine robes, bathed on a scaffold erected in the bazaar, while the criminal crouched beneath it. With the water which dripped from them on him their sins also were washed away and fell on the human scapegoat. To complete the transference the Rajah and his wife made over their fine robes to their substitute, while they themselves, clad in new raiment, mixed with the people till evening. But at the close of the day they entered into retreat and remained in seclusion for about a week, during which they were esteemed sacred or tabooed.[4] Further, in Manipur "they have a noteworthy system of keeping count of the years. Each year is named after some man, who—for a consideration—undertakes to bear the for- *Sins and misfortunes transferred to human scapegoats in New Zealand and Manipur.*

Annual eponyms in Manipur.

[1] J. G. Dalyell, *Darker Superstitions of Scotland* (Edinburgh, 1834), pp. 104 *sq.* I have modernised the spelling.

[2] J. Perham, "Sea Dyak Religion," *Journal of the Straits Branch of the Royal Asiatic Society,* No. 10 (December 1882), p. 232.

[3] Rev. Richard Taylor, *Te Ika A Maui, or New Zealand and its Inhabitants,* Second Edition (London, 1870), p. 101.

[4] T. C. Hodson, "The Native Tribes of Manipur," *Journal of the Anthropological Institute,* xxxi. (1901) p. 302; *id., The Meitheis* (London, 1908), pp. 106 *sq.*

tune good or bad of the year. If the year be good, if there be no pestilence and a good harvest, he gets presents from all sorts of people, and I remember hearing that in 1898, when the cholera was at its worst, a deputation came to the Political Agent and asked him to punish the name-giver, as it was obvious that he was responsible for the epidemic. In former times he would have got into trouble."[1] The nomination of the eponym, or man who is to give his name to the year, takes place at a festival called *Chirouba*, which falls about the middle of April. It is the priests who nominate the eponym, after comparing his horoscope with that of the Rajah and of the State generally. The retiring official, who gave his name to the past year, addresses his successor as follows : " My friend, I bore and took away all evil spirits and sins from the Rajah and his people during the last year. Do thou likewise from to-morrow until the next *Chirouba*." Then the incoming official, who is to give his name to the New Year, addresses the Rajah in these words : " O son of heaven, Ruler of the Kings, great and ancient Lord, Incarnation of God, the great Lord Pakhangba, Master of the bright Sun, Lord of the Plain and Despot of the Hills, whose kingdom is from the hills on the east to the mountains on the west, the old year perishes, the new cometh. New is the sun of the new year, and bright as the new sun shalt thou be, and mild withal as the moon. May thy beauty and thy strength grow with the growth of the new year. From to-day will I bear on my head all thy sins, diseases, misfortunes, shame, mischief, all that is aimed in battle against thee, all that threatens thee, all that is bad and hurtful for thee and thy kingdom." For these important services the eponym or vicar receives from the Rajah a number of gifts, including a basket of salt, and his grateful country rewards his self-sacrificing devotion by bestowing many privileges on him.[2] Elsewhere, perhaps, if we knew more about the matter, we might find that eponymous magistrates who give their names to the year have been similarly regarded as public scapegoats, who bore on their devoted

Eponymous magistrates as public scapegoats.

---

[1] T. C. Hodson, "The Native Tribes of Manipur," *Journal of the Anthropological Institute*, xxxi. (1901) p. 302.

[2] T. C. Hodson, *The Meitheis* (London, 1908), pp. 104-106.

heads the misfortunes, the sins, and the sorrows of the whole people.[1]

In the *Jataka*, or collection of Indian stories which narrate the many transmigrations of the Buddha, there is an instructive tale, which sets forth how sins and misfortunes can be transferred by means of spittle to a holy ascetic. A lady of easy virtue, we are told, had lost the favour of King Dandaki and bethought herself how she could recover it. As she walked in the park revolving these things in her mind, she spied a devout ascetic named Kisavaccha. A thought struck her. "Surely," said she to herself, "this must be Ill Luck. I will get rid of my sin on his person and then go and bathe." No sooner said than done. Chewing her toothpick, she collected a large clot of spittle in her mouth with which she beslavered the matted locks of the venerable man, and having hurled her toothpick at his head into the bargain she departed with a mind at peace and bathed. The stratagem was entirely successful ; for the king took her into his good graces again. Not long after it chanced that the king deposed his domestic chaplain from his office. Naturally chagrined at this loss of royal favour, the clergyman repaired to the king's light o' love and enquired how she had contrived to recapture the monarch's affection. She told him frankly how she had got rid of her sin and emerged without a stain on her character by simply spitting on the head of Ill Luck in the royal park. The chaplain took the hint, and hastening to the park bespattered in like manner the sacred locks of the holy man ; and in consequence he was soon reinstated in office. It would have been well if the thing had stopped there, but unfortunately it did not. By and bye it happened that there was a disturbance on the king's frontier, and the king put himself at the head of his army to go forth and fight. An unhappy idea occurred to his domestic chaplain. Elated by the success of the expedient which had restored him to royal favour, he asked the king, "Sire, do you wish for victory or defeat ?" "Why for victory, of course," replied the king. "Then you take my advice," said the chaplain ; "just go and spit on the head of Ill Luck, who dwells in the

Indian story of the transference of sins to a holy man.

---
[1] Compare *The Dying God*, pp. 116 *sq.*

royal park ; you will thus transfer all your sin to his person."
It seemed to the king a capital idea and he improved on it
by proposing that the whole army should accompany him
and get rid of their sins in like manner. They all did so,
beginning with the king, and the state of the holy man's
head when they had all done is something frightful to con-
template. But even this was not the worst. For after the
king had gone, up came the commander-in-chief and seeing
the sad plight of the pious ascetic, he took pity on him and
had his poor bedabbled hair thoroughly washed. The fatal
consequences of this kindly-meant but most injudicious
shampoo may easily be anticipated. The sins which had
been transferred with the saliva to the person of the devotee
were now restored to their respective owners ; and to punish
them for their guilt fire fell from heaven and destroyed the
whole kingdom for sixty leagues round about.[1]

Transfer-
ence of
evils to
human
scapegoats
in Uganda.
    A less harmless way of relieving an army from guilt or
misfortune used in former times to be actually practised by
the Baganda. When an army had returned from war, and
the gods warned the king by their oracles that some evil
had attached itself to the soldiers, it was customary to pick
out a woman slave from the captives, together with a cow,
a goat, a fowl, and a dog from the booty, and to send them
back under a strong guard to the borders of the country
from which they had come. There their limbs were broken
and they were left to die ; for they were too crippled to
crawl back to Uganda. In order to ensure the transference
of the evil to these substitutes, bunches of grass were rubbed
over the people and cattle and then tied to the victims.
After that the army was pronounced clean and was allowed
to return to the capital. A similar mode of transferring
evil to human and animal victims was practised by the
Baganda whenever the gods warned the king that his
hereditary foes the Banyoro were working magic against
him and his people.[2]

    In Travancore, when a rajah is near his end, they seek
out a holy Brahman, who consents to take upon himself the

[1] The Jataka or Stories of the
Buddha's former Births, vol. v., translated by H. T. Francis (Cambridge,
1905), pp. 71 sq.
[2] Rev. J. Roscoe, The Baganda
(London, 1911), p. 342.

sins of the dying man in consideration of the sum of ten
thousand rupees. Thus prepared to immolate himself on the
altar of duty as a vicarious sacrifice for sin, the saint is introduced into the chamber of death, and closely embraces the
dying rajah, saying to him, " O King, I undertake to bear
all your sins and diseases. May your Highness live long
and reign happily." Having thus, with a noble devotion,
taken to himself the sins of the sufferer, and likewise the
rupees, he is sent away from the country and never more
allowed to return.[1] Closely akin to this is the old Welsh
custom known as " sin-eating." According to Aubrey, " In
the County of Hereford was an old Custome at funeralls to
hire poor people, who were to take upon them all the sinnes
of the party deceased. One of them I remember lived in a
cottage on Rosse-high way. (He was a long, leane, ugly,
lamentable poor raskal.) The manner was that when the
Corps was brought out of the house and layd on the Biere ;
a Loafe of bread was brought out, and delivered to the
Sinne-eater over the corps, as also a Mazar-bowle of maple
(Gossips bowle) full of beer, which he was to drinke up, and
sixpence in money, in consideration whereof he took upon
him (ipso facto) all the Sinnes of the Defunct, and freed him
(or her) from walking after they were dead. . . . This
Custome (though rarely used in our dayes) yet by some
people was observed even in the strictest time of ye Presby-
terian government : as at Dynder, volens nolens the Parson
of ye Parish, the kinred of a woman deceased there had this
ceremonie punctually performed according to her Will : and
also the like was donne at ye City of Hereford in these times,
when a woman kept many yeares before her death a Mazard-
bowle for the Sinne-eater ; and the like in other places in
this Countie ; as also in Brecon, e.g. at Llangors, where Mr.
Gwin the minister about 1640 could no hinder ye performing
of this ancient custome. I believe this custom was hereto-
fore used over all Wales. . . . In North Wales the Sinne-
eaters are frequently made use of ; but there, instead of a
Bowle of Beere, they have a bowle of Milke."[2] According

Marginal notes:
Transference of sins to a Brahman in Travancore.

Transference of sins to a Sin-eater in England.

[1] Rev. S. Mateer, *Native Life in Travancore* (London, 1883), p. 136.

[2] J. Aubrey, *Remaines of Gentilisme and Judaisme* (Folk-lore Society, London, 1881), pp. 35 *sq.*

to a letter dated February 1, 1714-15, "within the memory of our fathers, in Shropshire, in those villages adjoyning to Wales, when a person dyed, there was notice given to an old sire (for so they called him), who presently repaired to the place where the deceased lay, and stood before the door of the house, when some of the family came out and furnished him with a cricket, on which he sat down facing the door. Then they gave him a groat, which he put in his pocket; a crust of bread, which he eat; and a full bowle of ale, which he drank off at a draught. After this he got up from the cricket and pronounced, with a composed gesture, the ease and rest of the soul departed for which he would pawn his own soul. This I had from the ingenious John Aubrey, Esq."[1] In modern times some doubt has been thrown on Aubrey's account of the custom.[2] The practice, however, is reported to have prevailed in a valley not far from Llandebie to a recent period. An instance was said to have occurred about sixty years ago.[3]

Transference of sins to a sin-eater in India.

Aubrey's statement is moreover supported by the analogy of similar customs in India. When the Rajah of Tanjore died in 1801, some of his bones and the bones of the two wives, who were burned with his corpse, were ground to powder and eaten, mixed with boiled rice, by twelve Brahmans. It was believed that the sins of the deceased passed into the bodies of the Brahmans, who were paid for the service.[4] A Brahman, resident in a village near Raipur, stated that he had eaten food (rice and milk) out of the hand of the dead Rajah of Bilaspur, and that in consequence he had been placed on the throne for the space of a year. At

---

[1] Bagford's letter in Leland's *Collectanea*, i. 76, quoted by J. Brand, *Popular Antiquities*, ii. 246 *sq.*, Bohn's edition (London, 1882–1883).

[2] In *The Academy*, 13th Nov. 1875, p. 505, Mr. D. Silvan Evans stated that he knew of no such custom anywhere in Wales; and the custom seems to be now quite unknown in Shropshire. See C. S. Burne and G. F. Jackson, *Shropshire Folk-lore* (London, 1883), pp. 307 *sq.*

[3] The authority for the statement is a Mr. Moggridge, reported in *Archaeologia Cambrensis*, second series, iii.

330. But Mr. Moggridge did not speak from personal knowledge, and as he appears to have taken it for granted that the practice of placing bread and salt upon the breast of a corpse was a survival of the custom of "sin-eating," his evidence must be received with caution. He repeated his statement, in somewhat vaguer terms, at a meeting of the Anthropological Institute, 14th December 1875. See *Journal of the Anthropological Institute*, v. (1876) pp. 423 *sq.*

[4] J. A. Dubois, *Mœurs des Peuples de l'Inde* (Paris, 1825), ii. 32 *sq.*

the end of the year he had been given presents and then
turned out of the territory and forbidden apparently to
return. He was an outcast among his fellows for having
eaten out of a dead man's hand.[1] A similar custom is
believed to obtain in the hill states about Kangra, and
to have given rise to a caste of "outcaste" Brahmans. At
the funeral of a Rani of Chamba rice and ghee were eaten out
of the hands of the corpse by a Brahman paid for the purpose.
Afterwards a stranger, who had been caught outside the
Chamba territory, was given the costly wrappings of the
corpse, then told to depart and never shew his face in the
country again.[2] In Oude when an infant was killed it used
to be buried in the room where it had been born. On the
thirteenth day afterwards the priest had to cook and eat his
food in that room. By doing so he was supposed to take
the whole sin upon himself and to cleanse the family from
it.[3] At Utch Kurgan in Turkestan Mr. Schuyler saw an old
man who was said to get his living by taking on himself the
sins of the dead, and thenceforth devoting his life to prayer
for their souls.[4]

In Tahiti, where the bodies of chiefs and persons of rank   Transfer-
were embalmed and preserved above ground in special sheds   ence of sins
or houses erected for them, a priest was employed at the   in Tahiti.
funeral rites who bore the title of the "corpse-praying
priest." His office was singular. When the house for the
dead had been prepared, and the corpse placed on the platform or bier, the priest ordered a hole to be made in the
floor, near the foot of the platform. Over this he prayed to
the god by whom it was supposed that the soul of the
deceased had been called away. The purport of his prayer

---

[1] R. Richardson, in *Panjab Notes and Queries*, i. p. 86, § 674 (May, 1884).

[2] *Panjab Notes and Queries*, i. p. 86, § 674, ii. p. 93, § 559 (March, 1885). Some of these customs have been already referred to in a different connexion. See *The Dying God*, p. 154. In Uganda the eldest son used to perform a funeral ceremony, which consisted in chewing some seeds which he took with his lips from the hand of his dead father ; some of these seeds

he then blew over the corpse and the rest over one of the childless widows who thereafter became his wife. The meaning of the ceremony is obscure. The eldest son in Uganda never inherited his father's property. See the Rev. J. Roscoe, *The Baganda* (London, 1911), p. 117.

[3] *Panjab Notes and Queries*, iii. p. 179, § 745 (July, 1886).

[4] E. Schuyler, *Turkistan* (London, 1876), ii. 28.

was that all the dead man's sins, especially the one for which his soul had been required of him, might be deposited there, that they might not attach in any degree to the survivors, and that the anger of the god might be appeased. He next addressed the corpse, usually saying, " With you let the guilt now remain." The pillar or post of the corpse, as it was called, was then planted in the hole, and the hole filled up. As soon as the ceremony of depositing the sins in the hole was over, all who had touched the body or the garments of the deceased, which were buried or destroyed, fled precipitately into the sea, to cleanse themselves from the pollution which they had contracted by touching the corpse. They also cast into the sea the garments they had worn while they were performing the last offices to the dead. Having finished their ablutions, they gathered a few pieces of coral from the bottom of the sea, and returning with them to the house addressed the corpse, saying, " With you may the pollution be." So saying they threw down the coral on the top of the hole which had been dug to receive the sins and the defilement of the dead.[1] In this instance the sins of the departed, as well as the pollution which the primitive mind commonly associates with death, are not borne by a living person, but buried in a hole. Yet the fundamental idea— that of the transference of sins—is the same in the Tahitian as in the Welsh and Indian customs ; whether the vehicle or receptacle destined to catch and draw off the evil be a person, an animal, or a thing, is for the purpose in hand a matter of little moment.[2]

---

[1] W. Ellis, *Polynesian Researches*, Second Edition (London, 1832–1836), i. 401 *sqq.*

[2] The Welsh custom of " sin-eating " has been interpreted by Mr. E. S. Hartland as a modification of an older custom of eating the corpse. See his article, " The Sin-eater," *Folk-lore*, iii. (1892) 145-157 ; *The Legend of Perseus*, ii. 291 *sqq.*, iii. p. ix. I cannot think his interpretation probable or borne out by the evidence. The Badaga custom of transferring the sins of the dead to a calf which is then let loose and never used again (above, pp. 36 *sq.*), the Tahitian custom of burying the sins of a person whose body is carefully preserved by being embalmed, and the Manipur and Travancore customs of transferring the sins of a Rajah before his death (pp. 39, 42 *sq.*) establish the practice of transferring sins in cases where there can be no question of eating the corpse. The original intention of such practices was perhaps not so much to take away the sins of the deceased as to rid the survivors of the dangerous pollution of death. This comes out to some extent in the Tahitian custom.

§ 5. *The Transference of Evil in Europe*

The examples of the transference of evil hitherto adduced have been mostly drawn from the customs of savage or barbarous peoples. But similar attempts to shift the burden of disease, misfortune, and sin from one's self to another person, or to an animal or thing, have been common also among the civilized nations of Europe, both in ancient and modern times. A Roman cure for fever was to pare the patient's nails, and stick the parings with wax on a neighbour's door before sunrise ; the fever then passed from the sick man to his neighbour.[1] Similar devices must have been resorted to by the Greeks ; for in laying down laws for his ideal state, Plato thinks it too much to expect that men should not be alarmed at finding certain wax figures adhering to their doors or to the tombstones of their parents, or lying at cross-roads.[2] Among the ruins of the great sanctuary of Aesculapius, which were excavated not very long ago in an open valley among the mountains of Epidaurus, inscriptions have been found recording the miraculous cures which the god of healing performed for his faithful worshippers. One of them tells how a certain Pandarus, a Thessalian, was freed from the letters which, as a former slave or prisoner of war, he bore tattooed or branded on his brow. He slept in the sanctuary with a fillet round his head, and in the morning he discovered to his joy that the marks of shame—the blue or scarlet letters—had been transferred from his brow to the fillet. By and by there came to the sanctuary a wicked man, also with brands or tattoo marks on his face, who had been charged by Pandarus to pay his debt of gratitude to the god, and had received the cash for the purpose. But the cunning fellow thought to cheat the god and keep the money all to himself. So when the god appeared to him in a dream and asked anxiously after the money, he boldly denied that he had it, and impudently prayed the god to remove the ugly marks from his own brazen brow. He was told to tie the fillet of Pandarus about his head, then to take it off, and look at his face in the water of the sacred well. He did so,

Transference of evils in ancient Greece.

[1] Pliny, *Nat. Hist.* xxviii. 86.   [2] Plato, *Laws*, xi. 12, p. 933 B.

and sure enough he saw on his forehead the marks of Pandarus in addition to his own.[1]   In the fourth century of our era Marcellus of Bordeaux prescribed a cure for warts, which has still a great vogue among the superstitious in various parts of Europe. Doubtless it was an old traditional remedy in the fourth, and will long survive the expiry of the twentieth, century. You are to touch your warts with as many little stones as you have warts ; then wrap the stones in an ivy leaf, and throw them away in a thoroughfare. Whoever picks them up will get the warts, and you will be rid of them.[2]   A similar cure for warts, with such trifling variations as the substitution of peas or barley for pebbles, and a rag or a piece of paper for an ivy leaf, has been prescribed in modern times in Italy, France, Austria, England, and Scotland.[3]   Another favourite way of passing on your warts to somebody else is to make as many knots in a string as you have warts ; then throw the string away or place it under a stone. Whoever treads on the stone or picks up the thread will get the warts instead of you ; sometimes to complete the transference it is thought necessary that he should undo the knots.[4]   Or you need only place the knotted thread before sunrise in the spout of a pump ; the next person who works the pump will be sure to get your warts.[5]   Equally

[1] Ἐφημερὶς ἀρχαιολογική, 1883, col. 213, 214 ; G. Dittenberger, Sylloge Inscriptionum Graecarum,[2] No. 802, lines 48 sqq. (vol. ii. pp. 652 sq.).

[2] Marcellus, De medicamentis, xxxiv. 102. A similar cure is described by Pliny (Nat. Hist. xxii. 149) ; you are to touch the warts with chick-peas on the first day of the moon, wrap the peas in a cloth, and throw them away behind you. But Pliny does not say that the warts will be transferred to the person who picks up the peas. On this subject see further J. Hardy, "Wart and Wen Cures," Folk-lore Record, i. (1878) pp. 216-228.

[3] Z. Zanetti, La Medicina delle nostre donne (Città di Castello, 1892), pp. 224 sq. ; J. B. Thiers, Traité des Superstitions (Paris, 1679), p. 321 ; B. Souché, Croyances, présages et traditions diverses (Niort, 1880), p. 19 ; J. W. Wolf, Beiträge zur deutschen

Mythologie (Göttingen, 1852-1857), i. 248, § 576 ; Dr. R. F. Kaindl, "Aus dem Volksglauben der Rutenen in Galizien," Globus, lxiv. (1893) p. 93 ; J. Harland and T. T. Wilkinson, Lancashire Folk-lore (Manchester and London, 1882), p. 157 ; G. W. Black, Folk-medicine (London, 1883), p. 41 ; W. Gregor, Folk-lore of the North-East of Scotland (London, 1881), p. 49 ; J. G. Campbell, Witchcraft and Second Sight in the Highlands and Islands of Scotland (Glasgow, 1902), pp. 94 sq.

[4] L. Strackerjan, Aberglaube und Sagen aus dem Herzogthum Oldenburg (Oldenburg, 1867), ii. 71, § 85 ; E. Monseur, Le Folklore Wallon (Brussels, N.D.), p. 29 ; H. Zahler, Die Krankheit im Volksglauben des Simmenthals (Bern, 1898), p. 93 ; R. Andree, Braunschweiger Volkskunde (Brunswick, 1896), p. 306.

[5] A. Birlinger, Volksthümliches aus

effective methods are to rub the troublesome excrescences with down or fat, or to bleed them on a rag, and then throw away the down, the fat, or the bloody rag. The person who picks up one or other of these things will be sure to release you from your warts by involuntarily transferring them to himself.[1] People in the Orkney Islands will some- Transfer-times wash a sick man, and then throw the water down at a ence of
sickness in gateway, in the belief that the sickness will leave the patient Scotland, and be transferred to the first person who passes through Germany,
and the gate.[2] A Bavarian cure for fever is to write upon a Austria. piece of paper, "Fever, stay away, I am not at home," and to put the paper in somebody's pocket. The latter then catches the fever, and the patient is rid of it.[3] Or the sufferer may cure himself by sticking a twig of the elder-tree in the ground without speaking. The fever then adheres to the twig, and whoever pulls up the twig will catch the disease.[4] A Bohemian prescription for the same malady is this. Take an empty pot, go with it to a cross-road, throw it down, and run away. The first person who kicks against the pot will catch your fever, and you will be cured.[5] In Oldenburg they say that when a person lies sweating with fever, he should take a piece of money to himself in bed. The money is afterwards thrown away on the street, and whoever picks it up will catch the fever, but the original patient will be rid of it.[6]

Often in Europe, as among savages, an attempt is made Sickness to transfer a pain or malady from a man to an animal. transferred
to asses, Grave writers of antiquity recommended that, if a man frogs, dogs, be stung by a scorpion, he should sit upon an ass with and other
animals. his face to the tail, or whisper in the animal's ear, "A scorpion has stung me"; in either case, they thought, the pain would be transferred from the man to the

---

Schwaben (Freiburg im Breisgau, 1861-1862), i. 483.

[1] Thiers, Souché, Strackerjan, Monseur, *ll.cc.*; J. G. Campbell, *Witchcraft and Second Sight in the Highlands and Islands of Scotland* (Glasgow, 1902), p. 95.

[2] Ch. Rogers, *Social Life in Scotland* (Edinburgh, 1884-1886), iii. 226.

[3] G. Lammert, *Volksmedizin und*

medizinischer Aberglaube in Bayern (Würzburg, 1869), p. 264.

[4] *Ibid.* p. 263.

[5] J. V. Grohmann, *Aberglauben und Gebräuche aus Böhmen und Mähren* (Prague and Leipsic, 1864), p. 167, § 1180.

[6] L. Strackerjan, *Aberglaube und Sagen aus dem Herzogthum Oldenburg* (Oldenburg, 1867), i. 71, § 85.

ass.[1]   Many cures of this sort are recorded by Marcellus. For example, he tells us that the following is a remedy for toothache.   Standing booted under the open sky on the ground, you catch a frog by the head, spit into its mouth, ask it to carry away the ache, and then let it go.   But the ceremony must be performed on a lucky day and at a lucky hour.[2]   In Cheshire the ailment known as aphtha or thrush, which affects the mouth or throat of infants, is not uncommonly treated in much the same manner.   A young frog is held for a few moments with its head inside the mouth of the sufferer, whom it is supposed to relieve by taking the malady to itself.   " I assure you," said an old woman who had often superintended such a cure, " we used to hear the poor frog whooping and coughing, mortal bad, for days after ; it would have made your heart ache to hear the poor creature coughing as it did about the garden." [3] Again Marcellus tells us that if the foam from a mule's mouth, mixed with warm water, be drunk by an asthmatic patient, he will at once recover, but the mule will die.[4]   An ancient cure for the gripes, recorded both by Pliny and Marcellus, was to put a live duck to the belly of the sufferer ; the pains passed from the man into the bird, to which they proved fatal.[5]   According to the same writers a stomachic complaint of which the cause was unknown might be cured by applying a blind puppy to the suffering part for three days.   The secret disorder thus passed into the puppy ; it died, and a post-mortem examination of its little body revealed the cause of the disease from which the man had suffered and of which the dog had died.[6]   Once more, Marcellus advises that when a man was afflicted with a disorder of the intestines the physician should catch a live hare, take the huckle-bone from one of its feet and the down

---

[1] *Geoponica*, xiii. 9, xv. 1 ; Pliny, *Nat. Hist.* xxviii. 155.   The authorities for these cures are respectively Apuleius and Democritus.   The latter is probably not the atomic philosopher. See J. G. Frazer, " The Language of Animals," *The Archæological Review*, vol. i. (May, 1888) p. 180, note [140].

[2] Marcellus, *De medicamentis*, xii. 24.

[3] W. G. Black, *Folk-medicine* (London, 1883), pp. 35 *sq.*

[4] Marcellus, *De medicamentis*, xvii. 18.

[5] Pliny, *Nat. Hist.* xxx. 61 ; Marcellus, *De medicamentis*, xxvii. 33. The latter writer mentions (*op. cit.* xxviii. 123) that the same malady might similarly be transferred to a live frog.

[6] Pliny, *Nat. Hist.* xxx. 64 ; Marcellus, *De medicamentis*, xxviii. 132.

from the belly, then let the hare go, pronouncing as he did so the words, "Run away, run away, little hare, and take away with you the intestine pain." Further, the doctor was to fashion the down into thread, with which he was to tie the huckle-bone to the patient's body, taking great care that the thread should not be touched by any woman.[1] A Northamptonshire, Devonshire, and Welsh cure for a cough is to put a hair of the patient's head between two slices of buttered bread and give the sandwich to a dog. The animal will thereupon catch the cough and the patient will lose it.[2] Sometimes an ailment is transferred to an animal by sharing food with it. Thus in Oldenburg, if you are sick of a fever you set a bowl of sweet milk before a dog and say, "Good luck, you hound! may you be sick and I be sound!" Then when the dog has lapped some of the milk, you take a swig at the bowl; and then the dog must lap again, and then you must swig again; and when you and the dog have done it the third time, he will have the fever and you will be quit of it. A peasant woman in Abbehausen told her pastor that she suffered from fever for a whole year and found no relief. At last somebody advised her to give some of her food to a dog and a cat. She did so and the fever passed from her into the animals. But when she saw the poor sick beasts always before her, she wished it undone. Then the fever left the cat and the dog and returned to her.[3]

A Bohemian cure for fever is to go out into the forest before the sun is up and look for a snipe's nest. When you have found it, take out one of the young birds and keep it beside you for three days. Then go back into the wood and set the snipe free. The fever will leave you at once. The snipe has taken it away. So in Vedic times the Hindoos of old sent consumption away with a blue jay. They said, "O consumption, fly away, fly away with the blue jay! With the wild rush of the storm and the whirlwind, oh, vanish away!"[4]

[1] Marcellus, *De medicamentis*, xxix. 35.

[2] W. Henderson, *Folk-lore of the Northern Counties* (London, 1879), p. 143; W. G. Black, *Folk-medicine*, p. 35; Marie Trevelyan, *Folk-lore and Folk-stories of Wales* (London, 1909), p. 226.

[3] L. Strackerjan, *Aberglaube und Sagen aus dem Herzogthum Oldenburg* (Oldenburg, 1867), i. 72, § 86.

[4] J. V. Grohmann, *Aberglauben und Gebräuche aus Böhmen und Mähren* (Prague and Leipsic, 1864), p. 166, § 1173, quoting Kuhn's translation of *Rig-veda*, x. 97. 13.   A

Sickness transferred to birds, snails, fish, and fowls.

In Oldenburg they sometimes hang up a goldfinch or a turtle-dove in the room of a consumptive patient, hoping that the bird may draw away the malady from the sufferer to itself.[1] A prescription for a cough in Sunderland is to shave the patient's head and hang the hair on a bush. When the birds carry the hair to their nests, they will carry the cough with it.[2] In the Mark of Brandenburg a cure for headache is to tie a thread thrice round your head and then hang it in a loop from a tree; if a bird flies through the loop, it will take your headache away with it.[3] A Saxon remedy for rupture in a child is to take a snail, thrust it at sunset into a hollow tree, and stop up the hole with clay. Then as the snail perishes the child recovers. But this cure must be accompanied by the recitation of a proper form of words; otherwise it has no effect.[4] A Bohemian remedy for jaundice is as follows. Take a living tench, tie it to your bare back and carry it about with you for a whole day. The tench will turn quite yellow and die. Then throw it into running water, and your jaundice will depart with it.[5] In the village of Llandegla in Wales there is a church dedicated to the virgin martyr St. Tecla, where the falling sickness is, or used to be, cured by being transferred to a fowl. The patient first washed his limbs in a sacred well hard by, dropped fourpence into it as an offering, walked thrice round the well, and thrice repeated the Lord's prayer. Then the fowl, which was a cock or a hen according as the patient was a man or a woman, was put into a basket and carried round first the well and afterwards the church. Next the sufferer entered the church and lay down under

---

slightly different translation of the verse is given by H. Grassmann, who here follows R. Roth (*Rig-veda übersetzt*, vol. ii. p. 379). Compare *Hymns of the Rigveda*, translated by R. T. H. Griffith (Benares, 1889-1892), iv. 312.

[1] L. Strackerjan, *op. cit.* i. **72**, § 87.

[2] W. Henderson, *Folk-lore of the Northern Counties* (London, 1879), p. 143.

[3] J. D. H. Temme, *Die Volkssagen der Altmark* (Berlin, 1839), p. 83; A. Kuhn, *Märkische Sagen und Märchen* (Berlin, 1843), p. 384, § 62.

[4] R. Wuttke, *Sächsische Volkskunde*[2] (Dresden, 1901), p. 372.

[5] J. V. Grohmann, *op. cit.* p. 230, § 1663. A similar remedy is prescribed in Bavaria. See G. Lammert, *Volksmedizin und medizinischer Aberglaube in Bayern* (Würzburg, 1869), p. 249.

the communion table till break of day. After that he offered sixpence and departed, leaving the fowl in the church. If the bird died, the sickness was supposed to have been transferred to it from the man or woman, who was now rid of the disorder. As late as 1855 the old parish clerk of the village remembered quite well to have seen the birds staggering about from the effects of the fits which had been transferred to them.[1] In South Glamorgan and West Pembrokeshire it is thought possible to get rid of warts by means of a snail. You take a snail with a black shell, you rub it on each wart and say,

> " *Wart, wart, on the snail's shell black,*
> *Go away soon, and never come back.*"

Then you put the snail on the branch of a tree or bramble and you nail it down with as many thorns as you have warts. When the snail has rotted away on the bough, your warts will have vanished. Another Welsh cure for warts is to impale a frog on a stick and then to rub the warts on the creature. The warts disappear as the frog expires.[2] In both these cases we may assume that the warts are transferred from the human sufferer to the suffering animal.

Often the sufferer seeks to shift his burden of sickness or ill-luck to some inanimate object. In Athens there is a little chapel of St. John the Baptist built against an ancient column. Fever patients resort thither, and by attaching a waxed thread to the inner side of the column believe that they transfer the fever from themselves to the pillar.[3] In the Mark of Brandenburg they say that if you suffer from giddiness you should strip yourself naked and run thrice round a flax-field after sunset ; in that way the flax will get the giddiness and you will be rid of it.[4] Sometimes an attempt is made to transfer the mischief, whatever it may be, to the moon. In Oldenburg a peasant related how he rid himself of a bony excrescence by stroking it thrice crosswise in the name of the Trinity, and then making a gesture as if

Sickness and ill-luck transferred to inanimate objects.

[1] J. Brand, *Popular Antiquities*, ii. 375 ; W. G. Black, *Folk-medicine*, p. 46.

[2] Marie Trevelyan, *Folk-lore and Folk-stories of Wales* (London, 1909),

pp. 229 *sq.*

[3] B. Schmidt, *Das Volksleben der Neugriechen* (Leipsic, 1871), p. 82.

[4] A. Kuhn, *Märkische Sagen und Märchen* (Berlin, 1843), p. 386.

he were seizing the deformity and hurling it towards the moon. In the same part of Germany a cure for warts is to stand in the light of a waxing moon so that you cannot see your own shadow, then hold the disfigured hand towards the moon, and stroke it with the other hand in the direction of the luminary. Some say that in doing this you should pronounce these words, " Moon, free me from these vermin." [1]

Sickness and trouble transferred to trees and bushes. But perhaps the thing most commonly employed in Europe as a receptacle for sickness and trouble of all sorts is a tree or bush. The modes of transferring the mischief to it are many. For example, the Esthonians say that you ought not to go out of the house on a spring morning before you have eaten or drunk; for if you do, you may chance to hear one of "the sounds which are not heard in winter," such as the song of a bird, and that would be unlucky. They think that if you thus let yourself be deceived or outwitted, as they call it, by a bird, you will be visited by all sorts of ill-luck during the year; indeed it may very well happen that you will fall sick and die before another spring comes round. However, there is a way of averting the evil. You have merely to embrace a tree or go thrice round it, biting into the bark each time or tearing away a strip of the bark with your teeth. Thus the bad luck passes from you to the tree, which accordingly withers away.[2] In Sicily it is believed that all kinds of marvellous cures can be effected on the night which precedes Ascension Day. For example, people who suffer from goitre bite the bark of a peach-tree just at the moment when the clocks are striking midnight. Thus the malady is transferred to the sap of the tree, and its leaves wither away in exact proportion as the patient recovers. But in order that the cure may be successful it is absolutely essential that the bark should be bitten at midnight precisely; a bite before or after that witching hour is labour thrown away.[3] On St. George's Day, South Slavonian lads and lasses

---

[1] L. Strackerjan, *Aberglaube und Sagen aus dem Herzogthum Oldenburg* (Oldenburg, 1867), i. 74, § 91.

[2] F. J. Wiedemann, *Aus dem inneren und äussern Leben der Ehsten*

(St. Petersburg, 1876), pp. 451 *sq.*

[3] *Le Tour du Monde*, lxvii. (1894) p. 308 ; *id.*, Nouvelle Série, v. (1899) p. 521.

climb thrice up and down a cornel-tree, saying, " My laziness and sleepiness to you, cornel-tree, but health and booty (?) to me." Then as they wend homewards they turn once more towards the tree and call out, " Cornel-tree ! cornel tree ! I leave you my laziness and sleepiness."[1] The same people attempt to cure fever by transferring it to a dwarf elder-bush. Having found such a bush with three shoots springing from the root, the patient grasps the points of the three shoots in his hand, bends them down to the ground, and fastens them there with a stone. Under the arch thus formed he creeps thrice ; then he cuts off or digs up the three shoots, saying, " In three shoots I cut three sicknesses out. When these three shoots grow young again, may the fever come back."[2] A Bulgarian cure for fever is to run thrice round a willow-tree at sunrise, crying, " The fever shall shake thee, and the sun shall warm me."[3] In the Greek island of Karpathos the priest ties a red thread round the neck of a sick person. Next morning the friends of the patient remove the thread and go out to the hillside, where they tie the thread to a tree, thinking that they thus transfer the sickness to the tree.[4] Italians attempt to cure fever in like manner by fastening it to a tree. The sufferer ties a thread round his left wrist at night, and hangs the thread on a tree next morning. The fever is thus believed to be tied up to the tree, and the patient to be rid of it ; but he must be careful not to pass by that tree again, otherwise the fever would break loose from its bonds and attack him afresh.[5] An old French remedy for fever was to bind the patient himself to a tree and leave him there for a time ; some said that the ceremony should be performed fasting and early in the morning, that the cord or straw rope with which the person was bound to the tree should be left there to rot, and that the sufferer should bite the bark of the tree before returning home.[6] In Bohemia the friends of a fever patient will sometimes carry him head

[1] F. S. Krauss, *Volksglaube und religiöser Brauch der Südslaven* (Münster i. W., 1890), pp. 35 *sq.*

[2] F. S. Krauss, *op. cit.* p. 39.

[3] A. Strausz, *Die Bulgaren* (Leipsic, 1898), p. 400, compare p. 401.

[4] *Blackwood's Magazine*, February 1886, p. 239.

[5] Z. Zanetti, *La medicina delle nostre donne* (Città di Castello, 1892), p. 73.

[6] J. B. Thiers, *Traité des Superstitions* (Paris, 1679), pp. 323 *sq.*

foremost, by means of straw ropes, to a bush, on which they dump him down. Then he must jump up and run home. The friends who carried him also flee, leaving the straw ropes and likewise the fever behind them on the bush.[1]

Sickness transferred to trees by means of knots.

Sometimes the sickness is transferred to the tree by making a knot in one of its boughs. Thus in Mecklenburg a remedy for fever is to go before sunrise to a willow-tree and tie as many knots in one of its branches as the fever has lasted days; but going and coming you must be careful not to speak a word.[2] A Flemish cure for the ague is to go early in the morning to an old willow, tie three knots in one of its branches, say, "Good-morrow, Old One, I give thee the cold; good-morrow, Old One," then turn and run away without looking round.[3] In Rhenish Bavaria the cure for gout is similar. The patient recites a spell or prayer while he stands at a willow-bush holding one of its boughs. When the mystic words have been spoken, he ties a knot in the bough and departs cured. But all his life long he must never go near that willow-bush again, or the gout will come back to him.[4] In Sonnenberg, if you would rid yourself of gout you should go to a young fir-tree and tie a knot in one of its twigs, saying, "God greet thee, noble fir. I bring thee my gout. Here will I tie a knot and bind my gout into it. In the name," etc.[5] Not far from Marburg, at a place called Neuhof, there is a wood of birches. Thither on a morning before sunrise, in the last quarter of the moon, bands of gouty people may often be seen hobbling in silence. Each of them takes his stand before a separate tree and pronounces these solemn words: " Here stand I before the judgment bar of God and tie up all my gout. All the disease in my body shall remain tied up in this birch-tree." Meanwhile the good physician ties a

---

[1] J. V. Grohmann, *Aberglauben und Gebräuche aus Böhmen und Mähren* (Prague and Leipsic, 1864), p. 167, § 1178. A Belgian cure of the same sort is reported by J. W. Wolf (*Beiträge zur deutschen Mythologie* (Göttingen, 1852–1857, i. 223 (wrongly numbered 219), § 256).

[2] L. Strackerjan, *Aberglaube und Sagen aus dem Herzogthum Oldenburg* (Oldenburg, 1867), i. 74, § 90.

[3] J. Grimm, *Deutsche Mythologie*[4] (Berlin, 1875–1878), ii. 979.

[4] *Bavaria, Landes- und Volkskunde des Königreichs Bayern*, iv. 2 (Munich, 1867), p. 406.

[5] A. Schleicher, *Volkstümliches aus Sonnenberg* (Weimar, 1858), p. 150; A. Witschel, *Sagen, Sitten und Gebräuche aus Thüringen* (Vienna, 1878), p. 283, § 82.

knot in a birch-twig, repeating thrice, " In the name of the Father," etc.[1]

Another way of transferring gout from a man to a tree is this. Pare the nails of the sufferer's fingers and clip some hairs from his legs. Bore a hole in an oak, stuff the nails and hair in the hole, stop up the hole again, and smear it with cow's dung. If, for three months thereafter, the patient is free of gout, you may be sure the oak has it in his stead.[2] A German cure for toothache is to bore a hole in a tree and cram some of the sufferer's hair into it.[3] In these cases, though no doubt the tree suffers the pangs of gout or toothache respectively, it does so with a sort of stoical equanimity, giving no outward and visible sign of the pains that rack it inwardly. It is not always so, however. The tree cannot invariably suppress every symptom of its suffering. It may hide its toothache, but it cannot so easily hide its warts. In Cheshire if you would be rid of warts, you have only to rub them with a piece of bacon, cut a slit in the bark of an ash-tree, and slip the bacon under the bark. Soon the warts will disappear from your hand, only however to reappear in the shape of rough excrescences or knobs on the bark of the tree.[4] Again in Beauce and Perche, two provinces of France, fever may be transferred to a young aspen by inserting the parings of the patient's nails in the tree and then plastering up the hole to prevent the fever from getting out. But the operation must be performed by night.[5] How subject an aspen is to fever must be obvious to the meanest capacity from the trembling of its leaves in every breath of wind ; nothing therefore can be easier or more natural than to transfer the malady, with its fits of shaking, to the tree. At Berkhampstead, in Hertfordshire, there used to be certain oak-trees which were long celebrated for the cure of ague. The transference of the malady to the tree was simple but painful. A lock of the sufferer's hair was

Sickness transferred to trees by means of the patient's hair or nails.

---

[1] W. Kolbe, *Hessische Volks-Sitten und -Gebrauche*[2] (Marburg, 1888), pp. 88 *sq.*

[2] C. Meyer, *Der Aberglaube des Mittelalters* (Bâle, 1884), p. 104.

[3] H. Zahler, *Die Krankheit im Volksglauben des Simmenthals* (Bern, 1898), p. 94.

[4] W. G. Black, *Folk-medicine*, p. 38.

[5] F. Chapiseau, *Le Folk-lore de la Beauce et du Perche* (Paris, 1902), i. 213.

pegged into an oak ; then by a sudden wrench he left his hair and his ague behind him in the tree.[1]

It seems clear that, though you may stow away your pain or sickness in a tree, there is a considerable risk of its coming out again. To obviate this danger common prudence suggests that you should plug or bung up the hole as tight as you can. And this, as we should naturally expect, is often done. A German cure for toothache or headache is to wrap some of the sufferer's cut hair and nails in paper, make a hole in the tree, stuff the parcel into it, and stop up the hole with a plug made from a tree which has been struck by lightning.[2] In Bohemia they say that, if you feel the fever coming on, you should pull out some of your hair, tear off a strip of a garment you are wearing, and bore a hole in a willow-tree. Having done so, you put the hair and the rag in the hole and stop it up with a wedge of hawthorn. Then go home without looking back, and if a voice calls to you, be sure not to answer. When you have complied with this prescription, the fever will cease.[3] In Oldenburg a common remedy for fever is to bore a hole in a tree, breathe thrice into the hole, and then plug it up. Once a man who had thus shut up his fever in a tree was jeered at by a sceptical acquaintance for his credulity. So he went secretly to the tree and drew the stopper, and out came that fever and attacked the sceptic.[4] Sometimes they say that the tree into which you thus breathe your fever or ague should be a hollow willow, and that in going to the tree you should be careful not to utter a word, and not to cross water.[5] Again, we read of a man who suffered acute pains in his arm. So " they beat up red corals with oaken leaves, and having kept them on the part affected till suppuration, they did in the morning put this mixture into an hole bored with an auger in the root of an oak, respecting the east, and stop up this hole with a peg made of the same tree ; from thenceforth the pain did altogether cease, and when they took out the

[1] W. G. Black, *Folk-medicine*, p. 39.

[2] A. Wuttke, *Der deutsche Volks-aberglaube*[2] (Berlin, 1869), p. 310, § 490.

[3] J. V. Grohmann, *Aberglauben und Gebräuche aus Böhmen und Mähren*, p.

165, § 1160.

[4] L. Strackerjan, *Aberglaube und Sagen aus dem Herzogthum Oldenburg*, ii. 74 *sq.*, § 89.

[5] J. Grimm, *Deutsche Mythologie*,[4] ii. 979.

amulet immediately the torments returned sharper than before." [1]   These facts seem to put it beyond the reach of reasonable doubt that the pain or malady is actually in the tree and waiting to pop out, if only it gets the chance.

§ 6. *The Nailing of Evils*

Often the patient, without troubling to bore a hole in the tree, merely knocks a wedge, a peg, or a nail into it, believing that he thus pegs or nails the sickness or pain into the wood.   Thus a Bohemian cure for fever is to go to a tree and hammer a wedge into it with the words " There, I knock you in, that you may come no more out to me." [2]   A German way of getting rid of toothache is to go in silence before sunrise to a tree, especially a willow-tree, make a slit in the bark on the north side of the tree, or on the side that looks towards the sunrise, cut out a splinter from the place thus laid bare, poke the splinter into the aching tooth till blood comes, then put back the splinter in the tree, fold down the bark over it, and tie a string round the trunk, that the splinter may grow into the trunk as before.   As it does so, your pain will vanish ; but you must be careful not to go near the tree afterwards, or you will get the toothache again. And any one who pulls the splinter out will also get the toothache.   He has in fact uncorked the toothache which was safely bottled up in the tree, and he must take the natural consequence of his rash act.[3]   A simpler plan, practised in Persia as well as in France and Germany, is merely to scrape the aching tooth with a nail or a twig till it bleeds, and then hammer the nail or the twig into a tree. In the Vosges, in Voigtland, and probably elsewhere, it is believed that any person who should draw out such a nail or twig would get the toothache.[4]   An old lime-tree at

Marginal note: Sickness and pain pegged or nailed into trees.

[1] T. J. Pettigrew, *On Superstitions connected with the History and Practice of Medicine and Surgery* (London, 1844), p. 77 ; W. G. Black, *Folk-medicine*, p. 37.

[2] J. V. Grohmann, *Aberglauben und Gebräuche aus Böhmen und Mähren*, p. 167, § 1182.

[3] L. Strackerjan, *Aberglaube und Sagen aus dem Herzogthum Oldenburg*, i. 73, § 89 ; A. Wuttke, *Der deutsche Volksaberglaube*,[2] pp. 309 *sq.*, § 490.

[4] L. F. Sauvé, *Le Folk-lore des Hautes-Vosges* (Paris, 1889), p. 40 ; A. Meyrac, *Traditions, Coutumes, Légendes et Contes des Ardennes* (Charleville, 1890), p. 174 ; A. Schleicher, *Volkstümliches aus Sonnen-*

Evessen, in Brunswick, is studded with nails of various shapes, including screw-nails, which have been driven into it by persons who suffered from aching teeth.[1] In the Mark of Brandenburg they say that the ceremony should be performed when the moon is on the wane, and that the bloody nail should be knocked, without a word being spoken, into the north side of an oak-tree, where the sun cannot shine on it; after that the person will have no more toothache so long as the tree remains standing.[2] Here it is plainly implied that the toothache is bottled up in the tree. If further proof were needed that in such cases the malady is actually transferred to the tree and stowed away in its trunk, it would be afforded by the belief that if the tree is cut down the toothache will return to the original sufferer.[3] Rupture as well as toothache can be nailed to an oak. For that purpose all that need be done is to take a coffin-nail and touch with it the injured part of the patient; then set the sufferer barefoot before an oak-tree, and knock the nail into the trunk above his head. That transfers the rupture to the tree, and that is why you may often see the boles of ancient oaks studded with nails.[4]

Such remedies are not confined to Europe. At Bilda in Algeria, there is a sacred old olive-tree, in which pilgrims, especially women, knock nails for the purpose of ridding themselves of their ailments and troubles.[5]

Ghosts and gods bunged up in India.

Again, the Majhwars, a Dravidian tribe in the hill country of South Mirzapur, believe that all disease is due to ghosts, but that ghosts, when they become troublesome, can be shut up in a certain tree, which grows on a little islet in a very deep pool of the Sukandar, a tributary of the Kanhar river. Accordingly, when the country is infested by ghosts, in other words when disease is raging, a

---

berg (Weimer, 1858), p. 149; J. A. E. Köhler, *Volksbrauch, Aberglauben, Sagen und andre alte Ueberlieferungen im Voigtlande* (Leipsic, 1867), p. 414; A. Witzschel, *Sagen, Sitten und Gebräuche aus Thüringen* (Vienna, 1878), p. 283, § 79; H. Zahler, *Die Krankheit im Volksglauben des Simmenthals* (Bern, 1898), p. 93.

[1] R. Andree, *Braunschweiger Volks-*

kunde (Brunswick, 1896), p. 307.

[2] A. Kuhn, *Märkische Sagen und Märchen* (Berlin, 1843), p. 384, § 66.

[3] H. Zahler, *loc. cit.*

[4] P. Wagler, *Die Eiche in alter und neuer Zeit*, i. (Wurzen, N.D.) p. 23.

[5] E. Doutté, *Magie et Religion dans l'Afrique du Nord* (Algiers, 1908), p. 436.

skilful wizard seeks for a piece of deer-horn in the jungle. When he has found it, he hammers it with a stone into the tree and thus shuts up the ghost. The tree is covered with hundreds of such pieces of horn.[1] Again, when a new settlement is being made in some parts of the North-Western Provinces of India, it is deemed necessary to apprehend and lay by the heels the local deities, who might otherwise do a deal of mischief to the intruders on their domain. A sorcerer is called in to do the business. For days he marches about the place mustering the gods to the tuck of drum. When they are all assembled, two men known as the Earthman and the Leafman, who represent the gods of the earth and of the trees respectively, become full of the spirit, being taken possession of bodily by the local deities. In this exalted state they shout and caper about in a fine frenzy, and their seemingly disjointed ejaculations, which are really the divine voice speaking through them, are interpreted by the sorcerer. When the critical moment has come, the wizard rushes in between the two incarnations of divinity, clutches at the spirits which are hovering about them in the air, and pours grains of sesame through their hands into a perforated piece of the wood of the sacred fig-tree. Then without a moment's delay he plasters up the hole with a mixture of clay and cow-dung, and carefully buries the piece of wood on the spot which is to be the shrine of the local deities. Needless to say that the gods themselves are bunged up in the wood and are quite incapable of doing further mischief, provided always that the usual offerings are made to them at the shrine where they live in durance vile.[2] In this case the source of mischief is imprisoned, not in a tree, but in a piece of one ; but the principle is clearly the same. Similarly in Corea an English lady observed at a cross-road a small log with several holes like those of a mouse-trap, one of which was plugged up doubly with bungs of wood. She was told that a demon, whose ravages spread

Demon plugged up and ghost nailed down.

---

[1] W. Crooke, *The Tribes and Castes of the North-Western Provinces and Oudh* (Calcutta, 1896), iii. 436 *sq.* ; compare *id.*, *Popular Religion and Folk-lore of Northern India* (Westminster, 1896), i. 43, 162. Compare E. Thurston, *Ethnographic Notes in Southern India* (Madras, 1906), pp. 313, 331.

[2] W. Crooke, *Popular Religion and Folk-lore of Northern India* (Westminster, 1896), i. 102 *sq.*

sickness in a family, had been inveigled by a sorceress into that hole and securely bunged up. It was thought proper for all passers-by to step over the incarcerated devil, whether to express their scorn and abhorrence of him, or more probably as a means of keeping him forcibly down.[1] In Cochinchina a troublesome ghost can be confined to the grave by the simple process of knocking a nail or thrusting a bar of iron into the earth at the point where the head of the corpse may be presumed to repose.[2]

<small>Evils nailed into stones, walls, door-posts, and so on.</small>
    From knocking the mischief into a tree or a log it is only a step to knocking it into a stone, a door-post, a wall, or such like. At the head of Glen Mor, near Port Charlotte, in Islay, there may be seen a large boulder, and it is said that whoever drives a nail into this stone will thereafter be secure from attacks of toothache. A farmer in Islay told an enquirer some years ago how a passing stranger once cured his grandmother of toothache by driving a horse-nail into the lintel of the kitchen door, warning her at the same time to keep the nail there, and if it should come loose just to tap it with a hammer till it had a grip again. She had no more toothache for the rest of her life.[3] In Brunswick it is open to any one to nail his toothache either into a wall or into a tree, as he thinks fit; the pain is cured quite as well in the one way as in the other.[4] So in Beauce and Perche a healer has been known to place a new nail on the aching tooth of a sufferer and then knock the nail into a door, a beam, or a joist.[5] The procedure in North Africa is similar. You write certain Arabic letters and numbers on the wall; then, while the patient puts a finger on the aching tooth, you knock a nail, with a light tap of a hammer, into the first letter on the wall, reciting a verse of the Coran as you do so. Next you ask the sufferer whether the pain is now abated, and if he says " Yes " you draw out the nail entirely. But if he says " No," you shift the nail to the next letter in the wall, and so on, till the pain goes away, which it always

[1] Mrs. Bishop, *Korea and her Neighbours* (London, 1898), ii. 143 *sq.*

[2] P. Giran, *Magie et Religion Annamites* (Paris, 1912), pp. 132 *sq.*

[3] R. C. Maclagan, " Notes on folk-lore Objects collected in Argyleshire,"

Folk-lore, vi. (1895) p. 158.

[4] R. Andree, *Braunschweiger Volks-kunde* (Brunswick, 1896), p. 307.

[5] F. Chapiseau, *Le Folk-lore de la Beauce et du Perche* (Paris, 1902), i. 170.

does, sooner or later.[1]   A Bohemian who fears he is about
to have an attack of fever will snatch up the first thing that
comes to hand and nail it to the wall.   That keeps the
fever from him.[2]

As in Europe we nail toothache or fever to a wall, so
in Morocco they nail devils.   A house in Mogador having
been infested with devils, who threw stones about it in
a way that made life a burden to the inmates, a holy man
was called in to exorcise them, which he did effectually
by pronouncing an incantation and driving a nail into the
wall; at every stroke of the hammer a hissing sound
announced that another devil had received his quietus.[3]
Among the modern Arabs the soul of a murdered man must
be nailed down.   Thus if a man be murdered in Egypt, his
ghost will rise from the ground where his blood was shed:
but it can be prevented from doing so by driving a new nail,
which has never been used, into the earth at the spot where
the murder was committed.   In Tripoli the practice is
similar.   Some years ago a native was murdered close to
the door of a little Italian inn.   Immediately the Arabs of
the neighbourhood thronged thither and effectually laid the
ghost with hammer and nail.   When the innkeeper rashly
attempted to remove the nail, he was warned that to do so
would be to set the ghost free.[4]   In modern Egypt numbers
of people afflicted with headache used to knock a nail into
the great wooden door of the old south gate of Cairo, for the
purpose of charming away the pain; others who suffered
from toothache used to extract a tooth and insert it in a
crevice of the door, or fix it in some other way, in order to
be rid of toothache for the future.   A holy and miraculous
personage, invisible to mortal eyes, was supposed to have

Devils and ghosts nailed down in Morocco, Tunis, and Egypt.

Headache nailed into a door or a wall.

[1] E. Doutté, *Magie et Religion dans l'Afrique du Nord* (Algiers, 1908), pp. 228 *sq.*

[2] J. V. Grohmann, *Aberglauben und Gebräuche aus Böhmen und Mähren*, p. 116, § 1172.

[3] A. Leared, *Morocco and the Moors* (London, 1876), pp. 275 *sqq.*

[4] R. C. Thompson, *Semitic Magic* (London, 1908), p. 17.   It would seem

that in Macedonia demons and ghosts can be hammered into walls.   See G. F. Abbott, *Macedonian Folklore* (Cambridge, 1903), p. 221.   In Chittagong, as soon as a coffin has been carried out of the house, a nail is knocked into the threshold "to prevent death from entering the dwelling, at least for a time."   See Th. Bérengier, "Les funérailles à Chittagong," *Les Missions Catholiques*, xiii. (1881) p. 504.

one of his stations at this gate.[1] In Mosul also a
sheikh can cure headache by first laying his hands on the
sufferer's head and then hammering a nail into a wall.[2]

Plague pegged into a hole. Not far from Neuenkirchen, in Oldenburg, there is a farm-
house to which, while the Thirty Years' War was raging,
the plague came lounging along from the neighbouring town
in the shape of a bluish vapour. Entering the house it
popped into a hole in the door-post of one of the rooms.
The farmer saw his chance, and quick as thought he seized
a peg and hammered it into the hole, so that the plague
could not possibly get out. After a time, however, thinking
the danger was past, he drew out the peg. Alas! with the
peg came creeping and curling out of the hole the blue
vapour once more. The plague thus let loose seized on
every member of the family in that unhappy house and left
not one of them alive.[3] Again, the great plague which devas-
tated the ancient world in the reign of Marcus Antoninus is
said to have originated in the curiosity and greed of some
Roman soldiers, who, pillaging the city of Seleucia, came
upon a narrow hole in a temple and incautiously enlarged
the opening in the expectation of discovering treasure. But
that which came forth from the hole was not treasure but
the plague. It had been pent up in a secret chamber by
the magic art of the Chaldeans ; but now, released from its
prison by the rash act of the spoilers, it stalked abroad and
spread death and destruction from the Euphrates to the
Nile and the Atlantic.[4]

Plague nailed down in ancient Rome. The simple ceremony, in which to this day the superstition of European peasants sees a sovereign remedy for
plague and fever and toothache, has come down to us from
a remote antiquity ; for in days when as yet Paris and
London were not, when France still revered the Druids as
the masters of all knowledge, human and divine, and when
our own country was still covered with virgin forests, the
home of savage beasts and savage men, the same ceremony

[1] E. W. Lane, *Manners and Customs
of the Modern Egyptians* (Paisley and
London, 1895), ch. x. p. 240.

[2] R. C. Thompson, *Semitic Magic*
(London, 1908), p. 18.

[3] L. Strackerjan, *Aberglaube und*

Sagen aus dem Herzogthum Oldenburg,
ii. 120, § 428a. A similar story is
told of a house in Neuenburg (*op. cit.*
ii. 182, § 512c).

[4] Ammianus Marcellinus, xxiii. 6.
24.

was solemnly performed from time to time by the highest
magistrate at Rome, to stay the ravages of pestilence or re-
trieve disaster that threatened the foundations of the national
life.   In the fourth century before our era the city of Rome
was desolated by a great plague which raged for three years,
carrying off some of the highest dignitaries and a great
multitude of common folk.   The historian who records the
calamity informs us that when a banquet had been offered
to the gods in vain, and neither human counsels nor divine
help availed to mitigate the violence of the disease, it was
resolved for the first time in Roman history to institute
dramatical performances as an appropriate means of ap-
peasing the wrath of the celestial powers.   Accordingly
actors were fetched from Etruria, who danced certain simple
and decorous dances to the music of a flute.   But even this
novel spectacle failed to amuse or touch, to move to tears
or laughter the sullen gods.   The plague still raged, and at
the very moment when the actors were playing their best in
the circus beside the Tiber, the yellow river rose in angry
flood and drove players and spectators, wading and splash-
ing through the fast-deepening waters, away from the show.
It was clear that the gods spurned plays as well as prayers
and banquets ; and in the general consternation it was felt
that some more effectual measure should be taken to put an
end to the scourge.   Old men remembered that a plague
had once been stayed by the knocking of a nail into a wall ;
and accordingly the Senate resolved that now in their extremity, when all other means had failed, a supreme magistrate
should be appointed for the sole purpose of performing this
solemn ceremony.   The appointment was made, the nail was
knocked, and the plague ceased, sooner or later.[1]   What
better proof could be given of the saving virtue of a nail ?

Twice more within the same century the Roman people
had recourse to the same venerable ceremony as a cure for
public calamities with which the ordinary remedies, civil and
religious, seemed unable to cope.   One of these occasions
was a pestilence ;[2] the other was a strange mortality among

*Pestilence
and civil
discord
nailed into
a wall in
Rome.*

---

[1] Livy, vii. 1-3.   The plague raged
from 365 to 363 B.C., when it was
happily stayed in the manner described

in the text.

[2] Livy, ix. 28.   This happened in
the year 313 B.C.

the leading men, which public opinion traced, rightly or wrongly, to a series of nefarious crimes perpetrated by noble matrons, who took their husbands off by poison. The crimes, real or imaginary, were set down to frenzy, and nothing could be thought of so likely to minister to minds diseased as the knocking of a nail into a wall. Search among the annals of the city proved that in a season of civil discord, when the state had been rent by party feud, the same time-honoured remedy, the same soothing balm, had been applied with the happiest results to the jarring interests and heated passions of the disputants. Accordingly the old nostrum was tried once more, and again success appeared to justify the experiment.[1]

The annual ceremony of knocking in a nail at Rome.

If the Romans in the fourth century before Christ thus deemed it possible to rid themselves of pestilence, frenzy, and sedition by hammering them into a wall, even as French and German peasants still rid themselves of fever and tooth-ache by knocking them into a tree, their prudent ancestors appear to have determined that so salutary a measure should not be restricted in its scope to meeting special and urgent emergencies as they arose, but should regularly diffuse its benefits over the community by anticipating and, as it were, nipping in the bud evils which, left unchecked, might grow to dangerous proportions. This, we may conjecture, was the original intention of an ancient Roman law which ordained that the highest magistrate of the republic should knock in a nail every year on the thirteenth day of September. The law might be seen, couched in old-fashioned language, engraved on a tablet which was fastened to a wall of the temple of Capitoline Jupiter ; and although the place where the nails were driven in is nowhere definitely stated by classical writers, there are some grounds for thinking that it may have been the same wall on which the law that sanctioned the custom was exhibited. Livy tells us that the duty of affixing the nail, at one time discharged by the consuls, was afterwards committed to dictators, whose higher rank consorted better with the dignity and importance of the function. At a later time the custom fell into abeyance, and the ancient ceremony was revived only from time to time in

---

[1] Livy, viii. 18. These events took place in 331 B.C.

seasons of grave peril or extraordinary calamity, which
seemed to attest the displeasure of the gods at modern ways,
and disposed men to bethink them of ancestral lore and to
walk in the old paths.[1]

In antiquity the annual practice of hammering a nail
into a wall was not confined to Rome. It was observed also
at Vulsinii, in Etruria, where the nails thus fixed in the
temple of the goddess Nortia served as a convenient means
of recording and numbering the years.[2] To Roman antiquaries of a later period it seemed, naturally enough, that
such a practice had indeed no other object than that of
marking the flight of time in ages when writing was but
little used.[3] Yet a little reflection will probably convince us
that this, though it was doubtless a useful consequence of the
custom, can hardly have been its original intention. For it
will scarcely be disputed that the annual observance of the
custom cannot be wholly dissociated from its occasional
observance in seasons of great danger or calamity, and that
whatever explanation we give of the one ought to apply to
the other also. Now it is plain that if we start from the
annual observance and regard it as no more than a time-
keeper or mode of recording the years, we shall never reach
an adequate explanation of the occasional observance. If
the nails were merely ready reckoners of the years, how
could they come to be used as supreme remedies for pesti-

*The cere-
mony was
probably
a purifi-
catory rite
designed
to disarm
and disable
all evils
that might
threaten
the Roman
state in the
course of
the year.*

---

[1] Livy, vii. 3. Livy says nothing
as to the place where the nails were
affixed ; but from Festus (p. 56 ed.
C. O. Müller) we learn that it was the
wall of a temple, and as the date of the
ceremony was also the date of the dedi-
cation of the temple of Jupiter on the
Capitol (Plutarch, *Publicola*, 14), we
may fairly conjecture that this temple
was the scene of the rite. It is the
more necessary to call attention to the
uncertainty which exists on this point
because modern writers, perhaps mis-
understanding the words of Livy, have
commonly stated as a fact what is at
best only a more or less probable
hypothesis. Octavian seems to have
provided for the knocking of a nail
into the temple of Mars by men who
had held the office of censor. See

Dio Cassius, lv. 10, ἧλόν τε αὐτῷ ὑπὸ
τῶν τιμητευσάντων προσπήγνυσθαι.
[2] Livy, vii. 3. Festus speaks (p. 56
ed. C. O. Müller) of "the annual nail,
which was fixed in the walls of temples
for the purpose of numbering the
years," as if the practice were common.
From Cicero's passing reference to the
custom ("*Ex hoc die clavum anni
movebis*," *Epist. ad Atticum*, v. 15. 1)
we see that it was matter of notoriety.
Hence we may safely reject Mommsen's theory, which Mr. W. Warde
Fowler is disposed to accept (*The
Roman Festivals of the period of the
Republic*, London, 1899, pp. 234 *sq.*),
that the supposed annual custom never
existed except in the brains of Roman
Dryasdusts.
[3] See Livy and Festus, *ll.cc.*

lence, frenzy, and sedition, resorted to by the state in desperate emergencies when all the ordinary resources of policy and religion had failed ?   On the other hand, if we start from the occasional observance and view it, in accordance with modern analogies, as a rude attempt to dispose of intangible evils as if they were things that could be handled and put away out of sight, we can readily understand how such an attempt, from being made occasionally, might come to be repeated annually for the sake of wiping out all the old troubles and misfortunes of the past year and enabling the community to start afresh, unencumbered by a fardel of ills, at the beginning of a new year.   Fortunately we can shew that the analogy which is thus assumed to exist between the Roman custom and modern superstition is not a merely fanciful one ; in other words, it can be proved that the Romans, like modern clowns, did believe in the possibility of nailing down trouble, in a literal and physical sense, into a material substance.   Pliny tells us that an alleged cure for epilepsy, or the falling sickness, was to drive an iron nail into the ground on the spot which was first struck by the patient's head as he fell.[1]   In the light of the modern instances which have come before us, we can hardly doubt that the cure was supposed to consist in actually nailing the disease into the earth in such a way that it could not get up and attack the sufferer again. Precisely parallel is a Suffolk cure for ague.   You must go by night alone to a cross-road, and just as the clock strikes the midnight hour you must turn yourself about thrice and drive a tenpenny nail up to the head into the ground. Then walk away backwards from the spot before the clock is done striking twelve, and you will miss the ague ; but the next person who passes over the nail will catch the malady in your stead.[2]   Here it is plainly assumed that the ague of

Marginal note: Roman cure for epilepsy.

---

[1] Pliny, *Nat. Hist.* xxviii. 63.

[2] *County Folk-lore, Suffolk*, edited by Lady E. C. Gurdon (London, 1893), p. 14.   In the north - west Highlands of Scotland it used to be customary to bury a black cock alive on the spot where an epileptic patient fell down.   Along with the cock were buried parings of the patient's nails

and a lock of his hair.   See (Sir) Arthur Mitchell, *On various Superstitions in the North-West Highlands and Islands of Scotland* (Edinburgh, 1862), p. 26 ; J. G. Campbell, *Witchcraft and Second Sight in the Highlands and Islands of Scotland* (Glasgow, 1902), p. 97.   Probably the disease was supposed to be buried with the cock which the patient is relieved has been left by him nailed down into the earth at the cross-road, and we may fairly suppose that a similar assumption underlay the Roman cure for epilepsy.   Further, we seem to be now justified in holding that originally, when a Roman dictator sought to stay a plague, to restore concord, or to terminate an epidemic of madness by knocking a nail into a wall, he was doing for the commonwealth exactly what any private man might do for an epileptic patient by knocking a nail into the ground on the spot where his poor friend had collapsed.   In other words, he was hammering the plague, the discord, or the madness into a hole from which it could not get out to afflict the community again.[1]

Different in principle from the foregoing customs appears to be the Loango practice of sticking nails into wooden idols or fetishes.   The intention of knocking a nail into a worshipful image is said to be simply to attract the notice of the deity in a forcible manner to the request of his worshipper ; it is like pinching a man or running a pin into his leg as a hint that you desire to speak with him.   Hence in order to be quite sure of riveting the god's attention the nails are sometimes made red-hot.[2]   Even the most absent-minded deity could hardly overlook a petition urged in so importunate a fashion.   The practice is resorted to in many emergencies.   For example, when a man has been robbed, he will go and get a priest to

Knocking nails into idols as a means of attracting the attention of the deity or spirit.

---

in the ground. The ancient Hindoos imagined that epilepsy was caused by a dog-demon. When a boy fell down in a fit, his father or other competent person used to wrap the sufferer in a net, and carry him into the hall, not through the door, but through an opening made for the purpose in the roof.   Then taking up some earth in the middle of the hall, at the place where people gambled, he sprinkled the spot with water, cast dice on it, and laid the boy on his back on the dice.   After that he prayed to the dog-demon, saying, "Doggy, let him loose ! Reverence be to thee, barker, bender ! Doggy, let him loose ! Reverence be to thee, barker, bender !" See *The Grihya Sutras*, translated by H. Oldenberg, Part i. (Oxford, 1886) pp.

296 *sq.* ; *id.* Part ii. (Oxford, 1892) pp. 219 *sq.*, 286 *sq.* (*Sacred Books of the East*, vols. xxix. and xxx.). Apparently the place where people gambled was for some reason supposed to be a spot where an epileptic could divest himself most readily of his malady. But the connexion of thought is obscure.

[1] The analogy of the Roman custom to modern superstitious practices has been rightly pointed out by Mr. E. S. Hartland (*Folk-lore*, iv. (1893) pp. 457, 464 ; *Legend of Perseus*, ii. 188), but I am unable to accept his general explanation of these and some other practices as modes of communion with a divinity.

[2] A. Bastian, *Die deutsche Expedition an der Loango-Küste* (Jena, 1874–1875), ii. 176.

knock a nail into an idol.   The sharp pang naturally exasperates the deity and he seeks to wreak his wrath on the thief, who is the real occasion of his suffering.   So when the thief hears of what has been done, he brings back the stolen goods in fear and trembling.   Similarly a nail may be knocked into an idol for the purpose of making somebody fall ill; and if a sick man fancies that his illness is due to an enemy who has played him this trick, he will send to the priest of the idol and pay him to remove the nail.[1]   This mode of refreshing the memory and stimulating the activity of a supernatural being is not confined to the negroes of Loango; it is practised also by French Catholics, as we learn from Sir John Rhys.   "Some years ago," he writes, "when I was on a visit at the late Ernest Renan's house at Rosmapamon, near Perros-Guirec on the north coast of Brittany, our genial host took his friends one day to see some of the sights of that neighbourhood.   Among other things which he showed us was a statue of St. Guirec standing at the head of an open creek.   It was of wood, and altogether a very rude work of art, if such it might be called ; but what attracted our attention most was the fact that it had innumerable pins stuck into it.   We asked M. Renan what the pins meant, and his explanation was exceedingly quaint.   He said that when any young woman in the neighbourhood made up her mind that she should marry, she came there and asked the saint to provide her with a husband, and to do so without undue delay.   She had every confidence in the willingness and ability of the saint to oblige her, but she was haunted by the fear that he might be otherwise engaged and forget her request.   So she would stick pins into him, and thus goad him, as she fancied, to exert himself on her behalf.   This is

[1] A. Bastian, *op. cit.* ii. 175-178. Compare Father Campana, "Congo, Mission Catholique de Landana," *Les Missions Catholiques*, xxvii. (1895) p. 93 ; *Notes Analytiques sur les Collections Ethnographiques du Musée du Congo*, i. (Brussels, 1902-1906) pp. 153, 246 ; B. H. Mullen, "Fetishes from Landana, South-West Africa," *Man*, v. (1905) pp. 102-104 ; R. E. Dennett, "Bavili Notes," *Folk-lore*, xvi. (1905) pp. 382 *sqq.* ; *id.*, At the

Back of the Black Man's Mind (London, 1906), pp. 85 *sqq.*, 91 *sqq.* The Ethnological Museum at Berlin possesses a number of rude images from Loango and Congo, which are thickly studded with nails hammered into their bodies.   The intention of the custom, as explained to me by Professor von Luschan, is to pain the fetish and so to refresh his memory, lest he should forget to do his duty.

why the saint's statue was full of pins."[1]   Similarly in Japan sufferers from toothache sometimes stick needles into a willow-tree, "believing that the pain caused to the tree-spirit will force it to exercise its power to cure."[2]

Thus it would seem that we must distinguish at least two uses of nails or pins in their application to spirits and spiritual influences.   In one set of cases the nails act as corks or bungs to bottle up and imprison a troublesome spirit ; in the other set of cases they act as spurs or goads to refresh his memory and stimulate his activity.   But so far as the evidence which I have cited allows us to judge, the use of nails as spiritual bungs appears to be commoner than their use as mental refreshers.

Two different spiritual applications of nails or pins.

---

[1] Sir John Rhys, "Celtae and Galli," *Proceedings of the British Academy*, ii. (1905–1906) pp. 114 *sq.*

[2] Lafcadio Hearn, *Glimpses of Unfamiliar Japan* (London, 1894), ii. 598 *sq.*, note.

CHAPTER II

THE OMNIPRESENCE OF DEMONS

Attempts to get rid of the accumulated sorrows of a whole people.

IN the foregoing chapter the primitive principle of the transference of ills to another person, animal, or thing was explained and illustrated. A consideration of the means taken, in accordance with this principle, to rid individuals of their troubles and distresses led us to believe that at Rome similar means had been adopted to free the whole community, at a single blow of the hammer, from diverse evils that afflicted it. I now propose to shew that such attempts to dismiss at once the accumulated sorrows of a people are by no means rare or exceptional, but that on the contrary they have been made in many lands, and that from being occasional they tend to become periodic and annual.

Sorrows conceived of as the work of demons.

It needs some effort on our part to realise the frame of mind which prompts these attempts. Bred in a philosophy which strips nature of personality and reduces it to the unknown cause of an orderly series of impressions on our senses, we find it hard to put ourselves in the place of the savage, to whom the same impressions appear in the guise of spirits or the handiwork of spirits. For ages the army of spirits, once so near, has been receding further and further from us, banished by the magic wand of science from hearth and home, from ruined cell and ivied tower, from haunted glade and lonely mere, from the riven murky cloud that belches forth the lightning, and from those fairer clouds that pillow the silver moon or fret with flakes of burning red the golden eve. The spirits are gone even from their last stronghold in the sky, whose blue arch no longer passes, except with children, for the screen that hides from mortal eyes the glories of the celestial world. Only in poets' dreams or impassioned flights of oratory is it given to catch a glimpse of the last flutter of the standards of the retreating host, to hear the beat of their invisible wings, the sound of their mocking laughter, or the swell of angel music dying away in the distance. Far otherwise is it with the savage. To his imagination the world still teems with those motley beings whom a more sober philosophy has discarded. Fairies and goblins, ghosts and demons, still hover about him both waking and sleeping. They dog his footsteps, dazzle his senses, enter into him, harass and deceive and torment him in a thousand freakish and mischievous ways. The mishaps that befall him, the losses he sustains, the pains he has to endure, he commonly sets down, if not to the magic of his enemies, to the spite or anger or caprice of the spirits. Their constant presence wearies him, their sleepless malignity exasperates him ; he longs with an unspeakable longing to be rid of them altogether, and from time to time, driven to bay, his patience utterly exhausted, he turns fiercely on his persecutors and makes a desperate effort to chase the whole pack of them from the land, to clear the air of their swarming multitudes, that he may breathe more freely and go on his way unmolested, at least for a time. Thus it comes about that the endeavour of primitive people to make a clean sweep of all their troubles generally takes the form of a grand hunting out and expulsion of devils or ghosts. They think that if they can only shake off these their accursed tormentors, they will make a fresh start in life, happy and innocent ; the tales of Eden and the old poetic golden age will come true again.

Hence, before we review some examples of these spirit-hunts, it may be well to adduce evidence of the deep hold which a belief in the omnipresence and malignity of spirits has upon the primitive mind. The reader will be better able to understand the savage remedy when he has an inkling of the nature of the evil which it is designed to combat. In citing the evidence I shall for the most part reproduce the exact words of my authorities lest I should incur the suspicion of deepening unduly the shadows in a gloomy picture.

Primitive belief in the omnipresence of demons.

Thus in regard to the aborigines of Australia we are
told that "the number of supernatural beings, feared if not
loved, that they acknowledge is exceedingly great; for not
only are the heavens peopled with such, but the whole face
of the country swarms with them; every thicket, most water-
ing-places, and all rocky places abound with evil spirits.
In like manner, every natural phenomenon is believed to be
the work of demons, none of which seem of a benign nature,
one and all apparently striving to do all imaginable mischief
to the poor blackfellow."[1] "The negro," says another writer,
"is wont to regard the whole world around him as peopled
with invisible beings, to whom he imputes every misfortune
that happens to him, and from whose harmful influence he
seeks to protect himself by all kinds of magic means."[2]
The Bantu negroes of Western Africa "regard their god as
the creator of man, plants, animals, and the earth, and they
hold that having made them, he takes no further interest in
the affair.   But not so the crowd of spirits with which the
universe is peopled, they take only too much interest, and
the Bantu wishes they would not and is perpetually saying
so in his prayers, a large percentage whereof amounts to,
'Go away, we don't want you.' 'Come not into this house,
this village, or its plantations.'"   Almost all these subordinate spirits are malevolent.[3]   A similar but fuller account of
the West African creed is given by a German writer, whose
statements apply particularly to the Ewe-speaking negroes
of the Slave Coast.   He says: "Thus the term fetishism
denotes the attitude of the Ewes, or of West African negro
tribes in general, towards magic; it forms one of the principal constituents of their religion.   The other main con-
stituent is their attitude to the gods, which is properly
demonolatry.   The Ewe names the gods *drowo*, that is,
intermediaries, namely, between a Supreme Being, whom he
calls *Mawu* ('the Unsurpassable'), and mankind.   The
drowo with whom the Ewe has to do, to whom his offerings

[1] A. Oldfield, "The Aborigines of
Australia," *Transactions of the Ethnological Society of London*, N.S., iii.
(1865) p. 228.
[2] J. Büttikoffer, "Einiges über die
Eingebornen von Liberia," *Interna-*

tionales Archiv für Ethnographie, i.
(1888) p. 85.

[3] Mary H. Kingsley, *Travels in
West Africa* (London, 1897) pp. 442
sq.

and his respects are paid, are thus subordinate deities, who
according to the etymological meaning of the word *dro* are
conceived as judging, composing disputes, and mediating
among men.   The existence of a Supreme Being is by no
means unfamiliar to the Ewe ; he has his *Mawu* often in
his mouth, especially in talking with the missionary, and he
willingly acknowledges that *Mawu* created him and the
gods.   But he can only conceive of this Supreme Being on
the analogy of his own personality and not as omnipresent and
so forth.   It is impossible that this Mawu can trouble himself
about details in the creation or even about every individual
man and his petty affairs ; what would be the use of the
many higher and lower spirits with which the world is filled
before his eyes ?   The West African perhaps conceives of
God as transcendant, but not as immanent; a creation he
possibly apprehends, but not an omnipresent government of
the world by the Supreme Being.   That government is
carried on by Mawu at a distance by means of the many
spirits or subordinate gods whom he has created for the
purpose. . . . A portion of the gods fills the air, wherefore
the forces and the phenomena of nature are deified as their
manifestations.   The elements are thought to be moved by
the gods of the air.   In the storm and the wind, in thunder
and lightning the Ewe sees the manifestation of particularly
powerful gods.   In the mysterious roll and roar of the deep
sea the Ewe, like the negro in general, beholds the sway of
a very mighty god or of a whole host of gods.   Further, the
earth itself is also the abode of a multitude of spirits or
gods, who have in it their sphere of activity.   They inhabit
certain great mountains, great hollow trees, caves, rivers, and
especially woods.   In such woods of the gods no timber
may be felled.   Thus the gods fill not only the air and the
sea, they also walk on earth, on all paths ; they lurk under
the trees, they terrify the lonely wayfarer, they disquiet and
plague even the sleeper.   When the negro rises from the
stool on which he has been sitting, he never fails to turn it
upside down, to prevent a spirit from sitting down on it. . . .
The spirit-world falls into two main classes: there are
good and kindly spirits, whose help is eagerly sought by
offerings ; but there are also gloomy and revengeful spirits,

whose approach and influence people eagerly endeavour to avert, and against whom all possible means are employed to ban them from the houses and villages. The people are much more zealous in their devotion to the evil spirits than in their devotion to the good. The reason is that the feeling of fear and the consciousness of guilt are much stronger than the emotions of love and gratitude for benefits received. Hence the worship of the false gods or spirits among this people, and among the West African negro tribes in general, is properly speaking a worship of demons or devils." [1]

Demons on the Congo.

Again, a missionary who spent fifteen years among the Boloki of the Upper Congo River tells us that "the religion of the Boloki has its basis in their fear of those numerous invisible spirits which surround them on every side, and are constantly trying to compass their sickness, misfortune and death ; and the Boloki's sole object in practising their religion is to cajole, or appease, cheat, or conquer and kill those spirits that trouble them—hence their *nganga* [medicine-men], their rites, their ceremonies and their charms. If there were no evil spirits to be circumvented there would be no need of their medicine men and their charms." [2] " The Boloki folk believe they are surrounded by spirits which try to thwart them at every twist and turn, and to harm them every hour of the day and night. The rivers and creeks are crowded with the spirits of their ancestors, and the forests and bush are full also of spirits, ever seeking to injure the living who are overtaken by night when travelling by road or canoe. I never met among them a man daring enough to go at night through the forest that divided Monsembe from the upper villages, even though a large reward was offered. Their invariable reply was : ' There

[1] G. Zündel, "Land und Volk der Eweer auf der Sclavenküste in Westafrika," *Zeitschrift der Gesellschaft für Erdkunde zu Berlin,* xii. (1877) pp. 412-414. Full details as to the religious creed of the Ewes, including their belief in a Supreme Being (*Mawu*), are given, to a great extent in the words of the natives themselves, by the German missionary Jakob Spieth in his elaborate and valuable works *Die Ewe-Stämme* (Berlin, 1906) and *Die Religion der Eweer in Süd-Togo* (Leipsic, 1911). As to *Mawu* in particular, the meaning of whose name is somewhat uncertain, see J. Spieth, *Die Ewe-Stämme,* pp. 421 *sqq.* ; *Die Religion der Eweer in Süd-Togo,* pp. 15 *sqq.*

[2] Rev. J. H. Weeks, "Anthropological Notes on the Bangala of the Upper Congo River," *Journal of the Royal Anthropological Institute,* xl. (1910) p. 377.

are too many spirits in the bush and forest.'"[1]   The spirits which these people dread so much are the *mingoli* or disembodied souls of the dead ; the life of the Boloki is described as " one long drawn out fear of what the *mingoli* may next do to them." These dangerous beings dwell everywhere, land and water are full of them ; they are ever ready to pounce on the living and carry them away or to smite them with disease and kill them. Though they are invisible to common eyes, the medicine-man can see them, and can cork them up in calabashes or cover them up with saucepans ; indeed, if it is made worth his while, he can even destroy them altogether.[2]   Again, of the Bantu tribes of South Africa we read that " nearer than the spirits of deceased chiefs or of their own ancestors was a whole host of hobgoblins, water sprites, and malevolent demons, who met the Bantu turn which way they would. There was no beautiful fairyland for them, for all the beings who haunted the mountains, the plains, and the rivers were ministers of evil. The most feared of these was a large bird that made love to women and incited those who returned its affection to cause the death of those who did not, and a little mis-

Demons in South Africa.

[1] Rev. John H. Weeks, *Among Congo Cannibals* (London, 1913), p. 261.

[2] Rev. J. H. Weeks, "Anthropological Notes on the Bangala of the Upper Congo River," *Journal of the Royal Anthropological Institute*, xl. (1910) pp. 368, 370. The singular form of *mingoli* is *mongoli*, " a disembodied spirit." Compare *id.*, *Among Congo Cannibals* (London, 1913), p. 252; and again *ibid.* p. 275. But great as is the fear of evil spirits among the natives of the Congo, their dread of witchcraft seems to be still more intense. See Rev. J. H. Weeks, "Notes on some Customs of the Lower Congo People," *Folk-lore*, xx. (1909) pp. 51 *sq.*: "The belief in witchcraft affects their lives in a vast number of ways, and touches them socially at a hundred different points. It regulates their actions, modifies their mode of thought and speech, controls their conduct towards each other, causes cruelty and callousness in a people not naturally cruel, and sets the various members of a family against each other. A man may believe any theory he likes about creation, about God, and about the abode of departed spirits, but he must believe in witches and their influence for evil, and must in unmistakable terms give expression to that belief, or be accused of witchcraft himself. . . . But for witchcraft no one would die, and the earnest longing of all right-minded men and women is to clear it out of the country by killing every discovered witch. It is an act of self-preservation. . . . Belief in witches is interwoven into the very fibre of every Bantu-speaking man and woman, and the person who does not believe in them is a monster, a witch, to be killed as soon as possible." Could we weigh against each other the two great terrors which beset the minds of savages all over the world, it seems probable that the dread of witches would be found far to outweigh the dread of evil spirits. However, it is the fear of evil spirits with which we are at present concerned.

chievous imp who was also amorously inclined. Many instances could be gathered from the records of magistrates' courts in recent years of demented women having admitted their acquaintance with these fabulous creatures, as well as of whole communities living in terror of them."[1] However, it would be no doubt a great mistake to imagine that the minds of the Bantu, or indeed of any savages, are perpetually occupied by a dread of evil spirits;[2] the savage and indeed the civilized man is incapable, at least in his normal state, of such excessive preoccupation with a single idea, which, if prolonged, could hardly fail to end in insanity.

Demons in South America.
Speaking of the spirits which the Indians of Guiana attribute to all objects in nature, Sir Everard F. im Thurn observes that "the whole world of the Indian swarms with these beings. If by a mighty mental effort we could for a moment revert to a similar mental position, we should find ourselves everywhere surrounded by a host of possibly hurtful beings, so many in number that to describe them as innumerable would fall ridiculously short of the truth. It is not therefore wonderful that the Indian fears to move beyond the light of his camp-fire after dark, or, if he is obliged to do so, carries a fire-brand with him that he may at least see among what enemies he walks; nor is it wonderful that occasionally the air round the settlement seems to the Indian to grow so full of beings, that a peaiman [sorcerer], who is supposed to have the power of temporarily driving them away, is employed to effect a general clearance of these beings, if only for a time. That is the main belief, of the kind that is generally called religious, of the Indians of Guiana."[3] The Lengua Indians of the Paraguayan Chaco believe in certain demons which they call *kilyikhama*. "The *kilyikhama* are confined to no particular

[1] G. McCall Theal, *Records of South-Eastern Africa*, vii. (1901) pp. 405 *sq.*

[2] On this subject Mr. Dudley Kidd has made some judicious observations (*Savage Childhood*, London, 1906, pp. 131 *sq.*). He says: "The Kafirs certainly do not live in everlasting dread of spirits, for the chief part of their life is not spent in thinking at all. A merrier set of people it would be hard to find. They are so easy-going that it would seem to them too much burden to be for ever thinking of spirits."

[3] (Sir) E. F. im Thurn, *Among the Indians of Guiana* (London, 1883), pp. 356 *sq.* As to the dread which the Brazilian Indians entertain of demons, see J. B. von Spix and C. F. Ph. von Martius, *Reise in Brasilien* (Munich, 1823–1831), iii. 1108-1111.

place. Time and distance do not seem to affect them in
the least. They are held in .great awe by the Indian, and
whithersoevèr he turns, whether by day or night, but particularly at night, he is subject to their malign influences.
. . . They live in constant dread of these supernatural beings,
and if nothing else contributed to make their life miserable,
this ever-present dread of the *kilyikhama* would be in itself
quite sufficient to rob it of most of its joy." [1]

Very different from the life of these Indians of the South
American forests and prairies is the life of the Esquimaux
on the desolate shores of Labrador; yet they too live in
like bondage to the evil creatures of their own imagination.
" All the affairs of life are supposed to be under the control
of spirits, each of which rules over a certain element, and all
of which are under the direction of a greater spirit. Each
person is supposed to be attended by a special guardian
who is malignant in character, ever ready to seize upon the
least occasion to work harm upon the individual whom it
accompanies. As this is an evil spirit, its good offices and
assistance can be obtained by propitiation only. The person
strives to keep the good-will of the evil spirit by offerings of
food, water, and clothing." " Besides this class of spirits,
there are the spirits of the sea, the land, the sky (for be it
understood that the Eskimo know nothing of the air), the
winds, the clouds, and everything in nature. Every cove of
the sea-shore, every point, island, and prominent rock has its
guardian spirit. All are of the malignant type, and to be
propitiated only by acceptable offerings from persons who
desire to visit the locality where it is supposed to reside.
Of course some of the spirits are more powerful than others,
and these are more to be dreaded than those able to inflict
less harm. These minor spirits are under the control of the
great spirit, whose name is Tung ak. This one great spirit
is more powerful than all the rest besides. The lesser spirits
are immediately under his control and ever ready to obey
his command. The shaman (or conjuror) alone is supposed
to be able to deal with the Tung ak. While the shaman
does not profess to be superior to the Tung ak, he is able to

Demons in Labrado

---

[1] W. Barbrooke Grubb, *An Unknown People in an Unknown Land* (London,
1911), pp. 118, 119.

enlist his assistance and thus be able to control all the undertakings his profession may call for.   This Tung ak is nothing more or less than death, which ever seeks to torment and harass the lives of people that their spirits may go to dwell with him."[1]

Demons in Polynesia.

Brighter at first sight and more pleasing is the mythology of the islanders of the Pacific, as the picture of it is drawn for us by one who seems to have felt the charm of those beliefs which it was his mission to destroy.   " By their rude mythology," he says, " each lovely island was made a sort of fairy-land, and the spells of enchantment were thrown over its varied scenes.   The sentiment of the poet that

> ' *Millions of spiritual creatures walk the earth,*
> *Unseen, both when we wake, and when we sleep,*'

was one familiar to their minds ; and it is impossible not to feel interested in a people who were accustomed to consider themselves surrounded by invisible intelligences, and who recognized in the rising sun—the mild and silver moon— the shooting star—the meteor's transient flame—the ocean's roar—the tempest's blast, or the evening breeze—the move- ments of mighty spirits.   The mountain's summit, and the fleecy mists that hang upon its brows—the rocky defile— the foaming cataract—and the lonely dell—were all regarded as the abode or resort of these invisible beings."[2]   Yet the spiritual powers which compassed the life of the islanders on every side appear to have been far from friendly to man. Speaking of their beliefs touching the souls of the dead, the same writer says that the Polynesians " imagined they lived in a world of spirits, which surrounded them night and day, watching every action of their lives, and ready to avenge the slightest neglect or the least disobedience to their injunc- tions, as proclaimed by their priests.   These dreaded beings were seldom thought to resort to the habitations of men on errands of benevolence."[3]   The Tahitians, when they were visited by Captain Cook, believed that " sudden deaths and all other accidents are effected by the immediate action of

---

[1] L. M. Turner, "Ethnology of the Ungava District, Hudson Bay Terri- tory," *Eleventh Annual Report of the Bureau of Ethnology* (Washington, 1894), pp. 193 *sq.*

[2] W. Ellis, *Polynesian Researches,* Second Edition (London, 1832–1836), i. 331.

[3] W. Ellis, *op. cit.* i. 406.

some divinity. If a man only stumble against a stone and hurt his toe, they impute it to an *Eatooa*; so that they may be literally said, agreeably to their system, to tread enchanted ground." [1] "The Maori gods," says a well-informed writer, "were demons, whose evil designs could only be counteracted by powerful spells and charms; these proving effectual, sacrifices and offerings were made to soothe the vanquished spirits and appease their wrath." "The gods in general appeared in the whirlwind and lightning, answering their votaries in the clap of thunder. The inferior beings made themselves visible in the form of lizards, moths, butterflies, spiders, and even flies; when they spoke it was in a low whistling tone. They were supposed to be so numerous as to surround the living in crowds, *kei te muia nga wairua penei nga wairoa,* 'the spirits throng like mosquitoes,' ever watching to inflict evil." [2]

Demons in New Zealand.

Again, we are informed that the popular religion of the Pelew Islanders "has reference to the gods (*kaliths*) who may be useful or harmful to men in all their doings. Their imagination peoples the sea, the wood, the earth with numerous gods, and whatever a man undertakes, be it to catch fish or fell a tree, he must first propitiate the deities, or rather guard himself against their spiteful anger, which can only be done by means of certain spells and incantations. The knowledge of these incantations is limited to a very few persons, and forms in fact the secret of the arts and industries which are plied in the islands. A master of his craft is not he who can build a good house or a faultless canoe, but he who possesses the *golay* or magic power to ban the tree-gods, that they may not prove hurtful to the workmen and to the people who afterwards use the things. All these gods of the earth, the woods, the mountains, the brooks are very mischievous and dangerous, and most diseases are caused by them. Hence the persons who possess the magic power are dreaded, frequently employed, and well paid; but in extreme cases they are regarded as sorcerers

Demons in the Pelew Islands.

[1] *The Voyages of Captain James Cook round the World* (London, 1809), vi. 152.
[2] R. Taylor, *Te Ika a Maui, or* New Zealand and its Inhabitants, Second Edition (London, 1870), p. 104.

and treated accordingly.   If one of them builds a house for somebody and is dissatisfied with his remuneration, he stirs up the tree-god to avenge him.   So the inhabitants of the house he has built fall sick, and if help is not forthcoming they die." [1]   Of the Mortlock Islanders we are told that " their imagination peopled the whole of nature with spirits and deities, of whom the number was past finding out." [2]

Demons in the Philippines.

Speaking of the natives of the Philippine Islands a writer observes that " the basis of all the superstitious beliefs of the Negritos, what might else be termed their religion, is the constant presence of the spirits of the dead near where they lived when alive.   All places are inhabited by the spirits.   All adverse circumstances, sickness, failure of crops, unsuccessful hunts, are attributed to them." [3]   As to the Melanesians of New Britain we read that " another deeply rooted belief which exercises an extraordinary influence on the life and customs of these people is a belief in demons.   To their thinking the demons, *tambaran* (a word synonymous with ' poor wretch,' ' sufferer ') are spirits entirely perverse, deceitful, maleficent, and ceaselessly occupied in injuring us. Diseases, death, the perturbations of nature, all unfortunate events are imputed to them.   The demons exist in legions ; they live everywhere, especially in the forests, desert places, and the depths of the sea." [4]   The beliefs and customs of one particular tribe of this great island—the Livuans, who occupy the eastern coast of the Gazelle Peninsula in New Britain—have been described by a Catholic missionary in similar terms.   " The distrustful natives," he tells us, " have not attained to a belief in a beneficent, compassionate deity. All the more numerous, however, are the evil spirits with which they people the universe.   These are legion.   The power which the natives ascribe to these spirits extends not merely to the property of mankind but also to life and death. The Livuan always believes that he can trace the pernicious

Demons in Melanesia.

[1] J. Kubary, "Die Religion der Pelauer," in A. Bastian's *Allerlei aus Volks- und Menschenkunde* (Berlin, 1888), i. 46.

[2] J. Kubary, " Die Bewohner der Mortlock-Inseln," *Mittheilungen der geographischen Gesellschaft in Hamburg*, 1878-79, p. 36.

[3] W. A. Reed, *Negritos of Zambales* (Manilla, 1904), p. 65 (*Ethnological Survey Publications*, vol. ii. Part i.).

[4] Mgr. Couppé, " En Nouvelle-Poméranie," *Les Missions Catholiques*, xxiii. (1891) pp. 355 *sq.*

influence of these *tambaran* (devils) on his actions.   In his conviction, the whole thoughts and endeavours of the evil spirits have no other object than to injure men in every possible way.   This dismal, comfortless superstition weighs heavy on the native."[1]   Again, another writer who lived for thirty years among the Melanesians of the Bismarck Archipelago, of which New Britain forms part, observes that " we often find the view expressed that the native is a being who lives only for the day, without cares of any kind. The view is very erroneous, for in fact he leads a life which is plagued by cares of all sorts.   Amongst the greatest plagues of his life is his bottomless superstition.   He sees himself surrounded at every step by evil spirits and their influences. He trusts nobody, for who knows whether his nearest neighbour, his professedly best friend, is not plotting to bring trouble, sickness, and even death on him by means of magic ? Everywhere he sees snares set for him, everywhere he scents treachery and guile.   We need not wonder, therefore, that mistrust is a leading feature in the character not only of the New Britons, but of the Melanesians generally. . . . The native is simply not accessible to rational motives.   The only motive he understands is sorcery on the part of malicious men or the influence of evil spirits."[2]

A Dutch missionary, who spent twenty-five years among the natives of Dutch New Guinea, tells us that "in their ignorance of a living God the Papuans people earth and air, land and sea with mysterious malignant powers, which take up their abode in stones and trees or in men and cause all kinds of misfortunes, especially sickness and death."[3] Again, speaking of the Bukaua, a tribe of German New Guinea, a German missionary writes that " the Bukaua knows himself to be surrounded by spirits (*balum*) at every step. An insight into the life and mode of thought of the natives,

Demons in Dutch New Guinea.

Demons in German New Guinea.

[1] P. A. Kleintitschen, *Die Küstenbewohner der Gazellehalbinsel* (Hiltrup bei Münster, preface dated 1906), pp. 336 *sq.* Compare Joachim Graf Pfeil, *Studien und Beobachtungen aus der Südsee* (Brunswick, 1899), p. 159 ; *id.*, in *Journal of the Anthropological Institute*, xxvii. (1898) pp. 183 *sq.*

[2] R. Parkinson, *Dreissig Jahre in der Südsee* (Stuttgart, 1907), pp. 120, 121.

[3] J. L. van Hasselt, " Die Papuastämme an der Geelvinkbai (Neuguinea)," *Mitteilungen der Geographischen Gesellschaft zu Jena*, ix. (1891) p. 98. As to Mr. van Hasselt's twenty-five years' residence among these savages, see *id.*, p. 22.

as the latter is expressed especially in their stories, confirms this view completely. What wonder that the fear of spirits dominates the whole existence of the Bukaua and causes him to tremble even in the hour of death? There are spirits of the beach, the water, the fields, the forests, spirits that reside in the villages and particular places, and a sort of vagabonds, who can take up their abode even in lifeless things." Then after describing the demons of the beach, the water, and the field, the writer proceeds as follows: "Of forest spirits the number is infinite; for it is above all in the mysterious darkness, the tangled wildernesses of the virgin forest that the spirits love to dwell. They hold their meetings in what are called evil places. They are never bent on good. Especially at nightfall the native fancies he hears the voice of the spirits in the hum and chirping of the insects in the forest. They lure hunting dogs from the trail. They make wild boars rabid; in the form of snakes they make inroads into human dwellings; they drive men crazy or into fits; they play roguish tricks of all sorts."[1]

Demons in British New Guinea.
Among the tribes who inhabit the south-eastern coasts of New Guinea "a death in a village is the occasion of bringing plenty of ghosts to escort their new companion, and perhaps fetch some one else. All night the friends of the deceased sit up and keep the drums going to drive away the spirits. When I was sleeping one night at Hood Bay, a party of young men and boys came round with sticks, striking the fences and posts of houses all through the village. This I found was always done when any one died, to drive back the spirits to their own quarters on the adjacent mountain tops. But it is the spirits of the inland tribes, the aborigines of the country, that the coast tribes most fear. The road from the interior to Port Moresby passed close to our house, and the natives told us that the barking of our English dog at night had frightened the evil spirits so effectually that they had had no ghostly visitors since we came. I was camping out one night in the bush with some coast natives, at a time when a number of the natives of the interior were hunting in the neighbourhood;

[1] Stefan Lehner, "Bukaua," in R. Neuhauss's *Deutsch Neu-Guinea*, iii. (Berlin, 1911) pp. 414-416.

noticing that the men with me did not go to sleep, I asked if they were afraid of the mountain men. ' No,' they replied, ' but the whole plain is full of the spirits who come with them.' All calamities are attributed to the power and malice of these evil spirits. Drought and famine, storm and flood, disease and death are all supposed to be brought by ' Vata ' and his hosts." [1]

The inhabitants of Timor, an island to the south-west of New Guinea, revere the lord of heaven, the sun, the mistress of the earth, and the spirits of the dead. " These last dwell, some with the mistress of the earth under ground, others on graves, others in stones and springs and woods, some on mountains and some in the habitations of their kinsfolk, where they take up their abode in the middle of the principal post of the house or in copper cymbals, in swords and pikes. Others again assume the shape of pigs and deer and bees ; men who have fallen in battle love especially to turn into bees, that they may roam over the earth at will. The ghosts who reside with the mistress of the earth are male and female, and their offspring swarm by myriads in the air, so that the people think you cannot stir without striking against one of them. According to their whim of the moment the ghosts are good or bad." " All diseases which are not due to infection or transmitted by inheritance are ascribed to the mistress of the earth, to the ghosts, and to their wicked offspring, who inflict them as punishments for insults and injuries, for insufficient food, for the killing of deer and of wild pigs, in which the ghosts take up their abode temporarily, and also for the sale of cymbals, swords and pikes, in which a ghost had settled." [2] The natives of Amboyna think that " woods, mountains, trees, stones, indeed the whole universe, is inhabited by a multitude of spirits, of whom many are the souls of the dead." [3] In Bolang Mongondo, a district of Celebes, " all calamities, great and small, of whatever kind, and by whatever name they are called, that befall men and animals, villages, gardens and so

Demons in Timor.

Demons in Celebes.

---

[1] W. G. Lawes, "Notes on New Guinea and its Inhabitants," *Proceedings of the Royal Geographical Society*, 1880, p. 615.

[2] J. G. F. Riedel, "Die Landschaft Dawan oder West-Timor," *Deutsche geographische Blätter*, x. 278 *sq.*

[3] G. W. W. C. Baron van Hoëvell, *Ambon en meer bepaaldelijk de Oeliasers* (Dordrecht, 1875), p. 148.

forth, are attributed to evil or angry spirits. The superstition is indescribably great. The smallest wound, the least indisposition, the most trifling adversity in the field, at the fishing, on a journey or what not, is believed by the natives to be traceable to the anger of their ancestors. The superstition cripples every effort to remedy the calamities except by sacrifice. There is perhaps no country the inhabitants of which know so little about simples as Bolang Mongondo. What a native of Bolang Mongondo calls medicine is nothing but sacrifice, magic, and talismans. And the method of curing a sick man always consists in the use of magic, or in the propitiation of angry ancestral spirits by means of offerings, or in the banishment of evil spirits. The application of one or other of these three methods depends again on the decision of the sorcerer, who plays a great part in every case of sickness." [1]

Demons in Bali and Java.

In the island of Bali "all the attention paid to the sick has its root solely in the excessive superstition of these islanders, which leads them to impute every unpleasantness in life, every adversity to the influence of evil spirits or of men who are in some way in league with them. The belief in witches and wizards is everywhere great in the Indies, but perhaps nowhere is it so universal and so strong as in Bali." [2] In Java, we are told, it is not merely great shady trees that are believed to be the abode of spirits. "In other places also, where the vital energy of nature manifests itself strikingly and impressively, a feeling of veneration is stirred, as on the sea-shore, in deep woods, on steep mountain sides. All such spots are supposed to be the abode of spirits of various kinds, whose mighty power is regarded with reverence and awe, whose anger is dreaded, and whose favour is hoped for. But wherever they dwell, whether in scenes of loveliness that move the heart, or in spots that affect the mind with fright and horror, the nature and disposition of these spirits appear not to differ. They are a source of fear and anxiety in the one case just as much as in the other. To none of them

[1] N. P. Wilken en J. A. Schwarz, "Het heidendom en de Islam in Bolaang Mongondou," *Mededeelingen van wege het Nederlandsche Zendeling-genootschap*, xi. (1867) p. 259.

[2] R. van Eck, "Schetsen van het eiland Bali," *Tijdschrift voor Nederlandsch Indië*, August, 1880, p. 83.

did I ever hear moral qualities ascribed. They are mighty, they are potentates, and therefore it is well with him who has their favour and ill with him who has it not ; this holds true of them all." " The number of the spirits is innumerable and inconceivable. All the phenomena of nature, which we trace to fixed laws and constant forces, are supposed by the Javanese to be wrought by spirits." [1]

The natives of the valley of the Barito in Borneo hold that " the air is filled with countless *hantoes* (spirits). Every object has such a spirit which watches over it and seeks to defend it from danger. It is these spirits especially that bring sickness and misfortune on men, and for that reason offerings are often made to them and also to the powerful *Sangsangs* (angels), whereas the supreme God, the original fountain of all good, is neglected." [2] Of the Battas or Bataks of Sumatra we are told that " the key-note of their religious mood is fear of the unknown powers, a childish feeling of dependence, the outcome of a belief in supernatural influences to which man is constantly exposed, in wonders and witchcraft, which hamper his free action. They feel themselves continually surrounded by unseen beings and dependent on them for everything." " Every misfortune bespeaks the ill-will of the hostile spirits. The whole world is a meeting-place of demons, and most of the phenomena of nature are an expression of their power. The only means of remedying or counteracting their baleful influence is to drive away the spirits by means of certain words, as well as by the use of amulets and the offering of sacrifices to the guardian spirits." [3] To the same effect another authority on the religion of the Battas remarks that " the common man has only a very dim and misty notion of his triune god, and troubles himself far more about the legions of spirits which people the whole world around him, and against which he must always be protected by

Demons in Borneo.

Demons in Sumatra.

[1] S. E. Harthoorn, "De Zending op Java en meer bepaald die van Malang," *Mededeelingen van wege het Nederlandsche Zendelinggenootschap,* iv. (1860) pp. 116 *sq.*

[2] C. A. L. M. Schwaner, *Borneo, Beschrijving van het stroomgebied van den Barito* (Amsterdam, 1853–54), i. 176.

[3] J. B. Neumann, "Het Pane- en Bila-stroomgebied," *Tijdschrift van het Nederlandsch Aardrijkskundig Genootschap,* Tweede Serie, iii. Afdeeling, meer uitgebreide artikelen, No. 2 (Amsterdam, 1886), p. 287.

magic spells." [1] Again, speaking of the same people, a Dutch missionary observes that " if there is still any adherent of Rousseau's superficial theories about the idyllically happy and careless life of people ' in a state of nature,' he ought to come and spend a little time among the Bataks and keep his eyes and ears open. He would soon be convinced of the hollowness and falsehood of these phrases and would learn to feel a deep compassion for human beings living in perpetual fear of evil spirits." [2]

Demons in the Nicobars.

The religion of the Nicobar Islanders " is an undisguised animism, and the whole of their very frequent and elaborate ceremonies and festivals are aimed at exorcising and scaring spirits (' devils,' as they have been taught to call them). Fear of spirits and ghosts (*iwi*) is the guide to all ceremonies, and the life of the people is *very* largely taken up with ceremonials and feasts of all kinds. These are usually held at night, and whether directly religious or merely convivial, seem all to have an origin in the overmastering fear of spirits that possesses the Nicobarese. It has so far proved ineradicable, for two centuries of varied and almost continuous missionary effort has had no appreciable effect on it." [3]

Demons in the Malay Peninsula.

The Mantras, an aboriginal race of the Malay Peninsula, " find or put a spirit everywhere, in the air they breathe, in the land they cultivate, in the forests they inhabit, in the trees they cut down, in the caves of the rocks. According to them, the demon is the cause of everything that turns out ill. If they are sick, a demon is at the bottom of it; if an accident happens, it is still the spirit who is at work; thereupon the demon takes the name of the particular evil of which he is supposed to be the cause. Hence the demon being assumed as the author of every ill, all their superstitions resolve themselves into enchantments and spells to

---

[1] B. Hagen, "Beiträge zur Kenntniss der Battareligion," *Tijdschrift voor Indische Taal- Land- en Volkenkunde*, xxviii. (1883) p. 508. The persons of the Batta Trinity are Bataraguru, Sori, and Balabulan. The most fundamental distinction between the persons of the Trinity appears to be that one of them is allowed to eat pork, while the others are not (*ibid.* p. 505).

[2] M. Joustra, "Het leven, de zeden en gewoonten der Bataks," *Mededeelingen van wege het Nederlandsche Zendelinggenootschap*, xlvi. (1902) p. 412.

[3] *The Census of India, 1901*, vol. iii. *The Andaman and Nicobar Islands*, by Lieut. - Colonel Sir Richard C. Temple (Calcutta, 1903), p. 206.

appease the evil spirit, to render mild and tractable the fiercest beasts." [1]   To the mind of the Kamtchatkan every corner of earth and heaven seemed full of spirits, whom he revered and dreaded more than God.[2]

Demons in Kamtchatka.

In India from the earliest times down to the present day the real religion of the common folk appears always to have been a belief in a vast multitude of spirits, of whom many, if not most, are mischievous and harmful.   As in Europe beneath a superficial layer of Christianity a faith in magic and witchcraft, in ghosts and goblins has always survived and even flourished among the weak and ignorant, so it has been and so it is in the East.   Brahmanism, Buddhism, Islam may come and go, but the belief in magic and demons remains unshaken through them all, and, if we may judge of the future from the past, is likely to survive the rise and fall of other historical religions.   For the great faiths of the world, just in so far as they are the outcome of superior intelligence, of purer morality, of extraordinary fervour of aspiration after the ideal, fail to touch and move the common man.   They make claims upon his intellect and his heart to which neither the one nor the other is capable of responding.   The philosophy they teach is too abstract, the morality they inculcate too exalted for him. The keener minds embrace the new philosophy, the more generous spirits are fired by the new morality ; and as the world is led by such men, their faith sooner or later becomes the professed faith of the multitude.   Yet with the common herd, who compose the great bulk of every people, the new religion is accepted only in outward show, because it is impressed upon them by their natural leaders whom they cannot choose but follow.   They yield a dull assent to it with their lips, but in their heart they never really abandon their old superstitions ; in these they cherish a faith such as they cannot repose in the creed which they nominally profess ; and to these, in the trials and emergencies of life, they have recourse as to infallible remedies,

Demons in India.

The high gods come and go, but demons remain.

[1] Borie, "Notice sur les Mantras, tribu sauvage de la péninsule Malaise," *Tijdschrift voor Indische Taal- Land- en Volkenkunde,* x. (1860) p. 434.

[2] S. Krascheninnikow, *Beschreibung des Landes Kamtschatka* (Lemgo, 1766), p. 215.

when the promises of the higher faith have failed them, as indeed such promises are apt to do.[1]

Demons in ancient India.

To establish for India in particular the truth of the propositions which I have just advanced, it may be enough to cite the evidence of two writers of high authority, one of whom deals with the most ancient form of Indian religion known to us, while the other describes the popular religion of the Hindoos at the present day. "According to the creed of the Vedic ages," says Professor Oldenberg, "the whole world in which man lives is animated. Sky and earth, mountain, forest, trees and beasts, the earthly water and the heavenly water of the clouds,—all is filled with living spiritual beings, who are either friendly or hostile to mankind. Unseen or embodied in visible form, hosts of spirits surround and hover about human habitations,— bestial or misshapen goblins, souls of dead friends and souls of foes, sometimes as kindly guardians, oftener as mischief-makers, bringing disease and misfortune, sucking the blood and strength of the living. A soul is attributed even to the object fashioned by human hands, whose functions are felt to be friendly or hostile. The warrior pays his devotion to the divine war-chariot, the divine arrow, the drum; the ploughman to the ploughshare; the gambler to the dice; the sacrificer, about whom naturally we have the most exact information, reveres the stone that presses out the juice of the Soma, the straw on which the gods recline, the post to which the sacrificial victim is bound, and the divine doors

---

[1] We may compare the instructive remarks made by Mr. W. E. Maxwell on the stratification of religious beliefs among the Malays ("The Folk-lore of the Malays," *Journal of the Straits Branch of the Royal Asiatic Society*, No. 7, June, 1881, pp. 11 *sq.*). He says: "Two successive religious changes have taken place among them, and when we have succeeded in identifying the vestiges of Brahmanism which underly the external forms of the faith of Muhammed, long established in all Malay kingdoms, we are only half-way through our task. There yet remain the powerful influences of the still earlier indigenous faith to be noted and accounted for. Just as the Buddhists of Ceylon turn, in times of sickness and danger, not to the consolations offered by the creed of Buddha, but to the propitiation of the demons feared and reverenced by their early progenitors, and just as the Burmese and Talaings, though Buddhists, retain in full force the whole of the *Nat* superstition, so among the Malays, in spite of centuries which have passed since the establishment of an alien worship, the Muhammedan peasant may be found invoking the protection of Hindu gods against the spirits of evil with which his primitive faith has peopled all natural objects."

through which the gods come forth to enjoy the sacrifice. At one time the beings in whose presence man feels himself are regarded by him as really endowed with souls ; at another time, in harmony with a more advanced conception of the world, they are imagined as substances or fluids invested with beneficent or maleficent properties : belief oscillates to and fro between the one mode of thought and the other. The art of turning to account the operations of these animated beings, the play of these substances and forces, is magic rather than worship in the proper sense of the word. The foundations of this faith and of this magic are an inheritance from the remotest past, from a period, to put it shortly, of shamanistic faith in spirits and souls, of shamanistic magic. Such a period has been passed through by the forefathers of the Indo-Germanic race as well as by other peoples." [1]

Coming down to the Hindoos of the present day, we find that their attitude towards the spiritual world is described as follows by Professor Monier Williams. "The plain fact undoubtedly is that the great majority of the inhabitants of India are, from the cradle to the burning-ground, victims of a form of mental disease which is best expressed by the term demonophobia. They are haunted and oppressed by a perpetual dread of demons. They are firmly convinced that evil spirits of all kinds, from malignant fiends to merely mischievous imps and elves, are ever on the watch to harm, harass, and torment them, to cause plague, sickness, famine, and disaster, to impede, injure, and mar every good work." [2] Elsewhere the same writer has expressed the same view somewhat more fully. "In fact," he says, "a belief in every kind of demoniacal influence has always been from the earliest times an essential ingredient in Hindu religious thought. The idea probably had its origin in the supposed peopling of the air by spiritual beings— the personifications or companions of storm and tempest. Certainly no one who has ever been brought into close contact with the Hindus in their own country can doubt the

Demons in modern India.

---

[1] H. Oldenberg, *Die Religion des Veda* (Berlin, 1894), pp. 39 *sq.*

[2] MonierWilliams, *Religious Thought*

and *Life in India* (London, 1883), pp. 210 *sq.*

fact that the worship of at least ninety per cent. of the people of India in the present day is a worship of fear. Not that the existence of good deities presided over by one Supreme Being is doubted; but that these deities are believed to be too absolutely good to need propitiation; just as in ancient histories of the Slav races, we are told that they believed in a white god and a black god, but paid adoration to the last alone, having, as they supposed, nothing to apprehend from the beneficence of the first or white deity. The simple truth is that evil of all kinds, difficulties, dangers and disasters, famines, diseases, pestilences and death, are thought by an ordinary Hindu to proceed from demons, or, more properly speaking, from devils, and from devils alone. These malignant beings are held, as we have seen, to possess varying degrees of rank, power, and malevolence. Some aim at destroying the entire world, and threaten the sovereignty of the gods themselves. Some delight in killing men, women, and children, out of a mere thirst for human blood. Some take a mere mischievous pleasure in tormenting, or revel in the infliction of sickness, injury, and misfortune. All make it their business to mar or impede the progress of good works and useful undertakings." [1]

It would be easy but tedious to illustrate in detail this general account of the dread of demons which prevails among the inhabitants of India at the present day. A very few particular statements must suffice. Thus, we are told that the Oraons, a Dravidian race in Bengal, " acknowledge a Supreme God, adored as Dharmi or Dharmesh, the Holy One, who is manifest in the sun, and they regard Dharmesh as a perfectly pure, beneficent being, who created us and would in his goodness and mercy preserve us, but that his benevolent designs are thwarted by malignant spirits whom mortals must propitiate, as Dharmesh cannot or does not interfere, if the spirit of evil once fastens upon us. It is, therefore, of no use to pray to Dharmesh or to offer

Demons in Bengal.

[1] Monier Williams, *op. cit.* pp. 230 sq. The views here expressed by the late Professor Monier Williams are confirmed from personal knowledge by Mr. E. T. Atkinson, *The Hima-layan Districts of the North-Western Provinces of India,* ii. (Allahabad, 1884) p. 840.

sacrifices to him ; so though acknowledged, recognised, and reverenced, he is neglected, whilst the malignant spirits are adored." Again, it is said of these Oraons that, " as the sole object of their religious ceremonies is the propitiation of the demons who are ever thwarting the benevolent intentions of Dharmesh, they have no notion of a service of thanksgiving." Once more, after giving a list of Oraon demons, the same writer goes on : " Besides this superstitious dread of the spirits above named, the Oraon's imagination tremblingly wanders in a world of ghosts. Every rock, road, river, and grove is haunted." [1]   Again, a missionary who spent many years among the Kacharis of Assam tells us that " the religion of the Kachári race is distinctly of the type commonly known as ' animistic ' and its underlying principle is characteristically one of fear or dread. The statement *Timor fecit deos* certainly holds good of this people in its widest and strictest sense ; and their religion thus stands in very marked, not to say violent, contrast with the teaching of the Faith in Christ. In the typical Kachári village as a rule neither idol nor place of worship is to be found ; but to the Kachári mind and imagination earth, air, and sky are alike peopled with a vast number of invisible spiritual beings, known usually as *Modai*, all possessing powers and faculties far greater than those of man, and almost invariably inclined to use these powers for malignant and malevolent, rather than benevolent, purposes. In a certain stage of moral and spiritual development men are undoubtedly influenced far more by what they fear than by what they love ; and this truth certainly applies to the Kachári race in the most unqualified way." [2]   Again, the Siyins, who inhabit the Chin Hills of north-eastern India, on the borders of Burma, " say that there is no Supreme God and no other world save this, which is full of evil spirits who inhabit the fields, infest the houses, and haunt the jungles. These spirits must be propitiated or bribed to refrain from doing the particular harm of which each is capable, for one can destroy crops, another can make women barren, and a third cause a lizard to enter

Demons in Assam.

Demons in the Chin Hills.

---

[1] E. T. Dalton, *Descriptive Ethnology of Bengal* (Calcutta, 1872), pp. 256, 257, 258.

[2] Rev. S. Endle, *The Kacharis* (London, 1911), p. 33.

the stomach and devour the bowels."[1] "Like most moun-
taineers, the people of Sikhim and the Tibetans are thorough-
going demon-worshippers. In every nook, path, big tree,
rock, spring, waterfall and lake there lurks a devil ; for which
reason few individuals will venture out alone after dark.
The sky, the ground, the house, the field, the country have
each their special demons, and sickness is always attributed
to malign demoniacal influence."[2] "Even the purest of all
the Lamaist sects—the Ge-lug-pa—are thorough-paced
devil-worshippers, and value Buddhism chiefly because it
gives them the whip-hand over the devils which everywhere
vex humanity with disease and disaster, and whose ferocity
weighs heavily on all."[3] The Lushais of Assam believe in
a beneficent spirit named Pathian, who made everything but
troubles himself very little about men. Far more important
in ordinary life are the numerous demons (huai), who inhabit
every stream, mountain, and forest, and are all malignant.
To their agency are ascribed all the illnesses and misfortunes
that afflict humanity, and a Lushai's whole life is spent in
propitiating them. It is the sorcerer (puithiam) who knows
what demon is causing any particular trouble, and it is he
who can prescribe the sort of sacrifice which will appease
the wrath of the fiend. Every form of sickness is set down
to the influence of some demon or other, and all the tales
about these spiritual foes begin or end with the recurrent
phrase, "There was much sickness in our village."[4] In
Travancore "the minor superstitions connected with demon-
worship are well-nigh innumerable ; they enter into all the
feelings, and are associated with the whole life of these people.
Every disease, accident, or misfortune is attributed to the
agency of the devils, and great caution is exercised to avoid
arousing their fury."[5]

With regard to the inhabitants of Ceylon we are told
that "the fiends which they conceive to be hovering around

[1] Bertram S. Carey and H. N.
Tuck, The Chin Hills, i. (Rangoon,
1896) p. 196.
[2] L. A. Waddell, "Demonolatry in
Sikhim Lamaism," The Indian Antiquary, xxiii. (1894) p. 197.
[3] L. A. Waddell, The Buddhism of

Tibet (London, 1895), p. 152.
[4] Lt.-Colonel J. Shakespear, The
Lushei Kuki Clans (London, 1912),
pp. 61, 65 sq., 67.
[5] Rev. S. Mateer, The Land of
Charity (London, 1883), p. 207.

them are without number. Every disease or trouble that
assails them is produced by the immediate agency of the
demons sent to punish them : while, on the other hand,
every blessing or success comes directly from the hands
of the beneficent and supreme God. To screen themselves
from the power of the inferior deities, who are all represented as wicked spirits, and whose power is by no means
irresistible, they wear amulets of various descriptions ; and
employ a variety of charms and spells to ward off the
influence of witchcraft and enchantments by which they
think themselves beset on all sides." " It is probable that,
by degrees, intercourse with Europeans will entirely do away
these superstitious fears, as the Cinglese of the towns
have already made considerable progress in subduing their
gloomy apprehensions. Not so the poor wretched peasants
who inhabit the more mountainous parts of the country, and
live at a distance from our settlements. These unhappy
people have never for a moment their minds free from
the terror of those demons who seem perpetually to hover
around them. Their imaginations are so disturbed by such
ideas that it is not uncommon to see many driven to madness from this cause. Several Cinglese lunatics have fallen
under my own observation ; and upon inquiring into the
circumstances which had deprived them of their reason,
I universally found that their wretched state was to be
traced solely to the excess of their superstitious fears. The
spirits of the wicked subordinate demons are the chief
objects of fear among the Ceylonese ; and impress their
minds with much more awe than the more powerful divinities who dispense blessings among them. They indeed
think that their country is in a particular manner delivered
over to the dominion of evil spirits." [1]

In Eastern as well as Southern Asia the same view Demons
of nature as pervaded by a multitude of spirits, mostly in Burma.
mischievous and malignant, has survived the nominal
establishment of a higher faith. " In spite of their long
conversion, their sincere belief in, and their pure form of,
Buddhism, which expressly repudiates and forbids such

---

[1] R. Percival, *Account of the Island of Ceylon*, Second Edition (London,
1805), pp. 211-213.

worship, the Burmans and Taleins (or Mons) have in a great measure kept their ancient spirit or demon worship. With the Taleins this is more especially the case. Indeed, with the country population of Pegu the worship, or it should rather be said the propitiation, of the 'nats' or spirits, enters into every act of their ordinary life, and Buddha's doctrine seems kept for sacred days and their visits to the kyoung (monastery) or to the pagoda."[1] Or, as another writer puts it, "the propitiating of the nats is a question of daily concern to the lower class Burman, while the worship at the pagoda is only thought of once a week. For the nat may prove destructive and hostile at any time, whereas the acquisition of *koothoh* [merit] at the pagoda is a thing which may be set about in a business-like way, and at proper and convenient seasons."[2]   But the term worship, we are informed, hardly conveys a proper notion of the attitude of the Burmese towards the nats or spirits. "Even the Karens and Kachins, who have no other form of belief, do not regard them otherwise than as malevolent beings who must be looked up to with fear, and propitiated by regular offerings. They do not want to have anything to do with the nats; all they seek is to be let alone. The bamboo pipes of spirit, the bones of sacrificial animals, the hatchets, swords, spears, bows and arrows that line the way to a Kachin village, are placed there not with the idea of attracting the spirits, but of preventing them from coming right among the houses in search of their requirements. If they want to drink, the rice spirit has been poured out, and the bamboo stoup is there in evidence of the libation; the blood-stained skulls of oxen, pigs, and the feathers of fowls show that there has been no stint of meat offerings; should the nats wax quarrelsome, and wish to fight, there are the axes and dahs with which to commence the fray. Only let them be grateful, and leave their trembling worshippers in peace and quietness."[3]

[1] C. J. F. S. Forbes, *British Burma* (London, 1878), pp. 221 *sq.*

[2] Shway Yoe, *The Burman, his Life and Notions* (London, 1882), i. 276 *sq.*

[3] Shway Yoe, *op. cit.* i. 278. "To the Burman," says A. Bastian, "the whole world is filled with nats. Mountains, rivers, waters, the earth, etc., have all their nat" (*Die Völker des östlichen Asien,* ii. 497).

Similarly the Lao or Laosians of Siam, though they are Demons in Siam. nominally Buddhists, and have monks and pagodas with images of Buddha, are said to pay more respect to spirits or demons than to these idols.[1] " The desire to propitiate the good spirits and to exorcise the bad ones is the prevailing influence upon the life of a Laosian. With *phees* [evil spirits] to right of him, to left of him, in front of him, behind him, all round him, his mind is haunted with a perpetual desire to make terms with them, and to ensure the assistance of the great Buddha, so that he may preserve both body and soul from the hands of the spirits." [2] " Independently of the demons who are in hell, the Siamese recognise another sort of devils diffused in the air : they call them *phi*; these are, they say, the demons who do harm to men and who appear sometimes in horrible shapes. They put down to the account of these malign spirits all the calamities which happen in the world. If a mother has lost a child, it is a *phi* who has done the ill turn ; if a sick man is given over, it is a *phi* that is at the bottom of it. To appease him, they invoke him and make him offerings which they hang up in desert places." [3] As to the Demons Thay, a widely spread race of Indo-China,[4] a French in Indo-China. missionary writes as follows : " It may be said that the Thay lives in constant intercourse with the invisible world. There is hardly an act of his life which is not regulated by some religious belief. There are two worships, the worship of the spirits and the worship of the dead, which, however, are scarcely distinguishable from each other, since the dead become spirits by the mere fact of their death. His simple imagination represents to him the world of spirits as a sort of double of the state of things here below. At the summit is Po Then, the father of the empyrean. Below him are the Then—Then Bun, Then Kum, Then Kom, of whom the chief is Then Luong, 'the great Then.' The dead go and cultivate his rice-fields in heaven and clear his mountains, just as they did their own in their life on earth. He has to

[1] Mgr. Pallegoix, *Description du royaume Thai ou Siam* (Paris, 1854), i. 42.

[2] C. Bock, *Temples and Elephants* (London, 1884), p. 198.

[3] Mgr. Bruguière, in *Annales de l'Association de la Propagation de la Foi*, v. (1831) p. 128.

[4] J. Deniker, *The Races of Man* (London, 1900), pp. 400 *sqq*.

wife a goddess Me Bau. Besides these heavenly spirits, the Thay reckons a multitude of others under the name of *phi*. His science being not very extensive, many things seem extraordinary to him. If he cannot explain a certain natural phenomenon, his perplexity does not last long. It is the work of a *phi*, he says, and his priests take care not to dissuade him. Hence he sees spirits everywhere. There are *phi* on the steep mountains, in the deep woods, the *phi bai* who, by night on the mountain, imitate the rain and the storms and leave no trace of their passage. If they shew themselves, they appear in the form of gigantic animals and cause terrible stomach troubles, such as diarrhœa, dysentery, and so on. . . . The large animals of the forest, wild oxen and buffaloes, rhinoceroses, elephants, and so on, have their guardian spirits. Hence the prudent hunter learns at the outset to exorcise them in order that, when he has killed these animals, he may be able to cut them up and eat their flesh without having to fear the vengeance of their invisible guardian. Spirits also guard the clearings whither the deer come by night to drink. The hunter should sacrifice a fowl to them from time to time, if he would bring down his game with ease. The gun itself has a spirit who looks to it that the powder explodes. In short, the Thay cannot take a single step without meeting a spirit on the path."[1] "Thus the life of the Thay seems regulated down to its smallest details by custom founded on his belief in the spirits. Spirits perpetually watch him, ready to punish his negligences, and he is afraid. Fear is not only for him the beginning of wisdom, it is the whole of his wisdom. Love has only a very moderate place in it. Even the respect in which he holds his dead, and the honours which he pays them on various occasions, seem to be dominated by a superstitious fear. It seems that the sacrifices which he offers to them aim rather at averting from himself the evils which he dreads than at honouring worthily the memory of his deceased kinsfolk and at paying them the tribute of his affection and gratitude. Once they sleep their last sleep yonder in the shadow of the great trees of the forest, none goes to shed a tear and murmur a prayer on their grave.

[1] A. Bourlet, "Les Thay," *Anthropos*, ii. (1907) p. 619.

Nothing but calamity suffices to rescue them from the oblivion into which they had fallen in the memory of the living." [1]

Demons in China.

" The dogma, prevailing in China from the earliest times, that the universe is filled in all its parts with *shen* and *kwei*, naturally implies that devils and demons must also swarm about the homes of men in numbers inestimable. It is, in fact, an axiom which constantly comes out in conversing with the people, that they haunt every frequented and lonely spot, and that no place exists where man is safe from them." [2] " The worship and propitiation of the gods, which is the main part of China's religion, has no higher purpose than that of inducing the gods to protect man against the world of evil, or, by descending among men, to drive spectres away by their intimidating presence.   This cult implies invocation of happiness ; but as happiness merely means absence of misfortune which the spectres cause, such a cult is tantamount to the disarming of spectres by means of the gods. . . . Taoism may then actually be defined as Exorcising Polytheism, a cult of the gods with which Eastern Asiatic imagination has filled the universe, connected with a highly developed system of magic, consisting for a great part in exorcism.   This cult and magic is, of course, principally in the hands of priests.   But, besides, the lay world, enslaved to the intense belief in the perilous omnipresence of spectres, is engaged every day in a restless defensive and offensive war against those beings." [3]

Demons in Corea.

In Corea, " among the reasons which render the shaman a necessity are these.   In Korean belief, earth, air, and sea are peopled by demons.   They haunt every umbrageous tree, shady ravine, crystal spring, and mountain crest.   On green hill-slopes, in peaceful agricultural valleys, in grassy dells, on wooded uplands, by lake and stream, by road and river, in north, south, east, and west, they abound, making

[1] A. Bourlet, *op. cit.* p. 632.
[2] J. J. M. de Groot, *The Religious System of China*, v. (Leyden, 1907) p. 470.
[3] J. J. M. de Groot, *op. cit.* vi. (Leyden, 1910) pp. 930-932.   This sixth volume of Professor de Groot's great work is mainly devoted to an account of the ceaseless war waged by the Chinese people on demons or spectres (*kwei*).   A more summary notice of this curious national delusion will be found in his work *The Religion of the Chinese* (New York, 1910), chapter ii., " The Struggle against Spectres," pp. 33-61.

malignant sport of human destinies.   They are on every
roof, ceiling, fireplace, *kang* and beam.   They fill the
chimney, the shed, the living-room, the kitchen—they are
on every shelf and jar.   In thousands they waylay the
traveller as he leaves his home, beside him, behind him,
dancing in front of him, whirring over his head, crying out
upon him from earth, air, and water.   They are numbered
by *thousands of billions*, and it has been well said that their
ubiquity is an unholy travesty of the Divine Omnipresence.
This belief, and it seems to be the only one he has, keeps
the Korean in a perpetual state of nervous apprehension, it
surrounds him with indefinite terrors, and it may truly be
said of him that he 'passes the time of his sojourning here
in fear.'   Every Korean home is subject to demons, here,
there, and everywhere.   They touch the Korean at every
point in life, making his well-being depend on a continual
series of acts of propitiation, and they avenge every omission
with merciless severity, keeping him under this yoke of
bondage from birth to death."   "Koreans attribute every
ill by which they are afflicted to demoniacal influence.   Bad
luck in any transaction, official malevolence, illness, whether
sudden or prolonged, pecuniary misfortune, and loss of
power or position, are due to the malignity of demons.   It
is over such evils that the *Pan-su* [shaman] is supposed to
have power, and to be able to terminate them by magical
rites, he being possessed by a powerful demon, whose
strength he is able to wield." [1]

Demons among the Koryaks.   Of the nomadic Koryaks of north-eastern Asia it is said
that "all their religious customs have only reference to the
evil spirits of the earth.   Their religion is thus a cunning
diplomacy or negotiation with these spirits in order, as far
as possible, to deter them from actions which would be
injurious to men.   Everywhere, on every mountain, in the
sea, by the rivers, in the forest, and on the plains their
fancy sees demons lurking, whom they picture to themselves
as purely malignant and very greedy.   Hence the frequent
offerings by which they seek to satisfy the greed of these

---

[1] Mrs. Bishop (Isabella L. Bird), *Korea and her Neighbours* (London, 1898), ii. 227 *sq.*, 229.   I have taken the liberty of changing the writer's "daemon" and "daemoniacal" into "demon" and "demoniacal."

insatiable beings, and to redeem that which they value and hold dear. Those of the people who are believed to be able to divine most easily the wishes of the evil ones and who enjoy their favour to a certain extent are called shamans, and the religious ceremonies which they perform are shamanism. In every case the shamans must give their advice as to how the devils are to be got rid of, and must reveal the wishes of the demons."[1] As to these demons of the earth, who infest the Koryaks, we are told that "when visiting the houses to cause diseases and to kill people, they enter from under ground, through the hearth-fire, and return the same way. It happens at times that they steal people, and carry them away. They are invisible to human beings, and are capable of changing their size. They are sometimes so numerous in houses, that they sit on the people, and fill up all corners. With hammers and axes they knock people over their heads, thus causing headaches. They bite, and cause swellings. They shoot invisible arrows, which stick in the body, causing death, if a shaman does not pull them out in time. The *kalau* [demons] tear out pieces of flesh from people, thus causing sores and wounds to form on their bodies."[2]

The Gilyaks of the Amoor valley in eastern Asia believe that besides the gods "there are evil supernatural beings who do him harm. They are devils, called *mil'k*, *kinr*. These beings appear in the most varied forms and are distinguished according to the degree of their harmfulness. They appear now in the form of a Gilyak, now in the form of an animal, from a bear down to a toad and a lizard. They exist on the land and in the sea, under the earth and in the sky. Some of them form special tribes of treacherous beings whose essential nature it is to be destructive. Others are isolated individuals, ruined beings, 'lost sons' of families of beneficent beings, who are exceptional in their hostility to man. The former class

Demons among the Gilyaks.

---

[1] C. von Dittmar, "Über die Koräken und die ihnen sehr nahe verwandten Tschuktschen," *Bulletin de la Classe Historico-philologique de l'Académie Impériale des Sciences de St. Pétersbourg*, xiii. (1856) coll. 123

sq.

[2] W. Jochelson, *The Koryak* (Leyden and New York, 1908), p. 28 (*The Jesup North Pacific Expedition, Memoir of the American Museum of Natural History*).

are naturally the most dangerous. Some are wholly occupied in robbing the Gilyak on the road (the spirits of loss—*gerniwuch-en*); others empty his barns, his traps, his pitfalls, and so on; lastly there are such also, the most dreadful of all, who lie in wait for his life and bring sickness and death. Were there no such beings, men would not die. A natural death is impossible. Death is the result of the wiles of these treacherous beings." [1]

Demons
in ancient
Babylonia
and
Assyria.

In the more westerly parts of the old world the same belief in the omnipresence and mischievous power of spirits has prevailed from antiquity to the present day. If we may judge from the fragments of their literature which have been deciphered, few people seem to have suffered more from the persistent assaults of demons than the ancient Babylonians and Assyrians, and the evil spirits that preyed on them were of a peculiarly cruel and malignant sort; even the gods themselves were not exempt from their attacks. These baleful beings lurked in solitary places, in graves, in the shadow of ruins and on the tops of mountains. They dwelt in the wilderness, in the holes and dens of the earth, they issued from the lower parts of the ground. Nothing could resist them in heaven above, nothing could withstand them on earth below. They roamed the streets, they leaped from house to house. The high and thick fences they penetrated like a flood, the door could not stay them, nor the bolt make them turn back. They glided through the door like a serpent, they pierced through the planks like the wind. There was no place, however small, which they could not invade, none so large that they could not fill. And their wickedness was equal to their power. "They are wicked, they are wicked," says an incantation. No prayers could move them, no supplications could make them relent; for they knew no pity, they hearkened not to reason, they knew no troth. To them all manner of evil was ascribed. Their presence was felt not only in the terrible winds that swept the land, in the fevers bred of the marshes, and in the diseases engendered by the damp heat of summer. All the petty annoyances of life—a sudden fall, an unlucky

---

[1] L. Sternberg, "Die Religion der Giljaken," *Archiv für Religionswissenschaft*, viii. (1905) pp. 460 *sq.*

word, a headache, a paltry quarrel—were set down to the agency of fiends ; and all the fierce emotions that rend the mind—love, hate, jealousy, and madness—were equally the work of these invisible tormentors. Men and women stood in constant danger of them. They tore the wife from the bosom of her husband, the son from the knees of his father. They ate the flesh and drank the blood of men, they prevented them from sleeping or taking food, and to adopt a metaphor from one of the texts, "they ground the country like flour." Almost every part of the human frame was menaced by a special fiend. One demon assailed the head, another the neck, another the hips, and so on. They bound a man's hands, they fettered his feet, they spat poison and gall on him. Day and night must he wander without rest ; sighs and lamentations were his food. They attacked even the animals. They drove doves from their dovecotes, and swallows from their nests ; they smote the bull and the ass. They pursued the cattle to their stalls : they lodged with the horses in the stable : they caused the she-ass to miscarry, and the young ass at its mother's dugs to pine away. Even lifeless things could be possessed by them ; for there were demons that rushed against houses and took walls by storm, that shut themselves up in doors, and hid themselves under bolts. Indeed they threatened the whole world with destruction, and there was none that could deliver from them save only the mighty god Marduk.[1]

In the opinion of the ancient Egyptians "there were good spirits as well as bad, but the *Book of the Dead* practically ignores the former, and its magical formulae were directed entirely against the operations of evil spirits. Though naturally of a gay and light-hearted disposition, the Egyptian must have lived in a perpetual state of fear of spirits of all kinds, spirits of calamity, disease, and sickness, spirits of angry gods and ancestors, and above all the spirit of Death. His imagination filled the world with spirits, whose acts

Demons in ancient Egypt.

[1] M. Jastrow, *The Religion of Babylonia and Assyria* (Boston, 1898), pp. 260 *sqq.* ; *id.*, *Die Religion Babyloniens und Assyriens*, i. (Giessen, 1905) pp. 278 *sqq.* ; C. Fossey, *La Magie Assyrienne* (Paris, 1902), pp. 27-30, 34 ; E. Schrader, *Die Keilinschriften und das Alte Testament*, Dritte Auflage, neu bearbeitet von H. Zimmern und H. Winckler (Berlin, 1902), pp. 458 *sqq.*

seemed to him to be generally malevolent, and his magical and religious literature and his amulets testify to the very real terror with which he regarded his future existence in the world of spirits. Escape from such spirits was impossible,

Demons in modern Egypt.

for they could not die."[1] In modern Egypt the jinn, a class of spiritual beings intermediate between angels and men, are believed to pervade the solid matter of the earth as well as the firmament, and they inhabit rivers, ruined houses, wells, baths, ovens, and so forth. So thickly do they swarm that in pouring water or other liquids on the ground an Egyptian will commonly exclaim or mutter "*Destoor!*" thereby asking the permission or craving the pardon of any jinn who might chance to be there, and who might otherwise resent being suddenly soused with water or unsavoury fluids. So too when people light a fire, let down a bucket into a well, or perform other necessary functions, they will say "Permission!" or "Permission, ye blessed!"[2] Again, in Egypt it is not considered proper to sweep out a house at night, lest in doing so you should knock against a jinnee, who might avenge the insult.[3]

Demons in ancient Greece.

The earliest of the Greek philosophers, Thales, held that the world is full of gods or spirits;[4] and the same primitive creed was expounded by one of the latest pagan thinkers of antiquity. Porphyry declared that demons appeared in the likeness of animals, that every house and every body was full of them, and that forms of ceremonial purification, such as beating the air and so forth, had no other object but that of driving away the importunate swarms of these invisible but dangerous beings. He explained that evil spirits delighted in food, especially in blood and impurities, that they settled like flies on us at meals, and that they could only be kept at a distance by ceremonial observances, which were directed, not to pleasing the gods, but simply and solely to beating off devils.[5] His theory of religious purification seems

[1] E. A. Wallis Budge, *Osiris and the Egyptian Resurrection* (London, 1911), ii. 150.

[2] E. W. Lane, *Manners and Customs of the Modern Egyptians* (Paisley and London, 1895), chap. x. pp. 231 *sq.*

[3] C. B. Klunzinger, *Bilder aus Oberägypten, der Wüste und dem Rothen Meere* (Stuttgart, 1877), p. 382; compare *ibid.* pp. 374 *sq.*

[4] Aristotle, *De anima*, i. 5. 17; Diogenes Laertius, i. 1. 27.

[5] Porphyry, quoted by Eusebius, *Praeparatio Evangelii*, iv. 23.

faithfully to reflect the creed of the savage on this subject,[1] but a philosopher is perhaps the last person whom we should expect to find acting as a mirror of savagery. It is less surprising to meet with the same venerable doctrine, the same world-wide superstition in the mouth of a mediaeval abbot; for we know that a belief in devils has the authority of the founder of Christianity and is sanctioned by the teaching of the church. No Esquimau on the frozen shores of Labrador, no Indian in the sweltering forests of Guiana, no cowering Hindoo in the jungles of Bengal, could well have a more constant and abiding sense of the presence of malignant demons everywhere about him than had Abbot Richalm, who ruled over the Cistercian monastery of Schönthal in the first half of the thirteenth century. In the curious work to which he gave the name of *Revelations*, he set forth how he was daily and hourly infested by devils, whom, though he could not see, he heard, and to whom he imputed all the ailments of his flesh and all the frailties of his spirit. If he felt squeamish, he was sure that the feeling was wrought in him by demoniacal agency. If puckers appeared on his nose, if his lower lip drooped, the devils had again to answer for it; a cough, a cold in the head, a hawking and spitting, could have none but a supernatural and devilish origin. If, pacing in his orchard on a sunny autumn morning, the portly abbot stooped to pick up the mellow fruit that had fallen in the night, the blood that mounted to his purple face was sent coursing thither by his invisible foes. If the abbot tossed on his sleepless couch, while the moonlight, streaming in at the window, cast the shadows of the stanchions like black bars on the floor of his cell, it was not the fleas and so forth that kept him awake—oh no! "Vermin," said he sagely, "do not really bite"; they seem to bite indeed, but it is all the work of devils. If a monk snored in the dormitory, the unseemly noise proceeded not from him, but from a demon lurking in his person. Especially dangerous were

---

[1] Elsewhere I have attempted to shew that a particular class of purifications—those observed by mourners—is intended to protect the living from the disembodied spirits of the dead ("On certain Burial Customs as illustrative of the Primitive Theory of the Soul," *Journal of the Anthropological Institute*, xv. (1886) pp. 64 *sqq.*).

the demons of intoxication. These subtle fiends commonly lodged at the taverns in the neighbouring town, but on feast days they were apt to slip through the monastery gates and glide unseen among the monks seated at the refectory table, or gathered round the roaring fire on the hearth, while the bleak wind whistled in the abbey towers, and a more generous vintage than usual glowed and sparkled in the flagons. If at such times a jolly, rosy-faced brother appeared to the carnal eye and ear to grow obstreperous or maudlin, to speak thick or to reel and stagger in his gait, be sure it was not the fiery spirit of the grape that moved the holy man; it was a spirit of quite a different order. Holding such views on the source of all bodily and mental indisposition, it was natural enough that the abbot should prescribe remedies which are not to be found in the pharmacopœia, and which would be asked for in vain at an apothecary's. They consisted chiefly of holy water and the sign of the cross; this last he recommended particularly as a specific for flea-bites.[1]

It is easy to suggest that the abbot's wits were unsettled, that he suffered from hallucinations, and so forth. This may have been so; yet a mode of thought like his seems to be too common over a great part of the world to allow us to attribute it purely to mental derangement. In the Middle Ages, when the general level of knowledge was low, a state of mind like Richalm's may have been shared by multitudes even of educated people, who have not, however, like him, left a monument of their folly to posterity. At the present day, through the advance and spread of knowledge, it might be difficult to find any person of acknowledged sanity holding the abbot's opinions on the subject of demons; but in remote parts of Europe a little research might shew that the creed of Porphyry and Richalm is still held, with but little variation, by the mass of the people. Thus we are told that the Roumanians of Transylvania "believe themselves to be surrounded on all sides by whole legions of evil spirits. These devils are furthermore assisted by *ismejus* (another sort of dragon), witches,

Demons in modern Europe.

---

[1] C. Meyer, *Der Aberglaube des Mittelalters* (Bâle, 1884), pp. 109-111, 191 *sq.*

and goblins, and to each of these dangerous beings are ascribed particular powers on particular days and at certain places. Many and curious are therefore the means by which the Roumanians endeavour to counteract these baleful influences ; and a whole complicated study, about as laborious as the mastering of an unknown language, is required in order to teach an unfortunate peasant to steer clear of the dangers by which he supposes himself to be beset on all sides."[1]

Similar beliefs are held to this day by the Armenians, who, though they are not a European people, have basked in the light of Christianity from a time when Central and Northern Europe was still plunged in heathen darkness. All the activities, we are told, of these professing Christians "are paralyzed after sunset, because at every step they quake with fear, believing that the evil demons are everywhere present in the air, in the water, on the earth. By day the evil ones are under the earth, therefore boiling hot water may not be poured on the ground, because it sinks into the earth and burns the feet of the children of the evil spirits. But in the evening the superstitious Armenian will pour no water at all on the earth, because the evil ones are everywhere present on the earth. Some of them are walking about, others are sitting at table and feasting, so that they might be disturbed by the pouring out of water, and they would take vengeance for it. Also by night you should not smite the ground with a stick, nor sweep out the house, nor remove the dung from the stable, because without knowing it you might hit the evil spirits. But if you are compelled to sweep by night, you singe the tip of the broom so as to frighten the evil ones away in time. You must not go out at night bareheaded, for the evil ones would smite you on the head. It is also dangerous to drink water out of a vessel in the dark, especially when the water is drawn from a brook or river ; for the evil ones in the water hit out, or they pass with the water into a man. Therefore in drinking you

Demons in modern Armenia.

---

[1] E. Gerard, *The Land beyond the Forest* (Edinburgh and London, 1888), i. 328. The superstitions of the Roumanians of Transylvania have been collected by W. Schmidt in his tract *Das Jahr und seine Tage in Meinung und Brauch der Romänen Siebenbürgens* (Hermannstadt, 1866).

should hold a knife with three blades or a piece of iron in the water. The baleful influence of the nocturnal demons extends also to useful objects; hence after sunset people do not lend salt or fire and do not shake out the tablecloth, because thereby the salt would lose its savour and the welfare of the house would depart." [1]

[1] Manuk Abeghian, *Der armenische Volksglaube* (Leipsic, 1899), pp. 31 *sq.*

CHAPTER III

THE PUBLIC EXPULSION OF EVILS

§ 1. *The Occasional Expulsion of Evils*

WE can now understand why those general clearances of evil, to which from time to time the savage resorts, should commonly take the form of a forcible expulsion of devils. In these evil spirits primitive man sees the cause of many if not of most of his troubles, and he fancies that if he can only deliver himself from them, things will go better with him. The public attempts to expel the accumulated ills of a whole community may be divided into two classes, according as the expelled evils are immaterial and invisible or are embodied in a material vehicle or scapegoat. The former may be called the direct or immediate expulsion of evils ; the latter the indirect or mediate expulsion, or the expulsion by scapegoat. We begin with examples of the former. *General clearances of evils take the form of expulsions of demons.*

In the island of Rook, between New Guinea and New Britain, when any misfortune has happened, all the people run together, scream, curse, howl, and beat the air with sticks to drive away the devil (*Marsába*), who is supposed to be the author of the mishap. From the spot where the mishap took place they drive him step by step to the sea, and on reaching the shore they redouble their shouts and blows in order to expel him from the island. He generally retires to the sea or to the island of Lottin.[1] The natives of New Britain ascribe sickness, drought, the failure of crops, and in short all misfortunes, to the influence of *General expulsions of demons in Melanesia.*

[1] Paul Reina, "Über die Bewohner der Insel Rook," *Zeitschrift für all-* *gemeine Erdkunde*, N.F., iv. (1858) p. 356.

wicked spirits. So at times when many people sicken and die, as at the beginning of the rainy season, all the inhabitants of a district, armed with branches and clubs, go out by moonlight to the fields, where they beat and stamp on the ground with wild howls till morning, believing that this drives away the devils; and for the same purpose they rush through the village with burning torches.[1] The natives of New Caledonia are said to believe that all evils are caused by a powerful and malignant spirit; hence in order to rid themselves of him they will from time to time dig a great pit, round which the whole tribe gathers. After cursing the demon, they fill up the pit with earth, and trample on the top with loud shouts. This they call burying the evil spirit.[2]

Expulsions of demons in Australia and South Africa.

Among the Dieri tribe of Central Australia, when a serious illness occurs, the medicine-men expel Cootchie or the devil by beating the ground in and outside of the camp with the stuffed tail of a kangaroo, until they have chased the demon away to some distance from the camp.[3] In some South African tribes it is a general rule that no common man may meddle with spirits, whether good or bad, except to offer the customary sacrifices. Demons may haunt him and make his life a burden to him, but he must submit to their machinations until the matter is taken up by the proper authorities. A baboon may be sent by evil spirits and perch on a tree within gunshot, or regale itself in his maize-field; but to fire at the beast would be worse than suicide. So long as a man remains a solitary sufferer, he has little chance of redress. It is supposed that he has committed some crime, and that the ancestors in their wrath have sent a demon to torment him. But should his neighbours also suffer; should the baboon from choice or necessity (for men do sometimes pluck up courage to scare the brutes) select a fresh field for its depredations, or the roof of another man's barn for its perch, the case begins to wear a different complexion. The magicians now deal with the matter seriously. One man may be haunted for his sins by a demon, but a

---

[1] R. Parkinson, *Im Bismarck-Archipel* (Leipsic, 1887), p. 142; *id.*, *Dreissig Jahre in der Südsee* (Stuttgart, 1907), p. 119.

[2] O. Opigez, "Aperçu général sur la Nouvelle-Calédonie," *Bulletin de la Société de Géographie* (Paris), VII. Série, vii. (1886) p. 443.

[3] S. Gason, in *Journal of the Anthropological Institute*, xxiv. (1895) p. 170.

whole community infested by devils is another matter. To shoot the baboon, however, would be useless ; it would merely enrage the demon and increase the danger. The first thing to do is to ascertain the permanent abode of the devil. It is generally a deep pool with overhanging banks and dark recesses. There the villagers assemble with the priests and magicians at their head, and set about pelting the demon with stones, men, women, and children all joining in the assault, while they load the object of their fear and hate with the foulest abuse. Drums too are beaten, and horns blown at intervals, and when everybody has been worked up to such a frenzy of excitement that some even fancy they see the imp dodging the missiles, he suddenly takes to flight, and the village is rid of him for a time. After that, the crops may be protected and baboons killed with impunity.[1]

When a village has been visited by a series of disasters or a severe epidemic, the inhabitants of Minahassa in Celebes lay the blame upon the devils who are infesting the village and who must be expelled from it. Accordingly, early one morning all the people, men, women, and children, quit their homes, carrying their household goods with them, and take up their quarters in temporary huts which have been erected outside the village. Here they spend several days, offering sacrifices and preparing for the final ceremony. At last the men, some wearing masks, others with their faces blackened, and so on, but all armed with swords, guns, pikes, or brooms, steal cautiously and silently back to the deserted village. Then, at a signal from the priest, they rush furiously up and down the streets and into and under the houses (which are raised on piles above the ground), yelling and striking on walls, doors, and windows, to drive away the devils. Next, the priests and the rest of the people come with the holy fire and march nine times round each house and thrice round the ladder

[marginal note:] General expulsion of demons in Minabassa, Halmahera, and the Kei Islands.

---

[1] Rev. James Macdonald, *Religion and Myth* (London, 1893), pp. 100-102. The writer, who describes the ceremony at first hand, remarks that "there is no periodic purging of devils, nor are more spirits than one expelled at a time." He adds : "I have noticed frequently a connection between the quantity of grain that could be spared for making beer, and the frequency of gatherings for the purging of evils."

that leads up to it, carrying the fire with them.   Then they
take the fire into the kitchen, where it must burn for three
days continuously.   The devils are now driven away, and
great and general is the joy.[1]   The Alfoors of Halmahera
attribute epidemics to the devil who comes from other
villages to carry them off.   So, in order to rid the village of
the disease, the sorcerer drives away the devil.   From all
the villagers he receives a costly garment and places it on
four vessels, which he takes to the forest and leaves at
the spot where the devil is supposed to be.   Then
with mocking words he bids the demon abandon the
place.[2]   In the Kei Islands to the south-west of New
Guinea, the evil spirits, who are quite distinct from the
souls of the dead, form a mighty host.   Almost every tree
and every cave is the lodging-place of one of these fiends,
who are moreover extremely irascible and apt to fly out on
the smallest provocation.   To speak loudly in passing their
abode, to ease nature near a haunted tree or cave, is enough
to bring down their wrath on the offender, and he must
either appease them by an offering or burn the scrapings of
a buffalo's horn or the hair of a Papuan slave, in order that
the smell may drive the foul fiends away.   The spirits
manifest their displeasure by sending sickness and other
calamities.   Hence in times of public misfortune, as when
an epidemic is raging, and all other remedies have failed,

---

[1] [P. N. Wilken], "De godsdienst
en godsdienstplegtigheden der Alfoeren
in de Menahassa op het eiland Celebes,"
Tijdschrift voor Nederlandsch Indië,
December 1849, pp. 392-394; *id.,*
"Bijdragen tot de kennis van de
zeden en gewoonten der Alfoeren in
de Minahassa," *Mededeelingen van wege
het Nederlandsche Zendelinggenootschap,*
vii. (1863) pp. 149 *sqq.*; J. G. F.
Riedel, "De Minahasa in 1825,"
*Tijdschrift voor Indische Taal- Land-
en Volkenkunde,* xviii. (1872) pp. 521
sq.   Wilken's first and fuller account
is reprinted in N. Graafland's *De
Minahasa* (Rotterdam, 1869), i. 117-
120.   A German translation of Wilken's earlier article is printed in *Zeitschrift für allgemeine Erdkunde,* N.F.,
x. (1861) pp. 43-61.

[2] J. G. F. Riedel, "Galela und
Tobeloresen," *Zeitschrift für Ethnologie,* xvii. (1885) p. 82; G. A.
Wilken, "Het Shamanisme bij de
Volken van de Indischen Archipel,"
*Bijdragen tot de Taal- Land- en Volken-
kunde van Nederlandsch Indie,* xxxvi.
(1887) p. 484; *id., Verspreide Ge-
schriften* (The Hague, 1912), iii. 383.
When smallpox is raging, the Toradjas of Central Celebes abandon the
village and live in the bush for seven
days in order to make the spirit of
smallpox believe that they are all
dead.   But it does not appear that they
forcibly expel him from the village.
See N. Adriani en Alb. C. Kruijt, *De
Bare'e-sprekende Toradja's van Midden-
Celebes,* i. (Batavia, 1912) p. 417.

the whole population go forth with the priest at their head
to a place at some distance from the village.   Here at sunset they erect a couple of poles with a cross-bar between
them, to which they attach bags of rice, wooden models
of pivot-guns, gongs, bracelets, and so on.   Then, when
everybody has taken his place at the poles and a
death-like silence reigns, the priest lifts up his voice and
addresses the spirits in their own language as follows:
" Ho! ho! ho! ye evil spirits who dwell in the trees, ye
evil spirits who live in the grottoes, ye evil spirits who
lodge in the earth, we give you these pivot-guns, these
gongs, etc.   Let the sickness cease and not so many people
die of it."   Then everybody runs home as fast as their legs
can carry them.[1]

In the island of Nias, when a man is seriously ill and
other remedies have been tried in vain, the sorcerer proceeds
to exorcise the devil who is causing the illness.   A pole is
set up in front of the house, and from the top of the pole a
rope of palm-leaves is stretched to the roof of the house.
Then the sorcerer mounts the roof with a pig, which he kills
and allows to roll from the roof to the ground.   The devil,
anxious to get the pig, lets himself down hastily from the
roof by the rope of palm-leaves, and a good spirit, invoked
by the sorcerer, prevents him from climbing up again.   If
this remedy fails, it is believed that other devils must still be
lurking in the house.   So a general hunt is made after them.
All the doors and windows in the house are closed, except a
single dormer-window in the roof.   The men, shut up in the
house, hew and slash with their swords right and left to the
clash of gongs and the rub-a-dub of drums.   Terrified at
this onslaught, the devils escape by the dormer-window, and
sliding down the rope of palm-leaves take themselves off.
As all the doors and windows, except the one in the roof,
are shut, the devils cannot get into the house again.   In the
case of an epidemic, the proceedings are similar.   All the
gates of the village, except one, are closed; every voice is

Demons of sickness expelled in Nias.

---

[1] C. M. Pleyte, " Ethnographische
Beschrijving der Kei - eilanden,"
*Tijdschrift van het Nederlandsch Aard-
rijkskundig Genootschap*, Tweede Serie,
x. (1893) pp. 834 *sq.*   A briefer

account of the custom had previously
been given by J. G. F. Riedel (*De
sluik- en kroesharige rassen tusschen
Selebes en Papua*, The Hague, 1886,
p. 239).

raised, every gong and drum beaten, every sword brandished. Thus the devils are driven out and the last gate is shut behind them. For eight days thereafter the village is in a state of siege, no one being allowed to enter it.[1]

Spiritual quarantine against demons of sickness in Nias.

The means adopted in Nias to exclude an epidemic from a village which has not yet been infected by it are somewhat similar; but as they exhibit an interesting combination of religious ritual with the purely magical ceremony of exorcism, it may be worth while to describe them. When it is known that a village is suffering from the ravages of a dangerous malady, the other villages in the neighbourhood take what they regard as effective measures for securing immunity from the disease. Some of these measures commend themselves to us as rational and others do not. In the first place, quarantine is established in each village, not only against the inhabitants of the infected village, but against all strangers; no person from outside is allowed to enter. In the second place, a feast is made by the people for one of their idols who goes by the name of *Fangeroe wŏchŏ*, or Protector from sickness. All the people of the village must participate in the sacrifice and bear a share of the cost. The principal idol, crowned with palm-leaves, is set up in front of the chief's house, and all the inhabitants who can do so gather about it. The names of those who cannot attend are mentioned, apparently as a substitute for their attendance in person. While the priest is reciting the spells for the banishment of the evil spirits, all persons present come forward and touch the image. A pig is then killed and its flesh furnishes a common meal. The mouth of the idol is smeared with the bloody heart of the pig, and a dishful of the cooked pork is set before him. Of the flesh thus consecrated to the idol none but priests and chiefs may

---

[1] J. T. Nieuwenhuisen en H. C. B. von Rosenberg, "Verslag omtrent het eiland Nias," *Verhandelingen van het Bataviaasch Genootschap van Kunsten en Wetenschapen*, xxx. (Batavia, 1863) pp. 116 *sq.*; H. von Rosenberg, *Der Malayische Archipel* (Leipsic, 1878), pp. 174 *sq.* Compare L. N. H. A. Chatelin, "Godsdienst en Bijgeloof der Niassers," *Tijdschrift voor Indische Taal- Land- en Volkenkunde*, xxvi. (1880) p. 139; E. Modigliani, *Un Viaggio a Nias* (Milan, 1890), pp. 195, 382. The Dyaks also drive the devil at the point of the sword from a house where there is sickness. See C. Hupe, "Korte verhandeling over de godsdienst, zeden, enz. der Dajakkers," *Tijdschrift voor Neêrlands Indië*, 1846, dl. iii. p. 149.

partake. Idols called *daha*, or branches of the principal idol,
are also set up in front of all the other houses in the village.
Moreover, bogies made of black wood with white eyes, to
which the broken crockery of the inhabitants has freely contributed, are placed at the entrances of the village to scare
the demon and prevent him from entering. All sorts of
objects whitened with chalk are also hung up in front of the
houses to keep the devil out. When eight days have elapsed,
it is thought that the sacrifice has taken effect, and the
priest puts an end to the quarantine. All boys and men
now assemble for the purpose of expelling the evil spirit.
Led by the priest, they march four times, with a prodigious
noise and uproar, from one end of the village to the other,
slashing the air with their knives and stabbing it with their
spears to frighten the devil away. If all these efforts prove
vain, and the dreaded sickness breaks out, the people think
it must be because they have departed from the ways of
their fathers by raising the price of victuals and pigs too
high or by enriching themselves with unjust gain. Accordingly a new idol is made and set up in front of the chief's
house ; and while the priest engages in prayer, the chief and
the magnates of the village touch the image, vowing as they
do so to return to the old ways and cursing all such as may
refuse their consent or violate the new law thus solemnly
enacted. Then all present betake themselves to the river
and erect another idol on the bank. In presence of this
latter idol the weights and measures are compared, and any
that exceed the lawful standard are at once reduced to it.
When this has been done, they rock the image to and fro to
signify, or perhaps rather to ensure, thereby that he who
does not keep the new law shall suffer misfortune, or fall
sick, or be thwarted in some way or other. Then a pig is
killed and eaten on the bank of the river. The feast being
over, each family contributes a certain sum in token that
they make restitution of their unlawful gains. The money
thus collected is tied in a bundle, and the priest holds the
bundle up towards the sky and down towards the earth to
satisfy the god of the upper and the god of the nether world
that justice has now been done. After that he either flings
the bag of money into the river or buries it in the ground

beside the idol. In the latter case the money naturally disappears, and the people explain its disappearance by saying that the evil spirit has come and fetched it.[1] A method like that which at the present day the people of Nias adopt for the sake of conjuring the demon of disease was employed in antiquity by the Caunians of Asia Minor to banish certain foreign gods whom they had imprudently established in their country. All the men of military age assembled under arms, and with spear-thrusts in the air drove the strange gods step by step from the land and across the boundaries.[2]

Demons of sickness expelled in the Solomon Islands.

The Solomon Islanders of Bougainville Straits believe that epidemics are always, or nearly always, caused by evil spirits ; and accordingly when the people of a village have been suffering generally from colds, they have been known to blow conch-shells, beat tins, shout, and knock on the houses for the purpose of expelling the demons and so curing their colds.[3]

Demons of sickness expelled in Burma.

When cholera has broken out in a Burmese village the able-bodied men scramble on the roofs and lay about them with bamboos and billets of wood, while all the rest of the population, old and young, stand below and thump drums, blow trumpets, yell, scream, beat floors, walls, tin pans, everything to make a din. This uproar, repeated on three successive nights, is thought to be very effective in driving away the cholera demons.[4] The Shans of Kengtung, a province of Upper Burma, imagine that epidemics are brought about by the prowling ghosts of wicked men, such as thieves and murderers, who cannot rest but go about doing all the harm they can to the living. Hence when sickness is rife, the people take steps to expel these dangerous spirits. The Buddhist priests exert themselves actively in the beneficent enterprise. They assemble in a body at the Town Court and read the scriptures. Guns are fired

[1] Fr. Kramer, "Der Götzendienst der Niasser," *Tijdschrift voor Indische Taal- Land- en Volkenkunde*, xxxiii. (1890) pp. 486-488.

[2] Herodotus, i. 172.

[3] G. C. Wheeler, "Sketch of the Totemism and Religion of the People of the Islands in the Bougainville Straits (Western Solomon Islands)," *Archiv für Religionswissenschaft*, xv. (1912) pp. 49, 51 *sq.*

[4] C. J. F. S. Forbes, *British Burma* (London, 1878), p. 233 ; Shway Yoe, *The Burman, his Life and Notions* (London, 1882), i. 282, ii. 105 *sqq.* ; A. Bastian, *Die Völker des östlichen Asien*, ii. 98 ; Max and Bertha Ferrars, *Burma* (London, 1900), p. 128.

and processions march to the city gates, by which the fiends
are supposed to take their departure.   There small trays of
food are left for them, but the larger offerings are deposited
in the middle of the town.[1]   When smallpox first appeared
amongst the Kumis of South-Eastern India, they thought it
was a devil come from Aracan.   The villages were placed
in a state of siege, no one being allowed to leave or enter
them.   A monkey was killed by being dashed on the
ground, and its body was hung at the village gate.   Its
blood, mixed with small river pebbles, was sprinkled on the
houses, the threshold of every house was swept with the
monkey's tail, and the fiend was adjured to depart.[2]   During
the hot summer cholera is endemic in Southern China, and
from time to time, when the mortality is great, vigorous
attempts are made to expel the demons who do all the
mischief.   For this salutary purpose processions parade the
streets by night ; images of the gods are borne in them,
torches waved, gongs beaten, guns fired, crackers popped,
swords brandished, demon-dispelling trumpets blown, and
priests in full canonicals trot up and down jingling hand-
bells, winding blasts on buffalo horns, and reciting exorcisms.
Sometimes the deities are represented in these processions
by living men, who are believed to be possessed by the divine
spirit.   Such a man-god may be seen naked to the waist with
his dishevelled hair streaming down his back ; long daggers
are stuck in his cheeks and arms, so that the blood drips
from them.   In his hand he carries a two-edged sword, with
which he deals doughty blows at the invisible foes in the
air ; but sometimes he inflicts bloody wounds on his own
back with the weapon or with a ball which is studded with
long sharp nails.   Other inspired men are carried in arm-
chairs, of which the seat, back, arms, and foot-rest are set
with nails or composed of rows of parallel sword-blades, that
cut into the flesh of the wretches seated on them : others
are stretched at full length on beds of nails.   For hours
these bleeding votaries are carried about the city.   Again,

Demons of sickness expelled in India and China.

---

[1] (Sir) J. George Scott and J. P.
Hardiman, *Gazetteer of Upper Burma
and the Shan States*, Part ii. vol. i.
(Rangoon, 1901) p. 440.

[2] T. H. Lewin, *Wild Tribes of
South-Eastern India* (London, 1870),
p. 226.

it is not uncommon to see in the procession a medium or man-god with a thick needle thrust through his tongue. His bloody spittle drips on sheets of paper, which the crowd eagerly scrambles for, knowing that with the blood they have absorbed the devil-dispelling power inherent in the man-god. The bloody papers, pasted on the lintel, walls, or beds of a house or on the bodies of the family, are supposed to afford complete protection against cholera. Such are the methods by which in Southern China the demons of disease are banished the city.[1]

Demons of sickness expelled in Japan.

In Japan the old-fashioned method of staying an epidemic is to expel the demon of the plague from every house into which he has entered. The treatment begins with the house in which the malady has appeared in the mildest form. First of all a Shinto priest makes a preliminary visit to the sick-room and extracts from the demon a promise that he will depart with him at his next visit. The day after he comes again, and, seating himself near the patient, beseeches the evil spirit to come away with him. Meanwhile red rice, which is used only on special occasions, has been placed at the sufferer's head, a closed litter made of pine boughs has been brought in, and four men equipped with flags or weapons have taken post in the four corners of the room to prevent the demon from seeking refuge there. All are silent but the priest. The prayer being over, the sick man's pillow is hastily thrown into the litter, and the priest cries, "All right now!" At that the bearers double with it into the street, the people within and without beat the air with swords, sticks, or anything that comes to hand, while others assist in the cure by banging away at drums and gongs. A procession is now formed in which only men take part, some of them carrying banners, others provided with a drum, a bell, a flute, a horn, and all of them wearing fillets and horns of twisted straw to keep the demon away from themselves. As the procession starts an old man chants, "What god are you bearing away?" To which the others respond in chorus, "The god of the pest we are bearing away!" Then to the music of the drum, the bell, the

---

[1] J. J. M. de Groot, *The Religious System of China*, vi. (Leyden, 1910) pp. 981 *sqq.* ; *id., The Religion of the Chinese* (New York, 1910), pp. 40 *sqq.*

flute, and the horn the litter is borne through the streets. During its passage all the people in the town who are not taking part in the ceremony remain indoors, every house along the route of the procession is carefully closed, and at the cross-roads swordsmen are stationed, who guard the street by hewing the air to right and left with their blades, lest the demon should escape by that way. The litter is thus carried to a retired spot between two towns and left there, while all who escorted it thither run away. Only the priest remains behind for half an hour to complete the exorcism and the cure. The bearers of the litter spend the night praying in a temple. Next day they return home, but not until they have plunged into a cold bath in the open air to prevent the demon from following them. The same litter serves to convey the evil spirit from every house in the town.[1] In Corea, when a patient is recovering from the smallpox, a farewell dinner is given in honour of the departing spirit of the disease. Friends and relations are invited, and the spirit's share of the good things is packed on the back of a hobby-horse and despatched to the boundary of the town or village, while respectful farewells are spoken and hearty good wishes uttered for his prosperous journey to his own place.[2] In Tonquin also a banquet is sometimes given to the demon of sickness to induce him to go quietly away from the house. The most honourable place at the festive board is reserved for the fiend ; prayers, caresses, and presents are lavished on him ; but if he proves obdurate, they assail him with coarse abuse and drive him from the house with musket-shots.[3]

Demons of sickness expelled in Corea and Tonquin.

---

[1] This description is taken from a newspaper-cutting, which was sent to me from the west of Scotland in October 1890, but without the name or date of the paper. The account, which is headed "Exorcism of the Pest Demon in Japan," purports to be derived from a series of notes on medical customs of the Japanese, which were contributed by Dr. C. H. H. Hall, of the U.S. Navy, to the *Sei-I Kwai Medical Journal*. Compare Lafcadio Hearn, *Glimpses of Unfamiliar Japan* (London, 1894), i. 147.

[2] Masanao Koike, "Zwei Jahren in Korea," *Internationales Archiv für Ethnographie*, iv. (1891) p. 10 ; Mrs. Bishop, *Korea and her Neighbours* (London, 1898), ii. 240.

[3] *Lettres édifiantes et curieuses*, Nouvelle Édition (Paris, 1780–1783), xvi. 206. It will be noticed that in this and the preceding case the principle of expulsion is applied for the benefit of an individual, not of a whole community. Yet the method of procedure in both is so similar to that adopted in the cases under consideration that I have allowed myself to cite them.

Demons
of sickness
expelled in
Africa.

When an epidemic is raging on the Gold Coast of West Africa, the people will sometimes turn out, armed with clubs and torches, to drive the evil spirits away. At a given signal the whole population begin with frightful yells to beat in every corner of the houses, then rush like mad into the streets waving torches and striking frantically in the empty air. The uproar goes on till somebody reports that the cowed and daunted demons have made good their escape by a gate of the town or village ; the people stream out after them, pursue them for some distance into the forest, and warn them never to return. The expulsion of the devils is followed by a general massacre of all the cocks in the village or town, lest by their unseasonable crowing they should betray to the banished demons the direction they must take to return to their old homes. For in that country the forest grows so thick or the grass so high that you can seldom see a village till you are close upon it ; and the first warning of your approach to human habitations is the crowing of the cocks.[1]   At Great Bassam, in Guinea, the French traveller Hecquard witnessed the exorcism of the evil spirit who was believed to make women barren. The women who wished to become mothers offered to the fetish wine-vessels or statuettes representing women suckling children. Then being assembled in the fetish hut, they were sprinkled with rum by the priest, while young men fired guns and brandished swords to drive away the demon.[2]   When smallpox breaks out in a village of the Cameroons, in West Africa, the spirit of the disease is driven out of the village by a " bushman " or member of the oppressed Bassa tribe, the members of which are reputed to possess high magical powers. The mode of expulsion consists in drumming and dancing for several days. Then the village is enclosed by ropes made of creepers in order that the disease may not return. Over the principal paths arches of bent poles are made, and fowls are buried as sacrifices. Plants of various sorts and the mushroom-shaped nests of termite ants are hung from the

---

[1] G. Zündel, "Land und Volk der Eweer auf der Sclavenküste in Westafrika," *Zeitschrift der Gesellschaft für Erdkunde zu Berlin*, xii. (1877) pp. 414 *sq.*

[2] H. Hecquard, *Reise an die Küste und in das Innere von West-Afrika* (Leipsic, 1854), p. 43.

arches, and a dog, freshly killed, is suspended over the middle of the entrance.[1] The Gallas try to drive away fever by firing guns, shouting, and lighting great fires.[2] When sickness was prevalent in a Huron village, and all other remedies had been tried in vain, the Indians had recourse to the ceremony called *Lonouyroya*, "which is the principal invention and most proper means, so they say, to expel from the town or village the devils and evil spirits which cause, induce, and import all the maladies and infirmities which they suffer in body and mind." Accordingly, one evening the men would begin to rush like madmen about the village, breaking and upsetting whatever they came across in the wigwams. They threw fire and burning brands about the streets, and all night long they ran howling and singing without cessation. Then they all dreamed of something, a knife, dog, skin, or whatever it might be, and when morning came they went from wigwam to wigwam asking for presents. These they received silently, till the particular thing was given them which they had dreamed about. On receiving it they uttered a cry of joy and rushed from the hut, amid the congratulations of all present. The health of those who received what they had dreamed of was believed to be assured ; whereas those who did not get what they had set their hearts upon regarded their fate as sealed.[3]

(marginal note: Demons of sickness expelled in America.*)*

---

[1] Dr. A. Plehn, "Beobachtungen in Kamerun, über die Anschauungen und Gebräuche einiger Negerstämme," *Zeitschrift für Ethnologie*, xxxvi. (1904) pp. 717 *sq.*

[2] Ph. Paulitschke, *Ethnographie Nordost-Afrikas : die materielle Cultur der Danâkil, Galla und Somâl* (Berlin, 1893), p. 177.

[3] F. Gabriel Sagard, *Le Grand Voyage du Pays des Hurons*, pp. 279 *sqq.* (195 *sq.* of the reprint, Paris, Libraire Tross, 1865). Compare *Relations des Jésuites*, 1639, pp. 88-92 (Canadian reprint, Quebec, 1858), from which it appears that each man demanded the subject of his dream in the form of a riddle, which the hearers tried to solve. The custom of asking riddles at certain seasons or on certain special occasions is curious and has not yet, so far as I know, been explained.

Perhaps enigmas were originally circumlocutions adopted at times when for certains reasons the speaker was forbidden the use of direct terms. They appear to be especially employed in the neighbourhood of a dead body. Thus in Bolang Mongondo (Celebes) riddles may never be asked except when there is a corpse in the village. See N. P. Wilken en J. A. Schwarz, "Allerlei over het land en volk van Bolaäng Mongondou," *Mededeelingen van wege het Nederlandsche Zendeling-genootschap*, xi. (1867) p. 357. In the Aru archipelago, while a corpse is uncoffined, the watchers propound riddles to each other, or rather they think of things which the others have to guess. See J. G. F. Riedel, *De sluik- en kroesharige rassen tusschen Selebes en Papua*, pp. 267 *sq.* In Brittany after a burial, when the rest

Sometimes, instead of chasing the demon of disease from their homes, savages prefer to leave him in peaceable possession, while they themselves take to flight and attempt to prevent him from following in their tracks. Thus when the Patagonians were attacked by smallpox, which they attributed to the machinations of an evil spirit, they used to abandon their sick and flee, slashing the air with their weapons and throwing water about in order to keep off the dreadful pursuer ; and when after several days' march they reached a place where they hoped to be beyond his reach, they used by way of precaution to plant all their cutting weapons with the sharp edges turned towards the quarter from which they had come, as if they were repelling a charge of cavalry.[1] Similarly, when the Lules or Tonocotes Indians of the Gran Chaco were attacked by an epidemic, they regularly sought to evade it by flight, but in so doing they always followed a

---

have gone to partake of the funeral banquet, old men remain behind in the graveyard, and having seated themselves on mallows, ask each other riddles. See A. de Nore, *Coutumes, Mythes et Traditions des Provinces de France* (Paris and Lyons, 1846), p. 199. Among the Akamba of British East Africa boys and girls at circumcision have to interpret certain pictographs cut on sticks : these pictographs are called "riddles." See C. W. Hobley, *Ethnology of A-Kamba and other East African Tribes* (Cambridge, 1910), pp. 71 *sq.* In Vedic times the priests proposed enigmas to each other at the great sacrifice of a horse. See *The Satapatha Brahmana*, translated by J. Eggeling, Part v. (Oxford, 1900), pp. 314-316 (*Sacred Books of the East*, vol. xliv.); H. Oldenberg, *Die Religion des Veda* (Berlin, 1894), p. 475. Compare O. Schrader, *Reallexikon der indogermanischen Altertumskunde* (Strasburg, 1901), pp. 647 *sq.* Among Turkish tribes of Central Asia girls publicly propound riddles to their wooers, who are punished if they cannot read them. See H. Vambery, *Das Türkenvolk* (Leipsic, 1885), pp. 232 *sq.* Among the Alfoors of Central Celebes riddles may only be asked during the season when the fields are

being tilled and the crops are growing. People meeting together at this time occupy themselves with asking riddles and telling stories. As soon as some one has found the answer to a riddle, they all cry out, "Make our rice to grow, make fat ears to grow both in the valleys and on the heights." But during the months which elapse between harvest and the preparation of new land for tillage the propounding of enigmas is strictly forbidden. The writer who reports the custom conjectures that the cry "Make our rice to grow" is addressed to the souls of the ancestors. See A. C. Kruijt, "Een en ander aangaande het geestelijk en maatschappelijk leven van den Poso-Alfoer," *Mededeelingen van wege het Nederlandsche Zendelinggenootschap*, xxxix. (1895) pp. 142 *sq.* Amongst the Toboongkoo of Central Celebes riddles are propounded at harvest and by watchers over a corpse. See A. C. Kruijt, "Eenige ethnografische aanteekeningen omtrent de Toboengkoe en de Tomori," *Mededeelingen van wege het Nederlandsche Zendelinggenootschap*, xliv. (1900) pp. 223, 228.

[1] A. d'Orbigny, *Voyage dans l'Amérique Méridionale*, ii. (Paris and Strasburg, 1839–1843) p. 190.

sinuous, not a straight, course ; because they said that when the disease made after them he would be so exhausted by the turnings and windings of the route that he would never be able to come up with them.[1]   When the Indians of New Mexico were decimated by smallpox or other infectious disease, they used to shift their quarters every day, retreating into the most sequestered parts of the mountains and choosing the thorniest thickets they could find, in the hope that the smallpox would be too afraid of scratching himself on the thorns to follow them.[2]   When some Chins on a visit to Rangoon were attacked by cholera, they went about with drawn swords to scare away the demon, and they spent the day hiding under bushes so that he might not be able to find them.[3]

§ 2. *The Periodic Expulsion of Evils*

The expulsion of evils, from being occasional, tends to become periodic. It comes to be thought desirable to have a general riddance of evil spirits at fixed times, usually once a year, in order that the people may make a fresh start in life, freed from all the malignant influences which have been long accumulating about them. Some of the Australian blacks annually expelled the ghosts of the dead from their territory. The ceremony was witnessed by the Rev. W. Ridley on the banks of the River Barwan. "A chorus of twenty, old and young, were singing and beating time with boomerangs. . . . Suddenly, from under a sheet of bark darted a man with his body whitened by pipeclay, his head and face coloured with lines of red and yellow, and a tuft of feathers fixed by means of a stick two feet above the crown of his head. He stood twenty minutes perfectly still, gazing upwards. An aboriginal who stood by told me he was looking for the ghosts of dead men. At last he began to move very slowly, and soon rushed to and fro at full

The periodic expulsion of evils.

Annual expulsion of ghosts in Australia.

[1] Pedro Lozano, *Descripcion Chorographica del Terreno, Rios, Arboles, y Animales de las dilatadissimas Provincias del Gran Chaco, Gualamba,* etc. (Cordova, 1733) p. 100.

[2] H. H. Bancroft, *Natives Races of the Pacific States* (London, 1875–1876), i. 589 note 259, quoting Arlegui, *Chrón. de Zacatecas,* pp. 152-3, 182.

[3] Bertram S. Carey and H. N. Tuck, *The Chin Hills,* i. (Rangoon, 1896) p. 198.

speed, flourishing a branch as if to drive away some foes invisible to us. When I thought this pantomime must be almost over, ten more, similarly adorned, suddenly appeared from behind the trees, and the whole party joined in a brisk conflict with their mysterious assailants. . . . At last, after some rapid evolutions in which they put forth all their strength, they rested from the exciting toil which they had kept up all night and for some hours after sunrise; they seemed satisfied that the ghosts were driven away for twelve months. They were performing the same ceremony at every station along the river, and I am told it is an annual custom."[1]

Annual expulsion of Tuña among the Esquimaux of Alaska.

Certain seasons of the year mark themselves naturally out as appropriate moments for a general expulsion of devils. Such a moment occurs towards the close of an Arctic winter, when the sun reappears on the horizon after an absence of weeks or months. Accordingly, at Point Barrow, the most northerly extremity of Alaska, and nearly of America, the Esquimaux choose the moment of the sun's reappearance to hunt the mischievous spirit Tuña from every house. The ceremony was witnessed by the members of the United States Polar Expedition, who wintered at Point Barrow. A fire was built in front of the council-house, and an old woman was posted at the entrance to every house. The men gathered round the council-house, while the young women and girls drove the spirits out of every house with their knives, stabbing viciously under the bunk and deer-skins, and calling upon Tuña to be gone. When they thought he had been driven out of every hole and corner, they thrust him down through the hole in the floor and chased him into the open air with loud cries and frantic gestures. Meanwhile the old woman at the entrance of the house made passes with a long knife in the air to keep him from returning. Each party drove the spirit towards the fire and invited him to go into it. All were by this time drawn up in a semicircle round the fire, when several of the leading men made specific charges against the spirit; and each after his speech brushed his clothes violently, calling on the spirit to leave

---

[1] Rev. W. Ridley, in J. D. Lang's *Queensland* (London, 1861), p. 441. Compare Rev. W. Ridley, *Kamilaroi* (Sydney, 1875), p. 149.

him and go into the fire. Two men now stepped forward
with rifles loaded with blank cartridges, while a third
brought a vessel of urine and flung it on the flames. At
the same time one of the men fired a shot into the fire; and as
the cloud of steam rose it received the other shot, which was
supposed to finish Tuña for the time being.[1]

In late autumn, when storms rage over the land and
break the icy fetters by which the frozen sea is as yet but
slightly bound, when the loosened floes are driven against
each other and break with loud crashes, and when the cakes
of ice are piled in wild disorder one upon another, the
Esquimaux of Baffin Land fancy they hear the voices of the
spirits who people the mischief-laden air. Then the ghosts
of the dead knock wildly at the huts, which they cannot
enter, and woe to the hapless wight whom they catch ; he
soon sickens and dies. Then the phantom of a huge hairless
dog pursues the real dogs, which expire in convulsions and
cramps at sight of him. All the countless spirits of evil are
abroad, striving to bring sickness and death, foul weather
and failure in hunting on the Esquimaux. Most dreaded
of all these spectral visitants are Sedna, mistress of the
nether world, and her father, to whose share dead Esquimaux
fall. While the other spirits fill the air and the water, she
rises from under ground. It is then a busy season for
the wizards. In every house you may hear them singing
and praying, while they conjure the spirits, seated in a
mystic gloom at the back of the hut, which is dimly lit by a
lamp burning low. The hardest task of all is to drive away
Sedna, and this is reserved for the most powerful enchanter.
A rope is coiled on the floor of a large hut in such a way
as to leave a small opening at the top, which represents the
breathing hole of a seal. Two enchanters stand beside it,
one of them grasping a spear as if he were watching a seal-
hole in winter, the other holding the harpoon-line. A third

*Annual
expulsion
of Sedna
among the
Esquimaux
of Baffin
Land.*

---

[1] *Report of the International Polar
Expedition to Point Barrow, Alaska*
(Washington, 1885), pp. 42 *sq.* It is
said that in Thule, where the sun disappeared below the horizon for forty
days every winter, the greatest festival
of the year was held when the luminary
reappeared. " It seems to me," says
Procopius, who records the fact, " that
though the same thing happens every
year, these islanders are very much
afraid lest the sun should fail them
altogether." See Procopius, *De bello
Gothico,* ii. 15.

sorcerer sits at the back of the hut chanting a magic song to lure Sedna to the spot. Now she is heard approaching under the floor of the hut, breathing heavily ; now she emerges at the hole ; now she is harpooned and sinks away in angry haste, dragging the harpoon with her, while the two men hold on to the line with all their might. The struggle is severe, but at last by a desperate wrench she tears herself away and returns to her dwelling in Adlivun. When the harpoon is drawn up out of the hole it is found to be splashed with blood, which the enchanters proudly exhibit as a proof of their prowess. Thus Sedna and the other evil spirits are at last driven away, and next day a great festival is celebrated by old and young in honour of the event. But they must still be cautious, for the wounded Sedna is furious and will seize any one she may find outside of his hut ; so they all wear amulets on the top of their hoods to protect themselves against her. These amulets consist of pieces of the first garments that they wore after birth.[1]

Annual expulsion of demons among the Koryaks.
The Koryaks of the Taigonos Peninsula, in north-eastern Asia, celebrate annually a festival after the winter solstice. Rich men invite all their neighbours to the festival, offer a sacrifice to " The-One-on-High," and slaughter many reindeer for their guests. If there is a shaman present he goes all round the interior of the house, beating the drum and driving away the demons (*kalau*). He searches all the people in the house, and if he finds a demon's arrow sticking in the body of one of them, he pulls it out, though naturally the arrow is invisible to common eyes. In this way he protects them against disease and death. If there is no

[1] Fr. Boas, "The Eskimo," *Proceedings and Transactions of the Royal Society of Canada for 1887*, vol. v. (Montreal, 1888) sect. ii. 36 *sq.* ; *id.*, " The Central Eskimo," *Sixth Annual Report of the Bureau of Ethnology* (Washington, 1888), pp. 603 *sq.* Elsewhere, however, the writer mentions a different explanation of the custom of harpooning Sedna. He says : " Sedna feels kindly towards the people if they have succeeded in cutting her. If there is no blood on the knife, it is an ill omen. As to the reason why Sedna must be cut, the people say that it is an old custom, and that it makes her feel better, that it is the same as giving a thirsty person a drink." See Fr. Boas, "The Eskimo of Baffin Land and Hudson Bay," *Bulletin of the American Museum of Natural History*, xv. (New York, 1901) p. 139. However, this explanation may well be an afterthought devised to throw light on an old custom of which the original meaning had been forgotten.

shaman present, the demons may be expelled by the host or by a woman skilled in incantations.[1]

The Iroquois inaugurated the new year in January, February, or March (the time varied) with a " festival of dreams " like that which the Hurons observed on special occasions.[2] The whole ceremonies lasted several days, or even weeks, and formed a kind of saturnalia. Men and women, variously disguised, went from wigwam to wigwam smashing and throwing down whatever they came across. It was a time of general license ; the people were supposed to be out of their senses, and therefore not to be responsible for what they did. Accordingly, many seized the opportunity of paying off old scores by belabouring obnoxious persons, drenching them with ice-cold water, and covering them with filth or hot ashes. Others seized burning brands or coals and flung them at the heads of the first persons they met. The only way of escaping from these persecutors was to guess what they had dreamed of. On one day of the festival the ceremony of driving away evil spirits from the village took place. Men clothed in the skins of wild beasts, their faces covered with hideous masks, and their hands with the shell of the tortoise, went from hut to hut making frightful noises ; in every hut they took the fuel from the fire and scattered the embers and ashes about the floor with their hands. The general confession of sins which preceded the festival was probably a preparation for the public expulsion of evil influences ; it was a way of stripping the people of their moral burdens, that these might be collected and cast out. This New Year festival is still celebrated by some of the heathen Iroquois, though it has been shorn of its former turbulence. A conspicuous feature in the ceremony is now the sacrifice of the White Dog, but this appears to have been added to the festival in comparatively modern times, and does not figure in the oldest descriptions of the ceremonies. We shall return to it later on.[3] A great annual festival of

Annual expulsion of demons among the Iroquois.

---

[1] W. Jochelson, *The Koryak* (Leyden and New York, 1908), p. 88 (*The Jesup North Pacific Expedition*, vol. vi., *Memoir of the American Museum of Natural History*).

[2] Above, p. 121.

[3] *Relations des Jésuites*, 1656, pp. 26 - 28 (Canadian reprint, Quebec, 1858) ; J. F. Lafitau, *Mœurs des Sauvages Ameriquains* (Paris, 1724), i. 367-369 ; Charlevoix, *Histoire de la Nouvelle France*, vi. 82 *sqq.* ; Timothy

the Cherokee Indians was the Propitiation, "Cementation,"
or Purification festival.   " It was celebrated shortly after the
first new moon of autumn, and consisted of a multiplicity of
rigorous rites, fastings, ablutions, and purifications.   Among
the most important functionaries on the occasion were seven
exorcisers or cleansers, whose duty it was, at a certain stage
of the proceedings, to drive away evil and purify the town.
Each one bore in his hand a white rod of sycamore.   ' The
leader, followed by the others, walked around the national
heptagon, and coming to the treasure or store-house to the
west of it, they lashed the eaves of the roofs with their rods.
The leader then went to another house, followed by the
others, singing, and repeated the same ceremony until every
house was purified.'   This ceremony was repeated daily
during the continuance of the festival.   In performing their
ablutions they went into the water, and allowed their old
clothes to be carried away by the stream, by which means
they supposed their impurities removed." [1]

Annual
expulsion
of evils
among the
Incas of
Peru.
In September the Incas of Peru celebrated a festival
called Situa, the object of which was to banish from the
capital and its vicinity all disease and trouble.   The festival
fell in September because the rains begin about this time,
and with the first rains there was generally much sickness.
And the melancholy begotten by the inclemency of the
weather and the sickliness of the season may well have been
heightened by the sternness of a landscape which at all
times is fitted to oppress the mind with a sense of desolation
and gloom.   For Cuzco, the capital of the Incas and the

Dwight, *Travels in New England and
New York* (London, 1823), iv. 201 *sq.*;
L. H. Morgan, *League of the Iroquois*
(Rochester, 1851), pp. 207 *sqq.*; Mrs.
E. A. Smith, " Myths of the Iroquois,"
*Second Annual Report of the Bureau
of Ethnology* (Washington, 1883), pp.
112 *sqq.* ; Horatio Hale, "Iroquois
Sacrifice of the White Dog," *American
Antiquarian*, vii. (1885) pp. 7 *sqq.*,
W. M. Beauchamp, "Iroquois White
Dog Feast," *ibid.* pp. 235 *sqq.* "They
had one day in the year which might
be called the Festival of Fools ; for in
fact they pretended to be mad, rushing
from hut to hut, so that if they ill-
treated any one or carried off anything,
they would say next day, ' I was mad ;
I had not my senses about me.'   And
the others would accept this explanation
and exact no vengeance " (L. Hennepin,
Description de la Louisiane, Paris,
1683, pp. 71 *sq.*).

[1] J. H. Payne, quoted in "Observa-
tions on the Creek and Cherokee
Indians, by W. Bartram, 1789, with
prefatory and supplementary notes by
E. G. Squier," *Transactions of the
American Ethnological Society*, vol. iii.
Part i. (1853) p. 78.

scene of the ceremony, lies in a high upland valley, bare and
treeless, shut in on every side by the most arid and forbidding mountaiñs.[1]   As a preparation for the festival the
people fasted on the first day of the moon after the
autumnal equinox.   Having fasted during the day, and
the night being come, they baked a coarse paste of
maize.   This paste was made of two sorts.   One was
kneaded with the blood of children aged from five to ten
years, the blood being obtained by bleeding the children
between the eyebrows.   These two kinds of paste were
baked separately, because they were for different uses.   Each
family assembled at the house of the eldest brother to
celebrate the feast ; and those who had no elder brother
went to the house of their next relation of greater age.   On
the same night all who had fasted during the day washed
their bodies, and taking a little of the blood-kneaded paste,
rubbed it over their head, face, breast, shoulders, arms, and
legs.   They did this in order that the paste might take away
all their infirmities.   After this the head of the family
anointed the threshold with the same paste, and left it there
as a token that the inmates of the house had performed their
ablutions and cleansed their bodies.   Meantime the High
Priest performed the same ceremonies in the temple of the
Sun.   As soon as the Sun rose, all the people worshipped
and besought him to drive all evils out of the city, and then
they broke their fast with the paste that had been kneaded
without blood.   When they had paid their worship and
broken their fast, which they did at a stated hour, in order
that all might adore the Sun as one man, an Inca of the
blood royal came forth from the fortress, as a messenger of
the Sun, richly dressed, with his mantle girded round his
body, and a lance in his hand.   The lance was decked with
feathers of many hues, extending from the blade to the
socket, and fastened with rings of gold.   He ran down the
hill from the fortress brandishing his lance, till he reached
the centre of the great square, where stood the golden urn,
like a fountain, that was used for the sacrifice of the fermented

---

[1] C. Gay, "Fragment d'un voyage
dans le Chili et au Cusco patrie des
anciens Incas," *Bulletin de la Société*
de Géographie (Paris), ii. Série, xix.
(1843) pp. 29 *sq.*

juice of the maize. Here four other Incas of the blood royal awaited him, each with a lance in his hand, and his mantle girded up to run. The messenger touched their four lances with his lance, and told them that the Sun bade them, as his messengers, drive the evils out of the city. The four Incas then separated and ran down the four royal roads which led out of the city to the four quarters of the world. While they ran, all the people, great and small, came to the doors of their houses, and with great shouts of joy and gladness shook their clothes, as if they were shaking off dust, while they cried, "Let the evils be gone. How greatly desired has this festival been by us. O Creator of all things, permit us to reach another year, that we may see another feast like this." After they had shaken their clothes, they passed their hands over their heads, faces, arms, and legs, as if in the act of washing. All this was done to drive the evils out of their houses, that the messengers of the Sun might banish them from the city ; and it was done not only in the streets through which the Incas ran, but generally in all quarters of the city. Moreover, they all danced, the Inca himself amongst them, and bathed in the rivers and fountains, saying that their maladies would come out of them. Then they took great torches of straw, bound round with cords. These they lighted, and passed from one to the other, striking each other with them, and saying, "Let all harm go away." Meanwhile the runners ran with their lances for a quarter of a league outside the city, where they found four other Incas ready, who received the lances from their hands and ran with them. Thus the lances were carried by relays of runners for a distance of five or six leagues, at the end of which the runners washed themselves and their weapons in rivers, and set up the lances, in sign of a boundary within which the banished evils might not return.[1]

[1] Garcilasso de la Vega, *Royal Commentaries of the Yncas*, translated by (Sir) Clements R. Markham (Hakluyt Society, London, 1869–1871), Part i. bk. vii. ch. 6, vol. ii. pp. 228 *sqq.* ; Molina, "Fables and Rites of the Yncas," in *Rites and Laws of the Yncas* (Hakluyt Society, 1873), pp. 20 *sqq.* ; J. de Acosta, *History of the Indies*, bk. v. ch. 28, vol. ii. pp. 375 *sq.* (Hakluyt Society, London, 1880). The accounts of Garcilasso and Molina are somewhat discrepant, but this may be explained by the statement of the latter that "in one year they added, and in another they reduced the number

The negroes of Guinea annually banish the devil from all their towns with much ceremony at a time set apart for the purpose.   At Axim, on the Gold Coast, this annual expulsion is preceded by a feast of eight days, during which mirth and jollity, skipping, dancing, and singing prevail, and " a perfect lampooning liberty is allowed, and scandal so highly exalted, that they may freely sing of all the faults, villanies, and frauds of their superiors as well as inferiors, without punishment, or so much as the least interruption."   On the eighth day they hunt out the devil with a dismal cry, running after him and pelting him with sticks, stones, and whatever comes to hand.   When they have driven him far enough out of the town, they all return.   In this way he is expelled from more than a hundred towns at the same time.   To make sure that he does not return to their houses, the women wash and scour all their wooden and earthen vessels, " to free them from all uncleanness and the devil."[1]   A later writer tells us that "on the Gold Coast there are stated occasions, when the people turn out *en masse* (generally at night) with clubs and torches to drive away the evil spirits from their towns.   At a given signal, the whole community start up, commence a most hideous howling, beat about in every nook and corner of their dwellings, then rush into the streets, with their torches and clubs, like so many frantic maniacs, beat the air, and scream at the top of their voices, until some one announces the departure of the spirits through some gate of the town, when they are pursued several miles into the woods, and warned not to come back.   After this the people breathe easier, sleep more quietly, have better health, and the town is once more cheered by an abundance of food."[2]

The ceremony as it is practised at Gatto, in Benin, has been described by an English traveller.   He says : " It was

---

of ceremonies, according to circumstances."   Molina places the festival in August, Garcilasso and Acosta in September.   According to Garcilasso there were only four runners in Cuzco ; according to Molina there were four hundred.   Acosta's account is very brief.   In the description given in the text features have been borrowed from all three accounts, where these seemed consistent with each other.

[1] W. Bosman, " Description of the Coast of Guinea," in J. Pinkerton's *Voyages and Travels,* xvi. (London, 1814) p. 402 ; Pierre Bouche, *La Côte des Esclaves* (Paris, 1885), p. 395.

[2] Rev. J. Leighton Wilson, *Western Africa* (London, 1856), p. 217.

about this time that I witnessed a strange ceremony, peculiar to this people, called the time of the 'grand devils.' Eight men were dressed in a most curious manner, having a dress made of bamboo about their bodies, and a cap on the head, of various colours and ornamented with red feathers taken from the parrot's tail ; round the legs were twisted strings of shells, which made a clattering noise as they walked, and the face and hands of each individual were covered with a net. These strange beings go about the town, by day and by night, for the term of one month, uttering the most discordant and frightful noises ; no one durst venture out at night for fear of being killed or seriously maltreated by these fellows, who are then especially engaged in driving the evil spirits from the town. They go round to all the chief's houses, and in addition to the noise they make, perform some extraordinary feats in tumbling and gymnastics, for which they receive a few cowries." [1]

Annual expulsion of demons at Cape Coast Castle.

At Cape Coast Castle, on the Gold Coast, the ceremony was witnessed on the ninth of October 1844 by an Englishman, who has described it as follows : " To-night the annual custom of driving the evil spirit, Abonsam, out of the town has taken place.   As soon as the eight o'clock gun fired in the fort the people began firing muskets in their houses, turning all their furniture out of doors, beating about in every corner of the rooms with sticks. etc., and screaming as loudly as possible, in order to frighten the devil.   Being driven out of the houses, as they imagine, they sallied forth into the streets, throwing lighted torches about, shouting, screaming, beating sticks together, rattling old pans, making the most horrid noise, in order to drive him out of the town into the sea.   The custom is preceded by four weeks' dead silence ; no gun is allowed to be fired, no drum to be beaten, no palaver to be made between man and man.   If, during these weeks, two natives should disagree and make a noise in the town, they are immediately taken before the king and fined heavily.   If a dog or pig, sheep or goat be found at large in the street, it may be killed, or taken by anyone, the former owner not being allowed to demand any compensation.

[1] *Narrative of Captain James Fawckner's Travels on the Coast of* *Benin, West Africa* (London, 1837), pp. 102 *sq.*

This silence is designed to deceive Abonsam, that, being off his guard, he may be taken by surprise, and frightened out of the place. If anyone die during the silence, his relatives are not allowed to weep until the four weeks have been completed." [1]

At Onitsha, on the Niger, Mr. J. C. Taylor witnessed the celebration of New Year's Day by the negroes. It fell on the twentieth of December 1858. Every family brought a firebrand out into the street, threw it away, and exclaimed as they returned, "The gods of the new year! New Year has come round again." Mr. Taylor adds, "The meaning of the custom seems to be that the fire is to drive away the old year with its sorrows and evils, and to embrace the new year with hearty reception." [2] Of all Abyssinian festivals that of Mascal or the Cross is celebrated with the greatest pomp. During the whole of the interval between St. John's day and the feast a desultory warfare is waged betwixt the youth of opposite sexes in the towns. They all sally out in the evenings, the boys armed with nettles or thistles and the girls with gourds containing a filthy solution of all sorts of abominations. When any of the hostile parties meet, they begin by reviling each other in the foulest language, from which they proceed to personal violence, the boys stinging the girls with their nettles, while the girls discharge their stink-pots in the faces of their adversaries. These hostilities may perhaps be regarded as a preparation for the festival of the Cross. The eve of the festival witnesses a ceremony which doubtless belongs to the world-wide class of customs we are dealing with. At sunset a discharge of fire-arms takes place from all the principal houses. "Then every one provides himself with a torch, and during the early part of the night bonfires are kindled, and the people parade the town, carrying their lighted torches in their hands. They go through their houses, too, poking a light into every dark corner in the hall, under the couches, in the stables, kitchen, etc., as if looking for something lost, and

Marginal notes:
Annual expulsion of evils on the Niger and in Abyssinia.

---

[1] "Extracts from Diary of the late Rev. John Martin, Wesleyan Missionary in West Africa, 1843–1848," *Man*, xii. (1912) pp. 138 *sq.* Compare Major A. J. N. Tremearne, *The Tailed Head-hunters of Nigeria* (London, 1912), pp. 202 *sq.*

[2] S. Crowther and J. C. Taylor, *The Gospel on the Banks of the Niger* (London, 1859), p. 320.

calling out, 'Akho, akhoky! turn out the spinage, and bring in the porridge; Mascal is come!' . . . After this they play, and poke fun and torches at each other." Next morning, while it is still dark, bonfires are kindled on the heights near the towns, and people rise early to see them. The rising sun of Mascal finds the whole population of Abyssinia awake.[1]

Annual expulsion of spirits at the yam harvest in New Guinea.

Sometimes the date of the annual expulsion of devils is fixed with reference to the agricultural seasons. Thus at Kiriwina, in South-Eastern New Guinea, when the new yams had been harvested, the people feasted and danced for many days, and a great deal of property, such as armlets, native money, and so forth, was displayed conspicuously on a platform erected for the purpose. When the festivities were over, all the people gathered together and expelled the spirits from the village by shouting, beating the posts of the houses, and overturning everything under which a wily spirit might be supposed to lurk. The explanation which the people gave to a missionary was that they had entertained and feasted the spirits and provided them with riches, and it was now time for them to take their departure. Had they not seen the dances, and heard the songs, and gorged themselves on the souls of the yams, and appropriated the souls of the money and all the other fine things set out on the platform? What more could the spirits want? So out they must go.[2]

Annual expulsion of demons among the Hos of West Africa before eating the new yams.

Among the Hos of Togoland in West Africa the expulsion of evils is performed annually before the people eat the new yams.[3] The chiefs meet together and summon the priests and magicians. They tell them that the people are now to eat the new yams and to be merry, therefore they must cleanse the town and remove the evils. For that purpose they take leaves of the *adzu* and *wo* trees, together with creepers and ashes. The leaves and creepers they bind fast to a pole of an *adzu* tree, while they pray that the evil spirits, the witches, and all the ills in the town may pass into the bundle and be bound. Then they make a paste out of the ashes and

[1] Mansfield Parkyns, *Life in Abyssinia*, Second Edition (London, 1868), pp. 285 *sq.*

[2] George Brown, D.D., *Melanesians and Polynesian* (London, 1910), pp. 413 *sq.*

[3] As to the ceremony of eating the new yams, see *Spirits of the Corn and of the Wild*, ii. 58 *sqq.*

smear it on the bundle, saying, " We smear it on the face of
all the evil ones who are in this bundle, in order that they
may not be able to see." With that they throw the bundle,
that is, the pole wrapt in leaves and creepers, on the ground
and they all mock at it. Then they prepare a medicine
and take the various leaf-wrapt poles, into which they have
conjured and bound up all mischief, carry them out of the
town, and set them up in the earth on various roads leading
into the town. When they have done this, they say that
they have banished the evils from the town and shut the
door in their face. With the medicine, which the elders
have prepared, all men, women, children and chiefs wash
their faces. After that everybody goes home to sweep out
his house and homestead. The ground in front of the
homesteads is also swept, so that the town is thoroughly
cleansed. All the stalks of grass and refuse of stock yams
that have been swept together they cast out of the town,
and they rail at the stock yams. In the course of the
night the elders assemble and bind a toad to a young palm-
leaf. They say that they will now sweep out the town and
end the ceremony. For that purpose they drag the toad
through the whole town in the direction of Mount Adaklu.
When that has been done, the priests say that they will now
remove the sicknesses. In the evening they give public
notice that they are about to go on the road, and that
therefore no one may light a fire on the hearth or eat food.
Next morning the women of the town sweep out their
houses and hearths and deposit the sweepings on broken
wooden plates. Many wrap themselves in torn mats and
tattered clothes ; others swathe themselves in grass and
creepers. While they do so, they pray, saying, " All ye
sicknesses that are in our body and plague us, we are come
to-day to throw you out." When they start to do so, the
priest gives orders that everybody is to scream once and at
the same time to smite his mouth. In a moment they all
scream, smite their mouths, and run as fast as they can in
the direction of Mount Adaklu. As they run, they say,
" Out to-day ! Out to-day ! That which kills anybody, out
to-day ! Ye evil spirits, out to-day ! and all that causes our
heads to ache, out to-day ! Anlo and Adaklu are the places

whither all ill shall betake itself!"   Now on Mount Adaklu there grows a *klo* tree, and when the people have come to the tree they throw everything away and return home.   On their return they wash themselves with the medicine which is set forth in the streets ; then they enter their houses.[1]

Annual expulsion of demons among the Hos of North-Eastern India at harvest.   Among the Hos of North-Eastern India the great festival of the year is the harvest home, held in January, when the granaries are full of grain, and the people, to use their own expression, are full of devilry.   "They have a strange notion that at this period, men and women are so overcharged with vicious propensities, that it is absolutely necessary for the safety of the person to let off steam by allowing for a time full vent to the passions."   The ceremonies open with a sacrifice to the village god of three fowls, a cock and two hens, one of which must be black.   Along with them are offered flowers of the Palas tree (*Butea frondosa*), bread made from rice-flour, and sesamum seeds.   These offerings are presented by the village priest, who prays that during the year about to begin they and their children may be preserved from all misfortune and sickness, and that they may have seasonable rain and good crops.   Prayer is also made in some places for the souls of the dead.   At this time an evil spirit is supposed to infest the place, and to get rid of it men, women, and children go in procession round and through every part of the village with sticks in their hands, as if beating for game, singing a wild chant, and shouting vociferously, till they feel assured that the evil spirit must have fled.   Then they give themselves up to feasting and drinking rice-beer, till they are in a fit state for the wild debauch which follows.   The festival now "becomes a saturnale, during which servants forget their duty to their masters, children their reverence for parents, men their

---

[1] J. Spieth, *Die Ewe - Stämme* (Berlin, 1906), pp. 305 - 307. At Kotedougou a French officer saw a number of disguised men called *dou* dancing and performing various antics about the houses, under the trees, and in the fields.   Hemp and palm leaves were sewn on their garments and they wore caps of hemp surmounted by a crest of red - ochred wood, sometimes by a wooden beak of a bird.   He gathered that the ceremony takes place at the beginning of winter, and he thought that the processions "are perhaps intended to drive away the evil spirits at the season of tillage or perhaps also to procure rain."   See Le Capitaine Binger, *Du Niger au Golfe de Guinée par le pays de Kong et le Mossi* (Paris, 1892), pp. 378-380.

respect for women, and women all notions of modesty, delicacy, and gentleness; they become raging bacchantes." Usually the Hos are quiet and reserved in manner, decorous and gentle to women. But during this festival "their natures appear to undergo a temporary change. Sons and daughters revile their parents in gross language, and parents their children; men and women become almost like animals in the indulgence of their amorous propensities." The festival is not held simultaneously in all the villages. The time during which it is celebrated in the different villages of a district may be from a month to six weeks, and by a pre-concerted arrangement the celebration begins at each village on a different date and lasts three or four days; so the inhabitants of each may take part in a long series of orgies. On these occasions the utmost liberty is given to the girls, who may absent themselves for days with the young men of another village; parents at such times never attempt to lay their daughters under any restraint. The Mundaris, kinsmen and neighbours of the Hos, keep the festival in much the same manner. "The resemblance to a Saturnale is very complete, as at this festival the farm labourers are feasted by their masters, and allowed the utmost freedom of speech in addressing them. It is the festival of the harvest home; the termination of one year's toil, and a slight respite from it before they commence again."[1]

Amongst some of the Hindoo Koosh tribes, as among the Hos and Mundaris, the expulsion of devils takes place after harvest. When the last crop of autumn has been got in, it is thought necessary to drive away evil spirits from the granaries. A kind of porridge called *mool* is eaten, and the head of the family takes his matchlock and fires it into the floor. Then, going outside, he sets to work loading and firing till his powder-horn is exhausted, while all his neighbours are similarly employed. The next day is spent in rejoicings. In Chitral this festival is called "devil-driving."[2]

Annual expulsion of demons among the Hindoo Koosh tribes at harvest.

---

[1] E. T. Dalton, *Descriptive Ethnology of Bengal* (Calcutta, 1872), pp. 196 *sq.* We have seen that among the Pondos of South Africa the harvest festival of first-fruits is in like manner a period of licence and debauchery. See *Spirits of the Corn and of the Wild*, ii. 66 *sq.*

[2] Major J. Biddulph, *Tribes of the Hindoo Koosh* (Calcutta, 1880), p. 103.

Annual
expulsion
of demons
among the
Khonds at
sowing.

On the other hand the Khonds of India expel the devils at seed-time instead of at harvest. At this time they worship Pitteri Pennu, the god of increase and of gain in every shape. On the first day of the festival a rude car is made of a basket set upon a few sticks, tied upon bamboo rollers for wheels. The priest takes this car first to the house of the lineal head of the tribe, to whom precedence is given in all ceremonies connected with agriculture. Here he receives a little of each kind of seed and some feathers. He then takes the car to all the other houses in the village, each of which contributes the same things. Lastly, the car is conducted to a field without the village, attended by all the young men, who beat each other and strike the air violently with long sticks. The seed thus carried out is called the share of the "evil spirits, spoilers of the seed." "These are considered to be driven out with the car ; and when it and its contents are abandoned to them, they are held to have no excuse for interfering with the rest of the seed-corn." Next day each household kills a hog over the seed for the year, and prays to Pitteri Pennu, saying, "O Pitteri Pennu! this seed we shall sow to-morrow. Some of us, your suppliants, will have a great return, some a small return. Let the least favoured have a full basket, let the most favoured have many baskets. Give not this seed to ant, or rat, or hog. Let the stems which shall spring from it be so stout that the earth shall tremble under them. Let the rain find no hole or outlet whereby to escape from our fields. Make the earth soft like the ashes of cow-dung. To him who has no iron wherewith to shoe his plough, make the wood of the *doh*-tree like iron. Provide other food than our seed for the parrot, the crow, and all the fowls and beasts of the jungle. Let not the white ant destroy the roots, nor the wild hog crush the stem to get at the fruit ; and make our crops of all kinds have a better flavour than that of those of any other country." The elders then feast upon the hogs. The young men are excluded from the repast, but enjoy the privilege of waylaying and pelting with jungle - fruit their elders as they return from the feast. Upon the third day the lineal head of the tribe goes out and sows his seed, after which all the rest may do so.[1]

In Ranchi, a district of Chota Nagpur in Bengal, a ceremony is performed every year by one of the clans to drive away disease. Should it prove ineffectual, all the villagers assemble by night and walk about the village in a body armed with clubs, searching for the disease. Everything they find outside of the houses they smash. Hence on that day the people throw out their chipped crockery, old pots and pans, and other trash into the courtyard, so that when the search party comes along they may belabour the heap of rubbish to their heart's content; the crash of shattered crockery and the clatter of shivered pans indicates, we are told, that the disease has departed; perhaps it might be more strictly accurate to say that they have frightened it away. At all events a very loud noise is made "so that the disease may not remain hidden anywhere."[2] In a village of the Mossos, an aboriginal tribe of south-western China, a French traveller witnessed the annual ceremony of the expulsion of devils. Two magicians, wearing mitres of red pasteboard, went from house to house, attended by a troop of children, their faces smeared with flour, some of whom carried torches and others cymbals, while all made a deafening noise. After dancing a wild dance in the courtyard of the house, they entered the principal room, where the performers were regaled with a draught of ardent spirits, of which they sprinkled a few drops on the floor. Then the magicians recited their spells to oblige the evil spirits to quit the chamber and the good spirits to enter it. At the end of each phrase, the children, speaking for the spirits, answered with a shout, " We go " or " We come." That concluded the ceremony in the house,

Annual expulsion of disease in Chota Nagpur.

Annual expulsion of demons among the Mossos of China.

----

[1] W. Macpherson, *Memorials of Service in India from the Correspondence of the late Major S. C. Macpherson* (London, 1865), pp. 357 *sq.* Possibly this case belongs more strictly to the class of mediate expulsions, the devils being driven out upon the car. Perhaps, however, the car with its contents is regarded rather as a bribe to induce them to go than as a vehicle in which they are actually carted away. Anyhow it is convenient to take this case along with those other expulsions of demons which are the accompaniment of an agricultural festival.

[2] H. C. Streatfield, " Ranchi," *Journal of the Asiatic Society of Bengal*, lxxii. Part iii. (Calcutta, 1904) p. 36.

and the noisy procession filed out to repeat it in the next.[1]

The people of Bali, an island to the east of Java, have periodical expulsions of devils upon a great scale. Generally the time chosen for the expulsion is the day of the "dark moon" in the ninth month. When the demons have been long unmolested the country is said to be "warm," and the priest issues orders to expel them by force, lest the whole of Bali should be rendered uninhabitable. On the day appointed the people of the village or district assemble at the principal temple. Here at a cross-road offerings are set out for the devils. After prayers have been recited by the priests, the blast of a horn summons the devils to partake of the meal which has been prepared for them. At the same time a number of men step forward and light their torches at the holy lamp which burns before the chief priest. Im- mediately afterwards, followed by the bystanders, they spread in all directions and march through the streets and lanes crying, "Depart! go away!" Wherever they pass, the people who have stayed at home hasten, by a deafening clatter on doors, beams, rice-blocks, and so forth, to take their share in the expulsion of devils. Thus chased from the houses, the fiends flee to the banquet which has been set out for them; but here the priest receives them with curses which finally drive them from the district. When the last devil has taken his departure, the uproar is succeeded by a dead silence, which lasts during the next day also. The devils, it is thought, are anxious to return to their old homes, and in order to make them think that Bali is not Bali but some desert island, no one may stir from his own abode for twenty-four hours. Even ordinary household work, including cooking, is dis- continued. Only the watchmen may shew themselves in the streets. Wreaths of thorns and leaves are hung at all the entrances to warn strangers from entering. Not till the third day is this state of siege raised, and even then it is forbidden to work at the rice-fields or to buy and sell

[1] *Le Tour du Monde*, iii. (Paris, 1897) pp. **227** *sq.*, quoting *Aux sources de l'Irraouaddi, d'Hanoï à* *Calcutta par terre*, par M. E. Roux, Troisième Partie.

in the market. Most people still stay at home, striving to while away the time with cards and dice.[1]

The Shans of Southern China annually expel the fire-spirit. The ceremony was witnessed by the English Mission under Colonel Sladen on the thirteenth of August 1868. Bullocks and cows were slaughtered in the market-place ; the meat was all sold, part of it was cooked and eaten, while the rest was fired out of guns at sundown. The pieces of flesh which fell on the land were supposed to become mosquitoes, those which fell in the water were believed to turn into leeches. In the evening the chief's retainers beat gongs and blew trumpets ; and when darkness had set in, torches were lit, and a party, preceded by the musicians, searched the central court for the fire-spirit, who is supposed to lurk about at this season with evil intent. They then ransacked all the rooms and the gardens, throwing the light of the torches into every nook and corner where the evil spirit might find a hiding-place.[2] In some parts of Fiji an annual ceremony took place which has much the aspect of an expulsion of devils. The time of its celebration was determined by the appearance of a certain fish or sea-slug (*balolo*) which swarms out in dense shoals from the coral reefs on a single day of the year, usually in the last quarter of the moon in November. The appearance of the sea-slugs was the signal for a general feast at those places where they were taken. An influential

Annual expulsion of the fire-spirit among the Shans.

Annual ceremony in Fiji.

---

[1] R. van Eck, "Schetsen van het eiland Bali," *Tijdschrift voor Neder-landsch Indië*, N.S., viii. (1879) pp. 58-60. Van Eck's account is reprinted in J. Jacobs's *Eenigen tijd onder de Baliërs* (Batavia, 1883), pp. 190 *sqq.* According to another writer, each village may choose its own day for expelling the devils, but the ceremony must always be performed at the new moon. A necessary preliminary is to mark exactly the boundaries of the village territory, and this is done by stretching the leaves of a certain palm across the roads at the boundaries. See F. A. Liefrinck, "Bijdrage tot de kennis van het eiland Bali," *Tijd-schrift voor Indische Taal- Land- en Volkenkunde*, xxxiii. (1890) pp. 246

sq. As to the "dark moon" it is to be observed that some eastern nations, particularly the Hindoos and the Burmese, divide the monthly cycle of the moon into two parts, which they call the light moon and the dark moon respectively. The light moon is the first half of the month, when the luminary is waxing ; the dark moon is the second half of the month, when the luminary is waning. See Francis Buchanan, "On the Religion and Literature of the Burmas," *Asiatick Researches*, vi. (London, 1801) p. 171. The Balinese have no doubt derived the distinction, like much else, from the Hindoos.

[2] J. Anderson, *Mandalay to Momien* (London, 1876), p. 308.

man ascended a tree and prayed to the spirit of the sky for good crops, fair winds, and so on. Thereupon a tremendous clatter, with drumming and shouting, was raised by all the people in their houses for about half an hour. This was followed by a dead quiet for four days, during which the people feasted on the sea-slug. All this time no work of any kind might be done, not even a leaf plucked nor the offal removed from the houses. If a noise was made in any house, as by a child crying, a forfeit was at once exacted by the chief. At daylight on the expiry of the fourth night the whole town was in an uproar; men and boys scampered about, knocking with clubs and sticks at the doors of the houses and crying " Sinariba !" This concluded the ceremony.[1] The natives of Tumleo, a small

---

[1] *United States Exploring Expedition, Ethnography and Philology*, by H. Hale (Philadelphia, 1846), pp. 67 *sq.*; Ch. Wilkes, *Narrative of the U.S. Exploring Expedition*, New Edition (New York, 1851), iii. 90 *sq.*, 342. According to the latter writer, the sea-slug was eaten by the men alone, who lived during the four days in the temple, while the women and boys remained shut up in their houses. As to the annual appearance and catch of the sea-slug in the seas of Fiji, see further B. Seeman, *Viti, an Account of a Government Mission to the Vitian or Fijian Islands in the Years 1860–1862* (Cambridge, 1862), pp. 59-61; Basil Thomson, *The Fijians* (London, 1908), pp. 324-327. A somewhat different account of the appearance of the slug (*Palolo veridis*) in the Samoan Sea is given from personal observation by Dr. George Brown. He says: "This annelid, as far as I can remember, is about 8 or 12 inches long, and somewhat thicker than ordinary piping-cord. It is found only on two mornings in the year, and the time when it will appear and disappear can be accurately predicted. As a general rule only a few *palolo* are found on the first day, though occasionally the large quantity may appear first; but, as a rule, the large quantity appears on the second morning. And it is only found on these mornings for a very limited period, viz. from early dawn to about seven o'clock, *i.e.* for about two hours. It then disappears until the following year, except in some rare instances, when it is found for the same limited period in the following month after its first appearance. I kept records of the time, and of the state of the moon, for some years, with the following result: that it always appeared on two out of the following three days, viz. the day before, the day of, and the day after the last quarter of the October moon." See George Brown, D.D., *Melanesians and Polynesians* (London, 1910), pp. 135 *sq.* The slug is also caught in the sea off Samoa, according to one account, at intervals of six months. One of its appearances takes place on the eighth day after the new moon of October. So regular are the appearances of the creature that the Samoans reckon their time by them. See E. Boisse, "Les Îles Samoa, Nukunono, Fakaafo, Wallis et Hoorn," *Bulletin de la Société de Géographie* (Paris), vi. Série, x. (1875) pp. 430 *sq.* In antiquity every year vast shoals of a small fish used to ascend the river Olynthiac from the lake of Bolbe in Macedonia, and all the people of the neighbourhood caught and salted great store of them. They thought that the fish were sent to them by Bolbe, the mother of Olynthus, and they noted it as a curious fact that

island off German New Guinea, also catch the sea-slug in the month of November, and at this season they observe a curious ceremony, which may perhaps be explained as an expulsion of evils or demons. The lads, and sometimes grown men with them, go in troops into the forest to search for grass-arrows (*räng*). When they have collected a store of these arrows, they take sides and, armed with little bows, engage in a regular battle. The arrows fly as thick as hail, and though no one is killed, many receive skin wounds and are covered with blood. The Catholic mission-ary who reports the custom could not ascertain the reasons for observing it. Perhaps one set of combatants represents the demons or embodied evils of the year, who are defeated and driven away by the champions of the people. The month in which these combats take place (November and the beginning of December) is sometimes named after the grass-arrows and sometimes after the sea-slug.[1]

On the last night of the year there is observed in most Japanese houses a ceremony called "the exorcism of the evil spirit." It is performed by the head of the family. Clad in his finest robes, with a sword, if he has the right of bearing one, at his waist, he goes through all the rooms at the hour of midnight, carrying in his left hand a box of roasted beans on a lacquered stand. From time to time he dips his right hand into the box and scatters a handful of beans on a mat, pronouncing a cabalistic form of words of which the meaning is, "Go forth, demons! Enter riches!"[2] According to another account, the ceremony takes place on the night before the beginning of spring, and the roasted beans are flung against the walls as well as on the floors of the houses.[3] While the duty of expelling the

---

the fish never swam higher up than the tomb of Olynthus, which stood on the bank of the river Olynthiac. The shoals always made their appear-ance in the months of Anthesterion and Elaphebolion, and as the people of Apollonia (a city on the bank of the lake) celebrated their festival of the dead at that season, formerly in the month of Elaphebolion, but afterwards in the month of Anthesterion, they imagined that the fish came at that

time on purpose. See Athenaeus, viii. 11, p. 334 F.

[1] M. J. Erdweg, "Die Bewohner der Insel Tumleo Berlinhafen, Deutsch-New-Guinea," *Mittheilungen der an-thropologischen Gesellschaft in Wien*, xxxii. (1902) pp. 329 *sq.*

[2] A. Humbert, *Le Japon illustré* (Paris, 1870), ii. 326.

[3] A. Bastian, *Die Völker des östlichen Asien*, v. (Jena, 1869) p. 367.

devils should, strictly speaking, be discharged by the head of the house, it is often delegated to a servant. Whether master or servant, the performer goes by the name of year-man (*toshi-otoko*), the rite being properly performed on the last day of the year. The words "Out with the devils" (*Oni ha soto*) are pronounced by him in a loud voice, but the words "In with the luck" (*fuku ha uchi*) in a low tone. In the Shogun's palace the ceremony was performed by a year-man specially appointed for the purpose, who scattered parched beans in all the principal rooms. These beans were picked up by the women of the palace, who wrapped as many of them in paper as they themselves were years old, and then flung them backwards out of doors. Sometimes people who had reached an unlucky year would gather these beans, one for each year of their life and one over, and wrap them in paper together with a small copper coin which had been rubbed over their body to transfer the ill-luck. The packet was afterwards thrown away at a cross-road. This was called "flinging away ill-luck" (*yaku sute*).[1] According to Lafcadio Hearn, the casting-out of devils from the houses is performed by a professional exorciser for a small fee, and the peas which he scatters about the house are afterwards swept up and carefully kept until the first peal of thunder is heard in spring, when it is customary to cook and eat some of them. After the demons have been thoroughly expelled from a house, a charm is set up over the door to prevent them from returning : it consists of a wooden skewer with a holly leaf and the dried head of a fish like a sardine stuck on it.[2]

Annual expulsion of poverty and demons in China, India, and Persia.

On the third day of the tenth month in every year the Hak-Ka, a native race in the province of Canton, sweep their houses and turn the accumulated filth out of doors, together with three sticks of incense and some mock money made of paper. At the same time they call out, "Let the devil of poverty depart! Let the devil of poverty depart!" By performing this ceremony they hope to preserve their homes from penury.[3] Among some of the Hindoos of the

[1] W. G. Aston, *Shinto* (London, 1905), p. 309.

[2] Lafcadio Hearn, *Glimpses of Unfamiliar Japan* (London, 1894), ii. 498 *sq.* The writer agrees with Mr. Aston as to the formula of exorcism— "*Oni wa soto ! fuku wa uchi*, "Devils out! Good fortune in!"

[3] Eitel, "Les Hak-ka," *L'Anthropologie*, iv. (1893) pp. 175 *sq.*

Punjaub on the morning after Diwali or the festival of lamps, at which the souls of ancestors are believed to visit the house, the oldest woman of the family takes a corn-sieve or winnowing basket and a broom, to both of which magical virtues are ascribed, and beats them in every corner of the house, exclaiming, "God abide, and poverty depart!" The sieve is then carried out of the village, generally to the east or north, and being thrown away is supposed to bear away with it the poverty and distress of the household. Or the woman flings all the sweepings and rubbish out of doors, saying, "Let all dirt and wretchedness depart from here, and all good fortune come in."[1] The Persians used annually to expel the demons or goblins (*Dives*) from their houses in the month of December. For this purpose the Magi wrote certain words with saffron on a piece of parchment or paper and then held the writing over a fire into which they threw cotton, garlic, grapes, wild rue, and the horn of an animal that had been killed on the sixteenth of September. The spell thus prepared was nailed or glued to the inside of the door, and the door was painted red. Next the priest took some sand and spread it out with a knife, while he muttered certain prayers. After that he strewed the sand on the floor, and the enchantment was complete. The demons now immediately vanished, or at least were deprived of all their malignant power.[2]

For ages it has been customary in China to expel the demons from house and home, from towns and cities, at the end of every year. Such general expulsions of devils go by the name of *no*. They are often mentioned and described in Chinese literature. For example, under the Han dynasty, in the second century of our era, "it was ordered that *fang-siang shi* with four eyes of gold, masked with bearskins, and wearing black coats with red skirts, bearing lances and brandishing shields, should always perform at the end of the year in the twelfth month the *no* of the season, in the rear of hundreds of official servants and boys, and search the interior

Annual expulsion of demons in China at the end of the year.

---

[1] *Panjab Notes and Queries*, ii. pp. 146 *sq.*, § 792 (June, 1885); D. C. J. Ibbetson, *Outlines of Panjab Ethnography* (Calcutta, 1883), p. 119; W. Crooke, *Popular Religion and Folk-* *lore of Northern India* (Westminster, 1896), ii. 188, 295 *sq.*

[2] John Richardson, *Dictionary of Persian, Arabic, and English*, New Edition (London, 1829), p. liii.

of the palace, in order to expel the demons of plague. With bows of peach wood and arrows of the thorny jujube they shoot at the spectres, and with porcelain drums they drum at them ; moreover they throw red balls and cereals at them, in order to remove disease and calamity." [1]   Again, in a poem of the same period we read that " at the end of the year the great *no* takes place for the purpose of driving off all spectres.   The *fang-siang* carry their spears, *wu* and *hih* hold their bundles of reed.   Ten thousand lads with red heads and black clothes, with bows of peach wood and arrows of thorny jujube shoot at random all around. Showers of potsherds and pebbles come down like rain, infallibly killing strong spectres as well as the weak. Flaming torches run after these beings, so that a sparkling and streaming glare chases the red plague to all sides ; thereupon they destroy them in the imperial moats and break down the suspension bridges (to prevent their return)." [2]   At a later period Chinese historians inform us that the house of Tsi caused the annual expulsion of demons to be performed on the last day of the year by two groups, each of one hundred and twenty lads, and twelve animals headed by drums and wind instruments.   The gates of the wards and of the city walls were flung open, and the emperor witnessed the ceremony seated on his throne in the midst of his officers.   With rolling drums the procession entered the palace through the western gate, and passed through all parts of it in two divisions, even ascending the towers, while they hopped, jumped and shrieked ; and on quitting the palace they spread out in six directions till they reached the city walls. [3]   At the present time it is customary in every part of China to fire off crackers on the last day and night of the year for the purpose of terrifying and expelling the devils : enormous quantities of the explosives are consumed at this season : the people seem to vie with one another as to who shall let off the most crackers and make the most noise.   Sometimes long strings of these fireworks hang from balconies and

[1] J. J. M. de Groot, *The Religious System of China*, vi. (Leyden, 1910) pp. 977 *sq.*

[2] J. J. M. de Groot, *op. cit.* vi. 978.

[3] J. J. M. de Groot, *op. cit.* vi. 979.

eaves and keep up a continuous crackling for half an hour together or more ; in great cities the prolonged and ear-splitting din is very annoying to foreigners. To the ears of the Chinese the noise appears to be agreeable, if not for its own sake, at least for the beneficial effect it is supposed to produce by driving demons away. Indeed they seem to be of opinion that any noise, provided it be sufficiently harsh and loud, serves this useful purpose. The sound of brass instruments is particularly terrifying to devils ; hence the great use which the Chinese make of gongs in rites of exorcism. The clash of gongs, we are told, resounds through the Chinese empire daily, especially in summer, when a rise in the death-rate, which ignorant Europeans attribute to mere climatic influences, stimulates the people to redouble their efforts for the banishment of the fiends, who are the real cause of all the mischief. At such times you may see and hear groups of benevolent and public-spirited men and women banging gongs, clashing cymbals, and drubbing drums for hours together. No protest is made by their neighbours, no complaint that they disturb the night's rest of the sick and the tired. People listen with resignation or rather with gratitude and complacency to the deafening uproar raised by these generous philanthropists, who thus devote their services gratuitously to the cause of the public health.[1] In Corea, also, the devils are driven out of the towns on New Year's Eve by the firing of guns and the popping of crackers.[2]

In Tonquin a *theckydaw* or general expulsion of malevolent spirits commonly took place once a year, especially if there was a great mortality amongst men, the elephants or horses of the general's stable, or the cattle of the country, " the cause of which they attribute to the malicious spirits of such men as have been put to death for treason, rebellion, and conspiring the death of the king, general, or princes, and that in revenge of the punishment they have suffered, they are bent to destroy everything and commit horrible violence. To

Annual expulsion of demons in Tonquin.

---

[1] J. J. M. de Groot, *The Religious System of China*, vi. 944 *sqq.* ; *id.*, *The Religion of China* (New York, 1910), pp. 38 *sq.* ; J. H. Gray, *China* (London, 1878), i. 251 *sq.*

[2] W. Woodville Rockhill, "Notes on some of the Laws, Customs, and Superstitions of Korea," *The American Anthropologist*, iv. (1891) p. 185.

prevent which their superstition has suggested to them the institution of this *theckydaw*, as a proper means to drive the devil away, and purge the country of evil spirits." The day appointed for the ceremony was generally the twenty-fifth of February, one month after the beginning of the new year, which fell on the twenty-fifth of January. The intermediate month was a season of feasting, merry-making of all kinds, and general licence. During the whole month the great seal was kept shut up in a box, face downwards, and the law was, as it were, laid asleep. All courts of justice were closed; debtors could not be seized; small crimes, such as petty larceny, fighting, and assault, escaped with impunity; only treason and murder were taken account of and the male-factors detained till the great seal should come into operation again. At the close of the saturnalia the wicked spirits were driven away. Great masses of troops and artillery having been drawn up with flying colours and all the pomp of war, "the general beginneth then to offer meat offerings to the criminal devils and malevolent spirits (for it is usual and customary likewise amongst them to feast the condemned before their execution), inviting them to eat and drink, when presently he accuses them in a strange language, by characters and figures, etc., of many offences and crimes committed by them, as to their having disquieted the land, killed his elephants and horses, etc., for all which they justly deserve to be chastised and banished the country. Whereupon three great guns are fired as the last signal; upon which all the artillery and musquets are discharged, that, by their most terrible noise the devils may be driven away; and they are so blind as to believe for certain, that they really and effectually put them to flight."[1]

---

[1] S. Baron, "Description of the Kingdom of Tonqueen," in J. Pinkerton's *Voyages and Travels*, ix. (London, 1811) pp. 673, 695 *sq.*; compare Richard, "History of Tonquin," *ibid.* p. 746. The account of the ceremony by Tavernier (whom Baron criticises very unfavourably) is somewhat different. According to him, the expulsion of wicked souls at the New Year is combined with sacrifice to the honoured dead. "At the beginning of every year they have a great solemnity in honour of the dead, who were in their lives renowned for their noble actions and valour, reckoning rebels among them. They set up several altars, some for sacrifices, others for the names of the persons they design to honour; and the king, princes, and mandarins are present at them, and make three profound reverences to the altars when the sacrifices are finished; but the king shoots five times against

In Cambodia the expulsion of evil spirits took place in March. Bits of broken statues and stones, considered as the abode of the demons, were collected and brought to the capital. Here as many elephants were collected as could be got together. On the evening of the full moon volleys of musketry were fired and the elephants charged furiously to put the devils to flight. The ceremony was performed on three successive days.[1] In Siam the banishment of demons is annually carried into effect on the last day of the old year. A signal gun is fired from the palace; it is answered from the next station, and so on from station to station, till the firing has reached the outer gate of the city. Thus the demons are driven out step by step. As soon as this is done a consecrated rope is fastened round the circuit of the city walls to prevent the banished demons from returning. The rope is made of tough couch-grass and is painted in alternate stripes of red, yellow, and blue.[2] According to a more recent account, the Siamese ceremony takes place at the New Year holidays, which are three in number, beginning with the first of April. For the feasting which accompanies these holidays a special kind of cake

Annual expulsion of demons in Cambodia.

Annual expulsion of demons in Siam.

---

the altars where the rebels' names are; then the great guns are let off, and the soldiers give vollies of small shot, to put the souls to flight. The altars and papers made use of at the sacrifices are burnt, and the bonzes and sages go to eat the meat made use of at the sacrifice " (Tavernier, in John Harris's *Collection of Voyages and Travels*, vol. i. (London, 1744) p. 823). The translation is somewhat abridged. For the French original, see J. B. Tavernier, *Voyages en Turquie, en Perse, et aux Indes* (The Hague, 1718), iii. 230 *sq.*

[1] É. Aymonier, *Notice sur le Cambodge* (Paris, 1875), p. 62.

[2] A. Bastian, *Die Völker des östlichen Asien*, iii. (Jena, 1867) pp. 237, 298, 314, 529 *sq.*; Mgr. Pallegoix, *Description du Royaume Thai ou Siam* (Paris, 1854), i. 252. Bastian (p. 314), with whom Pallegoix seems to agree, distinctly states that the

expulsion takes place on the last day of the year. Yet both say that it occurs in the fourth month of the year. According to Pallegoix (i. 253) the Siamese year is composed of twelve lunar months, and the first month usually begins in December. Hence the expulsion of devils would commonly take place in March, as in Cambodia. In Laos the year begins in the fifth month and it ends in the fifth month of the following year. See Lieutenant-Colonel Tournier, *Notice sur le Laos Français* (Hanoi, 1900), p. 187. According to Professor E. Seler the festival of Toxcatl, celebrated in the fifth month, was the old Mexican festival of the New Year. See E. Seler, *Altmexikanische Studien*, ii. (Berlin, 1899) pp. 153, 166 *sq.* (*Veröffentlichungen aus dem königlichen Museum für Völkerkunde*, vi. Heft 2/4). Hence it appears that in some calendars the year is not reckoned to begin with the first month.

is made, "which is as much in demand as our own Shrove-Tuesday pancakes or our Good-Friday hot cross-buns. The temples are thronged with women and children making offerings to Buddha and his priests. The people inaugurate their New Year with numerous charitable and religious deeds. The rich entertain the monks, who recite appropriate prayers and chants. Every departed soul returns to the bosom of his family during these three days, freed from any fetters that may have bound him in the regions of indefinable locality. On the third day the religious observances terminate, and the remaining hours are devoted to 'the world, the flesh, and the devil.' Gambling is not confined to the licensed houses, but may be indulged in anywhere. Games of chance hold powerful sway in every house as long as the licence to participate in them lasts. Priests in small companies occupy posts at regular intervals round the city wall, and spend their time in chanting away the evil spirits. On the evening of the second day, the ghostly visitors from the lower realms lose the luxury of being exorcised with psalms. Every person who has a gun may fire it as often as he pleases, and the noise thus made is undoubtedly fearful enough in its intensity to cause any wandering traveller from the far-off fiery land to retrace his steps with speed. The bang and rattle of pistols, muskets, shot-guns, and rifles cease not till the break of day, by which time the city is effectually cleared of all its infernal visitors."[1] From this account we learn that among the spirits thus banished are the souls of the dead, who revisit their living friends once a year. To the same effect, apparently, Bishop Bruguière, writing from Bangkok in 1829, tells us that "the three first days of the moon of April are days of solemn festivity for the pious Siamese. That day Lucifer opens all the gates of the abyss, the souls of the dead, which are shut up there, come forth and partake of a repast in the bosom of their family. They are treated splendidly. One of these three days a monk repairs to the palace to preach before the king. At the end of the sermon a preconcerted signal is given, and in a moment the cannons are fired in all the

---

[1] Ernest Young, *The Kingdom of the Yellow Robe* (Westminster, 1898), pp. 135 *sq.*

quarters of the city to chase the devil out of the walls or to kill him, if he dares to resist. On the first day a temporary king is named, who bears the title of *phaja-phollathep*; during these three days he enjoys all the royal prerogatives, the real king remaining shut up in his palace." [1]

A similar belief and a similar custom prevail in Japan. There, too, the souls of the departed return to their old homes once a year, and a festival called the Feast of Lanterns is made to welcome them. They come at evening on the thirteenth day of the seventh month of the old calendar, which falls towards the end of August. It is needful to light them on their way. Accordingly bamboos with pretty coloured lanterns attached to them are fastened on the tombs, and being thickly set they make an illumination on the hills, where the burying-grounds are generally situated. Lamps of many hues or rows of tapers are also lit and set out in front of the houses and in the gardens, and small fires are kindled in the streets, so that the whole city is in a blaze of light. After the sun has set, a great multitude issues from the town, for every family goes forth to meet its returning dead. When they come to the spot where they believe the souls to be, they welcome the unseen visiters and invite them to rest after their journey, and to partake of refreshments which they offer to them. Having allowed the souls time enough to satisfy their hunger and recover from their fatigue, they escort them by torchlight, chatting gaily with them, into the city and to the houses where they lived and died. These are also illuminated with brilliant lanterns; a banquet is spread on the tables; and the places of the dead, who are supposed to absorb the ethereal essence of the food, are laid for them as if they were alive. After the repast the living go from house to house to visit the souls of their dead friends and neighbours; and thus they spend the night running about the town. On the evening of the third day of the festival, which is the fifteenth day of the month, the time has come for the souls

Annual reception and expulsion of the spirits of the dead in Japan.

[1] "Lettre de Mgr. Bruguière, évêque de Capse, à M. Bousquet, vicaire-général d'Aire," *Annales de l'Association de la Propagation de la Foi*, v. (Paris and Lyons, 1831) p. 188. As to the temporary king of Siam, his privileges and the ceremony of ploughing which he performs, see *The Dying God*, pp. 149-151.

to return to their own place. Fires again blaze in the streets to light them on the road ; the people again escort them ceremoniously to the spot where they met them two days before ; and in some places they send the lanterns floating away on rivers or the sea in miniature boats, which are laden with provisions for the spirits on their way to their long home. But there is still a fear that some poor souls may have lagged behind, or even concealed themselves in a nook or corner, loth to part from the scenes of their former life and from those they love. Accordingly steps are taken to hunt out these laggards and send them packing after their fellow-ghosts. With this intention the people throw stones on the roofs of their houses in great profusion ; and going through every room armed with sticks they deal swashing blows all about them in the empty air to chase away the lingering souls. This they do, we are told, out of a regard for their own comfort quite as much as from the affection they bear to the dead ; for they fear to be disturbed by unseasonable apparitions if they suffered the airy visiters to remain in the house.[1]

Annual reception and expulsion of the spirits of the dead in ancient Greece. Thus in spite of the kindly welcome given to the souls, the fear which they inspire comes out plainly in the pains taken to ensure their departure ; and this fear justifies us in including such forced departures among the ceremonies for the expulsion of evils with which we are here concerned. It may be remembered that the annual banishment of ghosts has been practised by savages so low in the scale of humanity as the Australian aborigines.[2] At the other end of the scale it was observed in classical antiquity by the civilized Greeks and Romans. The Athenians believed that at the festival of the Anthesteria the souls of the dead came back from the nether world and went about the city. Accordingly ropes were fastened round the temples to keep out

---

[1] Charlevoix, *Histoire et description generale du Japon* (Paris, 1736), i. 128 *sq.* ; C. P. Thunberg, *Voyages au Japon* (Paris, 1796), iv. 18-20 ; A. Bastian, *Die Völker des östlichen Asien*, v. (Jena, 1869) p. 364 ; Beaufort, in *Journal of the Anthropological Institute*, xv. (1886) p. 102 ; A. Morgan, in *Journal of American Folk-lore*, x.

(1897) pp. 244 *sq.* ; Lafcadio Hearn, *Glimpses of Unfamiliar Japan* (London, 1894), i. 106-110, ii. 504 *sq.* The custom of welcoming the souls of the dead back to their old homes once a year has been observed in many lands. See *Adonis, Attis, Osiris*, Second Edition, pp. 301 *sqq.*

[2] Above, pp. 123 *sq.*

the wandering ghosts; and with a like intention the people chewed buckthorn in the morning and smeared the doors of their houses with pitch, apparently thinking that any rash spirits who might attempt to enter would stick fast in the pitch and be glued, like so many flies, to the door. But at the end of the festival the souls were bidden to depart in these words: "Out of the door with you, souls. The Anthesteria is over."[1] Yet for the entertainment of

---

[1] Hesychius, *s.v.* μιαραὶ ἡμέραι· τοῦ Ἀνθεστηριῶνος μηνός, ἐν αἷς τὰς ψυχὰς τῶν κατοιχομένων ἀνιέναι ἐδόκουν. Photius, *Lexicon, s.vv.* Θύραζε Κᾶρες· οὐκέτ' Ἀνθεστήρια . . . τινὲς δὲ οὕτως τὴν παροιμίαν φασί· θύραζε Κῆρες οὐκέτ' Ἀνθεστήρια· ὡς κατὰ τὴν πόλιν τοῖς Ἀνθεστηρίοις τῶν ψυχῶν περιερχομένων. *Id.*, *s.vv.* μιαρὰ ἡμέρα· ἐν τοῖς Χουσὶν Ἀνθεστηριῶνος μηνός, ἐν ᾧ δοκοῦσιν αἱ ψυχαὶ τῶν τελευτησάντων ἀνιέναι, ῥάμνῳ ἔωθεν ἐμασῶντο καὶ πίττῃ τὰς θύρας ἔχριον. Pollux, viii. 141: περισχοινίσαι τὰ ἱερὰ ἔλεγον ἐν ταῖς ἀποφράσι καὶ τὸ παραφράξαι. As to the closing of the temples, see further Athenaeus, x. 49, p. 447 C. As to the Anthesteria in general, see E. Rohde, *Psyche*[3] (Tübingen and Leipsic, 1903), i. 236 *sqq.*, who rightly adopts Hesychius's second explanation of Κῆρες. The reasons given by August Mommsen for rejecting that explanation betray an imperfect acquaintance with popular superstition (*Feste der Stadt Athen im Altertum*, Leipsic, 1898, p. 386, note 1). Compare Miss J. E. Harrison, *Prolegomena to the Study of Greek Religion*, Second Edition (Cambridge, 1908), pp. 32 *sqq.* The Greeks thought that branches of buckthorn (*rhamnus*) fastened to doors or windows kept out witches (Dioscorides, *De materia medica*, i. 119). A similar virtue was attributed to buckthorn or hawthorn by the ancient Romans and modern European peasants. See A. Kuhn, *Die Herabkunft des Feuers und des Göttertranks*[2] (Gütersloh, 1886), pp. 209 *sq.*; J. Murr, *Pflanzenwelt in der griechischen Mythologie* (Innsbruck, 1890), pp. 104-106; *The Magic Art and the Evolution of Kings*, ii. 54 *sq.*, 191. According to Mr. Murr, *rhamnus* is *Lycium europaeum* L. I learn from Miss J. E. Harrison that Sir Francis Darwin believes it to be buckthorn (*Rhamnus catharticus*). In some parts of Bosnia, when peasant women go to pay a visit in a house where a death has occurred they put a little hawthorn (*Weissdorn*) behind their headcloth, and on returning from the house they throw it away on the street. They think that if the deceased has turned into a vampyre, he will be so occupied in picking up the hawthorn, that he will not be able to follow them to their homes. See F. S. Krauss, "Vampyre im südslavischen Volksglauben," *Globus*, lxi. (1892) p. 326. At childbirth also the Greeks smeared pitch on their houses to keep out the demons (εἰς ἀπέλασιν τῶν δαιμόνων) who attack women at such times (Photius, *Lexicon, s.v.* ῥάμνος). To this day the Bulgarians try to keep wandering ghosts from their houses by painting crosses with tar on the outside of their doors, while on the inside they hang a tangled skein composed of countless broken threads. The ghost cannot enter until he has counted all the threads, and before he has done the sum the cock crows and the poor soul must return to the grave. See A. Strausz, *Die Bulgaren* (Leipsic, 1898), p. 454. The Servians paint crosses with tar on the doors of houses and barns to keep out vampyres. See F. S. Krauss, "Vampyre im südslavischen Volksglauben," *Globus*, lxi. (1892) p. 326. In the Highlands of Scotland it was believed that tar put on a door kept witches away. See J. G. Campbell, *Witchcraft and Second Sight in the Highlands and Islands of Scotland* (Glasgow, 1902), p. 13. The

the unseen guests during their short stay earthenware pots full of boiled food appear to have been everywhere prepared throughout the city ; but probably these were placed in the street outside the houses, in order to give the ghosts no excuse for entering and disturbing the inmates. No priest would eat of the food thus offered to the dead,[1] but prowling beggars probably had no such scruples. Similarly when the Sea Dyaks of Sarawak celebrate their great Festival of Departed Spirits at intervals which vary from one to three or four years, food is prepared for the dead and they are summoned from their far-off home to partake of it ; but it is put outside at the entrance of the house. And before the general arrival of the souls, while the people are busy brewing the drink for the feast, each family takes care to hang an earthenware pot full of the liquor outside of the single room which it occupies in the large common house, lest some thirsty soul should arrive prematurely from the other world, and, forcing his way into the domestic circle, should not merely slake his thirst but carry off one of the living.[2] During three days in May the Romans held a festival in honour of the ghosts. The temples were shut, doubtless to keep out the ghostly swarms ; but, as in Japan, every house seems to have been thrown open to receive the spirits of its own departed. When the recep-

Annual reception and expulsion of the spirits of the dead in ancient Rome.

Thompson Indians of British Columbia used to bar their houses against ghosts by means not unlike those adopted by the Athenians at the Anthesteria. When a death had happened, they hung a string of deer-hoofs across the inside of the house, and an old woman often pulled at the string to make the hoofs rattle. This kept the ghost out. They also placed branches of juniper at the door or burned them in the fire for the same purpose. See James Teit, "The Thompson Indians of British Columbia" (April 1900), p. 332 (*The Jesup North Pacific Expedition, Memoir of the American Museum of Natural History*). With the Athenian use of ropes to keep ghosts out of the temples at the Anthesteria we may compare the Siamese custom of roping demons out

of the city at the New Year (above, p. 149). Ropes of rice-straw, which are supposed to repel demoniacal and evil influences, are hung by the Japanese in front of shrines, and at the New Year they hang them also before ordinary houses. See W. G. Aston, *Shinto* (London, 1905), pp. 335 *sq.* Some of the Kayans of Borneo stretch ropes round their houses to keep out demons of disease ; in order to do so more effectually leaves of a certain plant or tree are fastened to the rope. See A. W. Nieuwenhuis, *Quer durch Borneo,* i. (Leyden, 1904) p. 448.

[1] Scholiast on Aristophanes, *Frogs,* 218.

[2] J. Perham, "Sea Dyak Religion," *Journal of the Straits Branch of the Royal Asiatic Society,* No. 14, December 1884, pp. 296-298.

tion was over, each head of a family arose at dead of night, washed his hands, and having made with fingers and thumb certain magic signs to ward off ghosts, he proceeded to throw black beans over his shoulder without looking behind him. As he did so, he said nine times, "With these beans I redeem me and mine"; and the ghosts, following unseen at his heels, picked up the beans and left him and his alone. Then he dipped his hands again in water, clashed bronze vessels together to make a din, and begged the ghosts to depart from his house, saying nine times, "Go forth, paternal shades!" After that he looked behind him, and the ceremony was over: the ghosts had taken their leave for another year.[1]

Annual expulsions of demons, witches, or evil influences appear to have been common among the heathen of Europe, if we may judge from the relics of such customs among their descendants at the present day. Thus among the heathen Wotyaks, a Finnish people of Eastern Russia, all the young girls of the village assemble on the last day of the year or on New Year's Day, armed with sticks, the ends of which are split in nine places. With these they beat every corner of the house and yard, saying, "We are driving Satan out of the village." Afterwards the sticks are thrown into the river below the village, and as they float down stream Satan goes with them to the next village, from which he must be driven out in turn. In some villages the expulsion is managed otherwise. The unmarried men receive from every house in the village groats, flesh, and brandy. These they take to the fields, light a fire under a fir-tree, boil the groats, and eat of the food they have brought with them, after pronouncing the words, "Go away into the wilderness, come not into the house." Then they return to the village and enter every house where there are young women. They take hold of the young women and throw them into the snow, saying, "May the spirits of disease leave you." The

Annual expulsion of Satan among the Wotyaks of Russia.

---

[1] Ovid, *Fasti*, v. 419-486; Varro, quoted by Nonius Marcellus, p. 135 (p. 142 ed. Quicherat), *s.v.* "Lemures"; Festus, p. 87 ed. C. O. Müller, *s.v.* "Fabam." Ovid, who is our chief authority for the ceremony, speaks as if the festival lasted only one day (the ninth of May). But we know from the inscribed calendars that it lasted three days. See W. Warde Fowler, *The Roman Festivals of the period of the Republic* (London, 1899), pp. 106 *sqq.*

remains of the groats and the other food are then distributed among all the houses in proportion to the amount that each contributed, and each family consumes its share. According to a Wotyak of the Malmyz district the young men throw into the snow whomever they find in the houses, and this is called "driving out Satan"; moreover, some of the boiled groats are cast into the fire with the words, "O god, afflict us not·with sickness and pestilence, give us not up as a prey to the spirits of the wood." But the most antique form of the ceremony is that observed by the Wotyaks of the Kasan Government. First of all a sacrifice is offered to the Devil at noon. Then all the men assemble on horseback in the centre of the village, and decide with which house they shall begin. When this question, which often gives rise to hot disputes, is settled, they tether their horses to the paling, and arm themselves with whips, clubs of lime-wood, and bundles of lighted twigs. The lighted twigs are believed to have the greatest terrors for Satan. Thus armed, they proceed with frightful cries to beat every corner of the house and yard, then shut the door, and spit at the ejected fiend. So they go from house to house, till the Devil has been driven from every one. Then they mount their horses and ride out of the village, yelling wildly and brandishing their clubs in every direction. Outside of the village they fling away the clubs and spit once more at the Devil.[1] The Cheremiss, another Finnish people of Eastern Russia, chase Satan from their dwellings by beating the walls with cudgels of lime-wood. For the same purpose they fire guns, stab the ground with knives, and insert burning chips of wood in the crevices. Also they leap over bonfires, shaking out their garments as they do so ; and in some districts they blow on long trumpets of lime-tree bark to frighten him away. When he has fled to the wood, they pelt the trees with some of the cheese-cakes and eggs which furnished the feast.[2]

Annual expulsion of Satan among the Cheremiss of Russia.

In Christian Europe the old heathen custom of expelling

[1] Max Buch, *Die Wotjäken* (Stuttgart, 1882), pp. 153 *sq.*

[2] A. Bastian, *Der Mensch in der Geschichte* (Leipsic, 1860), ii. 94; P. v. Stenin, "Ein neuer Beitrag zur Ethnographie der Tscheremissen," *Globus,* lviii. (1890) p. 204.

the powers of evil at certain times of the year has survived to modern times. Thus in some villages of Calabria the month of March is inaugurated with the expulsion of the witches. It takes place at night to the sound of the church bells, the people running about the streets and crying, "March is come." They say that the witches roam about in March, and the ceremony is repeated every Friday evening during the month.[1] Often, as might have been anticipated, the ancient pagan rite has attached itself to church festivals. For example, in Calabria at Eastertide every family provides itself in time with a supply of holy water, and when the church bells proclaim the resurrection of Christ the people sprinkle the house with the water, saying in a loud voice, "*Esciti fora sùrici uorvi, esciti fora tentaziuni, esca u malu ed entri u bene.*" At the same time they knock on doors and windows, on chests and other articles of furniture.[2] Again, in Albania on Easter Eve the young people light torches of resinous wood and march in procession, swinging them, through the village. At last they throw the torches into the river, crying, " Ha, Kore ! we throw you into the river, like these torches, that you may never return."[3] Silesian peasants believe that on Good Friday the witches go their rounds and have great power for mischief. Hence about Oels, near Strehlitz, the people on that day arm themselves with old brooms and drive the witches from house and home, from farmyard and cattle-stall, making a great uproar and clatter as they do so.[4]

The belief in the maleficent power and activity of witches and wizards would seem to have weighed almost as heavily on the heathen of Central and Northern Europe in prehistoric times as it still weighs on the minds of African negroes and other savages in many parts of the world. But while these unhallowed beings were always with our forefathers, there were times and seasons of the year when

---

[1] Vincenzo Dorsa, *La tradizione greco-latina negli usi e nelle credenze popolari della Calabria Citeriore* (Cosenza, 1884), pp. 42 *sq.*

[2] Vincenzo Dorsa, *La tradizione greco-latina negli usi e nelle credenze popolari della Calabria Citeriore*, p. 48.

[3] J. G. von Hahn, *Albanesische Studien* (Jena, 1854), i. 160. Compare *The Dying God*, pp. 264 *sq.*

[4] P. Drechsler, *Sitte, Brauch und Volksglaube in Schlesien* (Leipsic, 1903-1906), i. 86.

they were supposed to be particularly mischievous, and when accordingly special precautions had to be taken against them. Among such times were the twelve days from Christmas to Twelfth Night, the Eve of St. George, the Eve of May Day (Walpurgis Night), and Midsummer Eve.[1]

Annual expulsion of witches on Walpurgis Night (the Eve of May Day).

In Central Europe it was apparently on Walpurgis Night, the Eve of May Day, above all other times that the baleful powers of the witches were exerted to the fullest extent; nothing therefore could be more natural than that men should be on their guard against them at that season, and that, not content with merely standing on their defence, they should boldly have sought to carry the war into the enemy's quarters by attacking and forcibly expelling the uncanny crew. Amongst the weapons with which they fought their invisible adversaries in these grim encounters were holy water, the fumes of incense or other combustibles, and loud noises of all kinds, particularly the clashing of metal instruments, amongst which the ringing of church bells was perhaps the most effectual.[2] Some of these strong measures are still in use among the peasantry, or were so down to recent years, and there seems no reason to suppose that their magical virtue has been at all impaired by lapse of time.

Annual expulsion of witches on May Day in the Tyrol.

In the Tyrol, as in other places, the expulsion of the powers of evil at this season goes by the name of "Burning out the Witches." It takes place on May Day, but people have been busy with their preparations for days before. On a Thursday at midnight bundles are made up of resinous splinters, black and red spotted hemlock, caperspurge, rosemary, and twigs of the sloe. These are kept and burned on May Day by men who must first have received plenary absolution from the Church. On the last three days of April all the houses are cleansed and fumigated with juniper berries and rue. On May Day, when the evening bell has rung and the twilight is falling,

---

[1] As to the activity of the evil powers on the twelve days from Christmas to Twelfth Night, see Gustav Bilfinger, *Das germanische Julfest* (Stuttgart, 1901), pp. 74 *sqq.*; as to witches on St. George's Eve, May Eve, and Midsummer Eve, see *The Magic Art and the Evolution of Kings*, ii. 52 *sqq.*, 127, 334 *sqq.*

[2] G. Bilfinger, *Das germanische Julfest* (Stuttgart, 1901), p. 76.

the ceremony of "Burning out the Witches" begins. Men and boys make a racket with whips, bells, pots, and pans; the women carry censers; the dogs are unchained and run barking and yelping about. As soon as the church bells begin to ring, the bundles of twigs, fastened on poles, are set on fire and the incense is ignited. Then all the house-bells and dinner-bells are rung, pots and pans are clashed, dogs bark, every one must make a noise. And amid this hubbub all scream at the pitch of their voices,

> *" Witch flee, flee from here,*
> *Or it will go ill with thee."*

Then they run seven times round the houses, the yards, and the village. So the witches are smoked out of their lurking-places and driven away.[1]

The custom of expelling the witches on Walpurgis Night is still, or was down to thirty or forty years ago, observed in many parts of Bavaria and among the Germans of Bohemia. Thus in the Böhmerwald Mountains, which divide Bavaria from Bohemia, all the young fellows of the village assemble after sunset on some height, especially at a cross-road, and crack whips for a while in unison with all their strength. This drives away the witches; for so far as the sound of the whips is heard, these maleficent beings can do no harm. The peasants believe firmly in the efficacy of

Annual expulsion of witches on Walpurgis Night in Bavaria.

---

[1] J. M. Ritter von Alpenburg, *Mythen und Sagen Tirols* (Zurich, 1857), pp. 260 *sq.* Compare J. E. Wald-freund, "Volksgebräuche und Aberglauben," *Zeitschrift für deutsche Mythologie und Sittenkunde*, iii. (1855) p. 339. A Westphalian form of the expulsion of evil is the driving out the *Süntevögel, Sunnenvögel,* or *Sommervögel,* that is, the butterfly. On St. Peter's Day, 22nd February, children go from house to house knocking on them with hammers and singing doggerel rhymes in which they bid the *Sommervögel* to depart. Presents are given to them at every house. Or the people of the house themselves go through all the rooms, knocking on all the doors, to drive away the *Sunnenvögel.* If this ceremony is omitted, it is thought that various misfortunes will be the consequence. The house will swarm with rats, mice, and other vermin, the cattle will be sick, the butterflies will multiply at the milk-bowls, etc. See J. F. L. Woeste, *Volksüberlieferungen in der Grafschaft Mark* (Iserlohn, 1848), p. 24; J. W. Wolf, *Beiträge zur deutschen Mythologie,* i. (Göttingen and Leipsic, 1852) p. 87; A. Kuhn, *Westfälische Sagen, Gebräuche und Märchen* (Leipsic, 1859), ii. pp. 119-121, §§ 366-374; Montanus, *Die deutschen Volksfeste, Volksbräuche, und deutscher Volksglaube* (Iserlohn, N.D.), pp. 21 *sq.*; U. Jahn, *Die deutschen Opfergebräuche bei Ackerbau und Viehzucht* (Breslau, 1884), pp. 94-96.

this remedy. A yokel will tell his sons to be sure to crack their whips loudly and hit the witches hard ; and to give more sting to every blow the whip-lashes are knotted. On returning to the village the lads often sing songs and collect contributions of eggs, lard, bread, and butter. In some places, while the young fellows are cracking their whips, the herdsmen wind their horns, and the long-drawn notes, heard far-off in the silence of night, are very effectual for banning the witches. In other places, again, the youth blow upon so-called shawms made of peeled willow-wood in front of every house, especially in front of such houses as are

Annual
expulsion
of witches
on Wal-
purgis
Night in
Voigtland.

suspected of harbouring a witch.[1] In Voigtland, a bleak mountainous region of Central Germany [2] bordering on the Frankenwald Mountains, the belief in witchcraft is still widely spread. The time when the witches are particularly dreaded is Walpurgis Night, but they play their pranks also on Midsummer Eve, St. Thomas's Eve, and Christmas Eve. On these days they try to make their way into a neighbour's house and to borrow or steal something from it ; and woe betide the man in whose house they have succeeded in their nefarious errand ! It is on Walpurgis Night and Midsummer Eve that they ride through the air astride of pitchforks and churn-dashers. They also be-witch the cattle ; so to protect the poor beasts from their hellish machinations the people on these days chalk up three crosses on the doors of the cattle-stalls or hang up St. John's wort, marjoram, and so forth. Very often, too, the village youth turn out in a body and drive the witches away with the cracking of whips, the firing of guns, and the waving of burning besoms through the air, not to mention shouts and noises of all sorts.[3] Such customs appear to be observed generally in Thüringen, of which Voigt-land is a part. The people think that the blows of the whip actually fall on the witches hovering unseen in the air, and that so far as the cracking of the whips is heard, the crops will be good and nothing will be struck by

---

[1] *Bavaria, Landes- und Volkskunde des Königreichs Bayern* (Munich, 1860–1866), ii. 272, iii. 302 *sq.*, 934 ; O. Freiherr von Reinsberg-Düringsfeld, *Das festliche Jahr* (Leipsic, 1863), p. 137.

[2] *Encyclopaedia Britannica*, Ninth Edition, xx. 493.

[3] R. Eisel, *Sagenbuch des Voigtlandes* (Gera, 1871), p. 210.

lightning,[1] no doubt because the witches have been banished by the sound.

In Bohemia many are the precautions taken by the peasantry, both German and Czech, to guard themselves and their cattle against the witches on Walpurgis Night. Thorny branches are laid on the thresholds of cow-houses and dwellings to keep out the infernal crew, and after sunset boys armed with whips and guns drive them from the villages with a prodigious uproar and burn them in bonfires on the neighbouring heights. It is true that the witches themselves are not seen, though effigies of them are sometimes consumed in the bonfires. This " Burning of the Witches," as it is called; protects the crops from their ravages. German lads also employ goats' horns as a means of driving away the witches at the moment when they issue forth from kitchen-chimneys on their way to the witches' Sabbath.[2] Some minor variations in the mode of expelling the witches on Walpurgis Night have been noted in the German villages of Western Bohemia. Thus in Absrot the village youth go out to cross-roads and there beat the ground with boards, no doubt for the purpose of thrashing the witches who are commonly supposed to assemble at such spots. In Deslawen, after the evening bells have rung, people go through the houses beating the walls or floors with boards ; then they issue forth into the roads, headed by a boy who carries the effigy of a witch made up of rags. Thereupon grown-up folk crack whips and fire shots. In Schönwert the young people go in bands through the village and the meadows, making a great noise with bells, flutes, and whips, for the more noise they make the more effectual is the ceremony supposed to be. Meantime the older men are busy firing shots over the fields and the dungheaps. In Hochofen troops of children go from house to house on Walpurgis Evening, making a great clatter with tin cans and kettles, while they scream, " Witch, go out, your house is burning." This is called

---

[1] August Witzschel, *Sitten, Sagen und Gebräuche aus Thüringen* (Vienna, 1878), pp. 262 *sq.*

[2] O. Freiherr von Reinsberg-Düringsfeld, *Fest-Kalender aus Böhmen* (Prague, preface dated 1861), pp. 210-212 ; *id., Das festliche Jahr* (Leipsic, 1863), p. 137 ; Alois John, *Sitte, Brauch und Volksglaube im deutschen Westböhmen* (Prague, 1905), pp. 70-73.

"Driving out the Witches."[1]   The German peasants of
Moravia, also, universally believe that on Walpurgis Night
the witches ride through the air on broomsticks and pitchforks in order to revel with Satan, their master, at the old
heathen places of sacrifice, which are commonly on heights.
To guard the cattle and horses from their insidious attacks
it is usual to put knives under the thresholds and to stick
sprigs of birch in the dungheaps.   Formerly lads used to
gather on the heights where the witches were believed to
assemble ; and by hurling besoms, dipped in pitch and
ignited, they attempted to banish the invisible foe.[2]

Annual
" Burning
of the
Witches "
on Wal-
purgis
Night in
Silesia.

In Silesia also, we are told, the belief in witchcraft still
occupies a large space in the minds of the people.   It is
on Walpurgis Night that the witches are let loose and all
the powers of magic have full sway.   At that time the
cottagers not uncommonly see a witch astride a hayfork
or broomstick emerging from the chimney.   Hence people
are careful to remove all utensils from the fireplace, or the
witches would ride on them, when they go with the Evil
One to a cross-road or a gallows-hill, there to dance wild
dances in a circle on the snow or to cut capers on the corn-
fields.   Steps are taken to guard village, house, and farm-
yard against their incursions.   Three crosses are chalked
up on every door, and little birch-trees fastened over the
house-door, because the witches must count every leaf on
the tree before they can cross the threshold, and while they
are still counting, the day breaks and their power is gone.
On that evening the cattle are especially exposed to the
attacks of the witches, and prudent farmers resort to
many expedients for the sake of protecting the animals from
the wiles of these malignant beings.   No wise man would
sell milk or butter on Walpurgis Night ; if he did, his
cows would certainly be bewitched.   And all the work of the
byres should be finished and the cattle fed before sundown,
which is the time when the witches begin to swarm in the
air.   Besides the usual crosses chalked on the door of the
byre, it is customary to fasten over it three horse-shoes, or a
holed flint, or a goat's horns with four branches ; it is well,

[1] Alois John, *op. cit.* p. 71.
[2] Willibald Müller, *Beiträge zur*

Volkskunde der Deutschen in Mähren
(Vienna and Olmutz, 1893), p. 324.

too, to nail bits of buckthorn crosswise over every entrance, and to lean pitchforks and harrows against the doors with the sharp points turned outwards. A sod freshly cut from a meadow and sprinkled with marsh-marigolds has likewise a very good effect when it is placed before a threshold. Moreover in the Grünberg district young men go clanking chains through the village and farmyards, for iron scares the witches ; also they knock at the doors and they prance through the yards astride on pitchforks and broomsticks, all to drive away the witches, but in doing so they must be sure not to speak a word. A very powerful means of keeping witches at bay are the Walpurgis bonfires, which are still kindled in the Hoyerswerda district and the Iser Mountains. The fires are fed with the stumps of old brooms, and the people dance round them and wave burning besoms, just as they do at the Midsummer bonfires. About Hoyerswerda they call these fires, as usual, " Burning the Witches." [1]

The Wends of Saxony adopt very similar precautions against witches on the evening of Walpurgis Day. Any one who has been in Lusatia on the last day of April must remember the fires which he saw blazing on the mountains and in the valleys and the plains. That is the Witch-burning (*kuzlarnĭce palić*). For weeks before that the boys and lads have been collecting old brooms, and when the time comes they sally forth and dance with the burning besoms on the fields ; the fire is thought to ban the witches and foul fiends. Also on that day people march about the fields and meadows clinking stones on scythes ; for the noise is also deemed effectual in driving the witches away.[2]   At Penzance in Cornwall boys run about blowing horns on the thirtieth of April (Walpurgis Day), and when questioned why they do so they say that they are " scaring away the devil."

Annual " Burning of the Witches" on Walpurgis Night among the Wends of Saxony.

[1] P. Drechsler, *Sitte, Brauch und Volksglaube in Schlesien* (Leipsic, 1903–1906), i. 108-110. With regard to the dance of the witches in the snow, it is a common saying in the northern district of the Harz Mountains that the witches must dance the snow away on the top of the Blocksberg on the first of May. See A. Kuhn und W. Schwartz, *Norddeutsche Sagen, Märchen und Gebräuche* (Leipsic, 1848), p. 376. At Dabelow in Mecklenburg all utensils are removed from the fireplace on Walpurgis Night, lest the witches should ride on them to the Blocksberg. See A. Kuhn and W. Schwartz, *l.c.*

[2] R. Wuttke, *Sächsische Volkskunde* (Dresden, 1901), p. 359.

The horns used for this purpose are made of tin and shaped like a herald's trumpet ; they vary in length from a foot to a yard and can give forth a very loud blast.[1]   The custom is probably a relic of a general expulsion of witches and demons on that day.

Another witching time is the period of twelve days between Christmas (the twenty-fifth of December) and Epiphany (the sixth of January).   A thousand quaint superstitions cluster round that mystic season.   It is then that the Wild Huntsman sweeps through the air, the powers of evil are let loose, werewolves are prowling round, and the witches work their wicked will.   Hence in some parts of Silesia the people burn pine-resin all night long between Christmas and the New Year in order that the pungent smoke may drive witches and evil spirits far away from house and homestead ; and on Christmas Eve and New Year's Eve they fire shots over fields and meadows, into shrubs and trees, and wrap straw round the fruit-trees, to prevent the spirits from doing them harm.[2]   On New Year's Eve, which is Saint Sylvester's Day, Bohemian lads, armed with guns, form themselves into circles and fire thrice into the air.   This is called " Shooting the Witches " and is supposed to frighten the witches away.   While the young fellows are rendering this service to the community, the housewives go about their houses sprinkling holy water

---

[1] Lady Agnes Macdonell, in *The Times*, May 3rd, 1913, p. 6.   In a letter to me (dated 31, Kensington Park Gardens, May 5th [1913]) Lady Macdonell was kind enough to give me some further particulars as to the custom.   It seems that the boys use their horns on May Day as well as on the thirtieth of April.   Processions of boys and girls decorated with flowers and leaves, and carrying flags and horns, went about Penzance on May Day of the present year (1913).   The horns are straight ; some of them terminate in a bell-shaped opening, others have no such appendage.   The latter and plainer are the older pattern.

[2] P. Drechsler, *Sitte, Brauch und Volksglaube in Schlesien* (Leipsic, 1903–1906), i. 15-18.   With regard to the superstitions attached to these twelve days or twelve nights, as the Germans call them, see further A. Kuhn und W. Schwartz, *Norddeutsche Sagen, Märchen und Gebräuche* (Leipsic, 1848), pp. 408-418 ; A. Kuhn, *Sagen, Gebräuche und Märchen aus Westfalen* (Leipsic, 1859), ii. 111-117 ; L. Strackerjan, *Aberglaube und Sagen aus dem Herzogthum Oldenburg* (Oldenburg, 1867), ii. 28 *sqq.* ; M. Toeppen, *Aberglauben aus Masuren*[2] (Danzig, 1867), pp. 61 *sqq.* ; A. Wuttke, *Der deutsche Volksaberglaube*[2] (Berlin, 1869), pp. 61 *sqq.*, § 74 ; E. Mogk, "Mythologie," in H. Paul's *Grundriss der germanischen Philologie*,[2] iii. (Strasburg, 1900) pp. 260 *sq.* ; Alois John, *Sitte, Brauch und Volksglaube im deutschen Westböhmen* (Prague, 1905), pp. 11 *sqq.*

in all the rooms and chalking three crosses on every door,[1] no doubt to accelerate the departure of the witches, and to prevent their return. At Trieste on St. Sylvester's Eve people form processions and drive the evil spirits with sticks and brooms out of the houses, while they invite the good spirits and good luck to come and dwell there.[2] In the town of Biggar, in Lanarkshire, it has been customary from time immemorial to celebrate a custom called "burning out the Old Year" on the thirty-first of December. A large bonfire, to which all the onlookers think it their duty to contribute fuel, is kindled in the evening at the town cross, and fires are also lighted on the adjacent hills.[3] When we remember how common it is in Central Europe to kindle fires at critical seasons for the purpose of burning the witches, we may suspect that what the good people of Biggar originally intended to burn on the last night of the year was not the Old Year but the witches. It would have been well for Scotland and for Europe if the practice of burning witches had always been carried out in this harmless fashion. A visitor to Scotland in 1644 saw nine witches of flesh and blood burned at one time on Leith Links.[4]

" Burning out the Old Year " at Biggar.

The last of the mystic twelve days is Epiphany or Twelfth Night, and it has been selected as a proper season for the expulsion of the powers of evil in various parts of Europe. Thus at Brunnen on the Lake of Lucerne the boys go about in procession on Twelfth Night, carrying torches and lanterns, and making a great noise with horns, cowbells, whips, and so forth. This is said to frighten away the two female spirits of the wood, Strudeli and Strätteli. Of these two names Strudeli seems to mean "witch" and Strätteli "nightmare." The people believe that if they do not make enough noise, there will be little fruit that year.[5]

Annual expulsion of witches and demons in Switzerland and France.

---

[1] O. Freiherr von Reinsberg-Düringsfeld, *Fest-Kalender aus Böhmen* (Prague, preface dated 1861), p. 602.

[2] W. G. Aston, *Shinto* (London, 1905), p. 312, referring to Lady Burton's life of her husband.

[3] T. Thiselton Dyer, *British Popular Customs* (London, 1876), p. 506.

[4] J. G. Dalyell, *The Darker Super-*

stitions of Scotland (Edinburgh, 1834), p. 670.

[5] H. Usener, "Italische Mythen," *Rheinisches Museum*, N.F., xxx.(1875) p. 198; *id.*, *Kleine Schriften*, iv. (Leipzic and Berlin, 1913), p. 109 ;. E. Hoffmann-Krayer, *Feste und Bräuche des Schweizervolkes* (Zurich, 1913), p. 101.

On the same day the inhabitants of the Muota Valley, immediately to the east of Brunnen, used to make a similar racket, no doubt for a similar purpose. They collected chains, pots and pans, cow-bells, horns, and such like musical instruments. He who could borrow a number of horse's bells and wear them on his person so that the jangling sounded afar off was deemed uncommonly lucky. Thus equipped parties of people marched about making all the din they could; sometimes they would meet and joining all their efforts in one concerted burst of harmony or discord would raise such a hubbub that the surrounding rocks rang again with the sound.[1] In Labruguière, also, a canton of Southern France, the evil spirits are expelled at the same season. The canton lies in the picturesque and little-known region of the Black Mountains, which form a sort of link between the Pyrenees and the Cevennes, and have preserved in their remote recesses certain types of life which have long disappeared elsewhere. On the eve of Twelfth Day the inhabitants rush through the streets jangling bells, clattering kettles, and doing everything to make a discordant noise. Then by the light of torches and blazing faggots they set up a prodigious hue and cry, an ear-splitting uproar, hoping thereby to chase all the wandering ghosts and devils from the town.[2]

Befana in the Piazza Navona at Rome.

With this noisy ceremony we may compare a similar custom which is still observed year by year at the same season in the long and spacious Piazza Navona at Rome. There on the night before Epiphany a dense crowd assembles and diverts itself by raising a hideous uproar. Soon after supper troops of young folk and others march through the streets, preceded by puppets or pasteboard figures and all making the utmost possible din. They converge from different quarters on the Piazza Navona, there to unite in one prolonged and deafening outburst of clangorous discord. The favourite musical instruments employed in this cats' concert are penny trumpets, of which, together with tambourines, bells, and so forth, the shops take care to provide

---

[1] H. Herzog, *Schweizerische Volksfeste, Sitten und Gebräuche* (Aaran, 1884), pp. 212 *sq.*

[2] A. de Nore, *Coutumes, Mythes, et Traditions des Provinces de France* (Paris and Lyons, 1846), pp. 81, 85.

a large stock as a preparation for the pandemonium of the evening. The ceremony is supposed to be in honour of a certain mythical old hag called Befana, effigies of whom, made of rags, are put by women and children in the windows on Twelfth Night. Her name Befana is clearly a popular corruption of Epiphany, the ecclesiastical name of the festival ; but viewed in connexion with the popular celebrations which we have examined she may be suspected to be of heathen rather than Christian origin. In fact we may conjecture that she was of old a witch, and that the noisy rite in the Piazza Navona is nothing but a relic of an annual expulsion of witches at this season.[1] A ceremony of the same sort is annually observed on the same evening, the Eve of Epiphany, by the peasantry who inhabit the mountains of the Tuscan Romagna. A troop of lads parade the streets of the village making a fiendish noise by means of bells and kitchen utensils of tin and brass, while others blow blasts on horns and reed-pipes. They drag about a cart containing an effigy of an old woman made up of rags and tow, which represents Befana (Epiphany). When they come to the village square they put fire to the effigy, which soon vanishes in smoke and flames amid a chorus of cries, shrieks, and other forms of rustic melody.[2] Similar ceremonies are probably observed on the same evening in other parts of Italy.

Befana in the Tuscan Romagna.

In the Shetland Islands the Yule or Christmas holidays begin, or used to begin, seven days before Christmas and last till Artinmas, that is, the twenty-fourth day after Christmas.

Expulsion of the Trows in Shetland

---

[1] As to Befana and her connexion with Epiphany, see J. Grimm, *Deutsche Mythologie*,[4] i. 234. The personified Befana, an ugly but good-natured old woman, is known in Sicily as well as Italy. See G. Pitrè, *Spettacoli e Feste Popolari Siciliane* (Palermo, 1881), p. 167. As to the ceremony in the Piazza Navona, see H. Usener, "Italische Mythen," *Kleine Schriften*, iv. (Leipsic and Berlin, 1913) pp. 108 *sqq.*, who rightly compares it to the Swiss ceremonies observed at and near Brunnen on Twelfth Night. I witnessed the noisy scene in the Piazza Navona in January, 1901.

[2] P. Fabbri, "Canti popolari raccolti sui monti della Romagna-Toscana," *Archivio per lo Studio delle Tradizioni Popolari*, xxii. (1903) pp. 356 *sq.*; H. Usener, *Kleine Schriften*, iv. 108 note[62]. In the Abruzzi, on the evening before Epiphany, musicians go from house to house serenading the inmates with songs and the strains of fiddles, guitars, organs, and so forth. They are accompanied by others carrying lanterns, torches, or burning branches of juniper. See Antonio de Nino, *Usi e Costumi Abruzzesi* (Florence, 1879–1883), ii. 178-180 ; G. Finamore, *Credenze, Usi e Costumi Abruzzesi* (Palermo, 1890), pp. 88 *sq.* Such house to house visitations may be a relic of an old expulsion of witches and demons.

on Up-
helly-a',
the twenty-
fourth day
after
Christmas.
In the Shetland parlance these holidays are known as "the Yules." On the first night, called Tul-ya's e'en, seven days before Christmas, certain mischievous elves, whom the Shetlanders name Trows, "received permission to leave their homes in the heart of the earth and dwell, if it so pleased them, above ground. There seemed to have been no doubt that those creatures preferred disporting themselves among the dwellings of men to residing in their own subterranean abodes, for they availed themselves of every permission given, and created no little disturbance among the mortals whom they visited. One of the most important of all Yule-tide observances was the 'saining' required to guard life or property from the Trows. If the proper observances were omitted, the 'grey-folk' were sure to take advantage of the opportunity."[1]   On the last day of the holidays, the twenty-fourth day after Christmas, which in Shetland goes by the name of Up-helly-a', Uphellia, or Uphaliday, "the doors were all opened, and a great deal of pantomimic chasing and driving and dispersing of unseen creatures took place. Many pious ejaculations were uttered, and iron was ostentatiously displayed, 'for Trows can never abide the sight o' iron.' The Bible was read and quoted. People moved about in groups or couples, never singly, and infants were carefully guarded as well as sained by vigilant and learned 'wise women.' Alas, the poor Trows! their time of frolic and liberty was ended, and on Twenty-fourth night they retired to their gloomy abodes beneath the sod, seldom finding opportunity to reappear again, and never with the same licence, until the Yules returned. All that pantomime, all that invoking of holier Powers, were but methods of 'speeding the parting guest,' and mortals were rejoicing that the unbidden, unwelcome grey-folk must depart. When day

[1] Rev. Biot Edmondston and Jessie M. E. Saxby, *The Home of a Naturalist* (London, 1888), p. 136. Compare *County Folk-lore*, vol. iii. *Orkney and Shetland Islands*, collected by G. F. Black (London, 1903), p. 196. As to the Trows, whose name is doubtless identical with the Norse Trolls (Swedish *troll*, Norwegian *trold*), see Edmondston and Saxby, *op. cit.* pp. 189 *sqq.* ; John Jamieson, *Etymological Dictionary of the Scottish Language*, New Edition, edited by J. Longmuir and D. Donaldson (Paisley, 1879–1882), iv. 630 *sq.*, who observes that "while the Fairies are uniformly represented as social, cheerful, and benevolent beings, the *Trows* are described as gloomy and malignant, ever prone to injure men."

dawned after Twenty-fourth night the Trows had vanished and the Yules were ended." [1] Of late years Up-helly-a' has been celebrated in Lerwick with pompous and elaborate masquerades. The chief event of the evening is a torch-light procession of maskers or "guizers," as they are called, who escort the model of a Norse galley through the streets, and finally set it on fire by throwing their torches into it. But in this form the celebration seems to date only from the latter part of the nineteenth century ; in former times an old boat filled with tar and ignited was dragged about and blazing tar-barrels were drawn or kicked through the streets. [2] The fire, however procured, was probably in origin intended to chase away the lingering Trows from the town at the end of the holidays.

Thus it would seem that the custom of annually ban-ishing witches and demons on a day or night set apart for the purpose has not been confined to Central Europe, but can be traced from Calabria and Rome in the south to the Shetland Islands in the far north.

Annual expulsion of witches and demons in Europe.

[1] Rev. Biot Edmondston and Jessie M. E. Saxby, *The Home of a Naturalist* (London, 1888), p. 146. Compare *County Folk-lore*, vol. iii. *Orkney and Shetland Islands*, collected by G. F. Black (London, 1903), pp. 202 *sq.*

[2] *The Shetland News*, February 1st, 1913, p. 5. As January 5th is reckoned Christmas in Shetland, the celebration of Up-helly-a' falls on January 29th. See J. Nicolson, in *The World's Work and Play*, February, 1906, pp. 283 *sqq.* For further information relating to the ceremony I am indebted to the kind-ness of Sheriff-Substitute David J. Mackenzie (formerly of Lerwick, now of Kilmarnock). According to one of his correspondents, the Rev. Dr. J. Willcock of Lerwick, the present elaborate form of the ceremony dates only from 1882, when the Duke of Edinburgh visited Lerwick on naval business, and Up-helly-a' was celebrated in his honour on a grander scale than ever before. Yet Dr. Willcock ap-parently does not deny the antiquity of the festival in a simpler form, for in his letter he says : "In former times

an old boat filled with tar was set on fire and dragged about, as were also lighted tar-barrels." Another authority on Shetland antiquities, Mr. Gilbert Goudie, writes to Sheriff Mackenzie that "the kicking about and burning a tar-barrel is very old in Lerwick." Compare *County Folk-lore*, iii. *Orkney and Shetland Islands*, collected by G. F. Black (London, 1903), p. 205 : "Formerly, blazing tar-barrels were dragged about the town, and after-wards, with the first break of morning, dashed over the knab into the sea." Up-helly-a', the Shetland name for Antinmas, is no doubt the same with Uphalyday, which Dr. J. Jamieson (*Dictionary of the Scottish Language*, New Edition, iv. 676) defines as "the first day after the termination of the Christmas holidays," quoting two official documents of A.D. 1494 and 1541 respectively.

I have to thank my friend Miss Anderson of Barskimming, Mauchline, Ayrshire, for kindly calling my attention to this interesting relic of the past.

CHAPTER IV

PUBLIC SCAPEGOATS

§ 1. *The Expulsion of Embodied Evils*

The expulsion of embodied evils.

THUS far we have dealt with that class of the general expulsion of evils which I have called direct or immediate. In this class the evils are invisible, at least to common eyes, and the mode of deliverance consists for the most part in beating the empty air and raising such a hubbub as may scare the mischievous spirits and put them to flight. It remains to illustrate the second class of expulsions, in which the evil influences are embodied in a visible form or are at least supposed to be loaded upon a material medium, which acts as a vehicle to draw them off from the people, village, or town.

Expulsion of demons personified by men among the American Indians.

The Pomos of California celebrate an expulsion of devils every seven years, at which the devils are represented by disguised men. "Twenty or thirty men array themselves in harlequin rig and barbaric paint, and put vessels of pitch on their heads ; then they secretly go out into the surrounding mountains. These are to personify the devils. A herald goes up to the top of the assembly-house, and makes a speech to the multitude. At a signal agreed upon in the evening the masqueraders come in from the mountains, with the vessels of pitch flaming on their heads, and with all the frightful accessories of noise, motion, and costume which the savage mind can devise in representation of demons. The terrified women and children flee for life, the men huddle them inside a circle, and, on the principle of fighting the devil with fire, they swing blazing firebrands in the air, yell, whoop, and make frantic dashes at the marauding and bloodthirsty devils, so creating a terrific spectacle, and striking great fear into the hearts of the assembled hundreds of women, who are screaming and fainting and clinging to their valorous protectors. Finally the devils succeed in getting into the assembly-house, and the bravest of the men enter and hold a parley with them. As a conclusion of the whole farce, the men summon courage, the devils are expelled from the assembly-house, and with a prodigious row and racket of sham fighting are chased away into the mountains."[1]   In spring, as soon as the willow-leaves were full grown on the banks of the river, the Mandan Indians celebrated their great annual festival, one of the features of which was the expulsion of the devil. A man, painted black to represent the devil, entered the village from the prairie, chased and frightened the women, and acted the part of a buffalo bull in the buffalo dance, the object of which was to ensure a plentiful supply of buffaloes during the ensuing year. Finally he was chased from the village, the women pursuing him with hisses and gibes, beating him with sticks, and pelting him with dirt.[2]   The Mayas of Yucatan divided the year into eighteen months of twenty days each, and they added five supplementary days at the end of the year in order to make a total of three hundred and sixty-five days. These five supplementary days were deemed unlucky. In the course of them the people banished the evils that might threaten them in the year on which they were about to enter. For that purpose they made a clay image of the demon of evil Uuayayab, that is *u-uayab-haab,* " He by whom the year is poisoned," confronted it with the deity who had supreme power over the coming year, and then carried it out of the village in the direction of that cardinal point to which, on the system of the Mayan calendar, the particular year was supposed to belong. Having thus rid themselves of the demon, they looked forward to a happy New Year.[3]

Expulsion of a demon embodied in an image among the Mayas of Yucatan.

[1] Stephen Powers, *Tribes of California* (Washington, 1877), p. 159.

[2] G. Catlin, *North American Indians,* Fourth Edition (London, 1844), i. 166 sqq.; id., *O-kee-pa, a Religious Ceremony, and other Customs of the Mandans* (London, 1867).

[3] Diego de Landa, *Relation des Choses de Yucatan* (Paris, 1864), pp. 203-205, 211-215; E. Seler, " The

Some of the native tribes of Central Queensland believe
in a noxious being called Molonga, who prowls unseen and
would kill men and violate women if certain ceremonies
were not performed.   These ceremonies last for five nights
and consist of dances, in which only men, fantastically
painted and adorned, take part.   On the fifth night Molonga
himself, personified by a man tricked out with red ochre and
feathers and carrying a long feather-tipped spear, rushes
forth from the darkness at the spectators and makes as if
he would run them through.   Great is the excitement, loud
are the shrieks and shouts, but after another feigned attack
the demon vanishes in the gloom.[1]   On the last night of
the year the palace of the Kings of Cambodia is purged
of devils.   Men painted as fiends are chased by elephants
about the palace courts.   When they have been expelled,
a consecrated thread of cotton is stretched round the

palace to keep them out.[2]   In Munzerabad, a district
of Mysore in Southern India, when cholera or smallpox has broken out in a parish, the inhabitants assemble
and conjure the demon of the disease into a wooden
image, which they carry, generally at midnight, into the
next parish.   The inhabitants of that parish in like manner
pass the image on to their neighbours, and thus the
demon is expelled from one village after another, until he
comes to the bank of a river into which he is finally thrown.[3]
Russian villagers seek to protect themselves against epidemics,
whether of man or beast, by drawing a furrow with a plough
right round the village.   The plough is dragged by four
widows and the ceremony is performed at night ; all fires and
lights must be extinguished while the plough is going the
round.   The people think that no unclean spirit can pass
the furrow which has thus been traced.   In the village of

Mexican   Chronology,"   *Bureau   of
American   Ethnology,   Bulletin   28*
(Washington, 1904), p. 17.   As to
the Maya calendar see further Cyrus
Thomas, *The Maya Year* (Washing-
ton, 1894), pp. 19 *sqq.* (*Smithsonian
Institution, Bureau of Ethnology*).

[1] W. E. Roth, *Ethnological Studies
among the North-West-Central Queens-*

land Aborigines (Brisbane and London,
1897), pp. 120-125.

[2] J. Moura, *Le Royaume du Cambodge* (Paris, 1883), i. 172.   Compare
above, p. 149.

[3] R. H. Elliot, *Experiences of a
Planter in the Jungles of Mysore*
(London, 1871), i. 60 *sq.*

Dubrowitschi a puppet is carried before the plough with the cry, "Out of the village with the unclean spirit!" and at the end of the ceremony it is torn in pieces and the fragments scattered about.[1] No doubt the demon of the disease is supposed to be in the puppet and to be destroyed with it. Sometimes in an Esthonian village a rumour will get about that the Evil One himself has been seen in the place. Instantly the whole village is in an uproar, and the entire population, armed with sticks, flails, and scythes, turns out to give him chase. They generally expel him in the shape of a wolf or a cat, occasionally they brag that they have beaten the devil to death.[2] At Carmona, in Andalusia, on one day of the year, boys are stripped naked and smeared with glue in which feathers are stuck. Thus disguised, they run from house to house, the people trying to avoid them and to bar their houses against them.[3] The ceremony is probably a relic of an annual expulsion of devils.

Expulsion of demons embodied in animals or boys in Esthonia and Spain.

Some of the Khasis of Assam annually expel the demon of plague. The ceremony is called *Beh-dieng-khlam*, that is "Driving away (*beh*) the plague (*khlam*) with sticks (*dieng*)"; it takes place in the Deep-water month (June). On the day fixed for the expulsion the men rise early and beat the roof with sticks, calling upon the demon of the plague to leave the house. Later in the day they go down to the stream where the goddess Aitan dwells. Then long poles or bamboos, newly cut, are laid across the stream and the people jump on them, trying to break them; when they succeed, they give a great shout. Next a very large pole or bamboo is similarly laid across the stream, and the people divide themselves into two parties, one on each side of the stream, and pull against each other at opposite ends of the pole. According to one account the party which succeeds in dragging the pole to their side of the stream is supposed to gain health and prosperity during the coming year.

Annual expulsion of the demon of plague among the Khasis of Assam.

---

[1] A. C. Winter, "Russische Volksbräuche bei Seuchen," *Globus*, lxxix. (1901) p. 302. For the Russian ceremony of drawing a plough round a village to keep out the cattle plague, see also W. R. S. Ralston, *Songs of the Russian People*, Second Edition

(London, 1872), pp. 396 *sqq.*

[2] J. G. Kohl, *Die deutsch-russischen Ostseeprovinzen* (Dresden and Leipsic, 1841), ii. 278.

[3] *Folk-lore Journal*, vii. (1889) p. 174.

According to another account, if the people on the east bank win in the contest or "tug-of-war," good luck and prosperity are assured ; but if the people on the west bank are victorious, then everything will go wrong.   On this occasion the people disguise themselves as giants and wild beasts, and they parade images of serpents, elephants, tigers, peacocks, and so on.   The men dance with enthusiasm, and the girls, dressed in their best, look on.   Before the assembly breaks up, the men play a sort of game of hockey with wooden balls.[1]   In this ceremonial contest or "tug of war" between two parties of the people, we may conjecture that the one party represents the expelled demons of the plague ; and if that is so, we may perhaps assume that in the struggle the representatives of the demons generally allow themselves to be overcome by their adversaries, in order that the village may be free from pestilence in the coming year.   Similarly in autumn the Central Esquimaux divide themselves into two parties, representing summer and winter respectively, which pull at opposite ends of a rope ; and they draw omens of the weather to be expected in the coming winter according as the party of summer or of winter prevails in the struggle.[2]   That in such contests, resembling our English game of "French and English" or the "Tug of War," the one side may represent demons is proved by a custom observed by the Chukmas, a tribe of the Chittagong Hill Tracts in South-Eastern India.   "On the death of a Dewan or of a priest a curious sport is customary at the funeral.   The corpse is conveyed to the place of cremation on a car ; to this car ropes are attached, and the persons attending the ceremony are divided into two equal bodies and set to work to pull in opposite directions.   One side represents the good spirits ; the other, the powers of evil.   The contest is so arranged that the former are victorious.   Sometimes, however, the young men representing the demons are inclined to pull too vigorously, but a stick generally quells this un-

The Tug of War probably a contest with demons represented by human beings.

The Tug of War at funerals in Chittagong and Burma.

---

[1] Major P. R. T. Gurdon, *The Khasis* (London, 1907), p. 157 ; A. Bastian, in *Verhandlungen der Berliner Gesellschaft für Anthropologie, Ethnologie, und Urgeschichte*, 1881, p. 151 ; *id.*, *Völkerstämme am Brahmaputra* (Berlin, 1883), pp. 6 *sq.*

[2] Fr. Boas, "The Central Eskimo," *Sixth Annual Report of the Bureau of Ethnology* (Washington, 1888), p. 605. See *The Dying God*, p. 259.

seemly ardour in the cause of evil."[1]   The contest is like that
between the angels and devils depicted in the frescoes of the
Campo Santo at Pisa.   In Burma a similar struggle takes
place at the funeral of a Buddhist monk who passed for a
saint in the popular estimation : ropes are attached to
opposite ends of the car on which the coffin is placed, all
the able-bodied men of the neighbourhood hold on to one or
other of the two ends and pull as if for dear life against
each other ; even the women and girls sometimes join in the
tug of war, and policemen have been seen, in a state of
frantic excitement, waving their batons to encourage the
combatants and dragging back shirkers by main force into
the fighting line.   The struggle is sometimes prolonged for
hours or even days.[2]   With the example of the Chukmas
before us, we may conjecture that the original motive of this
internecine strife was a persuasion that the eternal happiness
or misery of the departed saint depended on the issue of this
contest between the powers of good and evil for the possession of his mortal remains.

But in Burma the tug of war has been employed for The Tug
more secular purposes than the salvation or perdition of of War as
souls.   " The inhabitants," we are told, "still have a custom making
of pulling a rope to produce rain.   A rain party and a ceremony
drought party tug against each other, the rain party being and else
allowed the victory, which in the popular notion is generally where.
followed by rain." [3]   The mode in which this salutary result
follows from tugging at a rope is explained by the Burmese
doctrine of *nats* or spirits who cause rain.   But it is only
when these spirits sport in the air that rain falls ; when they
shut themselves up in their houses there is drought.   Now
in some Burmese writings " it is said, that when the sun is
in the path of the goat, these *Nat* do not chuse to leave
their houses on account of the great heat, whence there is
then no rain.   For this reason, the inhabitants of the Burma

---

[1] Capt. T. H. Lewin, *Wild Races of South - Eastern India* (London, 1870), p. 185.

[2] Father Sangermano, *Description of the Burmese Empire* (Rangoon, 1885), p. 98 ; Capt. C. J. F. S. Forbes, *British Burma* (London, 1878), pp.

216 *sq.* ; Shway Yoe, *The Burman, his Life and Notions* (London, 1882), ii. 334 *sq.*, 342.

[3] F. E. Sawyer, "S. Swithin and Rainmakers," *The Folk-lore Journal*, i. (1883) p. 214.

empire, in times of drought, are wont to assemble in great numbers, with drums and a long cable. Dividing themselves into two parties, with a vast shouting and noise, they drag the cable contrary ways, the one party endeavouring to get the better of the other : and they think, by this means, to invite the *Nat* to come out from their houses, and to sport in the air. The thunder and lightning, which frequently precede rain, are the clashing and shining of the arms of these *Nat*, who sometimes sport in mock battles."[1] Apparently, therefore, in the tug of war, practised as a rain-charm, the one party represent the spirits who have to be dragged reluctantly from their houses in order to make rain in the sky. Similarly in the Timor-laut Islands, when the people want a rainy wind from the west, the population of the village, men, women, and children divide into two parties and pull against each other at the end of a long bamboo. But the party at the eastern end must pull the harder, in order to draw the desired wind out of the west.[2] We can now perhaps understand why among the Khasis the victory of the eastern side in the tug of war is thought to prognosticate good luck and prosperity, and why the victory of the western side is believed to portend the contrary ; the distinction is at once intelligible when we remember that in the country of the Khasis the rainy wind is the monsoon which blows from the south-west, whereas the wind which blows from the south-east is hot and dry.[3] Thus a victory of the eastern party in the tug of war means that they have drawn rain and consequently fertility into the country from the west ; whereas a victory of the western party signifies that they have dragged drought and consequently dearth into the country from the east.

However, a somewhat different turn is given to the

[1] Francis Buchanan, "On the Religion and Literature of the Burmas," *Asiatick Researches*, vi. (London, 1801) pp. 193 *sq.* Compare Lieut.-General A. Fytche, *Burma Past and Present* (London, 1878), i. 248 note[1]; Max and Bertha Ferrars, *Burma* (London, 1900), p. 184 ; (Sir) J. G. Scott and J. P. Hardiman, *Gazetteer of Upper Burma and the Shan States* (Rangoon, 1900–

1901), Part ii. vol. ii. pp. 95, 279.

[2] J. G. F. Riedel, *De sluik- en kroesharige rassen tusschen Celebes en Papua* (The Hague, 1886), p. 282.

[3] For particulars as to the winds of Assam I am indebted to my friend Mr. J. D. Anderson, formerly of the Indian Civil Service, who resided many years in that country.

ceremony of rope-pulling in the East Indies by another writer, who informs us, that while the contest only takes place in some of these islands when rain is wanted, it is closely connected with those licentious rites performed for the fertilization of the ground which have been described in another part of this work.[1]   According to this account the men and women appear to take opposite sides in the tug of war, and in pulling against each other they imitate by their movements the union of the sexes.[2]   If that is so, it would seem that the rite is a magical ceremony designed to promote the fertility of the ground by means of homoeopathic or imitative magic.   The same may perhaps be the intention of the tug of war as it is practised for the benefit of the crops by some of the Naga tribes of Assam, and this is the more likely because in the case of these tribes we are definitely told that the sexes take opposite sides, the women and girls tugging against the men and boys.   This is done by the Tangkhuls of Assam a month after the rice has been sown ; the ceremony is performed " in order to take the omens for the future of the crops," and it " is followed by considerable license."   The tug of war between the sexes with its attendant license is repeated before the first-fruits are cut by the sacred headman.[3]   In Corea about the fifteenth day of the first month villages engage in the same kind of contest with each other, and it is thought that the village which wins will have a good harvest.   The rope which they pull is made of straw, two feet in diameter, with its ends divided into branches.   The men lay hold of the main stem, while the women grasp the branches, and they often tug harder than the men, for they load their skirts with stones,

---

[1] *The Magic Art and the Evolution of Kings*, ii. 98 *sq.*

[2] G. W. W. C. Baron van Hoevell, "Leti - eilanden," *Tijdschrift voor Indische Taal- Land- en Volkenkunde*, xxxiii. (1890) p. 207.   However, it is not quite clear from the writer's words ("*Immers de mannen en vrouwen in twee partijeen verdeelt en elk een stuk van de roten in de hande houdende bootsen toch ook door't voor- en achter-overbuigen van't lichaam de bewegingen van cohabitie na*") whether the men and women take opposite sides or are distributed between the two.

[3] T. C. Hodson, *The Naga Tribes of Manipur* (London, 1911), p. 168 ; compare 64.   "The Chirus have six crop festivals, one of which, that before the crops are cut, is marked by a rope-pulling ceremony of the same nature as that observed among the Tangkhuls" (*op. cit.* p. 172).   The headman (*khullākpa*) " is a sacrosanct person, the representative of the village in all religious rites, and surrounded by special alimentary, social and conjugal *gennas* " or taboos (*op. cit.* p. 110).

The Tug
of War in
Kamt-
chatka
and New
Guinea.
which adds weight to the force of their muscles.[1]　In
Kamtchatka, when the fishing season is over, the people
used to divide into two parties, one of which tried to pull a
birch-tree by a strap through the smoke-hole into their
subterranean winter dwelling, while the other party outside,
pulling at the end of the tree, endeavoured to hinder them.
If the party in the house succeeded, they raised shouts of
joy and set up a grass effigy of a wolf, which they preserved
carefully throughout the year, believing that it espoused
their young women and prevented them from giving birth to
twins.　For they deem the birth of twins a dreadful misfortune and a horrible sin ; they put it down to the wolf in
the forest, and all who chance to be in the house at the
time shew a clean pair of heels, leaving the mother and her
infants to shift for themselves.　Should the twins be both
girls, the calamity is even greater.[2]　In the village of Doreh,
in Dutch New Guinea, when some of the inhabitants have
gone on a long journey, the people who stay at home
engage in a Tug of War among themselves to determine
whether the journey will be prosperous or not.　One side
represents the voyagers and the other side those who are
left behind.　They pull at opposite ends of a long bamboo,
and if the bamboo breaks or the side which represents the
people at home is obliged to let go, the omen is favourable.[3]

The Tug
of War in
Morocco
to procure
rain or
sunshine.
In Morocco, also, the Tug of War is resorted to as a
means of influencing the weather, sometimes in order to
procure rain and sometimes to procure sunshine ; and here
men and women appear usually to take opposite sides in
the contest.　For example, among the Igliwa, a Berber
people of the Great Atlas, when rain is wanted, they take a
rope and the men pull at one end and women at the other.
While they are tugging away, a man suddenly cuts the rope
and the women fall down.　The same device for procuring
rain in time of drought is practised by the Ait Warain,
another Berber tribe of Morocco ; but among them in the
heat of the contest the women as well as the men will some-

---

[1] Stewart Culin, *Korean Games*
(Philadelphia, 1895), p. 35 ; A. C.
Haddon, *The Study of Man* (London
and New York, 1898), p. 274.

[2] G. W. Steller, *Beschreibung von*

dem Lande Kamtschatka (Frankfort
and Leipsic, 1774), pp. 327 *sq.*

[3] H. von Rosenberg, *Der malayische
Archipel* (Leipsic, 1878), p. 462.

times let go the rope and allow the opposite party to fall on their backs. However, the Tsûl, another Berber tribe of Morocco, employ the Tug of War for the opposite purpose of ensuring a supply of sunshine and heat in autumn, when they wish to dry their figs and grapes ; the contest takes place at night by the light of the moon.[1] The apparent contradiction of employing the same procedure for opposite purposes vanishes if we suppose that, as the Assamese custom seems to indicate, the intention is to draw either a rainy or a dry wind out of the quarters from which the breezes that bring rain or sunshine usually blow, and which will usually be on opposite sides of the sky. Hence in order fully to understand the Tug of War, when it is practised for the purpose of influencing the weather, we should know, first, the directions from which the rainy and the dry winds respectively come in the country under consideration, and second, the direction in which the rope is stretched between the contending parties. If, for example, as happens in Assam, the rainy wind blows from the west, and a victory of the eastern party in the Tug of War is an omen of prosperity, we may conclude with a fair degree of probability that the intention of the contest is to draw the rain from the quarter of the sky in which it is lingering. But these niceties of observation have usually escaped the attention of those who have described the Tug of War.

In various parts of Morocco games of ball are played for the sake now of procuring rain and now of procuring dry weather ; the ball is sometimes propelled with sticks and sometimes with the feet of the competitors. An Arab questioned as to why a game of ball should bring on rain explained that the ball is dark like a rain-cloud.[2] Perhaps the answer furnishes the clue to the meaning of the rite. If in such games played to influence the weather the ball represents a rain-cloud, the success or failure of the charm

Games of ball in Morocco to procure rain or sunshine.

[1] Edward Westermarck, "The Popular Ritual of the Great Feast in Morocco," *Folk-lore*, xxii. (1911) pp. 158 *sq.* ; *id.*, *Ceremonies and Beliefs connected with Agriculture, Certain Dates of the Solar Year, and the Weather in Morocco* (Helsingfors, 1913), p. 122.

[2] E. Westermarck, *Ceremonies and Beliefs connected with Agriculture, Certain Dates of the Solar Year, and the Weather in Morocco* (Helsingfors, 1913), pp. 121 *sq.*

will depend on which side contrives to get the ball home in the enemy's quarters. For example, if rain is desired and the rainy wind blows in Morocco, as may perhaps be assumed, from the west, then should the western side succeed in driving the ball through the eastern goal, there will be rain; but if the eastern party wins, then the rain is driven away and the drought will continue. Thus a game of ball would in theory and practice answer exactly to the Tug of War practised for the same purposes.

The Tug of War in Morocco to ensure prosperity. In Morocco, however, the Tug of War is apparently used also for the purpose of ensuring prosperity in general without any special reference to the weather. Dr. Westermarck was informed by an old Arab from the Hiaina that the Tug of War " is no longer practised at the Great Feast, as it was in his childhood, but that it is performed in the autumn when the threshing is going on and the fruits are ripe. Then men and women have a tug of war by moonlight so that the *bäs*, or evil, shall go away, that the year shall be good, and that the people shall live in peace. Some man secretly cuts two of the three cords of which the rope is made, with the result that both parties tumble down."[1] In this contest one party perhaps represents the powers of good and the other the powers of evil in general. But why in these Moroccan cases of the Tug of War the rope should be so often cut and one or both sides laid on their backs, is not manifest. Perhaps the simple device of suddenly slacking the rope in order to make the opposite side lose their footing, and so to haul the rope away from them before they can recover themselves, may have led to the more trenchant measure of cutting it with a knife for the same purpose.

Spiritual significance of the Tug of War. These examples make it probable that wherever the Tug of War is played only at certain definite seasons or on certain particular occasions, it was originally performed, not as a mere pastime, but as a magical ceremony designed to work some good for the community. Further, we may surmise that in many cases the two contending parties represent respectively the powers of good and evil struggling against each other for the mastery, and

[1] E. Westermarck, "The Popular Ritual of the Great Feast in Morocco," *Folk-lore,* xxii. (1911) p. 159.

as the community has always an interest in the prevalence of the powers of good, it may well happen that the
powers of evil do not always get fair play in these conflicts;
though no doubt when it comes to be "pull devil, pull
baker," the devil is apt, in the spirit of a true sportsman,
to tug with as hearty good will as his far more deserving
adversary the baker.   To take cases in which the game is
played without any alleged practical motive, the Roocooyen
Indians of French Guiana engage in the Tug of War as a
sort of interlude during the ceremonial tortures of the youth.[1]
Among the Cingalese the game "is connected with the
superstitious worship of the goddess Patiné; and is more
intended for a propitiation to that deity, than considered
as an indulgence, or pursued as an exercise.   Two opposite
parties procure two sticks of the strongest and toughest
wood, and so crooked as to hook into one another without
slipping; they then attach strong cords or cable-rattans of
sufficient length to allow of every one laying hold of them.
The contending parties then pull until one of the sticks
gives way."   The victorious piece of wood is gaily decorated, placed in a palanquin, and borne through the village
amid noisy rejoicings, often accompanied with coarse and
obscene expressions.[2]   The use of foul language on this
occasion suggests that the ceremony is here, as elsewhere,
observed for the purpose of ensuring fertility.   In the
North-Western provinces of India the game is played on
the fourteenth day of the light half of the month Kuar.
The rope (*barra*) is made of the grass called *makra*, and
is thicker than a man's arm.   The various quarters of a
village pull against each other, and the one which is
victorious keeps possession of the rope during the ensuing
year.   It is chiefly in the east of these provinces that the
game is played; in the west it is unknown.[3]   Sometimes
the contest is between the inhabitants of neighbouring
villages, and the rope is stretched across the boundary;

The Tug of War in French Guiana.

The Tug of War in North-Western India.

---

[1] H. Coudreau, *Chez nos Indiens, Quatre Années dans la Guayane Fran-çaise* (Paris, 1895), p. 234.

[2] Major Forbes, *Eleven Years in Ceylon* (London, 1840), i. 358.

[3] Sir Henry M. Elliot, *Memoirs on the History, Folk-lore, and Distribu-tion of the Races of the North-Western Provinces of India,* edited, revised, and re-arranged by John Beames (Lon-don, 1869), i. 235.

plenty is supposed to attend the victorious side.[1] At the Great Feast, a yearly sacrificial festival of the Mohammedan world, some tribes in Morocco practise a Tug of War. Thus among the Ait Sadden it is observed on the first day of the festival before the sacrifice ; among the Ait Yusi it is performed either before the religious service or in the afternoon of the same day, and also in the morning of the Little Feast. Both sexes generally take part in the contest, the men tugging at one end of the rope and ·the women at the other, and sometimes the weaker party applies for help to persons of the same sex in a neighbouring village. When they are all hard at it, the men may suddenly let go the rope and so send the women sprawling on their backs.[2]

The Tug of War in Shropshire and Radnorshire. At Ludlow in Shropshire a grand Tug of War used to take place on Shrove Tuesday between the inhabitants of Broad Street Ward on the one side and of Corve Street Ward on the other. The rope was three inches thick and thirty-six yards long, with a red knob at one end and a blue knob at the other. The rope was paid out by the Mayor in person from a window in the Market Hall at four o'clock in the. afternoon. The shops then put up their shutters, and the population engaged in the struggle with enthusiasm, gentle and simple, lawyers and parsons bearing a hand on one side or the other, till their clothes were torn to tatters on their backs. The injured were carried into the neighbouring houses, where their hurts were attended to. If the party of the Red Knob won, they carried the rope in triumph to the River Leme and dipped it in the water. Finally, the rope was sold, the money which it brought in was devoted to the purchase of beer, and drinking, squabbling, and fighting ended the happy day. This ancient and highly popular pastime was suppressed in 1851 on the frivolous pretext that it gave rise to disorderly scenes and dangerous accidents.[3] A similar custom has long been observed on Shrove Tuesday at Presteign in Radnorshire.

---

[1] W. Crooke, *Popular Religion and Folk-lore of Northern India* (Westminster, 1896), ii. 321.

[2] E. Westermarck, "The Popular Ritual of the Great Feast in Morocco," *Folk-lore*, xxii. (1911) p. 158.

[3] John Brand, *Popular Antiquities of Great Britain*, New Edition (London, 1883), i. 92 ; Miss C. S. Burne and Miss G. F. Jackson, *Shropshire Folk-lore* (London, 1883), pp. 319-321.

The rope is pulled by two parties representing the upper and the lower portions of the town, who strive to drag it either to a point in the west wall or to another point in Broad Street, where the River Lugg is reached.[1] In the Contests for a ball (*soule*) in Normandy. Bocage of Normandy most desperate struggles used to take place between neighbouring parishes on Shrove Tuesday for the possession of a large leathern ball stuffed with bran and called a *soule*. The ball was launched on the village green and contended for by representatives of different parishes, who sometimes numbered seven or eight hundred, while five or six thousand people might assemble to witness the combat ; for indeed it was a fight rather than a game. The conflict was maintained with the utmost fury ; old scores were paid off between personal enemies ; there were always many wounded, and sometimes there were deaths. The aim of each side was to drive the ball over a stream and to lodge it in a house of their own parish. It was thought that the parish which was victorious in the struggle would have a better crop of apples that year than its neighbours. At Lande-Patry the ball was provided by the bride who had been last married, and she had the honour of throwing it into the arena. The scene of the fiercest battles was St. Pierre d'Entremont, on the highroad between Condé and Tinchebray. After several unsuccessful attempts the custom was suppressed at that village in 1852 with the help of four or five brigades of police. It is now everywhere extinct.[2] The belief that the parish which succeeded in carrying the ball home would have a better crop of apples that year raises a presumption that these conflicts were originally practised as magical rites to ensure fertility. The local custom of Lande-Patry, which required that the ball should be provided and thrown by the last bride,[3] points in the

---

[1] C. S. Burne and G. F. Jackson, *op. cit.* p. 321.

[2] Jules Lecœur, *Esquisses du Bocage Normand* (Condé-sur-Noireau, 1883–1887), i. 13, ii. 153-165. Compare Laisnel de la Salle, *Croyances et Légendes du Centre de la France* (Paris, 1875), i. 86 *sqq.* ; and as to the game of *soule*, see Guerry, in *Mémoires des Antiquaires de France*, viii. (1829) pp.

459-461.

[3] In the parish of Vieux-Pont, in the department of Orne, the man who is last married before the first Sunday in Lent must throw a ball from the foot of the cross. The village lads compete with each other for its possession. To win it the lad must carry it through three parishes without being overtaken by his rivals. See A. de

same direction. It is possible that the popular English, or
rather Scotch, game of football had a similar origin : the
winning side may have imagined that they secured good
crops, good weather, or other substantial advantages to their
village or ward.

Annual
sham fights
may repre-
sent con-
tests with
demons.In like manner, wherever a sham or a real conflict
takes place between two parties annually, above all at the
New Year, we may suspect that the old intention was
to ensure prosperity in some form for the people throughout
the following year, whether by obtaining possession of a
material object in which the luck of the year was supposed
to be embodied, or by defeating and driving away a band
of men who personated the powers of evil. For example,
among the Tenggerese of eastern Java the New Year festival
regularly includes a sham fight fought between two bands
of men, who are armed with spears and swords and advance
against each other again and again at a dancing step, thrusting at their adversaries with their spears, but always taking
care to miss their aim.[1] Again, in Ferghana, a province of
Turkestan, it is or used to be customary on the first day
of the year for the king and chiefs to divide into two parties,
each of which chose a champion. Then the two champions,
clad in armour, engaged in a combat with each other, while
the crowd joined in with bricks and stones. When one of
them was slain the scrimmage stopped, and omens were
drawn as to whether the year on which they had entered
would be prosperous or the reverse.[2] In these combats it
seems probable that one side represents the demons or other
powers of evil whom the people hope to vanquish and expel
at the beginning of the New Year.

Oftener, however, the expelled demons are not represented at all, but are understood to be present invisibly in
the material and visible vehicle which conveys them away.
Here, again, it will be convenient to distinguish between occasional and periodical expulsions. We begin with the former.

Nore, *Coutumes, Mythes, et Traditions
des Provinces de France* (Paris and
Lyons, 1846), pp. 244 *sq.*

[1] J. H. F. Kohlbrugge, " Die
Tenggeresen, ein alter Javanischer
Volksstamm," *Bijdragen tot de Taal-*

*Land- en Volkenkunde van Neder-
landsch-Indië*, liii. (1901) pp. 140
sq.

[2] Edouard Chavannes, *Documents
sur les Tou-Kiue (Turcs) Occidentaux*
(St. Petersburg, 1903), p. 148.

§ 2. *The Occasional Expulsion of Evils in a Material Vehicle*

The vehicle which conveys away the demons may be of various kinds. A common one is a little ship or boat. Thus, in the southern district of the island of Ceram, when a whole village suffers from sickness, a small ship is made and filled with rice, tobacco, eggs, and so forth, which have been contributed by all the people. A little sail is hoisted on the ship. When all is ready, a man calls out in a very loud voice, "O all ye sicknesses, ye smallpoxes, agues, measles, etc., who have visited us so long and wasted us so sorely, but who now cease to plague us, we have made ready this ship for you and we have furnished you with provender sufficient for the voyage. Ye shall have no lack of food nor of betel-leaves nor of areca nuts nor of tobacco. Depart, and sail away from us directly ; never come near us again ; but go to a land which is far from here. Let all the tides and winds waft you speedily thither, and so convey you thither that for the time to come we may live sound and well, and that we may never see the sun rise on you again." Then ten or twelve men carry the vessel to the shore, and let it drift away with the land-breeze, feeling convinced that they are free from sickness for ever, or at least till the next time. If sickness attacks them again, they are sure it is not the same sickness, but a different one, which in due time they dismiss in the same manner. When the demon-laden bark is lost to sight, the bearers return to the village, whereupon a man cries out, " The sicknesses are now gone, vanished, expelled, and sailed away." At this all the people come running out of their houses, passing the word from one to the other with great joy, beating on gongs and on tinkling instruments.[1]

Similar ceremonies are commonly resorted to in other East Indian islands. Thus in Timor-laut, to mislead the demons who are causing sickness, a small proa, containing the image of a man and provisioned for a long voyage, is allowed to drift away with wind and tide. As it is being

Marginal notes: Demons of sickness expelled in a small ship in Ceram. — Demons of sickness expelled in a small ship in Timor-laut.

----

[1] François Valentyn, *Oud- en nieuw Ost-Indiën* (Dordrecht and Amsterdam, 1724–1726), iii. 14. L. de Backer (*L'Archipel Indien*, Paris, 1874, pp. 377 *sq.*) copies from Valentyn.

launched, the people cry, " O sickness, go from here ; turn back ; what do you here in this poor land ? " Three days after this ceremony a pig is killed, and part of the flesh is offered to Dudilaa, who lives in the sun. One of the oldest men says, " Old sir, I beseech you make well the grand-children, children, women, and men, that we may be able to eat pork and rice and to drink palm-wine. I will keep my promise. Eat your share, and make all the people in the village well." If the proa is stranded at any inhabited spot, the sickness will break out there. Hence a stranded proa excites much alarm amongst the coast population, and they

Demons of sickness expelled in a ship in Buru. immediately burn it, because demons fly from fire.[1] In the island of Buru the proa which carries away the demons of disease is about twenty feet long, rigged out with sails, oars, anchor, and so on, and well stocked with provisions. For a day and a night the people beat gongs and drums, and rush about to frighten the demons. Next morning ten stalwart young men strike the people with branches, which have been previously dipped in an earthen pot of water. As soon as they have done so, they run down to the beach, put the branches on board the proa, launch another boat in great haste, and tow the disease-burdened bark far out to sea. There they cast it off, and one of them calls out, " Grand-father Smallpox, go away—go willingly away—go visit another land ; we have made you food ready for the voyage, we have now nothing more to give." When they have

Demons of sickness removed from the persons of the suf-ferers. landed, all the people bathe together in the sea.[2] In this ceremony the reason for striking the people with the branches is clearly to rid them of the disease-demons, which are then supposed to be transferred to the branches. Hence the haste with which the branches are deposited in the proa and towed away to sea. So in the inland districts of Ceram, when smallpox or other sickness is raging, the priest strikes all the houses with consecrated branches, which are then thrown into the river, to be carried down to the sea ;[3] exactly as amongst the Wotyaks of Russia the sticks which have been used for expelling the devils from the village are thrown

---

[1] J. G. F. Riedel, *De sluik- en kroesharige rassen tusschen Selebes en Papua* (The Hague, 1886), pp. 304 *sq.*

[2] J. G. F. Riedel, *op. cit.* pp. 25 *sq.*

[3] *Ibid.* p. 141.

into the river, that the current may sweep the baleful burden away.[1]   In Amboyna, for a similar purpose, the whole body of the patient is rubbed with a live white cock, which is then placed on a little proa and committed to the waves ;[2] and in the Babar archipelago the bark which is to carry away to sea the sickness of a whole village contains a bowl of ashes taken from every kitchen in the village, and another bowl into which all the sick people have spat.[3]   The plan of putting puppets in the boat to represent sick persons, in order to lure the demons after them, is not uncommon.[4]   For example, most of the pagan tribes on the coast of Borneo seek to drive away epidemic disease as follows.   They carve one or more rough human images from the pith of the sago palm and place them on a small raft or boat or full-rigged Malay ship together with rice and other food.   The boat is decked with blossoms of the areca palm and with ribbons made from its leaves, and thus adorned the little craft is allowed to float out to sea with the ebb-tide, bearing, as the people fondly think or hope, the sickness away with it.[5]

In Selangor, one of the native states in the Malay Peninsula, the ship employed in the export of disease is, or used to be, a model of a special kind of Malay craft called a *lanchang*. This was a two-masted vessel with galleries fore and aft, armed with cannon, and used by Malay rajahs on the coast of Sumatra.   So gallant a ship would be highly acceptable to the spirits, and to make it still more beautiful in their eyes it was not uncommonly stained yellow with turmeric or saffron, for among the Malays yellow is the royal colour. Some years ago a very fine model of a *lanchang*, with its cargo of sickness, was towed down the river to sea by the Government steam launch.   A common spell uttered at the launching of one of these ships runs as follows :—

Demons of disease expelled in a ship in Selangor.

> " *Ho, elders of the upper reaches,*
> *Elders of the lower reaches,*
> *Elders of the dry land,*

---

[1] See above, p. 155.

[2] J. G. F. Riedel, *op. cit.* p. 78.

[3] *Ibid.* p. 357.

[4] *Ibid.* pp. 266, 304 *sq.*, 327, 357 ; H. Ling Roth, *Natives of Sarawak*

and British North Borneo (London, 1896), i. 284.

[5] Ch. Hose and W. McDougall, *The Pagan Tribes of Borneo* (London, 1912), ii. 122 *sq.*

Elders of the river-flats,
Assemble ye, O people, lords of hill and hill-foot,
Lords of cavern and hill-locked basin,
Lords of the deep primeval forest,
Lords of the river-bends,
Come on board this lanchang, *assembling in your multitudes.*
So may ye depart with the ebbing stream,
Depart on the passing breeze,
Depart in the yawning earth,
Depart in the red-dyed earth.
Go ye to the ocean which has no wave,
And the plain where no green herb grows,
And never return hither.
But if ye return hither,
Ye shall be consumed by the curse.
At sea ye shall get no drink,
Ashore ye shall get no food,
But gape in vain about the world." [1]

Demons of sickness expelled in small ships in New Guinea, the Philippines, Tikopia, and the Nicobar Islands. The practice of sending away diseases in boats is known outside the limits of the Malay region. Thus when smallpox raged among the Yabim of German New Guinea, they used to make a little model of a canoe with mast, sail, and rudder. Then they said to the small vessel, on which the spirit of smallpox was supposed to have taken his passage, " Bear him away to another village. When the people come forth to draw you ashore, give them ' the thing ' and do to them what you have done to us." Lest the spirit should be hungry on the voyage, they put some taro on board, and to make sure of getting rid of the disease, they wiped their hands on the tiny canoe, after which they let it drift away. It often happened that the wind or

---

[1] W.W. Skeat, *Malay Magic* (London, 1900), pp. 433-435. For other examples of sending away plague-laden boats in the Malay region see J. G. F. Riedel, *op. cit.* pp. 181, 210 ; R. van Eck, " Schetsen van het eiland Bali," *Tijdschrift voor Nederlandsch Indië*, N.S., viii. (1879) p. 104 ; A. Bastian, *Indonesien*, i. 147 ; C. Hupe, " Korte verhandeling over de godsdienst, zeden, enz. der Dajakkers," *Tijdschrift voor Neêrlands Indië*, 1846, dl. iii. 150 ; C. F. H. Campen, " De godsdienstbegrippen der Halmaherasche Alfoeren," *Tijdschrift voor Indische Taal- Land- en Volkenkunde*, xxvii. (1882) p. 441 ; *Journal of the*

Straits Branch of the Royal Asiatic Society, No. 12, pp. 229-231 ; A. L. van Hasselt, *Volksbeschrijving van Midden-Sumatra* (Leyden, 1882), p. 98 ; C. M. Pleyte, " Ethnographische Beschrijving der Kei-Eilanden," *Tijdschrift van het Nederlandsch Aardrijkskundig Genootschap*, Tweede Serie, x. (1893) p. 835 ; H. Ling Roth, " Low's Natives of Sarawak," *Journal of the Anthropological Institute*, xxii, (1893) p. 25 ; C. Snouck Hurgronje, *De Atjehers* (Batavia and Leyden, 1893-1894),i. 461 *sq.*; J. A. Jacobsen, *Reisen in der Inselwelt des Banda-Meeres* (Berlin, 1896), p. 110.

tide drove the vessel back to the place from which it started. Then there would be a deafening rub-a-dub of drums and blowing of shell-trumpets ; and the little ship, or rather its invisible passenger, would be again apostrophized, " Do go away, you have already raged among us so that the air is poisoned with the stench of corpses." If this time it sailed away, they would stand on the shore and watch it with glad hearts disappearing ; then they would climb the trees to get a last glimpse of it till it vanished in the distance. After that they came down joyfully and said to each other, " We have had enough of it. The sickness has happily gone away." [1] When the Tagbanuas and other tribes of the Philippines suffered from epidemics, they used to make little models of ships, supply them with rice and fresh drinking water, and launch them on the sea, in order that the evil spirits might sail away in them.[2] When the people of Tikopia, a small island in the Pacific, to the north of the New Hebrides, were attacked by an epidemic cough, they made a little canoe and adorned it with flowers. Four sons of the principal chiefs carried it on their shoulders all round the island, accompanied by the whole population, some of whom beat the bushes, while others uttered loud cries. On returning to the spot from which they had set out, they launched the canoe on the sea.[3] In the Nicobar Islands, in the Bay of Bengal, when there is much sickness in a village or no fish are caught, the blame is laid upon the spirits. They must be propitiated with offerings. All relations and friends are invited, a huge pig is roasted, and the best of it is eaten, but some parts are offered to the shades. The heap of offerings remains in front of the house till it is carried away by the rising tide. Then the priests, their faces reddened with paint and swine's blood, pretend to catch the demon of disease, and after a hand-to-hand tussle, force him into a model boat, made of leaves and decked with garlands, which is then towed so far to sea that neither wind nor tide is

---

[1] H. Zahn, " Die Jabim," in R. Neuhauss's *Deutsch Neu-Guinea*, iii. (1911) pp. 329 *sq.*

[2] F. Blumentritt, " Über die Eingeborenen der Insel Palawan und der Inselgruppe der Talamianen," *Globus*, lix.

(1891) p. 183.

[3] J. Dumont D'Urville, *Voyage autour du monde et à la recherche de La Pérouse, sur la corvette Astrolabe* (Paris, 1832–1833), v. 311.

likely to drive it back to the shore.[1]　In Annam, when the population of a village has been decimated by cholera, they make a raft and lade it with offerings of money and food, such as a sucking pig, bananas, and oranges.　Sticks of incense also smoke on the floating altar ; and when all is ready and earnest prayers have been uttered, the raft is abandoned to the current of the river.　The people hope that the demon of cholera, allured and gratified by these offerings, will float away on the raft and trouble them no more.[2]

Demons of sickness expelled in the form of animals in India.

Often the vehicle which carries away the collected demons or ills of a whole community is an animal or scapegoat. In the Central Provinces of India, when cholera breaks out in a village, every one retires after sunset to his house.　The priests then parade the streets, taking from the roof of each house a straw, which is burnt with an offering of rice, ghee, and turmeric, at some shrine to the east of the village. Chickens daubed with vermilion are driven away in the direction of the smoke, and are believed to carry the disease with them.　If they fail, goats are tried, and last of all pigs.[3] When cholera rages among the Bhars, Mallans, and Kurmis of India, they take a goat or a buffalo—in either case the animal must be a female, and as black as possible—then having tied some grain, cloves, and red lead in a yellow cloth on its back they turn it out of the village.　The animal is conducted beyond the boundary and not allowed to return.[4] Sometimes the buffalo is marked with a red pigment and driven to the next village, where he carries the plague with him.[5]　The people of the city and cantonments of Sagar being

---

[1] Roepstorff, "Ein Geisterboot der Nicobaresen," *Verhandlungen der Berliner Gesellschaft für Anthropologie, Ethnologie und Urgeschichte* (1881), p. 401 ; W. Svoboda, "Die Bewohner des Nikobaren - Archipels," *Internationales Archiv für Ethnographie*, vi. (1893) pp. 10 *sq.*

[2] P. Denjoy, "An-nam, Médecins et Sorciers, Remèdes et Superstitions," etc., *Bulletins de la Société d'Anthropologie de Paris*, v. (1894) pp. 409 *sq.* Compare É. Aymonier, *Voyage dans le Laos* (Paris, 1895–1897), i. 121. For Siamese applications of the same

principle to the cure of individuals, see A. Bastian, *Die Völker des östlichen Asien*, iii. (Jena, 1867) pp. 295 *sq.*, 485 *sq.*

[3] *Panjab Notes and Queries*, i. p. 48, § 418 (January, 1884).

[4] *Id.*, iii. p. 81, § 373 (February 1886).

[5] W. Crooke, *Popular Religion and Folk-lore of Northern India* (Westminster, 1896), i. 142.　Bulls are used as scapegoats for cholera in Cashmeer (H. G. M. Murray-Aynsley, in *Folk-lore*, iv. (1893) pp. 398 *sq.*).

afflicted with a violent influenza, General Sir William Slee-
man received a request from the old Queen Dowager of
Sagar " to allow of a noisy religious procession for the purpose
of imploring deliverance from this great calamity.   Men,
women, and children in this procession were to do their
utmost to add to the noise by 'raising their voices in
psalmody,' beating upon their brass pots and pans with all
their might, and discharging firearms where they could get
them ; and before the noisy crowd was to be driven a
buffalo, which had been purchased by general subscription,
in order that every family might participate in the merit.
They were to follow it out for eight miles, where it was to be
turned loose for any man who would take it.   If the animal
returned, the disease, it was said, must return with it, and
the ceremony be performed over again. . . . It was, however, subsequently determined that the animal should be a
goat, and he was driven before the crowd accordingly.   I
have on several occasions been requested to allow of such
noisy *pūjās* in cases of epidemics."[1]   Once, when influenza
was raging in Pithoria, a village to the north-west of Sagar,
a man had a small carriage made, after a plan of his own,
for a pair of scapegoats, which were harnessed to it and
driven to a wood at some distance, where they were let loose.
From that hour the disease entirely ceased in the town.   The
goats never returned ; had they done so, it was affirmed that
the disease must have come back with them.[2]

The use of a scapegoat is not uncommon in the hills of the
Eastern Ghats.   In 1886, during a severe outbreak of smallpox, the people of Jepur did reverence to a goat, marched it to
the Ghats, and let it loose on the plains.[3]   In Southern
Konkan, on the appearance of cholera, the villagers went in
procession from the temple to the extreme boundaries of the
village, carrying a basket of cooked rice covered with red
powder, a wooden doll representing the pestilence, and a
cock.   The head of the cock was cut off at the village

Goats and cocks employed as scapegoats in various parts of India.

---

[1] Major-General Sir W. H. Slee-
mann, *Rambles and Recollections of
Indian Official*, New Edition (Westminster, 1893), i. 203.

[2] Major-General Sir W. H. Slee-
man, *op. cit.* i. 198.

[3] F. Fawcett, " On the Saoras (or
Savaras), an Aboriginal Hill People of
the Eastern Ghats," *Journal of the
Anthropological Society of Bombay*, i.
213, note.

boundary, and the body was thrown away. When cholera had thus been transferred from one village to another, the second village observed the same ceremony and passed on the scourge to its neighbours, and so on through a number of villages.[1] Among the Korwas of Mirzapur, when cholera has broken out, the priest offers a black cock or, if the disease is very malignant, a black goat, at the shrine of the local deity, and then drives the animal away in the direction of some other village. But it has not gone far before he overtakes it, kills it, and eats it; which he may do with perfect safety in virtue of his sacred office. Again, when cholera is raging among the Pataris, an aboriginal Dravidian race of South Mirzapur, the wizard and the village elders feed a black cock with grain and drive it beyond the boundaries, ordering the fowl to take the disease away with it. A little oil, red lead, and a spangle worn by a woman on her forehead are usually fastened to the bird's head before it is let loose. The cost of purchasing the cock is defrayed by public subscription. When such a bird of ill-omen appears in a village, the priest takes it to the shrine of the local deity and sacrifices it there; but sometimes he merely bows before it at the shrine and passes it on to some other village. If a murrain attacks their cattle, the Kharwars of Northern India take a black cock and put red lead on its head, antimony on its eyes, a spangle on its forehead, and a pewter bangle on its leg; thus arrayed they let it loose, calling out to the disease, " Mount on the fowl and go elsewhere into the ravines and thickets; destroy the sin." Perhaps, as has been suggested, this tricking out of the bird with women's ornaments may be a relic of some grosser form of expiation in which a human being was sacrificed or banished.[2] Charms of this sort in India no doubt date from a remote antiquity. An ancient Indian book of magic, known as the *Kausika Sutra*, describes a ceremony of letting loose against a hostile army a white-footed ewe in which the power of disease was believed to be

---

[1] Mr. Y. V. Athalye, in *Journal of the Anthropological Society of Bombay*, i. 37.

[2] W. Crooke, *Popular Religion and*

Folk-lore of Northern India (Westminster, 1896), i. 169 *sq.*; *id., Tribes and Castes of the North-Western Provinces and Oudh* (Calcutta, 1896), iii. 445.

incarnate.[1] In the same treatise we read of a mode of getting rid of ill-luck by fastening a hook to the left leg of a crow, attaching a sacrificial cake to the hook, and then letting the bird fly away in a south-westerly direction, while the priest or magician recites as usual the appropriate formula.[2]

Amongst the Dinkas, a pastoral people of the White Nile, each family possesses a sacred cow. When the country is threatened with war, famine, or any other public calamity, the chiefs of the village require a particular family to surrender their sacred cow to serve as a scapegoat. The animal is driven by the women to the brink of the river and across it to the other bank, there to wander in the wilderness and fall a prey to ravening beasts. Then the women return in silence and without looking behind them ; were they to cast a backward glance, they imagine that the ceremony would have no effect.[3] When influenza broke out in a virulent form among the negroes of Togoland during the winter of 1892, the natives set the trouble down to the machinations of evil spirits, who must be expelled the country. The principal instrument of expulsion was a fat toad, which was dragged through the streets of every town or village, followed by an elder who sprinkled holy water to right and left. All the evil was thus concentrated in the toad, which was finally thrown away into the forest. Thus the natives expected to rid the village of the influenza.[4] In 1857, when the Aymara Indians of Bolivia and Peru were suffering from a plague, they loaded a black llama with the clothes of the plague-stricken people, sprinkled brandy on the clothes, and then turned the animal loose on the mountains, hoping that it would carry the pest away with it.[5]

In some parts of India a principal means of expelling

Cows, toads, and llamas as scapegoats in Africa and America.

---

[1] *Kausika Sutra*, xiv. 22 (W. Caland, *Altindisches Zauberritual*, Amsterdam, 1900, p. 29) ; H. Oldenberg, *Die Religion des Veda* (Berlin, 1894), p. 498.

[2] *Kausika Sutra*, xviii. 16 (W. Caland, *Altindisches Zauberritual*, pp. 44 *sq.*).

[3] Dom Daniel Sour Dharim Dena (a Dinka convert), in *Annales de la*

Propagation de la Foi, lx. (1888) pp. 57 *sq.*

[4] H. Seidel, "Krankheit, Tod, und Begräbnis bei den Togonegern," *Globus*, lxxii. (1897) p. 24.

[5] D. Forbes, "On the Aymara Indians of Bolivia and Peru," *Journal of the Ethnological Society of London*, vol. ii. No. 3 (October, 1870), p. 237.

O

Goddess of disease expelled in a toy chariot. an epidemic is a little toy chariot called a *ratha* or *rath,* in which the goddess of the disease is supposed to be carted away. It is carried or drawn in procession to the next village, the inhabitants of which pass it on in like manner, with great alacrity, to their neighbours. Thus the goddess and the plague are transferred from village to village, until at last they come to one which is so far away from its next neighbour that the people do not care to undertake the long weary journey. In that case they content themselves with conveying the chariot to a place so shut in by hills that the disease cannot possibly escape, and there they leave it to die. Or if the village is near the sea, they drown the sickness by throwing the chariot into the water. However, in Central India the real home of the goddess of cholera is at Unkareshwar ; and accordingly the chariot in which she is politely escorted out of a village is finally deposited at or near that place. It is usual and proper for the people of a village to give a friendly notice to their neighbours that they are going to cart the cholera, smallpox, or whatever it may be, to their village, so that the inhabitants may be ready to receive the goddess with due honour and to escort her on her progress. But some unneighbourly folk, without giving notice, go by night and stealthily deposit the chariot on the outskirts of the next village. If the inhabitants are not on the watch, and suffer the fatal little vehicle to remain there, the disease will naturally cleave to them. Sometimes, perhaps generally, the procession with the chariot is accompanied by a goat, a cock, and a pot of native beer or wine, which serve as additional attractions to the goddess to set out on her travels.[1]

Human scapegoats in Uganda. Occasionally the scapegoat is a man. For example, from time to time the gods used to warn the King of Uganda that his foes the Banyoro were working magic against him and his people to make them die of disease. To avert such a catastrophe the king would send a scape-

[1] Jivangi Jimshedji Modi, B.A., "On the Chariot of the Goddess, a Supposed Remedy for driving out an Epidemic," *Journal of the Anthropological Society of Bombay,* vol. iv. No. 8 (Bombay, 1899), pp. 420-424 ; Captain C. Eckford Luard, in *Census of India, 1901,* vol. xix., *Central India* (Lucknow, 1902), p. 78.

goat to the frontier of Bunyoro, the land of the enemy. The scapegoat consisted of either a man and a boy or a woman and her child, chosen because of some mark or bodily defect, which the gods had noted and by which the victims were to be recognized. With the human victims were sent a cow, a goat, a fowl, and a dog; and a strong guard escorted them to the land which the god had indicated. There the limbs of the victims were broken and they were left to die a lingering death in the enemy's country, being too crippled to crawl back to Uganda. The disease or plague was thought to have been thus transferred to the victims and to have been conveyed back in their persons to the land from which it came. So, too, after a war the gods sometimes advised the king to send back a scapegoat in order to free the warriors from some evil that had attached itself to the army. One of the women slaves, a cow, a goat, a fowl, and a dog would be chosen from among the captives and sent back to the borders of the country whence they had come; there they were maimed and left to die. After that the army would be pronounced clean and allowed to return to the capital. In each case a bundle of herbs would be rubbed over the people and the cattle, and would then be tied to the victims, who would thus carry back the evil with them.[1] A similar use of scapegoats, human and animal, was regularly made after a King of Uganda had been crowned. Two men were brought to the king; one of them he wounded slightly with an arrow shot from a bow. The man was then sent away, under a strong guard, as a scapegoat to Bunyoro, the enemy's country, and with him were sent a cow, a goat, and a dog. On his sad journey he took with him the dust and ashes of the sacred fire, which had burned day and night at the entrance to the late king's enclosure and had been extinguished, as usual, at his death. Arrived at their destination, the man and the animals were maimed and left to die. They were believed to bear away with them any uncleanness that might cleave to the new King or Queen.[2]

[1] Rev. J. Roscoe, *The Baganda* (London, 1911), p. 342.
[2] Rev. J. Roscoe, *The Baganda*, pp. 109, 200. As to the perpetual fire at the entrance to a king's enclosure, see *id.* pp. 103, 197, 202 *sq.*

Human scapegoats in China and India.

Some of the aboriginal tribes of China, as a protection against pestilence, select a man of great muscular strength to act the part of scapegoat. Having besmeared his face with paint, he performs many antics with the view of enticing all pestilential and noxious influences to attach themselves to him only. He is assisted by a priest. Finally the scapegoat, hotly pursued by men and women beating gongs and tom-toms, is driven with great haste out of the town or village.[1] In the Punjaub a cure for the murrain is to hire a man of the Chamar caste, turn his face away from the village, brand him with a red-hot sickle, and let him go out into the jungle taking the murrain with him. He must not look back.[2] When disease breaks out among a herd, the Oraons take the herdsman himself, tie a wooden bell from one of the cows round his neck, beat him with sticks, and drive him out of the village to a cross-road, where the bell and sticks are deposited.[3]

Indian ceremony of sliding down a rope.

In the territory of Kumaon, lying on the southern slopes of the Western Himalayas, the custom of employing a human scapegoat appears to have taken a somewhat peculiar form in the ceremony known as Barat. First of all a thick rope of grass is stretched from the top of a cliff to the valley beneath, where it is made fast to posts driven into the ground. Next a wooden saddle, with a very sharp ridge and unpadded, is attached by thongs to the cable, along which it runs in a deep groove. A man now seats himself on the saddle and is strapped to it, while sand-bags or heavy stones are suspended from his feet to secure his balance. Then, after various ceremonies have been performed and a kid sacrificed, he throws himself as far back in the saddle as he can go, and is started off to slide down the rope into the valley. Away he shoots at an ever-increasing speed; the saddle under him, however well greased, emits volumes of smoke during the greater part of his progress; and he is nearly senseless when he reaches the bottom.

---

[1] J. H. Gray, *China* (London, 1878), ii. 306.

[2] *Panjab Notes and Queries*, i. p. 75, § 598 (April, 1884); W. Crooke, *Popular Religion and Folk-lore of Northern India* (Westminster, 1896),

i. 170.

[3] Rev. F. Hahn, "Some Notes on the Religion and Superstitions of the Oraõs," *Journal of the Asiatic Society of Bengal*, lxxii. Part iii. (Calcutta, 1904) p. 17; compare H. C. Streatfield, *ibid.* p. 37.

Here men are waiting to catch him and run forward with him some distance in order to break gradually the force of his descent. This ceremony, regarded as a propitiation of Mahadeva, is performed as a means of delivering a community from present or impending calamity. Thus, for example, it was performed when cholera was raging at Almora, and the people traced the immunity they enjoyed to the due observance of the rite. Each district has its hereditary Badi, as the performer is called ; he is supported by annual contributions in grain from the inhabitants, as well as by special payments for each performance. When the ceremony is over, the grass rope is cut up and distributed among the villagers, who hang the pieces as charms at the eaves of their houses ; and they preserve the hair of the Badi for a similar purpose. Yet while his severed locks bring fertility to other people's lands, he entails sterility on his own ; and it is firmly believed that no seed sown by his hand could ever sprout. Formerly the rule prevailed that, if a Badi had the misfortune to fall from the rope in the course of his flying descent, he was immediately despatched with a sword by the spectators. The rule has naturally been abolished by the English Government ; but its former observance seems to indicate that the custom of letting a man slide down a rope as a charm to avert calamity is only a mitigation of an older custom of putting him to death.[1]

A somewhat similar ceremony is annually performed at Lhasa a few days after the beginning of the Tibetan New Year, which falls in spring. The scene of the performance is Potala Hill, on the summit and slope of which is built the superb castle of the Grand Lama of Tibet, a massive and imposing pile of buildings which attracts the eye and dominates the landscape from afar. On the day in question a rope of hide is stretched from the top to the bottom of the steep hill, and men from a distant province of Tibet climb up it with the agility of monkeys. They are called Flying

Tibetan New Year ceremony of sliding down a rope.

---

[1] *North Indian Notes and Queries,* i. pp. 55, 74 *sq.,* 77, §§ 417, 499, 516 (July and August, 1891), quoting G. W. Traill, *Statistical Sketch of Kumaun,* pp. 68 *sq.,* and Moorcroft and Trebeck, *Travels in the Himalayan Provinces of Hindustan and the Panjáb,* i. 17 *sq.* Compare E. T. Atkinson, *The Himalayan Districts of the North-Western Provinces of India,* ii. (Allahabad, 1884), pp. 834 *sq.*

Spirits.   Arrived at the top, each of them places a piece of wood on his breast, stretches out his hands and feet, and letting himself go shoots down the rope (in the words of a Chinese writer) "like the bolt flying from the bow, or the swallow skimming the water.   'Tis a wondrous sight!" Considering that these performers are called Spirits, and that the performance takes place a few days after the New Year, a season so commonly selected for the expulsion of demons, we may conjecture that the Flying Spirits represent the powers of evil who are thus shot out of the Tibetan pope's palace at the beginning of the year.[1]

§ 3. *The Periodic Expulsion of Evils in a Material Vehicle*

Periodic expulsion of evils in a material vehicle.

Periodic expulsion of spirits in rafts from Perak.

In this last case the expulsion of evils, if I am right in so interpreting the ceremony, is periodic, not occasional, being repeated every spring at the beginning of a new year. It brings us accordingly to the consideration of a whole class of such cases, for the mediate expulsion of evils by means of a scapegoat or other material vehicle, like the immediate expulsion of them in invisible form, tends to become periodic, and for a like reason.   Thus in Perak, a state on the west coast of the Malay Peninsula, it was in ancient times the custom to perform periodically a ceremony intended to ensure the prosperity of the country by the propitiation of friendly spirits and the expulsion of evil influences.   The writer who records the custom is uncertain as to the period which elapsed between two successive celebrations ; he suggests with hesitation that the rite was performed once in seven years or once in a Rajah's reign. The name of the ceremony was *pĕlas negri*, which means "the cleansing of the country from evils."   When the time came, the Rajah, the chiefs, and a great following of people assembled at a point as far up the river as possible, but short of the rapids which further up impede navigation.

---

[1] W. Woodville Rockhill, "Tibet, A Geographical, Ethnographical, and Historical Sketch, derived from Chinese Sources," *Journal of the Royal Asiatic Society for 1891* (London, 1891), p. 209.   Compare Huc, *Souvenirs d'un Voyage dans la Tartarie et le Thibet*, Sixième Édition (Paris, 1878), ii. 379 *sq*.   For a description of Potala Hill and its grand palace, see L. Austine Waddell, *Lhasa and its Mysteries* (London, 1905), pp. 330 *sqq.*, 387 *sqq.*

There a number of rafts were prepared, some of them elaborately built with houses on them. Four of them were devoted to the four great classes of spirits which are found in Perak, namely the *Hantu Blian* or "Tiger-spirits," the *Hantu Sungkei*, the *Hantu Malayu*, and the *Jin Raja*. In each of these rafts a number of wizards (*pawangs*) took up their post, according to the particular class of demon which they affected. The procession was headed by the raft devoted to the Tiger-spirits; and in it was set up a *prah* tree with all its branches, kept erect by stays. It was followed by the three rafts dedicated to the other three classes of spirits, and behind them came a train of other rafts bearing mere common mortals, the royal bandsmen, the Rajah himself, the chiefs, and the people. As the long procession floated down the river with the current, the wizards, standing on sheets of tin, waved white cloths and shouted invocations to the spirits and demons who inhabited the country through which the rafts were drifting seaward. The burden of the invocations was to invite the spirits and demons to come aboard the rafts and partake of the food which had been considerately made ready for them. At every village on the bank large enough to possess a mosque (for the Malays of Perak are professing Mohammedans) the procession halted; a buffalo, subscribed for by the inhabitants, was slaughtered, and its head placed on one of the spirit-barks, while people feasted on the flesh. The ceremony ended at Bras Basah, a village on the left bank of the Perak river, not far from its mouth. There the rafts were abandoned to the current, which swept them out to sea,[1] doubtless bearing with them the hapless demons who had been lured by the tempting viands to embark and were now left to toss forlorn on the great deep at the mercy of the waves and the winds.

Again, every year, generally in March, the people of Leti, Moa, and Lakor, islands of the Indian Archipelago, send away all their diseases to sea. They make a proa about six feet long, rig it with sails, oars, rudder, and other gear, and every family deposits in it some rice,

Annual expulsion of evils in small ships in the Indian Archipelago.

---

[1] *Straits Branch of the Royal Asiatic Society, Notes and Queries*, No. 3 (Singapore, 1886), pp. 80 *sq.*

fruit, a fowl, two eggs, insects that ravage the fields, and
so on.   Then they let it drift away to sea, saying, " Take
away from here all kinds of sickness, take them to other
islands, to other lands, distribute them in places that lie
eastward, where the sun rises." [1]   The Biajas of Borneo
annually send to sea a little bark laden with the sins and
misfortunes of the people.   The crew of any ship that falls
in with the ill-omened bark at sea will suffer all the sorrows
with which it is laden. [2]   A like custom is annually observed
by the Dusuns of the Tuaran district in British North Borneo.
The ceremony is the most important of the whole year.   Its
aim is to bring good luck to the village during the ensuing
year by solemnly expelling all the evil spirits that may
have collected in or about the houses throughout the last
twelve months.   The task of routing out the demons and
banishing them devolves chiefly on women, who indeed play
the principal part in all religious ceremonies among the
Dusuns, while the humble duty of beating drums and
banging gongs is discharged by members of the inferior sex.
On this momentous occasion a procession of women, in full
ceremonial dress, goes from house to house, stopping at each
to go through their performances.   At the head of the
procession marches a boy carrying a spear on which is
impaled a bundle of palm leaves containing rice.   He is
followed by two men, who carry a large gong and a drum
slung on a pole between them.   Then come the women.
One of them carries a small sucking pig in a basket on her
back ; and all of them bear wands, with which they belabour
the little pig at the appropriate moment; its squeals help
to attract the vagrant spirits.   At every house the women
dance and sing, clashing castanets or cymbals of brass and
jingling bunches of little brass bells in both hands.   When
the performance has been repeated at every house in the
village, the procession defiles down to the river and all the
evil spirits, which the performers have chased from the
houses, follow them to the edge of the water.   There a raft
has been made ready and moored to the bank.   It contains

---

[1] J. G. F. Riedel, *De sluik- en kroesharige rassen tusschen Selebes en Papua*
(The Hague, 1886), p. 393.

[2] A. Bastian, *Der Mensch in der
Geschichte* (Leipsic, 1860), ii. 93.

offerings of food, cloth, cooking-pots, and swords; and the deck is crowded with figures of men, women, animals, and birds, all made out of the leaves of the sago palm. The evil spirits now embark on the raft, and when they are all aboard, it is pushed off and allowed to float down with the current, carrying the demons with it. Should the raft run aground near the village, it is shoved off with all speed, lest the invisible passengers should seize the opportunity of landing and returning to the village. Finally, the sufferings of the little pig, whose squeals served to decoy the demons from their lurking-places, are terminated by death, for it is killed and its carcase thrown away.[1]

Every year, at the beginning of the dry season, the Nicobar Islanders carry the model of a ship through their villages. The devils are chased out of the huts, and driven on board the little ship, which is then launched and suffered to sail away with the wind.[2] The ceremony has been described by a catechist, who witnessed it at Car Nicobar in July 1897. For three days the people were busy preparing two very large floating cars, shaped like canoes, fitted with sails, and loaded with certain leaves, which possessed the valuable property of expelling devils. While the young people were thus engaged, the exorcists and the elders sat in a house singing songs by turns; but often they would come forth, pace the beach armed with rods, and forbid the devil to enter the village. The fourth day of the solemnity bore the name of *Intō-nga-Sīya*, which means "Expelling the Devil by Sails." In the evening all the villagers assembled, the women bringing baskets of ashes and bunches of devil-expelling leaves. These leaves were then distributed to everybody, old and young. When all was ready, a band of robust men, attended by a guard of exorcists, carried one of the cars down to the sea on the right side of the village graveyard, and set it floating in the water. As soon as they had returned, another band of men carried the other car to the beach and floated it similarly in the sea to the left of the graveyard. The demon-laden

Annual expulsion of demons in little ships in the Nicobar Islands.

---

[1] Ivor H. N. Evans, "Notes on the Religious Beliefs, Superstitions, Ceremonies and Tabus of the Dusuns of the Tuaran and Tempassuk Districts, British North Borneo," *Journal of the Royal Anthropological Institute*, xlii. (1912) pp. 382-384.

[2] A. Bastian, *op. cit.* ii. 91.

barks being now launched, the women threw ashes from the shore, and the whole crowd shouted, saying, "Fly away, devil, fly away, never come again!" The wind and the tide being favourable, the canoes sailed quickly away; and that night all the people feasted together with great joy, because the devil had departed in the direction of Chowra. A similar expulsion of devils takes place once a year in other Nicobar villages; but the ceremonies are held at different times in different places.[1]

Annual expulsion of embodied evils in India, China, and Corea.

At Sucla-Tirtha, in India, an earthen pot containing the accumulated sins of the people is (annually?) set adrift on the river. Legend says that the custom originated with a wicked priest who, after atoning for his guilt by a course of austerities and expiatory ceremonies, was directed to sail upon the river in a boat with white sails. If the white sails turned black, it would be a sign that his sins were forgiven him. They did so, and he joyfully allowed the boat to drift with his sins to sea.[2] Amongst many of the aboriginal tribes of China, a great festival is celebrated in the third month of every year. It is held by way of a general rejoicing over what the people believe to be a total annihilation of the ills of the past twelve months. The destruction is supposed to be effected in the following way. A large earthenware jar filled with gunpowder, stones, and bits of iron is buried in the earth. A train of gunpowder, communicating with the jar, is then laid; and a match being applied, the jar and its contents are blown up. The stones and bits of iron represent the ills and disasters of the past year, and the dispersion of them by the explosion is believed to remove the ills and disasters themselves. The festival is attended with much revelling and drunkenness.[3] On New Year's Day people in Corea seek to rid themselves of all their distresses by painting images on paper, writing against them their troubles of body or mind, and afterwards giving the papers to a boy to burn. Another method of effecting the same object at the same season is to make rude dolls of

[1] V. Solomon, "Extracts from Diaries kept in Car Nicobar," *Journal of the Anthropological Institute*, xxxii. (1902) pp. 228 *sq.*

[2] Captain F. Wilford, "An Essay on the Sacred Isles in the West," *Asiatic Researches*, ix. (London, 1809) pp. 96 *sq.*

[3] J. H. Gray, *China* (London, 1878), ii. 306 *sq.*

straw, stuff them with a few copper coins, and throw them into the street. Whoever picks up such an effigy gets all the troubles and thereby relieves the original sufferer.[1] Again, on the fourteenth day of the first month the Coreans fly paper kites inscribed with a wish that all the ills of the year may fly away with them.[2] Mr. George Bogle, the English envoy sent to Tibet by Warren Hastings, witnessed the celebration of the Tibetan New Year's Day at Teshu Lumbo, the capital of the Teshu Lama. Monks walked in procession round the court to the music of cymbals, tabors, trumpets, hautboys and drums. Then others, clad in masquerade dress and wearing masks which represented the heads of animals, mostly wild beasts, danced with antic motions. "After this, the figure of a man, chalked upon paper, was laid upon the ground. Many strange ceremonies, which to me who did not understand them appeared whimsical, were performed about it ; and a great fire being kindled in a corner of the court, it was at length held over it, and being formed of combustibles, vanished with much smoke and explosion. I was told it was a figure of the devil."[3] Another Tibetan mode of expelling demons from a dwelling is to make a paste image, into which the lamas by their incantations conjure all the evil spirits that may be lurking in the house. This image is carried to a distance by a runner and thrown away. He is attended by men, who shout at the top of their voices, brandish swords, and fire guns, all to frighten the demons and drive them far from human habitations.[4]

Annual expulsion or destruction of demons embodied in images in Tibet.

At Old Calabar on the coast of Guinea, the devils and ghosts are, or used to be, publicly expelled once in two years. Among the spirits thus driven from their haunts are the souls of all the people who died since the last lustration of the town. About three weeks or a month before the expulsion, which according to one account takes place in

Biennial expulsion of demons embodied in effigies at Old Calabar.

[1] W. Woodville Rockhill, "Notes on some of the Laws, Customs, and Superstitions of Corea," *The American Anthropologist,* iv. (1891) p. 185 ; Mrs. Bishop, *Korea and her Neighbours* (London, 1898), ii. 56.

[2] Stewart Culin, *Korean Games* (Philadelphia, 1895), p. 12.

[3] *Narratives of the Mission of George Bogle to Tibet and of the Journey of Thomas Manning to Lhasa,* edited by (Sir) Clements R. Markham (London, 1876), pp. 106 *sq.* Compare Sarat Chandra Das, *Journey to Lhasa and Central Tibet* (London, 1902), p. 116.

[4] Missionary Fage, in *Annales de la Propagation de la Foi,* xxix. (1857) p. 321.

the month of November, rude effigies representing men and animals, such as crocodiles, leopards, elephants, bullocks, and birds, are made of wicker-work or wood, and being hung with strips of cloth and bedizened with gew-gaws, are set before the door of every house.   About three o'clock in the morning of the day appointed for the ceremony the whole population turns out into the streets, and proceeds with a deafening uproar and in a state of the wildest excitement to drive all lurking devils and ghosts into the effigies, in order that they may be banished with them from the abodes of men.   For this purpose bands of people roam through the streets knocking on doors, firing guns, beating drums, blowing on horns, ringing bells, clattering pots and pans, shouting and hallooing with might and main, in short making all the noise it is possible for them to raise.   The hubbub goes on till the approach of dawn, when it gradually subsides and ceases altogether at sunrise.   By this time the houses have been thoroughly swept, and all the frightened spirits are supposed to have huddled into the effigies or their fluttering drapery.   In these wicker figures are also deposited the sweepings of the houses and the ashes of yesterday's fires.   Then the demon-laden images are hastily snatched up, carried in tumultuous procession down to the brink of the river, and thrown into the water to the tuck of drums. The ebb-tide bears them away seaward, and thus the town is swept clean of ghosts and devils for another two years.   This biennial expulsion of spirits goes by the name of *Ndok*, and the effigies by which it is effected are called *Nabikem* or *Nabikim*.[1]

[1] T. J. Hutchinson, *Impressions of Western Africa* (London, 1858), p. 162 ; Rev. J. Macdonald, *Religion and Myth* (London, 1893), pp. 105-107 ; Hugh Goldie, *Calabar and its Mission*, New Edition (Edinburgh and London, 1901), pp. 49 *sq.*; Miss Mary H. Kingsley, *Travels in West Africa* (London, 1897), p. 495 ; Major A. G. Leonard, *The Lower Niger and its Tribes* (London, 1906), pp. 449-451. The ceremony takes place both in Creek Town and Duke Town.   The date of it, according to Miss Kingsley, is either every November or every second November ; but with the exception of Mr. Macdonald, who does not mention the period, the other authorities agree in describing the ceremony as biennial.   According to Major Leonard it is celebrated usually towards the end of the year.   Miss Kingsley speaks of the effigies being set up in the houses themselves ; but all the other writers say or imply that they are set up at the doors of the houses in the streets.   According to Mr. Goldie the spirits expelled are "all the ghosts of those who have died since the last lustration."   He makes no mention of devils.

Further to the west similar ceremonies are or were till recently enacted at Porto Novo, the seaport of Dahomey. One of them has been described by an eye-witness, a Catholic missionary, who interpreted the rites as a Funeral of Death. He says : " Some time ago a curious event took place : the King had commanded to celebrate the funeral of Death. Every year, at the season of the rains, the predecessors of his sable Majesty, in order to preserve the life of their dear subjects, had caused the fetish of that terrible and pitiless enemy, who spares not even kings, to be drowned in the lagoon. Toffa wished to comply with the traditions of his ancestors." However, the ceremony as described by the missionary seems to conform closely to the type of the expulsion of ghosts and demons. Two days before the crowning act of the celebration the streets were carefully swept and all the filth which usually encumbered them was removed, " lest Death should there find a refuge." All the people from the neighbouring villages assembled ; their fetishes, daubed with red paint, were carried in great pomp through the streets of the capital attended by noisy processions of mummers. A great multitude passed the night in the public square, drinking, singing, and shouting. Finally, a number of rude and hideous effigies were escorted by a noisy crowd to the shore of the lagoon ; there canoes were waiting to receive them and paddle them out to deep water, where they were flung overboard. These effigies the missionary regarded as so many images of Death, who thus received his passport and was dismissed from the territory of Porto Novo. But more probably they represented the hosts of demons and ghosts who were believed to lurk about the town and to massacre people under the form of sickness and disease. Having made a clean sweep of the whole baleful crew the inhabitants no doubt thought that they had removed the principal, if not the only, cause of death, and that accordingly they had taken out a new lease of life.[1] It is not without interest to observe that in cleansing their streets the people did actually retrench one of the most fruitful sources of disease and death, especially in the sweltering

[1] Missionary F. Terrien, in *Annales de la Propagation de la Foi*, liv. (1882) pp. 375-377.

heat of a damp tropical climate ; hence the measures they took for the prolongation of their lives were really to a certain extent effectual, though they did not accomplish their object in the precise way they imagined. So curiously does it often happen that the savage reaches the goal of his wishes by a road which to civilized man might appear at first sight to lead far away from it.

Annual expulsion of embodied evils among the Hos of Togoland.

Before the Hos of Togoland, to the west of Dahomey, celebrate their festival of the new yams, which has been described in another part of this work,[1] they say that it is necessary to clean the town and to put it in order. The way in which they do so is this. They take leaves of two particular sorts of trees (the *adzu* and the *wo*), together with creepers and ashes, and bind all the leaves fast to a pole of the *adzu* tree. As they do so they pray or command the evil spirits, the witches, and all other evils in the town to enter into the band and be bound with it. Then they make a paste out of the ashes mixed with urine and smear it on the bundle of leaves, saying, " We smear it on the face of the Evil Ones who are in this bundle, in order that they may not be able to see any more." Then they throw the bundle on the ground and mock at it. Next they take all the similar poles, wrapt in creepers, in which they have bound up all the evil powers, and carry them out of the town and stick them in the ground on the various roads leading into the town. When they have done this, they say that they have driven the evils out of the town and shut the door against them. After that they wash the faces of all the people with a medicine which has been prepared by the oldest men. Thereupon they all return home to sweep out their houses and yards ; they sweep even the ground in front of the yards, so that the whole town is thoroughly clean. All the grass-stalks and refuse of stock-yams which have been swept together are carried out of the town, and the people rail at the stock-yams. In the course of the night the oldest men assemble and tie a toad to a young palm-leaf. They say that they wish now to sweep the town and finish the ceremony. So they drag the toad behind them through the whole town in the direction of Mount

[1] *Spirits of the Corn and of the Wild,* ii. 58 *sqq.*

Adaklu. When that has been done, the priests say that they will now remove the sicknesses. In the evening they give public notice that they are about to take to the road, so nobody may light a fire on the hearth or eat. At dead of night, when people are asleep, three men go through the town. One of them drags behind them a toad fastened to a bunch of herbs ; another carries a calabash of holy herbs and water, with which he sprinkles the streets ; and the third whistles softly. As soon as they have thus passed through the whole town, they throw away the toad and the holy herbs in the direction of Mount Adaklu. Next morning the women sweep out their houses and hearths and set the sweepings on broken wooden plates. Many put on torn mats or torn clothes ; others tie grasses and creepers about them. While they do so, they pray, saying, " All ye sicknesses which are in our body and plague us, we are come this day to cast you out ! " When they set out so to do, the priest commands every man to cry out thrice and thereby to smite himself on the mouth. In a moment they all cry out, smite themselves on the mouth, and run as fast as their legs can carry them in the direction of Mount Adaklu. As they run, they say, " Out to-day ! Out to-day ! What kills anybody, out to-day ! Ye evil spirits, out to-day ! And all that makes our heads to ache, out to-day ! Anlo and Adaklu are the places whither all evil ought to go." Now on Mount Adaklu there stands a *klo* tree ; and when they have come thither they throw everything away and return home. After their return every man washes himself with the medicine which is set forth for that purpose in the public street ; then he goes into his house. Such is the ceremony by which the Hos prepare themselves to eat the new yams.[1] Thus among the Hos the public expulsion of evils is definitely connected with the crops and therefore takes place every year, not every two years, as at Old Calabar.

Similar annual expulsions of embodied evils are not unknown in Europe. On the evening of Easter Sunday

---

[1] Jakob Spieth, *Die Ewe-Stämme* (Berlin, 1906), pp. 305-307. We have seen (above, p. 193) that these people used a toad as a scapegoat to free them from the influenza.

Annual
expulsion
of em-
bodied
evils
among the
gypsies.
the gypsies of Southern Europe take a wooden vessel like a band-box, which rests cradle-wise on two cross pieces of wood. In this they place herbs and simples, together with the dried carcase of a snake, or lizard, which every person present must first have touched with his fingers. The vessel is then wrapt in white and red wool, carried by the oldest man from tent to tent, and finally thrown into running water, not, however, before every member of the band has spat into it once, and the sorceress has uttered some spells over it. They believe that by performing this ceremony they dispel all the illnesses that would otherwise have afflicted them in the course of the year ; and that if any one finds the vessel and opens it out of curiosity, he and his will be visited by all the maladies which the others have escaped.[1]

Annual
expulsion
of evils in
an animal
scapegoat
among the
Garos of
Assam.
The scapegoat by means of which the accumulated ills of a whole year are publicly expelled is sometimes an animal. For example, among the Garos of Assam, " besides the sacrifices for individual cases of illness, there are certain ceremonies which are observed once a year by a whole community or village, and are intended to safeguard its members from dangers of the forest, and from sickness and mishap during the coming twelve months. The principal of these is the Asongtata ceremony. Close to the outskirts of every big village a number of stones may be noticed stuck into the ground, apparently without order or method. These are known by the name of *asong*, and on them is offered the sacrifice which the Asongtata demands. The sacrifice of a goat takes place, and a month later, that of a *langur* (*Entellus* monkey) or a bamboo-rat is considered necessary. The animal chosen has a rope fastened round its neck and is led by two men, one on each side of it, to every house in the village. It is taken inside each house in turn, the assembled villagers, meanwhile, beating the walls from the outside, to frighten and drive out any evil spirits which may have taken up their residence within. The round of the village having been made in this manner, the monkey or rat is led to the outskirts of the village, killed by a blow of a *dao*, which disembowels it, and then crucified on bamboos set up in the

---

[1] H. von Wlislocki, *Volksglaube und religiöser Brauch der Zigeuner* (Münster i. W., 1891), pp. 65 *sq.*

ground.   Round the crucified animal long, sharp bamboo
stakes are placed, which form *chevaux de frise* round about it.
These commemorate the days when such defences surrounded
the villages on all sides to keep off human enemies, and they
are now a symbol to ward off sickness and dangers to life
from the wild animals of the forest.   The *langur* required
for the purpose is hunted down some days before, but should
it be found impossible to catch one, a brown monkey may
take its place; a hulock may not be used."[1]   Here the
crucified ape or rat is the public scapegoat, which by its
vicarious sufferings and death relieves the people from all
sickness and mishap in the coming year.

Again, on one day of the year the Bhotiyas of Juhar, in the
Western Himalayas, take a dog, intoxicate him with spirits
and bhang or hemp, and having fed him with sweetmeats,
lead him round the village and let him loose.   They then
chase and kill him with sticks and stones, and believe that,
when they have done so, no disease or misfortune will visit
the village during the year.[2]   In some parts of Breadalbane
it was formerly the custom on New Year's Day to take a
dog to the door, give him a bit of bread, and drive him out,
saying, "Get away, you dog!   Whatever death of men or
loss of cattle would happen in this house to the end of the
present year, may it all light on your head!"[3]   It appears
that the white dogs annually sacrificed by the Iroquois
at their New Year Festival are, or have been, regarded
as scapegoats.   According to Mr. J. V. H. Clark, who
witnessed the ceremony in January 1841, on the first day
of the festival all the fires in the village were extinguished,
the ashes scattered to the winds, and a new fire kindled
with flint and steel.   On a subsequent day, men dressed in
fantastic costumes went round the village, gathering the sins
of the people.   When the morning of the last day of the
festival was come,   wo white dogs, decorated with red paint,

Marginal note: Dogs as scapegoats in India, Scotland, and America.

---

[1] Major A. Playfai   *The Garos*
(London, 1909), p. 92.

[2] E. T. Atkinson, ' Notes on the
History of Religion in t ; Himalaya of
the North-West Provinces," *Journal of
the Asiatic Society of Bengal*, liii. Pt. i.
(1884) p. 62 ; *id.*, *The Himalayan*

*Districts of the North-Western Prov-
inces of India*, ii. (Allahabad, 1884) p.
871.

[3] *Scotland and Scotsmen in the Eigh-
teenth Century*, from the MSS. of John
Ramsay of Ochtertyre, edited by Alex.
Allardyce (Edinburgh, 1888), ii. 439.

wampum, feathers, and ribbons, were led out. They were soon strangled, and hung on a ladder. Firing and yelling succeeded, and half an hour later the animals were taken into a house, " where the people's sins were transferred to them." The carcases were afterwards burnt on a pyre of wood.[1] According to the Rev. Mr. Kirkland, who wrote in the eighteenth century, the ashes of the pyre upon which one of the white dogs was burnt were carried through the village and sprinkled at the door of every house.[2] Formerly, however, as we have seen, the Iroquois expulsion of evils was immediate and not by scapegoat.[3] On the Day of Atonement, which was the tenth day of the seventh month, the Jewish high-priest laid both his hands on the head of a live goat, confessed over it all the iniquities of the Children of Israel, and, having thereby transferred the sins of the people to the beast, sent it away into the wilderness.[4]

The Jewish scapegoat.

The scapegoat upon whom the sins of the people are periodically laid, may also be a human being. At Onitsha, on the Niger, two human beings used to be annually sacrificed to take away the sins of the land. The victims were purchased by public subscription. All persons who, during the past year, had fallen into gross sins, such as

Human scapegoats formerly put to death every year in Africa.

[1] W. M. Beauchamp, "The Iroquois White Dog Feast," *American Antiquarian*, vii. (1885) p. 237.

[2] *Ibid.* p. 236; T. Dwight, *Travels in New England and New York* (London, 1823), iv. 202.

[3] Above, p. 127.

[4] Leviticus xvi. The word translated "scapegoat" in the Authorised Version is Azazel, which appears rather to be the name of a bad angel or demon, to whom the goat was sent away. "In later Jewish literature (Book of Enoch) Azazel appears as the prince of the fallen angels, the offspring of the unions described in Gen. vi. 1 ff. The familiar rendering 'scapegoat,' *i.e.* the goat which is allowed to escape, goes back to the *caper emissarius* of the Vulgate, and is based on an untenable etymology" (Professor A. R. S. Kennedy, in his commentary on Leviticus xvi. 8, in the *Century*

Bible). There is some ground for thinking that the animal was killed by being thrown over a certain crag that overhangs a rocky chasm not far from Jerusalem. See *Encyclopædia Biblica*, ed. T. K. Cheyne and J. S. Black, vol. i. (London, 1899) coll. 394 *sqq.*, *s.v.* "Azazel." Modern Jews sacrifice a white cock on the eve of the Day of Atonement, nine days after the beginning of their New Year. The father of the family knocks the cock thrice against his own head, saying, "Let this cock be a substitute for me, let it take my place, let death be laid upon this cock, but a happy life bestowed on me and on all Israel." Then he cuts its throat and dashes the bird violently on the ground. The intestines are thrown on the roof of the house. The flesh of the cock was formerly given to the poor. See J. Buxtorf, *Synagoga Judaica* (Bâle, 1661), ch. xxv. pp. 508 *sqq.*

incendiarism, theft, adultery, witchcraft, and so forth, were expected to contribute 28 *ngugas*, or a little over £2. The money thus collected was taken into the interior of the country and expended in the purchase of two sickly persons "to be offered as a sacrifice for all these abominable crimes —one for the land and one for the river." A man from a neighbouring town was hired to put them to death. On the twenty-seventh of February 1858 the Rev. J. C. Taylor witnessed the sacrifice of one of these victims. The sufferer was a woman, about nineteen or twenty years of age. They dragged her alive along the ground, face downwards, from the king's house to the river, a distance of two miles, the crowds who accompanied her crying, " Wickedness ! wickedness ! " The intention was " to take away the iniquities of the land. The body was dragged along in a merciless manner, as if the weight of all their wickedness was thus carried away." [1] Similar customs are said to be still secretly practised every year by many tribes on the delta of the Niger in spite of the vigilance of the British Government.[2] Among the Yoruba negroes of West Africa "the human victim chosen for sacrifice, and who may be either a free-born or a slave, a person of noble or wealthy parentage, or one of humble birth, is, after he has been chosen and marked out for the purpose, called an *Oluwo*. He is always well fed and nourished and supplied with whatever he should desire during the period of his confinement. When the occasion arrives for him to be sacrificed and offered up, he is commonly led about and paraded through the streets of the town or city of the Sovereign who would sacrifice him for the well-being of his government and of every family and individual under it, in order that he might carry off the sin, guilt, misfortune and death of all without exception. Ashes and chalk would be employed to hide his identity by the one being freely thrown over his head, and his face painted with the latter, whilst individuals would often rush out of their

---

[1] S. Crowther and J. C. Taylor, *The Gospel on the Banks of the Niger* (London, 1859), pp. 343-345. Compare J. F. Schön and S. Crowther, *Journals* (London, 1848), pp. 48 *sq.* The account of the custom by J. Africanus

B. Horton (*West African Countries and Peoples*, pp. 185 *sq.*) is taken entirely from Taylor.

[2] Major A. G. Leonard, *The Lower Niger and its Tribes* (London, 1906), pp. 446 *sqq.*

houses to lay their hands upon him that they might thus transfer to him their sin, guilt, trouble, and death. This parading done, he is taken through a temporary sacred shed of palm and other tree branches, and especially of the former, the Igbodu [1] and to its first division, where many persons might follow him, and through a second where only the chiefs and other very important persons might escort and accompany him to, and to a third where only the Babalawo [priest] and his official assistant, the Ajigbona, are permitted to enter with him. Here, after he himself has given out or started his last song, which is to be taken up by the large assembly of people who will have been waiting to hear his last word or his last groan, his head is taken off and his blood offered to the gods. The announcement of his last word or his last groan heard and taken up by the people, would be a signal for joy, gladness, and thanksgiving, and for drum beating and dancing, as an expression of their gratification because their sacrifice has been accepted, the divine wrath is appeased, and the prospect of prosperity or increased prosperity assured." [2]

Human scapegoats formerly put to death every year in Siam.

In Siam it used to be the custom on one day of the year to single out a woman broken down by debauchery, and carry her on a litter through all the streets to the music of drums and hautboys. The mob insulted her and pelted her with dirt ; and after having carried her through the whole city, they threw her on a dunghill or a hedge of thorns outside the ramparts, forbidding her ever to enter the walls again. They believed that the woman thus drew upon herself all the malign influences of the air and of evil spirits. [3]

Annual human scapegoats in Japan.

In Japan the " *tsuina* or *oni-yarahi*, that is to say, demon expelling, is a sort of drama in which disease, or more generally ill-luck, is personified, and driven away with threats

---

[1] An Igbodu is a sacred grove in which oracles are given. It is divided into three compartments by fences of palm branches and the *omu* shrub. Into the first compartment women and uninitiated men may enter ; into the other two only priestly officials are permitted, according to their rank in the hierarchy, to enter. See Bishop James Johnson, "Yoruba Heathenism," quoted by R. E. Dennett, *At the Back of the Black Man's Mind* (London, 1906), p. 254.

[2] Bishop James Johnson, *op. cit.* p. 263. Bishop Johnson is a native African. It does not appear whether the sacrifice which he describes is occasional or periodical.

[3] Turpin, "History of Siam," in J. Pinkerton's *Voyages and Travels* (London, 1808–1814), ix. 579.

and a show of violence. Like the *oho-harahi*,[1] it was performed on the last day of the year. This association is
only natural. The demons of the *tsuina* are personified
wintry influences, with the diseases which they bring with
them, while the *oho-harahi* is intended to cleanse the people
from sin and uncleanness, things closely related to disease,
as well as from disease itself. Though probably of Chinese
origin, the *tsuina* is a tolerably ancient rite. It is alluded to
in the *Nihongi* under the date A.D. 689. It was at one time
performed at Court on an imposing scale. Four bands of
twenty youths, each wearing a four-eyed mask, and each
carrying a halberd in the left hand, marched simultaneously
from the four gates of the palace, driving the devils before
them. Another account of this ceremony says that a man
disguised himself as the demon of pestilence, in which garb
he was shot at and driven off by the courtiers armed with
peach-wood bows and arrows of reed. Peach-wood staves
were used for the same purpose. There was formerly a
practice at Asakusa in Tokio on the last day of the year for
a man got up as a devil to be chased round the pagoda
there by another wearing a mask. After this 3,000 tickets
were scrambled for by the spectators. These were carried
away and pasted up over the doors as a charm against pestilence."[2] The Battas of Sumatra offer either a red horse or a
buffalo as a public sacrifice to purify the land and obtain the
favour of the gods. Formerly, it is said, a man was bound
to the same stake as the buffalo, and when they killed the
animal, the man was driven away; no one might receive
him, converse with him, or give him food.[3] Doubtless he

Human
scapegoats
in
Sumatra.

---

[1] The *oho-harahi* or "Great Purification" is a ceremony, which used to
be performed in the Japanese capital
twice every year, namely on the
last days of the sixth and twelfth
month. It included a preliminary
lustration, expiatory offerings, and the
recital of a *norito* or formula (not a
prayer), in which the Mikado, by
virtue of an authority transmitted to
him from the Sun-goddess, pronounced
to his ministers and people the absolution and remission of their sins. See
W. G. Aston, *Shinto* (London, 1905),
pp. 294 *sqq.* The writer adds (p.

295): "The Chinese had an *oho-
harahi*, defined by Mr. Giles in his
Chinese Dictionary as 'a religious
ceremony of purification performed in
spring and autumn, with a view to
secure divine protection for agricultural
interests.'" The popular celebrations
of the first of May and the first of
November in Europe seem to be relics
of similar biennial purifications.

[2] W. G. Aston, *Shinto*, pp. 308 *sq.*

[3] W. Ködding, "Die Batakschen
Götter und ihr Verhältnis zum Brah-
manismus," *Allgemeine Missions-Zeitschrift*, xii. (1885) pp. 476, 478.

was supposed to carry away the sins and misfortunes of the people.

Annual human scapegoats in Europe. Human scapegoats, as we shall see presently, were well known in classical antiquity, and even in mediæval Europe the custom seems not to have been wholly extinct. In the town of Halberstadt, in Thüringen, there was a church said to have been founded by Charlemagne. In this church every year they chose a man, who was believed to be stained with heinous sins. On the first day of Lent he was brought to the church, dressed in mourning garb, with his head muffled up. At the close of the service he was turned out of the church. During the forty days of Lent he perambulated the city barefoot, neither entering the churches nor speaking to any one. The canons took it in turn to feed him. After midnight he was allowed to sleep in the streets. On the day before Good Friday, after the consecration of the holy oil, he was readmitted to the church and absolved from his sins. The people gave him money. He was called Adam, and was now believed to be in a state of innocence.[1]   At

The expulsion of Posterli in Switzerland. Entlebuch, in Switzerland, down to the close of the eighteenth century, the custom of annually expelling a scapegoat was preserved in the ceremony of driving "Posterli" from the village into the lands of the neighbouring village. "Posterli" was represented by a lad disguised as an old witch or as a goat or an ass. Amid a deafening noise of horns, clarionets, bells, whips, and so forth, he was driven out. Sometimes "Posterli" was represented by a puppet, which was drawn on a sledge and left in a corner of the neighbouring village. The ceremony took place on the Thursday evening of the last week but one before Christmas.[2]

Annual expulsion of the devil, personified by a man, from Munich on Ascension Day. In Munich down to about a hundred years ago the expulsion of the devil from the city used to be annually enacted on Ascension Day. On the Eve of Ascension Day a man disguised as a devil was chased through the streets,

---

[1] Aeneas Sylvius, *Opera* (Bâle, 1571), pp. 423 *sq.*

[2] H. Usener, "Italische Mythen," *Rheinisches Museum*, N.F.,xxx. (1875) p. 198; *id.*, *Kleine Schriften*, iv. (Leipsic and Berlin, 1913) pp. 109 *sq.* The custom seems to have been revived in the latter part of the nineteenth century; perhaps it may still be observed. See H. Herzog, *Schweizerische Volksfeste, Sitten und Gebräuche* (Aarau, 1884), pp. 293 *sq.*; E. Hoffmann-Krayer, *Feste und Bräuche des Schweizervolkes* (Zurich, 1913), p. 101.

which were then narrow and dirty in contrast to the broad, well-kept thoroughfares, lined with imposing buildings, which now distinguish the capital of Bavaria. His pursuers were dressed as witches and wizards and provided with the indispensable crutches, brooms, and pitchforks which make up the outfit of these uncanny beings. While the devil fled before them, the troop of maskers made after him with wild whoops and halloos, and when they overtook him they ducked him in puddles or rolled him on dunghills. In this way the demon at last succeeded in reaching the palace, where he put off his hideous and now filthy disguise and was rewarded for his vicarious sufferings by a copious meal. The devilish costume which he had thrown off was then stuffed with hay and straw and conveyed to a particular church (the Frauenkirche), where it was kept over night, being hung by a rope from a window in the tower. On the afternoon of Ascension Day, before the Vesper service began, an image of the Saviour was drawn up to the roof of the church, no doubt to symbolize the event which the day commemorates. Then burning tow and wafers were thrown on the people. Meantime the effigy of the devil, painted black, with a pair of horns and a lolling red tongue, had been dangling from the church tower, to the delight of a gaping crowd of spectators gathered before the church. It was now flung down into their midst, and a fierce struggle for possession of it took place among the rabble. Finally, it was carried out of the town by the Isar gate and burned on a neighbouring height, "in order that the foul fiend might do no harm to the city." The custom died out at Munich towards the end of the eighteenth century; but it is said that similar ceremonies are observed to this day in some villages of Upper Bavaria.[1]

This quaint ceremony suggests that the pardoned criminal who used to play the principal part in a solemn religious procession on Ascension Day at Rouen[2] may in like manner have originally served, if not as a representative

The pardoned criminal at Rouen on Ascension Day may have been a public scapegoat.

---

[1] L. Curtius, "Christi Himmelfahrt," *Archiv für Religionswissenschaft*, xiv. (1911) p. 307, quoting the *Münchener Neuesten Nachrichten*, No. 235, May 21st, 1909.

[2] *The Magic Art and the Evolution of Kings*, ii. 164 *sqq.*

of the devil, at least as a public scapegoat, who relieved the whole people of their sins and sorrows for a year by taking them upon himself. This would explain why the gaol had to be raked in order to furnish one who would parade with the highest ecclesiastical dignitaries in their gorgeous vestments through the streets of Rouen, while the church bells pealed out, the clergy chanted, banners waved, and every circumstance combined to enhance the pomp and splendour of the pageant. It would add a pathetic significance to the crowning act of the ceremony, when on a lofty platform in the public square, with the eyes of a great and silent multitude turned upon him, the condemned malefactor received from the Church the absolution and remission of his sins ; for if the rite is to be interpreted in the way here suggested, the sins which were thus forgiven were those not of one man only but of the whole people. No wonder, then, that when the sinner, now a sinner no more, rose from his knees and thrice lifted the silver shrine of St. Romain in his arms, the whole vast assembly in the square broke out into joyous cries of " *Noel! Noel! Noel!* " which they understood to signify, " God be with us ! " In Christian countries no more appropriate season could be selected for the ceremony of the human scapegoat than Ascension Day, which commemorates the departure from earth of Him who, in the belief of millions, took away the sins of the world.[1]

Divine animals as scapegoats in India and ancient Egypt.

Sometimes the scapegoat is a divine animal. The people of Malabar share the Hindoo reverence for the cow, to kill and eat which " they esteem to be a crime as heinous as homicide or wilful murder." Nevertheless the " Bramans transfer the sins of the people into one or more Cows, which are then carry'd away, both the Cows and the Sins wherewith these Beasts are charged, to what place the Braman shall appoint." [2] When the ancient Egyptians sacrificed a bull, they invoked upon its head all the evils that might otherwise befall themselves and the land of Egypt, and thereupon they either sold the bull's head to the Greeks or cast it into the river.[3] Now, it cannot be said that in the

---

[1] On the use of eponymous magistrates as annual scapegoats see above, pp. 39-41.

[2] J. Thomas Phillips, *Account of the* *Religion, Manners, and Learning of the People of Malabar* (London, 1717), pp. 6, 12 *sq.*

[3] Herodotus, ii. 39.

times known to us the Egyptians worshipped bulls in general, for they seem to have commonly killed and eaten them.[1] But a good many circumstances point to the conclusion that originally all cattle, bulls as well as cows, were held sacred by the Egyptians. For not only were all cows esteemed holy by them and never sacrificed, but even bulls might not be sacrificed unless they had certain natural marks ; a priest examined every bull before it was sacrificed ; if it had the proper marks, he put his seal on the animal in token that it might be sacrificed ; and if a man sacrificed a bull which had not been sealed, he was put to death. Moreover, the worship of the black bulls Apis and Mnevis, especially the former, played an important part in Egyptian religion ; all bulls that died a natural death were carefully buried in the suburbs of the cities, and their bones were afterwards collected from all parts of Egypt and interred in a single spot ; and at the sacrifice of a bull in the great rites of Isis all the worshippers beat their breasts and mourned.[2] On the whole, then, we are perhaps entitled to infer that bulls were originally, as cows were always, esteemed sacred by the Egyptians, and that the slain bull upon whose head they laid the misfortunes of the people was once a divine scapegoat. It seems not improbable that the lamb annually slain by the Madis of Central Africa is a divine scapegoat, and the same supposition may partly explain the Zuni sacrifice of the turtle.[3]

Lastly, the scapegoat may be a divine man. Thus, in November the Gonds of India worship Ghansyam Deo, the protector of the crops, and at the festival the god himself is said to descend on the head of one of the worshippers, who is suddenly seized with a kind of fit and, after staggering about, rushes off into the jungle, where it is believed that, if left to himself, he would die mad. However, they bring him back, but he does not recover his senses for one or two days. The people think that one man is thus singled out as a scape-

Divine men as scapegoats among the Gonds of India and the Albanians of the Caucasus.

---

[1] Herodotus, ii. 38-41 ; Sir J. Gardner Wilkinson, *Manners and Customs of the Ancient Egyptians*, New Edition (London, 1878), iii. 403 *sqq.*

[2] Herodotus, *l.c.* As to the worship of sacred bulls in ancient Egypt, see further *Spirits of the Corn and of the Wild*, ii. 34 *sqq.*

[3] *Spirits of the Corn and of the Wild*, ii. 175 *sqq.*, 314 *sq.*

goat for the sins of the rest of the village.[1] In the temple of the Moon the Albanians of the Eastern Caucasus kept a number of sacred slaves, of whom many were inspired and prophesied. When one of these men exhibited more than usual symptoms of inspiration or insanity, and wandered solitary up and down the woods, like the Gond in the jungle, the high priest had him bound with a sacred chain and maintained him in luxury for a year. At the end of the year he was anointed with unguents and led forth to be sacrificed. A man whose business it was to slay these human victims and to whom practice had given dexterity, advanced from the crowd and thrust a sacred spear into the victim's side, piercing his heart. From the manner in which the slain man fell, omens were drawn as to the welfare of the commonwealth. Then the body was carried to a certain spot where all the people stood upon it as a purificatory ceremony.[2] This last circumstance clearly indicates that the sins of the people were transferred to the victim, just as the Jewish priest transferred the sins of the people to the scapegoat by laying his hands on the animal's head ; and since the man was believed to be possessed by the divine spirit, we have here an undoubted example of a man-god slain to take away the sins and misfortunes of the people.

Annual human scapegoats in Tibet.

In Tibet the ceremony of the scapegoat presents some remarkable features. The Tibetan new year begins with the new moon which appears about the fifteenth of February. For twenty-three days afterwards the government of Lhasa, the capital, is taken out of the hands of the ordinary rulers and entrusted to the monk of the Debang monastery who offers to pay the highest sum for the privilege. The successful bidder is called the Jalno, and he announces his accession to power in person, going through the streets of Lhasa with a silver stick in his hand. Monks from all the neighbouring monasteries and temples assemble to pay him homage. The Jalno exercises his authority in the most arbitrary manner for his own benefit, as all the fines which

The Jalno, the temporary ruler of Lhasa.

[1] *Panjab Notes and Queries*, ii. p. 54, § 335 (December, 1884).

[2] Strabo, xi. 4. 7, p. 503. For the custom of standing upon a sacrificed victim, compare Demosthenes, *Or.* xxiii. 68, p. 642 ; Pausanias, iii. 20. 9.

he exacts are his by purchase. The profit he makes is
about ten times the amount of the purchase money. His
men go about the streets in order to discover any conduct
on the part of the inhabitants that can be found fault with.
Every house in Lhasa is taxed at this time, and the slightest
offence is punished with unsparing rigour by fines. This
severity of the Jalno drives all working classes out of the
city till the twenty-three days are over. But if the laity
go out, the clergy come in. All the Buddhist monasteries
of the country for miles round about open their gates and
disgorge their inmates. All the roads that lead down into
Lhasa from the neighbouring mountains are full of monks
hurrying to the capital, some on foot, some on horseback,
some riding asses or lowing oxen, all carrying their prayer-
books and culinary utensils. In such multitudes do they
come that the streets and squares of the city are encumbered
with their swarms, and incarnadined with their red cloaks.
The disorder and confusion are indescribable. Bands of the
holy men traverse the streets chanting prayers or uttering
wild cries. They meet, they jostle, they quarrel, they fight ;
bloody noses, black eyes, and broken heads are freely given
and received. All day long, too, from before the peep of
dawn till after darkness has fallen, these red-cloaked monks
hold services in the dim incense-laden air of the great
Machindranath temple, the cathedral of Lhasa ; and thither
they crowd thrice a day to receive their doles of tea and
soup and money. The cathedral is a vast building, standing
in the centre of the city, and surrounded by bazaars and
shops. The idols in it are richly inlaid with gold and
precious stones.

Twenty-four days after the Jalno has ceased to have
authority, he assumes it again, and for ten days acts in
the same arbitrary manner as before. On the first of the
ten days the priests again assemble at the cathedral,
pray to the gods to prevent sickness and other evils
among the people, " and, as a peace-offering, sacrifice one
man. The man is not killed purposely, but the ceremony
he undergoes often proves fatal.[1] Grain is thrown against

The Jalno and the King of the Years.

---

[1] The ceremony referred to is perhaps the one performed on the tenth day,
as described in the text.

his head, and his face is painted half white, half black."
Thus grotesquely disguised, and carrying a coat of skin on
his arm, he is called the King of the Years, and sits daily in
the market-place, where he helps himself to whatever he
likes and goes about shaking a black yak's tail over the
people, who thus transfer their bad luck to him.   On the
tenth day, all the troops in Lhasa march to the great
temple and form in line before it.   The King of the Years
is brought forth from the temple and receives small
donations from the assembled multitude.   He then ridicules
the Jalno, saying to him, "What we perceive through the
five senses is no illusion.   All you teach is untrue," and
the like.   The Jalno, who represents the Grand Lama
for the time being, contests these heretical opinions ; the
dispute waxes warm, and at last both agree to decide
the questions at issue by a cast of the dice, the Jalno
offering to change places with the scapegoat should the
throw be against him.   If the King of the Years wins,
much evil is prognosticated ; but if the Jalno wins, there
is great rejoicing, for it proves that his adversary has
been accepted by the gods as a victim to bear all the
sins of the people of Lhasa.   Fortune, however, always
favours the Jalno, who throws sixes with unvarying success,
while his opponent turns up only ones.   Nor is this so
extraordinary as at first sight it might appear ; for the
Jalno's dice are marked with nothing but sixes and his
adversary's with nothing but ones.   When he sees the finger
of Providence thus plainly pointed against him, the King of
the Years is terrified and flees away upon a white horse, with
a white dog, a white bird, salt, and so forth, which have all
been provided for him by the government.   His face is still
painted half white and half black, and he still wears his
leathern coat.   The whole populace pursues him, hooting,
yelling, and firing blank shots in volleys after him.   Thus
driven out of the city, he is detained for seven days in the
great chamber of horrors at the Samyas monastery, surrounded by monstrous and terrific images of devils and skins
of huge serpents and wild beasts.   Thence he goes away
into the mountains of Chetang, where he has to remain
an outcast for several months or a year in a narrow den.

Expulsion of the King of the Years.

If he dies before the time is out, the people say it is an auspicious omen ; but if he survives, he may return to Lhasa and play the part of scapegoat over again the following year.[1]

This quaint ceremonial, still annually observed in the secluded capital of Buddhism—the Rome of Asia—is interesting because it exhibits, in a clearly marked religious stratification, a series of divine redeemers themselves redeemed, of vicarious sacrifices vicariously atoned for, of gods undergoing a process of fossilization, who, while they retain the privileges, have disburdened themselves of the pains and penalties of divinity. In the Jalno we may without undue straining discern a successor of those temporary kings, those mortal gods, who purchase a short lease of power and glory at the price of their lives. That he is the temporary substitute of the Grand Lama is certain ; that he is, or was once, liable to act as scapegoat for the people is made nearly certain by his offer to change places with the real scapegoat—the King of the Years—if the arbitrament of the dice should go against him. It is true that the conditions under which the question is now put to the hazard have reduced the offer to an idle form. But such forms are no mere mushroom growths, springing up of

The Grand Lama, the Jalno, and the King of the Years in their relations to each other.

---

[1] "Report of a Route Survey by Pundit — from Nepal to Lhasa," etc., *Journal of the Royal Geographical Society*, xxxviii. (1868) pp. 167, 170 *sq.* ; "Four Years' Journeying through Great Tibet, by one of the Trans-Himalayan Explorers," *Proceedings of the Royal Geographical Society*, N.S. vii. (1885) pp. 67 *sq.* ; W. Woodville Rockhill, "Tibet, a Geographical, Ethnographical, and Historical Sketch, derived from Chinese Sources," *Journal of the Royal Asiatic Society for 1891* (London, 1891), pp. 211 *sq.* ; L. A. Waddell, *The Buddhism of Tibet* (London, 1895), pp. 504 *sqq.*, 512 *sq.* ; J. L. Dutreuil de Rhins, *Mission Scientifique dans la Haute Asie 1890–1895 : Récit du Voyage* (Paris, 1897), pp. 257 *sq.* The accounts supplement each other, though they differ in some particulars. I have endeavoured to combine them. According to Mr.

Rockhill's account, which is drawn from Chinese sources, at one point of the ceremonies the troops march thrice round the temple and fire volleys of musketry to drive away the devil. With the like intent they discharge a great old cannon, which bears the inscription, "My power breaks up and destroys rebellion." The same account speaks of a fencing with battle-axes by a troop of boy-dancers, a great illumination of the cathedral with lanterns, and its decoration with figures made out of butter and flour to represent men, animals, dragons, etc. ; also it makes mention of a horse-race and a foot-race, both run by boys. The clerical invasion of the capital at this season is graphically described by an eye-witness. See Huc, *Souvenirs d'un Voyage dans la Tartarie et le Thibet*, Sixième Édition (Paris, 1878), ii. 380 *sq.*

Probability that of old the Tibetan scapegoat was put to death as a substitute for the Grand Lama. themselves in a night. If they are now lifeless formalities, empty husks devoid of significance, we may be sure that they once had a life and a meaning; if at the present day they are blind alleys leading nowhere, we may be certain that in former days they were paths that led somewhere, if only to death. That death was the goal to which of old the Tibetan scapegoat passed after his brief period of licence in the market-place, is a conjecture that has much to commend it. Analogy suggests it; the blank shots fired after him, the statement that the ceremony often proves fatal, the belief that his death is a happy omen, all confirm it. We need not wonder then that the Jalno, after paying so dear to act as deputy-deity for a few weeks, should have preferred to die by deputy rather than in his own person when his time was up. The painful but necessary duty was accordingly laid on some poor devil, some social outcast, some wretch with whom the world had gone hard, who readily agreed to throw away his life at the end of a few days if only he might have his fling in the meantime. For observe that while the time allowed to the original deputy—the Jalno—was measured by weeks, the time allowed to the deputy's deputy was cut down to days, ten days according to one authority, seven days according to another. So short a rope was doubtless thought a long enough tether for so black or sickly a sheep; so few sands in the hour-glass, slipping so fast away, sufficed for one who had wasted so many precious years. Hence in the jack-pudding who now masquerades with motley countenance in the market-place of Lhasa, sweeping up misfortune with a black yak's tail, we may fairly see the substitute of a substitute, the vicar of a vicar, the proxy on whose back the heavy burden was laid when it had been lifted from nobler shoulders. But the clue, if we have followed it aright, does not stop at the Jalno; it leads straight back to the pope of Lhasa himself, the Grand Lama, of whom the Jalno is merely the temporary vicar. The analogy of many customs in many lands points to the conclusion that, if this human divinity stoops to resign his ghostly power for a time into the hands of a substitute, it is, or rather was once, for no other reason than that the substitute might die in his stead. Thus through the mist of ages unillumined by the lamp of history, the tragic figure of the pope of Buddhism—God's vicar on earth for Asia— looms dim and sad as the man-god who bore his people's sorrows, the Good Shepherd who laid down his life for the sheep.

CHAPTER V

ON SCAPEGOATS IN GENERAL

General remarks. THE foregoing survey of the custom of publicly expelling the accumulated evils of a village or town or country suggests a few general observations.

First, the immediate and the mediate expulsions of evil are identical in intention. In the first place, it will not be disputed that what I have called the immediate and the mediate expulsions of evil are identical in intention; in other words, that whether the evils are conceived of as invisible or as embodied in a material form, is a circumstance entirely subordinate to the main object of the ceremony, which is simply to effect a total clearance of all the ills that have been infesting a people. If any link were wanting to connect the two kinds of expulsion, it would be furnished by such a practice as that of sending the evils away in a litter or a boat. For here, on the one hand, the evils are invisible and intangible; and, on the other hand, there is a visible and tangible vehicle to convey them away. And a scape-goat is nothing more than such a vehicle.

Second, the annual expulsion of evil generally coincides with some well-marked change of season, such as the beginning or end of winter, the beginning In the second place, when a general clearance of evils is resorted to periodically, the interval between the celebrations of the ceremony is commonly a year, and the time of year when the ceremony takes place usually coincides with some well-marked change of season, such as the beginning or end of winter in the arctic and temperate zones, and the beginning or end of the rainy season in the tropics. The increased mortality which such climatic changes are apt to produce, especially amongst ill-fed, ill-clothed, and ill-housed savages, is set down by primitive man to the agency of demons, who must accordingly be expelled. Hence, in the tropical regions

of New Britain and Peru, the devils are or were driven out
at the beginning of the rainy season ; hence, on the dreary
coasts of Baffin Land, they are banished at the approach of
the bitter arctic winter.   When a tribe has taken to husbandry, the time for the general expulsion of devils is
naturally made to agree with one of the great epochs of the
agricultural year, as sowing, or harvest ; but, as these epochs
themselves naturally coincide with changes of season, it does
not follow that the transition from the hunting or pastoral
to the agricultural life involves any alteration in the time of
celebrating this great annual rite.   Some of the agricultural
communities of India and the Hindoo Koosh, as we have
seen, hold their general clearance of demons at harvest,
others at sowing-time.   But, at whatever season of the year
it is held, the general expulsion of devils commonly marks
the beginning of the new year.   For, before entering on a
new year, people are anxious to rid themselves of the troubles
that have harassed them in the past ; hence it comes about
that in so many communities the beginning of the new year
is inaugurated with a solemn and public banishment of evil
spirits.

In the third place, it is to be observed that this public
and periodic expulsion of devils is commonly preceded or
followed by a period of general license, during which the
ordinary restraints of society are thrown aside, and all
offences, short of the gravest, are allowed to pass unpunished.
In Guinea and Tonquin the period of license precedes the
public expulsion of demons ; and the suspension of the
ordinary government in Lhasa previous to the expulsion of
the scapegoat is perhaps a relic of a similar period of universal
license.   Amongst the Hos of India the period of license
follows the expulsion of the devil.   Amongst the Iroquois it
hardly appears whether it preceded or followed the banishment of evils.   In any case, the extraordinary relaxation of
all ordinary rules of conduct on such occasions is doubtless
to be explained by the general clearance of evils which precedes or follows it.   On the one hand, when a general riddance of evil and absolution from all sin is in immediate
prospect, men are encouraged to give the rein to their
passions, trusting that the coming ceremony will wipe out

the score which they are running up so fast.   On the other hand, when the ceremony has just taken place, men's minds are freed from the oppressive sense, under which they generally labour, of an atmosphere surcharged with devils; and in the first revulsion of joy they overleap the limits commonly imposed by custom and morality.   When the ceremony takes place at harvest-time, the elation of feeling which it excites is further stimulated by the state of physical wellbeing produced by an abundant supply of food.[1]

Fourth, the use of a divine man or animal as a scape-goat is remarkable.

Fourthly, the employment of a divine man or animal as a scapegoat is especially to be noted ; indeed, we are here directly concerned with the custom of banishing evils only in so far as these evils are believed to be transferred to a god who

[1] In the Dassera festival, as celebrated in Nepaul, we seem to have another instance of the annual expulsion of demons preceded by a time of license.   The festival occurs at the beginning of October and lasts ten days.   "During its continuance there is a general holiday among all classes of the people.   The city of Kathmandu at this time is required to be purified, but the purification is effected rather by prayer than by water-cleansing.   All the courts of law are closed, and all prisoners in jail are removed from the precincts of the city. . . .   The Kalendar is cleared, or there is a jail-delivery always at the Dassera of all prisoners."   This seems a trace of a period of license.   At this time "it is a general custom for masters to make an annual present, either of money, clothes, buffaloes, goats, etc., to such servants as have given satisfaction during the past year.   It is in this respect, as well as in the feasting and drinking which goes on, something like our 'boxing-time' at Christmas."   On the seventh day at sunset there is a parade of all the troops in the capital, including the artillery.   At a given signal the regiments begin to fire, the artillery takes it up, and a general firing goes on for about twenty minutes, when it suddenly ceases.   This probably represents the expulsion of the demons.   "The grand cutting of the rice-crops is always postponed till the Dassera is over, and commences all over the valley the very day afterwards."   See the description of the festival in H. A. Oldfield's *Sketches from Nipal* (London, 1880), ii. 342-351.   On the Dassera in India, see J. A. Dubois, *Mœurs, Institutions et Cérémonies des Peuples de l'Inde* (Paris, 1825), ii. 329 *sqq.*   The Besisi of the Malay Peninsula hold a regular carnival at the end of the rice-harvest, when they are said to be allowed to exchange wives.   See W. W. Skeat and C. O. Blagden, *Pagan Races of the Malay Peninsula* (London, 1906), ii. 70, 76, 145, compare 120 *sq.*   Amongst the Swahili of East Africa New Year's Day was formerly a day of general license, "every man did as he pleased.   Old quarrels were settled, men were found dead on the following day, and no inquiry was instituted about the matter."   See Ch. New, *Life, Wanderings, and Labours in Eastern Africa* (London, 1873), p. 65 ; and *The Golden Bough*,[2] iii. 250.   An annual period of anarchy and license, lasting three days, is reported by Borelli to be observed by some of the Gallas.   See Ph. Paulitschke, *Ethnographie Nordost-Afrikas : die geistige Cultur der Danâkil, Galla und Somal* (Berlin, 1896), p. 158.   In Ashantee the annual festival of the new yams is a time of general license.   See *Spirits of the Corn and of the Wild*, ii. 62.

is afterwards slain. It may be suspected that the custom of employing a divine man or animal as a public scapegoat is much more widely diffused than appears from the examples cited. For, as has already been pointed out, the custom of killing a god dates from so early a period of human history that in later ages, even when the custom continues to be practised, it is liable to be misinterpreted. The divine character of the animal or man is forgotten, and he comes to be regarded merely as an ordinary victim. This is especially likely to be the case when it is a divine man who is killed. For when a nation becomes civilized, if it does not drop human sacrifices altogether, it at least selects as victims only such wretches as would be put to death at any rate. Thus the killing of a god may sometimes come to be confounded with the execution of a criminal.

If we ask why a dying god should be chosen to take upon himself and carry away the sins and sorrows of the people, it may be suggested that in the practice of using the divinity as a scapegoat we have a combination of two customs which were at one time distinct and independent. On the one hand we have seen that it has been customary to kill the human or animal god in order to save his divine life from being weakened by the inroads of age. On the other hand we have seen that it has been customary to have a general expulsion of evils and sins once a year. Now, if it occurred to people to combine these two customs, the result would be the employment of the dying god as a scapegoat. He was killed, not originally to take away sin, but to save the divine life from the degeneracy of old age ; but, since he had to be killed at any rate, people may have thought that they might as well seize the opportunity to lay upon him the burden of their sufferings and sins, in order that he might bear it away with him to the unknown world beyond the grave. *Why a dying god should serve as a scapegoat.*

The use of the divinity as a scapegoat clears up the ambiguity which, as we saw, appears to hang about the European folk-custom of " carrying out Death." [1] Grounds have been shewn for believing that in this ceremony the so-called Death was originally the spirit of vegetation, who *The use of a divinity as scapegoat explains an ambiguity in the ceremony*

[1] See *The Dying God*, pp. 233 *sqq.*, 264.

of "Carrying out Death." was annually slain in spring, in order that he might come to life again with all the vigour of youth. But, as I pointed out, there are certain features in the ceremony which are not explicable on this hypothesis alone. Such are the marks of joy with which the effigy of Death is carried out to be buried or burnt, and the fear and abhorrence of it manifested by the bearers. But these features become at once intelligible if we suppose that the Death was not merely the dying god of vegetation, but also a public scapegoat, upon whom were laid all the evils that had afflicted the people during the past year. Joy on such an occasion is natural and appropriate ; and if the dying god appears to be the object of that fear and abhorrence which are properly due not to himself, but to the sins and misfortunes with which he is laden, this arises merely from the difficulty of distinguishing, or at least of marking the distinction, between the bearer and the burden. When the burden is of a baleful character, the bearer of it will be feared and shunned just as much as if he were himself instinct with those dangerous properties of which, as it happens, he is only the vehicle. Similarly we have seen that disease-laden and sin-laden boats are dreaded and shunned by East Indian peoples.[1] Again, the view that in these popular customs the Death is a scapegoat as well as a representative of the divine spirit of vegetation derives some support from the circumstance that its expulsion is always celebrated in spring and chiefly by Slavonic peoples. For the Slavonic year began in spring ;[2] and thus, in one of its aspects, the ceremony of " carrying out Death " would be an example of the widespread custom of expelling the accumulated evils of the old year before entering on a new one.

---

[1] Above, pp. 186, 189, 201.

[2] H. Usener, "Italische Mythen," *Rheinisches Museum*, N.F. (1875) xxx. 194 ; *id., Kleine Schriften*, iv. (Leipsic and Berlin, 1913) p. 105.

CHAPTER VI

HUMAN SCAPEGOATS IN CLASSICAL ANTIQUITY

§ 1. *The Human Scapegoat in Ancient Rome*

WE are now prepared to notice the use of the human scape- Annual goat in classical antiquity. Every year on the fourteenth of expulsion of " the March a man clad in skins was led in procession through the Old Mars " streets of Rome, beaten with long white rods, and driven out in the month of of the city. He was called Mamurius Veturius,[1] that is, "the March in old Mars,"[2] and as the ceremony took place on the day preced- ancient Rome. ing the first full moon of the old Roman year (which began on the first of March), the skin-clad man must have represented the Mars of the past year, who was driven out at the beginning of a new one. Now Mars was originally not a god of war but of vegetation. For it was to Mars that the Roman husbandman prayed for the prosperity of his corn and his vines, his fruit-trees and his copses ;[3] it was to Mars that the

---

[1] Joannes Lydus, *De mensibus*, iii. 29, iv. 36. Lydus places the expulsion on the Ides of March, that is 15th March. But this seems to be a mistake. See H. Usener, "Italische Mythen," *Rheinisches Museum*, xxx. (1875) pp. 209 *sqq.* ; *id., Kleine Schriften*, iv. (Leipsic and Berlin, 1913) pp. 122 *sqq.* Again, Lydus does not expressly say that Mamurius Veturius was driven out of the city, but he implies it by mentioning the legend that his mythical prototype was beaten with rods and expelled the city. Lastly, Lydus only mentions the name Mamurius. But the full name Mamurius Veturius is preserved by Varro, *De lingua latina*, vi. 45 ; Festus, ed. C. O. Müller, p. 131 ; Plutarch, *Numa*, 13. Mr. W. Warde Fowler

is disposed to be sceptical as to the antiquity of the ceremony of expelling Mamurius. See his *Roman Festivals of the period of the Republic* (London, 1899), pp. 44-50.

[2] H. Usener, "Italische Mythen," pp. 212 *sq.* ; *id., Kleine Schriften*, iv. 125 *sq.* ; W. H. Roscher, *Apollon una Mars* (Leipsic, 1873), p. 27 ; L. Preller, *Römische Mythologie*[3] (Berlin, 1881–1883), i. 360 ; A. Vaniček, *Griechisch-lateinisches etymologisches Wörterbuch* (Leipsic, 1877), p. 715. The three latter scholars take Veturius as = *annuus*, because *vetus* is etymologically equivalent to ἔτος. But, as Usener argues, it seems quite unallowable to take the Greek meaning of the word instead of the Latin.

[3] Cato, *De agri cultura*, 141.

priestly college of the Arval Brothers, whose business it was to sacrifice for the growth of the crops,[1] addressed their petitions almost exclusively;[2] and it was to Mars, as we saw,[3] that a horse was sacrificed in October to secure an abundant harvest. Moreover, it was to Mars, under his title of " Mars of the woods " (*Mars Silvanus*), that farmers offered sacrifice for the welfare of their cattle.[4] We have already seen that cattle are commonly supposed to be under the special patronage of tree-gods.[5] Once more, the consecration of the vernal month of March to Mars seems to point him out as the deity of the sprouting vegetation. Thus the Roman custom of expelling the old Mars at the beginning of the new year in spring is identical with the Slavonic custom of " carrying out Death," if the view here taken of the latter custom is correct. The similarity of the Roman and Slavonic customs has been already remarked by scholars, who appear, however, to have taken Mamurius Veturius and the corresponding figures in the Slavonic ceremonies to be representatives of the old year rather than of the old god of vegetation.[6] It is possible that ceremonies of this kind may have come to be thus interpreted in later times even by the people who practised them. But the personification of a period of time is too abstract an idea to be primitive.[7]

---

[1] Varro, *De lingua latina*, v. 85.

[2] See the song of the Arval Brothers in *Acta Fratrum Arvalium*, ed. G. Henzen (Berlin, 1874), pp. 26 *sq.* ; J. Wordsworth, *Fragments and Specimens of Early Latin* (Oxford, 1874), p. 158; H. Dessau, *Inscriptiones Latinae Selectae*, ii. Pars i. (Berlin, 1902) p. 276.

[3] *Spirits of the Corn and of the Wild*, ii. 42 *sqq.*

[4] Cato, *De agri cultura*, 83.

[5] *The Magic Art and the Evolution of Kings*, ii. 50 *sq.*, 55, 124 *sq.*

[6] L. Preller, *Römische Mythologie*,[3] i. 360; W. H. Roscher, *Apollon und Mars*, p. 49; *id.*, *Lexikon der griech. und röm. Mythologie*, ii. 2408 *sq.* ; H. Usener, *op. cit.* The ceremony also closely resembles the Highland New Year ceremony already described. See *Spirits of the Corn and of the Wild*, ii. 322 *sqq.*

[7] But the Biyârs, a mixed tribe of North-Western India, observe an annual ceremony which they call " burning the old year." The old year is represented by a stake of the wood of the cotton-tree, which is planted in the ground at an appointed place outside of the village, and then burned on the day of the full moon in the month of Pûs. Fire is first put to it by the village priest, and then all the people follow his example, parch stalks of barley in the fire, and afterwards eat them. Next day they throw the ashes of the burnt wood in the air; and on the morrow the festival ends with a regular saturnalia, at which decency and order are forgotten. See W. Crooke, *Tribes and Castes of the North-Western Provinces and Oudh* (Calcutta, 1896), ii. 137 *sq.* Compare *id.*, *Popular Religion and Folk-lore of Northern India* (Westminster, 1896), ii. 319.

However, in the Roman, as in the Slavonic, ceremony, the representative of the god appears to have been treated not only as a deity of vegetation but also as a scapegoat. His expulsion implies this; for there is no reason why the god of vegetation, as such, should be expelled the city. But it is otherwise if he is also a scapegoat; it then becomes necessary to drive him beyond the boundaries, that he may carry his sorrowful burden away to other lands. And, in fact, Mamurius Veturius appears to have been driven away to the land of the Oscans, the enemies of Rome.[1]

The blows with which the "old Mars" was expelled the city seem to have been administered by the dancing priests of Mars, the Salii. At least we know that in their songs these priests made mention of Mamurius Veturius;[2] and we are told that on a day dedicated to him they beat a hide with rods.[3] It is therefore highly probable that the hide which they drubbed on that day was the one worn by the representative of the deity whose name they simultaneously chanted. Thus on the fourteenth day of March every year Rome witnessed the curious spectacle of the human incarnation of a god chased by the god's own priests with blows from the city. The rite becomes at least intelligible on the theory that the man so beaten and expelled stood for the outworn deity of vegetation, who had to be replaced by a fresh and vigorous young divinity at the beginning of a New Year, when everywhere around in field and meadow, in wood and thicket the vernal flowers, the sprouting grass, and the opening buds and blossoms testified to the stirring of new life in nature after the long torpor and stagnation of

---

[1] Propertius, v. 2. 61 *sq.*; H. Usener, "Italische Mythen," p. 210; *id.*, *Kleine Schriften*, iv. 123.

[2] Varro, *De lingua latina*, vi. 45 ed. C. O. Müller; Festus, *s.v.* "Mamuri Veturi," p. 131 ed. C. O. Müller; Ovid, *Fasti*, iii. 389 *sqq.*; Plutarch, *Numa*, 13.

[3] Servius, on Virgil, *Aen.* vii. 188, "*Cui* [*scil. Mamurio*] *et diem consecrarunt, quo pellem virgis feriunt*"; Minucius Felix, *Octavius*, 24, "*Nudi cruda hieme discurrunt, alii incedunt pilleati, scuta vetera circumferunt, pelles*

caedunt." Neither Servius nor Minucius Felix expressly mentions the Salii, but the description given by the latter writer ("*pilleati, scuta vetera circumferunt*") proves that he alludes to them. The expression of Minucius Felix *pelles caedunt* is conclusive in favour of *pellem* in the passage of Servius, where some would wrongly substitute *peltam*, the reading of a single MS. That the beating of the skin-clad representative of Mamurius was done by the Salii was long ago rightly pointed out by Dr. W. H. Roscher (*Apollon und Mars*, p. 49).

winter. The dancing priests of the god derived their name of Salii from the leaps or dances which they were bound to execute as a solemn religious ceremony every year in the Comitium, the centre of Roman political life.[1] Twice a year, in the spring month of March and the autumn month of October, they discharged this sacred duty;[2] and as they did so they invoked Saturn, the Roman god of sowing.[3] As the Romans sowed the corn both in spring and autumn,[4] and as down to the present time in Europe superstitious rustics are wont to dance and leap high in spring for the purpose of making the crops grow high,[5] we may conjecture that the leaps and dances performed by the Salii, the priests of the old Italian god of vegetation, were similarly supposed to quicken the growth of the corn by homoeopathic or imitative magic. The Salii were not limited to Rome; similar colleges of dancing priests are known to have existed in many towns of ancient Italy;[6] everywhere, we may conjecture, they were supposed to contribute to the fertility of the earth by their leaps and dances. At Rome they were divided into two colleges, each composed of twelve members; and it is not impossible that the number twelve was fixed with reference to the twelve months of the old lunar year;[7] the *Fratres Arvales*, or "Brethren of the Ploughed Fields," another Roman college of priests, whose functions were purely agricultural, and who wore as a badge of their office a wreath of corn-ears, were also twelve in number,

The dances of the Salii in spring and autumn were perhaps intended to quicken the growth of the corn sown at these seasons.

---

[1] Varro, *De lingua latina*, v. 85, "*Salii a salitando, quod facere in comitio in sacris quotannis et solent et debent.*" Compare Ovid, *Fasti*, iii. 387, "*Iam dederat Saliis a saltu nomina dicta*"; Plutarch, *Numa*, 13; Dionysius Halicarnasensis, *Antiquitates Romanae*, ii. 70.

[2] J. Marquardt, *Römische Staatsverwaltung*, iii.[2] (Leipsic, 1885) p. 431; G. Wissowa, *Religion und Kultus der Römer*[2] (Munich, 1912), p. 144; W. Warde Fowler, *The Religious Experience of the Roman People* (London, 1911), pp. 96 *sq.*

[3] Festus, ed. C. O. Müller, p. 325, "*Qui deus in saliaribus Saturnus nominatur, videlicet a sationibus.*" In this passage Ritschl reads *Saeturnus*

for *Saturnus*. The best MSS. of the epitome read *Sateurnus*. See J. Wordsworth, *Fragments and Specimens of Early Latin* (Oxford, 1884), p. 405. As to Saturn in this capacity see below, p. 306.

[4] Columella, *De re rustica*, ii. 9. 6 *sq.*

[5] *The Magic Art and the Evolution of Kings*, i. 137 *sqq.*

[6] J. Marquardt, *Römische Staatsverwaltung*, iii.[2] (Leipsic, 1885) pp. 427 *sq.*

[7] L. Preller, *Römische Mythologie*[3] (Berlin, 1881–1883), i. 359. As to the lunar year of the old Roman Calendar see L. Ideler, *Handbuch der mathematischen und technischen Chronologie* (Berlin, 1825–1826), ii. 38 *sqq.*

perhaps for a similar reason.[1]   Nor was the martial equipment of the Salii so alien to this peaceful function as a
modern reader might naturally suppose.   Each of them
wore on his head a peaked helmet of bronze, and at his side
a sword ; on his left arm he carried a shield of a peculiar
shape, and in his right hand he wielded a staff with which
he smote on the shield till it rang again.[2]   Such weapons in
priestly hands may be turned against spiritual foes ; in the
preceding pages we have met with many examples of the
use of material arms to rout the host of demons who oppress
the imagination of primitive man, and we have seen that the
clash and clangour of metal is often deemed particularly
effective in putting these baleful beings to flight.[3]   May it
not have been so with the martial priests of Mars ?   We
know that they paraded the city for days together in a
regular order, taking up their quarters for the night at a
different place each day ; and as they went they danced in
triple time, singing and clashing on their shields and taking
their time from a fugleman, who skipped and postured at
their head.[4]   We may conjecture that in so doing they were
supposed to be expelling the powers of evil which had
accumulated during the preceding year or six months, and
which the people pictured to themselves in the form of
demons lurking in the houses, temples, and the other edifices
of the city.   In savage communities such tumultuous and
noisy processions often parade the village for a similar purpose.   Similarly, we have seen that among the Iroquois men
in fantastic costume used to go about collecting the sins of
the people as a preliminary to transferring them to the
scapegoat dogs ; and we have met with many examples of

The armed processions of the Salii may have been intended to rout out and expel the demons lurking in the city.

---

[1] As to their number and badge see
Aulus Gellius, vi. (vii., ed. M. Hertz)
7. 8 ; as to their function see Varro,
De lingua latina, v. 85, "*Fratres
Arvales dicti sunt, qui sacra publica
faciunt propterea ut fruges ferant arva,
a ferendo et arvis fratres arvales dicti.*"
[2] Livy, i. 20. 4 ; Plutarch, *Numa*,
13 ; Dionysius Halicarnasensis, *Antiquitates Romanae*, ii. 70.   Livy only
mentions the shields.   From an ancient
relief we learn that the staves of the
Salii terminated in a knob at each end.
Hence we may correct the statement

of Dionysius, who describes the weapon
doubtfully as λόγχην ἢ ῥάβδον ἤ τι
τοιοῦθ' ἕτερον. See J. Marquardt,
Römische Staatsverwaltung, iii.[2] 432,
note [6].
[3] See above, pp. 113, 116, 117, 132,
139, 141, 147, 158, 159, 161, 163,
165, 166, 186, 191, 196, 200, 204,
214.
[4] Livy, i. 20. 4 ; J. Marquardt, *op.
cit.* iii.[2] 432 *sq.* ; W. Smith, *Dictionary of Greek and Roman Antiquities*,
Third Edition (London, 1891), vol. ii.
p. 590, *s.v.* "Salii."

armed men rushing about the streets and houses to drive out demons and evils of all kinds.[1] Why should it not have been so also in ancient Rome? The religion of the old Romans is full of relics of savagery.

The demons expelled by the Salii may have been above all the demons of blight and infertility. This conjecture is supported by analogous ceremonies performed by savages for the purpose of driving off the demons that would harm the crops.

If there is any truth in this conjecture, we may suppose that, as priests of a god who manifested his power in the vegetation of spring, the Salii turned their attention above all to the demons of blight and infertility, who might be thought by their maleficent activity to counteract the genial influence of the kindly god and to endanger the farmer's prospects in the coming summer or winter. The conjecture may be supported by analogies drawn from the customs of modern European peasants as well as of savages. Thus, to begin with savages, we have seen that at the time of sowing the Khonds drive out the "evil spirits, spoilers of the seed" from every house in the village, the expulsion being effected by young men who beat each other and strike the air violently with long sticks.[2] If I am right in connecting the vernal and the autumnal processions of the Salii with the vernal and the autumnal sowing, the analogy between the Khond and the Roman customs would be very close. In West Africa the fields of the King of Whydah, according to an old French traveller, "are hoed and sowed before any of his subjects has leave to hoe and sow a foot of his own lands. These labours are performed thrice a year. The chiefs lead their people before the king's palace at daybreak, and there they sing and dance for a full quarter of an hour. Half of these people are armed as in a day of battle, the other half have only their farm tools. They go all together singing and dancing to the scene of their labours, and there, keeping time to the sound of the instruments, they work with such speed and neatness that it is a pleasure to behold. At the end of the day they return and dance before the king's palace. This exercise refreshes them and does them more good than all the repose they could take."[3] From this account we might infer that the dancing was merely a recreation of the field-labourers, and that the music of the

---

[1] See above, pp. 111 *sqq.*

[2] See above, p. 138.

[3] Labat, *Voyage du Chevalier Des* *Marchais en Guinée, Isles voisines, et à Cayenne* (Amsterdam, 1731), ii. 80 (p. 99 of the Paris edition).

band had no other object than to animate them in their work by enabling them to ply their mattocks in time to its stirring strains.   But this inference, though it seems to have been drawn by the traveller who has furnished the account, would probably be erroneous.   For if half of the men were armed as for war, what were they doing in the fields all the time that the others were digging?   A clue to unravel the mystery is furnished by the description which a later French traveller gives of a similar scene witnessed by him near Timbo in French Guinea.   He saw some natives at work preparing the ground for sowing.   "It is a very curious spectacle: fifty or sixty blacks in a line, with bent backs, are smiting the earth simultaneously with their little iron tools, which gleam in the sun.   Ten paces in front of them, marching backwards, the women sing a well marked air, clapping their hands as for a dance, and the hoes keep time to the song.   Between the workers and the singers a man runs and dances, crouching on his hams like a clown, while he whirls about his musket and performs other manœuvres with it. Two others dance, also pirouetting and smiting the earth here and there with their little hoe.   All that is necessary for exorcising the spirits and causing the grain to sprout."[1] Here, while the song of the women gives the time to the strokes of the hoes, the dances and other antics of the armed man and his colleagues are intended to exorcise or ward off the spirits who might interfere with the diggers and so prevent the grain from sprouting.

Again, an old traveller in southern India tells us that "the men of Calicut, when they wish to sow rice, observe this practice.   First, they plough the land with oxen as we do, and when they sow the rice in the field they have all the instruments of the city continually sounding and making merry.   They also have ten or twelve men clothed like devils, and these unite in making great rejoicing with the players on the instruments, in order that the devil may make that rice very productive."[2]   We may suspect that the

Dances of masked men in India, Borneo, and South America to promote the growth of the crops.

---

[1] Olivier de Sanderval, *De l'Atlantique au Niger par le Foutah-Djallon* (Paris, 1883), p. 230. The phrase which I have translated "for exorcising the spirits" is "*pour conjurer les esprits.*"

[2] Ludovico di Varthema, *Travels in Egypt, Syria*, etc., translated by J. W. Jones (Hakluyt Society, London, 1863), pp. 166 *sq.*

noisy music is played and the mummers cut their capers for the purpose rather of repelling demons than of inducing them to favour the growth of the rice. However, where our information is so scanty it would be rash to dogmatize. Perhaps the old traveller was right in thinking that the mummers personated devils. Among the Kayans of Central Borneo men disguised in wooden masks and great masses of green foliage certainly play the part of demons for the purpose of promoting the growth of the rice just before the seed is committed to the ground ; and it is notable that among the performances which they give on this occasion are war dances.[1] Again, among the Kaua and Kobeua Indians of North-Western Brazil masked men who represent spirits or demons of fertility perform dances or rather pantomimes for the purpose of stimulating the growth of plants, quickening the wombs of women, and promoting the multiplication of animals.[2]

Dances in Aracan for the sake of the crops.

Dances of the Tara-humare Indians of Mexico to procure rain for their crops.

Further, we are told that "the natives of Aracan dance in order to render propitious the spirits whom they believe to preside over the sowing and over the harvest. There are definite times for doing it, and we may say that in their eyes it is, as it were, an act of religion."[3] Another people who dance diligently to obtain good crops are the Tarahumare Indians of Mexico. They subsist by agriculture and their thoughts accordingly turn much on the supply of rain, which is needed for their fields. According to them, "the favour of the gods may be won by what for want of a better term may be called dancing, but what in reality is a series of monotonous movements, a kind of rhythmical exercise, kept up sometimes for two nights. By dint of such hard work they think to prevail upon the gods to grant their prayers. The dancing is accompanied by the song of the shaman, in which he communicates his wishes to the unseen world, describing the beautiful effect of the rain, the fog, and the mist on the vegetable world. He invokes the aid of all the animals, mentioning each by name, and also calls on them, especially the deer and the rabbit, to multiply that the people

---

[1] *Spirits of the Corn and of the Wild*, i. 95, 186 *sq.*

[2] *Spirits of the Corn and of the*

Wild, i. 111 *sq.*

[3] *Annales de la Propagation de la Foi*, liii. (1881) p. 178.

may have plenty to eat. As a matter of fact, the Tarahumares assert that the dances have been taught them by
the animals. Like all primitive people, they are close
observers of nature. To them the animals are by no means
inferior creatures ; they understand magic and are possessed
of much knowledge, and may assist the Tarahumares in
making rain. In spring, the singing of the birds, the cooing
of the dove, the croaking of the frog, the chirping of the
cricket, all the sounds uttered by the denizens of the green-
sward, are to the Indian appeals to the deities for rain. For
what other reason should they sing or call ? For the strange
behaviour of many animals in the early spring the Tarahumares can find no other explanation but that these
creatures, too, are interested in rain. And as the gods grant
the prayers of the deer expressed in its antics and dances,
and of the turkey in its curious playing, by sending the rain,
they easily infer that to please the gods they, too, must
dance as the deer and play as the turkey. From this it will
be understood that dance with these people is a very serious
and ceremonious matter, a kind of worship and incantation
rather than amusement." [1]

The two principal dances of these Indians, the *rutuburi*
and the *yumari*, are supposed to have been taught them by
the turkey and the deer respectively. They are danced by
numbers of men and women, the two sexes keeping apart
from each other in the dance, while the shaman sings and
shakes his rattle. But " a large gathering is not necessary in
order to pray to the gods by dancing. Sometimes the family
dances alone, the father teaching the boys. While doing
agricultural work, the Indians often depute one man to dance
yumari near the house, while the others attend to the work
in the fields. It is a curious sight to see a lone man taking
his devotional exercise to the tune of his rattle in front of
an apparently deserted dwelling. The lonely worshipper is
doing his share of the general work by bringing down the
fructifying rain and by warding off disaster, while the rest of
the family and their friends plant, hoe, weed, or harvest. In
the evening, when they return from the field, they may join
him for a little while ; but often he goes on alone, dancing

Dances of the Tara-humare Indians to cause rain to fall, corn to sprout, grass to grow, and animals to multiply.

[1] C. Lumholtz, *Unknown Mexico* (London, 1903), i. 330 *sq.*

all night, and singing himself hoarse, and the Indians told me that this is the very hardest kind of work, and exhausting even to them. Solitary worship is also observed by men who go out hunting deer or squirrels for a communal feast. Every one of them dances *yumari* alone in front of his house for two hours to insure success on the hunt ; and when putting corn to sprout for the making of *tesvino* the owner of the house dances for a while, that the corn may sprout well." Another dance is thought to cause the grass and funguses to grow, and the deer and rabbits to multiply ; and another is supposed to draw the clouds together from the north and south, so that they clash and descend in rain.[1]

Dance of the Cora Indians at the sowing festival.

The Cora Indians of Mexico celebrate a festival of sowing shortly before they commit the seed of the maize to the ground. The festival falls in June, because that is the month when the rainy season sets in, supplying the moisture needed for the growth of the maize. At the festival two old women, who represent the goddesses of sowing, dance side by side and imitate the process of sowing by digging holes in the earth with long sticks and inserting the seed of the maize in the holes ; whereupon a man who represents the Morning Star pours water on the buried seeds. This solemn dance is accompanied by the singing of an appropriate hymn, which may be compared to the song of the Arval Brothers in ancient Rome.[2]

Dances and leaps of European peasants to make the corn grow tall.

We have seen that in many parts of Germany, Austria, and France the peasants are still, or were till lately, accustomed to dance and leap high in order that the crops may grow tall. Such leaps and dances are sometimes performed by the sower immediately before or after he sows the seed ; but often they are executed by the people on a fixed day of the year, which in some places is Twelfth Night (the sixth of January), or Candlemas (the second of February) or Walpurgis Night, that is, the Eve of May Day ; but apparently the favourite season for these per-

---

[1] C. Lumholtz, *Unknown Mexico* (London, 1903), i. 335 *sqq.*, 352 *sq.*

[2] K. Th. Preuss, *Die Nayarit-Expedition*, I. *Die Religion der Cora-Indianer* (Leipsic, 1912), pp. xcviii. *sq.*, 61-63. As to the sowing festival

of the Mexican Indians, compare K. Th. Preuss, "Die religiösen Gesänge und Mythen einiger Stämme der mexikanischen Sierra Madre," *Archiv für Religionswissenschaft*, xi. (1908) pp. 374 *sqq.*

formances is the last day of the Carnival, namely Shrove Tuesday.[1] In such cases the leaps and dances are performed by every man for his own behoof; he skips and jumps merely in order that his own corn, or flax, or hemp may spring up and thrive. But sometimes in modern Europe, as (if I am right) in ancient Rome, the duty of dancing for the crops was committed to bands or troops of men, who cut their capers for the benefit of the whole community. For example, at Grub, in the Swiss canton of the Grisons (Graubünden), the practice used to be as follows. " The peasants of Grub," we are informed, "have still some hereditary customs, in that they assembled in some years, mostly at the time of the summer solstice, disguised themselves as maskers so as to be unrecognizable, armed themselves with weapons defensive and offensive, took every man a great club or cudgel, marched in a troop together from one village to another, and executed high leaps and strange antics. They ran full tilt at each other, struck every man his fellow with all his might, so that the blow resounded, and clashed their great staves and cudgels. Hence they were called by the country folk the *Stopfer*. These foolish pranks they played from a superstitious notion that their corn would thrive the better; but now they have left off, and these *Stopfer* are no longer in any repute." Another authority, after describing the custom, remarks : " With this custom was formerly connected the belief that its observance brought a fruitful year." [2]

[1] *The Magic Art and the Evolution of Kings*, i. 137-139.

[2] Dr. F. J. Vonbun, *Beiträge zur deutschen Mythologie gesammelt in Churrhaetien* (Chur, 1862), p. 21, quoting J. Stumpf and Ulr. Campell. As the passage is curious and the work probably rare, I will quote the original in full : " *Sicherlich auch im zusammenhange mit Donarcultus war ein brauch der leute in der Grub* (*in Graubünden*). ' *Die landleute in der Grub haben noch etwas anererbte bräuche, indem dass sie sich zu etlichen jahren* (*meistens zur zeit der sonnenwende*) *besammelten, verbutzten* (*sich als masken vermummten*) *und einander unbekannt machten, legten harnisch und geweer an, und nahm jeder ein grossen kolben oder knüttel, zugen in einer rott mit einander von einem dorf zum andern, triben hohe sprünge und seltsame abentheur.—Sie luffen gestracks laufs aneinander, stiessen mit kräften je einer den andern, dass es erhillt, stiessen laut mit ihren grossen stöcken und knütteln, deswegen sie vom landvolk genannt werden die Stopfer. Diese thorechte abentheuer triben sie zum aberglauben, dass ihnen das korn destobas gerathen sölle, haben aber anjetzo abgelassen, und sind diese Stopfer in keiner achtung mehr.*' (Joh. Stumpf). *Auch Ulr. Campell erwähnt dieses volksbrauch* (*s. 11*) *und bemerkt : ' mit diesem gebrauche hing früher der glaube zusammen, dass dessen ausübung ein fruchtbares jahr bringe.*'" The word *Stopfer* means " stopper," " rammer," " crammer," etc.

In the Austrian provinces of Salzburg and Tyrol bands
of mummers wearing grotesque masks, with bells jingling on
their persons, and carrying long sticks or poles in their
hands, used formerly to run and leap about on certain days
of the year for the purpose of procuring good crops. They
were called *Perchten*, a name derived from Perchta, Berchta,
or Percht, a mythical old woman, whether goddess or elf, who
is well known all over South Germany ; Mrs. Perchta (*Frau
Perchta*), as they call her, is to be met with in Elsace,
Swabia, Bavaria, Austria, and Switzerland, but nowhere,
perhaps, so commonly as in Salzburg and the Tyrol. In
the Tyrol she appears as a little old woman with a very
wrinkled face, bright lively eyes, and a long hooked nose ;
her hair is dishevelled, her garments tattered and torn.
Hence they say to a slatternly wench, " You are a regular
Perchta." She goes about especially during the twelve
days from Christmas to Twelfth Night (Epiphany), above
all on the Eve of Twelfth Night, which is often called
Perchta's Day. Many precautions must be observed during
these mystic days in order not to incur her displeasure, for
she is mischievous to man and beast. If she appears in the
byre, a distemper breaks out among the cows. That is why
during these days the byres must be kept very clean and
straw laid on the threshold ; otherwise you will find bald
patches on your sheep and goats next morning, and next
summer the hair which has been filched from the animals
will descend in hail-stones from the sky. Old Mrs. Perchta
also keeps a very sharp eye on spinners during the twelve
days ; she inspects all distaffs and spinning-wheels in the
houses, and if she finds any flax or tow unspun on them, she
tears it to bits, and she does not spare the lazy spinner, for
she scratches her and smacks her fingers so that they bear
the marks of it for the rest of her life. Indeed she sometimes does much more ; for she rips up the belly of the
sluggard and stuffs it with flax. That is the punishment
with which a Bavarian mother will threaten an idle jade of
a girl who has left some flax on her distaff on New Year's
Eve. However, they say in Bavaria that if you only eat
plenty of the rich juicy cakes which are baked for Mrs.
Perchta on her day, the old woman's knife will glance off

your body without making any impression on it. Perchta
often comes not alone but attended by many little children,
who follow her as chickens waddle after the mother hen ;
and if you should see any little child lagging behind the rest
and blubbering, you may be quite sure that that child has
been baptized. On the Eve of Twelfth Night everybody
should eat pancakes baked of meal and milk or water. If
anybody does not do so, old Mrs. Perchta comes and slits
up his stomach, takes out the other food, fills up the vacuity
so created with a tangled skein and bricks, and then sews
up the orifice neatly, using, singularly enough, a ploughshare for a needle and an iron chain for thread. In
other or the same places she does the same thing to anybody who does not eat herrings and dumplings on Twelfth
Night. Some say that she rides on the storm like the Wild
Huntsman, followed by a boisterous noisy pack, and carrying off people into far countries. Yet withal old Mrs.
Perchta has her redeeming qualities. Good children who
spin diligently and learn their lessons she rewards with nuts
and sugar plums. It has even been affirmed that she makes
the ploughed land fruitful and causes the cattle to thrive.
When a mist floats over the fields, the peasants see her
figure gliding along in a white mantle. On the Eve of
Twelfth Night good people leave the remains of their supper
for her on the table, and when they have gone to bed and
all is quiet in the house, she comes in the likeness of an
old wizened little woman, with all the children about her,
and partakes of the broken victuals. But woe to the prying
wight who peeps at her through the key-hole ! Many a
man has been blinded by her for a whole year as a punishment for his ill-timed curiosity.[1]

[1] J. Grimm, *Deutsche Mythologie*[4]
(Berlin, 1875–1878), i. 226 *sqq.*, iii.
88 *sq.* ; Fr. Panzer, *Beitrag zur
deutschen Mythologie* (Munich, 1848–
1855), i. 247 *sq.*, ii. 381 ; I. V.
Zingerle, " Perahta in Tirol," *Zeitschrift für deutsche Mythologie*, iii.
(Göttingen, 1855), pp. 203-206 ; *id.*,
*Sitten, Bräuche und Meinungen des
Tiroler Volkes*[2] (Innsbruck, 1871), pp.
128 *sq.*, 138 *sq.* ; J. M. Ritter von Al-
penburg, *Mythen und Sagen Tirols*
(Zürich, 1857), pp. 46-51, 63-65 ;
*Bavaria, Landes- und Volkskunde des
Königreichs Bayern* (Munich, 1860–
1867), i. 365 ; A. Wuttke, *Der deutsche
Volksaberglaube*[2] (Berlin, 1869), § 25,
pp. 25-27 ; W. Mannhardt, *Der Baum-
kultus der Germanen und ihrer Nach-
barstämme* (Berlin, 1875), pp. 542 *sq.* ;
Karl Weinhold, *Weinacht-Spiele und
Lieder aus Süddeutschland und Schlesien*
(Vienna, 1875), pp. 19 *sqq.* ; E. Mogk,
in H. Paul's *Grundriss der germani-*

The running and leaping of the *Perchten* mummers on Twelfth Night.

The processions of maskers who took their name of *Perchten* from this quaint creation of the popular fancy were known as *Perchten*-running or *Perchten*-leaping from the runs and leaps which the men took in their wild headlong course through the streets and over the fields. They appear to have been held in all the Alpine regions of Germany, but are best known to us in the Tyrol and Salzburg. The appropriate season for the celebration of the rite was Perchta's Day, that is, Twelfth Night or Epiphany, the sixth of January, but in some places it was held on Shrove Tuesday, the last day of the Carnival, the very day when many farmers of Central Europe jump to make the crops grow tall. Corresponding to the double character of Perchta as a power for good and evil, the maskers are divided into two sets known respectively as the Beautiful and the Ugly *Perchten*. At Lienz in the Tyrol, where the maskers made their appearance on Shrove Tuesday, the Beautiful *Perchten* were decked with ribbons, galloons, and so forth, while the ugly *Perchten* made themselves as hideous as they could by hanging rats and mice, chains and bells about their persons. All wore on their heads tall pointed caps with bells attached to them ; their faces were concealed by masks, and in their hands they all carried long sticks. The sticks of the Beautiful *Perchten* were adorned with ribbons ; those of the Ugly *Perchten* ended in the heads of devils. Thus equipped they leaped and ran about the streets and went into the houses. Amongst them was a clown who blew ashes and soot in people's faces through a blow-pipe. It was all very merry and frolicsome, except when " the wild Perchta " herself came, invisible to ordinary eyes, upon the scene. Then her namesakes the *Perchten* grew wild and furious too ; they scattered and fled for their lives to the nearest house, for as soon as they got under the gutter of a roof they were safe. But if she caught them, she tore them in pieces. To this

The Beautiful *Perchten* and the Ugly *Perchten*.

---

schen Philologie,[2] iii. (Strasburg, 1900), pp. 280 *sq.* (where it is said that Perchta " *spendet dem Acker Fruchtbarkeit und lässt das Vieh gedeihen* ") ; E. H. Meyer, *Mythologie der Germanen* (Strasburg, 1903), pp. 424 *sqq.* ; P. Herrmann, *Deutsche Mythologie* (Leipsic, 1906), pp. 303 *sqq.* ; M. Andree-Eysen, *Volkskundliches aus dem bayrisch-österreichischen Alpengebiet* (Brunswick, 1910), pp. 156 *sqq.* ; E. Hoffmann-Krayer, *Feste und Bräuche des Schweizervolkes* (Zürich, 1913), pp. 118 *sqq.*

day you may see the graves where the mangled bodies of her victims lie buried. When no such interruption took place, the noisy rout of maskers rushed madly about, with jingling bells and resounding cracks of whips, entering the houses, dancing here, drinking there, teasing wayfarers, or racing from village to village like the Wild Hunt itself in the sky ; till at the close of the winter day the church bells rang the *Ave Maria*. Then at last the wild uproar died away into silence. Such tumultuous masquerades were thought to be very beneficial to the crops ; a bad harvest would be set down to the omission of the *Perchten* to skip and jump about in their usual fashion.[1]

In the province of Salzburg the *Perchten* mummers are also divided into two sets, the Beautiful *Perchten* and the Ugly *Perchten*. The Ugly *Perchten* are properly speaking twelve young men dressed in black sheepskins and wearing hoods of badger-skins and grotesque wooden masks, which represent either coarse human features with long teeth and horns, or else the features of fabulous animals with beaks and bristles or movable jaws. They all carry bells, both large and small, fastened to broad leathern girdles. The procession was headed by a man with a big drum, and after him came lads bearing huge torches and lanterns fastened to tall poles ; for in Salzburg or some parts of it these mummers played their pranks by night. Behind the torch-bearers came two Fools, a male and a female, the latter acted by a lad in woman's clothes. The male Fool carried a sausage-like roll, with which he struck at all women or girls of his acquaintance when they shewed themselves at the open doors or windows. Along with the *Perchten* themselves went a train of young fellows cracking whips, blowing horns, or jingling bells. The ways might be miry and the night pitch dark, but with flaring lights the procession swept rapidly by, the men leaping along with the help of their long sticks and waking the echoes of the slumbering valley by their loud uproar. From

The Ugly Perchten in Salzburg.

[1] J. Grimm, *Deutsche Mythologie,*[4] i. 231 ; I. V. Zingerle, *Sitten, Bräuche und Meinungen des Tiroler Volkes*[2] (Innsbruck, 1871), pp. 138 *sq.* ; W. Mannhardt, *Baumkultus*, pp. 542 *sq.* ; J. M. Ritter von Alpenburg, *Mythen und Sagen Tirols* (Zürich, 1857), pp. 50 *sq.* ; K. Weinhold, *Weinacht-Spiele und Lieder aus Süddeutschland und Schlesien* (Vienna, 1875), pp. 21 *sqq.*

time to time they stopped at a farm, danced and cut their
capers before the house, for which they were rewarded by
presents of food and strong drink ; to offer them money
would have been an insult.   By midnight the performance
came to an end, and the tired maskers dispersed to their
homes.

The Beautiful *Perchten* in Salzburg.   The Beautiful *Perchten* in Salzburg are attired very
differently from the Ugly *Perchten*, but their costume varies
with the district.   Thus in the Pongau district the distinctive
feature of their costume is a tall and heavy framework covered
with bright red cloth and decorated with a profusion of silver
jewelry and filagree work.   This framework is sometimes
nine or ten feet high and forty or fifty pounds in weight.
The performer carries it above his head by means of iron
supports resting on his shoulders or his back.   To run or
jump under the weight of such an encumbrance is impossible ; the dancer has to content himself with turning round
and round slowly and clumsily.   Very different is the head-
dress of the Beautiful *Perchten* in the Pinzgau district of
Salzburg.   There the performers are dressed in scarlet and
wear straw hats, from which bunches of white feathers,
arranged like fans, nod and flutter in the wind.   Red shoes
and white stockings complete their attire.   Thus lightly
equipped they hop and jump and stamp briskly in the
dance.   Unlike their Ugly namesakes, who seem now to be
extinct, the Beautiful *Perchten* still parade from time to time
among the peasantry of the Salzburg highlands ; but the
intervals between their appearances are irregular, varying
from four to seven years or more.   Unlike the Ugly
Perchten, they wear no masks and appear in full daylight,
always on · Perchta's Day (Twelfth Night, the sixth of
January) and the two following Sundays.   They are attended
by a train of followers who make a great din with bells,
whips, pipes, horns, rattles, and chains.   Amongst them one
or two clowns, clothed in white and wearing tall pointed
hats of white felt with many jingling bells attached to them,
play a conspicuous part.   They carry each a sausage-
shaped roll stuffed with tow, and with this instrument they
strike lightly such women and girls among the spectators
as they desire particularly to favour.   Another attendant

carries the effigy of a baby in swaddling bands, made of linen rags, and fastened to a string ; this effigy he throws at women and girls and then pulls back again, but he does this only to women and girls whom he respects and to whom he wishes well.   At St. Johann the *Perchten* carry drawn swords ; each is attended by a lad dressed as a woman ; and they are followed by men clad in black sheepskins, wearing the masks of devils, and holding chains in their hands.[1]

What is the meaning of the quaint performances still enacted by the *Perchten* and their attendants in the Austrian highlands ?   The subject has been carefully investigated by a highly competent enquirer, Mrs. Andree-Eysn.   She has visited the districts, witnessed the performances, collected information, and studied the costumes.   It may be well to quote her conclusion : " If we enquire into the inner meaning which underlies the *Perchten*-race and kindred processions, we must confess that it is not at first sight obvious, and that the original meaning appears blurred and indistinct.   Nevertheless from many features which they present in common it can be demonstrated that the processions were held for the purpose of driving away demons and had for their object to promote fertility. In favour of this view it may be urged, first of all, that their appearance is everywhere greeted with joy, because it promises fertility and a good harvest.   ' It is a good year,' they say in Salzburg.   If the processions are prevented from taking place, dearth and a bad harvest are to be apprehended. The peasants of the Tyrol still believe that the more *Perchten* run about, the better will the year be, and therefore they treat them to brandy and cakes.   In Lienz, when the harvest turns out ill, they say that they omitted to let the *Perchten* run over the fields, and for that reason the peasant in the Sarn valley gets the *Perchten* to leap about on his fields, for then there will be a good year.

" If fertility and blessing are to be poured out on field, house, and homestead, it is obvious that everything that could hinder or harm must be averted and driven away. When we consider how even at the present time, and still

Mrs. Andree-Eysn on the Perchten ; according to her, the processions of Perchten are intended to promote fertility by banishing the demons that would thwart it.

---

[1] Marie Andree - Eysn, *Volkskund-liches aus dem bayrisch-österreichischen Alpengebiet* (Brunswick, 1910), pp. 156-175.

more in times gone by, much that is harmful is attributed to the malevolence of invisible powers, we can readily understand why people should resort to measures which they deem effective for the purpose of disarming these malevolent beings. Now it is a common belief that certain masks possess the virtue of banning demons, and that loud noise and din are a means of keeping off evil spirits or hindering their activity. In the procession of the *Perchten* we see the principle of the banishment of evil carried out in practice. The people attack the evil spirits and seek to chase them away by putting on frightful masks, with which they confront the demon. For one sort of malevolent spirits one kind of mask appears suitable, and for another another; this spirit is daunted by this mask, and that spirit by that; and so they came to discriminate. Originally, particular masks may have been used against particular evil spirits, but in course of time they were confused, the individual taste of the maker of the mask counted for something, and so gradually it resulted in carving all kinds of horrible, fantastic, and hideous masks which had nothing in common but their general tendency to frighten away all evil spirits." [1]

The bells worn by the *Perchten* mummers may be intended to ban demons.

In support of her view that the procession of the *Perchten* aims chiefly at banishing demons who might otherwise blight the crops, Mrs. Andree-Eysn lays stress on the bells which figure so prominently in the costume of these maskers; for the sound of bells, as she reminds us, is commonly believed to be a potent means of driving evil spirits away. The notion is too familiar to call for proof,[2] but a single case from Central Africa may be cited as an illustration. The Teso people, who inhabit a land of rolling plains between Mount Elgon and Lake Kioga, "make use of bells to exorcise the storm fiend; a person who has been injured by a flash or in the resulting fire wears bells round his ankles for weeks

---

[1] Marie Andree-Eysn, *Volkskundliches aus dem bayrisch-österreichischen Alpengebiet* (Brunswick, 1910), pp. 179 *sq.* The authoress kindly presented me with a copy of her valuable work in May 1910, when I had the pleasure of visiting her and her husband, the eminent anthropologist, the late Dr. Richard Andree, in their home at Munich.

[2] See P. Sartori, "Glockensagen und Glockenaberglaube," *Zeitschrift des Vereins für Volkskunde*, vii. (1897) pp. 360 *sqq.* The use in classical antiquity of bells, gongs, and the clash of bronze generally to ban the demon host has been learnedly illustrated by Mr. A. B. Cook in his article, "The Gong at Dodona," *Journal of Hellenic Studies*, xxii. (1902) pp. 14 *sqq.*

afterwards.   Whenever rain threatens, and rain in Uganda almost always comes in company with thunder and lightning, this person will parade the village for an hour, with the jingling bells upon his legs and a wand of papyrus in his hand, attended by as many of his family as may happen to be at hand and not employed in necessary duties."[1]   The resemblance of such men, with their bells and wands, to the Austrian *Perchten* with their bells and wands is, on the theory in question, fairly close; both of them go about to dispel demons by the sound of their bells and probably also by the blows of their rods.   Whatever may be thought of their efficacy in banning fiends, certain it is that in the Tyrol, where the *Perchten* play their pranks, the chime of bells is used for the express purpose of causing the grass to grow in spring.   Thus in the lower valley of the Inn, especially at Schwaz, on the twenty-fourth of April (there reckoned St. George's Day) troops of young fellows go about ringing bells, some of which they hold in their hands, while others are attached to their persons; and the peasants say, " Wherever the Grass-ringers come, there the grass grows well, and the corn bears abundant fruit."   Hence the bell-ringers are welcomed and treated wherever they go.   Formerly, it is said, they wore masks, like the *Perchten*, but afterwards they contented themselves with blackening their faces with soot.[2]   In other parts of the Tyrol the bell-ringing processions take place at the Carnival, but their object is the same; for " it is believed that by this noisy procession growth in general, but especially the growth of the meadows, is promoted."[3]   Again, at Bergell, in the Swiss canton of the Grisons, children go in procession on the first of March ringing bells, " in order that the grass may grow."[4]   So in Hildesheim, on the afternoon of Ascension Day, young girls ascend the church tower and ring all the church bells, " in order that they may get a good harvest of flax; the girl who, hanging on to the bell-rope, is swung highest by the swing

Bells rung to make the grass grow in spring.

Bells rung to make the flax grow.

---

[1] Rev. A. L. Kitching, *On the Backwaters of the Nile* (London, 1912), p. 264.   As to the country of the Teso people, who do not belong to the Bantu stock, see *id.*, pp. 26 *sq.*

[2] Marie Andree-Eysn, *op. cit.* pp. 180-182.   As to the custom of "ring-ing-out the grass," see further W. Mannhardt, *Baumkultus*, p. 540; *The Magic Art and the Evolution of Kings*, ii. 343 *sq.*

[3] Marie Andree-Eysn, *op. cit.* p. 182.

[4] Marie Andree-Eysn, *l.c.*

of the bell, will get the longest flax." [1]   Here the sound of the bells as a means of promoting the growth of the flax is reinforced by the upward swing of the bell, which, carrying with it the bell-ringer at the end of the rope, naturally causes the flax in like manner to rise high in the air.   It is a simple piece of imitative magic, like the leaps and bounds which the peasants of Central Europe often execute for precisely the same purpose.   Once more, in various parts of the Tyrol on Senseless Thursday, which is the last Thursday in Carnival, young men in motley attire, with whips and brooms, run about cracking their whips and making believe to sweep away the onlookers with their brooms.   They are called *Huttler* or *Huddler*.   The people say that if these fellows do not run about, the flax will not thrive, and that on the contrary the more of them run about, the better will the flax grow.   And where there are many of them, there will be much maize.[2]   In this custom the cracking of the whips may be supposed to serve the same purpose as the ringing of the bells by frightening and banishing the demons of infertility and dearth.   About Hall, in the northern Tyrol, the ceremony of the *Hudel*-running, as it is called, is or used to be as follows.   A peasant-farmer, generally well-to-do and respected, rigs himself out in motley and hides his face under a mask ; round his waist he wears a girdle crammed with rolls, while in his hand he wields a long whip, from which more than fifty cracknels dangle on a string.   Thus arrayed he suddenly bursts from the ale-house door into the public view, solicited thereto by the cries of the street urchins, who have been anxiously waiting for his appearance.   He throws amongst them the string of cracknels, and while they are scrambling for these dainties, he lays on to them most liberally with his whip.   Having faithfully discharged this public duty, he marches down between rows of peasants, who have meantime taken up their position in a long street.   Amongst them he picks out one who is to run

[1] K. Seifart, *Sagen, Märchen, Schwänke und Gebräuche aus Stadt und Stift Hildesheim* [2] (Hildesheim, 1889), p. 180.   For more evidence of the supposed fertilizing influence of bells, see P. Sartori, "Glockensagen und Glockenaberglaube," *Zeitschrift des Vereins für Volkskunde,* vii. (1897) pp. 363 *sq.*

[2] I. V. Zingerle, *Sitten, Bräuche und Meinungen des Tiroler Volkes* [2] (Innsbruck, 1871), pp. 135 *sq.*, 139, § 1196, 1211, 1212.

before him.   The man selected for the honour accordingly takes to his heels, hotly pursued by the other with the whip, who lashes the feet of the fugitive till he comes up with him. Having run him down, he leads him back to the alehouse, where he treats him to a roll and a glass of wine.   After that the masker runs a similar race with another man ; and so it goes on, one race after another, till the sun sets.   Then the mummer doffs his mask and leads the dance in the ale-house.   The object of these races is said to be to ensure a good crop of flax and maize.[1]

In these races of mummers, whether known as *Perchten* or *Huttler*, there are certain features which it is difficult to explain on the theory that the aim of the performers is simply to drive away demons, and that the hideous masks which they assume have no other intention than that of frightening these uncanny beings.   For observe that in the last example the blows of the whip fall not on the airy swarms of invisible spirits, but on the solid persons of street urchins and sturdy yokels, who can hardly be supposed to receive the chastisement vicariously for the demons.   Again, what are we to make of the rolls and cracknels with which in this case the mummer is laden, and which he distributes among his victims, as if to console them in one part of their person for the pain which he has inflicted on another? Surely this bounty seems to invest him with something more than the purely negative character of an exorciser of evil ; it appears to raise him to the positive character of a dispenser of good.   The same remark applies to the action of the *Perchten* who strike women lightly, as a mark of friendship and regard, with the sausage-like rolls which they carry in their hands, or throw them, as a mark of favour, the effigy of a baby.   The only probable explanation of these practices, as Mrs. Andree-Eysn rightly points out, is that the mummers thereby intend to fertilize the women whom they honour by these attentions.[2]   Here, again, therefore the maskers appear as the actual dispensers of good, the bestowers of fruitful-ness, not merely the averters of evil.   If that is so, we seem bound to infer that these masked men represent or

Certain features in these processions or races of mummers seem to shew that the mummers represent beneficent spirits of fertility, who quicken the seed in the ground and offspring in the wombs of women.

[1] W. Mannhardt, *Baumkultus*, pp. 268 *sq.*

[2] Marie Andree-Eysn, *op. cit.* pp. 182 *sq.*

embody the spirits who quicken the seed both in the earth
and in the wombs of women.   That was the view of W.
Mannhardt, the highest authority on the agricultural superstitions of European peasantry.   After reviewing these and
many more similar processions, he concludes that if the
comparison which he has instituted between them holds
good, all these various mummers " were intended by the
original founders of the processions to represent demons of
vegetation, who by their mere appearance and cries drove
away the powers that hinder growth and woke to new life
the slumbering spirits of the grasses and corn-stalks." [1]   Thus
Mannhardt admitted that these noisy processions of masked
men are really supposed to dispel the evil spirits of blight
and infertility, while at the same time he held that the men
themselves originally personated vegetation-spirits.   And he
thought it probable that the original significance of these
performances was in later times misunderstood and interpreted as a simple expulsion of witches and other uncanny
beings that haunt the fields. [2]

On the whole this conclusion of an enquirer remarkable
for a rare combination of learning, sobriety, and insight, is
perhaps the most probable that can now be reached with the
evidence at our disposal.   It is confirmed by some of the
savage masquerades in which the maskers definitely represent
spirits of fertility in order to promote the fruitfulness of the
earth and of women ; [3] and it is supported by the evidence
of many other rustic mummeries in Europe, for example, by
the English rites of Plough Monday, in which the dancers,
or rather jumpers, who wore bunches of corn in their hats
as they leaped into the air, are most naturally interpreted as
agents or representatives of the corn-spirit. [4]   It is, therefore,
worth observing that in some places the dancers of Plough
Monday, who attended the plough in its peregrinations
through the streets and fields, are described as morris-
dancers. [5]   If the description is correct, it implies that they

The view of W. Mannhardt.

Confirmations of this view.

---

[1] W. Mannhardt, *Baumkultus*, p. 548.

[2] W. Mannhardt, *l.c.*

[3] See above, p. 236.

[4] *Spirits of the Corn and of the Wild,* ii. 325 *sqq.*

[5] T. F. Thiselton Dyer, *British Popular Customs* (London, 1876), p. 32; *County Folk-lore, Printed Extracts, No. 3, Leicestershire and Rutlandshire,* collected and edited by C. J. Billson (London, 1895), pp. 93 *sq.*

had bells attached to their costume, which would further The use
assimilate them to the *Perchten* and other masqueraders of of bells in
these cere-
Central Europe ; for the chief characteristic of the morris- monies.
dance is that the performers wear bells fastened to their legs
which jingle at every step.[1]   We may suppose that if the
men who ran and capered beside the plough on Plough
Monday really wore bells, the original intention of this
appendage to their costume was either to dispel the demons
who might hinder the growth of the corn, or to waken the
spirits of vegetation from their long winter sleep.   In favour The use of
of the view which sees in all these dances and mummeries swords in
these cere-
rather the banishment of what is evil than the direct promo- monies.
tion of what is good, it may be urged that some of the
dancers wear swords,[2] a weapon which certainly seems better
fitted to combat demons than to prune fruit-trees or turn up
the sod.   Further, it deserves to be noted that many of the
performances take place either on Twelfth Day or, like the
celebration of Plough Monday, very shortly after it ; and
that in the Lord of Misrule, who reigned from Christmas to
Twelfth Day,[3] we have a clear trace of one of those periods
of general licence and suspension of ordinary government,
which so commonly occur at the end of the old year or the
beginning of the new one in connexion with a general
expulsion of evils.

Surveying these masquerades and processions, as they These mas-
have been or still are celebrated in modern Europe, we may querades
originally
say in general that they appear to have been originally intended
intended both to stimulate the growth of vegetation in spring both to
stimulate
and to expel the demoniac or other evil influences which vegetation
were thought to have accumulated during the preceding in spring
and to
winter or year ; and that these two motives of stimulation expel
and expulsion, blended and perhaps confused together, appear demons.
to explain the quaint costumes of the mummers, the multi-

---

[1] Mrs. Lilly Grove (Mrs. J. G. Frazer), *Dancing* (London, 1895), pp. 147 *sqq.* ; E. K. Chambers, *The Mediaeval Stage* (Oxford, 1903), i. 195 *sqq.*

[2] As to the swords carried by the *Perchten* see above, p. 245 ; as to those carried by the dancers on Plough Monday, see J. Brand, *Popular Antiquities of Great Britain* (London, 1882–

1883), i. 505.   As to the sword-dance in general, see K. Müllenhoff, " Über den Schwerttanz," in *Festgaben für Gustav Homeyer* (Berlin, 1871), pp. 111-147 (who compares the dances of the Salii) ; Mrs. Lilly Grove, *op. cit.* pp. 189 *sqq.*, 211 *sqq.* ; E. K. Chambers, *op. cit.* i. 182 *sqq.*

[3] See below, pp. 331 *sqq.*

tudinous noises which they make, and the blows which they
direct either at invisible foes or at the visible and tangible
persons of their fellows. In the latter case the beating
may be supposed to serve as a means of forcibly freeing the
sufferers from the demons or other evil things that cling to
them unseen.

Application of these conclusions to the expulsion of " the Old Mars " in ancient Rome.

To apply these conclusions to the Roman custom of
expelling Mamurius Veturius or " the Old Mars " every year
in spring, we may say that they lend some support to the
theory which sees in " the Old Mars " the outworn deity of
vegetation driven away to make room, either for a younger
and more vigorous personification of vernal life, or perhaps
for the return of the same deity refreshed and renovated by
the treatment to which he had been subjected, and particularly by the vigorous application of the rod to his sacred
person. For, as we shall see presently, King Solomon was
by no means singular in his opinion of the refreshing
influence of a sound thrashing. So far as " the Old Mars "
was supposed to carry away with him the accumulated
weaknesses and other evils of the past year, so far would he
serve as a public scapegoat, like the effigy in the Slavonic
custom of " Carrying out Death," which appears not only to
represent the vegetation-spirit of the past year, but also to
act as a scapegoat, carrying away with it a heavy load
of suffering, misfortune, and death.

§ 2. *The Human Scapegoat in Ancient Greece*

Human scapegoats in ancient Greece. The " Ex- pulsion of Hunger " at Chaer- onea.

The ancient Greeks were also familiar with the use of a
human scapegoat. In Plutarch's native town of Chaeronea a
ceremony of this kind was performed by the chief magistrate
at the Town Hall, and by each householder at his own home.
It was called the " expulsion of hunger." A slave was beaten
with rods of the *agnus castus*, and turned out of doors with
the words, " Out with hunger, and in with wealth and health."
When Plutarch held the office of chief magistrate of his
native town he performed this ceremony at the Town Hall,
and he has recorded the discussion to which the custom
afterwards gave rise.[1] The ceremony closely resembles

---

[1] Plutarch, *Quaest. conviv.* vi. 8.

the Japanese, Hindoo, and Highland customs already described.[1]

But in civilized Greece the custom of the scapegoat took darker forms than the innocent rite over which the amiable and pious Plutarch presided. Whenever Marseilles, one of the busiest and most brilliant of Greek colonies, was ravaged by a plague, a man of the poorer classes used to offer himself as a scapegoat. For a whole year he was maintained at the public expense, being fed on choice and pure food. At the expiry of the year he was dressed in sacred garments, decked with holy branches, and led through the whole city, while prayers were uttered that all the evils of the people might fall on his head. He was then cast out of the city or stoned to death by the people outside of the walls.[2] The Athenians regularly maintained a number of degraded and useless beings at the public expense ; and when any calamity, such as plague, drought, or famine, befell the city, they sacrificed two of these outcasts as scapegoats. One of the victims was sacrificed for the men and the other for the women. The former wore round his neck a string of black, the latter a string of white figs. Sometimes, it seems, the victim slain on behalf of the women was a woman. They were led about the city and then sacrificed, apparently by being stoned to death outside the city.[3] But such sacrifices were not confined to extraordinary occasions of public calamity ; it

Human scapegoats at Marseilles.

Human scapegoats put to death at Athens.

---

[1] See above, pp. 143 *sqq.*, 209.

[2] Servius on Virgil, *Aen.* iii. 57, following Petronius ; Lactantius Placidius, *Commentarii in Statii Thebaida* x. 793, p. 452, ed. R. Jahnke (Leipsic, 1898). According to the former writer, the scapegoat was cast out ("*projiciebatur*") ; according to the latter, he was stoned to death by the people outside of the walls ("*extra pomeria saxis occidebatur a populo*"). The statement of some modern writers that he was killed by being hurled from a height rests on a reading ("*praecipitabatur*" for "*projiciebatur*") in the text of Servius, which appears to have no manuscript authority and to be merely a conjecture of R. Stephan's. Yet the conjecture has been inserted in the text by F. Buecheler in his edition of Petronius (Third Edition, Berlin, 1882, p. 109) without any intimation that all the MSS. present a different reading. See the critical edition of Servius edited by G. Thilo and H. Hagen, vol. i. (Leipsic, 1881), p. 346.

[3] Helladius, in Photius, *Bibliotheca*, p. 534 A, ed. Im. Bekker (Berlin, 1824) ; Scholiast on Aristophanes, *Frogs*, 734, and on *Knights*, 1136 ; Hesychius, *Lexicon*, *s.v.* φαρμακοί; compare Suidas, *Lexicon*, *s.vv.* κάθαρμα, φαρμακός, and φαρμακούς ; Lysias, *Orat.* vi. 53. That they were stoned is an inference from Harpocration. See next note. When the people of Cyrene sacrificed to Saturn (Cronus), they wore crowns of fresh figs on their heads. See Macrobius, *Saturn.* i. 7. 25.

appears that every year, at the festival of the Thargelia in May, two victims, one for the men and one for the women,

were led out of Athens and stoned to death.[1] The city of Abdera in Thrace was publicly purified once a year, and one of the burghers, set apart for the purpose, was stoned to death as a scapegoat or vicarious sacrifice for the life of all the others ; six days before his execution he was excommunicated, " in order that he alone might bear the sins of all the people." [2]

From the Lover's Leap, a white bluff at the southern end of their island, the Leucadians used annually to hurl a criminal into the sea as a scapegoat. But to lighten his fall they fastened live birds and feathers to him, and a flotilla of small boats waited below to catch him and convey him beyond the boundary. Probably these humane precautions were a mitigation of an earlier custom of flinging the scapegoat into the sea to drown, just as in Kumaon the custom of letting a man slide down a rope from the top of a cliff appears to be a modification of an older practice of putting him to death. The Leucadian ceremony took place at the time of a sacrifice to Apollo, who had a temple or sanctuary on the spot.[3] Elsewhere it was customary to cast

---

[1] Harpocration, *Lexicon, s.v.* φαρμακός, who says δύο ἄνδρας Ἀθήνῃσιν ἐξῆγον καθάρσια ἐσομένους τῆς πόλεως ἐν τοῖς Θαργηλίοις, ἕνα μὲν ὑπὲρ τῶν ἀνδρῶν, ἕνα δὲ ὑπὲρ τῶν γυναικῶν. He does not expressly state that they were put to death ; but as he says that the ceremony was an imitation of the execution of a mythical Pharmacus who was stoned to death, we may infer that the victims were killed by being stoned. Suidas (*s.v.* φαρμακός) copies Harpocration. As to the human scapegoats employed by the Greeks at the Thargelia and on other occasions see W. Mannhardt, *Mythologische Forschungen* (Strasburg, 1884), pp. 124 *sqq.* ; J. Töpffer, *Beiträge zur griechischen Altertumswissenschaft* (Berlin, 1897), pp. 130 *sqq.* ; August Mommsen, *Feste der Stadt Athen im Altertum* (Leipsic, 1898), pp. 468 *sqq.* ; Miss J. E. Harrison, *Prolegomena to the Study of Greek Religion*, Second Edition (Cambridge, 1908), pp. 95 *sqq.* ; M. P.

Nilsson, *Griechische Feste* (Leipsic, 1906), pp. 105 *sqq.* ; W. R. Paton, "The φαρμακοί and the Story of the Fall," *Revue Archéologique*, iv. Série ix. (1907) pp. 51-57.

[2] Ovid, *Ibis*, 467 *sq.* :

" *Aut te devoveat certis Abdera diebus*
    Saxaque devotum grandine plura
        petant,"

with the two scholia quoted respectively by M. P. Nilsson, *Griechische Feste*, p. 108 note[6], and by O. Schneider, in his *Callimachea* (Leipsic, 1870-1873), ii. 684. The scholiast refers to Callimachus as his authority.

[3] Strabo, x. 2. 9, p. 542 ; Photius, *Lexicon, s.v.* Λευκάτης ; L. Ampelius, *Liber Memorialis*, viii. 4 ; Servius, on Virgil, *Aen.* iii. 279 ; Ptolemaeus Hephaest., *Nov. Histor.* in Photius, *Bibliotheca*, cod. 190, p. 153, ed. Im. Bekker ; *Mythographi Graeci*, ed. A. Westermann (Brunswick, 1843), pp. 198 *sq.* According to the manuscript

a young man every year into the sea, with the prayer, " Be thou our offscouring." This ceremony was supposed to rid the people of the evils by which they were beset, or according to a somewhat different interpretation it redeemed them by paying the debt they owed to the sea-god.[1] As practised by the Greeks of Asia Minor in the sixth century before our era, the custom of the scapegoat was as follows. When a city suffered from plague, famine, or other public calamity, an ugly or deformed person was chosen to take upon himself all the evils which afflicted the community. He was brought to a suitable place, where dried figs, a barley loaf, and cheese were put into his hand. These he ate. Then he was beaten seven times upon his genital organs with squills and branches of the wild fig and other wild trees, while the flutes played a particular tune. Afterwards he was burned on a pyre built of the wood of forest trees ; and his ashes were cast into the sea.[2] A similar custom appears to have been annually celebrated by the Asiatic Greeks at the harvest festival of the Thargelia.[3]

Human scapegoats annually put to death at the festival of the Thargelia in Asia Minor.

In the ritual just described the scourging of the victim with squills, branches of the wild fig, and so forth, cannot have been intended to aggravate his sufferings, otherwise any stick would have been good enough to beat him with. The true meaning of this part of the ceremony has been explained by W. Mannhardt.[4] He points out that the ancients attributed to squills a magical power of averting evil influences, and that accordingly they hung them up at the doors of their houses and made use of them in purificatory rites.[5]

Mannhardt's interpretation of the custom of beating the human scapegoat on the genitals : it was intended to free his repro-

<hr>

reading in Photius, *l.c.*, the priests flung themselves into the sea ; but the reading has been altered by the editors. As to the Kumaon ceremony see above, pp. 196 *sq.*

[1] Suidas and Photius, *Lexicon, s.v.* περίψημα. The word which I have translated " offscouring " (περίψημα) occurs in 1 Corinthians iv. 13, where it is similarly translated in the English version. It means properly that on which something is wiped off, like a sponge or a duster.

[2] J. Tzetzes, *Chiliades*, v. 726-761 (ed. Th. Kiesseling, Leipsic, 1826). Tzetzes's authority is the satirical poet Hipponax. The tune which was played

by the flutes while the man was being beaten is mentioned by Hesychius, *s.v.* Κραδίης νόμος. Compare *id., s.v.* Κραδησίτης ; Plutarch, *De musica*, 8.

[3] This may be inferred from the verse of Hipponax, quoted by Athenaeus, ix. 9, p. 370 B, where for φαρμάκου we should perhaps read φαρμακοῦ with Schneidewin (*Poetae lyrici Graeci*,[3] ed. Th. Bergk, ii. 763).

[4] W. Mannhardt, *Mythologische Forschungen* (Strasburg, 1884), pp. 113 *sqq.*, especially 123 *sq.*, 133.

[5] Pliny, *Nat. Hist.* xx. 101 ; Dioscorides, *De materia medica*, ii. 202 ; Lucian, *Necyom.* 7 ; *id., Alexander*, 47 ; Theophrastus, *Superstitious Man*.

ductive
energies
from any
restraint
laid on
them by
demoniacal
or other
malignant
agency.

Hence the Arcadian custom of whipping the image of Pan with squills at a festival, or whenever the hunters returned empty-handed,[1] must have been meant, not to punish the god, but to purify him from the harmful influences which were impeding him in the exercise of his divine functions as a god who should supply the hunter with game. Similarly the object of beating the human scapegoat on the genital organs with squills and so on, must have been to release his reproductive energies from any restraint or spell under which they might be laid by demoniacal or other malignant agency ; and as the Thargelia at which he was annually sacrificed was an early harvest festival celebrated in May,[2] we must recognize in him a representative of the creative and fertilizing god of vegetation. The representative of the god was annually slain for the purpose I have indicated, that of maintaining the divine life in perpetual vigour, untainted by the weakness of age ; and before he was put to death it was not unnatural to stimulate his reproductive powers in order that these might be transmitted in full activity to his successor, the new god or new embodiment of the old god, who was doubtless supposed immediately to take the place of the one slain.[3] Similar reasoning would lead to a similar treatment of the scapegoat on special occasions, such as drought or famine. If the crops did not answer to the expectation of the husbandman, this would be attributed to some failure in the generative powers of the god whose function it was to produce the fruits of the earth. It might be thought that he was under a spell or was growing old and feeble. Accordingly he was slain in the person of his representative, with all the ceremonies already described, in order that, born young again, he might infuse his own youthful vigour into the stagnant energies of nature. On the

---

[1] Theocritus, vii. 106 *sqq.* with the scholiast.

[2] Compare Aug. Mommsen, *Heortologie* (Leipsic, 1864), pp. 414 *sqq.*, id., *Feste der Stadt Athen im Altertum* (Leipsic, 1898), pp. 468 *sq.*, 479 *sqq.* ; M. P. Nilsson, *Griechische Feste* (Leipsic, 1906), pp. 105, 111 *sqq.* ; W. Mannhardt, *Antike Wald- und Feldkulte* (Berlin, 1877), p. 215.

[3] At certain sacrifices in Yucatan blood was drawn from the genitals of a human victim and smeared on the face of the idol. See Diego de Landa, *Relation des choses de Yucatan,* texte espagnol et traduction française par l'Abbé Brasseur de Bourbourg (Paris, 1864), p. 167. Was the original intention of this rite to transfuse into the god a fresh supply of reproductive energy ?

same principle we can understand why Mamurius Veturius was beaten with rods, why the slave at the Chaeronean ceremony was beaten with the *agnus castus* (a tree to which magical properties were ascribed),[1] why the effigy of Death in some parts of Europe is assailed with sticks and stones,[2] and why at Babylon the criminal who played the god was scourged before he was crucified.[3]   The purpose of the scourging was not to intensify the agony of the divine sufferer, but on the contrary to dispel any malignant influences by which at the supreme moment he might conceivably be beset.

Thus far I have assumed that the human victims at the Thargelia represented the spirits of vegetation in general,[4] but it has been well remarked by Mr. W. R. Paton that these poor wretches seem to have masqueraded as the spirits of fig-trees in particular.   He points out that the process of caprification, as it is called, that is, the artificial fertilization of the cultivated fig-trees by hanging strings of wild figs among the boughs, takes place in Greece and Asia Minor in June about a month after the date of the Thargelia, and he suggests that the hanging of the black and white figs round the necks of the two human victims, one of whom represented the men and the other the women, may have been a direct imitation of the process of caprification designed, on the principle of imitative magic, to assist the fertilization of the fig-trees.   And since caprification is in fact a marriage of the male fig-tree with the female fig-tree, Mr. Paton further supposes that the loves of the trees may, on the same principle of imitative magic, have been simulated by a mock or even a real marriage between the two human victims, one of whom appears sometimes to have been a woman.   On this view the practice of beating the human victims on their genitals with branches of wild fig-trees and with squills was a charm intended to stimulate the generative powers of the man and woman who for the time being personated the male and the female fig-trees

[marginal note:] W. R. Paton's view that the human scapegoats at the Thargelia personated the spirits of fig-trees, and that the ceremony was a magical rite for the fertilization of fig-trees, being copied from the process of caprification.

---

[1] Aelian, *Nat. Anim.* ix. 26.
[2] *The Dying God*, pp. 239 *sq.*
[3] *The Dying God*, p. 114.
[4] On the other hand, W. Mannhardt regarded the victims as representing the demons of infertility, dearth, and sickness, who in the persons of their representatives were thus hounded with blows out of the city. See his *Mythologische Forschungen*, p. 129.

respectively, and who by their union in marriage, whether real or pretended, were believed to help the trees to bear fruit.[1]

This theory is confirmed by a comparison with the Roman rites of the *Nonae Caprotinae.*

The theory is ingenious and attractive ; and to some extent it is borne out by the Roman celebration of the *Nonae Caprotinae,* which I have described in an earlier part of this work.[2]   For on the *Nonae Caprotinae,* the ninth of July, the female slaves, in the attire of free women, feasted under a wild fig-tree, cut a rod from the tree, beat each other, perhaps with the rod, and offered the milky juice of the tree to the goddess Juno Caprotina, whose surname seems to point her out as the goddess of the wild fig-tree (*caprificus*).   Here the rites performed in July by women under the wild fig-tree, which the ancients rightly regarded as a male and employed to fertilize the cultivated female fig-tree, can hardly be dissociated from the caprification or artificial marriage of the fig-trees which, according to Columella, was best performed in July ; and if the blows which the women gave each other on this occasion were administered, as seems highly probable, by the rod which they cut from the wild fig-tree, the parallel between the Roman and the Greek ceremony would be still closer ; since the Greeks, as we saw, beat the genitals of the human victims with branches of wild fig-trees.   It is true that the human sacrifices, which formed so prominent a feature in the Greek celebration of the Thargelia, do not figure in the Roman celebration of the *Nonae Caprotinae* within historical times ; yet a trace of them may perhaps be detected in the tradition that Romulus himself mysteriously disappeared on that very day in the midst of a tremendous thunder-storm, while he was reviewing his army outside the walls of Rome at the Goat's Marsh ("*ad Caprae paludem*"), a name which suggests that the place was not far distant from the wild fig-tree or the goat-fig (*caprificus*), as the Romans called it, where the slave women performed their curious ceremonies.   The legend that he was cut in pieces by the patricians, who carried away the morsels of his body under their robes and buried them in the earth,[3]

[1] W. R. Paton, "The φαρμακοί and the Story of the Fall," *Revue Archéologique,* iv. Série, ix. (1907) pp. 51 *sqq.*

[2] *The Magic Art and the Evolu-*tion of Kings, ii. 313 *sqq.*

[3] Dionysius Halicarnasensis, *Antiquitates Romanae,* ii. 56. 4. Compare Livy, i. 16. 4 ; Plutarch, *Romulus,* 27.

exactly describes the treatment which the Khonds used to accord to the bodies of the human victims for the purpose of fertilizing their fields.[1]   Can the king have played at Rome the same fatal part in the fertilization of fig-trees which, if Mr. Paton is right, was played in Greece by the male victim ? The traditionary time, place, and manner of his death all suggest it.   So many coincidences between the Greek and Roman ceremonies and traditions can hardly be wholly accidental ; and accordingly I incline to think that there may well be an element of truth in Mr. Paton's theory, though it must be confessed that the ancient writers who describe the Greek custom appear to regard it merely as a purification of the city and not at all as a mode of fertilizing fig-trees.[2]   In similar ceremonies, which combine the elements of purification and fertilization, the notion of purification apparently tends gradually to overshadow the notion of fertilization in the minds of those who practise the rites. It seems to have been so in the case of the annual expulsion of Mamurius Veturius from ancient Rome and in the parallel processions of the *Perchten* in modern Europe ; it may have been so also in the case of the human sacrifices at the Thargelia.[3]

The interpretation which I have adopted of the custom of beating the human scapegoat with certain plants is supported by many analogies.   We have already met with examples of a practice of beating sick people with the leaves of certain plants or with branches in order to rid them of noxious influences.[4]   Some of the Dravidian tribes of Northern India,

Beating as a mode of dispelling evil influences.

---

[1] *Spirits of the Corn and of the Wild*, i. 248. Compare *Adonis, Attis, Osiris*, Second Edition, pp. 331 *sqq.*

[2] See, for example, Helladius, cited by Photius, *Bibliotheca*, p. 534 *a*, ed. Im. Bekker, καὶ ἐκράτει τὸ ἔθος ἀεὶ καθαίρειν τὴν πόλιν τοῖς φαρμακοῖς ; Harpocration, *s.v.* φαρμακός (vol. i. p. 298, ed. G. Dindorf), δύο ἄνδρας Ἀθήνησιν ἐξῆγον καθάρσια ἐσομένους τῆς πόλεως ; Scholiast on Aristophanes, *Knights*, 1136, δημοσίους δέ, τοὺς λεγομένους φαρμακούς, οἵπερ καθαίρουσι τὰς πόλεις τῷ ἑαυτῶν φόνῳ.

[3] Mr. Paton ingeniously suggests that in the Biblical narrative of Adam and Eve, who for eating a

particular fruit were condemned to death and driven out of the happy garden with aprons of fig-leaves about their loins (Genesis iii.), we have a reminiscence of a custom of fertilizing fig-trees by a pair of human scapegoats, who, like the victims at the Thargelia, assimilated themselves to the tree by wearing its foliage or fruit. See W. R. Paton, "The φαρμακοί and the Story of the Fall," *Revue Archéologique*, iv. Série, ix. (1907) pp. 55 *sq.*

[4] Above, pp. 2, 186. Compare Plutarch, *Parallela*, 35, where a woman is represented as going from house to house striking sick people with a hammer and bidding them be whole.

who attribute epilepsy, hysteria, and similar maladies to demoniacal possession, endeavour to cure the sufferer by thrashing him soundly with a sacred iron chain, which is believed to have the effect of immediately expelling the demon.[1]   When a herd of camels refuses to drink, the Arabs will sometimes beat the male beasts on the back to drive away the jinn who are riding them and frightening the females.[2]   In Bikol, the south-western part of Luzon, it was generally believed that if the evil spirit Aswang were not properly exorcised he took possession of the bodies of the dead and tormented them.   Hence to deliver a corpse from his clutches the native priestesses used to beat it with a brush or whisk made of the leaves of the aromatic China orange, while they chanted a certain song, throwing their bodies into contortions and uttering shrill cries, as if the evil spirit had entered into themselves.   The soul of the deceased, thus delivered from the cruel tyranny of Aswang, was then free to roam at pleasure along the charming lanes or in the thick shade of the forest.[3]

Beating people to rid them of clinging ghosts.

Sometimes it appears that a beating is administered for the purpose of ridding people of a ghost who may be clinging too closely to their persons ; in such cases the blows, though they descend on the bodies of the living, are really aimed at the spirit of the dead, and have no other object than to drive it away, just as a coachman will flick the back of a horse with his whip to rid the beast of a fly.   At a funeral in the island of Halmahera, before the coffin is lowered into the grave, all the relations whip themselves on the head and shoulders with wands made of plants which

[1] W. Crooke, *Popular Religion and Folk-lore of Northern India* (Westminster, 1896), i. 99, 155 ; *id.*, *Tribes and Castes of the North-Western Provinces and Oudh* (Calcutta, 1896), iii. 333, 441, 445.

[2] A. Certeux et E. H. Carnoy, *L'Algérie Traditionnelle* (Paris and Algiers, 1884), p. 189.

[3] H. Kern, " Een Spanisch schrijver over den godsdienst der heidensche Bikollers," *Bijdragen tot de Taal-Land- en Volkenkunde van Nederlandsch-Indië*, xlvii. (1897) pp. 232

sq. The Spanish authority is Father José Castaño.   An ancient Egyptian relief from Saqqarah represents a mummy at the entrance of the tomb, while the women tear out their hair and the men wave palm-branches, apparently to drive away evil spirits away. The custom has been inherited by the modern Arabs, who similarly beat off the invisible foes with palm-branches. See A. Wiedemann, *Herodots Zweites Buch* (Leipsic, 1890), p. 347.   However, in these cases the blows seem to be administered to the demons and not to the corpse.

are believed to possess the power of keeping off evil spirits. The intention of the custom is said to be to bring back their own spectres or souls and to prevent them from following the ghost; but this may fairly be interpreted to mean that the blows are directed to brushing off the ghost, who would otherwise abstract the soul of the person on whose body he was allowed to settle. This interpretation is strongly confirmed by the practice, observed by the same people on the same occasion, of throwing the trunk of a banana-tree into the grave, and telling the dead man that it is a companion for him; for this practice is expressly intended to prevent the deceased from feeling lonely, and so coming back to fetch away a friend.[1]   When Mr. Batchelor returned to a hut after visiting the grave of an old Aino woman, her relations brought him a bowl of water to the door and requested him to wash his face and hands. While he did so, the women beat him and brushed him down with sacred whittled sticks (*inao*). On enquiring into the meaning of this treatment, he discovered that it was intended to purify him from all uncleanness contracted at the grave through contact with the ghost of the deceased, and that the beating and brushing with the whittled sticks had for its object to drive away all evil influences and diseases with which the ghost of the old woman might have attempted to infect him out of spite for his trespassing on her domain.[2]   The Banmañas of Senegambia think that the soul of a dead infant becomes for a time a wandering and maleficent spirit. Accordingly when a baby dies, all the uncircumcised children of the same sex in the village run about the streets in a band, each armed with three or four supple rods. Some of them enter every house to beg, and while they are doing so, one of the troop, propping himself against the wall with his hands, is lashed by another of the children on his back or legs till the blood flows. Each of the children takes it in turn to be thus whipped. The object of the whipping, we are told, "appears to be to preserve the uncircumcised child

[1] J. M. van Baarda, "Ile de Halmaheira," *Bulletins de la Société d'Anthropologie de Paris*, Quatrième Série, iii. (1892) p. 545. As to throwing a banana-trunk into the grave, see *Spirits of the Corn and of the Wild*, ii. 97.

[2] Rev. J. Batchelor, *The Ainu and their Folk-lore* (London, 1901), p. 550.

from being carried off by its comrade who has just died."[1]
The severe scourgings inflicted on each other by some South
American Indians at ceremonies connected with the dead
may be similarly intended to chase away the dangerous
ghost, who is conceived as sticking like a leech or a bur
to the skin of the living.[2] The ancient Greeks employed
the laurel very commonly as an instrument of ceremonial
purification ;[3] and from the monuments which represent the
purgation of Orestes from the guilt of matricide[4] it seems
probable that the regular rite of cleansing a homicide consisted essentially in sprinkling him with pig's blood and
beating him with a laurel bough, for the purpose, as we may
conjecture, of whisking away the wrathful ghost of his victim,
who was thought to buzz about him like an angry wasp
in summer.   If that was so, the Greek ritual of purification
singularly resembles the Nicobarese ceremony of exorcism ;
for when a man is supposed to be possessed by devils, the
Nicobarese rub him all over with pig's blood and beat him
with bunches of certain leaves, to which a special power of
exorcising demons is attributed.   As fast as each devil is
thus disengaged from his person, it is carefully folded up
in leaves, to be afterwards thrown into the sea at daybreak.[5]

Exorcism of ghosts by means of leaves and pig's blood.

At the autumn festival in Peru people used to strike
each other with torches, saying, "Let all harm go
away."[6]   Every year when the Pleiades reappeared in the
sky, the Guaycurus, an Indian nation of the Gran Chaco,
held a festival of rejoicing, at which men, women, and
children all thrashed each other, expecting thereby to procure health, abundance, and victory over their enemies.[7]

Beating practised by South American Indians and others as a mode of convey-ing good qualities.

---

[1] *Revue d'Ethnographie*, iii. (1885)
pp. 395 *sq.*
[2] R. Schomburgk, *Reisen in
Britisch-Guiana* (Leipsic, 1847–1848),
ii. 457 *sqq.*; Rev. J. H. Bernau,
Missionary Labours in British Guiana
(London, 1847), p. 52 ; C. F. Ph. von
Martius, *Zur Ethnographie Amerika's,
zumal Brasiliens* (Leipsic, 1867), pp.
694 *sq.*; J. Crevaux, *Voyages dans
l'Amérique du Sud* (Paris, 1883), p.
548.
[3] Servius, on Virgil, *Aen.* i. 329.
For more evidence see C. Boetticher,
Der Baumkultus der Hellenen (Berlin,

1856), pp. 369 *sqq.*
[4] See my note on Pausanias, ii. 31.
8, vol. ii. pp. 276 *sqq.*
[5] V. Solomon, "Extracts from
Diaries kept in Car Nicobar," *Journal
of the Anthropological Institute*, xxxii.
(1902) p. 227.
[6] J. de Acosta, *History of the Indies*,
vol. ii. p. 375 (Hakluyt Society, London, 1880).   See above, pp. 128 *sqq.*
[7] P. Lozano, *Descripcion Chorographica del terreno, rios, arboles, y
animales de las dilatadissimas provincias del Gran Chaco, Gualamba,
etc.* (Cordova, 1733), p. 67.   The

Indians of the Quixos, in South America, before they set out on a long hunting expedition, cause their wives to whip them with nettles, believing that this renders them fleeter, and helps them to overtake the peccaries. They resort to the same proceeding as a cure for sickness.[1]   The Roocooyen Indians of French Guiana train up young people in the way they should go by causing them to be stung by ants and wasps ; and at the ceremony held for this purpose the grown-up people improve the occasion by allowing themselves to be whacked by the chief with a stick over the arms, the legs, and the chest. They appear to labour under an impression that this conveys to them all sorts of moral and physical excellences. One of the tribe, ambitious of acquiring the European virtues, begged a French traveller to be so kind as to give him a good hiding. The traveller obligingly did his best to gratify him, and the face of the Indian beamed with gratitude as the blows fell on his naked back.[2] The Delaware Indians had two sovereign remedies for sin ; one was an emetic, the other a thrashing. In the latter case, the remedy was administered by means of twelve different sticks, with which the sinner was belaboured from the soles of his feet up to his neck. In both cases the sins were supposed to be expelled from the body, and to pass out through the throat.[3] At the inauguration of a king in ancient India it was customary for the priests to strike him lightly on the back with sticks. "By beating him with sticks," it was said, "they guide him safely over judicial punishment ; whence the king is exempt from punishment, because they guide him safely over judicial punishment."[4] On the thirtieth of December the heathen of Harran used to receive three, five, or seven blows apiece from a priest with a tamarisk branch. After the beating had been duly admin-

---

reappearance of the Pleiades probably marked the beginning of the year for these people. See *Spirits of the Corn and of the Wild*, i. 307 *sqq.*

[1] G. Osculati, *Esplorazione delle regioni equatoriali lungo il Napo ed il fiume delle Amazzoni* (Milan, 1850), p. 118.

[2] H. Coudreau, *Chez nos Indiens : quatre années dans la Guyane Fran-*

çaise (Paris, 1895), p. 544.

[3] G. H. Loskiel, *History of the Mission of the United Brethren among the Indians in North America* (London, 1794), Part i. p. 37.

[4] *The Satapatha Brahmana*, v. 4. 4. 7, translated by J. Eggeling, Part iii. (Oxford, 1894) p. 108 (*Sacred Books of the East*, vol. xli.).

istered the priest on behalf of the whole community prayed for long life, much offspring, power and glory over all peoples, and the restoration of their ancient kingdom.[1]

Beating people with instruments which possess and impart special virtues.

Sometimes, in the opinion of those who resort to it, the effect of a beating is not merely the negative one of dispelling demoniac or other baneful influences; it confers positive benefits by virtue of certain useful properties supposed to inhere in the instrument with which the beating is administered.[2] Thus among the Kai of German New Guinea, when a man wishes to make his banana shoots bear fruit quickly, he beats them with a stick cut from a banana-tree which has already borne fruit.[3] Here it is obvious that fruitfulness is believed to inhere in a stick cut from a fruitful tree and to be imparted by contact to the young banana plants. Similarly in New Caledonia a man will beat his taro plants lightly with a branch, saying as he does so, "I beat this taro that it may grow," after which he plants the branch in the ground at the end of the field.[4] Among the Indians of Brazil at the mouth of the Amazon, when a man wishes to increase the size of his generative organ, he strikes it with the fruit of a white aquatic plant called an *aninga*, which grows luxuriantly on the banks of the river. The fruit, which is inedible, resembles a banana, and is clearly chosen for this purpose on account of its shape. The ceremony should be performed three days before or after the new moon.[5] In the county of Bekes, in Hungary, barren women are fertilized by being struck with a stick which has first been used to separate pairing dogs.[6] Here a fertilizing virtue

[1] D. Chwolsohn, *Die Ssabier und der Ssabismus* (St. Petersburg, 1856), ii. 34.

[2] On the positive benefits supposed in certain cases to flow from a beating compare S. Reinach, "La flagellation rituelle," *Cultes, Mythes et Religions*, i. (Paris, 1905) pp. 180 *sqq.*; E. S. Hartland, *Primitive Paternity* (London, 1909–1910), i. 102 *sqq.*

[3] Ch. Keysser, "Aus dem Leben der Kaileute," in R. Neuhauss's *Deutsch Neu-Guinea*, iii. (Berlin, 1911) p. 124.

[4] Father Lambert, "Mœurs et Superstitions de la tribu Bélep," *Les Missions Catholique*, xii. (1880) p. 273; *id.*, *Mœurs et Superstitions des Néo-Calédoniens* (Nouméa, 1900), p. 218.

[5] F. J. de Santa-Anna Nery, *Folklore Brésilien* (Paris, 1889), p. 253.

[6] R. Temesváry, *Volksbräuche und Aberglauben in der Geburtshilfe und der Pflege des Neugeborenen in Ungarn* (Leipsic, 1900), p. 8. Compare E. S. Hartland, *Primitive Paternity* (London, 1909–1910), i. 106.

is clearly supposed to be inherent in the stick and to be conveyed by contact to the women.   The Toradjas of Central Celebes think that the plant *Dracaena terminalis* has a strong soul, because when it is lopped, it soon grows up again.   Hence when a man is ill, his friends will sometimes beat him on the crown of the head with *Dracaena* leaves in order to strengthen his weak soul with the strong soul of the plant.[1]   At Mowat in British New Guinea small boys are beaten lightly with sticks during December " to make them grow strong and hardy." [2]

Among the Arabs of Morocco the Great Feast, which is the annual sacrificial festival of Mohammedan peoples, is the occasion when men go about beating people with the kindly intention of healing or preventing sickness and benefiting the sufferers generally.   In some tribes the operator is muffled in the bloody skins of sacrificed sheep, and he strikes everybody within reach of him with a flap of the skin or a foot of the sheep which dangles loose from his arm ; sick people present themselves to him in order to receive the health-giving blows, and mothers bring their little children to him for the same purpose.   Anybody whom he hits on the head will be free from headache.   Nor does he confine his attention to people ; he goes about striking the tents also, in order that they too may receive their share of the blessed influence (*baraka*) that radiates like sunshine from a bloody sheepskin.   From the costume which he wears the masker is known as the " Lion with Sheepskins " ; and he himself participates in the blessings which he diffuses so liberally around him.   Hence in at least one tribe he is generally a person who suffers from some illness, because he expects to be healed by the magic virtue or holiness of the bloody skins.[3]   Similarly, as we shall see presently, in ancient Mexico the men who masqueraded in the skins of the human victims were commonly persons who suffered

[1] A. C. Kruyt, " Het koppensnellen der Toradja's van Midden-Celebes, en zijne beteekenis," *Verslagen en Mededeelingen der Koninklijke Akademie van Wetenschappen*, Afdeeling Letterkunde, iv. Reeks, iii. (Amsterdam, 1899) p. 199.

[2] E. Beardmore, "The Natives of Mowat, Daudai, New Guinea," *Journal of the Anthropological Institute*, xix. (1890) p. 464.
[3] E. Westermarck, "The Popular Ritual of the Great Feast in Morocco," *Folk-lore*, xxii. (1911) pp. 163-165.

from skin disease, because they thought that the bleeding skin of a man who had been killed in the character of a god must surely possess a sovereign virtue for the healing of disease.[1]   In Morocco the skin-clad mummer sometimes operates with sticks instead of a flap of the skin, and some-times the skins in which he is muffled are those of goats instead of sheep, but in all cases the effect, or at least the intention, is probably the same.[2]

European custom of beating · cattle with branches to make them healthy or drive away the witches from them.

In some parts of Eastern and Central Europe a similar custom is very commonly observed in spring.   On the first of March the Albanians strike men and beast with cornel branches, believing that this is very good for their health.[3] In March the Greek peasants of Cos ·switch their cattle, saying, " It is March, and up with your tail ! "   They think that the ceremony benefits the animals, and brings good luck.   It is never observed at any other time of the year.[4] In some parts of Mecklenburg it is customary to beat the cattle before sunrise on the morning of Good Friday with rods of buckthorn, which are afterwards concealed in some secret place where neither sun nor moon can shine on them. The belief is that though the blows light upon the animals, the pain of them is felt by the witches who are riding the beasts.[5]   In the neighbourhood of Iserlohn, in Westphalia, the herdsman rises at peep of dawn on May morning, climbs a hill, and cuts down the young rowan-tree which is the first to catch the beams of the rising sun.   With this he returns to the farm-yard.   The heifer which the farmer desires to "quicken" is then led to the dunghill, and the herdsman strikes it over the hind-quarters, the haunches, and the udders with a branch of the rowan-tree, saying,

> " Quick, quick, quick !
> Bring milk into the dugs.
> The sap is in the birches.
> The heifer receives a name.

---

[1] See below, pp. 298, 302, 304.

[2] E. Westermarck, op. cit. pp. 165 sq., 170, 178. The purificatory character of the rite is duly recognised by Dr. Westermarck (op. cit. p. 178).

[3] J. G. v. Hahn, Albanesische Studien (Jena, 1854), i. 155.

[4] W. H. D. Rouse, " Folk-lore from the Southern Sporades," Folk-lore, x. (1899) p. 179.

[5] K. Bartsch, Sagen, Märchen und Gebräuche aus Mecklenburg (Vienna, 1879–1880), ii. p. 258, § 1348.

> " *Quick, quick, quick !*
> *Bring milk into the dugs.*
> *The sap comes in the beeches,*
> *The leaf comes on the oak.*

> " *Quick, quick, quick !*
> *Bring milk into the dugs.*
> *In the name of the sainted Greta,*
> *Gold-flower shall be thy name,*"

and so on.[1] The intention of the ceremony appears to be
to make sure that the heifer shall in due time yield a
plentiful supply of milk ; and this is perhaps supposed to
be brought about by driving away the witches, who are
particularly apt, as we have seen,[2] to rob the cows of their
milk on the morning of May Day. Certainly in the north-
east of Scotland pieces of rowan-tree and woodbine used to
be placed over the doors of the byres on May Day to keep
the witches from the cows ; sometimes a single rod of rowan,
covered with notches, was found to answer the purpose.
An even more effectual guard against witchcraft was to tie
a small cross of rowan-wood by a scarlet thread to each
beast's tail ; hence people said,

The rowan-tree as a protection against witchcraft.

> " *Rawn-tree in red-threed*
> *Pits the witches t' their speed.*" [3]

In Germany also the rowan-tree is a protection against
witchcraft ;[4] and Norwegian sailors and fishermen carry a
piece of it in their boats for good luck.[5] Thus the benefit
to young cows of beating them with rowan appears to be
not so much the positive one of pouring milk into their
udders, as merely the negative one of averting evil influence ;
and the same may perhaps be said of most of the beatings
with which we are here concerned.

---

[1] J. F. L. Woeste, *Volksüberlie-
ferungen in der Grafschaft Mark*
(Iserlohn, 1848), pp. 25 *sq.* ; A. Kuhn,
*Die Herabkunft des Feuers und des
Göttertranks* [2] (Gütersloh, 1886), pp.
161 *sqq.* The ceremony takes its
name of " quickening " from *Quieke* or
Quickenbaum, a German name for the
rowan-tree. Quicken-tree is also an
English name for the rowan.

[2] *The Magic Art and the Evolution
of Kings,* ii. 52 *sqq.*

[3] Rev. W. Gregor, *Notes on the
Folk-lore of the North-east of Scotland*
(London, 1881), p. 188.

[4] A. Wuttke, *Der deutsche Volksaberglaube* [2] (Berlin, 1869), p. 106,
§ 145.

[5] J. F. L. Woeste, *Volksüberlieferungen in der Grafschaft Mark*
(Iserlohn, 1848), p. 26. Compare
A. Kuhn, *Die Herabkunft des Feuers
und des Göttertranks* [2](Gütersloh, 1886),
p. 179.

European
custom of
beating
people with
branches
at Easter
to do them
good :
" Easter
Smacks."

On Good Friday and the two previous days people in Croatia and Slavonia take rods with them to church, and when the service is over they beat each other "fresh and healthy."[1]   In some parts of Russia people returning from the church on Palm Sunday beat the children and servants who have stayed at home with palm branches, saying, "Sickness into the forest, health into the bones."[2]   A similar custom is widely known under the name of *Schmeckostern* or "Easter Smacks" in some parts of Germany and Austria. The regions in which the practice prevails are for the most part districts in which the people either are or once were predominantly of Slavonic blood, such as East and West Prussia, Voigtland, Silesia, Bohemia, and Moravia.   While the German population call the custom *Schmeckostern*, the Slavonic inhabitants give it, according to their particular language or dialect, a variety of names which signify to beat or scourge.   It is usually observed on Easter Monday, less frequently on Easter Saturday or Easter Sunday.   Troops of boys or lads go from house to house on the morning of Easter Monday beating every girl or woman whom they meet ; they even make their way into the bedrooms, and if they find any girls or women still abed, they compel them with blows to get up.   Even grown-up men indulge themselves in the pastime of going to the houses of friends and relations to inflict the "Easter Smacks."   In some places, for example in the Leobschütz district of Silesia, the boys and men further claim and exercise the right of drenching all the girls and women with water on Easter Monday ; and for this purpose they generally go about armed with squirts, which are not always charged with eau de Cologne.   Next day, Easter Tuesday, the women have the right to retaliate on the men ; however, they do not as a rule go about the streets but confine their operations to their own houses, beating and chasing from their beds any lads or men they can find lying in them.   Children are less discriminating in their "Easter Smacks," which they bestow impartially on parents and relations, friends and strangers, without observing the subtle distinction of sex.   In many places it is only

[1] F. S. Krauss, *Kroatien und Slavonien* (Vienna, 1889), p. 108.

[2] W. Mannhardt, *Baumkultus*, p. 257.

the women who are privileged to receive the smacks. The instrument with which the beating is administered is in some districts, such as Lithuania, Samland, and Neumark, a twig or branch of birch on which the fresh green leaves have just sprouted. If the birch-trees have not budded in time, it is customary to keep the rods in pickle for days or even weeks, nursing them tenderly in warm water ; and if that measure also fails, they are heated in the stove-pipe. But more commonly the instrument of torture is a branch of willow with catkins on it, which has also been nursed in warm water or the chimney so as to be ripe for execution on Easter Monday. A number of these birch or willow twigs are usually tied together into a switch, and ornamented with motley ribbons and pieces of silk paper, so that they present the appearance of a nosegay ; indeed, in northern Bohemia spring flowers form part of the decoration. In some places, particularly in Silesia and Moravia, pieces of licorice root are substituted for willow twigs ; or again in the vine-growing districts of Bohemia vine-branches are used for the same purpose. Sometimes a scourge made of leather straps of various colours takes the place of a green bough. The blows are commonly inflicted on the hands and feet ; and in some places, particularly in Bohemia, the victims are expected to reward their tormentors with a present of red Easter eggs ; nay sometimes a woman is bound to give an egg for every blow she receives. In the afternoon the lads carry their eggs to high ground and let them roll down the slope ; he whose egg reaches the bottom first, wins all the rest. The beating is supposed to bring good luck to the beaten, or to warrant them against flies and vermin during the summer, or to save them from pains in their back throughout the whole year. At Gilgenburg in Masuren the rods or bundles of twigs are afterwards laid by and used to drive the cattle out to pasture for the first time after their winter confinement.[1]

---

[1] Th. Vernaleken, *Mythen und Bräuche des Volkes in Österreich* (Vienna, 1859), pp. 300 *sq.* ; O. Freiherr von Reinsberg - Düringsfeld, *Fest-Kalender aus Böhmen* (Prague, preface dated 1861), pp. 163-167 ; A. Peter, *Volksthümliches aus Öster-reichisch-Schlesien* (Troppau, 1865–1867), ii. 285 ; J. A. E. Köhler, *Volks-brauch, Aberglauben, Sagen und andre alte Überlieferungen im Voigtlande* (Leipsic, 1867), pp. 173 *sq.* ; M.

European
custom of
beating
people with
branches
in the
Christmas
holidays
(Holy
Innocents'
Day, etc.)
to do them
good.

In some parts of Germany and Austria a custom like that of " Easter Smacks " is observed at the Christmas holidays, especially on Holy Innocents' Day, the twenty-eighth of December. Young men and women beat each other mutually, but on different days, with branches of fresh green, whether birch, willow, or fir. Thus, for example, among the Germans of western Bohemia it is customary on St. Barbara's Day (the fourth of December) to cut twigs or branches of birch and to steep them in water in order that they may put out leaves or buds. They are afterwards used by each sex to beat the other on subsequent days of the Christmas holidays. In some villages branches of willow or cherry-trees or rosemary are employed for the same purpose. With these green boughs, sometimes tied in bundles with red or green ribbons, the young men go about beating the young women on the morning of St. Stephen's Day (the twenty-sixth of December) and also on Holy Innocents' Day (the twenty-eighth of December). The beating is inflicted on the hands, feet, and face ; and in Neugramatin it is said that she who is not thus beaten with fresh green will not herself be fresh and green. As the blows descend, the young men recite verses importing that the beating is administered as a compliment and in order to benefit the health of the victim. For the service

Toeppen, *Aberglauben aus Masuren*[2] (Danzig, 1867), pp. 69 *sq.* ; A. Wuttke, *Der deutsche Volksaberglaube*[2] (Berlin, 1869), p. 70, § 83 ; W. Mannhardt, *Der Baumkultus* (Berlin, 1875), pp. 258-263 ; W. Müller, *Beiträge zur Volkskunde der Deutschen in Mähren* (Vienna and Olmütz, 1893), pp. 322, 399 *sq.* ; Dr. F. Tetzner, "Die Tschechen und Mährer in Schlesien," *Globus*, lxxviii. (1900) p. 340 ; P. Drechsler, *Sitte, Brauch und Volksglaube in Schlesien* (Leipsic, 1903-1906), pp. 100 *sq.* ; Alois John, *Sitte, Brauche und Volksglaube im deutschen Westböhmen* (Prague, 1905), pp. 67 *sq.* Mannhardt's whole discussion of what he calls "the Blow with the Rod of Life" (" *Der Schlag mit der Lebensrute* ") deserves to be studied. See his *Baumkultus*, pp.

251-303 ; and compare his treatment of the same theme, " Der Schlag mit dem Februum," *Mythologische Forschungen* (Strasburg, 1884), pp. 113-153. The custom of "Easter Smacks" can be traced back to the twelfth century, when the practice was for women to beat their husbands on Easter Monday and for husbands to retaliate on their wives on Easter Tuesday. See J. Belethus, *Rationale Divinorum Officiorum*, cap. 120, appended to G. Durandus's *Rationale Divinorum Officiorum* (Lyons, 1584), p. 546 recto : " *Notandum quoque est in plerisque regionibus secundo die post Pascha mulieres maritos suos verberare, ac vicissim viros eas tertio die quemadmodum licebat servis in Decembri dominos suos impune accusare.*"

which they thus render the damsels they are rewarded by them with cakes, brandy, or money. Early in the morning of New Year's Day the lasses pay off the lads in the same kind.[1] A similar custom is also observed iŋ central and south-west Germany, especially in Voigtland. Thus in Voigtland and the whole of the Saxon Erz-gebirge the lads beat the lasses and women on the second day of the Christmas holidays with something green, such as rosemary or juniper ; and if possible the beating is inflicted on the women as they lie in bed. As they beat them, the lads say

"Fresh and green ! Pretty and fine !
Gingerbread and brandy-wine !"

The last words refer to the present of gingerbread and brandy which the lads expect to receive from the lasses for the trouble of thrashing them. Next day the lasses and women retaliate on the lads and men.[2] In Thüringen on Holy Innocents' Day (the twenty-eighth of December) children armed with rods and green boughs go about the streets beating passers-by and demanding a present in return ; they even make their way into the houses and beat the maidservants. In Orlagau the custom is called "whipping with fresh green." On the second day of the Christmas holidays the girls go to their parents, godparents, relations, and friends, and beat them with fresh green branches of fir ; next day the boys and lads do the same. The words spoken while the beating is being administered are " Good morning ! fresh green ! Long life ! You must give us a bright thaler," and so on.[3]

In these European customs the intention of beating persons, especially of the other sex, with fresh green leaves appears unquestionably to be the beneficent one of renewing

The intention of beating people with

[1] Alois John, *Sitte, Brauch und Volksglaube im deutschen Westböhmen* (Prague, 1905), pp. 5, 23 *sq.*, 25, 28. Compare Th. Vernaleken, *Mythen und Bräuche des Volkes in Österreich* (Vienna, 1859), pp. 301 *sq.*

[2] J. A. E. Köhler, *Volksbrauch, Aberglauben, Sagen und andre alte Überlieferungen im Voigtlande* (Leipsic, 1867), p. 174 ; W. Mannhardt, *Baum-*

kultus, pp. 264 *sq.*

[3] August Witzschel, *Sagen, Sitten und Gebräuche aus Thüringen* (Vienna, 1878), pp. 181 *sq.* ; W. Mannhardt, *Baumkultus*, p. 265. Compare G. Bilfinger, *Untersuchungen über die Zeitrechnung der alten Germanen*, ii., *Das Germanische Julfest* (Stuttgart, 1901), pp. 85 *sq.*

fresh green
leaves is
to renew
their life
and vigour.
their life and vigour, whether the purpose is supposed to be accomplished directly and positively by imparting the vital energy of the fresh green to the persons, or negatively and indirectly by dispelling any injurious influences, such as the machinations of witches and demons, by which the persons may be supposed to be beset. The application of the blows by the one sex to the other, especially by young men to young women, suggests that the beating is or was originally intended above all to stimulate the reproductive powers of the men or women who received it ; and the pains taken to ensure that the branches with which the strokes are given should have budded or blossomed out just before their services are wanted speak strongly in favour of the view that in these customs we have a deliberate attempt to transfuse a store of vital energy from the vegetable to the animal world.

Hence the
custom of
beating
the human
victims
at the
Thargelia
with fig-
branches
and squills
was prob-
ably a
charm to
increase
their re-
productive
energies.
These analogies, accordingly, support the interpretation which, following my predecessors W. Mannhardt and Mr. W. R. Paton, I have given of the beating inflicted on the human victims at the Greek harvest festival of the Thargelia. That beating, being administered to the generative organs of the victims by fresh green plants and branches, is most naturally explained as a charm to increase the reproductive energies of the men or women either by communicating to them the fruitfulness of the plants and branches, or by ridding them of maleficent influences ; and this interpretation is confirmed by the observation that the two victims represented the two sexes, one of them standing for the men in general and the other for the women. The season of the year when the ceremony was performed, namely the time of the corn harvest, tallies well with the theory that the rite had an agricultural significance. Further, that it was above all intended to fertilize the fig-trees is strongly suggested by the strings of black and white figs which were hung round the necks of the victims, as well as by the blows which were given their genital organs with the branches of a wild fig-tree ; since this procedure closely resembles the procedure which ancient and modern husbandmen in Greek lands have regularly resorted to for the purpose of actually fertilizing their fig-trees. When we remember what an important part the artificial fertilization of the date palm-tree appears

to have played of old not only in the husbandry but in the religion of Mesopotamia,[1] there seems no reason to doubt that the artificial fertilization of the fig-tree may in like manner have vindicated for itself a place in the solemn ritual of Greek religion.

If these considerations are just, we must apparently conclude that while the human victims at the Thargelia certainly appear in later classical times to have figured chiefly as public scapegoats, who carried away with them the sins, misfortunes, and sorrows of the whole people, at an earlier time they may have been looked on as embodiments of vegetation, perhaps of the corn but particularly of the fig-trees ; and that the beating which they received and the death which they died were intended primarily to brace and refresh the powers of vegetation then beginning to droop and languish under the torrid heat of the Greek summer.

Hence the human victims at the Thargelia may have primarily represented spirits of vegetation.

The view here taken of the Greek scapegoat, if it is correct, obviates an objection which might otherwise be brought against the main argument of this book. To the theory that the priest of Aricia was slain as a representative of the spirit of the grove,[2] it might have been objected that such a custom has no analogy in classical antiquity. But reasons have now been given for believing that the human being periodically and occasionally slain by the Asiatic Greeks was regularly treated as an embodiment of a divinity of vegetation. Probably the persons whom the Athenians kept to be sacrificed were similarly treated as divine. That they were social outcasts did not matter. On the primitive view a man is not chosen to be the mouth-piece or embodiment of a god on account of his high moral qualities or social rank. The divine afflatus descends equally on the good and the bad, the lofty and the lowly. If then the civilized Greeks

Parallel between the human sacrifices at the Thargelia and the bloody ritual of the Arician Grove.

---

[1] *The Magic Art and the Evolution of Kings*, ii. 24 *sq.* It is highly significant that the heathen of Harran celebrated the marriage festival of all the gods and goddesses in the very month (March) in which the artificial fertilization of the date-palm was effected (D. Chwolsohn, *Die Ssabier und der Ssabismus*, St. Petersburg, 1856, ii. 36, 251). The frequency with which the artificial fertilization of the palm-tree by a mythical winged figure is represented on Assyrian monuments furnishes strong evidence of the religious and economic importance of the ceremony.

[2] *The Magic Art and the Evolution of Kings*, i. 40 *sqq.*, ii. 376 *sqq.*

of Asia and Athens habitually sacrificed men whom they regarded as incarnate gods, there can be no inherent improbability in the supposition that at the dawn of history a similar custom was observed by the semi-barbarous Latins in the Arician Grove.

CHAPTER VII

KILLING THE GOD IN MEXICO

BY no people does the custom of sacrificing the human The custom of sacrificing human represent- atives of the gods among the Aztecs of Mexico. representative of a god appear to have been observed so commonly and with so much solemnity as by the Aztecs of ancient Mexico. With the ritual of these remarkable sacrifices we are well acquainted, for it has been fully described by the Spaniards who conquered Mexico in the sixteenth century, and whose curiosity was naturally excited by the discovery in this distant region of a barbarous and cruel religion which presented many curious points of analogy to the doctrine and ritual of their own church. " They took a captive," says the Jesuit Acosta, " such as they thought good ; and afore they did sacrifice him unto their idols, they gave him the name of the idol, to whom he should be sacrificed, and apparelled him with the same ornaments like their idol, saying, that he did represent the same idol. And during the time that this representation lasted, which was for a year in some feasts, in others six months, and in others less, they reverenced and worshipped him in the same manner as the proper idol ; and in the meantime he did eat, drink, and was merry. When he went through the streets, the people came forth to worship him, and every one brought him an alms, with children and sick folks, that he might cure them, and bless them, suffering him to do all things at his pleasure, only he was accompanied with ten or twelve men lest he should fly. And he (to the end he might be reverenced as he passed) sometimes sounded upon a small flute, that the people might prepare to worship him. The feast being come, and he grown fat, they killed

275

him, opened him, and ate him, making a solemn sacrifice of him." [1]

Sacrifice
of a man
in the
character
of the
great god
Tezcat-
lipoca at
the festival
of Toxcatl
in the
fifth Aztec
month.

This general description of the custom may now be illustrated by particular examples. Thus at the festival called Toxcatl, the greatest festival of the Mexican year, a young man was annually sacrificed in the character of Tezcatlipoca, "the god of gods," after having been maintained and worshipped as that great deity in person for a whole year. According to the old Franciscan monk Sahagun, our best authority on the Aztec religion, the sacrifice of the human god fell at Easter or a few days later, so that, if he is right, it would correspond in date as well as in character to the Christian festival of the death and resurrection of the Redeemer.[2] More exactly he tells us that the sacrifice took place on the first day of the fifth Aztec month, which according to him began on the twenty-third or twenty-seventh day of April.[3] However, according to other Spanish authorities of the sixteenth century the festival lasted from the ninth to the nineteenth day of May, and the sacrifice of the human victim in the character of the

---

[1] J. de Acosta, *The Natural and Moral History of the Indies* (London, Hakluyt Society, 1880), ii. 323. I have modernized the spelling of the old English translator, whose version was originally published in 1604. Acosta resided both in Peru and Mexico, and published his work at Seville in 1590. It was reprinted in a convenient form at Madrid in 1894. Compare A. de Herrera, *General History of the Vast Continent and Islands of America*, translated by Captain John Stevens (London, 1725–1726), iii. 207 *sq.*

[2] B. de Sahagun, *Histoire Générale des Choses de la Nouvelle - Espagne*, traduite par D. Jourdanet et R. Siméon (Paris, 1880), pp. 61 *sq.*: "*On appelait le cinquième moi* toxcatl. *Au premier jour on faisait une grande fête en l'honneur du dieu appelé* Titlacauan, *autrement dit* Tezcatlipoca, *que l'on croyait être le dieu des dieux. C'était en son honneur que l'on tuait, le jour de sa fête, un jeune homme choisi. . . . Cette fête était la principale de*

toutes, comme qui dirait la Pâque, et, en réalité, elle se célébrait aux environs de la Pâque de résurrection, ou quelques jours après." Compare J. de Torquemada, *Monarquia Indiana*, lib. x. cap. 14, vol. ii. p. 256 (Madrid, 1723). As to Tezcatlipoca, the greatest of the Mexican gods, see J. G. Müller, *Geschichte der amerikanischen Urreligionen* (Bâle, 1867), pp. 613 *sqq.*; H. H. Bancroft, *The Native Races of the Pacific States* (London, 1875–1876), iii. 199 *sqq.*, 237 *sqq.*; E. Seler, *Altmexikanische Studien*, ii. (Berlin, 1899) pp. 125 *sqq.* (*Veröffentlichungen aus dem königlichen Museum für Völkerkunde*, vol. vi. Heft 2/4).

[3] On the twenty-third of April according to the Spanish text of Sahagun's work as translated in French by D. Jourdanet and R. Simeon (p. 52); the twenty-seventh of April according to the Aztec text of Sahagun's work as translated into German by Professor E. Seler (*Altmexikanische Studien*, ii. 194).

god was performed on the last of these days.[1]   An eminent
modern authority, Professor E. Seler, is of opinion that the
festival originally celebrated the beginning of the year, and
that it fell on the day when the sun on his passage north-
ward to the tropic of Cancer stood in the zenith over the
city of Mexico, which in the early part of the sixteenth
century would be the ninth or tenth day of May (old style)
or the nineteenth or twentieth day of May (new style).[2]
Whatever the exact date of the celebration may have been,
we are told that the " feast was not made to any other end,
but to demand rain, in the same manner that we solemnize
the Rogations ; and this feast was always in May, which is
the time that they have most need of rain in those countries." [3]

At this festival the great god died in the person of one
human representative and came to life again in the person
of another, who was destined to enjoy the fatal honour of
divinity for a year and to perish, like all his predecessors, at
the end of it.   The young man singled out for this high dignity
was carefully chosen from among the captives on the ground
of his personal beauty.   He had to be of unblemished body,
slim as a reed and straight as a pillar, neither too tall nor
too short.   If through high living he grew too fat, he was
obliged to reduce himself by drinking salt water.   And in
order that he might behave in his lofty station with
becoming grace and dignity he was carefully trained to
comport himself like a gentleman of the first quality, to
speak correctly and elegantly, to play the flute, to smoke

*The train-
ing and
equipment
of the
human
god.*

[1] J. de Acosta, *Natural and Moral
History of the Indies* (Hakluyt Society,
London, 1880), ii. 378, 380 ; Diego
Duran, *Historia de las Indias de
Nueva España* (Mexico, 1867–1880),
ii. 99, 101 ; *Manuscrit Ramirez, Histoire de l'Origine des Indiens qui
habitent la Nouvelle Espagne selon
leurs traditions*, publié par D. Charnay
(Paris, 1903), pp. 159, 160 *sq.* According to Clavigero, the fifth Mexican
month, in which the sacrifice of the
human representative of Tezcatlipoca
took place, began on the 17th of May
(*History of Mexico*, translated by C.
Cullen, London, 1807, i. 299) ; but
this must be an error.

[2] E. Seler, *Altmexikanische Studien*,
ii. (Berlin, 1899) pp. 117 note,[1] 121-
125, 153 *sq.*, 166 *sq.* (*Veröffentlichungen aus dem königlichen Museum
für Völkerkunde*, vol. vi. Heft 2/4).

[3] J. de Acosta, *op. cit.* ii. 380 ;
Diego Duran, *op. cit.* ii. 101 ; *Manuscrit Ramirez, Histoire de l'Origine
des Indiens qui habitent la Nouvelle
Espagne selon leurs traditions*, publié
par D. Charnay (Paris, 1903), p. 160 ;
J. de Torquemada, *Monarquia Indiana*,
lib. x. cap. 14, vol. ii. p. 257 (Madrid,
1723).   I have modernized the spelling
of Acosta's old translator (Edward
Grimston).

cigars and to snuff at flowers with a dandified air.   He was
honourably lodged in the temple where the nobles waited on
him and paid him homage, bringing him meat and serving
like a prince.   The king himself saw to it that he was
apparelled in gorgeous attire, "for already he esteemed him
as a god."   Eagle down was gummed to his head and white
cock's feathers were stuck in his hair, which drooped to his
girdle.   A wreath of flowers like roasted maize crowned
his brows, and a garland of the same flowers passed over
his shoulders and under his arm-pits.   Golden ornaments
hung from his nose, golden armlets adorned his arms,
golden bells jingled on his legs at every step he took ;
earrings of turquoise dangled from his ears, bracelets
of turquoise bedecked his wrists ; necklaces of shells
encircled his neck and depended on his breast ; he wore
a mantle of network, and round his middle a rich waist-
cloth.   When this bejewelled exquisite lounged through the
streets playing on his flute, puffing at a cigar, and smell-
ing at a nosegay, the people whom he met threw themselves on the earth before him and prayed to him with
sighs and tears, taking up the dust in their hands and
putting it in their mouths in token of the deepest humilia-
tion and subjection.   Women came forth with children in
their arms and presented them to him, saluting him as a
god.   For "he passed for our Lord God ; the people
acknowledged him as the Lord."   All who thus worshipped
him on his passage he saluted gravely and courteously.
Lest he should flee, he was everywhere attended by a guard of
eight pages in the royal livery, four of them with shaven crowns
like the palace-slaves, and four of them with the flowing
locks of warriors ; and if he contrived to escape, the captain
of the guard had to take his place as the representative of
the god and to die in his stead.   Twenty days before he
was to die, his costume was changed, and four damsels,
delicately nurtured and bearing the names of four goddesses
—the Goddess of Flowers, the Goddess of the Young Maize,
the Goddess "Our Mother among the Water," and the
Goddess of Salt—were given him to be his brides, and with
them he consorted.   During the last five days divine
honours were showered on the destined victim.   The king

remained in his palace while the whole court went after the human god. Solemn banquets and dances followed each other in regular succession and at appointed places. On the last day the young man, attended by his wives and pages, embarked in a canoe covered with a royal canopy and was ferried across the lake to a spot where a little hill rose from the edge of the water. It was called the Mountain of Parting, because here his wives bade him a last farewell. Then, accompanied only by his pages, be repaired to a small and lonely temple by the wayside. Like the Mexican temples in general, it was built in the form of a pyramid ; and as the young man ascended the stairs he broke at every step one of the flutes on which he had played in the days of his glory. On reaching the summit he was seized and held down by the priests on his back upon a block of stone, while one of them cut open his breast, thrust his hand into the wound, and wrenching out his heart held it up in sacrifice to the sun. The body of the dead god was not, like the bodies of common victims, sent rolling down the steps of the temple, but was carried down to the foot, where the head was cut off and spitted on a pike. Such was the regular end of the man who personated the greatest god of the Mexican pantheon.[1]

But he was not the only man who played the part of a

---

[1] B. de Sahagun, *Histoire Générale des Choses de la Nouvelle Espagne*, traduite par D. Jourdanet, et R. Siméon (Paris, 1880), pp. 61 *sq.*, 96-99, 103 ; E. Seler, *Altmexikanische Studien*, ii. (Berlin, 1899), pp. 116-165, 194-209 (the latter passage contains the Aztec text of Sahagun's account with a German translation) ; J. de Acosta, *The Natural and Moral History of the Indies* (Hakluyt Society, London, 1880), pp. 350 *sq.* ; *Manuscrit Ramirez, Histoire de l'Origine des Indiens qui habitent la Nouvelle Espagne selon leurs traditions*, publié par D. Charnay (Paris, 1903), pp. 157 *sqq.*, 180 *sq.* ; Diego Duran, *Historia de las Indias de Nueva España* (Mexico, 1867-1880), ii. 98-105 ; J. de Torquemada, *Monarquia Indiana*, lib. x. cap. 14, vol. ii. pp. 256 *sqq.* (Madrid, 1723) ; F. S. Clavigero, *History of Mexico*, translated by Charles Cullen, Second Edition (London, 1807), i. 300 ; Brasseur de Bourbourg, *Histoire des Nations civilisées du Mexique et de l'Amérique-Centrale* (Paris, 1857-1859), iii. 510-512 ; H. H. Bancroft, *The Native Races of the Pacific States* (London, 1875 – 1876), iii. 319 *sq.* According to Torquemada the flesh of the human victim was eaten by the elders " as a sacred and divine flesh " ; but this is not mentioned by the other authorities of the sixteenth century cited above. Elsewhere (*Spirits of the Corn and of the Wild*, ii. 92 *sq.*) I cited this cannibal banquet as an example of a sacramental communion with the deity ; but the silence of most early writers on the point makes it doubtful whether the custom has been correctly reported by Torquemada and later writers.

Sacrifice of a man in the character of the great Mexican god Vitzilo-pochtli (Huitzilo-pochtli) in the month of May.

god and was sacrificed as such in the month of May. The great god Vitzilopochtli or Huitzilopochtli was also worshipped at the same season. An image of him was made out of dough in human shape, arrayed in all the ornaments of the deity, and set up in his temple. But the god had also his living representative in the person of a young man, who, like the human representative of Tezcatlipoca, personated the divinity for a whole year and was sacrificed at the end. In the month of May it was the duty of the divine man, destined so soon to die, to lead the dances which formed a conspicuous feature of the festivities. Courtiers and warriors, old and young, danced in winding figures, holding each other by the hand ; and with them danced young women, who had taken a vow to dance with roasted maize. On their heads these damsels wore crowns of roasted maize ; festoons of maize hung from their shoulders and crossed on their breasts ; their faces were painted, and their arms and legs were covered with red feathers. Dancing in this attire the damsels were said to hold the god Vitzilopochtli in their arms ; but they conducted themselves with the utmost gravity and decorum. If any man so far forgot himself as to toy with one of the maidens, the elder warriors dealt with him promptly and severely, reproaching him for the sacrilege of which he had been guilty. Sahagun compares these May dances to the dances of peasant men and women in old Castile, and the crowns of maize worn by the girls he compares to the garlands of flowers worn by rustic Castilian maidens in the month of May. So they danced till nightfall. Next morning they danced again, and in the course of the day the man who represented the god Vitzilopochtli was put to death. He had the privilege of choosing the hour when he was to die. When the fatal moment drew near, they clothed him in a curious dress of paper painted all over with black circles ; on his head they clapped a paper mitre decked with eagle feathers and nodding plumes, among which was fastened a blood-stained obsidian knife. Thus attired, with golden bells jingling at his ankles, he led the dance at all the balls of the festival, and thus attired he went to his death. The priests seized him, stretched him out, gripped him tight, cut out his heart, and held it up to the sun. His head was severed from the trunk and spiked beside the head of the other human god, who had been sacrificed not long before.[1]

In Cholula, a wealthy trading city of Mexico, the merchants worshipped a god named Quetzalcoatl. His image, set upon a richly decorated altar or pedestal in a spacious temple, had the body of a man but the head of a bird, with a red beak surmounted by a crest, the face dyed yellow, with a black band running from the eyes to below the beak, and the tongue lolling out. On its head was a paper mitre painted black, white, and red ; on its neck a large golden jewel in the shape of butterfly wings ; about its body a feather mantle, black, red, and white ; golden socks and golden sandals encased its legs and feet. In the right hand the image wielded a wooden instrument like a sickle, and in the left a buckler covered with the black and white plumage of sea-birds.[2] The festival of this god was celebrated on the third day of February. Forty days before the festival " the merchants bought a slave well proportioned, without any fault or blemish, either of sickness or of hurt, whom they did attire with the ornaments of the idol, that he might represent it forty days. Before his clothing they did cleanse him, washing him twice in a lake, which they called the lake of the gods ; and being purified, they attired him like the idol. During these forty days, he was much respected for his sake whom he represented. By

Sacrifice of a man in the character of the great Mexican god Quetzalcoatl in the month of February.

[1] B. de Sahagun, *Histoire Générale des Choses de la Nouvelle Espagne*, traduite par D. Jourdanet et R. Siméon (Paris, 1880), pp. 99-104 ; E. Seler, *Altmexikanische Studien*, ii. (Berlin, 1899) pp. 159-165, 202-209 ; F. S. Clavigero, *History of Mexico*, translated by Ch. Cullen, Second Edition (London, 1807), i. 301-303 ; Brasseur de Bourbourg, *Histoire des Nations civilisées du Mexique et de l'Amérique-Centrale*, iii. 512-516 ; H. H. Bancroft, *The Native Races of the Pacific States*, ii. 321-324. As to the dances of the maidens wearing garlands of maize, see also J. de Acosta, *Natural and Moral History of the Indies* (London, 1880), ii. 380.

[2] J. de Acosta, *The Natural and*

Moral History of the Indies (Hakluyt Society, London, 1880), ii. 321 ; Diego Duran, *Historia de las Indias de Nueva España* (Mexico, 1867–1880), ii. 118-120 ; *Manuscrit Ramirez, Histoire de l'Origine des Indiens qui habitent la Nouvelle Espagne selon leurs traditions*, publié par D. Charnay (Paris, 1903), pp. 182 *sq.* Acosta's description of the idol is abridged. As to the Mexican god Quetzalcoatl, worshipped especially by the people of Cholula, see J. G. Müller, *Geschichte der amerikanischen Urreligionen* (Bâle, 1867), pp. 577 *sqq.* ; H. H. Bancroft, *The Native Races of the Pacific States* (London, 1875–1876), iii. 248 *sqq.*

night they did imprison him (as hath been said) lest he
should fly, and in the morning they took him out of prison,
setting him upon an eminent place, where they served him,
giving him exquisite meats to eat.   After he had eaten, they
put a chain of flowers about his neck, and many nosegays
in his hands.   He had a well-appointed guard, with much
people to accompany him.   When he went through the city,
he went dancing and singing through all the streets, that he
might be known for the resemblance of their god, and when
he began to sing, the women and little children came forth
of their houses to salute him, and to offer unto him as to
their god.   Two old men of the ancients of the temple came
unto him nine days before the feast, and humbling themselves before him, they said with a low and submissive voice,
'Sir, you must understand that nine days hence the exercise
of dancing and singing doth end, and thou must then die';
and then he must answer, 'In a good hour.'   They call this
ceremony *Neyòlo Maxilt Ileztli*, which is to say, the adver-
tisement; and when they did thus advertise him, they took
very careful heed whether he were sad, or if he danced as
joyfully as he was accustomed, the which if he did not as
cheerfully as they desired, they made a foolish superstition
in this manner.   They presently took the sacrifizing razors,
the which they washed and cleansed from the blood of men
which remained of the former sacrifices.   Of this washing
they made a drink mingled with another liquor made of
cacao, giving it him to drink; they said that this would
make him forget what had been said unto him, and would
make him in a manner insensible, returning to his former
dancing and mirth.   They said, moreover, that he would
offer himself cheerfully to death, being enchanted with this
drink.   The cause why they sought to take from him this
heaviness, was, for that they held it for an ill augury, and a
fore-telling of some great harm.   The day of the feast
being come, after they had done him much honour, sung,
and given him incense, the sacrificers took him about midnight and did sacrifice him, as hath been said, offering his
heart unto the Moon, the which they did afterwards cast
against the idol, letting the body fall to the bottom of the
stairs of the temple, where such as had offered him took him

up, which were the merchants, whose feast it was. Then having carried him into the chiefest man's house amongst them, the body was drest with diverse sauces, to celebrate (at the break of day) the banquet and dinner of the feast, having first bid the idol good morrow, with a small dance, which they made whilst the day did break, and that they prepared the sacrifice. Then did all the merchants assemble at this banquet, especially those which made it a trafick to buy and sell slaves, who were bound every year to offer one, for the resemblance of their god. This idol was one of the most honoured in all the land ; and therefore the temple where he was, was of great authority." [1]

The honour of living for a short time in the character of a god and dying a violent death in the same capacity was not restricted to men in Mexico ; women were allowed, or rather compelled, to enjoy the glory and to share the doom as representatives of goddesses. Thus in the seventh month of their year, which corresponded roughly to June, the Aztecs celebrated a festival in honour of Huixtocihuatl, the Goddess of Salt. She was said to be a sister of the Rain Gods, but having quarrelled with them she was banished and driven to take up her abode in the salt water. Being of an ingenious turn of mind, she invented the process of extracting salt by means of pans ; hence she was worshipped by all salt-makers as their patron goddess. Her garments were yellow ; on her head she wore a mitre surmounted by bunches of waving green plumes, which shone with greenish iridescent hues in the sun. Her robe and petticoats were embroidered with patterns simulating the waves of the sea.

Sacrifice of a woman in the character of the Mexican Goddess of Salt in the month of June.

---

[1] J. de Acosta, *The Natural and Moral History of the Indies* (Hakluyt Society, London, 1880), ii. 384-386. I have modernized the old translator's spelling. The accounts of Duran and the anonymous author of the Ramirez manuscript agree verbally with that of Acosta. It is plain that Acosta and Duran drew on the same source, which may be the Ramirez manuscript. However, Duran is the only one of the three who gives the date of the festival (the third of February). See Diego Duran, *Historia de las Indias de Nueva España* (Mexico, 1867 – 1880), ii. 120 *sq.* ; *Manuscrit Ramirez, Histoire de l'Origine des Indiens qui habitent la Nouvelle Espagne selon leurs traditions*, publié par de Charnay (Paris, 1903), pp. 182 *sqq.* Compare A. de Herrera, *The General History of the Vast Continent and Islands of America*, translated by Captain John Stevens (London, 1725 – 1726), iii. 218 *sq.* ; J. G. Müller, *Geschichte der amerikanischen Urreligionen* (Bâle, 1867), pp. 589 *sq.* ; H. H. Bancroft, *The Native Races of the Pacific States* (London, 1875–1876), iii. 286.

Golden ear-rings in the form of flowers dangled at her ears ; golden bells jingled at her ankles.   In one hand she carried a round shield painted with the leaves of a certain plant and adorned with drooping fringes of parrots' feathers ; in the other hand she carried a stout baton ending in a knob and bedecked with paper, artificial flowers, and feathers.   For ten days before her festival a woman personated the goddess and wore her gorgeous costume.   It was her duty during these days to lead the dances which at this season were danced by the women and girls of the salt-makers.   They danced, young, old, and children, in a ring, all holding a cord, their heads crowned with garlands of a fragrant flower (*Artemisia laciniata*) and singing airs in a shrill soprano.   In the middle of the ring danced the woman who represented the goddess, with her golden bells jingling at every step, brandishing her shield, and marking the time of the dance and song with her baton.   On the last day, the eve of the festival, she had to dance all night without resting till break of day, when she was to die.   Old women supported her in the weary task, and they all danced together, arm in arm. With her, too, danced the slaves who were to die with her in the morning.   When the hour was come, they led her, still personating the goddess, up the steps of the temple of Tlaloc, followed by the doomed captives.   Arrived at the summit of the pyramid, the butchery began with the captives, while the woman stood looking on.   Her turn being come, they threw her on her back on the block, and while five men held her down and two others compressed her throat with a billet of wood or the sword of a sword-fish to prevent her from screaming, the priest cut open her breast with his knife, and thrusting his hand into the wound tore out her heart and flung it into a bowl.   When all was over, the salt-makers who had witnessed the sacrifice went home to drink and make merry.[1]

[1] B. de Sahagun, *Histoire Générale des Choses de la Nouvelle Espagne*, traduite par D. Jourdanet et R. Siméon (Paris, 1880), pp. 64, 115-117 ; J. de Torquemada, *Monarquia Indiana* (Madrid, 1723), lib. x. cap. 18, vol. ii. p. 268.   Compare F. S. Clavigero, *History of Mexico*, translated by C. Cullen (London, 1807), i. 305 ; Brasseur de Bourbourg, *Histoire des Nations Civilisées du Mexique et de l'Amérique-Centrale*, iii. 517 *sq.* ; H. H. Bancroft, *The Native Races of the Pacific States*, ii. 325-327.

Again, in the eighth month of the Mexican year, which answered to the latter end of June and the early part of July, the Aztecs sacrificed a woman who personated Xilonen, the goddess of the young maize-cobs (*xilotl*). The festival at which the sacrifice took place was held on the tenth day of the month about the time when the maize is nearly ripe, and when fibres shooting forth from the green ear shew that the grain is fully formed. For eight days before the festival men and women, clad in rich garments and decked with jewels, danced and sang together in the courts of the temples, which were brilliantly illuminated for the purpose. Rows of tall braziers sent up a flickering blaze, and torchbearers held aloft huge torches of pinewood. Some of the dancers themselves carried heavy torches, which flared and spluttered as they danced. The dances began at sundown and lasted till about nine o'clock. None but tried and distinguished warriors might take part in them. The women wore their long hair hanging loose on their back and shoulders, in order that the tassels of the maize might likewise grow long and loose, for the more tassels the more grain in the ear. Men and women danced holding each other by the hand or with their arms round each other's waists, marking time exactly with their feet to the music of the drums and moving out and in among the flaming braziers and torches. The dances were strictly decorous. If any man was detected making love to one of the women dancers, he was publicly disgraced, severely punished, and never allowed to dance and sing in public again. On the eve of the festival the woman who was to die in the character of the Goddess of the Young Maize was arrayed in the rich robes and splendid jewels of the divinity whom she personated. The upper part of her face was painted red and the lower part yellow, probably to assimilate her to the ruddy and orange hues of the ripe maize. Her legs and arms were covered with red feathers. She wore a paper crown decked with a bunch of feathers ; necklaces of gems and gold encircled her neck ; her garments were embroidered with quaint figures ; her shoes were striped with red. In her left hand she held a round shield, in her right a crimson baton. Thus arrayed, she was led by other women to offer incense in four different places. All

Sacrifice of a woman in the character of the Mexican Goddess of the Young Maize about Midsummer.

the rest of the night she and they danced and sang in front of the temple of the goddess Xilonen, whose living image she was supposed to be. In the morning the nobles danced a solemn dance by themselves, leaning, or making believe to lean, on stalks of maize. The women, pranked with garlands and festoons of yellow flowers, danced also by themselves along with the victim. Among the priests the one who was to act as executioner wore a fine bunch of feathers on his back. Another shook a rattle before the doomed woman as she mounted up the steps of the temple of Cinteotl, the Goddess of the Maize. On reaching the summit she was seized by a priest, who threw her on his back, while the sacrificer severed her head from her body, tore out her heart, and threw it in a saucer. When this sacrifice had been performed in honour of Xilonen, the Goddess of the Young Maize, the people were free to eat the green ears of maize and the bread that was baked of it. No one would have dared to eat of these things before the sacrifice.[1]

---

[1] B. de Sahagun, *Histoire Générale des Choses de la Nouvelle Espagne*, traduite par D. Jourdanet et R. Siméon (Paris, 1880), pp. 65 *sq.*, 118-126; J. de Torquemada, *Monarquia Indiana* (Madrid, 1723), lib. x. cap. 19, vol. ii. pp. 269-271; E. J. Payne, *History of the New World called America*, i. (Oxford, 1892) pp. 421-423. Compare Brasseur de Bourbourg, *Histoire des Nations civilisées du Mexique et de l'Amérique-Centrale*, iii. 518-520; H. H. Bancroft, *The Native Races of the Pacific States*, ii. 326 *sq.* I have followed Torquemada (vol. ii. p. 269) and the French translators of Sahagun (p. 65, note [2]) in deriving the name of Xilonen from *xilotl* in the sense of "young cobs of maize." But according to E. J. Payne, the word *xilotl* means "hair," and Xilonen is "Hairy Mother" (*Mater comata*) with reference to the hair-like fibres or tassels that shoot from the maize-cobs. See E. J. Payne, *op. cit.* i. 417. On either interpretation the goddess is a personification of the young maize. The goddess of the maize in general was called Cinteotl or Centeotl (Centeutl), a name which, according to Torque-

mada, is derived from *centli*, "maize-cob" (*Monarquia Indiana*, lib. vi. cap. 25, vol. ii. p. 52). But E. J. Payne, while he regards Cinteotl as the maize-goddess, explains her name differently. He says (*op. cit.* i. 416 *sq.*): "The Totonacs worshipped the corn-spirit under names which were translated into Mexican as Tzinteotl (goddess of beginning or origin) and Tonacayohua (provider of our food). They considered her to be the wife of the sun, their supreme god. Theoretically subordinated to him, the maize-goddess was in practice the chief deity of the Totonacs : it was to her service that the principal warriors, quitting their wives and children, dedicated themselves in their old age." Similarly Clavigero, who lived many years in Mexico and learned the Mexican language, explains Cinteotl (Tzinteotl) to mean "original goddess"; he adds that the Maize Goddess changed her name "according to the different states of the grain in the progress of its growth" (*History of Mexico*, translated by C. Cullen, i. 253 note [(p)]). Another name applied to the Maize Goddess Cinteotl was Chicomecohuatl

Again, in the seventeenth month of the Mexican year,[1] which corresponded to the latter part of December and the early part of January, the Aztecs sacrificed a woman, who personated the goddess Ilamatecutli or Tonan, which means "Our Mother." Her festival fell on Christmas Day, the twenty-fifth of December. The image of the goddess wore a two-faced mask with large mouths and protruding eyes. The woman who represented her was dressed in white robes and shod with white sandals. Over her white mantle she wore a leathern jerkin, the lower edge of which was cut into a fringe of straps, and to the end of each strap was fastened a small shell. As she walked, the shells clashed together and made a noise which was heard afar off. The upper half of her face was painted yellow and the lower half black ; and she wore a wig. In her hand she carried a round whitewashed shield decorated in the middle with a circle of eagle feathers, while white heron plumes, ending in eagle feathers, drooped from it. Thus arrayed and personating the goddess, the woman danced alone to music played by old men, and as she danced she sighed and wept at the thought of the death that was so near. At noon or a little later the dance ceased ; and when the sun was declining in the west, they led her up the long ascent to the summit of Huitzilo-pochtli's temple. Behind her marched the priests clad in the trappings of all the gods, with masks on their faces. One of them wore the costume and the mask of the goddess Ilamatecutli, whom the victim also represented. On reaching the lofty platform which crowned the pyramidal temple, they slew her in the usual fashion, wrenched out her heart, and cut off her head. The dripping head was given

Sacrifice of a woman in the character of the Mexican goddess "Our Mother" on Christmas Day.

---

or "Seven Snakes." See J. de Torquemada, *Monarquia Indiana*, lib. x. cap. 13, vol. ii. p. 255; J. G. Müller, *Geschichte der amerikanischen Urreligionen* (Bâle, 1867), pp. 491 *sqq.*; E. Seler, *Altmexikanische Studien*, ii. (Berlin, 1899) pp. 108 *sq.*, 112. Some have held that Cinteotl was a Maize God rather than a Maize Goddess. See H. H. Bancroft, *The Native Races of the Pacific States*, iii. 349 *sqq.*

[1] The Mexican year of three hundred and sixty-five days was divided into eighteen months of twenty days each, with five supplementary days over. See J. de Torquemada, *Monarquia Indiana*, lib. x. cap. 36, vol. ii. p. 300 (Madrid, 1723); B. de Sahagun, *Histoire Générale des Choses de la Nouvelle Espagne*, traduite par D. Jourdanet et R. Simeon (Paris, 1880), p. lxvii.; F. S. Clavigero, *History of Mexico*, translated by C. Cullen (London, 1807), i. 290 *sq.*

to the priest who wore the costume and mask of the goddess and waving it up and down he danced round the platform, followed by all the other priests in the attire and masks of the gods. When the dance had lasted a certain time, the leader gave the signal, and they all trooped down the long flight of stairs to disrobe themselves and deposit the masks and costumes in the chapels where they were usually kept. Next day the people indulged in a certain pastime. Men and boys furnished themselves with little bags or nets stuffed with paper, flowers of galingale, or green leaves of maize, which they tied to strings, and used them as instruments to strike any girl or woman they might meet in the streets. Sometimes three or four urchins would gather round one girl, beating her till she cried ; but some shrewd wenches went about that day armed with sticks, with which they retaliated smartly on their assailants. It was a penal offence to put stones or anything else that could hurt in the bags.[1]

Sacrifice of a woman in the character of the Mexican goddess the Mother of the Gods at the end of August or beginning of September.   In the preceding custom, what are we to make of the sacrifice of a woman, who personated the goddess, by a man who also wore the costume and mask of the goddess, and who immediately after the sacrifice danced with the bleeding head of the victim ? Perhaps the intention of the strange rite was to represent the resurrection of the slain goddess in the person of the priest who wore her costume and mask and dangled the severed head of her slaughtered representative. If that was so, it would explain another and still ghastlier rite, in which the Mexicans seem to have set forth the doctrine of the divine resurrection. This was to skin the slain woman who had personated the goddess and then to clothe in the bloody skin a man, who pranced about in it, as if he were the dead woman or rather goddess come to life again. Thus in the eleventh Mexican month, which corresponded to the latter part of August and the early part of September, they celebrated a festival in honour of a

---

[1] B. de Sahagun, *Histoire Générale des Choses de la Nouvelle Espagne*, traduite par D. Jourdanet et R. Simeon (Paris, 1880), pp. 75, 158-160 ; J. de Torquemada, *Monarquia Indiana*, lib. x. cap. 29, vol. ii. pp. 284 *sq.* (Madrid, 1723). Compare F. S. Clavigero, *History of* *Mexico*, translated by C. Cullen (London, 1807), i. 312 ; Brasseur de Bourbourg, *Histoire des Nations Civilisées du Mexique et de l'Amérique-Centrale*, iii. 535 *sq.* ; H. H. Bancroft, *The Native Races of the Pacific States*, ii. 337 *sq.*

goddess called the Mother of the Gods (*Teteo innan*) or Our Ancestress (*Toci*), or the Heart of the Earth, and they sacrificed a woman clad in the costume and ornaments of the goddess. She was a slave bought for the purpose by the guilds of physicians, surgeons, blood-letters, midwives, and fortune-tellers, who particularly worshipped this deity. When the poor wretch came forth decked in all the trappings of the goddess, the people, we are told, looked on her as equivalent to the Mother of the Gods herself and paid her as much honour and reverence as if she had indeed been that great divinity. For eight days they danced silently in four rows, if dance it could be called in which the dancers scarcely stirred their legs and bodies, but contented themselves with moving their hands, in which they held branches of blossoms, up and down in time to the tuck of drum. These dances began in the afternoon and lasted till the sun went down. No one might speak during their performance ; only some lively youths mimicked by a booming murmur of the lips the rub-a-dub of the drums. When the dances were over, the medical women, young and old, divided themselves into two parties and engaged in a sham fight before the woman who acted the part of the Mother of the Gods. This they did to divert her and keep her from being sad and shedding tears ; for if she wept, they deemed it an omen that many men would die in battle and many women in childbed. The fight between the women consisted in throwing balls of moss, leaves, or flowers at each other ; and she who personated the goddess led one of the parties to the attack. These mock battles lasted four days.

After that they led the woman who was to die to the market-place, that she might bid it farewell ; and by way of doing so she scattered the flour of maize wherever she went. The priests then attended her to a building near the temple in which she was to be sacrificed. The knowledge of her doom was kept from her as far as possible. The medical women and the midwives comforted her, saying, " Be not cast down, sweetheart ; this night thou shalt sleep with the king ; therefore rejoice." Then they put on her the ornaments of the goddess, and at midnight led her to the temple where she was to die. On the passage not a word was

The farewell to the market.

spoken, not a cough was heard; crowds were gathered to
see her pass, but all kept a profound silence. Arrived at the
summit of the temple she was hoisted on to the back of one
priest, while another adroitly cut off her head. The body,
still warm, was skinned, and a tall robust young man clothed
himself in the bleeding skin and so became in turn a living
image of the goddess. One of the woman's thighs was
flayed separately, and the skin carried to another temple,
where a young man put it over his face as a mask and so
personated the maize-goddess Cinteotl, daughter of the
Mother of the Gods. Meantime the other, clad in the rest
of the woman's skin, hurried down the steps of the temple.
The nobles and warriors fled before him, carrying blood-
stained besoms of couchgrass, but turned to look back at
him from time to time and smote upon their shields as if to
bid him come on. He followed hard after them and all who
saw that flight and pursuit quaked with fear. On arriving
at the foot of the temple of Huitzilopochtli, the man who
wore the skin of the dead woman and personated the Mother
of the Gods, lifted up his arms and stood like a cross before
the image of the god; this action he repeated four times.
Then he joined the man who personated the maize-goddess
Cinteotl, and together they went slowly to the temple of the
Mother of the Gods, where the woman had been sacrificed.
All this time it was night. Next morning at break of day
the man who personated the Mother of the Gods took up
his post on the highest point of the temple; there they
decked him in all the gorgeous trappings of the goddess and
set a splendid crown on his head. Then the captives were
set in a row before him, and arrayed in all his finery he
slaughtered four of them with his own hand: the rest he
left to be butchered by the priests. A variety of ceremonies
and dances followed. Amongst others, the blood of the
human victims was collected in a bowl and set before the
man who personated the Mother of the Gods. He dipped
his finger into the blood and then sucked his bloody finger;
and when he had sucked it he bowed his head and uttered a
dolorous groan, whereat the Indians believed the earth itself
shook and trembled, as did all who heard it. Finally the
skin of the slain woman and the skin of her thigh were

The skin
of the
sacrificed
woman
flayed and
worn by a
man who
personated
the god-
dess.

carried away and deposited separately at two towers, one of which stood on the border of the enemy's country.[1]

This remarkable festival in honour of the Mother of the Gods is said to have been immediately preceded by a similar festival in honour of the Maize Goddess Chicomecohuatl.[2] The image of this goddess was of wood and represented her as a girl of about twelve years of age wearing feminine ornaments painted in gay colours.   On her head was a pasteboard mitre ; her long hair fell on her shoulders; in her ears she had golden earrings ; round her neck she wore a necklace of golden maize-cobs strung on a blue ribbon, and in her hands she held the likeness of maize-cobs made of feathers and garnished with gold.   Her festival, which was observed throughout the whole country with great devotion on the fifteenth day of September, was preceded by a strict fast of seven days, during which old and young, sick and

Young girl chosen to personate the Mexican Goddess of the Maize, Chicome-cohuatl.

---

[1] B. de Sahagun, *Histoire Générale des Choses de la Nouvelle Espagne*, traduite par D. Jourdanet et R. Simeon (Paris, 1880), pp. 18 *sq.*, 68 *sq.*, 133-139 : J. de Torquemada, *Monarquia Indiana* (Madrid, 1723), lib. x. cap. 23, vol. ii. pp. 275 *sq.* ; Diego Duran, *Historia de las Indias de Nueva España* (Mexico, 1867-1880), ii. 185-191. Compare Brasseur de Bourbourg, *Histoire des Nations civilisées du Mexique et de l'Amérique-Centrale*, iii. 523-525 ; H. H. Bancroft, *The Native Races of the Pacific States*, iii. 353-359 ; E. J. Payne, *History of the New World called America*, i. (Oxford, 1892), pp. 470 *sq.* A statue of basalt, about half the size of life, said to have come from Tezcuco, represents a man clothed in a human skin which he wears on his body, his arms, and his face ; his own skin is painted bright red, the other skin a dirty white. See H. H. Bancroft, *op. cit.* iv. 522 ; Marquis de Nadaillac, *L'Amérique Préhistorique* (Paris, 1883), p. 295, fig. 119. In the Art Museum (*Kunst-Museum*) at Bâle there is a statuette of the same sort.   It is labelled : "*Xipe. Der in einer Menschenhaut gekleidete Gott. Gesch. v. H. Luk. Vischer* (1828–1837)." The figure is about eighteen inches high and appears

to be made of a porous stone. It represents a man seated on his haunches with his feet crossed in front of him and his hands resting on his knees. His own skin, of which the legs, feet, hands, wrists, neck and part of the face are visible, is coloured a terra-cotta red.   The rest of his body is covered by the representation of the skin of a human victim, of a greyish colour, quite distinct from that of the wearer, and this skin is also worn like a mask on his face.   At his back the jacket of human skin only partially meets, displaying the wearer's red skin under it for some distance ; it is as if the skin of the human victim had been split up the back and then drawn together and fastened at the back of the wearer like an ill-fitting and imperfectly buttoned coat.   The hands of the human victim are represented dangling at the wrists of the seated figure.   I saw this remarkable statuette in the Museum at Bâle on July 25th, 1912, but I was not able to remove it from the case for closer examination.   As to Xipe, the Mexican god clad in a human skin, whom the statuette represents, see below, pp. 296 *sqq.*

[2] As to this name for the Maize Goddess, see above, p. 286, note [1].

whole, ate nothing but broken victuals and dry bread and drank nothing but water, and did penance by drawing blood from their ears. The blood so drawn was kept in vessels, which were not scoured, so that a dry crust formed over it. On the day before the fast began the people ate and drank to their heart's content, and they sanctified a woman to represent Atlatatonan, the Goddess of Lepers, dressing her up in an appropriate costume. When the fast was over, the high priest of the temple of Tlaloc sacrificed the woman in the usual way by tearing out her heart and holding it up as an offering to the sun. Her body, with all the robes and ornaments she had worn, was cast into a well or vault in the temple, and along with the corpse were thrown in all the plates and dishes out of which the people had eaten, and all the mats on which they had sat or slept during the fast, as if, says the historian, they had been infected with the plague of leprosy. After that the people were free to eat bread, salt, and tomatoes; and immediately after the sacrifice of the woman who personated the Goddess of Leprosy they sanctified a young slave girl of twelve or thirteen years, the prettiest they could find, to represent the Maize Goddess Chicomecohuatl. They invested her with the ornaments of the goddess, putting the mitre on her head and the maize-cobs round her neck and in her hands, and fastening a green feather upright on the crown of her head to imitate an ear of maize. This they did, we are told, in order to signify that the maize was almost ripe at the time of the festival, but because it was still tender they chose a girl of tender years to play the part of the Maize Goddess. The whole long day they led the poor child in all her finery, with the green plume nodding on her head, from house to house dancing merrily to cheer people after the dulness and privations of the fast.

Adoration of the girl who personated the Goddess of the Maize. In the evening all the people assembled at the temple, the courts of which they lit up by a multitude of lanterns and candles. There they passed the night without sleeping, and at midnight, while the trumpets, flutes, and horns discoursed solemn music, a portable framework or palanquin was brought forth, bedecked with festoons of maize-cobs and peppers and filled with seeds of all sorts. This the bearers

set down at the door of the chamber in which the wooden
image of the goddess stood. Now the chamber was adorned
and wreathed, both outside and inside, with wreaths of
maize-cobs, peppers, pumpkins, roses, and seeds of every
kind, a wonder to behold ; the whole floor was covered
deep with these verdant offerings of the pious. When the
music ceased, a solemn procession came forth of priests and
dignitaries, with flaring lights and smoking censers, leading
in their midst the girl who played the part of the goddess.
Then they made her mount the framework, where she stood
upright on the maize and peppers and pumpkins with which
it was strewed, her hands resting on two bannisters to keep
her from falling. Then the priests swung the smoking
censers round her ; the music struck up again, and while it
played, a great dignitary of the temple suddenly stepped up
to her with a razor in his hand and adroitly shore off the
green feather she wore on her head, together with the hair
in which it was fastened, snipping the lock off by the root.
The feather and the hair he then presented to the wooden
image of the goddess with great solemnity and elaborate
ceremonies, weeping and giving her thanks for the fruits of
the earth and the abundant crops which she had bestowed
on the people that year ; and as he wept and prayed, all the
people, standing in the courts of the temple, wept and prayed
with him. When that ceremony was over, the girl descended
from the framework and was escorted to the place where she
was to spend the rest of the night. But all the people kept
watch in the courts of the temple by the light of torches till
break of day.

The morning being come, and the courts of the temple
being still crowded by the multitude, who would have
deemed it sacrilege to quit the precincts, the priests again
brought forth the damsel attired in the costume of the
goddess, with the mitre on her head and the cobs of maize
about her neck. Again she mounted the portable framework or palanquin and stood on it, supporting herself by her
hands on the bannisters. Then the elders of the temple
lifted it on their shoulders, and while some swung burning
censers and others played on instruments or sang, they
carried it in procession through the great courtyard to the

The girl
who per-
sonated the
Goddess of
the Maize
carried in
procession
and wor-
shipped
with offer-
ings of
human
blood.

hall of the god Huitzilopochtli and then back to the chamber, where stood the wooden image of the Maize Goddess, whom the girl personated. There they caused the damsel to descend from the palanquin and to stand on the heaps of corn and vegetables that had been spread in profusion on the floor of the sacred chamber. While she stood there all the elders and nobles came in a line, one behind the other, carrying the saucers of dry and clotted blood which they had drawn from their ears by way of penance during the seven days' fast. One by one they squatted on their haunches before her, which was the equivalent of falling on their knees with us, and scraping the crust of blood from the saucer cast it down before her as an offering in return for the benefits which she, as the embodiment of the Maize Goddess, had conferred upon them. When the men had thus humbly offered their blood to the human representative of the goddess, the women, forming a long line, did so likewise, each of them dropping on her hams before the girl and scraping her blood from the saucer. The ceremony lasted a long time, for great and small, young and old, all without exception had to pass before the incarnate deity and make their offering. When it was over, the people returned home with glad hearts to feast on flesh and viands of every sort as merrily, we are told, as good Christians at Easter partake of meat and other carnal mercies after the long abstinence of Lent. And when they had eaten and drunk their fill and rested after the night watch, they returned quite refreshed to the temple to see the end of the festival. And the end of the festival was this. The multitude being assembled, the priests solemnly incensed the girl who personated the goddess; then they threw her on her back on the heap of corn and seeds, cut off her head, caught the gushing blood in a tub, and sprinkled the blood on the wooden image of the goddess, the walls of the chamber, and the offerings of corn, peppers, pumpkins, seeds, and vegetables which cumbered the floor. After that they flayed the headless trunk, and one of the priests made shift to squeeze himself into the bloody skin. Having done so they clad him in all the robes which the girl had worn; they put the mitre on his head, the necklace of golden maize-cobs about his neck, the maize-

The human representative of the Maize Goddess put to death on a heap of corn and her skin flayed and worn by a priest.

cobs of feathers and gold in his hands; and thus arrayed
they led him forth in public, all of them dancing to the tuck
of drum, while he acted as fugleman, skipping and posturing
at the head of the procession as briskly as he could be expected to do, incommoded as he was by the tight and
clammy skin of the girl and by her clothes, which must have
been much too small for a grown man.[1]

In the foregoing custom the identification of the young
girl with the Maize Goddess appears to be complete. The
golden maize cobs which she wore round her neck, the artificial maize cobs which she carried in her hands, the green
feather which was stuck in her hair in imitation (we are told)
of a green ear of maize, all set her forth as a personification
of the corn-spirit; and we are expressly informed that she
was specially chosen as a young girl to represent the young
maize, which at the time of the festival had not yet fully
ripened.   Further, her identification with the corn and the
corn-goddess was clearly announced by making her stand on
the heaps of maize and there receive the homage and blood-
offerings of the whole people, who thereby returned her
thanks for the benefits which in her character of a divinity
she was supposed to have conferred upon them.   Once
more, the practice of beheading her on a heap of corn and
seeds and sprinkling her blood, not only on the image of
the Maize Goddess, but on the piles of maize, peppers,
pumpkins, seeds, and vegetables, can seemingly have had no
other object but to quicken and strengthen the crops of corn

*Identifi-
cation of
the human
victim
with the
Goddess
of Maize
whom she
personated.*

---

[1] Diego Duran, *Historia de las
Indias de Nueva España* (Mexico,
1867–1880), ii. 179-184.   This remarkable festival appears not to be
noticed by the other early Spanish
writers such as Sahagun, Acosta, and
Torquemada, who have given us de-
tailed descriptions of the Mexican
festivals.   It might perhaps have been
conjectured that Duran was here describing the similar festival of the
Mother of the Gods (see above, pp. 288
sqq.), which fell about the same time of
the year.   But the conjecture is excluded by the simple fact that Duran
describes both festivals, the one immediately after the other, assigning as
their dates the fifteenth and sixteenth
of September respectively (*op. cit.* ii.
180, 185 *sq.*).   Almost nothing is
known about Duran except that he
was a Spanish monk, apparently a
native of Mexico, who had weak health
and died in 1588.   His work remained
in manuscript till it was edited at
Mexico in 1867–1880 by José F.
Ramirez.   The original manuscript is
preserved in the National Library at
Madrid.   The accounts contained in
his history bear internal marks of
authenticity and are in general supported by the independent testimony of
the other early Spanish authorities.

and the fruits of the earth in general by infusing into their representatives the blood of the Corn Goddess herself. The analogy of this Mexican sacrifice, the meaning of which appears to be indisputable, may be allowed to strengthen the interpretation which I have given of other human sacrifices offered for the crops.[1] If the Mexican girl, whose blood was sprinkled on the maize, indeed personated the Maize Goddess, it becomes more than ever probable that the girl whose blood the Pawnees similarly sprinkled on the seed corn personated in like manner the female Spirit of the Corn ; and so with the other human beings whom other races have slaughtered for the sake of promoting the growth of the crops.

The resurrection of the Maize Goddess set forth by the wearing of the skin of her human representative.
Lastly, the concluding act of the sacred drama, in which the body of the dead Maize Goddess was flayed and her skin worn, together with all her sacred insignia, by a man who danced before the people in this grim attire, seems to be best explained on the hypothesis that it was intended to ensure that the divine death should be immediately followed by the divine resurrection. If that was so, we may infer with some degree of probability that the practice of killing a human representative of a deity has commonly, perhaps always, been regarded merely as a means of perpetuating the divine energies in the fulness of youthful vigour, untainted by the weakness and frailty of age, from which they must have suffered if the deity had been allowed to die a natural death.

Xipe, the Flayed God, and the Mexican festival of the Flaying of Men.
This interpretation of the Mexican custom of flaying human beings and permitting or requiring other persons to parade publicly in the skins of the victims may perhaps be confirmed by a consideration of the festival at which this strange rite was observed on the largest scale, and which accordingly went by the name of the Festival of the Flaying of Men (*Tlacaxipeualiztli*). It was celebrated in the second month of the Aztec year, which corresponded to the last days of February and the early part of March. The exact day of the festival was the twentieth of March, according to one pious chronicler, who notes with unction that the bloody rite fell only one day later than the feast which

[1] *Spirits of the Corn and of the Wild*, i. 236 *sqq.*

Holy Church solemnizes in honour of the glorious St. Joseph. The god whom the Aztecs worshipped in this strange fashion was named Xipe, " the Flayed One," or Totec, " Our Lord." On this occasion he also bore the solemn name of Youallauan, " He who drinks in the Night." His image was of stone and represented him in human form with his mouth open as if in the act of speaking ; his body was painted yellow on the one side and drab on the other ; he wore the skin of a flayed man over his own, with the hands of the victim dangling at his wrists. On his head he had a hood of various colours, and about his loins a green petticoat reaching to his knees with a fringe of small shells. In his two hands he grasped a rattle like the head of a poppy with the seeds in it ; while on his left arm he supported a yellow shield with a red rim. At his festival the Mexicans killed all the prisoners they had taken in war, men, women, and children. The number of the victims was very great. A Spanish historian of the sixteenth century estimated that in Mexico more people used to be sacrificed on the altar than died a natural death. All who were sacrificed to Xipe, " the Flayed God," were themselves flayed, and men who had made a special vow to the god put on the skins of the human victims and went about the city in that guise for twenty days, being everywhere welcomed and revered as living images of the deity. Forty days before the festival, according to the historian Duran, they chose a man to personate the god, clothed him in all the insignia of the divinity, and led him about in public, doing him as much reverence all these days as if he had really been what he pretended to be. Moreover, every parish of the capital did the same ; each of them had its own temple and appointed its own human representative of the deity, who received the homage and worship of the parishioners for the forty days.

On the day of the festival these mortal gods and all the other prisoners, with the exception of a few who were reserved for a different death, were killed in the usual way. The scene of the slaughter was the platform on the summit of the god Huitzilopochtli's temple. Some of the poor wretches fainted when they came to the foot of the steps

The human shambles.

and had to be dragged up the long staircase by the hair of
their heads.   Arrived at the summit they were slaughtered
one by one on the sacrificial stone by the high priest, who
cut open their breasts, tore out their hearts, and held them
up to the sun, in order to feed the great luminary with these
bleeding relics.   Then the bodies were sent rolling down the
staircase, clattering and turning over and over like gourds
as they bumped from step to step till they reached the
bottom.   There they were received by other priests, or rather
human butchers, who with a dexterity acquired by practice
slit the back of each body from the nape of the neck to the
heels and peeled off the whole skin in a single piece as neatly
as if it had been a sheepskin.   The skinless body was then
fetched away by its owner, that is, by the man who had
captured the prisoner in war.   He took it home with him,
carved it, sent one of the thighs to the king, and other joints
to friends, or invited them to come and feast on the carcase
in his house.   The skins of the human victims were also a
perquisite of their captors, and were lent or hired out by
them to men who had made a vow of going about clad in
the hides for twenty days.   Such men clothed in the
reeking skins of the butchered prisoners were called
Xixipeme or Tototectin after the god Xipe or Totec, whose
living image they were esteemed and whose costume they
wore.   Among the devotees who bound themselves to this
pious exercise were persons who suffered from loathsome
skin diseases, such as smallpox, abscesses, and the itch ; and
among them there was a fair sprinkling of debauchees, who
had drunk themselves nearly blind and hoped to recover the
use of their precious eyes by parading for a month in this
curious mantle.   Thus arrayed, they went from house to house
throughout the city, entering everywhere and asking alms for
the love of God.   On entering a house each of these reverend
palmers was made to sit on a heap of leaves ; festoons of maize
and wreaths of flowers were placed round his body ; and he
was given wine to drink and cakes to eat.   And when a
mother saw one of these filthy but sanctified ruffians passing
along the street, she would run to him with her infant and
put it in his arms that he might bless it, which he did with
unction, receiving an alms from the happy mother in return.

The earnings of these begging-friars on their rounds were sometimes considerable, for the rich people rewarded them hand-
somely. Whatever they were, the collectors paid them in to
the owners of the skins, who thus made a profit by hiring out
these valuable articles of property. Every night the wearers
of the skins deposited them in the temple and fetched them
again next morning when they set out on their rounds. At
the end of the twenty days the skins were dry, hard,
shrivelled and shrunken, and they smelt so villainously that
people held their noses when they met the holy beggars
arrayed in their fetid mantles. The time being come to
rid themselves of these encumbrances, the devotees walked
in solemn procession, wearing the rotten skins and stinking
like dead dogs, to the temple called Yopico, where they
stripped themselves of the hides and plunged them into a
tub or vat, after which they washed and scrubbed themselves
thoroughly, while their friends smacked their bare bodies loudly
with wet hands in order to squeeze out the human grease
with which they were saturated. Finally, the skins were
solemnly buried, as holy relics, in a vault of the temple.
The burial service was accompanied by chanting and
attended by the whole people ; and when it was over, one of
the high dignitaries preached a sermon to the assembled
congregation, in which he dwelt with pathetic eloquence on
the meanness and misery of human existence and exhorted
his hearers to lead a sober and quiet life, to cultivate the
virtues of reverence, modesty, humility and obedience, to be
kind and charitable to the poor and to strangers ; he warned
them against the sins of robbery, fornication, adultery, and
covetousness ; and kindling with the glow of his oratory, he
passionately admonished, entreated, and implored all who
heard him to choose the good and shun the evil, drawing
a dreadful picture of the ills that would overtake the wicked
here and hereafter, while he painted in alluring colours the
bliss in store for the righteous and the rewards they might
expect to receive at the hands of the deity in the life to
come.

While most of the men who masqueraded in the skins
of the human victims appear to have personated the Flayed
God Xipe, whose name they bore in the form Xixipeme,

the men
clad in the
skins of
the human
victims.

others assumed the ornaments and bore the names of other Mexican deities, such as Huitzilopochtli and Quetzalcoatl; the ceremony of investing them with the skins and the insignia of divinity was called *netcotoquiliztli*, which means "to think themselves gods." Amongst the gods thus personated was Totec. His human representative wore, over the skin of the flayed man, all the splendid trappings of the deity. On his head was placed a curious crown decorated with rich feathers. A golden crescent dangled from his nose, golden earrings from his ears, and a necklace of hammered gold encircled his neck. His feet were shod in red shoes decorated with quail's feathers; his loins were begirt with a petticoat of gorgeous plumage; and on his back three small paper flags fluttered and rustled in the wind. In his left hand he carried a golden shield and in his right a rattle, which he shook and rattled as he walked with a majestic dancing step. Seats were always prepared for this human god; and when he sat down, they offered him a paste made of uncooked maize-flour. Also they presented to him little bunches of cobs of maize chosen from the seed-corn; and he received as offerings the first fruits and the first flowers of the season.[1]

Men
roasted
alive as
images of
the Fire-
god.

In the eighteenth and last month of their year, which fell in January, the Mexicans held a festival in honour of the god of fire. Every fourth year the festival was celebrated on a grand scale by the sacrifice of a great many men and women, husbands and wives, who were dressed in the

---

[1] B. de Sahagun, *Histoire Générale des Choses de la Nouvelle Espagne*, traduite par D. Jourdanet et R. Simeon (Paris, 1880), pp. 37 *sq.*, 58-60, 87-94, 584 *sq.*; E. Seler, *Altmexikanische Studien*, ii. (Berlin, 1899) pp. 76-100, 171-188 (the latter passage gives the Aztec text of Sahagun's account with a German translation); Diego Duran, *Historia de las Indias de Nueva España* (Mexico, 1867-1880), ii. 147-155; J. de Torquemada, *Monarquia Indiana*, lib. x. cap. 11, vol. ii. pp. 252 *sq.* (Madrid, 1723). Compare F. S. Clavigero, *History of Mexico*, translated by C. Cullen, Second Edition (London, 1807), i. 297 *sq.*; Brasseur de Bourbourg, *Histoire des Nations civilisées du Mexique*

et de l'Amérique-Centrale (Paris, 1857-1859), iii. 503 *sq.*; H. H. Bancroft, *The Native Races of the Pacific States* (London, 1875-1876), ii. 306 *sqq.* According to Torquemada, the prisoners were flayed alive, but this statement is not, so far as I know, supported by the other early Spanish authorities. It is Duran who gives the 20th of March as the date of the festival at which the captives were killed and skinned; but this is inconsistent with the evidence of Sahagun, according to whom the second Aztec month, in which the festival fell, ended with the 13th of March. See B. de Sahagun, *Histoire Générale des Choses de la Nouvelle Espagne*, p. 51.

trappings of the fire-god and regarded as his living images.
Bound hand and foot, they were thrown alive into a great
furnace, and after roasting in it for a little were raked
out of the fire before they were dead in order to allow the
priest to cut the hearts out of their scorched, blistered, and
still writhing bodies in the usual way.[1] The intention of the
sacrifice probably was to maintain the Fire-god in full
vigour, lest he should grow decrepit or even die of old age,
and mankind should thus be deprived of his valuable services. This important object was attained by feeding the
fire with live men and women, who thus as it were poured
a fresh stock of vital energy into the veins of the Fire-god
and perhaps of his wife also. But they had to be raked out
of the flames before they were dead ; for clearly it would
never do to let them die in the fire, else the Fire-god whom
they personated would die also. For the same reason their
hearts had to be torn from their bodies while they were still
palpitating ; what use could the Fire-god make of human
hearts that were burnt to cinders ?

This was the ordinary mode of sacrificing the human
representatives of the Fire-god every fourth year. But in
Quauhtitlan, a city distant four leagues from the city of
Mexico, the custom was different. On the eve of the festival
two women were beheaded on the altar of the temple and
afterwards flayed, faces and all, and their thigh bones
extracted. Next morning two men of high rank clothed
themselves in the skins, including the skins of the women's
faces, which they put over their own ; and thus arrayed
and carrying in their hands the thigh bones of the victims
they came down the steps of the temple roaring like wild
beasts. A vast crowd of people had assembled to witness
the spectacle, and when they saw the two men coming

*Women
flayed in
honour of
the Fire-
god and
their skiris
worn by
men who
personated
gods.*

---

[1] J. de Torquemada, *Monarquia
Indiana*, lib. x. cap. 30, vol. ii. pp.
285 *sq.* (Mexico, 1723); B. de Sahagun, *Histoire Générale des Choses de la
Nouvelle Espagne*, traduite par D.
Jourdanet et R. Simeon (Paris, 1880),
pp. 164 *sq.* The latter writer does
not describe the mode in which the
victims were sacrificed at this quadri-
ennial festival ; but he describes as in
the text the annual sacrifice of victims
in honour of the fire-god in the tenth
month of the Mexican year (*op. cit.*
pp. 67 *sq.*, 129 *sqq.*). Compare F. S.
Clavigero, *History of Mexico*, translated by C. Cullen, Second Edition
(London, 1807), i. 306 *sq.* ; H. H.
Bancroft, *The Native Races of the
Pacific States*, ii. 329 *sq.*

down the steps in the dripping skins, brandishing the bones, and bellowing like beasts, they were filled with fear and said, "There come our gods!" Arrived at the foot of the staircase these human gods engaged in a dance, which they kept up for the rest of the day, never divesting themselves of the bloody skins till the festival was over.[1]

The personation of a god by a man wearing the skin of a human victim is probably intended to represent and ensure the resurrection of the deity.

The idea of resurrection from the dead is suggested by the observation of snakes and other creatures that cast their skins.

The theory that the custom of wearing the skin of a flayed man or woman and personating a god in that costume is intended to represent the resurrection of the deity derives some support from the class of persons who made a vow to masquerade in the skins. They were, as we have seen, especially men who suffered from diseases of the skin and the eyes: they hoped, we are told, by wearing the skins to be cured of their ailments, and the old Spanish monk who records the belief adds dryly that some were cured and some were not.[2] We may conjecture that by donning the skins of men who had acted the part of gods they expected to slough off their own diseased old skins and to acquire new and healthy skins, like those of the deities. This notion may have been suggested to them by the observation of certain animals, such as serpents and lizards, which seem to renew their youth by casting their skins and appear refreshed and renovated in new integuments. That many savages have noticed such transformations in the animal world is proved by the tales which some of them tell to account for the origin of death among mankind. For example, the Arawaks of British Guiana say that man was created by a good being whom they call Kururumany. Once on a time this kindly creator came to earth to see how his creature man was getting on. But men were so ungrateful that they tried to kill their Maker. Hence he took from them the gift of immortality and bestowed it upon animals that change their skins, such as

[1] J. de Torquemada, *Monarquia Indiana*, lib. x. cap. 30, vol. ii. p. 286 (Madrid, 1723). Compare F. S. Clavigero, *History of Mexico*, translated by C. Cullen, Second Edition (London, 1807), i. 283 *sq.* ; Brasseur de Bourbourg, *Histoire des Nations civilisées du Mexique et de l'Amérique-*

Centrale, iii. 539 *sq.*

[2] B. de Sahagun, *Histoire Générale des Choses de la Nouvelle Espagne*, traduite par D. Jourdanet et R. Simeon, pp. 37, 93; E. Seler, *Alt-mexikanische Studien*, ii. (Berlin, 1889) pp. 96, 185 (quoting the Aztec text of Sahagun).

snakes, lizards, and beetles.[1]   Again, the Tamanachiers,. an
Indian tribe of the Orinoco, tell how the creator kindly
intended to make men immortal by telling them that they
should change their skins.   He meant to say that by so doing
they should renew their youth like serpents and beetles.
But the glad tidings were received with such incredulity by
an old woman that the creator in a huff changed his tune
and said very curtly, " Ye shall die." [2]

In Annam they say that Ngoc hoang sent a messenger
from heaven to inform men that when they reached old age
they should change their skins and live for ever, but that
when serpents grew old, they must die.   Unfortunately for
the human race the message was perverted in the transmis-
sion, so that men do not change their skins and are therefore mortal, whereas serpents do cast their old skins and
accordingly live for ever.[3]   According to the natives of Nias
the personage who was charged by the creator with the duty
of putting the last touches to man broke his fast on bananas
instead of on river-crabs, as he should have done ; for had
he only eaten river-crabs, men would have changed their
skins like crabs, and like crabs would have never died.
But the serpents, wiser in their generation than men, ate
the crabs, and that is why they too are immortal.[4]   Stories
of the same sort are current among the Melanesians.
Thus the natives of the Gazelle Peninsula in New Britain
account for the origin of death by a tale very like that told
in Annam.   The Good Spirit, they say, loved men and
wished to make them immortal, but he hated serpents and
wished to kill them.   So he despatched his brother to mankind with this cheering message : " Go to men and take them
the secret of immortality.   Tell them to cast their skin every
year.   So will they be protected from death, for their life

*Savage
notion that
men would
have been
immortal,
if only they
could have
cast their
skins like
serpents
and crabs.*

---

[1] R. Schomburgk, *Reisen in Britisch-
Guiana* (Leipsic, 1847–1848), ii. 319.
I have already noticed this and the
following stories of the origin of death
in *The Belief in Immortality*, i. 69
sqq.

[2] R. Schomburgk, *op. cit.* ii. 320.

[3] A. Landes, " Contes et Légendes
Annamites," *Cochinchine française,
Excursions et Reconnaissances*, No. 25

(Saigon, 1886), pp. 108 *sq.*

[4] H.   Sundermann,   " Die Insel
Nias und die Mission daselbst," *Allgemeine Missions-Zeitschrift*, xi. (1884)
p. 451 ; *id.*, *Die Insel Nias und die
Mission daselbst* (Barmen, 1905), p.
68 ; E. Modigliani, *Un Viaggio a Nías*
(Milan, 1890), p. 295 ; A. Fehr, *Der
Niasser im Leben und Sterben* (Barmen, 1901), p. 8.

will be constantly renewed. But tell the serpents that they must henceforth die." Through the carelessness or treachery of the messenger this message was reversed; so that now, as we all know, men die and serpents live for ever by annually casting their skins.[1] Again, if we can trust the traditions of the Banks' Islanders and New Hebrideans, there was a time when men did really cast their skins and renew their youth. The melancholy change to mortality was brought about by an old woman, who most unfortunately resumed her old cast-off skin to please an infant, which squalled at seeing her in her new integument.[2] The Gallas of East Africa say that God sent a certain bird (*holawaka*, "the sheep of God") to tell men that they would not die, but that when they grew old they would slough their skins and so renew their youth. But the bird foolishly or maliciously delivered the message to serpents instead of to men, and that is why ever since men have been mortal and serpents immortal. For that evil deed God punished the bird with a painful malady from which it suffers to this day, and it sits on the tops of trees and moans and wails perpetually.[3]

Hence the Mexicans apparently thought that they could renew their own skins by putting on those of other people.

Thus it appears that some peoples have not only observed the curious transformations which certain animals undergo, but have imagined that by means of such transformations the animals periodically renew their youth and live for ever. From such observations and fancies it is an easy step to the conclusion that man might similarly take a fresh lease of life and renew the lease indefinitely, if only he could contrive like the animals to get a new skin. This desirable object the Mexicans apparently sought to accomplish by

[1] P. Kleintitschen, *Die Küstenbewohner der Gazellehalbinsel* (Hiltrup bei Münster, preface dated Christmas, 1906), p. 334.

[2] R. H. Codrington, *The Melanesians* (Oxford, 1891), pp. 260, 265; W. Gray, "Some Notes on the Tannese," *Internationales Archiv für Ethnographie*, vii. (1894) p. 232. The same story of the origin of death has been recorded in the Shortlands Islands and among the Kai of German New Guinea. See C. Ribbe, *Zwei Jahre*

unter den Kannibalen der Salomo-Inseln (Dresden-Blasowitz, 1903), p. 148; Ch. Keysser, "Aus dem Leben der Kaileute," in R. Neuhauss's *Deutsch Neu-Guinea*, iii. (Berlin, 1911) pp. 161 *sq*. It is also told with some variations by the natives of the Admiralty Islands. See Josef Meier, "Mythen und Sagen der Admiralitäts-insulaner," *Anthropos*, iii. (1908) p. 193.

[3] Miss A. Werner, "Two Galla Legends," *Man*, xiii. (1913) pp. 90 *sq*.

flaying men and wearing their bleeding skins like garments thrown over their own. By so doing persons who suffered from cutaneous diseases hoped to acquire a new and healthy skin ; and by so doing the priests attempted not merely to revive the gods whom they had just slain in the persons of their human representatives, but also to restore to their wasting and decaying frames all the vigour and energy of youth.

The rites described in the preceding pages suffice to prove that human sacrifices of the sort I suppose to have prevailed at Aricia [1] were, as a matter of fact, systematically offered on a large scale by a people whose level of culture was probably not inferior, if indeed it was not distinctly superior, to that occupied by the Italian races at the early period to which the origin of the Arician priesthood must be referred. The positive and indubitable evidence of the prevalence of such sacrifices in one part of the world may reasonably be allowed to strengthen the probability of their prevalence in places for which the evidence is less full and trustworthy. Taken all together, the facts which we have passed in review seem to shew that the custom of killing men whom their worshippers regard as divine has prevailed in many parts of the world. But to clinch the argument, it is clearly desirable to prove that the custom of putting to death a human representative of a god was known and practised in ancient Italy elsewhere than in the Arician Grove. This proof I now propose to adduce.

General conclusion: the custom of putting human beings to death in the character of gods has prevailed in many parts of the world.

[1] *The Magic Art and the Evolution of Kings*, i. 40 *sqq.*, ii. 376 *sqq.*

CHAPTER VIII

THE SATURNALIA AND KINDRED FESTIVALS

§ 1. *The Roman Saturnalia*

Annual periods of license.

IN an earlier part of this book we saw that many peoples have been used to observe an annual period of license, when the customary restraints of law and morality are thrown aside, when the whole population give themselves up to extravagant mirth and jollity, and when the darker passions find a vent which would never be allowed them in the more staid and sober course of ordinary life. Such outbursts of the pent-up forces of human nature, too often degenerating into wild orgies of lust and crime, occur most commonly at the end of the year, and are frequently associated, as I have had occasion to point out, with one or other of the agricultural seasons, especially with the time of sowing or of harvest. Now, of all these periods of license the one which is best known and which in modern languages has given its name to the rest, is the Saturnalia. This famous festival fell in December, the last month of the Roman year, and was popularly supposed to commemorate the merry reign of Saturn, the god of sowing and of husbandry, who lived on earth long ago as a righteous and beneficent king of Italy, drew the rude and scattered dwellers on the mountains together, taught them to till the ground, gave them laws, and ruled in peace. His reign was the fabled Golden Age: the earth brought forth abundantly: no sound of war or discord troubled the happy world: no baleful love of lucre worked like poison in the blood of the industrious and contented peasantry. Slavery and private property were alike unknown: all men had all things in

The Roman Saturnalia.

common. At last the good god, the kindly king, vanished suddenly; but his memory was cherished to distant ages, shrines were reared in his honour, and many hills and high places in Italy bore his name.[1] Yet the bright tradition of his reign was crossed by a dark shadow: his altars are said to have been stained with the blood of human victims, for whom a more merciful age afterwards substituted effigies.[2] Of this gloomy side of the god's religion there is little or no trace in the descriptions which ancient writers have left us of the Saturnalia. Feasting and revelry and all the mad pursuit of pleasure are the features that seem to have especially marked this carnival of antiquity, as it went on for seven days in the streets and public squares and houses of ancient Rome from the seventeenth to the twenty-third of December.[3]

But no feature of the festival is more remarkable, nothing in it seems to have struck the ancients themselves more than the license granted to slaves at this time. The distinction between the free and the servile classes was temporarily abolished. The slave might rail at his master, intoxicate himself like his betters, sit down at table with them, *The license granted to slaves at the Saturnalia.*

---

[1] Virgil, *Georg.* ii. 536-540, *Aen.* viii. 319-327, with the comments of Servius; Tibullus, i. 3. 35-48; Ovid, *Fasti*, i. 233 *sqq.*; Lucian, *Saturnalia*, 7; Macrobius, *Saturn.* i. 7. 21-26; Justin, xliii. 1. 3-5; Aurelius Victor, *Origo gentis Romanae*, 3; Dionysius Halicarnasensis, *Antiquit. Rom.* i. 34. On Saturn and the Saturnalia see especially L. Preller, *Römische Mythologie*,[3] ii. 10 *sqq.* Compare J. Marquardt, *Römische Staatsverwaltung*, iii.[2] (Leipsic, 1885) pp. 586 *sqq.*; W. Warde Fowler, *The Roman Festivals of the Period of the Republic* (London, 1899), pp. 268-273; G. Wissowa, *Religion und Kultus der Römer*[2] (Munich, 1912), pp. 204 *sqq.*; *id.*, in W. H. Roscher's *Ausführliches Lexikon der griech. und röm. Mythologie*, iv. 427 *sqq.* A good account of the Saturnalia, based on the texts of the classical writers, is given by Dezobry (*Rome au siècle d'Auguste*,[3] iii. 143 *sqq.*). The name Saturn seems to be etymologically akin to *satus* and *satio*,

" a sowing " or " planting." Compare Varro, *De lingua Latina*, v. 64, " *Ab satu est dictus Saturnus*"; Festus, *s.v.* "Opima spolia," p. 186 ed. C. O. Müller: "*ipse [Saturnus] agrorum cultor habetur, nominatus a satu, tenensque falcem effingitur, quae est insigne agricolae.*" Compare Tertullian, *Ad Nationes*, ii. 12; Arnobius, *Adversus Nationes*, iv. 9; Augustine, *De civitate Dei*, vii. 2, 3, 13, 15, 18, 19. The god's name appears in the form Saeturnus inscribed on an ancient bowl (H. Dessau, *Inscriptiones Latinae Selectae*, vol. ii. pars i. p. 2, No. 2966).

[2] Dionysius Halicarnasensis, *Ant. Rom.* i. 38; Macrobius, *Saturn.* i. 7. 31; Lactantius, *Divin. Inst.* i. 21; Arnobius, *Adversus Nationes*, ii. 68.

[3] For the general dissipation of the Saturnalia see Seneca, *Epist.* 18; for the seven days of the popular festival see Martial, xiv. 72. 2; Macrobius, *Sat.* i. 10. 2; Lucian, *Saturnalia*, 21.

and not even a word of reproof would be administered to him for conduct which at any other season might have been punished with stripes, imprisonment, or death.[1]   Nay, more, masters actually changed places with their slaves and waited on them at table ; and not till the serf had done eating and drinking was the board cleared and dinner set for his master.[2]   So far was this inversion of ranks carried, that each household became for a time a mimic republic in which the high offices of state were discharged by the slaves, who gave their orders and laid down the law as if they were indeed invested with all the dignity of the consulship, the

The mock King of the Saturnalia.

praetorship, and the bench.[3]   Like the pale reflection of power thus accorded to bondsmen at the Saturnalia was the mock kingship for which freemen cast lots at the same season.   The person on whom the lot fell enjoyed the title of king, and issued commands of a playful and ludicrous nature to his temporary subjects.   One of them he might order to mix the wine, another to drink, another to sing, another to dance, another to speak in his own dispraise, another to carry a flute-girl on his back round the house.[4]

Persona-tion of Saturn at the Saturn-alia by a soldier who afterwards suffered death.

Now, when we remember that the liberty allowed to slaves at this festive season was supposed to be an imitation of the state of society in Saturn's time, and that in general the Saturnalia passed for nothing more or less than a temporary revival or restoration of the reign of that merry monarch, we are tempted to surmise that the mock king who presided over the revels may have originally represented Saturn himself.   The conjecture is strongly confirmed, if not established, by a very curious and interesting account of the way in which the Saturnalia was celebrated by the Roman soldiers stationed on the Danube in the reign of Maximian and Diocletian.   The account is preserved in a narrative of the martyrdom of St. Dasius, which was unearthed from a Greek manuscript in the Paris library, and published by

---

[1] Horace, *Sat.* ii. 7. 4 *sq.* ; Macro-bius, *Saturn.* i. 7. 26 ; Justin, xliii. 1. 4 ; Plutarch, *Sulla,* 18 ; Lucian, *Saturnalia,* 5, 7 ; Porphyry, *De antro nympharum,* 23.

[2] Macrobius, *Saturn.* i. 12. 7, i. 24. 23 ; Solinus, i. 35 ; Joannes Lydus,

De mensibus, iii. 15 ; Athenaeus, xiv. 44, p. 639 B ; Dio Cassius, lx. 19.

[3] Seneca, *Epist.* 47. 14.   Compare Porphyry, *De abstinentia,* ii. 23.

[4] Tacitus, *Annals,* xiii. 15 ; Arrian, *Epicteti Dissert.* i. 25. 8 ; Lucian, *Saturnalia,* 4.

Professor Franz Cumont of Ghent. Two briefer descriptions of the event and of the custom are contained in manuscripts at Milan and Berlin ; one of them had already seen the light in an obscure volume printed at Urbino in 1727, but its importance for the history of the Roman religion, both ancient and modern, appears to have been overlooked until Professor Cumont drew the attention of scholars to all three narratives by publishing them together some years ago.[1] According to these narratives, which have all the appearance of being authentic, and of which the longest is probably based on official documents, the Roman soldiers at Durostorum in Lower Moesia celebrated the Saturnalia year by year in the following manner. Thirty days before the festival they chose by lot from amongst themselves a young and handsome man, who was then clothed in royal attire to resemble Saturn. Thus arrayed and attended by a multitude of soldiers he went about in public with full license to indulge his passions and to taste of every pleasure, however base and shameful. But if his reign was merry, it was short and ended tragically ; for when the thirty days were up and the festival of Saturn had come, he cut his own throat on the altar of the god whom he personated.[2] In the year 303 A.D. the lot fell upon the Christian soldier Dasius, but he refused to play the part of the heathen god and soil his last days by debauchery. The threats and arguments of his commanding officer Bassus failed to shake his constancy, and accordingly he was beheaded, as the Christian martyrologist records with minute accuracy, at Durostorum by the soldier John on Friday the twentieth day of November, being the twenty-fourth day of the moon, at the fourth hour.

Since this narrative was published by Professor Cumont,

[1] "Les Actes de S. Dasius," *Analecta Bollandiana,* xvi. (1897) pp. 5-16. I have to thank Prof. Cumont for courteously sending me a copy of this important paper. The bearing of the new evidence on the Saturnalia has been further discussed by Messrs. Parmentier and Cumont ("Le roi des Saturnales," *Revue de Philologie,* xxi. (1897) pp. 143-153).

[2] The phrase of the Paris MS. is ambiguous (τοῖς ἀνωνύμοις καὶ μυσαροῖς εἰδώλοις προσεκόμιξεν ἑαυτὸν σπουδήν, ἀναιρούμενος ὑπὸ μαχαίρας) ; but the other two versions say plainly that the mock king perished by his own hand (μέλλοντα ἑαυτὸν ἐπισφάξαι τῷ βωμῷ τοῦ Κρόνου, Berlin MS. ; ἑαυτὸν ἐπισφάξαι αὐτοχείρως τῷ Κρόνῳ, Milan MS.).

The sarco-
phagus of
St. Dasius,
the martyr
on whom
the lot fell
to play the
part of
Saturn.

its historical character, which had been doubted or denied, has received strong confirmation from an interesting discovery. In the crypt of the cathedral which crowns the promontory of Ancona there is preserved, among other remarkable antiquities, a white marble sarcophagus bearing a Greek inscription, in characters of the age of Justinian, to the following effect: "Here lies the holy martyr Dasius, brought from Durostorum." The sarcophagus was transferred to the crypt of the cathedral in 1848 from the church of San Pellegrino, under the high altar of which, as we learn from a Latin inscription let into the masonry, the martyr's bones still repose with those of two other saints. How long the sarcophagus was deposited in the church of San Pellegrino, we do not know ; but it is recorded to have been there in the year 1650. We may suppose that the saint's relics were transferred for safety to Ancona at some time in the troubled centuries which followed his martyrdom, when Moesia was occupied and ravaged by successive hordes of barbarian invaders.[1] At all events it appears certain from the independent and mutually confirmatory evidence of the martyrology and the monuments that Dasius was no mythical saint, but a real man, who suffered death for his faith at Durostorum in one of the early centuries of the Christian era. Finding the narrative of the nameless martyrologist thus established as to the principal fact recorded, namely, the martyrdom of St. Dasius, we may reasonably accept his testimony as to the manner and cause of the martyrdom, all the more because his narrative is precise, circumstantial, and entirely free from the miraculous element. Accordingly I conclude that the account which he gives of the celebration of the Saturnalia among the Roman soldiers is trustworthy.

This account sets in a new and lurid light the office of

---

[1] Franz Cumont, "Le tombeau de S. Dasius de Durostorum," *Analecta Bollandiana*, xxvii. (Brussels, 1908) pp. 369-372. The inscription on the sarcophagus runs thus : Ἐνταῦθα κατακεῖται ὁ ἅγιος μάρτυς Δάσιος ἐνεχθεὶς ἀπὸ Δωροστόλου. The inscription on the altar runs thus : " *Vetere diruta nobiliorem FF. Karmelitani excalciati aram* extruxerunt subter qua sanctorum martyrum Peregrini Flaviani Dasii corpora et infantium ab Herode necatorum ossa minus decenter antiquitus recondita honorificentius et populo spectanda reponi curaverunt die virgini et matri Theresiae sacro anno MDCCCIV."

the King of the Saturnalia, the ancient Lord of Misrule,
who presided over the winter revels at Rome in the time of
Horace and of Tacitus. It seems to prove that his business
had not always been that of a mere harlequin or merry-
andrew whose only care was that the revelry should run
high and the fun grow fast and furious, while the fire blazed
and crackled on the hearth, while the streets swarmed with
festive crowds, and through the clear frosty air, far away to
the north, Soracte shewed his coronal of snow. When we
compare this comic monarch of the gay, the civilized
metropolis with his grim counterpart of the rude camp on
the Danube, and when we remember the long array of
similar figures, ludicrous yet tragic, who in other ages and
in other lands, wearing mock crowns and wrapped in sceptred
palls, have played their little pranks for a few brief hours or
days, then passed before their time to a violent death, we
can hardly doubt that in the King of the Saturnalia at
Rome, as he is depicted by classical writers, we see only a
feeble emasculated copy of that original, whose strong
features have been fortunately preserved for us by the
obscure author of the *Martyrdom of St. Dasius*. In other
words, the martyrologist's account of the Saturnalia agrees
so closely with the accounts of similar rites elsewhere, which
could not possibly have been known to him, that the
substantial accuracy of his description may be regarded as
established ; and further, since the custom of putting a mock
king to death as a representative of a god cannot have
grown out of a practice of appointing him to preside over a
holiday revel, whereas the reverse may . very well have
happened, we are justified in assuming that in an earlier
and more barbarous age it was the universal practice in
ancient Italy, wherever the worship of Saturn prevailed, to
choose a man who played the part and enjoyed all the
traditionary privileges of Saturn for a season, and then died,
whether by his own or another's hand, whether by the knife
or the fire or on the gallows-tree, in the character of the
good god who gave his life for the world. In Rome itself
and other great towns the growth of civilization had probably mitigated this cruel custom long before the Augustan
age, and transformed it into the innocent shape it wears in.

the writings of the few classical writers who bestow a passing notice on the holiday King of the Saturnalia. But in remoter districts the older and sterner practice may long have survived ; and even if after the unification of Italy the barbarous usage was suppressed by the Roman government, the memory of it would be handed down by the peasants and would tend from time to time, as still happens with the lowest forms of superstition among ourselves, to lead to a recrudescence of the practice, especially among the rude soldiery on the outskirts of the empire over whom the once iron hand of Rome was beginning to relax its grasp.[1]

The modern Carnival perhaps the equivalent of the ancient Saturnalia.   The resemblance between the Saturnalia of ancient and the Carnival of modern Italy has often been remarked ; but in the light of all the facts that have come before us, we may well ask whether the resemblance does not amount to identity. We have seen that in Italy, Spain, and France, that is, in the countries where the influence of Rome has been deepest and most lasting, a conspicuous feature of the Carnival is a burlesque figure personifying the festive season, which after a short career of glory and dissipation is publicly shot, burnt, or otherwise destroyed, to the feigned grief or genuine delight of the populace.[2] If the view here suggested of the Carnival is correct, this grotesque personage is no other than a direct successor of the old King of the Saturnalia, the master of the revels, the real man who personated Saturn and, when the revels were over, suffered a real death in his assumed character. The King of the Bean on Twelfth Night and the mediaeval Bishop of Fools, Abbot of Unreason, or Lord of Misrule are figures of the same sort and may perhaps have had a similar origin. We will consider them in the following section.

---

[1] The opinion that at Rome a man used to be sacrificed at the Saturnalia cannot be regarded as in itself improbable, when we remember that down apparently to the establishment of Christianity a human victim was slaughtered every year at Rome in honour of Latian Jupiter. See Tertullian, *Apologeticus*, 9, *Contra Gno-* *sticos Scorpiace*, 7 ; Minucius Felix, *Octavius*, 22 and 30 ; Lactantius, *Divin. Instit.* i. 21 ; Porphyry, *De abstinentia*, ii. 56. We may conjecture that at first the sacrifice took place on the top of the Alban Mountain, and was offered to Saturn, to whom, as we have seen, high places were sacred.

[2] *The Dying God*, pp. 220 *sqq.*

§ 2. *The King of the Bean and the Festival of Fools*

The custom of electing by lot a King and often also a Queen of the Bean on Twelfth Night (Epiphany, the sixth of January) or on the eve of that festival used to prevail in France, Belgium, Germany, and England, and it is still kept up in some parts of France. It may be traced back to the first half of the sixteenth century at least, and no doubt dates from a very much more remote antiquity. At the French court the Kings themselves did not disdain to countenance the mock royalty, and Louis XIV. even supported with courtly grace the shadowy dignity in his own person. Every family as a rule elected its own King. On the eve of the festival a great cake was baked with a bean in it; the cake was divided in portions, one for each member of the family, together with one for God, one for the Virgin, and sometimes one also for the poor. The person who obtained the portion containing the bean was proclaimed King of the Bean. Where a Queen of the Bean was elected as well as a King, a second bean was sometimes baked in the cake for the Queen. Thus at Blankenheim, near Neuerburg, in the Eifel, a black and a white bean were baked in the cake; he who drew the piece with the black bean was King, and she who drew the white bean was Queen. In Franche-Comté, at the beginning of the nineteenth century, they used to put as many white haricot beans in a hat as there were persons present, and two coloured beans were added; the beans were drawn at haphazard from the hat by a child, and they who got the coloured beans were King and Queen. In England and perhaps elsewhere the practice was to put a bean in the cake for the King and a pea for the Queen. But in some places only the King was elected by lot, and after his election he chose his Queen for himself. Sometimes a coin was substituted for the bean in the cake; but though this usage was followed in southern Germany as early as the first half of the sixteenth century, it is probably an innovation on the older custom of employing a bean as the lot. In France the distribution of the pieces of the cake among the persons present was made in accordance with the directions of a child, the youngest boy present, who was placed under or on the table and addressed by the name of " Phoebe " or " Tébé " ; he answered in Latin " *Domine*." The master of the house, holding a piece of the cake in his hand, asked the child to whom he should give it, and the child named any person he pleased. Sometimes the first slice of cake was regularly assigned to "the good God" and set aside for the poor. In the name " Phoebe " or " Tébé," by which the child was addressed, learned antiquaries have detected a reference to the oracle of Apollo ; but more probably the name is a simple corruption of the Latin or French word for bean (Latin *faba*, French *fève*). Immediately on his election the King of the Bean was enthroned, saluted by all, and thrice lifted up, while he made crosses with chalk on the beams and rafters of the ceiling. Great virtue was attributed to these white crosses. They were supposed to protect the house for the whole year against

" all injuryes and harmes
Of cursed devils, sprites, and bugges, of conjurings and charmes."

Then feasting and revelry began and were kept up merrily without respect of persons. Every time the King or Queen drank, the whole company was expected to cry, "The King drinks!" or "The Queen drinks!" Any person who failed to join in the cry was punished by having his face blackened with soot or a burned cork or smeared with the lees of wine. In some parts of the Ardennes the custom was to fasten great horns of paper in the hair of the delinquent and to put a huge pair of spectacles on his nose ; and he had to wear these badges of infamy till the end of the festival.[1]

Marginal note: Crosses made by the King of the Bean to protect the house against demons and witchcraft.

<hr>

[1] Joannes Boemus, *Mores, Leges, et Ritus Omnium Gentium* (Lyons, 1541), p. 122 ; *The Popish Kingdome or reigne of Antichrist, written in Latin verse by Thomas Naogeorgus and Englyshed by Barnabe Googe, 1570*, edited by R. C. Hope (London, 1880), pp. 45 *sq.*; E. Pasquier, *Recherches de la France* (Paris, 1633), pp. 375 *sq.*; R. Herrick, "Twelfth Night, or King and Queene," *The Works of Robert Herrick* (Edinburgh, 1823), ii. 171 *sq.*; J. Brand, *Popular Antiquities of Great Britain* (London, 1883), i. 21 *sqq.*; T. F. Thiselton Dyer, *British Popular Customs* (London, 1876), pp. 24-28; R. Chambers, *The Book of Days* (London and Edinburgh, 1886), i. 61 *sqq.*; Desgranges, "Usages du Canton de Bonneval," *Mémoires de la Société Royale des Antiquaires de France*, i. (Paris, 1817) pp. 233-236; L. Beaulieu, *Archéologie de la Lorraine* (Paris, 1840–1843), i. 255 *sq.*; Reins-

The custom of electing a King and Queen of the Bean on Twelfth Day is still kept up all over the north of France. A miniature porcelain figure of a child is sometimes substituted for the bean in the cake. If the lot, whether bean or doll, falls to a boy he becomes King and chooses his Queen; if it falls to a girl she becomes Queen and chooses her King.[1]

So far, apart from the crosses chalked up to ban hobgoblins, witches, and bugs, the King and Queen of the Bean might seem to be merely playful personages appointed at a season of festivity to lead the revels. However, a more serious significance was sometimes attached to the office and to the ceremonies of Twelfth Day in general. Thus in Lorraine the height of the hemp crop in the coming year was prognosticated from the height of the King and Queen; if the King was the taller of the two, it was supposed that the male hemp would be higher than the female, but that the contrary would happen if the Queen were taller than the King.[2] Again, in the Vosges Mountains, on the borders of Franche-Comté, it is customary on Twelfth Day for people to dance on the roofs in order to make the hemp grow tall.[3]

Serious significance of the King of the Bean and Twelfth Night.

berg - Düringsfeld, *Calendrier Belge* (Brussels, 1861–1862), i. 23 *sqq.*; *id.*, *Das festliche Jahr* (Leipsic, 1863), pp. 20-23; E. Cortet, *Essai sur les Fêtes religieuses* (Paris, 1867), pp. 29-50; J. H. Schmitz, *Sitten und Sagen, Lieder, Sprüchwörter und Räthsel des Eifler Volkes* (Trèves, 1856–1858), i. 6; Laisnel de la Salle, *Croyances et Légendes du Centre de la France* (Paris, 1875), i. 19-29; J. Lecœur, *Esquisses du Bocage Normand* (Condé-sur-Noireau, 1883–1887), ii. 125; L. Bonnemère, "Le Jour des Rois en Normandie," *Revue des Traditions populaires*, ii. (1887) pp. 55 *sq.*; P. Sébillot, "La Fête des Rois," *Revue des Traditions populaires*, iii. (1888) pp. 7-12; A. Meyrac, *Traditions, Coutumes, Légendes et Contes des Ardennes* (Charleville, 1890), pp. 74 *sq.*; J. L. M. Noguès, *Les Mœurs d'autrefois en Saintonge et en Aunis* (Saintes, 1891), pp. 49 *sqq.*; L. F. Sauvé, *Le Folk-lore des Hautes-Vosges* (Paris, 1889), pp. 16 *sq.*; Ch. Beauquier,

Les Mois en Franche-Comté (Paris, 1900), pp. 16 *sq.*; F. Chapiseau, *Le Folk-lore de la Beauce et du Perche* (Paris, 1902), i. 312-315; Anatole France, "Le roy boit," *Annales Politiques et Littéraires*, 5 Janvier, 1902, pp. 4 *sq.*; *La Bresse Louhannaise*, Janvier, 1906, pp. 42-46. The custom of making white crosses on the ceiling is reported for Germany and Switzerland, but apparently not for France. It is mentioned in the earliest of the works cited above, namely that of Joannes Boemus, whose description applies especially to Franconia (Franken).

[1] This I learn from my friend M. Léon Chouville of Rouen and Cambridge. The custom is also kept up in Bresse (*La Bresse Louhannaise*, Janvier, 1906, pp. 44-46).

[2] L. Beaulieu, *Archéologie de la Lorraine* (Paris, 1840–1843), i. 256 note[1]; E. Cortet, *Essai sur les Fêtes religieuses* (Paris, 1867), p. 43.

[3] L. F. Sauvé, *op. cit.* pp. 17 *sq.*

Further, in many places the beans used in the cake were carried to the church to be blessed by the clergy, and people drew omens from the cake as to the good or ill that would Divination on Twelfth Night. befall them throughout the year.   Moreover, certain forms of divination were resorted to on Twelfth Night for the purpose of ascertaining in which month of the year wheat would be dearest.[1]

Bonfires on the Eve of Twelfth Night. In Franche-Comté, particularly in the Montagne du Doubs, it is still the custom on the Eve of Twelfth Night (the fifth of January) to light bonfires, which appear to have, in the popular mind, some reference to the crops. The whole population takes part in the festivity.   In the afternoon the young folk draw a cart about the street collecting fuel.   Some people contribute faggots, others bundles of straw or of dry hemp stalks.   Towards evening the whole of the fuel thus collected is piled up a little way from the houses and set on fire.   While it blazes, the people dance round it, crying, "Good year, come back !   Bread and wine, come back !"   In the district of Pontarlier the young folk carry lighted torches about the fields, shaking sparks over the sowed lands and shouting, "Couaille, couaille, blanconnie !"—words of which the meaning has been for- Fire applied to the fruit-trees on the Eve of Twelfth Night in Normandy and the Ardennes. gotten.[2]   A similar custom is commonly observed on the same day (the Eve of Twelfth Night, the fifth of January) in the Bocage of Normandy, except that it is the fruit-trees rather than the sowed fields to which the fire is applied. When the evening shadows have fallen on the landscape, the darkness begins to be illuminated here and there by twinkling points of fire, which multiply as the night grows late, till they appear as numerous on earth as the stars in the sky.   About every village, in the fields and orchards, on the crests of the hills, wandering lights may be discerned, vanishing and suddenly reappearing, gathering together and

---

[1] Anatole France, "Le roy boit," *Annales Politiques et Littéraires*, 5 Janvier, 1902, p. 5.   In some parts of France divination was practised for this purpose on Christmas Day.   Twelve grains of wheat, each representing a month of the year, were placed, one after the other, on a hot fire-shovel ; if the grain bounced up from the shovel, wheat would be dear in the corresponding month, but it would be cheap if the grain remained still.   See J. B. Thiers, *Traité des Superstitions* (Paris, 1679), p. 268.   See further P. Sébillot, *Le Folk-lore de France*, iii. (Paris, 1906) pp. 510 *sq.*

[2] Ch. Beauquier, *Les Mois en Franche-Comté* (Paris, 1900), p. 12.

then dispersing, pursuing each other capriciously, and tracing broken lines, sparkling arabesques of fire in the gloom of night. The peasants are observing the ceremony of the " Moles and Field-mice " (*Taupes et Mulots*); and that evening there is not a hamlet, not a farm, hardly a solitary cottage that does not contribute its flame to the general illumination, till the whole horizon seems in a blaze, and houses, woods, and hills stand out in dark relief against the glow of the sky. The villages vie with each other in the number and brilliancy of the fires they can exhibit on this occasion. Woods and hedges are scoured to provide the materials for the blaze. Torches of straw wound about poles are provided in abundance; and armed with them men and women, lads and lasses, boys and girls, pour forth from the houses at nightfall into the fields and orchards. There they run about among the trees, waving the lighted torches under the branches and striking the trunks with them so that the sparks fly out in showers. And as they do so they sing or scream at the top of their voices certain traditional curses against the animals and insects that injure the fruit-trees. They bid the moles and field-mice to depart from their orchards, threatening to break their bones and burn their beards if they tarry. The more they do this, the larger, they believe, will be the crop of fruit in the following autumn. When everybody has rushed about his own orchard, meadow or pasture in this fashion, they all assemble on a height or crest of a hill, where they picnic, each bringing his share of provisions, cider, or brandy to the feast. There, too, they kindle a huge bonfire, and dance round it, capering and brandishing their torches in wild enthusiasm.[1] Customs of the same sort used to be observed on the same day (the Eve of Epiphany, the fifth of January) in the Ardennes. People ran about with burning torches, commanding the moles and field-mice to go forth. Then they threw the torches on the ground, and believed that by this proceeding they purified the earth and made it fruitful.[2]

---

[1] J. Lecœur, *Esquisses du Bocage Normand* (Condé-sur-Noireau, 1883–1887), ii. 126-129. Compare Amélie Bosquet, *La Normandie Romanesque et Merveilleuse* (Paris and Rouen, 1845), pp. 295 *sq.*; W. Mannhardt, *Der Baumkultus* (Berlin, 1875), pp. 536 *sqq.*

[2] A. Meyrac, *Traditions, Coutumes, Légendes et Contes des Ardennes* (Charleville, 1890), pp. 75 *sq.*

Fires
kindled
on Twelfth
Night or
the Eve of
Twelfth
Night in
England
for the
sake of
the crops.
This ceremony appears to be intended to ensure a good
crop of fruit by burning out the animals and insects that
harm the fruit-trees.   In some parts of England it used to
be customary to light fires at the same season for the
purpose, apparently, of procuring a plentiful crop of wheat
in the ensuing autumn.   Thus, "in the parish of Pauntley,
a village on the borders of the county of Gloucester, next
Worcestershire, and in the neighbourhood, a custom prevails,
which is intended to prevent the smut in wheat.   On the
Eve of Twelfth-day, all the servants of every farmer assemble
together in one of the fields that has been sown with wheat.
At the end of twelve lands, they make twelve fires in a
row with straw, around one of which, much larger than the
rest, they drink a cheerful glass of cider to their master's
health, and success to the future harvest ; then, returning
home, they feast on cakes soaked in cider, which they claim
as a reward for their past labours in sowing the grain." [1]
Similarly in Herefordshire, "on the Eve of Twelfth Day, at
the approach of evening, the farmers, their friends, servants,
etc., all assemble, and, near six o'clock, all walk together
to a field where wheat is growing.   The highest part of the
ground is always chosen, where twelve small fires, and one
large one are lighted up.   The attendants, headed by the
master of the family, pledge the company in old cyder,
which circulates freely on these occasions.   A circle is
formed round the large fire, when a general shout and
hallooing takes place, which you hear answered from all
the villages and fields near ; as I have myself counted fifty
or sixty fires burning at the same time, which are generally
placed on some eminence.   This being finished, the company
all return to the house, where the good housewife and her
maids are preparing a good supper, which on this occasion
is very plentiful.   A large cake is always provided, with a
hole in the middle.   After supper, the company all attend the
bailiff (or head of the oxen) to the wain-house, where the
following particulars are observed.   The master, at the head
of his friends, fills the cup (generally of strong ale), and

[1] J. Brand, *Popular Antiquities of
Great Britain*, New Edition (London,
1883), i. 33.   In many parishes of
Gloucestershire it used to be customary on Twelfth Day to light twelve
small fires and one large one (J. Brand,
op. cit. i. 28).

stands opposite the first or finest of the oxen (twenty-four of which I have often seen tied up in their stalls together); he then pledges him in a curious toast; the company then follow his example with all the other oxen, addressing each by their name. This being over, the large cake is produced, and is, with much ceremony, put on the horn of the first ox, through the hole in the cake; he is then tickled to make him toss his head: if he throws the cake behind, it is the mistress's perquisite; if before (in what is termed the *boosy*), the bailiff claims this prize. This ended, the company all return to the house, the doors of which are in the meantime locked, and not opened till some joyous songs are sung. On entering, a scene of mirth and jollity commences, and reigns thro' the house till a late, or rather an early, hour, the next morning."[1]

The custom was known as Wassailing and it was believed to have a beneficial effect on the crops.[2] According to one Herefordshire informant, "on Twelfth Day they make twelve fires of straw and one large one to burn the old witch; they sing, drink, and dance round it; without this festival they think they should have no crop."[3] This explanation of the large fire on Twelfth Day is remarkable and may supply the key to the whole custom of kindling fires on the fields or in the orchards on that day. We have seen that witches and fiends of various sorts are believed to be let loose during the Twelve Days and that in some places they are formally driven away on Twelfth Night.[4] It may well be that the fires lighted on that day were everywhere primarily intended to burn the witches and other maleficent beings swarming invisible in the mischief-laden air, and that the benefit supposed to be conferred by the fires on the crops was not so much the positive one of quickening the growth of vegetation by genial warmth as the negative one of destroying the baleful influences which would otherwise

[marginal note:] One of the fires on Twelfth Day said to be intended "to burn the old witch."

---

[1] *The Gentleman's Magazine*, vol. lxi., February, 1791, p. 116. The article is signed J. W. and dated "Hereford, Jan. 24." The passage is quoted, correctly in substance, but with many verbal changes, by J. Brand, *Popular Antiquities of Great Britain*, i. 30 *sq.*, and by (Mrs.) E. M. Leather, *The Folk-lore of Herefordshire* (Hereford and London, 1912), p. 93.

[2] (Mrs.) Ella Mary Leather, *The Folk-lore of Herefordshire* (Hereford and London, 1912), pp. 93 *sq.*

[3] (Mrs.) E. M. Leather, *op. cit.* pp. 94 *sq.*

[4] See above, pp. 164 *sqq.*

Parallel
custom
observed
in Mace-
donia on
the Eve of
Twelfth
Night.
blast the fruits of the earth and of the trees.   This interpretation of the English and French custom of lighting fires
in fields and orchards on Twelfth Night is confirmed by a
parallel custom observed by Macedonian peasants for the
express purpose of burning up certain malicious fiends, who
are believed to be abroad at this season.   These noxious
beings are known as *Karkantzari* or *Skatsantzari*.   They are
thought to be living people, whether men or women, who during
the Twelve Days are transformed into horrible monsters,
with long nails, red faces, bloodshot eyes, snottering noses,
and slobbering mouths.   In this hideous guise they roam
about by night haunting houses and making the peasant's
life well-nigh unbearable ; they knock at the doors and
should they be refused admittance they will scramble down
the chimney and pinch, worry, and defile the sleepers in
their beds.   The only way to escape from these tormenters
is to seize and bind them fast with a straw rope.   If you
have no such rope or your heart fails you, there is nothing
for it but to shut yourself up in the house before dark, fasten
the door tight, block up the chimney, and wait for daylight ;
for it is only at night that the monsters are on the prowl,
during the day they resume their ordinary human shape.
However, in some places strenuous efforts are made during
the Twelve Days to destroy these hateful nocturnal goblins
by fire.   For example, on Christmas Eve some people
burn the *Karkantzari* by lighting faggots of holm-oak
and throwing them out into the streets at early dawn.   In
other places, notably at Melenik, they scald the fiends to
death on New Year's Eve by means of pancakes frizzling
and hissing in a pan.   While the goodwife is baking
the cakes, the goodman disguises himself as one of the
fiends in a fur coat turned inside out, and in his assumed
character dances and sings outside the door, while he invites
his wife to join him in the dance.   In other districts people
collect faggots during the whole of the Twelve Days and
lay them up on the hearth.   Then on the Eve of Twelfth
Night they set fire to the pile in order that the goblins, who are supposed to be lurking under the ashes,
may utterly perish.[1]   Thus the view that the large fire in

---

[1] G. F. Abbott, *Macedonian Folk-lore* (Cambridge, 1903), pp. 73-75.

Herefordshire on Twelfth Night is intended "to burn the
old witch" is far more probable than the opinion that it
represents the Virgin Mary, and that the other twelve fires
stand for the twelve apostles.[1]   This latter interpretation is
in all probability nothing more than a Christian gloss put
upon an old heathen custom of which the meaning was
forgotten.

The Gloucestershire custom was described by the
English traveller Thomas Pennant in the latter part of the
eighteenth century.   He says: "A custom savouring of
the Scotch Bel-tien prevales in Gloucestershire, particularly
about Newent and the neighbouring parishes, on the
twelfth day, or on the Epiphany, in the evening.   All
the servants of every particular farmer assemble together
in one of the fields that has been sown with wheat; on
the border of which, in the most conspicuous or most
elevated place, they make twelve fires of straw, in a
row; around one of which, made larger than the rest,
they drink a cheerful glass of cyder to their master's
health, success to the future harvest, and then returning
home, they feast on cakes made of carraways, etc., soaked
in cyder, which they claim as a reward for their past
labours in sowing the grain."[2]   In Shropshire also it used
to be customary to kindle festal fires on the tops of hills and
other high places on Twelfth Night.[3]   Again, in Ireland "on
Twelfth-Eve in Christmas, they use to set up as high as
they can a sieve of oats, and in it a dozen of candles set
round, and in the centre one larger, all lighted.   This in
memory of our Saviour and his Apostles, lights of the
world."[4]   Down to the present time, apparently, in the
county of Roscommon, "Twelfth Night, which is Old
Christmas Day, is a greater day than Christmas Day itself.
Thirteen rushlights are made in remembrance of the numbers
at the Last Supper, and each is named after some member

Other
accounts
of the fires
on Twelfth
Night in
England
and
Ireland.

[1] This opinion is mentioned by
(Mrs.) E. M. Leather, *The Folk-lore
of Herefordshire*, p. 95.
[2] Thomas Pennant, "A Tour in
Scotland, 1769," in John Pinkerton's
Voyages and Travels (London, 1808–
1814), iii. 49.

[3] Thomas Hyde, *Historia religionis
veterum Persarum* (Oxford, 1700), p.
257.
[4] Sir Henry Piers, *Description of
the County of Westmeath*, quoted by
J. Brand, *Popular Antiquities of
Great Britain* (London, 1883), i. 25.

of the family. If there are not enough in the household other relations' names are added. The candles are stuck in a cake of cow-dung and lighted, and as each burns out, so will be the length of each person's life. Rushlights are only used for this occasion." [1]

Belief of the Germanic peoples that the weather for the twelve months of the year is determined by the weather of the Twelve Days.

In these English and Irish customs observed on Twelfth Night the twelve fires or candles probably refer either to the twelve days from Christmas to Epiphany or to the twelve months of the year. In favour of this view it may be said that according to a popular opinion, which has been reported in England [2] and is widely diffused in Germany and the German provinces of Austria, the weather of the twelve days in question determines the weather of the twelve following months, so that from the weather on each of these days it is possible to predict the weather of the corresponding month in the ensuing year. [3] Hence in Swabia the days are called "the Twelve Lot Days"; and many people seek to pry into the future with scientific precision by means of twelve circles, each subdivided into four quadrants, which they chalk up over the parlour door or inscribe on paper. Each circle represents a month, and each quadrant represents a quarter

[1] H. J. Byrne, " All Hallows Eve and other Festivals in Connaught," *Folk-lore*, xviii. (1907) p. 439.

[2] C. S. Burne and G. F. Jackson, *Shropshire Folk-lore* (London, 1883), p. 408.

[3] *The Popish Kingdome or reigne of Antichrist, written in Latin verse by Thomas Naogeorgus and Englyshed by Barnabe Googe, 1570*, edited by R. C. Hope (London, 1880), p. 46; E. Meier, *Deutsche Sagen, Sitten und Gebräuche aus Schwaben* (Stuttgart, 1852), p. 473, § 237; A. Birlinger, *Volksthümliches aus Schwaben* (Freiburg im Breisgau, 1861–1862), i. 468, § 696; A. Kuhn und W. Schwartz, *Norddeutsche Sagen, Märchen und Gebräuche* (Leipsic, 1848), p. 411; A. Kuhn, *Sagen, Gebräuche und Märchen aus Westfalen* (Leipsic, 1859), ii. 115, § 354; A. Wuttke, *Der deutsche Volksaberglaube* [2] (Berlin, 1869), p. 61, § 74; Montanus, *Die deutschen Volksfeste*,

Volksbräuche und deutscher Volksglaube (Iserlohn, N.D.), p. 18; M. Toeppen, *Aberglauben aus Masuren* [2] (Danzig, 1867), p. 61; L. Strackerjan, *Aberglaube und Sagen aus dem Herzogthum Oldenburg* (Oldenburg, 1867), ii. 29, § 294; August Witzschel, *Sagen, Sitten und Gebräuche aus Thüringen* (Vienna, 1878), p. 175; K. Bartsch, *Sagen, Märchen und Gebräuche aus Mecklenburg* (Vienna, 1880), p. 250, § 1292; Christian Schneller, *Märchen und Sagen aus Wälschtirol* (Innsbruck, 1867), p. 231; J. Haltrich, *Zur Volkskunde der Siebenbürger Sachsen* (Vienna, 1885), p. 282; Willibald Müller, *Beiträge zur Volkskunde der Deutschen in Mähren* (Vienna and Olmutz, 1893), p. 317; Alois John, *Sitte, Brauch und Volksglaube im deutschen Westböhmen* (Prague, 1905), p. 12; P. Drechsler, *Sitte, Brauch und Volksglaube in Schlesien* (Leipsic, 1903–1906), i. 16 sq.

of a month ; and according as the sky is overcast or clear during each quarter of a day from Christmas to Epiphany, you shade the corresponding quadrant of a circle or leave it a blank. By this contrivance, as simple as it is ingenious, you may forecast the weather for the whole year with more or less of accuracy.[1] At Hosskirch in Swabia they say that you can predict the weather for the twelve months from the weather of the twelve hours of Twelfth Day alone.[2] A somewhat different system of meteorology is adopted in various parts of Switzerland, Germany, and Austria. On Christmas, New Year's Day, or another of the twelve days you take an onion, slice it in two, peel off twelve coats, and sprinkle a pinch of salt in each of them. The twelve coats of the onion stand for the twelve months of the year, and from the amount of moisture which has gathered in each of them next morning you may foretell the amount of rain that will fall in the corresponding month.[3]

But the belief that the weather of the twelve months can be predicted from the weather of the twelve days is not confined to the Germanic peoples. It occurs also in France and among the Celts of Brittany and Scotland. Thus in the Bocage of Normandy "the village old wives have a very simple means of divining the general temperature of the coming season. According to them, the twelve days between Christmas and Epiphany, including Epiphany, represent the twelve months of the year. So the thing to do is to mark the temperature of each of these days, for the temperature of the corresponding month will be relatively the same. Some people say that this experience is rarely at fault, and more trust is put in it than in the predictions of the *Double-Liégois*."[4] In Cornouaille, Brittany, it is popularly believed that the weather of the last six days of December and the first six of January prognosticates the weather of the twelve

[margin note:] Belief of the Celtic peoples that the weather for the twelve months of the year is determined by the weather of the Twelve Days.

[1] E. Meier, *Deutsche Sagen, Sitten und Gebräuche aus Schwaben* (Stuttgart, 1852), p. 473, § 237 ; A. Birlinger, *Volksthümliches aus Schwaben* (Freiburg im Breisgau, 1861-1862), i. 468, § 696.

[2] A. Birlinger, *op. cit.* i. 470.

[3] F. J. Vonbun, *Beiträge zur deut-*

schen Mythologie (Chur, 1862), p. 131 ; A. Birlinger, *Volksthümliches aus Schwaben*, i. 469 ; Chr. Schneller, *Märchen und Sagen aus Wälschtirol* (Innsbruck, 1867), p. 231.

[4] Jules Lecoeur, *Esquisses du Bocage Normand* (Condé-sur-Noireau, 1883-1887), ii. 20 *sq.*

months ; but in other parts of Brittany it is the first twelve days of January that are supposed to be ominous of the weather for the year. These days are called *gour-deziou*, which is commonly interpreted " male days," but is said to mean properly " additional or supplementary days." [1]   Again, in the Highlands of Scotland the twelve days of Christmas (*Da latha dheug na Nollaig*) " were the twelve days commencing from the Nativity or Big *Nollaig*, and were deemed to represent, in respect of weather, the twelve months of the year. Some say the days should be calculated from New Year's Day." [2]   Others again reckon the Twelve Days from the thirty-first of December. Thus Pennant tells us that " the Highlanders form a sort of almanack or presage of the weather of the ensuing year in the following manner : they make observation on twelve days, beginning at the last of December, and hold as an infallible rule, that whatsoever weather happens on each of those days, the same will prove to agree in the correspondent months. Thus, January is to answer to the weather of December 31st ; February to that of January 1st ; and so with the rest. Old people still pay great attention to this augury." [3]   It is interesting to observe that in the Celtic regions of Scotland and France popular opinion hesitates as to the exact date of the twelve days, some people dating them from Christmas, others from the New Year, and others again from the thirty-first of December. This hesitation has an important bearing on the question of the origin of the twelve days' period, as I shall point out immediately.

The Twelve Nights among the ancient Aryans of India.

Thus in the popular mind the twelve days from Christmas to Epiphany are conceived as a miniature of the whole year, the character of each particular day answering to the character of a particular month. The conception appears to be very ancient, for it meets us again among the Aryans of the Vedic age in India. They, too, appear to have invested

---

[1] J. Loth, " Les douze jours supplémentaires (*gourdeziou*) des Bretons et les douze jours des Germains et des Indous," *Revue Celtique*, xxiv. (1903) pp. 310 *sq.*

[2] J. G. Campbell, *Witchcraft and Second Sight in the Highlands and*

Islands of Scotland (Glasgow, 1902), p. 243.

[3] Thomas Pennant, " A Tour in Scotland and Voyage to the Hebrides in 1772," in John Pinkerton's *Voyages and Travels* (London, 1808–1814), iii. 384.

twelve days in midwinter with a sacred character as a time when the three Ribhus or genii of the seasons rested from their labours in the home of the sun-god ; and these twelve rest-days they called " an image or copy of the year." [1]

This curious coincidence, if such it is, between the winter festivals of the ancient Aryans of India and their modern kinsfolk in Europe seems to be best explained on the theory that the twelve days in question derive their sanctity from the position which they occupied in the calendar of the primitive Aryans. The coincidence of the name for month with the name for moon in the various Aryan languages [2] points to the conclusion that the year of our remote ancestors was primarily based on observation of the moon rather than of the sun ; but as a year of twelve lunar months or three hundred and fifty-four days (reckoning the months at twenty-nine and thirty days alternately) falls short of the solar year of three hundred and sixty-five and a quarter days by roundly twelve days, the discrepancy could not fail to attract the attention of an intelligent people, such as the primitive Aryans must be supposed to have been, who had made some progress in the arts of life ; and the most obvious way of removing the discrepancy and equating the lunar with the solar year is to add twelve days at the end of each period of twelve lunar months so as to bring the total days of the year up to three hundred and sixty-six. The equation is not indeed perfectly exact, but it may well have been sufficiently so for the rudimentary science of the primitive Aryans.[3] As many

The Twelve Nights are an ancient intercalary period introduced to equate twelve lunar months to the solar year.

[1] *The Hymns of the Rigveda*, translated by R. T. H. Griffith (Benares, 1889–1892), book iv. hymn 33, vol. ii. pp. 150 *sqq.* ; H. Zimmer, *Altindisches Leben* (Berlin, 1879), pp. 365-367 ; A. Hillebrandt, *Ritual-Litteratur, Vedische Opfer und Zauber* (Strasburg, 1897), pp. 5 *sq.* However, the Ribhus are very obscure figures in Vedic mythology. Compare H. Oldenberg, *Die Religion des Veda* (Berlin, 1894), pp. 235 *sq.* ; A. A. Macdonnell, *Vedic Mythology* (Strasburg, 1897), pp. 131 *sqq.*

[2] F. Max Müller, *Lectures on the Science of Language*, Sixth Edition (London, 1871), i. 6 *sq.* ; O. Schrader, *Reallexikon der indogermanischen Alter-*

tumskunde (Strasburg, 1901), p. 547 ; *id.*, *Sprachvergleichung und Urgeschichte* [3] (Jena, 1906–1907), ii. 228.

[3] This explanation of the sacredness of the twelve days among the Indo-European peoples of the East and West is due to A. Weber. See O. Schrader, *Reallexikon der indogermanischen Altertumskunde* (Strasburg, 1901), pp. 391-394 ; *id.*, *Sprachvergleichung und Urgeschichte*[3] (Jena, 1906–1907), ii. 2. pp. 228-234. It is accepted by J. Loth (in *Revue Celtique*, xxiv. 1903, pp. 311 *sq.*), Professor H. Hirt (*Die Indogermanen*, Strasburg, 1905-1907, ii. 537, 544), Professor J. H. Moulton (*Two Lectures on the Science of Language*, Cambridge, 1903, pp. 47 *sq.*), and

savage races in modern times have observed the discrepancy between solar and lunar time and have essayed to correct it by observations of the sun or the constellations, especially the Pleiades,[1] there seems no reason to doubt that the ancestors of the Indo-European peoples in prehistoric times were able to make similar observations, and that they were not, as has been suggested, reduced to the necessity of borrowing the knowledge of such simple and obvious facts from the star-gazers of ancient Babylonia. Learned men who make little use of their eyes except to read books are too apt to underrate the observational powers of the savage, who lives under totally different conditions from us, spending most of his time in the open air and depending for his very existence on the accuracy with which he notes the varied and changing aspects of nature.

The superstitions attaching to the Twelve Nights are not of Christian origin. It has been proposed to explain the manifold superstitions which cluster round the Twelve Days, or rather the Twelve Nights, as they are more popularly called,[2] by reference to the place which they occupy in the Christian calendar, beginning as they do immediately after Christmas and ending with Epiphany.[3] But, in the first place, it is difficult to see why the interval between these two particular festivals should have attracted to itself a greater mass of superstitious belief and custom than the interval between any other two Christian

---

J. A. MacCulloch (in Dr. J. Hastings's *Encyclopaedia of Religion and Ethics*, iii. 81 *sq.*), but is rejected on what seem to me insufficient grounds by Professor O. Schrader (*ll.cc.*).

[1] *Spirits of the Corn and of the Wild*, i. 307 *sqq.*

[2] *Die gestriegelte Rockenphilosophie* (Chemnitz, 1759), pp. 860, 861; *Bavaria, Landes- und Volkskunde des Königreichs Bayern* (Munich, 1860–1867), i. 365; A. Wuttke, *Der deutsche Volksaberglaube*[2] (Berlin, 1869), p. 61; P. Drechsler, *Sitte, Brauch und Volksglaube in Schlesien* (Leipsic, 1903–1906), i. 15; A. John, *Sitte, Brauch und Volksglaube im deutschen Westböhmen* (Prague, 1905), p. 11. The phrase "the Twelve Nights" in the sense of "the Twelve Days and Nights" is doubtless derived from the

ancient Aryan custom of counting by nights instead of by days and of regarding the period of the earth's revolution on its axis as beginning with the night rather than with the day. See Caesar, *De bello Gallico*, vi. 18; Tacitus, *Germania*, 11; O. Schrader, *Reallexikon der indogermanischen Altertumskunde* (Strasburg, 1901), pp. 844 *sqq.*; J. Loth, "L'Année celtique," *Revue Celtique*, xxv. (1904) pp. 115 *sqq.* The Athenians reckoned a day from sunset to sunset, and the Romans reckoned it from midnight to midnight (Censorinus, *De die natali*, xxiii. 3).

[3] A. Tille, *Die Geschichte der deutschen Weihnacht* (Leipsic, preface dated 1893), pp. 3 *sq.*, 281 *sqq.*; O. Schrader, *Reallexikon der indogermanischen Altertumskunde* (Strasburg, 1901), p. 392.

festivals in the calendar ; if it really did so, the ground of
its special attraction is still to seek, and on this essential
point the advocates of the Christian origin of the Twelve
Nights throw no light. In the second place, the superstitious
beliefs and customs themselves appear to have no relation to
Christianity but to be purely pagan in character. Lastly, a
fatal objection to the theory in question is that the place
of the Twelve Days in the calendar is not uniformly fixed
to the interval between Christmas and Epiphany ; it varies
considerably in popular opinion in different places, but it is
significant that the variations never exceed certain comparatively narrow limits. The twelve-days' festival, so to
speak, oscillates to and fro about a fixed point, which is
either the end of the year or the winter solstice. Thus in
Silesia the Twelve Days are usually reckoned to fall before
Christmas instead of after it ; though in the Polish districts
and the mountainous region of the country the ordinary
German opinion prevails that the days immediately follow
Christmas.[1] In some parts of Bavaria the Twelve Days are
counted from St. Thomas's Day (the twenty-first of December)
to New Year's Day; while in parts of Mecklenburg they
begin with New Year's Day and so coincide with the first
twelve days of January,[2] and this last mode of reckoning
finds favour, as we saw, with some Celts of Brittany and
Scotland.[3] These variations in the dating of the Twelve
Days seem irreconcilable with the theory that they derive
their superstitious character purely from the accident that
they fall between Christmas and Epiphany ; accordingly we
may safely dismiss the theory of their Christian origin and
recognize, with many good authorities,[4] in the Twelve Days
the relics of a purely pagan festival, which was probably

---

[1] P. Drechsler, *Sitte, Brauch und Volksglaube in Schlesien* (Leipsic, 1903–1906), i. 15.

[2] A. Wuttke, *Der deutsche Volks-aberglaube*[2] (Berlin, 1869), p. 61, § 74. As to the varying dates of the Twelve Nights see further E. Mogk, "Mytho-logie," in H. Paul's *Grundriss der germanischen Philologie*, iii.[2] (Stras-burg, 1900), p. 260.

[3] See above, p. 324.

[4] Thus A. Wuttke observes that by far the greater part of the superstitions attaching to the Twelve Nights are of purely heathen origin (*Der deutsche Volksaberglaube*,[2] p. 61); and K. Weinhold similarly remarks that the superstitions in question cannot have originated in Christian dogmas, and that they point to the sacredness of the winter solstice among the heathen tribes of Germany (*Weinacht-Spiele und Lieder aus Süddeutschland und Schlesien*, Vienna, 1875, p. 4).

celebrated long before the foundation of Christianity. In truth the hypothesis of the Christian derivation of the Twelve Days in all probability exactly inverts the historical order of the facts. On the whole the evidence goes to shew that the great Christian festivals were arbitrarily timed by the church so as to coincide with previously existing pagan festivals for the sake of weaning the heathen from their old faith and bringing them over to the new religion. To make the transition as easy as possible the ecclesiastical authorities, in abolishing the ancient rites, appointed ceremonies of some-what similar character on the same days, or nearly so, thus filling up the spiritual void by a new creation which the worshipper might accept as an adequate substitute for what he had lost. Christmas and Easter, the two pivots on which the Christian calendar revolves, appear both to have been instituted with this intention: the one superseded a mid-winter festival of the birth of the sun-god, the other super-seded a vernal festival of the death and resurrection of the vegetation-god.[1]

An intercalary period a natural subject of supersti-tion to primitive peoples.

If the twelve days from Christmas to Epiphany were indeed an ancient intercalary period inserted for the purpose of equating the lunar to the solar year, we can better under-stand the curious superstitions that have clustered round them and the quaint customs that have been annually observed during their continuance. To the primitive mind it might well seem that an intercalary period stands outside of the regular order of things, forming part neither of the lunar nor of the solar system; it is an excrescence, inevitable but unaccountable, which breaks the smooth surface of ordinary existence, an eddy which interrupts the even flow of months and years. Hence it may be inferred that the ordinary rules of conduct do not apply to such extraordinary periods, and that accordingly men may do in them what they would never dream of doing at other times. Thus intercalary days tend to degenerate into seasons of unbridled license; they form an interregnum during which the customary restraints of law

[1] See *Adonis, Attis, Osiris*, Second Edition, pp. 254 *sqq.*; and for Easter in particular see my letter " Attis and Christ," *The Athenaeum*, No. 4184, January 4th, 1908, pp. 19 *sq.*; Franz Cumont, *Les Religions orientales dans le Paganisme romain*[2] (Paris, 1909), pp. 106 *sq.*, 333 *sq.*

and morality are suspended and the ordinary rulers abdicate their authority in favour of a temporary regent, a sort of puppet king, who bears a more or less indefinite, capricious, and precarious sway over a community given up for a time to riot, turbulence, and disorder. If that is so—though it must be confessed that the view here suggested is to a great extent conjectural—we may perhaps detect the last surviving representatives of such puppet kings in the King of the Bean and other grotesque figures of the same sort who used to parade with the mimic pomp of sovereignty on one or other of the twelve days between Christmas and Epiphany. For the King of the Bean was by no means the only such ruler of the festive season, nor was Twelfth Night the only day on which he and his colleagues played their pranks. We will conclude this part of our subject with a brief notice of some of these mummers.

In the first place it deserves to be noticed that in many parts of the continent, such as France, Spain, Belgium, Germany, and Austria, Twelfth Day is regularly associated with three mythical kings named Caspar, Melchior, and Balthasar, and derives its popular appellation from them, being known in Germany and Austria as the Day of the Three Kings (*Dreikönigstag*) and in France as the Festival of the Kings (*Fête des Rois*). Further, it has been customary in many places to represent the three kings by mummers, who go about arrayed in royal costume from door to door, singing songs and collecting contributions from the households which they visit.[1] The custom may very well be older than Christianity, though it has received a Christian colouring; for the mythical kings are commonly identified with the wise men of the East, who are said to have been attracted

The Three Kings of Twelfth Night.

---

[1] J. Brand, *Popular Antiquities of Great Britain* (London, 1883), i. 21 *sq.* ; E. Cortet, *Essai sur les Fêtes religieuses* (Paris, 1867), pp. 32, 38, 39-42 ; Reinsberg-Düringsfeld, *Calendrier Belge* (Brussels, 1861–1862), i. 21 *sq.*, 30 *sq.*; *id.*, *Fest-Kalender aus Böhmen* (Prague, N.D.), p. 18 ; *id.*, *Das festliche Jahr* (Leipsic, 1863), pp. 23-26 ; *Bavaria, Landes- und Volkskunde des Königreichs Bayern* (Munich, 1860–1867), ii. 262 *sq.* ; L. F. Sauvé, *Le Folk-lore des Hautes-Vosges* (Paris, 1889), pp. 15-18 ; Ch. Beauquier, *Les Mois en Franche-Comté* (Paris, 1900), pp. 13-15 ; *La Bresse Louhannaise*, Janvier, 1906, p. 42 ; P. Drechsler, *Sitte, Brauch und Volksglaube in Schlesien* (Leipsic, 1903-1906), i. 51 ; A. John, *Sitte, Brauch und Volksglaube im deutschen Westböhmen* (Prague, 1905), pp. 32-34 ; E. Hoffmann-Krayer, *Feste und Bräuche des Schweizervolkes* (Zürich, 1913), pp. 104, 121.

to the infant Christ at Bethlehem by the sight of his star in the sky.[1] Yet there is no Biblical authority for regarding these wise men as kings or for fixing their number at three. In Franche-Comté the old custom is still observed, or at all events it was so down to recent years. The Three Kings are personated by three boys dressed in long white shirts with coloured sashes round their waists ; on their heads they wear pointed mitres of pasteboard decorated with a gilt star and floating ribbons. Each carries a long wand topped by a star, which he keeps constantly turning. The one who personates Melchior has his face blackened with soot, because Melchior is supposed to have been a negro king. When they enter a house, they sing a song, setting forth that they are three kings who have come from three different countries, led by a star, to adore the infant Jesus at Bethlehem. After the song the negro king solicits contributions by shaking his money-box or holding out a basket, in which the inmates of the house deposit eggs, nuts, apples and so forth. By way of thanks for this liberality the three kings chant a stave in which they call down the blessing of God on the household.[2] The custom is similar in the Vosges Mountains, where the Three Kings are held in great veneration and invoked by hedge doctors to effect various cures. For example, if a man drops to the ground with the falling sickness, you need only whisper in his right ear, " *Gaspard fert myrrham, thus Melchior, Balthasar aurum,*" and he will get up at once. But to make the cure complete you must knock three nails into the earth on the precise spot where he fell ; each nail must be exactly of the length of the patient's little finger, and as you knock it in you must take care to utter the sufferer's name.[3] In many Czech villages of Bohemia the children who play the part of the Three Kings assimilate themselves to the wise men of the East in the gospel by carrying gilt paper, incense, and myrrh with them on their rounds, which they distribute as gifts in the houses they visit, receiving in return money or presents in kind. Moreover they fumigate

---

[1] Matthew ii. 1-12.

[2] Ch. Beauquier, *Les Mois en Franche-Comté* (Paris, 1900), pp. 13-16.

[3] L. F. Sauvé, *Le Folk-lore des Hautes-Vosges* (Paris, 1889), pp. 15-17. Compare the old Roman cure for the falling sickness (above, p. 68).

and sprinkle the houses and describe crosses and letters on the doors. Amongst the Germans of West Bohemia it is the schoolmaster who, accompanied by some boys, goes the round of the village on Twelfth Day. He chalks up the letters C. M. B. (the initials of Caspar, Melchior, and Balthasar), together with three crosses, on every door, and fumigates the house with a burning censer in order to guard it from evil influences and infectious diseases.[1] Some people used to wear as an amulet a picture representing the adoration of the Three Kings with a Latin inscription to the following effect: " Holy three kings, Caspar, Melchior, Balthasar, pray for us, now and in the hour of our death." The picture was thought to protect the wearer not only from epilepsy, headache, and fever, but also from the perils of the roads, from the bite of mad dogs, from sudden death, from sorcery and witchcraft.[2] Whatever its origin, the festival of the Three Kings goes back to the middle ages, for it is known to have been celebrated with great pomp at Milan in 1336. On that occasion the Three Kings appeared wearing crowns, riding richly caparisoned horses, and surrounded by pages, bodyguards, and a great retinue of followers. Before them was carried a golden star, and they offered gifts of gold, frankincense, and myrrh to the infant Christ cradled in a manger beside the high altar of the church of St. Eustorgius.[3]

In our own country a popular figure during the Christmas holidays used to be the Lord of Misrule, or, as he was called in Scotland, the Abbot of Unreason, who led the revels at that merry season in the halls of colleges, the Inns of Court, the palace of the king, and the mansions of nobles.[4] Writing at the end of the sixteenth century, the antiquary John Stow tells us that, " in the feast of Christmas, there was in the King's house, wheresoever he was lodged, a Lord of Misrule, or Master of Merry Disports ; and the like had ye in the

The Lord of Misrule in England.

---

[1] O. Freiherr von Reinsberg-Düringsfeld, *Fest-Kalender aus Böhmen* (Prague, N.D.), pp. 17 *sq.*

[2] Reinsberg-Düringsfeld, *Calendrier Belge* (Brussels, 1861–1862), i. 22. The mere names of the three kings worn on the person were believed to be a cure for epilepsy. See J. B. Thiers, *Traité des Superstitions* (Paris, 1679),

pp. 350 *sq.*

[3] R. Chambers, *The Book of Days* (London and Edinburgh, 1886), i. 62, referring to Warton's *History of English Poetry*.

[4] J. Brand, *Popular Antiquities of Great Britain* (London, 1883), i. 497 *sqq.* ; E. K. Chambers, *The Mediaeval Stage* (Oxford, 1903), i. 403 *sqq.*

house of every nobleman of honour or good worship, were he spiritual or temporal. Amongst the which the Mayor of London, and either of the Sheriffs, had their several Lords of Misrule, ever contending, without quarrel or offence, who should make the rarest pastimes to delight the beholders. These Lords beginning their rule on Alhollon eve, continued the same til the morrow after the Feast of the Purification, commonly called Candlemas day. In all which space there were fine and subtle disguisings, masks and mummeries, with playing at cards for counters, nails, and points, in every house, more for pastime than for gain."[1] Again, in the seventeenth century the ardent royalist Sir Thomas Urquhart wrote that "they may be likewise said to use their king . . . as about Christmas we do the King of Misrule; whom we invest with that title to no other end, but to countenance the Bacchanalian riots and preposterous disorders of the family, where he is installed."[2] From the former passage it appears that the Lords of Misrule often or even generally reigned for more than three months in winter, namely from Allhallow Even (the thirty-first of October, the Eve of All Saints' Day) till Candlemas (the second of February). Sometimes, however, their reign seems to have

Reign of the Lord of Misrule during the Twelve Days. been restricted to the Twelve Nights. Thus we are told that George Ferrers of Lincoln's Inn was Lord of Misrule for twelve days one year when King Edward VI. kept his Christmas with open house at Greenwich.[3] At Trinity College, Cambridge, a Master of Arts used to be appointed to this honourable office, which he held for the twelve days from Christmas to Twelfth Day, and he resumed office on Candlemas Day. His duty was to regulate the games and diversions of the students, particularly the plays which were acted in the college hall. Similar masters of the revels were commonly instituted in the colleges at Oxford; for example, at Merton College the fellows annually elected about St. Edmund's Day, in November a Lord of Misrule or, as he was called in the registers, a King of the Bean (*Rex Fabarum*),

[1] John Stow, *A Survey of London, written in the year 1598*, edited by William J. Thoms (London, 1876), p. 37.

[2] Sir Thomas Urquhart, *The Discovery of a most Exquisite Jewel, more precious than Diamonds inchased in Gold* (Edinburgh, 1774), p. 146.

[3] J. Brand, *op. cit.* i. 499.

who held office till Candlemas and sometimes assumed a
number of ridiculous titles. In the Inner Temple a Lord of Lord of
Misrule used to be appointed on St. Stephen's Day (the Misrule in
the Temple.
twenty-sixth of December); surrounded by his courtiers, who
were dubbed by various derogatory or ribald names, he
presided at the dancing, feasting, and minstrelsy in the hall.
Of the mock monarch who in the Christmas holidays of 1635
held office in the Middle Temple the jurisdiction, privileges,
and parade have been minutely described. He was attended
by his lord keeper, lord treasurer, with eight white staves,
a band of gentleman pensioners with poleaxes, and two
chaplains. He dined under a canopy of state both in the
hall and in his own chambers. He received many petitions,
which he passed on in regal style to his Master of Requests;
and he attended service in the Temple church, where his
chaplains preached before him and did him reverence. His
expenses, defrayed from his own purse, amounted to no
less than two thousand pounds.[1] "I remember to have
heard a Bencher of the Temple tell a story of a tradition in
their house, where they had formerly a custom of choosing
kings for such a season, and allowing him his expences at
the charge of the society: One of our kings, said my friend,
carried his royal inclination a little too far, and there was a
committee ordered to look into the management of his
treasury. Among other things it appeared, that his Majesty
walking *incog.* in the cloister, had overheard a poor man say
to another, Such a small sum would make me the happiest
man in the world. The king out of his royal compassion
privately inquired into his character, and finding him a
proper object of charity, sent him the money. When the
committee read the report, the house passed his accounts
with a plaudite without further examination, upon the
recital of this article in them, 'For making a man happy,
£10:0:0.'"[2]

At the English court the annual Lord of Misrule is not
to be confounded with the Master of the Revels, who was a

[1] J. Brand, *Popular Antiquities of
Great Britain* (London, 1883), i. 497
sqq. As to the Lords of Misrule in colleges and the Inns of Court see further

E. K. Chambers, *The Mediaeval Stage*,
i. 407 *sqq.*
[2] Sir Richard Steele, in *The Spec-
tator*, Friday, 14th December 1711.

permanent official and probably despised the temporary Lord
as an upstart rival and intruder.   Certainly there seems to
have been at times bad blood between them.   Some correspondence which passed between the two merry monarchs
in the reign of Edward VI. has been preserved, and from it
we learn that on one occasion the Lord of Misrule had much
difficulty in extracting from the Master of the Revels the
fool's coat, hobby-horses, and other trumpery paraphernalia
which he required for the proper support of his dignity.
Indeed the costumes furnished by his rival were so shabby
that his lordship returned them with a note, in which he
informed the Master of the Revels that the gentlemen of
rank and position who were to wear these liveries stood too
much on their dignity to be seen prancing about the streets
of London rigged out in such old slops.   The Lords of Council
had actually to interpose in the petty squabble between the
two potentates.[1]

In France the counterparts of these English Lords of
Misrule masqueraded in clerical attire as mock Bishops,
Archbishops, Popes, or Abbots.   The festival at which they
disported themselves was known as the Festival of Fools
(*Fête des Fous*), which fell in different places at different
dates, sometimes on Christmas Day, sometimes on St.
Stephen's Day (the twenty-sixth of December), sometimes
on New Year's Day, and sometimes on Twelfth Day.
According to one account "on the first day, which was the
festival of Christmas, the lower orders of clergy and monks
cried in unison *Noël* (Christmas) and gave themselves up
to jollity.   On the morrow, St. Stephen's Day, the deacons
held a council to elect a Pope or Patriarch of Fools, a Bishop
or Archbishop of Innocents, an Abbot of Ninnies ; next day,
the festival of St. John, the subdeacons began the dance in
his honour ; afterwards, on the fourth day, the festival of the
Holy Innocents, the choristers and minor clergy claimed the
Pope or Bishop or Abbot elect, who made his triumphal
entry into the church on Circumcision Day (the first of
January) and sat enthroned pontifically till the evening of
Epiphany.   It was then the joyous reign of this Pope or
this Bishop or this Abbot of Folly which constituted the

---

[1] E. K. Chambers, *The Mediaeval Stage*, i. 405-407.

Festival of Fools and dominated its whimsical phases, the grotesque and sometimes impious masquerades, the merry and often disgusting scenes, the furious orgies, the dances, the games, the profane songs, the impudent parodies of the catholic liturgy." [1]   At these parodies of the most solemn rites of the church the priests, wearing grotesque masks and sometimes dressed as women, danced in the choir and sang obscene chants: laymen disguised as monks and nuns mingled with the clergy: the altar was transformed into a tavern, where the deacons and subdeacons ate sausages and black-puddings or played at dice and cards under the nose of the celebrant; and the censers smoked with bits of old shoes instead of incense, filling the church with a foul stench. After playing these pranks and running, leaping, and cutting capers through the whole church, they rode about the town in mean carts, exchanging scurrilities with the crowds of laughing and jeering spectators. [2]

Amongst the buffooneries of the Festival of Fools one of the most remarkable was the introduction of an ass into the church, where various pranks were played with the animal. At Autun the ass was led with great ceremony to the church under a cloth of gold, the corners of which were held by four canons; and on entering the sacred edifice the animal was wrapt in a rich cope, while a parody of the mass was performed.   A regular Latin liturgy in glorification of the ass was chanted on these occasions, and the celebrant priest imitated the braying of an ass.   At Beauvais the ceremony

Buffooneries in the churches at the Festival of Fools.

---

[1] L. J. B. Bérenger-Feraud, *Superstitions et Survivances*, iv. (Paris, 1896) pp. 4 *sq.*, quoting Jacob, *Mœurs et Coutumes du Moyen-Age*. Compare E. Cortet, *Essai sur les Fêtes religieuses* (Paris, 1867), pp. 50 *sqq.* In some places the festival was held on the octave of Epiphany. See E. K. Chambers, *The Mediaeval Stage* (Oxford, 1903), i. 323.

[2] E. Cortet, *op. cit.* p. 51; Papon, *Histoire Générale de la Provence*, iii. p. 212, quoted by L. J. B. Bérenger-Feraud, *op. cit.* iv. 9 *sq.*; E. K. Chambers, *The Mediaeval Stage* (Oxford, 1903), i. 293 *sq.*, quoting a circular

letter which was addressed by the Faculty of Theology at Paris to the bishops and chapters of France on March 12th, 1445. Many details as to the mode of celebrating the Festival of Fools in different parts of France are on record. See A. de Nore, *Coutumes, Mythes, et Traditions des Provinces de France* (Paris and Lyons, 1846), pp. 293-295; E. Cortet, *op. cit.* pp. 52 *sqq.*; L. J. B. Bérenger-Feraud, *op. cit.* iv. 5 *sqq.*; G. Bilfinger, *Untersuchungen über die Zeitrechnung der alten Germanen*, ii. *Das germanische Julfest* (Stuttgart, 1901), pp. 72 *sq.*; and especially E. K. Chambers, *The Mediaeval Stage*, i. 274 *sqq.*

was performed every year on the fourteenth of January. A young girl with a child in her arms rode on the back of the ass in imitation of the Flight into Egypt. Escorted by the clergy and the people she was led in triumph from the cathedral to the parish church of St. Stephen. There she and her ass were introduced into the chancel and stationed on the left side of the altar ; and a long mass was performed which consisted of scraps borrowed indiscriminately from the services of many church festivals throughout the year. In the intervals the singers quenched their thirst : the congregation imitated their example ; and the ass was fed and watered. The services over, the animal was brought from the chancel into the nave, where the whole congregation, clergy and laity mixed up together, danced round the animal and brayed like asses. Finally, after vespers and compline, the merry procession, led by the precentor and preceded by a huge lantern, defiled through the streets to wind up the day with indecent farces in a great theatre erected opposite the church.[1]

Festival of the Innocents and the Boy Bishop in France.

A pale reflection or diminutive copy of the Festival of Fools was the Festival of the Innocents, which was celebrated on Childermas or Holy Innocents' Day, the twenty-eighth of December. The custom was widely observed both in France and England. In France on Childermas or the eve of the festival the choristers assembled in the church and chose one of their number to be a Boy Bishop, who officiated in that character with mock solemnity. Such burlesques of ecclesiastical ritual appear to have been common on that day in monasteries and convents, where the offices performed by the clergy and laity were inverted for the occasion. At the Franciscan monastery of Antibes, for example, the lay

[1] E. Cortet, *Essai sur les Fêtes religieuses* (Paris, 1867), pp. 53-56 ; L. J. B. Bérenger-Feraud, *Superstitions et Survivances*, iv. 28-41 ; E. K. Chambers, *The Mediaeval Stage* (Oxford, 1903), i. 330-334. While the Festival of Fools appears to have been most popular in France, it is known to have been celebrated also in Germany, Bohemia, and England. See E. K. Chambers, *op. cit.* i. 318 *sqq.* In his youth the Bohemian reformer John Huss

took part in these mummeries. The revellers wore masks. " A clerk, grotesquely vested, was dubbed ' bishop,' set on an ass with his face to the tail, and led to mass in the church. He was regaled on a platter of broth and a bowl of beer, and Huss recalls the unseemly revel which took place. Torches were borne instead of candles, and the clergy turned their garments inside out and danced " (E. K. Chambers, *op. cit.* i. 320 *sq.*).

brothers, who usually worked in the kitchen and the garden, took the place of the priests on Childermas and celebrated mass in church, clad in tattered sacerdotal vestments turned inside out, holding the books upside down, wearing spectacles made of orange peel, mumbling an unintelligible jargon, and uttering frightful cries.   These buffooneries were kept up certainly as late as the eighteenth century,[1] and probably later.   In the great convent of the Congrégation de Notre Dame at Paris down to the latter part of the nineteenth century the nuns and their girl pupils regularly exchanged parts on Holy Innocents' Day.   The pupils pretended to be nuns and a select few of them were attired as such, while the nuns made believe to be pupils, without however changing their dress.[2]

In England the Boy Bishop was widely popular during the later Middle Ages and only succumbed to the austerity of the Reformation.   He is known, for example, to have officiated in St. Paul's, London, in the cathedrals of Salisbury, Exeter, Hereford, Gloucester, Lichfield, Norwich, Lincoln, and York, in great collegiate churches such as Beverley minster, St. Peter's, Canterbury, and Ottery St. Mary's, in college chapels such as Magdalen and All Souls' at Oxford, in the private chapels of the king, and in many parish churches throughout the country.   The election was usually made on St. Nicholas's Day (the sixth of December), but the office and authority lasted till Holy Innocents' Day (the twenty-eighth of December).   Both days were appropriate, for St. Nicholas was the patron saint of school children, and Holy Innocents' Day commemorates the slaughter of the young children by Herod.   In cathedrals the Bishop was chosen from among the choir boys.   After his election he was completely apparelled in the episcopal vestments, with a mitre and crosier, bore the title and displayed the state of

The Boy Bishop in England.

---

[1] E. Cortet, *Essai sur les Fêtes religieuses*, p. 58; E. K. Chambers, *The Mediaeval Stage* (Oxford, 1903), i. 317 *sq.*, 336 *sqq.* Compare L. J. B. Bérenger-Feraud, *Superstitions et Survivances*, iv. 25-28. From the evidence collected by the latter writer it appears that in some places the election of the Boy Bishop took place on other days

than Childermas. At Alençon the election took place on the sixth of December; at Vienne, in Dauphiné, on the fifteenth, and at Soissons on St. Thomas's Day (the twenty-first of December).

[2] This I learn from my wife, who as a girl was educated in the convent.

a Bishop, and exacted ceremonial obedience from his fellows,
who were dressed like priests.   They took possession of the
church and, with the exception of mass, performed all the
ceremonies and offices.   The Boy Bishop preached from
the pulpit.   At Salisbury the ceremonies at which he presided are elaborately regulated by the statutes of Roger de
Mortival, enacted in 1319; and two of the great service-
books of the Sarum use, the Breviary and the Processional,
furnish full details of the ministrations of the Boy Bishop and
his fellows.   He is even said to have enjoyed the right of dis-
posing of such prebends as happened to fall vacant during
the days of his episcopacy.   But the pranks of the mock
bishop were not confined to the church.   Arrayed in full
canonicals he was led about with songs and dances from
house to house, blessing the grinning people and collecting
money in return for his benedictions.   At York in the year
1396 the Boy Bishop is known to have gone on his rounds
to places so far distant as Bridlington, Leeds, Beverley,
Fountains Abbey, and Allerton ; and the profits which he
made were considerable.   William of Wykeham ordained in
1400 that a Boy Bishop should he chosen at Winchester
College and another at New College, Oxford, and that he
should recite the office at the Feast of the Innocents.   His
example was followed some forty years afterwards in the
statutes of the royal foundations of Eton College and of
King's College, Cambridge.   From being elected on St.
Nicholas's Day the Boy Bishop was sometimes called a
Nicholas Bishop (*Episcopus Nicholatensis*).[1]   In Spanish
cathedrals, also, it appears to have been customary on St.
Nicholas's Day to elect a chorister to the office of Bishop.
He exercised a certain jurisdiction till Holy Innocents' Day,
and his prebendaries took secular offices, acting in the capacity
of alguazils, catchpoles, dog-whippers, and sweepers.[2]

On the whole it seems difficult to suppose that the
curious superstitions and quaint ceremonies, the outbursts

---

[1] J. Brand, *Popular Antiquities of Great Britain* (London, 1883), i. 421-431 ; E. K. Chambers, *The Mediaeval Stage* (Oxford, 1903), i. 352 *sqq.* ; (Mrs.) Ella Mary Leather, *The Folk-lore of Herefordshire* (Hereford and London, 1912), pp. 138 *sq.* ; *County Folk-lore*, II. *North Riding of York-shire, York and the Ainsty*, edited by Mrs. Gutch (London, 1901), pp. 352 *sq.*

[2] J. Brand, *op. cit.* i. 426.

of profanity and the inversions of ranks, which characterize
the popular celebration of the twelve days from Christmas
to Epiphany, have any connexion with the episodes of
Christian history believed to be commemorated by these
two festivals. More probably they are relics of an old
heathen festival celebrated during the twelve intercalary
days which our forefathers annually inserted in their
calendar at midwinter in order to equalize the short lunar
year of twelve months with the longer solar year of three
hundred and sixty-five or sixty-six days. We need not
assume that the license and buffooneries of the festive season
were borrowed from the Roman Saturnalia; both celebrations
may well have been parallel and independent deductions from
a like primitive philosophy of nature. There is not indeed,
so far as I am aware, any direct evidence that the Saturnalia
at Rome was an intercalary festival; but the license which
characterized it, and the temporary reign of a mock king,
who personated Saturn, suggest that it may have been so.
If we were better acquainted with the intercalary periods
of peoples at a comparatively low level of culture, we might
find that they are commonly marked by similar outbreaks
of lawlessness and similar reigns of more or less nominal
and farcical rulers. But unfortunately we know too little
about the observance of such periods among primitive
peoples to be warranted in making any positive affirmation
on the subject.

However, there are grounds for thinking that intercalary
periods have commonly been esteemed unlucky. The Aztecs
certainly regarded as very unlucky the five supplementary
days which they added at the end of every year in order to
make up a total of three hundred and sixty-five days.[1] These
five supplementary days, corresponding to the last four of
January and the first of February, were called *nemontemi*,
which means "vacant," "superfluous," or "useless." Being
dedicated to no god, they were deemed inauspicious, equally
unfit for the services of religion and the transaction of civil
business. During their continuance no sacrifices were
offered by the priests and no worshippers frequented the
temples. No cases were tried in the courts of justice. The

The customs and superstitions associated with the Twelve Days or Nights are probably relics of an old heathen festival of intercalation at midwinter.

Superstitions associated with intercalary periods among the Aztecs of Mexico and the Mayas of Yucatan.

---

[1] As to the Aztec year see above, p. 287 note [1].

houses were not swept. People abstained from all actions of importance and confined themselves to performing such as could not be avoided, or spent the time in paying visits to each other. In particular they were careful during these fatal days not to fall asleep in the daytime, not to quarrel, and not to stumble ; because they thought that if they did such things at that time they would continue to do so for ever. Persons born on any of these days were deemed unfortunate, destined to fail in their undertakings and to live in wretchedness and poverty all their time on earth.[1] The Mayas of Yucatan employed a calendar like that of the Aztecs, and they too looked upon the five supplementary days at the end of the year as unlucky and of evil omen ; hence they gave no names to these days, and while they lasted the people stayed for the most part at home ; they neither washed themselves, nor combed their hair, nor loused each other; and they did no servile or fatiguing work lest some evil should befall them.[2]

The five supplementary days of the year in ancient Egypt. The ancient Egyptians like the Aztecs considered a year to consist of three hundred and sixty ordinary days divided into months and eked out with five supplementary days so as to bring the total number of days in the year up to three hundred and sixty-five ; but whereas the Aztecs divided the three hundred and sixty ordinary days into eighteen arbitrary divisions or months of twenty days each, the Egyptians, keeping much closer to the natural periods marked by the phases of the moon, divided these days into twelve months of thirty days each.[3] This mode of regulating the calendar appears to be exceedingly ancient in Egypt and may even date from the prehistoric period ; for the five days over and above the year (*haru duaït hiru ronpit*) are expressly mentioned in the texts of the pyramids.[4] The myth told to explain their

---

[1] B. de Sahagun, *Histoire Générale des Choses de la Nouvelle Espagne*, traduite par D. Jourdanet et R. Simeon (Paris, 1880), pp. 77, 283 ; E. Seler, " The Mexican Chronology," in *Bureau of American Ethnology, Bulletin No. 28* (Washington, 1904), p. 16 (where some extracts from the Aztec text of Sahagun are quoted and translated) ; J. de Acosta, *Natural and Moral History of the Indies* (Hakluyt Society, London, 1880), ii. 392.

[2] Diego de Landa, *Relation des Choses de Yucatan* (Paris, 1864), pp. 204 *sq.*, 276 *sq.*

[3] Geminus, *Elementa Astronomiae*, viii. 18, p. 106, ed. C. Manitius (Leipsic, 1898).

[4] G. Foucart, in Dr. J. Hastings's *Encyclopaedia of Religion and Ethics*, iii. (1910) p. 93. Professor Ed. Meyer adduces astronomical and other grounds for thinking that the ancient Egyptian calendar, as we know it, began on the

origin was as follows. Once on a time the earth-god Keb lay secretly with the sky-goddess Nut, and the sun-god Ra in his anger cursed the goddess, saying that she should give birth to her offspring neither in any month nor in any year. He thought, no doubt, by this imprecation to prevent her from bringing forth the fruit of her womb. But he was out-witted by the wily Thoth, who engaged the goddess of the moon in a game of draughts and having won the game took as a forfeit from her the seventieth part of every day in the year, and out of the fractions thus abstracted he made up five new days, which he added to the old year of three hundred and sixty days. As these days formed no part either of a month or of a year, the goddess Nut might be delivered in them without rendering the sun-god's curse void and of no effect. Accordingly she bore Osiris on the first of the days, Horus on the second, Set or Typhon on the third, Isis on the fourth, and Nephthys on the fifth. Of these five supplementary or intercalary days the third, as the birth-day of the evil deity Set or Typhon, was deemed unlucky, and the Egyptian kings neither transacted business on it nor attended to their persons till nightfall.[1] Thus it appears that the ancient Egyptians regarded the five supplementary or intercalary days as belonging neither to a month nor to a year, but as standing outside of both and forming an extraordinary period quite apart and distinct from the ordinary course of time. It is probable, though we cannot prove it, that in all countries intercalary days or months have been so considered

19th of July, 4241 B.C., which accord-ingly he calls "the oldest sure date in the history of the world." See Ed. Meyer, *Geschichte des Altertums*[2], i. 2. (Stuttgart and Berlin, 1909), pp. 101 *sq.*, § 197 ; and against this view C. F. Lehmann-Haupt, in the *English His-torical Review*, April 1913, p. 348.

[1] Plutarch, *Isis et Osiris*, 12. Compare Diodorus Siculus, i. 13. 4 *sq.* As to Keb and Nut, the parents of Osiris, Isis, and the rest, see A. Erman, *Die ägyptische Religion* (Berlin, 1905), p. 29. The Egyptian deities Keb, Nut, and Thoth are called by Plutarch by the Greek names of Cronus, Rhea, and Hermes. On account of these Greek names the

myth was long thought to be of comparatively recent date ; "but the Leyden Papyrus (i. 346) has shown that the legend existed in its essential features in the time of the Thebans, and the Texts of the Pyramids have carried it back to the very beginnings of Egyptian mythology " (G. Foucart, *l.c.*). As five days are the seventy-second, not the seventieth, part of three hundred and sixty days, it was proposed by Wyttenbach to read τὸ ἑβδομηκοστὸν δεύτερον instead of τὸ ἑβδομηκοστὸν in Plutarch's text. See D. Wyttenbachius, *Animadversiones in Plutarchi Moralia* (Leipsic, 1820–1834), iii. 143 *sq.*

by the primitive astronomers who first observed the discrepancy between solar and lunar time and attempted to reconcile it by the expedient of intercalation.

Early attempts of the Aryan peoples to correct the lunar year by intercalating a month at intervals of several years instead of intercalating twelve days in every year.

Thus we infer with some probability that the sacred Twelve Days or Nights at midwinter derive their peculiar character in popular custom and superstition from the circumstance that they were originally an intercalary period inserted annually at the end of a lunar year of three hundred and fifty-four days for the purpose of equating it to a solar year reckoned at three hundred and sixty-six days. However, there are grounds for thinking that at a very early time the Aryan peoples sought to correct their lunar year, not by inserting twelve supplementary days every year, but by allowing the annual deficiency to accumulate for several years and then supplying it by a whole intercalary month. In India the Aryans of the Vedic age appear to have adopted a year of three hundred and sixty days, divided into twelve months of thirty days each, and to have remedied the annual deficiency of five days by intercalating a whole month of thirty days every fifth year, thus regulating their calendar according to a five years' cycle.[1] The Celts of Gaul, as we learn from the Coligny calendar, also adopted a five years' cycle, but they managed it differently. They retained the old lunar year of three hundred and fifty-four days divided into twelve months, six of thirty days and six of twenty-nine days; but instead of intercalating twelve days every year to restore the balance between lunar and solar time they intercalated a month of thirty days every two and a half years, so that in each cycle of five years the total number of intercalary days was sixty, which was equivalent to intercalating twelve days annually. Thus the result at the end of each cycle of five years was precisely the same as it would have been if they had followed the old system of annual intercalation.[2] Why they abandoned the simple and obvious

[1] H. Zimmer, *Altindisches Leben* (Berlin, 1879), pp. 365-370. Compare *The Hymns of the Rigveda*, translated by R. T. H. Griffith (Benares, 1889-1892), Book i. Hymn 164, stanza 48 (vol. i. p. 293), Book iii. Hymn 55, stanza 18 (vol. ii. pp. 76 *sq.*).

[2] J. A. MacCulloch, in Dr. J. Hastings's *Encyclopaedia of Religion and Ethics*, iii. (Edinburgh, 1910) pp. 78 *sqq.* Compare S. de Ricci, "Le calendrier Gaulois de Coligny," *Revue Celtique*, xix. (1898) pp. 213-223; *id.*, "Le calendrier Celtique de Coligny," *Revue Celtique*, xxi. (1900) pp. 10-27; *id.*,

expedient of annually intercalating twelve days, and adopted instead the more recondite system of intercalating a month of thirty days every two and a half years, is not plain. It may be that religious or political motives unknown to us concurred with practical considerations to recommend the change. One result of the reform would be the abolition of the temporary king who, if I am right, used to bear a somewhat tumultuary sway over the community during the saturnalia of the Twelve Days. Perhaps the annually recurring disorders which attended that period of license were not the least urgent of the reasons which moved the rulers to strike the twelve intercalary days out of the year and to replace them by an intercalary month at longer intervals.

However that may be, the equivalence of the new intercalary month to the old intercalary Twelve Days multiplied by two and a half is strongly suggested by a remarkable feature of the Coligny calendar ; for in it the thirty days of the intercalary month, which bore the name of Ciallos, are named after the ordinary twelve months of the year. Thus the first day of the intercalary month is called Samon, which is the name of the first month of the year ; the second day of the month is called Dumannos, which is the name of the second month of the year ; the third day of the month is called Rivros, which is the name of the third month of the year ; the fourth day of the month is called Anacan, which is the name of the fourth month of the year ; and so on with

[margin note: Equivalence of the new intercalary month to the old intercalary Twelve Days multiplied by two and a half.]

" Un passage remarquable du calendrier de Coligny," *Revue Celtique*, xxiv. (1903) pp. 313-316; J. Loth, "L'année Celtique," *Revue Celtique*, xxv. (1904) pp. 113-162 ; Sir John Rhys, "The Coligny Calendar, *Proceedings of the British Academy, 1909-1910*, pp. 207 *sqq*. As the calendar stands, the number of days in the ordinary year is 355, not 354, seven of the months having thirty days and five of them twenty-nine days. But the month Equos has attached to it the sign ANM, which is attached to all the months of twenty-nine days but to none of the months of thirty days except Equos, all of which, except Equos, are marked with the sign MAT. Hence, following a suggestion of M. S. de Ricci (*Revue Celtique*, xxi. 25), I suppose that the month Equos had regularly twenty-nine days instead of thirty, and that the attribution of thirty days to it is an error of the scribe or mason who engraved the calendar.

In the Coligny calendar the summer solstice seems to be marked by the word *trinouxtion* affixed to the seventeenth day of the first month (Samonios, nearly equivalent to our June). As interpreted by Sir John Rhys (*op. cit.* p. 217), the word means "a period of three nights of equal length." If he is right, it follows that the Celts who constructed the calendar had observed the summer solstice.

all the rest, so that the thirty days of the intercalary month bear the names of the twelve months of the year repeated two and a half times.[1]   This seems to shew that, just as our modern peasants regard the Twelve Days as representing each a month of the year in their chronological order, so the old Celts of Gaul who drew up the Coligny calendar regarded the thirty days of the intercalary month as representing the thirty ordinary months which were to follow it till the next intercalation took place.   And we may conjecture that just as our modern peasants still draw omens from the Twelve Days for the twelve succeeding months, so the old Celts drew omens from the thirty days of the intercalary month for the thirty months of the two and a half succeeding years. Indeed we may suppose that the reformers of the calendar transferred, or attempted to transfer, to the new intercalary month the whole of the quaint customs and superstitions which from time immemorial had clustered round the twelve

The intercalary month may have been a period of license, during which the reins of government were held by a temporary king. intercalary days of the old year.   Thus, like the old Twelve Days of midwinter, the thirty days of the new intercalary month may have formed an interregnum or break in the ordinary course of government, a tumultuary period of general license, during which the ordinary rules of law and morality were suspended and the direction of affairs committed to a temporary and more or less farcical ruler or King of the Bean, who may possibly have had to pay with his life for his brief reign of thirty days.   The floating traditions of such merry monarchs and of the careless happy-go-lucky life under them may have crystallized in after ages into the legend of Saturn and the Golden Age.   If that was so— and I put forward the hypothesis for no more than a web of conjectures woven from the gossamer threads of popular superstition—we can understand why the Twelve Days, intercalated every year in the old calendar, should have survived to the present day in the memory of the people, whereas the thirty days, intercalated every two and a half years in the new calendar, have long been forgotten.   It is the simplest ideas that live longest in the simple minds

---

[1] J. A. MacCulloch, in Dr. J. Hastings's *Encyclopaedia of Religion and Ethics*, iii. 79. Compare Sir J. Rhys, " The Coligny Calendar," *Proceedings of the British Academy, 1909 1910*, pp. 292 *sq.*

of the peasantry; and since the intercalation of twelve days in every year to allow the lagging moon to keep pace with the longer stride of the sun is certainly an easier and more obvious expedient than to wait for two and a half years till he has outrun her by thirty days, we need not wonder that this ancient mode of harmonizing lunar and solar time should have lingered in the recollection and in the usages of the people ages after the more roundabout method, which reflective minds had devised for accomplishing the same end, had faded alike from the memory of the peasant and the page of the historian.

§ 3. *The Saturnalia and Lent*

As the Carnival is always held on the last three days before the beginning of Lent, its date shifts somewhat from year to year, but it invariably falls either in February or March. Hence it does not coincide with the date of the Saturnalia, which within historical times seems to have been always celebrated in December even in the old days, before Caesar's reform of the calendar, when the Roman year ended with February instead of December.[1] Yet if the Saturnalia, like many other seasons of license, was originally celebrated as a sort of public purification at the end of the old year or the beginning of the new one, it may at a still more remote period, when the Roman year began with March, have been regularly held either in February or March and therefore at approximately the same date as the modern Carnival. So strong and persistent are the conservative instincts of the peasantry in respect to old custom, that it would be no matter for surprise if, in rural districts of Italy, the ancient festival continued to be celebrated at the ancient time long

The modern Carnival is perhaps the equivalent of the ancient Saturnalia.

[1] We know from Livy (xxii. 1. 19 sq.) that the Saturnalia was celebrated in December as early as the year 217 B.C.; and in his learned discussion of the proper date of the festival the antiquary Macrobius gives no hint that it ever fell at any other time than in December (*Saturnal.* i. 10). It would be a mistake to infer from Livy's account of the Saturnalia in the year 217 B.C. that he supposed the festival to have been first instituted in that year; for elsewhere (ii. 21. 1) he tells us that it was established at the time when the temple of Saturn was dedicated, namely in the year 497 B.C. Macrobius (*Saturn.* i. 8. 1) refers the institution of the Saturnalia to King Tullus Hostilius. More probably the festival was of immemorial antiquity.

after the official celebration of the Saturnalia in the towns had been shifted from February to December. Latin Christianity, which struck at the root of official or civic paganism, has always been tolerant of its rustic cousins, the popular festivals and ceremonies which, unaffected by political and religious revolutions, by the passing of empires and of gods, have been carried on by the people with but little change from time immemorial, and represent in fact the original stock from which the state religions of classical antiquity were comparatively late offshoots. Thus it may very well have come about that while the new faith stamped out the Saturnalia in the towns, it suffered the original festival, disguised by a difference of date, to linger unmolested in the country ; and so the old feast of Saturn, under the modern name of the Carnival, has reconquered the cities, and goes on merrily under the eye and with the sanction of the Catholic Church.

The Saturnalia may have originally fallen at the end of February, which would be an appropriate time for a festival of sowing.   The opinion that the Saturnalia originally fell in February or the beginning of March receives some support from the circumstance that the festival of the Matronalia, at which mistresses feasted their slaves just as masters did theirs at the Saturnalia, always continued to be held on the first of March, even when the Roman year began with January.[1] It is further not a little recommended by the consideration that this date would be eminently appropriate for the festival of Saturn, the old Italian god of sowing and planting. It has always been a puzzle to explain why such a festival should have been held at midwinter ; but on the present hypothesis the mystery vanishes. With the Italian farmer February and March were the great season of the spring sowing and planting ;[2] nothing could be more natural than that the husbandman should inaugurate the season with the worship of the deity to whom he ascribed the function of

---

[1] Macrobius, *Sat.* i. 12. 7 ; Solinus, i. 35, p. 13 ed. Th. Mommsen (Berlin, 1864) ; Joannes Lydus, *De Mensibus*, iii. 15. On the other hand, we know that the ceremony of renewing the laurels, which originally took place on the first of March, was long afterwards transferred to the first of January. See Ovid, *Fasti*, iii. 135 *sqq.*, and Macro-bius, *Saturn.* i. 12. 6, compared with *Geoponica*, xi. 2. 6, where the note of the commentator Niclas may be consulted. This transference is strictly analogous to the change which I conjecture to have been made in the date of celebrating the Saturnalia.

[2] Palladius, *De re rustica*, books iii. and iv. *passim*.

quickening the seed. It is no small confirmation of this theory that the last day of the Carnival, namely Shrove Tuesday, is still, or was down to recent times, the customary season in Central Europe for promoting the growth of the crops by means of leaps and dances.[1] The custom fits in very well with the view which derives the Carnival from an old festival of sowing such as the Saturnalia probably was in its origin. Further, the orgiastic character of the festival is readily explained by the help of facts which met us in a former part of our investigation. We have seen that between the sower and the seed there is commonly supposed to exist a sympathetic connexion of such a nature that his conduct directly affects and can promote or retard the growth of the crops.[2] What wonder then if the simple husbandman imagined that by cramming his belly, by swilling and guzzling just before he proceeded to sow his fields, he thereby imparted additional vigour to the seed?[3]

But while his crude philosophy may thus have painted gluttony and intoxication in the agreeable colours of duties which he owed to himself, to his family, and to the commonwealth, it is possible that the zest with which he acquitted himself of his obligations may have been whetted by a less comfortable reflection. In modern times the indulgence of the Carnival is immediately followed by the abstinence of Lent; and if the Carnival is the direct descendant of the Saturnalia, may not Lent in like manner be merely the continuation, under a thin disguise, of a period of temperance which was annually observed, from superstitious motives, by Italian farmers long before the Christian era? Direct evidence of this, so far as I am aware, is not forthcoming; but we have seen that a practice of abstinence from fleshly lusts has been observed by various peoples as a sympathetic charm to foster the growth of the seed;[4] and such an

The Lenten fast in spring may be an old heathen period of abstinence intended to promote the growth of the seed.

---

[1] *The Magic Art and the Evolution of Kings*, i. 137-139.

[2] *The Magic Art and the Evolution of Kings*, i. 136-144, ii. 97 *sqq.*

[3] Compare C. Lumholtz, *Unknown Mexico* (London, 1903), ii. 268 : "To the Huichol so closely are corn, deer, and hikuli associated that by consuming the broth of the deer-meat and the

hikuli they think the same effect is produced—namely, making the corn grow. Therefore when clearing the fields they eat hikuli before starting the day's work."

[4] *The Magic Art and the Evolution of Kings*, ii. 104 *sqq.* The Indians of Santiago Tepehuacan abstain from flesh, eggs, and grease while they are

observance would be an appropriate sequel to the Saturnalia, if that festival was indeed, as I conjecture it to have been, originally held in spring as a religious or magical preparation for sowing and planting. When we consider how widely diffused is the belief in the sympathetic influence which human conduct, and especially the intercourse of the sexes, exerts on the fruits of the earth, we may be allowed to conjecture that the Lenten fast, with the rule of continence which is recommended, if not strictly enjoined, by the Catholic and Coptic churches during that season,[1] was in its origin intended, not so much to commemorate the sufferings of a dying god, as to foster the growth of the seed, which in the bleak days of early spring the husbandman commits with anxious care and misgiving to the bosom of the naked earth. Ecclesiastical historians have been puzzled to say why after much hesitation and great diversity of usage in different places the Christian church finally adopted forty days as the proper period for the mournful celebration of Lent.[2] Perhaps in coming to this decision the authorities were guided, as so often, by a regard for an existing pagan celebration of similar character and duration which they hoped by a change of name to convert into a Christian solemnity. Such a heathen Lent they may have found to hand in the rites of Persephone, the Greek goddess of the corn, whose image, carved out of a tree, was annually brought into the cities and mourned for forty nights, after which it was

---

engaged in sowing cotton and chilis, because they believe that were they to partake of these viands at that time, the blossoms would fall and the crop would suffer. See " Lettre du curé de Santiago Tepehuacan à son évêque sur les mœurs et coutumes des Indiens," *Bulletin de la Société de Géographie* (Paris), Deuxième Série, ii. (1834) p. 181.

[1] In Franche-Comté not only husbands and wives were expected to be continent from the first Sunday of Lent to the first Sunday after Easter, but even sweethearts separated during that time, bidding each other a formal farewell on the first of these days and meeting again with similar formality on the last. See C. Beauquier, *Les Mois en Franche-Comté* (Paris, 1900), p. 35.

I am informed that the observance of chastity during Lent is enjoined generally by the Catholic church. As to its injunction by the Coptic church see F. Wüstenfeld, *Macrizi's Geschichte der Copten* (Göttingen, 1845), p. 84; *Il Fetha Nagast, o Legislazione dei Re, codice ecclesiastico e civile di Abissinia,* tradotto e annotato da Ignazio Guidi (Rome, 1899), p. 164.

[2] Socrates, *Historia Ecclesiastica,* v. 22; Sozomenus, *Historia Ecclesiastica,* vii. 19 (Migne, *Patrologia Graeca,* lxvii. coll. 632-636, 1477); W. Smith and S. Cheetham, *Dictionary of Christian Antiquities, s.v.* "Lent," vol. ii. pp. 972 *sq.*; Mgr. L. Duchesne, *Origines du Culte Chrétien* (Paris, 1903), pp. 241-243.

burned.[1] The time of year when these lamentations took
place is not mentioned by the old Christian writer who
records them ; but they would fall most appropriately at the
season when the seed was sown or, in mythical language,
when the corn-goddess was buried, which in ancient Italy, as
we saw, was done above all in the months of February and
March. We know that at the time of the autumnal sowing Autumnal
Greek women held a sad and serious festival because the rites of
mourning
Corn-goddess Persephone or the Maiden, as they called and fasting
her, then went down into the earth with the sown grain, for the sake
of the seed.
and Demeter fondly mourned her daughter's absence ;
hence in sympathy with the sorrowful mother the women
likewise mourned and observed a solemn fast and abstained
from the marriage bed.[2]   It is reasonable, therefore, to
suppose that they practised similar rules of mourning
and abstinence for a like reason at the time of the
spring sowing, and that the ancient ritual survives in the
modern Lent, which preserves the memory of the *Mater
Dolorosa*, though it has substituted a dead Son for a dead
Daughter.

Be that as it may, it is worthy of note that in The
Burma a similar fast, which English writers call the Buddhist
Lent.
Buddhist Lent, is observed for three months every year
while the ploughing and sowing of the fields go forward ;
and the custom is believed to be far older than Buddhism,
which has merely given it a superficial tinge like the
veneer of Christianity which, if I am right, has over-
laid an old heathen observance in Lent.   This Burmese
Lent, we are told, covers the rainy season from the full
moon of July to the full moon of October.   " This is the
time to plough, this is the time to sow ; on the villagers'
exertions in these months depends all their maintenance for
the rest of the year.   Every man, every woman, every child,
has hard work of some kind or another.   And so, what with

---

[1] Firmicus Maternus, *De errore
profanarum religionum*, 27.

[2] Plutarch, *Isis et Osiris*, 69 : καὶ
γὰρ Ἀθήνῃσι νηστεύουσιν αἱ γυναῖκες ἐν
θεσμοφορίοις χαμαὶ καθήμεναι, καὶ Βοιωτοὶ
τὰ τῆς Ἀχαιᾶς μέγαρα κινοῦσιν, ἐπαχθῆ
τὴν ἑορτὴν ἐκείνην ὀνομάζοντες, ὡς διὰ

τὴν τῆς Κόρης κάθοδον ἐν ἄχει τῆς
Δήμητρος οὔσης. Ἔστι δὲ ὁ μὴν οὗτος
περὶ πλειάδα σπόριμος, ὃν Ἀθὺρ Αἰγύπτιοι,
Πυανεψιῶνα δ' Ἀθηναῖοι, Βοιωτοὶ δὲ
Δαμάτριον καλοῦσι. As to the festival
and the rule of chastity observed at it,
see further *Spirits of the Corn and of
the Wild*, i. 116, ii. 17 *sq.*

the difficulties of travelling, what with the work there is to do, and what with the custom of Lent, every one stays at home. It is the time for prayer, for fasting, for improving the soul. Many men during these months will live even as the monks live, will eat but before midday, will abstain from tobacco. There are no plays during Lent, and there are no marriages. It is the time for preparing the land for the crop ; it is the time for preparing the soul for eternity. The congregations on the Sundays will be far greater at this time than at any other ; there will be more thought of the serious things of life." [1]

§ 4. *Saturnalia in Ancient Greece*

Inversion of social ranks at ancient Greek festivals held in Crete, Troezen, and Thessaly.

Beyond the limits of Italy festivals of the same general character as the Saturnalia appear to have been held over a considerable area of the ancient world. A characteristic feature of the Saturnalia, as we saw, was an inversion of social ranks, masters changing places with their slaves and waiting upon them, while slaves were indulged with a semblance not merely of freedom but even of power and office. In various parts of Greece the same hollow show of granting liberty to slaves was made at certain festivals. Thus at a Cretan festival of Hermes the servants feasted and their masters waited upon them. In the month of Geraestius the Troezenians observed a certain solemnity lasting many days, on one of which the slaves played at dice with the citizens and were treated to a banquet by their lords. The Thessalians held a great festival called Peloria, which Baton of Sinope identified with the Saturnalia, and of which the antiquity is vouched for by a tradition that it originated with the Pelasgians. At this festival sacrifices were offered to Pelorian Zeus, tables splendidly adorned were set out, all strangers were invited to the feast, all prisoners released, and the slaves sat down to the banquet,

<hr/>

[1] H. Fielding, *The Soul of a People* (London, 1898), pp. 172 *sq.* The orthodox explanation of the custom is that during these three months the Buddha retired to a monastery. But "the custom was far older even than that—so old that we do not know how it arose. Its origin is lost in the mists of far-away time." Compare C. J. F. S. Forbes, *British Burma* (London, 1878), pp. 170 *sq.* ; Shway Yoe, *The Burman, his Life and Notions* (London, 1882), i. 257, 262 *sqq.*

enjoyed full freedom of speech, and were served by their masters.[1]

But the Greek festival which appears to have corre- *The Greek festival of the Cronia compared to the Roman Saturnalia.* sponded most closely to the Italian Saturnalia was the Cronia or festival of Cronus, a god whose barbarous myth and cruel ritual clearly belong to a very early stratum of Greek religion, and who was by the unanimous voice of antiquity identified with Saturn. We are told that his festival was celebrated in most parts of Greece, but especially at Athens, where the old god and his wife Rhea had a shrine near the stately, but far more modern, temple of Olympian Zeus. A joyous feast, at which masters and slaves sat down together, formed a leading feature of the solemnity. At Athens the festival fell in the height of summer, on the twelfth day of the month Hecatombaeon, formerly called the month of Cronus, which answered nearly to July ; and tradition ran that Cecrops, the first king of Attica, had founded an altar in honour of Cronus and Rhea, and had ordained that master and man should share a common meal when the harvest was got in.[2] Yet there are indications that at Athens the Cronia may once have been a spring festival. For a cake with twelve knobs, which perhaps referred to the twelve months of the year, was offered to Cronus by the Athenians on the fifteenth day of the month Elaphebolion, which corresponded roughly to March,[3] and there are traces of a

[1] Athenaeus, xiv. 44 *sq.*, pp. 639 B-640 A.

[2] Macrobius, *Saturn.* i. 7. 37 and i. 10. 22 ; Demosthenes, *Or.* xxiv. 26, p. 708. As to the temple of Cronus and Rhea, see Pausanias, i. 18. 7 ; Im. Bekker's *Anecdota Graeca* (Berlin, 1814–1821), i. p. 273, lines 20 *sq.* That the Attic month Hecatombaeon was formerly called Cronius is mentioned by Plutarch (*Theseus*, 12). Other Greek states, including Samos, Amorgos, Perinthus, and Patmos, had a month called Cronion, that is, the month of Cronus, which seems to have coincided with June or July. See G. Dittenberger, *Sylloge Inscriptionum Graecarum*[2] (Leipsic, 1898–1901), Nos. 644 and 645 ; E. Bischoff, " De fastis Graecorum antiquioribus," *Leipziger Studien für classischen*

Philologie, vii. (1884) p. 400. At Magnesia on the Maeander the month of Cronion was the time of sowing (Dittenberger, *op. cit.* No. 553, lines 15 *sq.*), which cannot have fallen in the height of summer. Compare *Spirits of the Corn and of the Wild*, ii. 8.

[3] *Corpus Inscriptionum Atticarum*, iii. No. 77 ; Ch. Michel, *Recueil d'Inscriptions Grecques* (Brussels, 1900), No. 692, pp. 595 *sq.* ; I. de Prott et L. Ziehen, *Leges Graecorum Sacrae*, i. (Leipsic, 1896), No. 3, pp. 7 *sq.* ; E. S. Roberts and E. A. Gardner, *Introduction to Greek Epigraphy*, Part II. (Cambridge, 1905), No. 142, pp. 387 *sq.* From the same inscription we learn that cakes with twelve knobs were offered to other deities, including Apollo and Artemis, Zeus, Poseidon, and Hercules.

license accorded to slaves at the Dionysiac festival of the opening of the wine-jars, which fell on the eleventh day of the preceding month Anthesterion.[1]   At Olympia the festival of Cronus undoubtedly occurred in spring; for here a low but steep hill, now covered with a tangled growth of dark holly-oaks and firs, was sacred to him, and on its top certain magistrates, who bore the title of kings, offered sacrifice to the old god at the vernal equinox in the Elean month Elaphius.[2]

In this last ceremony, which probably went on year by year long before the upstart Zeus had a temple built for himself at the foot of the hill, there are two points of special interest, first the date of the ceremony, and second the title of the celebrants.   First, as to the date, the spring equinox, or the twenty-first of March, must have fallen so near the fifteenth day of the Athenian month Elaphebolion, that we may fairly ask whether the Athenian custom of offering a cake to Cronus on that day may not also have been an equinoctial ceremony.   In the second place, the title of kings borne by the magistrates who sacrificed to Cronus renders it probable that, like magistrates with similar high-sounding titles elsewhere in republican Greece, they were the lineal descendants of sacred kings whom the superstition of their subjects invested with the attributes of divinity.[3]   If that was so, it would be natural enough that one of these

The Olympian Cronia held at the spring equinox.

The magistrates called Kings who celebrated the Cronia at Olympia may have personated King Cronus himself.

[1] Scholiast on Hesiod, *Works and Days*, 370 (p. 170 ed. E. Vollbehr, Kiel, 1844): Καὶ ἐν τοῖς πατρίοις ἐστὶν ἑορτὴ Πιθοιγία, καθ᾽ ἣν οὔτε οἰκέτην οὔτε μισθωτὸν εἴργειν τῆς ἀπολαύσεως τοῦ οἴνου θεμιτὸν ἦν, ἀλλὰ θύσαντας πᾶσι μεταδιδόναι τοῦ δώρου τοῦ Διονύσου. As to the festival of the opening of the wine-jars see August Mommsen, *Heortologie* (Leipsic, 1864), pp. 349 *sqq.*; *id.*, *Feste der Stadt Athen im Altertum* (Leipsic, 1898), pp. 384 *sqq.*   "When the slaves," says Plutarch, "feast at the Cronia or go about celebrating the festival of Dionysus in the country, the shouts they raise and the tumult they make in their rude merriment are intolerable" (*Non posse suaviter vivi secundum Epicurum*, 26). That the original festival of Cronus fell at Athens in Anthesterion is the view of Aug. Mommsen (*Heortologie*, pp. 22, 79;

Feste der Stadt Athen, p. 402).

[2] Pausanias, vi. 20. 1.   Compare Dionysius Halicarnasensis, *Antiquit. Rom.* i. 34.   The magistrates called "kings" (βασιλαι) by Pausanias are doubtless identical with "the kings" (τοὶ βασιλᾶες) mentioned in a law of Elis, which was found inscribed on a bronze plate at Olympia.   See H. Roehl, *Inscriptiones Graecae Antiquissimae* (Berlin, 1882), No. 112, p. 39; C. Cauer, *Delectus Inscriptionum Graecarum propter dialectum memorabilium*[2] (Leipsic, 1883), No. 253, p. 175; H. Collitz, *Sammlung der griechischen Dialekt-Inschriften*, No. 1152 (vol. i. Göttingen, 1884, p. 321); Ch. Michel, *Recueil d'Inscriptions Grecques*, No. 195, p. 179.

[3] See *The Magic Art and the Evolution of Kings*, i. 44 *sqq.*, ii. 177, 361.

nominal kings should pose as the god Cronus in person. For, like his Italian counterpart Saturn, the Greek Cronus was believed to have been a king who reigned in heaven or on earth during the blissful Golden Age, when men passed their days like gods without toil or sorrow, when life was a long round of festivity, and death came like sleep, sudden but gentle, announced by none of his sad forerunners, the ailments and infirmities of age.[1] Thus the analogy of the Olympian Cronia, probably one of the oldest of Greek festivals, to the Italian Saturnalia would be very close if originally, as I conjecture, the Saturnalia fell in spring and Saturn was personated at it, as we have good reason to believe, by a man dressed as a king. May we go a step further and suppose that, just as the man who acted King Saturn at the Saturnalia was formerly slain in that character, so one of the kings who celebrated the Cronia at Olympia not only played the part of Cronus, but was sacrificed, as god and victim in one, on the top of the hill? Cronus certainly bore a sinister reputation in antiquity. He passed for an unnatural parent who had devoured his own offspring, and he was regularly identified by the Greeks with the cruel Semitic Baals who delighted in the sacrifice of human victims, especially of children.[2] A legend which savours strongly of infant sacrifice is reported of a shrine that stood at the very foot of the god's own hill at Olympia ;[3] and a quite unambiguous story was told of the sacrifice of a babe to Lycaean Zeus on Mount Lycaeus in Arcadia, where the worship of Zeus was probably nothing but a continuation, under a new name, of the old worship of Cronus, and where human victims appear to have been regularly offered down to the Christian era.[4] The Rhodians annually sacrificed a

Perhaps the man who annually personated King Cronus was put to death.

---

[1] Hesiod, *Works and Days*, 111, 169 ; Plato, *Politicus*, p. 269 A ; Diodorus Siculus, iii. 61, v. 66 ; Julian, *Epistola ad Themistium*, p. 258 c (pp. 334 *sq.*, ed. F. C. Hertlein, Leipsic, 1875–1876) ; " Anonymi Chronologica," printed in L. Dindorf's edition of J. Malalas (Bonn, 1831), p. 17. See further M. Mayer's article " Kronos," in W. H. Roscher's *Lexikon der griech. und röm. Mythologie*, ii. (Leipsic, 1890–1897) col. 1458.

[2] See M. Mayer, *op. cit.* ii. 1501 *sqq.*

[3] Pausanias, vi. 20. 4 *sq.*

[4] Plato, *Republic*, ix. p. 565 D E ; pseudo-Plato, *Minos*, p. 315 C ; Pliny, *Nat. Hist.* viii. 81 ; Pausanias, viii. 2 and 38 ; Porphyry, *De abstinentia*, ii. 27 ; Augustine, *De civitate Dei*, xviii. 17. The suggestion that Lycaean Zeus may have been merely a successor of Cronus is due to my friend Professor W. Ridgeway.

A man
annually
sacrificed
to Cronus
at the
Cronia in
Rhodes.

man to Cronus in the month Metageitnion; at a later time they kept a condemned criminal in prison till the festival of the Cronia was come, then led him forth outside the gates, made him drunk with wine, and cut his throat.[1] With the parallel of the Saturnalia before our eyes, we may surmise that the victim who thus ended his life in a state of intoxication at the Cronia perhaps personated King Cronus himself, the god who reigned in the happy days of old when men had nothing to do but to eat and drink and make merry. At least the Rhodian custom lends some countenance to the conjecture that formerly a human victim may have figured at the sacrifice which the so-called kings offered to Cronus on his hill at Olympia. In this connexion it is to be remembered that we have already found well-attested examples of a custom of sacrificing the scions of royal houses in ancient Greece.[2] If the god to whom, or perhaps rather in whose character, the princes were sacrificed, was Cronus, it would be natural that the Greeks of a later age should identify him with Baal or Moloch, to whom in like manner Semitic kings offered up their children. The Laphystian Zeus of Thessaly and Boeotia, whom tradition associated with these human sacrifices, was probably, like the Lycaean Zeus of Arcadia, nothing but the aboriginal deity, commonly known as Cronus, whose gloomy rites the Greek invaders suffered the priests of the vanquished race to continue after the ancient manner, while they quieted their scruples of conscience or satisfied their pride as conquerors by investing the bloodthirsty old savage with the name, if not with the character, of their own milder deity, the humane and gracious Zeus.

§ 5. *Saturnalia in Western Asia*

The
Babylonian
festival of
the Sacaea.

When we pass from Europe to western Asia, from ancient Greece to ancient Babylon and the regions where Babylonian influence penetrated, we are still met with festivals which bear the closest resemblance to the oldest form of the Italian Saturnalia. The reader may remember the festival of the Sacaea, on which I had occasion to touch in

---

[1] Porphyry, *De abstinentia*, ii. 54.   [2] *The Dying God*, pp. 161 *sqq.*

an earlier part of this work.[1] It was held at Babylon during five days of the month Lous, beginning with the sixteenth day of the month. During its continuance, just as at the Saturnalia, masters and servants changed places, the servants issuing orders and the masters obeying them ; and in each house one of the servants, dressed as a king and bearing the title of Zoganes, bore rule over the household. Further, just as at the Saturnalia in its original form a man was dressed as King Saturn in royal robes, allowed to indulge his passions and caprices to the full, and then put to death, so at the Sacaea a condemned prisoner, who probably also bore for the time being the title of Zoganes, was arrayed in the king's attire and suffered to play the despot, to use the king's concubines, and to give himself up to feasting and debauchery without restraint, only however in the end to be stript of his borrowed finery, scourged, and hanged or crucified.[2] From Strabo we learn that this Asiatic counterpart of the Saturnalia was celebrated in Asia Minor wherever the worship of the Persian goddess Anaitis had established itself. He describes it as a Bacchic orgy, at which the revellers were disguised as Scythians, and men and women drank and dallied together by day and night.[3]

As the worship of Anaitis, though of Persian origin, appears to have been deeply leavened with coarse elements which it derived from the religion of Babylon,[4] we may perhaps regard Mesopotamia as the original home from which the Sacaean festival spread westward into other parts of Asia Minor. Now the Sacaean festival, described by the Babylonian priest Berosus in the first book of his history of Babylon, has been plausibly identified [5] with the great

The Sacaea by some identified with Zakmuk or Zagmuk, the Babylonian festival of the New Year, which was held

---

[1] *The Dying God*, pp. 113 *sqq.*

[2] Athenaeus, xiv. 44, p. 639 C ; Dio Chrysostom, *Or.* iv. 69 *sq.* (vol. i. p. 76 ed. L. Dindorf, Leipsic, 1857). From Athenaeus we learn that the festival was described or mentioned by Berosus in his first book and by Ctesias in his second.

[3] Strabo, xi. 8. 5, p. 512.

[4] Strabo, xi. 14. 16, pp. 532 *sq.* ; Ed. Meyer's article "Anaitis," in W. H. Roscher's *Lexikon der griech. und röm. Mythologie*, i. (Leipsic, 1884–

1890) pp. 330 *sqq.*

[5] By A. H. Sayce, *Religion of the Ancient Babylonians* (London and Edinburgh, 1887), p. 68 ; Bruno Meissner, "Zur Entstehungsgeschichte des Purimfestes," *Zeitschrift der deutschen morgenländischen Gesellschaft*, l. (1896) pp. 296-301 ; H. Winckler, *Altorientalische Forschungen*, Zweite Reihe, ii. Heft 3 (Leipsic, 1900), p. 345 ; C. Brockelmann, "Wesen und Ursprung des Eponymats in Assyrien," *Zeitschrift für Assyriologie*, xvi. (1902) pp. 391 *sq.*

about the spring equinox in March.

Babylonian festival of the New year called Zakmuk, Zagmuk, Zakmuku, or Zagmuku, which has become known to us in recent times through inscriptions.   The Babylonian year began with the spring month of Nisan, which seems to have covered the second half of March and the first half of April. Thus the New Year festival, which occupied at least the first eleven days of Nisan, probably included the spring equinox. It was held in honour of Marduk or Merodach, the chief god of Babylon, whose great temple of Esagila in the city formed the religious centre of the solemnity.   For here, in a splendid chamber of the vast edifice, all the gods were believed to assemble at this season under the presidency of Marduk for the purpose of determining the fates for the new year,

Annual renewal of the king of Babylon's power at the Zakmuk festival.

especially the fate of the king's life.   On this occasion the king of Babylon was bound annually to renew his regal power by grasping the hands of the image of Marduk in his temple, as if to signify that he received the kingdom directly from the deity and was unable without the divine assistance and authority to retain it for more than a year.   Unless he thus formally reinstated himself on the throne once a year, the king ceased to reign legitimately.   When Babylonia was conquered by Assyria, the Assyrian monarchs themselves used to come to Babylon and perform the ceremony of grasping the god's hands in order to establish by this solemn act their title to the kingdom which they had won for themselves by the sword ; until they had done so, they were not recognized as kings by their Babylonian subjects.   Some of them indeed found the ceremony either so burdensome or so humiliating to their pride as conquerors, that rather than perform it they renounced the title of king of Babylon altogether and contented themselves with the more modest title of regent.   Another notable feature of the Babylonian festival of the New Year appears to have been a ceremonial marriage of the god Marduk ; for in a hymn relating to the solemnity it is said of the deity that " he hastened to his bridal."   The festival was of hoar antiquity, for it was known to Gudea, an old king of Southern Babylonia who flourished between two and three thousand years before the beginning of our era, and it is mentioned in an early account of the Great Flood.   At a much later period it is repeatedly referred to by King Nebuchadnezzar and his successors. Nebuchadnezzar records how he built of bricks and bitumen a chapel or altar, "a thing of joy and rejoicing," for the great festival of Marduk, the lord of the gods ; and we read of the rich and abundant offerings which were made by the high priest at this time.[1]

Unfortunately the notices of this Babylonian festival of the New Year which have come down to us deal chiefly with its mythical aspect and throw little light on the mode of its celebration. Hence its identity with the Sacaea must remain for the present a more or less probable hypothesis. In favour of the hypothesis may be alleged in the first place the resemblance of the names Sacaea and Zoganes to Zakmuk or Zagmuku, if that was the real pronunciation of the name,[2] and in the second place the very significant statement that the fate of the king's life was supposed to be determined by the gods, under the presidency of Marduk, at the Zakmuk or New Year's festival.[3]   When

Reasons for identifying the Sacaea with Zakmuk.

---

[1] P. Jensen, *Die Kosmologie der Babylonier* (Strasburg, 1890), pp. 84 *sqq.*; H. Zimmern, "Zur Frage nach dem Ursprunge des Purimfestes," *Zeitschrift für die alttestamentliche Wissenschaft*, xi. (1891) pp. 159 *sqq.*; A. Jeremias, *s.v.* "Marduk," in W. H. Roscher's *Lexicon der griech. und röm. Mythologie*, ii. 2347 *sq.*; M. Jastrow, *Religion of Babylonia and Assyria* (Boston, U.S.A., 1898), pp. 186, 677 *sqq.*; R. F. Harper, *Assyrian and Babylonian Literature* (New York, 1901), pp. 136 *sq.*, 137, 140, 149 ; C. Brockelmann, "Wesen und Ursprung des Eponymats in Assyrien," *Zeitschrift für Assyriologie*, xvi. (1902) pp. 391 *sqq.*; H. Zimmern, in E. Schrader's *Die Keilinschriften und das Alte Testament*[3] (Berlin, 1902), pp. 370 *sqq.*, 374, 384 *n.*[4], 402, 514 *sqq.*; *id.*, "Zum Babylonischen Neujahrsfest," *Berichte über die Verhandlungen der königlich Sächsischen Gesellschaft der Wissenschaften zu Leipzig, Philologisch-historische Klasse*, lviii. (1906) pp. 126-156; M. J. Lagrange, *Études sur les Religions Sémitiques*[2] (Paris, 1905), pp. 285 *sqq.* King Gudea is thought to have flourished about 2340 B.C. See Ed. Meyer, *Geschichte des*

Altertums,[2] i. 2. (Stuttgart and Berlin, 1909) pp. 488 *sq.* As to the ceremony of grasping the hands of Marduk's image, see also C. F. Lehmann (-Haupt), *Šamaššumukin, König von Babylonien* (Leipsic, 1892), pp. 50 *sqq.*; Sir G. Maspero, *Histoire Ancienne des Peuples de l'Orient Classique*, iii. *Les Empires* (Paris, 1899), pp. 381 *sq.*

[2] On this subject the Master of St. Catharine's College, Cambridge (the Rev. C. H. W. Johns), has kindly furnished me with the following note : "ZAG is the name of the ideogram meaning 'head or beginning.' MU is the sign for 'year.' When put together ZAG-MU means 'beginning of year.' But ZAG-MU-KU means ZAG MU-d, *i.e.* ZAG with MU suffixed. Therefore it is the name of the ideogram, and there is as yet no *proof* that it was ever read Zakmuk. Hence any similarity of sound with either Sacaea or Zoganes is precarious. I cannot prove that the signs were *never* read Zakmuku, but that is not a Semitic word nor a Sumerian word."

[3] The statement occurs in an inscription of Nebuchadnezzar. See P. Jensen, *Die Kosmologie der Babylonier*,

we remember that the central feature of the Sacaea appears to have been the saving of the king's life for another year by the vicarious sacrifice of a criminal on the cross or the gallows, we can understand that the season was a critical one for the king, and that it may well have been regarded as determining his fate for the ensuing twelve months. The annual ceremony of renewing the king's power by contact with the god's image, which formed a leading feature of the Zakmuk festival, would be very appropriately performed immediately after the execution or sacrifice of the temporary king who died in the room of the real monarch.

A difficulty, however, in the way of identifying the Sacaea with the Zakmuk arises from the statement of Berosus that the Sacaea fell on the sixteenth day of Lous, which was the tenth month of the Syro-Macedonian calendar and appears to have nearly coincided with July. Thus if the Sacaea occurred in July and the Zakmuk in March, the theory of their identity could not be maintained. But the dating of the months of the Syro-Macedonian calendar is a matter of some uncertainty; the month of Lous in particular appears to have fallen at different times of the year in different places,[1] and until we have ascertained beyond the reach of doubt when Lous fell at Babylon in the time of Berosus, it would be premature to allow much weight to the seeming discrepancy in the dates of the two festivals. At all events, whether the festivals were the same or different, we are confronted with difficulties which in the present state of our knowledge may be pronounced insoluble. If the festivals were the same, we cannot explain their apparent difference of date : if they were different, we cannot explain their apparent similarity of character. In what follows I

---

p. 85 ; H. Zimmern, in E. Schrader's *Die Keilinschriften und das Alte Testament*[3] (Berlin, 1902), p. 402. The title of the president of the divine synod, "king of the gods of heaven and earth," is believed by Professor Zimmern to have originally referred to the god Nabu, though at a later time it was applied to Marduk.

[1] See *The Dying God*, p. 116 note [1].

In Egypt the Macedonian calendar seems to have fallen into great confusion. See W. Dittenberger, *Orientis Graeci Inscriptiones Selectae* (Leipsic, 1903–1905), ii. pp. 649 *sq.* I would remind the reader that while the *dates* of the Syro-Macedonian months varied in different places, their *order* was the same everywhere.

shall, with some eminent Oriental scholars,[1] provisionally assume the identity of Zakmuk and Sacaea, but I would ask the reader to bear clearly in mind that the hypothesis leaves the apparent discrepancy of their dates unexplained. Towards a solution of the problem I can only suggest conjecturally either that the date of the festival had been for some reason shifted in the time of Berosus, or that two different festivals of the same type may have been held at different seasons of the year, one in spring and one in summer, perhaps by two distinct but kindred tribes, who retained their separate religious rites after they had coalesced in the Babylonian empire. Both conjectures might be supported by analogies. On the one hand, for example, in the Jewish calendar New Year's Day was shifted under Babylonian influence from autumn to spring,[2] and in a later part of this work we shall see that the Chinese festival of new fire, at first celebrated in spring, was afterwards shifted to the summer solstice, only however to be brought back at a later time to its original date. On the other hand, the popular festivals of our European peasantry afford many examples of rites which appear to be similar in character, though they fall at different times of the year; such, for instance, are the ceremonies concerned with vegetation on May Day, Whitsuntide, and Midsummer Day,[3] and the fire festivals which are distributed at still wider intervals throughout the months.[4] Similarly in ancient Italy the agricultural festival of the Ambarvalia was celebrated by Italian farmers at different dates in different places.[5] These cases may warn us against the danger of hastily inferring an essential difference between Zakmuk and Sacaea on the ground of a real or apparent difference in their dates.

A fresh and powerful argument in favour of the identity

Suggested ways of meeting the difficulty.

---

[1] See above, p. 355, note [5]. On the other hand Prof. H. Zimmern prefers to suppose that the Sacaea was quite distinct from Zakmuk, and that it fell in July at the time of the heliacal rising of Sirius, which seems to have been associated with the goddess Ishtar. See H. Zimmern, in E. Schrader's *Die Keilinschriften und das Alte Testament*[3] (Berlin, 1902), pp. 426 *sq.*

[2] *Encyclopaedia Biblica, s.v.* "Year," vol. iv. (London, 1903) coll. 5365 *sqq.*

[3] *The Magic Art and the Evolution of Kings,* ii. 59 *sqq.*

[4] *The Golden Bough,* Second Edition, iii. 237 *sqq.*

[5] J. Marquardt, *Römische Staatsverwaltung*[2] (Leipsic, 1885), pp. 200 *sq.*

An argument for identifying Sacaea and Zakmuk is the apparent connexion of both with the Jewish festival of Purim. of the two festivals is furnished by the connexion which has been traced between both of them and the Jewish feast of Purim.[1] There are good grounds for believing that Purim was unknown to the Jews until after the exile, and that they learned to observe it during their captivity in the East. The festival is first mentioned in the book of Esther, which by the majority of critics is assigned to the fourth or third century B.C.,[2] and which certainly cannot be older than the Persian period, since the scene of the narrative is laid in Susa at the court of a Persian king Ahasuerus, whose name appears to be the Hebrew equivalent of Xerxes. The next reference to Purim occurs in the second book of Maccabees, a work written probably about the beginning of our era.[3] Thus from the absence of all notice of Purim in the older books of the Bible, we may fairly conclude that the festival was instituted or imported at a comparatively late date among the Jews. The same conclusion is supported by the book of Esther itself, which was manifestly written to explain the origin of the feast and to suggest motives for its observance. For, according to the author of the book, the festival was established to commemorate the deliverance of the Jews from a great danger which threatened them in Persia under the reign of King Xerxes. Thus the opinion of modern scholars that the feast of Purim, as celebrated by the Jews, was of late date and oriental origin, is borne out by the tradition of the Jews themselves. An examination of that tradition and the mode of celebrating the feast renders

---

[1] H. Zimmern, "Zur Frage nach dem Ursprunge des Purimfestes," *Zeitschrift für die alttestamentliche Wissenschaft*, xi. (1891) pp. 157-169; W. Nowack, *Lehrbuch der hebräischen Archäologie* (Freiburg i. B. and Leipsic, 1894), ii. 198 *sqq.*; Br. Meissner, "Zur Entstehungsgeschichte des Purimfestes,"*Zeitschrift der deutschen morgenländischen Gesellschaft*, l. (1896) pp. 296-301; Fr. Cumont, "Le roi des Saturnales," *Revue de Philologie*, xxi. (1897) p. 150; P. Haupt, *Purim* (Leipsic, 1906). The various theories which have been propounded as to the origin of Purim are stated and discussed by Prof. L. B. Paton in his *Commentary on the Book of Esther* (Edinburgh, 1908), pp. 77-94. See also *EncyclopaediaBiblica, s.v.* "Purim," vol. iii. (London, 1902) coll. 3976 *sqq.*

[2] S. R. Driver, *Introduction to the Literature of the Old Testament*[8] (Edinburgh, 1909), p. 484. Professor T. Witton Davies would date the book about 130 B.C. See *Ezra, Nehemiah and Esther*, edited by Rev. T. Witton Davies (Edinburgh and London, N.D.), pp. 299-301 (*The Century Bible*).

[3] 2 Maccabees xv. 36. As to the date of this book, see S. R. Driver, *op. cit.* p. 481.

it probable that Purim is nothing but a more or less disguised form of the Babylonian festival of the Sacaea or Zakmuk.

In the first place, the feast of Purim was and is held on the fourteenth and fifteenth days of Adar, the last month of the Jewish year, which corresponds roughly to March.[1] Thus the date agrees nearly, though not exactly, with the date of the Babylonian Zakmuk, which fell a fortnight later in the early days of the following month Nisan. A trace of the original celebration of Purim in Nisan may perhaps be found in the statement that "they cast Pur, that is, the lot, before Haman" in Nisan, the first month of the year.[2] It has been suggested with some plausibility that the Jews may have shifted the date of Purim in order that the new and foreign festival might not clash with their own old festival of the Passover, which began on the fourteenth day of Nisan. Another circumstance which speaks at once for the alien origin of Purim and for its identity with Zakmuk is its name. The author of the book of Esther derives the name Purim from *pur*, "a lot,"[3] but no such word with this signification exists in Hebrew, and hence we are driven to look for the meaning and etymology of Purim in some other language. A specious theory is that the name was derived from an Assyrian word *puhru*, "an assembly," and referred primarily to the great assembly of the gods which, as we have seen, formed a chief feature of the festival of Zakmuk, and was held annually in the temple of Marduk at Babylon for the purpose of determining the fates or lots of the new year;[4] the august assembly appears to have been occasionally, if not regularly, designated by the very name *puhru*.[5] On this hypothesis the traditional Jewish explanation of the name Purim preserved a genuine

The Jewish festival of Purim seems to be derived from the Babylonian festival of Zakmuk.

---

[1] We know from Josephus(*Antiquit.* iii. 10. 5) that in the month Nisan, the first month of the Jewish year, the sun was in Aries. Now the sun is in Aries from March 20th or 21st to April 19th or 20th; hence Nisan answers approximately to April, and Adar to March.

[2] Esther iii. 7.

[3] Esther iii. 7, ix. 26.

[4] This is the view of H. Zimmern (*Zeitschrift für die alttestamentliche Wissenschaft*, xi. (1891) pp. 157 *sqq.*), and it is favoured by W. Nowack (*Lehrbuch der hebräischen Archäologie*, ii. 198 *sq.*). Compare H. Zimmern, in E. Schrader's *Die Keilinschriften und das Alte Testament*[3] (Berlin, 1902), p. 518.

[5] P. Jensen, *Die Kosmologie der Babylonier*, pp. 240 *sq.*

kernel of historical truth, or at least of mythical fancy, under the husk of a verbal error ; for the name, if this derivation of it is correct, really signified, not "the lots," but the assembly for drawing or otherwise determining the lots. Another explanation which has been offered is "that *pūr* or *būr* seems to be an old Assyrian word for 'stone,' and that therefore it is possible that the word was also used to signify 'lot,' like the Hebrew גּוֹרָל 'lot,' which originally, no doubt, meant 'little stone.'"[1]   Either of these explanations of the name Purim, by tracing it back to the New Year assembly of the gods at Babylon for settling the lots, furnishes an adequate explanation of the traditional association of Purim with the casting of lots—an association all the more remarkable and all the more likely to be ancient because there is nothing to justify it either in the Hebrew language or in the Jewish mode of celebrating the festival. When to this we add the joyous, nay, extravagant festivity which has always been characteristic of Purim, and is entirely in keeping with a New Year celebration, we may perhaps be thought to have made out a fairly probable case for holding that the Jewish feast is derived from the Babylonian New Year festival of Zakmuk.   Whether the Jews borrowed the feast directly from the Babylonians or indirectly through the Persian conquerors of Babylon is a question which deserves to be considered ; but the Persian colouring of the book of Esther speaks strongly for the view that Purim came to Israel by way of Persia, or at all events from Babylon under Persian rule, and this view is confirmed by other evidence, to which I shall have to ask the reader's attention a little later on.

Connexion of Purim with the Sacaea.

If the links which bind Purim to Zakmuk are reasonably strong, the chain of evidence which connects the Jewish festival with the Sacaea is much stronger.   Nor is this surprising when we remember that, while the popular mode of celebrating Zakmuk is unknown, we possess important and trustworthy details as to the manner of holding the

---

[1] The explanation is that of P. Jensen, quoted by Th. Nöldeke in *Encyclopaedia Biblica*, s.v. "Esther," vol. ii. (London, 1901) col. 1404 note[1]. In Greek, for a similar reason, the word for "pebble" and "vote" is identical ($\psi\hat\eta\phi os$). As to this etymology see also C. H. W. Johns, s.v. "Purim," *Encyclopaedia Biblica*, iii. (London, 1902) coll. 3979 *sq.*

Sacaea. We have seen that the Sacaea was a wild Bacchanalian revel at which men and women disguised themselves and drank and played together in a fashion that was
more gay than modest. Now this is, or used to be, precisely the nature of Purim. The two days of the festival,   The joyous
according to the author of the book of Esther, were to be   nature of
Purim.
kept for ever as " days of feasting and gladness, and of sending portions one to another, and gifts to the poor." [1]   And
this joyous character the festival seems always to have
retained. The author of a tract in the Talmud lays it down
as a rule that at the feast of Purim every Jew is bound to
drink until he cannot distinguish between the words " Cursed
be Haman " and " Blessed be Mordecai " ; and he tells how
on one occasion a certain Rabba drank so deep at Purim
that he murdered a rabbi without knowing what he was
about. Indeed Purim has been described as the Jewish
Bacchanalia, and we are told that at this season everything is lawful which can contribute to the mirth and
gaiety of the festival.[2] Writers of the seventeenth century
assert that during the two days, and especially on the evening of the second day, the Jews did nothing but feast and
drink to repletion, play, dance, sing, and make merry ; in
particular they disguised themselves, men and women exchanging clothes, and thus attired ran about like mad, in
open defiance of the Mosaic law, which expressly forbids
men to dress as women and women as men.[3] Among the
Jews of Frankfort, who inhabited the squalid but quaint and
picturesque old street known as the Judengasse, which many
of us still remember, the revelry at Purim ran as high as
ever in the eighteenth century. The gluttony and intoxication began punctually at three o'clock in the afternoon of
the first day and went on until the whole community seemed
to have taken leave of their senses. They ate and drank,
they frolicked and cut capers, they reeled and staggered

---

[1] Esther x. 22.

[2] J. Buxtorf, *Synagoga Judaica*
(Bâle, 1661), pp. 554 *sq.*, 559 *sq.*

[3] J. Buxtorf, *op. cit.* p. 559 ; Schick-
ard, quoted by Lagarde, " Purim,"
Abhandlungen der kön. Gesellschaft

der Wissenschaften zu Göttingen,
xxxiv. (1887) pp. 54 *sq.* Compare J.
Chr. G. Bodenschatz, *Kirchliche Verfassung der heutigen Juden* (Erlangen,
1748), ii. 256. For the rule forbidding men and women to exchange
garments, see Deuteronomy xxii. 5.

about, they shrieked, yelled, stamped, clattered, and broke each other's heads with wooden hammers till the blood flowed. On the evening of the first day the women were allowed, as a special favour, to open their latticed window and look into the men's synagogue, because the great deliverance of the Jews from their enemies in the time of King Ahasuerus was said to have been effected by a woman. A feature of the festival which should not be overlooked was the acting of the story of Esther as a comedy, in which Esther, Ahasuerus, Haman, Mordecai, and others played their parts after a fashion that sometimes degenerated from farce into ribaldry.[1] Thus on the whole we may take it that Purim has always been a Saturnalia, and therefore corresponds in character to the Sacaea as that festival has been described for us by Strabo.

The origin of Purim according to the book of Esther.

But further, when we examine the narrative which professes to account for the institution of Purim, we discover in it not only the strongest traces of Babylonian origin, but also certain singular analogies to those very features of the Sacaean festival with which we are here more immediately concerned. The book of Esther turns upon the fortunes of two men, the vizier Haman and the despised Jew Mordecai, at the court of a Persian king. Mordecai, we are told, had given mortal offence to the vizier, who accordingly prepares a tall gallows on which he hopes to see his enemy hanged, while he himself expects to receive the highest mark of the king's favour by being allowed to wear the royal crown and the royal robes, and thus attired to parade the streets mounted on the king's own horse and attended by one of the noblest princes, who should proclaim to the multitude his temporary exaltation and glory. But the artful intrigues of the wicked vizier miscarried and resulted in precisely the opposite of what he had hoped and expected; for the royal honours which he had looked for fell to his rival Mordecai, and he himself was hanged on the gallows which he had made ready for his foe. In this story we seem to detect a reminiscence, more or less confused, of the Zoganes of the Sacaea, in other words, of the custom of investing a private man with the insignia of royalty for a few days and then putting him to; death on the gallows or the cross. It is true that in the narrative the part of the Zoganes is divided between two actors, one of whom hopes to play the king but is hanged instead, while the other acts the royal part and escapes the gallows to which he was destined by his enemy. But this bisection, so to say, of the Zoganes may have been deliberately invented by the Jewish author of the book of Esther for the sake of setting the origin of Purim, which it was his purpose to explain, in a light that should reflect glory on his own nation. Or, perhaps more probably, it points back to a custom of appointing two mock kings at the Sacaea, one of whom was put to death at the end of the festival, while the other was allowed to go free, at least for a time. We shall be the more inclined to adopt the latter hypothesis when we observe that corresponding to the two rival aspirants to the temporary kingship there appear in the Jewish narrative two rival queens, Vashti and Esther, one of whom succeeds to the high estate from which the other has fallen. Further, it is to be noted that Mordecai, the successful candidate for the mock kingship, and Esther, the successful candidate for the queenship, are linked together by close ties both of interest and blood, the two being said to be cousins. This suggests that in the original story or the original custom there may have figured two pairs of kings and queens, of whom one pair is represented in the Jewish narrative by Mordecai and Esther and the other by Haman and Vashti.

The rival pairs Mordecai and Esther on the one side, Haman and Vashti on the other.

Some confirmation of this view is furnished by the names of two at least out of the four personages. It seems to be now generally recognized by Biblical scholars that the name Mordecai, which has no meaning in Hebrew, is nothing but a slightly altered form of Marduk or Merodach, the name of the chief god of Babylon, whose great festival was the Zakmuk ; and further, it is generally admitted that Esther in like manner is equivalent to Ishtar, the great Babylonian goddess whom the Greeks called Astarte, and who is more familiar to English readers

Analysis of the names Mordecai and Esther, Haman and Vashti.

Jensen's
theory that
Haman
and Vashti
were
Elamite
deities in
opposition
to the
Babylonian
deities
Mordecai
(Marduk)
and Esther
(Ishtar).

as Ashtaroth. The derivation of the names of Haman and Vashti is less certain, but some high authorities are disposed to accept the view of Jensen that Haman is identical with Humman or Homman, the national god of the Elamites, and that Vashti is in like manner an Elamite goddess whose name Jensen read as Mashti in inscriptions. Now, when we consider that the Elamites were from time immemorial the hereditary foes of the Babylonians and had their capital at Susa, the very place in which the scene of the book of Esther is laid, we can hardly deny the plausibility of the theory that Haman and Vashti on the one side and Mordecai and Esther on the other represent the antagonism between the gods of Elam and the gods of Babylon, and the final victory of the Babylonian deities in the very capital of their rivals.[1] " It is therefore possible," says Professor Nöldeke, " that we here have to do with a feast whereby the Babylonians commemorated a victory gained by their gods over the gods of their neighbours the Elamites, against whom they had so often waged war. The Jewish feast of Purim is an annual merrymaking of a wholly secular kind, and it is known that there were similar feasts among the Babylonians. That the Jews in Babylonia should have adopted a festival of this sort cannot be deemed improbable, since in modern Germany, to cite an analogous

---

[1] P. Jensen, "Elamitische Eigennamen," *Wiener Zeitschrift für die Kunde des Morgenlandes*, vi. (1892) pp. 47-70; compare *ib.* pp. 209-212. All Jensen's etymologies are accepted by W. Nowack (*Lehrbuch der hebräischen Archäologie*, Freiburg i. Baden and Leipsic, 1894, ii. 199 *sq.*); H. Gunkel (*Schöpfung und Chaos*, Göttingen, 1895, pp. 310 *sq.*); D. G. Wildeboer (in his commentary on Esther, pp. 173 *sqq.*, forming part of K. Marti's *Kurzer Hand-Commentar zum alten Testament*, Freiburg i. B. 1898); Th. Nöldeke (*s.v.* "Esther," *Encyclopaedia Biblica*, vol. ii. coll. 1404 *sq.*); and H. Zimmern (in E. Schrader's *Die Keilinschriften und das Alte Testament*,[3] Berlin, 1902, pp. 485, 516 *sq.*). On the other hand, Br. Meissner (*Zeitschrift der deutschen morgenländischen Gesellschaft*, l. (1896) p. 301) and M. Jastrow (*The Religion of Babylonia*

and Assyria, p. 686, note 2) suspend their judgment as to the identification of Haman and Vashti with Elamite deities, though they apparently regard the identification of Mordecai and Esther with Marduk and Ishtar as quite certain. The doubt which these scholars felt as to the derivation of one at least of these names (Vashti) is now known to be well founded. See below, p. 367, note [3].

It deserves to be noted that on the twenty-seventh day of the month Tammuz the heathen of Harran used to sacrifice nine male lambs to Haman, "the supreme God, the father of the gods," and they ate and drank on that day. Chwolsohn suggests a comparison of the festival with the Athenian Cronia. See D. Chwolsohn, *Die Ssabier und der Ssabismus* (St. Petersburg, 1856), ii. 27 *sq.*, 211 *sqq.*

case, many Jews celebrate Christmas after the manner of their Christian fellow-countrymen, in so far at least as it is a secular institution. It is true that hitherto no Babylonian feast coinciding, like Purim, with the full moon of the twelfth month has been discovered; but our knowledge of the Babylonian feasts is derived from documents of an earlier period. Possibly the calendar may have undergone some change by the time when the Jewish feast of Purim was established. Or it may be that the Jews intentionally shifted the date of the festival which they borrowed from the heathen." [1]

However, the theory of an opposition between the gods of Babylon and the gods of Elam at the festival appears to break down at a crucial point; for the latest and most accurate reading of the Elamite inscriptions proves, I am informed, that the name of the goddess which Jensen read as Mashti, and which on that assumption he legitimately compared to the Hebrew Vashti,[2] must really be read as Parti, between which and Vashti there is no connexion. Accordingly, in a discussion of the origin of Purim it is safer at present to lay no weight on the supposed religious antagonism between the deities of Babylon and Elam.[3]

But the proposed etymology of Vashti is untenable.

[1] Th. Nöldeke, *s.v.* "Esther," in *Encyclopaedia Biblica*, vol. ii. (London, 1901) coll. 1405. But in a letter, written to me (20th May 1901) since the publication of the last edition of this book, Professor Nöldeke expresses a doubt whether he has not followed Jensen's mythological identifications in the book of Esther too far.

[2] "The change of *m* to *w* or *v* (the Hebrew ו=*waw*) is frequent and certain" (the Rev. C. H. W. Johns in a letter to me, May 19th, 1913). The change is vouched for also by my friend Professor A. A. Bevan, who cites as an instance the name of the Babylonian king Amel-Marduk, which in Hebrew is changed into Evil-Merodach (2 Kings xxv. 27; Jeremiah lii. 31). See E. Schrader, *Die Keilinschriften und das Alte Testament* [3] (Berlin, 1902), p. 396.

[3] The name of the Elamite goddess is read as Parti by the Rev. Father Scheil. See E. Cosquin, *Le Prologue-cadre des Mille et Une Nuits,*

les Légendes Perses, et le Livre d'Esther (Paris, 1909), p. 68 (extract from the *Revue Biblique International*, Janvier et Avril, 1909, published by the Dominicans of Jerusalem). The Master of St. Catharine's College, Cambridge (the Rev. C. H. W. Johns), has kindly examined the facsimile of the inscriptions for me. He informs me that Father Scheil's reading is correct and that the reading Mashti is quite wrong. He further tells me that Jensen was misled by an incorrect edition of the inscriptions to which alone he had access. The signs for *par* (or *bar*) and *mash* in the inscriptions resemble each other and therefore might easily be confused by a copyist. All Jensen's etymologies, except that of Mordecai, are adversely criticized by M. Emile Cosquin in the work to which I have referred (pp. 67 *sqq.*). He prefers with Oppert to derive all the names except Mordecai (the identity of which with Marduk he does not dispute) from the old Persian. However,

The mock
king of the
Sacaea
seems
to have
personated
a god.

The
view of
Movers.

If we are right in tracing the origin of Purim to the Babylonian Sacaea and in finding the counterpart of the Zoganes in Haman and Mordecai, it would appear that the Zoganes during his five days of office personated not merely a king but a god, whether that god was the Babylonian Marduk or some other deity not yet identified. The union of the divine and royal characters in a single person is so common that we need not be surprised at meeting with it in ancient Babylon. And the view that the mock king of the Sacaea died as a god on the cross or the gallows is no novelty. The acute and learned Movers long ago observed that " we should be overlooking the religious significance of oriental festivals and the connexion of the Sacaea with the worship of Anaitis, if we were to treat as a mere jest the custom of disguising a slave as a king. We may take it for certain that with the royal dignity the king of the Sacaea assumed also the character of an oriental ruler as representative of the divinity, and that when he took his pleasure among the women of the king's harem, he played the part of Sandan or Sardanapalus himself. For according to ancient oriental ideas the use of the king's concubines constituted a claim to the throne, and we know from Dio that the five-days' king received full power over the harem. Perhaps he began his reign by publicly cohabiting with the king's concubines, just as Absalom went in to his father's concubines in a tent spread on the roof of the palace before all Israel, for the purpose of thereby making known and strengthening his claim to the throne." [1]

Whatever may be thought of this latter conjecture, there

these derivations from the Persian are rejected by Professor Th. Nöldeke, whose opinion on such a point is entitled to carry great weight. See *Encyclopaedia Biblica*, ii. (London, 1901) col. 1402, *s.v.* " Esther."

[1] F. C. Movers, *Die Phoenizier*, i. (Bonn, 1841) pp. 490 *sq.* ; 2 Samuel xvi. 21 *sq.*, compare xii. 8. It was a well-attested custom of the Assyrian kings, when they had conquered a city, to take into their harem the daughters of the vanquished princes

and rulers. See C. F. Lehmann (-Haupt), *Šamaššumukîn König von Babylonien* (Leipsic, 1892), p. 31. The Persian and Scythian kings seem also to have married the wives of their predecessors. See Herodotus, iii. 68 and 88, iv. 78 ; K. Neumann, *Die Hellenen im Skythenlande*, i. (Berlin, 1855) p. 301. Such a custom points to an old system of mother-kin under which the royal dignity was transmitted through women. See *The Magic Art and the Evolution of Kings*, ii. 268 *sqq.*

can be no doubt that Movers is right in laying great stress both on the permission given to the mock king to invade the real king's harem, and on the intimate connexion of the Sacaea with the worship of Anaitis. That connexion is vouched for by Strabo, and when we consider that in Strabo's time the cult of the old Persian goddess Anaitis was thoroughly saturated with Babylonian elements and had practically merged in the sensual worship of the Babylonian Ishtar or Astarte,[1] we shall incline to view with favour Movers's further conjecture, that a female slave may have been appointed to play the divine queen to the part of the divine king supported by the Zoganes, and that reminiscences of such a queen have survived in the myth or legend of Semiramis. According to tradition, Semiramis was a fair courtesan beloved by the king of Assyria, who took her to wife. She won the king's heart so far that she persuaded him to yield up to her the kingdom for five days, and having assumed the sceptre and the royal robes she made a great banquet on the first day, but on the second day she shut up her husband in prison or put him to death and thenceforward reigned alone.[2] Taken with Strabo's evidence as to the association of the Sacaea with the worship of Anaitis, this tradition seems clearly to point to a custom of giving the Zoganes, during his five days' reign, a queen who represented the goddess Anaitis or Semiramis or Astarte, in short the great Asiatic goddess of love and fertility, by whatever name she was called. For that in Eastern legend Semiramis was a real queen of Assyria, who had absorbed many of the attributes of the goddess Astarte, appears to be established by the researches of modern scholars ; in particular it has been shewn by Robertson Smith that the worship of Anaitis is not only

The mock king of the Sacaea may have mated with a woman who played the part of a goddess, whether Anaitis, Astarte, or Semiramis.

Identity of the mythical Semiramis with Astarte.

---

[1] Ed. Meyer, *s.v.* "Anaitis," in W. H. Roscher's *Lexikon der griech. und röm. Mythologie*, i. (Leipsic, 1884–1890) coll. 352 *sq.* At the temple of Anaitis in Acilisena, a city of Armenia, the daughters of the noblest families regularly prostituted themselves for a long time before marriage (Strabo, xi. 14. 16, p. 532). Agathias identified Anaitis with Aphrodite (*Hist.* ii. 24), and when the Greeks spoke of the Oriental Aphrodite, they meant

Astarte or one of her equivalents. Jensen proposes to identify Anaitis with an Elamite goddess Nahuntí, whom he takes to have been equivalent to Ishtar or Astarte, especially in her quality of the Evening Star. See his article, "Elamitische Eigennamen," *Wiener Zeitschrift für die Kunde des Morgenlandes*, vi. (1892) pp. 64-67, 70.

[2] Diodorus Siculus, ii. 20 ; Aelian, *Var. Hist.* vii. 1.

modelled on Astarte worship in general, but corresponds to that particular type of it which was specially associated with the name of Semiramis.[1]   The identity of Anaitis and the mythical Semiramis is clearly proved by the circumstance that the great sanctuary of Anaitis at Zela in Pontus was actually built upon a mound of Semiramis;[2] probably the old worship of the Semitic goddess always continued there even after her Semitic name of Semiramis or Astarte had been exchanged for the Persian name of Anaitis, perhaps in obedience to a decree of the Persian king Artaxerxes II., who first spread the worship of Anaitis in the west of Asia.[3] It is highly significant, not only that the Sacaean festival was annually held at this ancient seat of the worship of Semiramis or Astarte ; but further, that the whole city of Zela was formerly inhabited by sacred slaves and harlots, ruled over by a supreme pontiff, who administered it as a sanctuary rather than as a city.[4]   Formerly, we may suppose, this priestly king himself died a violent death at the Sacaea

[1] W. Robertson Smith, "Ctesias and the Semiramis Legend," *English Historical Review*, ii. (1887) pp. 303-317.   Amongst other evidence, Smith refers to Diodorus Siculus, from whose account (ii. 4) of the birth of Semiramis he infers that she "is the daughter of Derceto, the fish goddess of Ascalon, and is herself the Astarte whose sacred doves were honoured at Ascalon and throughout Syria."   It seems probable that the legendary Semiramis is to be identified with Shammuramat, the "palace wife" of Samsi-Adad, king of Assyria, and mother of King Adad-Nirari ; she lived towards the end of the ninth century B.C., and is known to us from Assyrian inscriptions.   See C. F. Lehmann-Haupt, *Die historische Semiramis und ihre Zeit* (Tübingen, 1910), pp. 1 *sqq.* ; *id.*, *s.v.* "Semiramis," in W. H. Roscher's *Lexicon der griech. und röm. Mythologie*, iv. coll. 678 *sqq.*

[2] Strabo, xii. 3. 37, p. 559, compare xi. 8. 4, p. 512.   Zela is the modern Zileh, a town of about 20,000 inhabitants clustered at the foot of the so-called mound of Semiramis, which is an inconsiderable protuberance of natural rock crowned by the walls of an old citadel.   The place is singularly destitute of ancient remains, but every year in the first fortnight of December a fair is held in the town, to which merchants come not only from the whole of Asia Minor, but also from the Caucasus, Armenia, and Persia.   This fair may very well be a direct descendant of a great festival held in honour of Anaitis or Astarte.   See G. Perrot et Ch. Chipiez, *Histoire de l'Art dans l'Antiquité*, iv. (Paris, 1887) p. 649 ; F. Cumont et E. Cumont, *Voyage d'Exploration archéologique dans le Pont et la Petite Arménie* (Brussels, 1906), pp. 188 *sqq.*

[3] Berosus, cited by Clement of Alexandria, *Protrept.* v. 65, p. 57 ed. Potter (where for Ταναῖδος we should read Ἀναΐτιδος, as is done by C. Müller, *Fragmenta Historicorum Graecorum*, ii. 509).

[4] Strabo, xi. 8. 4, p. 512, xii. 3. 37, p. 559.   The nature of the ἱερόδουλοι at Zela is indicated by Strabo in a passage (xii. 3. 36) where he describes a similar state of things at Comana, a city not far from Zela.   His words are πλῆθος γυναικῶν τῶν ἐργαζομένων ἀπὸ τοῦ σώματος, ὧν αἱ πλείους εἰσὶν ἱεραί.

in the character of the divine lover of Semiramis, while the The
part of the goddess was played by one of the sacred prosti- lovers of
Semiramis
tutes. The probability of this is greatly strengthened by and Ishtar
the existence of the so-called mound of Semiramis under the (Astarte).
sanctuary. For the mounds of Semiramis, which were
pointed out all over Western Asia,[1] were said to have been
the graves of her lovers whom she buried alive.[2] The
tradition ran that the great and lustful queen Semiramis,
fearing to contract a lawful marriage lest her husband should
deprive her of power, admitted to her bed the handsomest of
her soldiers, only, however, to destroy them all afterwards.[3]
Now this tradition is one of the surest indications of the
identity of the mythical Semiramis with the Babylonian
goddess Ishtar or Astarte. For the famous Babylonian epic
which recounts the deeds of the hero Gilgamesh tells how,
when he clothed himself in royal robes and put his crown on
his head, the goddess Ishtar was smitten with love of him
and wooed him to be her mate. But Gilgamesh rejected her
insidious advances, for he knew the sad fate that had overtaken all her lovers, and he reproached the cruel goddess,
saying :—

" *Tammuz, the lover of thy youth,*
Thou causest to weep every year.
The bright-coloured allallu *bird thou didst love.*
Thou didst crush him and break his pinions.
In the woods he stands and laments, ' O my pinions !'
Thou didst love the lion of perfect strength,
Seven and seven times thou didst dig pit-falls for him.
Thou didst love the horse that joyed in the fray,
With whip and spur and lash thou didst urge him on.
Thou didst force him on for seven double hours,
Thou didst force him on when wearied and thirsty ;
His mother the goddess Silili thou madest weep.
Thou didst also love a shepherd of the flock,
Who continually poured out for thee the libation,
And daily slaughtered kids for thee ;
But thou didst smite him, and didst change him into a wolf,
So that his own sheep-boys hunted him,
And his own hounds tore him to pieces."

---

[1] Herodotus, i. 184 ; Strabo, xvi.
i. 2, p. 737 ; Diodorus Siculus, ii.
14.

[2] Ctesias, cited by John of Antioch,
in C. Müller's *Fragmenta Historicorum*

Graecorum, iv. 539.

[3] Diodorus Siculus, ii. 13. Note
that the first husband of Semiramis is
said to have hanged himself (Diodorus
Siculus, ii. 6).

The hero also tells the miserable end of a gardener in the service of the goddess's father.   The hapless swain had once been honoured with the love of the goddess, but when she tired of him she changed him into a cripple so that he could not rise from his bed.   Therefore Gilgamesh fears to share the fate of all her former lovers and spurns her proffered favours.[1]   But it is not merely that the myth of Ishtar thus tallies with the legend of Semiramis; the worship of the goddess was marked by a profligacy which has found its echo in the loose character ascribed by tradition to the queen.   Inscriptions, which confirm and supplement the evidence of Herodotus, inform us that Ishtar was served by harlots of three different classes all dedicated to her worship. Indeed, there is reason to think that these women personated the goddess herself, since one of the names given to them is applied also to her.[2]

Thus we can hardly doubt that the mythical Semiramis is substantially a form of Ishtar or Astarte, the great Semitic goddess of love and fertility ; and if this is so, we may assume with at least a fair degree of probability that the high pontiff of Zela or his deputy, who played the king of the Sacaea at the sanctuary of Semiramis, perished as one

The sacred harlots of Ishtar.

The myth of Ishtar (Astarte) and her lovers acted at the Sacaea in Zela.

---

[1] A. Jeremias, *Izdubar - Nimrod*, (Leipsic, 1891), pp. 23 *sqq.*; M. Jastrow, *The Religion of Babylonia and Assyria* (Boston, U.S.A., 1898), p. 482 ; L. W. King, *Babylonian Religion and Mythology* (London, 1899), pp. 159 *sqq.* ; P. Jensen, *Assyrisch-Babylonische Mythen und Epen* (Berlin, 1900), pp. 169, 171 ; R. F. Harper, *Assyrian and Babylonian Literature* (New York, 1901), pp. 338 *sq.*; *Das Gilgamesch-Epos, neu übersetzt von* Arthur Ungnad *und gemeinverständlich erklärt von* Hugo Gressmann (Göttingen, 1911), pp. 31 *sq.* The true name of the Babylonian hero, which used to be read as Izdubar, has been found to be Gilgamesh. See M. Jastrow, *op. cit.* pp. 468 *sq.* ; H. Zimmern, in E. Schrader's *Die Keilinschriften und das Alte Testament*[3] (Berlin, 1902), p. 566 note[4] ; A. Ungnad, *Das Gilgamesch-Epos*, pp. 76 *sq.* Aelian mentions (*De natura animalium*, xii. 21) a Babylonian king, Gilgamus, whose name is

doubtless identical with that of the hero.

[2] A. Jeremias, *op. cit.* pp. 59 *sq.* ; M. Jastrow, *op. cit.* pp. 475 *sq.*, 484 *sq.* ; Herodotus, i. 199. The name which Herodotus gives to the goddess is Mylitta, but this is only a corruption of one of her Semitic titles, whether Baalath (Hebrew בַּעֲלָה), "mistress," or perhaps rather *Mullittu*, from *Mu'allidtu* (Hebrew מְיַלֶּדֶת), "she who helps to the birth." See E. Meyer, *s.v.* "Astarte," in W. H. Roscher's *Lexicon der griech. und röm. Mythologie*, i. 648; H. Zimmern, in E. Schrader's *Die Keilinschriften und das Alte Testament*[3] (Berlin, 1902), p. 423 note[7]. The female "votaries of Marduk" are repeatedly mentioned in the code of Hammurabi. See C. H. W. Johns, *Babylonian and Assyrian Laws, Contracts, and Letters* (Edinburgh, 1904), pp. 54, 55, 59, 60, 61 ; *Adonis, Attis, Osiris*, Second Edition, p. 63.

of the unhappy lovers of the goddess, perhaps as Tammuz, whom she caused "to weep every year." When he had run his brief meteoric career of pleasure and glory, his bones would be laid in the great mound which covered the mouldering remains of many mortal gods, his predecessors, whom the goddess had honoured with her fatal love.[1]

Here then at the great sanctuary of the goddess in Zela it appears that her myth was regularly translated into action ; the story of her love and the death of her divine lover was performed year by year as a sort of mystery-play by men and women who lived for a season and sometimes died in the character of the visionary beings whom they personated. The intention of these sacred dramas, we may be sure, was

Such sacred dramas are magical rites intended to influence the course of nature.

---

[1] Along with Anaitis at Zela there were worshipped two deities named Omanos and Anadates ; Strabo says that they were Persian divinities, and certainly their ritual as described by him was purely Persian. See Strabo, xi. 8. 4, p. 512, xv. 3. 15, p. 733 ; Franz Cumont, *Les Religions orientales dans le Paganisme romain*[2] (Paris, 1909), pp. 214 *sq.* It has been proposed to identify their names, first, with those of the two Persian archangels (Amshaspands), Vohumano or Vohu Manah ("Good Thought") and Ameretât ("Immortality"), and, second, with those of Haman and his father Hammedatha in the book of Esther (iii. 1). In order to support the identification of Anadates with Ameretât and Hammedatha it has been further proposed to alter Anadates into Amadates or Amardates in the text of Strabo, which would assimilate the name to Amurdâd, a late form of Ameretât. See P. Jensen, *Hittiter und Armenier* (Strasburg, 1898), p. 181 ; Franz Cumont, *Textes et Monuments figurés relatifs aux Mystères de Mithra*, i. (Brussels, 1899) pp. 130, 131 ; H. Winckler, *Altorientalische Forschungen*, Dritte Reihe, i. (Leipsic, 1901) p. 4 ; H. Zimmern, in E. Schrader's *Die Keilinschriften und das Alte Testament*[3] (Berlin, 1902), p. 516 note[3] ; P. Haupt, *Purim* (Leipsic, 1906), p. 26 ; L. B. Paton, *Critical and Exegetical Commentary on the Book of Esther* (Edinburgh, 1908), pp. 88, 92.

As to the Persian archangels (Amshaspands) see C. P. Tiele, *Geschichte der Religion im Altertum* (Gotha, 1896–1903), ii. 200 *sqq.* ; L. H. Gray, "The Double Nature of the Iranian Archangels," *Archiv für Religionswissenschaft*, vii. (1904) pp. 345 *sqq.*; J. H. Moulton, *Early Religious Poetry of Persia* (Cambridge, 1911), pp. 58 *sqq.* But apart from the philological difficulty created by the forcible alteration of Strabo's text in order to bring it into conformity with the theory, it is difficult to see how the highly abstract conceptions of the archangels "Good Thought" and "Immortality" could have passed into the highly concrete and by no means angelic figures of Haman and Hammedatha. This latter difficulty has been pointed out to me in a letter (8th June, 1901) by my friend the Rev. Professor J. H. Moulton, who further informs me that in Persian religion Vohu Manah is never linked with Ameretât, whereas Ameretât is constantly linked with another archangel Haurvatât ("Health"). Professor Theodor Nöldeke in a letter to me (20th May, 1901) also expresses himself sceptical as to the proposed identifications ; he tells me that the name of a Persian god cannot end in *data*, just as the name of a Greek god cannot end in -δωρος or -δοτος. On the whole it seems better to leave Omanos and Anadates out of the present discussion.

neither to amuse nor to instruct an idle audience, and as little were they designed to gratify the actors, to whose baser passions they gave the reins for a time. They were solemn rites which mimicked the doings of divine beings, because man fancied that by such mimicry he was able to arrogate to himself the divine functions and to exercise them for the good of his fellows. The operations of nature, to his thinking, were carried on by mythical personages very like himself; and if he could only assimilate himself to them completely he would be able to wield all their powers. This is probably the original motive of most religious dramas or mysteries among rude peoples. The dramas are played, the mysteries are performed, not to teach the spectators the doctrines of their creed, still less to entertain them, but for the purpose of bringing about those natural effects which they represent in mythical disguise; in a word, they are magical ceremonies and their mode of operation is mimicry or sympathy. We shall probably not err in assuming that many myths, which we now know only as myths, had once their counterpart in magic; in other words, that they used to be acted as a means of producing in fact the events which they describe in figurative language. Ceremonies often die out while myths survive, and thus we are left to infer the dead ceremony from the living myth. If myths are, in a sense, the reflections or shadows of men cast upon the clouds, we may say that these reflections continue to be visible in the sky and to inform us of the doings of the men who cast them, long after the men themselves are not only beyond our range of vision but sunk beneath the horizon.

Magical intention of sacred dramas and masked dances among savages.

The principle of mimicry is implanted so deep in human nature and has exerted so far-reaching an influence on the development of religion as well as of the arts that it may be well, even at the cost of a short digression, to illustrate by example some of the modes in which primitive man has attempted to apply it to the satisfaction of his wants by means of religious or magical dramas. For it seems probable that the masked dances and ceremonies, which have played a great part in the social life of savages in many quarters of the world, were primarily designed to subserve practical purposes rather than simply to stir the emotions of the spectators and to while away the languor and tedium of idle hours. The actors sought to draw down blessings on the community by mimicking certain powerful superhuman beings and in their assumed character working those benefi- cent miracles which in the capacity of mere men they would have confessed themselves powerless to effect. In fact the aim of these elementary dramas, which contain in germ the tragedy and comedy of civilized nations, was the acquisition of superhuman power for the public good. That this is the real intention of at least many of these dramatic perform- ances will appear from the following accounts, which for the sake of accuracy I will quote for the most part in the words of the original observers.

A conspicuous feature in the social life of the Indian tribes of North-Western America are the elaborate masked dances or pantomimes in which the actors personate spirits or legendary animals. Most of them appear designed to bring before the eyes of the people the guardian spirits of the clans. " Owing to the fact that these spirits are hereditary, their gifts are always contained in the legend detailing their acquisition by the ancestor of a clan. The principal gifts in these tales are the magic harpoon which insures success in sea-otter hunting ; the death bringer which, when pointed against enemies, kills them ; the water of life which resuscitates the dead ; the burning fire which, when pointed against an object, burns it ; and a dance, a song, and cries which are peculiar to the spirit. The gift of this dance means that the protégé of the spirit is to perform the same dances which have been shown to him. In these dances he personates the spirit. He wears his mask and his ornaments. Thus the dance must be considered a dramatic performance of the myth relating to the acquisition of the spirit, and shows to the people that the performer by his visit to the spirit has obtained his powers and desires. When nowadays a spirit appears to a young Indian, he gives him the same dance, and the youth also returns from the initiation filled with the powers and desires of the spirit. He authenticates his initiation by his dance in the same way as his mythical ancestor did. The obtaining of the magical gifts from these spirits is

Masked dances among the Indians of North-West America.

called *lokoala*, while the person who has obtained them becomes *naualaku*, supernatural, which is also the quality of the spirit himself. The ornaments of all these spirits are described as made of cedar bark, which is dyed red in the juice of alder bark. They appear to their devotees only in winter, and therefore the dances are also performed only in winter."[1] In some of the dances the performers imitate animals, and the explanation which the Indians give of these dances is that "the ceremonial was instituted at the time when men had still the form of animals; before the transformer had put everything into its present shape. The present ceremonial is a repetition of the ceremonial performed by the man animals or, as we may say, a dramatization of the myth. Therefore the people who do not represent spirits, represent these animals."[2]

These masked dances represent mythical incidents and are supposed to have been revealed to the Indians by their guardian spirits.

Another observer of these Indians writes on the same subject as follows: "The *dukwally* (*i.e. lokoala*) and other *tamanawas*[3] performances are exhibitions intended to represent incidents connected with their mythological legends. There are a great variety, and they seem to take the place, in a measure, of theatrical performances or games during the season of the religious festivals. There are no persons especially set apart as priests for the performance of these ceremonies, although some, who seem more expert than others, are usually hired to give life to the scenes, but these performers are quite as often found among the slaves or common people as among the chiefs, and excepting during the continuance of the festivities are not looked on as of any particular importance. On inquiring the origin of these ceremonies, I was informed that they did not originate with the Indians, but were revelations of the guardian spirits, who made known what they wished to be performed. An Indian,

[1] Franz Boas, "The Social Organization and the Secret Societies of the Kwakiutl Indians," *Report of the United States National Museum for 1895* (Washington, 1897), p. 396.

[2] Franz Boas, *op. cit.* pp. 420 *sq.* The description applies specially to the masked dances of the Kwakiutl tribe, but probably it holds good for the similar dances of the other Indian tribes on the same coast. Thus among

the Bella Coola Indians "the masks used in the dances represent mythical personages, and the dances are pantomimic representations of myths. Among others, the thunder bird and his servant . . . appear in the dances" (F. Boas, *op. cit.* p. 651).

[3] *Tamanawas* or *tamanous* is a Chinook term signifying "guardian spirits." See *Totemism and Exogamy*, iii. 405 *sqq.*

for instance, who has been consulting with his guardian spirit, which is done by going through the washing and fasting process before described, will imagine or think he is called upon to represent the owl.   He arranges in his mind the style of dress, the number of performers, the songs and dances or other movements, and, having the plan perfected, announces at a *tamanawas* meeting that he has had a revelation which he will impart to a select few.   These are then taught and drilled in strict secrecy, and when they have perfected themselves, will suddenly make their appearance and perform before the astonished tribe.   Another Indian gets up the representation of the whale, others do the same of birds, and in fact of everything that they can think of. If any performance is a success, it is repeated, and gradually comes to be looked upon as one of the regular order in the ceremonies ; if it does not satisfy the audience, it is laid aside.   Thus they have performances that have been handed down from remote ages, while others are of a more recent date." [1]

Another writer, who travelled among the Indians of North - Western America, has expressed himself on this subject as follows : "The task of representing the gods is undertaken in every tribe by some intelligent and, according to their own account, inspired men ; they form the Secret Societies, in order that their secret arts and doctrines, their mummeries and masquerades may not be revealed to the uninitiated and to the public.   The intention of these exhibitions is to confirm the faith of the young people and the women in the ancient traditions as to the intercourse of the gods with men and as to their own intimate relations to the gods.   In order to convince possible doubters, the members of the Secret Societies have had recourse to all kinds of mysterious means, which to a civilized man must appear the height of savagery ; for example, they mutilate their bodies, rend corpses in pieces and devour them, tear pieces out of the bodies of living men, and so on.   Further, the almost morbid vanity of the North - Western Indians and their desire to win fame, respect, and distinction may have served

Gods or spirits personated by the actors in the masked dances.

---

[1] James G. Swan, *The Indians of Cape Flattery*, p. 66, quoted by Franz Boas, *op. cit.* pp. 637 *sq.*

as a motive for joining the Secret Societies; since every member of them enjoys great respect.

"There were and still are hundreds of masks in use, every one of which represents a spirit who occurs in their legends. In the exhibitions they appear singly or in groups, according as the legend to be represented requires, and the masked men are then looked upon by the astonished crowd, not only as actors representing the gods, but as the very gods themselves who have come down from heaven to earth. Hence every such representative must do exactly what legend says the spirit did. If the representative wears no mask, as often happens with the *Hametzes* (the Cannibals or Biters) or the *Pakwalla* (Medicine-men), then the spirit whom he represents has passed into his body, and accordingly the man possessed by the spirit is not responsible for what he does amiss in this condition. As the use of masks throws a sort of mysterious glamour over the performance and at the same time allows the actor to remain unknown, the peculiarly sacred festivals are much oftener celebrated with masks than without them. In every Secret Society there are definite rules as to how often and how long a mask may be used. Amongst the Kwakiutl the masks may not, under the heaviest penalties, be disposed of for four winters, the season when such festivals are usually celebrated. After that time they may be destroyed or hidden in the forest, that no uninitiated person may find them, or they may be finally sold. The masks are made only in secret, generally in the deep solitude of the woods, in order that no uninitiated person may detect the maker at work. . . .

The dances accompanied by songs.

"The dance is accompanied by a song which celebrates in boastful words the power of the gods and the mighty deeds represented in the performance. At the main part of the performance all present join in the song, for it is generally known to everybody and is repeated in recitative again and again. It seems that new songs and new performances are constantly springing up in one or other of the villages through the agency of some intelligent young man, hitherto without a song of his own, who treats in a poetical fashion some legend which has been handed down orally from their forefathers. For every man who takes part in the performances and festivals must make his *début* with a song composed by himself.   In this way new songs and dances are constantly originating, the material for them being, of course, always taken from the tribal deities of the particular singer and poet." [1]

Similar masquerades are in vogue among the neighbours of these Indians, the Esquimaux of Bering Strait, and from the following account it will appear that the performances are based on similar ideas and beliefs. " Shamans make masks representing grotesque faces of supernatural beings which they claim to have seen.   These may be *yu-ă*, which are the spirits of the elements, of places, and of inanimate things in general ; the *tunghät*, or wandering genii, or the shades of people and animals.   The first-named are seen in lonely places, on the plains and mountains or at sea, and more rarely about the villages, by the clairvoyant vision of the shamans.   They are usually invisible to common eyes, but sometimes render themselves visible to the people for various purposes.

Spirits personated by masked performers among the Esquimaux of Bering Strait.

" Many of them, especially among the *tunghät*, are of evil character, bringing sickness and misfortune upon people from mere wantonness or for some fancied injury.   The Eskimo believe that everything, animate or inanimate, is possessed of a shade, having semihuman form and features, enjoying more or less freedom of motion ; the shamans give form to their ideas of them in masks, as well as of others which they claim inhabit the moon and the sky-land.   In their daily life, if the people witness some strange occurrence, are curiously affected, or have a remarkable adventure, during which they seem to be influenced or aided in a supernatural manner, the shamans interpret the meaning and describe the appearance of the being that exerted its power.

" Curious mythological beasts are also said to inhabit both land and sea, but to become visible only on special occasions.   These ideas furnish material upon which their fancy works, conjuring up strange forms that are usually modifications of known creatures.   It is also believed that

The animal masks worn by the actors.

---

[1] J. Adrian Jacobsen, " Geheim-bünde der Küstenbewohner Nordwest-America's," *Verhandlungen der Berliner Gesellschaft für Anthropologie, Ethno-* *logie und Urgeschichte* (1891), pp. 384 *sq.* The passage has been already quoted by me in *Totemism and Exo-gamy*, iii. 500-502.

in early days all animate beings had a dual existence, becoming at will either like man or the animal forms they now wear. In those early days there were but few people; if an animal wished to assume its human form, the forearm, wing, or other limb was raised and pushed up the muzzle or beak as if it were a mask, and the creature became manlike in form and features. This idea is still held, and it is believed that many animals now possess this power. The manlike form thus appearing is called the *inua*, and is supposed to represent the thinking part of the creature, and at death becomes its shade. Shamans are believed to have the power of seeing through the animal mask to the manlike features behind. The ideas held on this subject are well illustrated in the Raven legends, where the changes are made repeatedly from one form to another.

Identification of the masked actor with the mythical being whom he represents. "Masks may also represent totemic animals, and the wearers during the festivals are believed actually to become the creature represented or at least to be endowed with its spiritual essence. Some of the masks of the lower Yukon and the adjacent territory to the Kuskokwim are made with double faces. This is done by having the muzzle of the animal fitted over and concealing the face of the *inua* below, the outer mask being held in place by pegs so arranged that it can be removed quickly at a certain time in the ceremony, thus symbolizing the transformation. Another style of mask from the lower Kuskokwim has the under face concealed by a small hinged door on each side, which opens out at the proper time in a ceremony, indicating the metamorphosis. When the mask represents a totemic animal, the wearer needs no double face, since he represents in person the shade of the totemic animal.

"When worn in any ceremonial, either as a totem mask or as representing the shade, *yu-ă* or *tunghăk*, the wearer is believed to become mysteriously and unconsciously imbued with the spirit of the being which his mask represents, just as the namesakes are entered into and possessed by the shades at certain parts of the Festival to the Dead.[1] . . .

---

[1] As to the belief of these Esquimaux that at the Festival of the Dead the spirits of the departed enter into and animate their human namesakes, see *Taboo and the Perils of the Soul*, p. 371.

" Mask festivals are usually held as a species of thanksgiving to the shades and powers of earth, air, and water for giving the hunter success. The *inuas* or shades of the powers and creatures of the earth are represented that they may be propitiated, thus insuring further success." [1]

The religious ritual of the Cora Indians of Mexico comprises elaborate dramatic ceremonies or dances, in which the actors or dancers identify themselves with the gods, such as the god of the Morning Star, the goddess of the Moon, and the divinities of the Rain. These dances form the principal part of the Cora festivals and are accompanied by liturgical songs, the words of which the Indians believe to have been revealed to their forefathers by the gods and to exercise a direct magical influence upon the deities themselves and through them upon nature.[2]

Dramatic ceremonies of the Cora Indians of Mexico in which the actors personate gods.

The Kobeua and Kaua Indians of North-Western Brazil perform masked dances at their festivals in honour of the dead. The maskers imitate the actions and the habits of birds, beasts, and insects. For example, there is a large azure - blue butterfly which delights the eye with the splendour of its colour, like a fallen fragment of the sky ; and in the butterfly dance two men represent the play of these brilliant insects in the sunshine, fluttering on the wing and settling on sandbanks and rocks. Again, the sloth is acted by a masker who holds on to a cross-beam of the house by means of a hooked stick, in imitation of the sluggish creature which will hang by its claws from the bough of a tree for hours together without stirring. Again, the darting of swallows, as they flit to and fro across a river, is mimicked by masked men dancing side by side : the swarming of sandflies in the air is acted by a swarm of maskers ; and so with the movements of the black vulture, the owl, the jaguar, the *aracu* fish, the house-spider, and the dung-beetle. Yet these representations are not simple dramas designed to amuse and divert the mourners in their hour of sorrow ; the Indian attributes to them a much deeper

Masked dances of the Brazilian Indians to ensure fertility and abundance.

---

[1] E. W. Nelson, "The Eskimo about Bering Strait," *Eighteenth Annual Report of the Bureau of American Ethnology*, Part i. (Washington, 1899) pp. 394 *sq.*

[2] K. Th. Preuss, *Die Nayarit Expedition*, I. *Die Religion der Cora Indianer* (Leipsic, 1912), pp. xcii. *sqq.*, xcv. *sqq.*

significance, for under the outer husk of beasts and birds and insects he believes that there lurk foul fiends and powerful spirits. " All these mimicries are based on an idea of magical efficiency. They are intended to bring blessing and fertility to the village and its inhabitants, to the plantations, and to the whole of surrounding nature, thereby compensating, as it were, for the loss of the dead man in whose honour the festival is held. By copying as faithfully as possible the movements and actions of the being whom he personates, the actor identifies himself with him. The mysterious force which resides in the mask passes into the dancer, turns the man himself into a mighty demon, and endows him with the power of banning demons or earning their favour. Especially is it the intention by means of mimicry to obtain for man control over the demons of growth and the spirits of game and fish." When the festival is over, the masks are burned, and the demons, which are thought to have animated them, take flight to their own place, it may be to the other world or to a mountain top, or to the side of a thundering cascade.[1]

Masked dances of the Monumbo in German New Guinea. The Monumbo of German New Guinea perform masked dances in which the dancers personate supernatural beings or animals, such as kangaroos, dogs, and cassowaries. They consecrate the masks by fumigating them with the smoke of a certain creeper, and believe that by doing so they put life into them. Accordingly they afterwards treat the masks with respect, talk to them as if they were alive, and refuse to part with them to Europeans. Certain of the masks they even regard as guardian spirits and appeal to them for fine weather, help in the chase or in war, and so forth. Every clan owns some masks and the head man of the clan makes all the arrangements for a masquerade. The dances are accompanied by songs of which the words are unintelligible even to the natives themselves.[2] Again, the Kayans of Masked dances of the Kayans of Borneo. Central Borneo perform masked dances for the purpose of ensuring abundant crops of rice. The actors personate demons, wearing grotesque masks on their faces, their bodies

---

[1] Th. Koch-Grünberg, *Zwei Jahre unter den Indianern* (Berlin, 1909–1910), i. 130-140, ii. 169-201. The passage translated in the text occurs in vol. ii. p. 196.

[2] F. Vormann, " Tänze und Tanz-festlichkeiten der Monumbo - Papua (Deutsch-Neuguinea)," *Anthropos*, vi. (1911) pp. 415 *sq.*, 418 *sqq.*, 426 *sq.*

swathed in cumbrous masses of green leaves. " In accordance with their belief that the spirits are more powerful than men, the Kayans assume that when they imitate the form of spirits and play their part, they acquire superhuman power. Hence just as their spirits can fetch back the souls of men, so they imagine that they can lure to themselves the souls of the rice."[1]

When the Sea Dyaks of Borneo have taken a human head, they hold a Head-feast (*Gawè Pala*) in honour of the war-god or bird-chief Singalang Burong, who lives far away above the sky. At this festival a long liturgy called *mengap* is chanted, the god is invoked, and is believed to be present in the person of an actor, who poses as the deity and blesses the people in his name. " But the invocation is not made by the human performer in the manner of a prayer direct to this great being ; it takes the form of a story, setting forth how the mythical hero Kling or Klieng made a head-feast and fetched Singalang Burong to it. This Kling, about whom there are many fables, is a spirit, and is supposed to live somewhere or other not far from mankind, and to be able to confer benefits upon them. The Dyak performer or performers then, as they walk up and down the long verandah of the house singing the *mengap*, in reality describe Kling's *Gawè Pala* [head-feast], and how Singalang Burong was invited and came. In thought the Dyaks identify themselves with Kling, and the resultant signification is that the recitation of this story is an invocation to Singalang Burong, who is supposed to come not to Kling's house only, but to the actual Dyak house where the feast is celebrated ; and he is received by a particular ceremony, and is offered food or sacrifice." At the close of the ceremony " the performer goes along the house, beginning with the head man, touches each person in it, and pronounces an invocation upon him. In this he is supposed to personate Singalang Burong and his sons-in-law, who are believed to be the real actors. Singalang Burong himself *nenjangs* the headmen, and his sons-in-law,

Dramatic performances of the Sea Dyaks of Borneo, in which the actor personates a god.

---

[1] A. W. Nieuwenhuis, *Quer durch Borneo* (Leyden, 1904–1907), i. 324. As to these masquerades of the Kayans see *Spirits of the Corn and of the Wild*, i. 95 *sq.*, 186 *sq.*

the birds, bless the rest. The touch of the human performer, and the accompanying invocation are thought to effect a communication between these bird-spirits from the skies and each individual being. The great bird-chief and his dependants come from above to give men their charms and their blessings. Upon the men the performer invokes physical strength and bravery in war ; and upon the women luck with paddy, cleverness in Dyak feminine accomplishments, and beauty in form and complexion." [1]

Religious or magical origin of the drama.

Thus the dramatic performances of these primitive peoples are in fact religious or oftener perhaps magical ceremonies, and the songs or recitations which accompany them are spells or incantations, though the real character of both is apt to be overlooked by civilized man, accustomed as he is to see in the drama nothing more than an agreeable pastime or at best a vehicle of moral instruction. Yet if we could trace the drama of the civilized nations back to its origin, we might find that it had its roots in magical or religious ideas like those which still mould and direct the masked dances of many savages. Certainly the Athenians in the heyday of their brilliant civilization retained a lively sense of the religious import of dramatic performances ; for they associated them directly with the worship of Dionysus and allowed them to be enacted only during the festivals of the god. [2] In India,

[1] Rev. J. Perham, "Mengap, the Song of the Dyak Sea Feast," *Journal of the Straits Branch of the Royal Asiatic Society*, No. 2 (Singapore, December, 1878), pp. 123 *sq.*, 134 ; H. Ling Roth, *The Natives of Sarawak and British North Borneo* (London, 1896), ii. 174 *sq.*, 183. Compare E. H. Gomes, *Seventeen Years among the Sea Dyaks of Borneo* (London, 1911), pp. 213 *sq.* : " This song of the head feast takes the form of a story setting forth how the mythical hero Klieng held a head feast on his return from the warpath, and invited the god of war, Singalang Burong, to attend it. It describes at great length all that happened on that occasion. The singing of this song takes up the whole night. It begins before 8 P.M., and lasts till next morning. Except for a short interval for rest in the middle of

the night, the performers are marching and singing all the time." On the third day of the festival the people go out on the open-air platform in front of the house and sacrifice a pig. "The people shout together (*manjong*) at short intervals until a hawk is seen flying in the heavens. That hawk is Singalang Burong, who has taken that form to manifest himself to them. He has accepted their offerings and has heard their cry" (E. H. Gomes, *op. cit.* p. 214).

[2] A. E. Haigh, *The Attic Theatre* (Oxford, 1889), pp. 4 *sqq.* The religious origin of Greek tragedy is maintained by Professor W. Ridgeway (*The Origin of Tragedy*, Cambridge, 1910), but he finds its immediate inspiration in the worship of the dead rather than in the worship of Dionysus.

also, the drama appears to have been developed out of religious dances or pantomimes, in which the actors recited the deeds and played the parts of national gods and heroes.[1] Hence it is at least a legitimate hypothesis that the criminal, who masqueraded as a king and perished in that character at the Bacchanalian festival of the Sacaea, was only one of a company of actors, who figured on that occasion in a sacred drama of which the substance has been preserved to us in the book of Esther.

When once we perceive that the gods and goddesses, the heroes and heroines of mythology have been represented officially, so to say, by a long succession of living men and women who bore the names and were supposed to exercise the functions of these fabulous creatures, we have attained a point of vantage from which it seems possible to propose terms of peace between two rival schools of mythologists who have been waging fierce war on each other for ages. On the one hand it has been argued that mythical beings are nothing but personifications of natural objects and natural processes ; on the other hand, it has been maintained that they are nothing but notable men and women who in their lifetime, for one reason or another, made a great impression on their fellows, but whose doings have been distorted and exaggerated by a false and credulous tradition. These two views, it is now easy to see, are not so mutually exclusive as their supporters have imagined. The personages about whom all the marvels of mythology have been told may have been real human beings, as the Euhemerists allege ; and yet they may have been at the same time personifications of natural objects or processes, as the adversaries of Euhemerism assert. The doctrine of incarnation supplies the missing link that was needed to unite the two seemingly inconsistent theories. If the powers of nature or a certain department of nature be conceived as personified in a deity, and that deity can become incarnate in a man or woman, it is obvious that the incarnate deity is at the same time a real human being and a personification of nature. To take the

The representation of mythical beings by living men and women may furnish a common ground where two rival schools of mythology can meet and be reconciled.

[1] H. Oldenberg, *Die Literatur des alten Indien* (Stuttgart and Berlin, 1903), pp. 236 *sqq.* Professor Oldenberg holds that the evolution of the Indian drama was probably not influenced by that of Greece.

instance with which we are here concerned, Semiramis may have been the great Semitic goddess of love, Ishtar or Astarte, and yet she may be supposed to have been incarnate in a woman or even in a series of real women, whether queens or harlots, whose memory survives in ancient history. Saturn, again, may have been the god of sowing and planting, and yet may have been represented on earth by a succession or dynasty of sacred kings, whose gay but short lives may have contributed to build up the legend of the Golden Age. The longer the series of such human divinities, the greater, obviously, the chance of their myth or legend surviving ; and when moreover a deity of a uniform type was represented, whether under the same name or not, over a great extent of country by many local dynasties of divine men or women, it is clear that the stories about him would tend still further to persist and be stereotyped.

The legend of Semiramis and her lovers a duplicate of the myth of Aphrodite and Adonis, of Cybele and Attis, of Isis and Osiris.

The conclusions which we have reached in regard to the legend of Semiramis and her lovers probably holds good of all the similar tales that were current in antiquity throughout the East ; in particular, it may be assumed to apply to the myths of Aphrodite and Adonis in Syria, of Cybele and Attis in Phrygia, and of Isis and Osiris in Egypt. If we could trace these stories back to their origin, we might find that in every case a human couple acted year by year the parts of the loving goddess and the dying god. We know that down to Roman times Attis was personated by priests who bore his name ;[1] and if within the period of which we have knowledge the dead Attis and the dead Adonis were represented only by effigies, we may surmise that it had not always been so, and that in both cases the dead god was once represented by a dead man. Further, the license accorded to the man who played the dying god at the Sacaea speaks strongly in favour of the hypothesis that before the incarnate deity was put to a public death he was in all cases allowed, or rather required, to enjoy the embraces of a woman who played the goddess of love. The reason for such an enforced union of the human god and goddess is not hard to divine. If primitive man believes that the growth of the crops can be stimulated by the intercourse of

[1] *Adonis, Attis, Osiris,* Second Edition, pp. 239 *sq.*

common men and women,[1] what showers of blessings will he not anticipate from the commerce of a pair whom his fancy invests with all the dignity and powers of deities of fertility ?

Thus the theory of Movers, that at the Sacaea the Zoganes represented a god and paired with a woman who personated a goddess, turns out to rest on deeper and wider foundations than that able scholar was aware of. He thought that the divine couple who figured by deputy at the ceremony were Semiramis and Sandan or Sardanapalus. It now appears that he was substantially right as to the goddess ; but we have still to enquire into the god. There seems to be no doubt that the name Sardanapalus is only the Greek way of representing Ashurbanapal, the name of the greatest and nearly the last king of Assyria. But the records of the real monarch which have come to light within recent years give little support to the fables that attached to his name in classical tradition. For they prove that, far from being the effeminate weakling he seemed to the Greeks of a later age, he was a warlike and enlightened monarch, who carried the arms of Assyria to distant lands and fostered at home the growth of science and letters.[2] Still, though the historical reality of King Ashurbanapal is as well attested as that of Alexander or Charlemagne, it would be no wonder if myths gathered, like clouds, round the great figure that loomed large in the stormy sunset of Assyrian glory. Now the two features that stand out most prominently in the legends of Sardanapalus are his extravagant debauchery and his violent death in the flames of a great pyre, on which he burned himself and his concubines to save them from falling into the hands of his victorious enemies. It is said that the womanish king, with painted face and arrayed in female attire, passed his days in the seclusion of the harem, spinning purple wool among his concubines and wallowing in sensual delights ; and that in the epitaph

Sardana-palus and Ashur-banapal.

The legendary death of Sardana-palus in the fire.

---

[1] *The Magic Art and the Evolution of Kings*, ii. 97 *sqq.*
[2] C. P. Tiele, *Babylonisch-Assyrische Geschichte* (Gotha, 1886–1888), pp. 351 *sqq.* ; M. Jastrow, *Religion of Babylonia and Assyria* (Boston, U.S.A., 1898), p. 43 ; Sir G. Maspero, *Histoire Ancienne des Peuples de l'Orient Classique*, iii. *Les Empires* (Paris, 1899), pp. 378 *sqq.* ; C. F. Harper, *Assyrian and Babylonian Literature* (New York, 1901), pp. 94 *sqq.*

which he caused to be carved on his tomb he recorded that
all the days of his life he ate and drank and toyed, remembering that life is short and full of trouble, that fortune is
uncertain, and that others would soon enjoy the good things
which he must leave behind.[1]   These traits bear little
resemblance to the portrait of Ashurbanapal either in life or
in death ; for after a brilliant career of conquest the Assyrian
king died in old age, at the height of human ambition, with
peace at home and triumph abroad, the admiration of his
subjects and the terror of his foes.   But if the traditional
characteristics of Sardanapalus harmonize but ill with what
we know of the real monarch of that name, they fit well
enough with all that we know or can conjecture of the mock
kings who led a short life and a merry during the revelry
of the Sacaea, the Asiatic equivalent of the Saturnalia.
We can hardly doubt that for the most part such men, with
death staring them in the face at the end of a few days,
sought to drown care and deaden fear by plunging madly into
all the fleeting joys that still offered themselves under the
sun.   When their brief pleasures and sharp sufferings were
over, and their bones or ashes mingled with the dust, what
more natural that on their tomb—those mounds in which
the people saw, not untruly, the graves of the lovers of
Semiramis—there should be carved some such lines as those
which tradition placed in the mouth of the great Assyrian
king, to remind the heedless passer-by of the shortness and
vanity of life ?

The
burning
of Sandan,
a mythical
god or
hero of
Western
Asia.

When we turn to Sandan, the other legendary or mythical
being whom Movers thought that the Zoganes may have personated, we find the arguments in support of his theory still
stronger.   The city of Tarsus in Cilicia is said to have been
founded by a certain Sandan whom the Greeks identified
with Hercules ; and at the festival of this god or hero an
effigy of him was burned on a great pyre.[2]   This Sandan is

---

[1] Athenaeus, xii. 38 *sq.*, pp. 528 F–
530 C ; Diodorus Siculus, ii. 23 and 27 ;
Justin, i. 3.   Several different versions
of the king's epitaph have come down
to us.   I have followed the version of
Choerilus, the original of which is said
to have been carved in Chaldean letters
on a tombstone that surmounted a

great barrow at Nineveh.   This
barrow may, as I suggest in the text,
have been one of the so-called mounds
of Semiramis.

[2] Ammianus Marcellinus, xiv. 8 ; Dio
Chrysostom, *Or.* xxxiii. p. 408 (vol. ii. p.
16 ed. L. Dindorf, Leipsic, 1857).   Coins
of Tarsus exhibit the effigy on the pyre,

doubtless the same with the Sandes whom Agathias calls the old Persian Hercules. Professing to give a list of the gods whom the Persians worshipped before the days of Zoroaster, the Byzantine historian mentions Bel, Sandes, and Anaitis, whom he identifies with Zeus, Hercules, and Aphrodite respectively.[1] As we know that Bel was a Babylonian, not a Persian deity, and that in later times Anaitis was practically equivalent to the Babylonian Ishtar or Astarte, a strong presumption is raised that Sandes also was a Babylonian or at all events Semitic deity, and that in speaking of him as Persian the historian confused the ancient Persians with the Babylonians and perhaps other stocks of Western Asia. The presumption is strengthened when we find that in Lydia the surname of Sandon, doubtless equivalent to Sandan, is said to have been borne by Hercules because he wore a woman's garment called a *sandyx*, fine and diaphanous as gossamer, at the bidding of Queen Omphale, whom the hero served for three years in the guise of a female slave, clad in purple, humbly carding wool and submitting to be slapped by the saucy queen with her golden slipper.[2] The familiar legend that Hercules burned himself alive on a great pyre completes the parallel between the effeminate Hercules Sandon of Lydia and the Assyrian Sardanapalus. So exact a parallel must surely rest on a common base of custom as well as of myth. That base, according to the conjecture of the admirable scholar K. O. Müller, may have been a custom of dressing up an effigy of an effeminate Asiatic deity in the semblance of a reveller, and then publicly burning it on a pyre. Such a custom appears to have prevailed not only at Tarsus in Cilicia, but also in Lydia; for a coin of the Lydian Philadelphia, a city which lay not far from the old royal capital Sardes, exhibits a device like that on coins of Tarsus, consisting of a figure stretched on a pyre. "We may suppose," says Müller, "that in the old Assyrian mythology a certain being called Sandan, or per-

K. O. Müller's description of the burning of Sandan.

---

which seems to be composed of a pyramid of great beams resting on a cubical base. See K. O. Müller, "Sandon und Sardanapal," *Kunstarchäologische Werke* (Berlin, 1873), iii. 8 *sqq.*, whose valuable essay I follow. For fuller details see *Adonis, Attis, Osiris*, Second Edition, pp. 91 *sqq.*, 139 *sqq.*

[1] Agathias, *Hist.* ii. 24.

[2] Joannes Lydus, *De magistratibus*, iii. 64; Apollodorus, *Bibliotheca*, ii. 6. 2 *sq.*; Lucian, *Dial. deorum*, xiii. 2.

haps Sardan, figured beside Baal and Mylitta or Astarte.
The character of this mythical personage is one which often
meets us in oriental religion—the extreme of voluptuousness
and sensuality combined with miraculous force and heroic
strength. We may imagine that at the great festivals of
Nineveh this Sandan or Sardan was exhibited as a buxom
figure with womanish features, the pale face painted with
white lead, the eyebrows and eyelashes blackened with kohl,
his person loaded with golden chains, rings, and earrings,
arrayed in a bright red transparent garment, grasping a
goblet in one hand and perhaps, as a symbol of strength, a
double axe in the other, while he sat cross-legged and surrounded by women on a splendidly adorned couch under a
purple canopy, altogether not unlike the figure of Adonis at
the court festivals of Alexandria. Then the people of 'mad
Nineveh,' as the poet Phocylides called it, 'the well-favoured
harlot,' as the prophet Nahum has it, would rejoice and
make merry with this their darling hero. Afterwards there
may have been another show, when this gorgeous Sandan or
Sardan was to be seen on a huge pyre of precious wood,
draped in gold-embroidered tapestry and laden with incense
and spices of every sort, which being set on fire, to the
howling of a countless multitude and the deafening din
of shrill music, sent up a monstrous pillar of fire whirling
towards heaven and flooded half Nineveh with smoke and
smell." [1]

Death
in the fire
of men who
personate
gods or
heroes.

The distinguished scholar whom I have just quoted does
not fail to recognize the part which imagination plays in the
picture he has set before us ; but he reminds us very properly
that in historical enquiries imagination must always supply
the cement that binds together the broken fragments of tradition. One thing, he thinks, emerges clearly from the present
investigation : the worship and legend of an effeminate hero
like Sandan appear to have spread, by means of an early
diffusion of the Semitic stock, first to the neighbourhood of

---

[1] K. O. Müller, "Sandon und Sardanapal," *Kunstarchäologische Werke*
(Berlin, 1873), iii. 16 *sq.* The writer
adds that there is authority for every
stroke in the picture. His principal
source is the sixty-second speech of
Dio Chrysostom (vol. ii. p. 202 ed.
L. Dindorf), where the unmanly Sardanapalus, seated cross-legged on a
gilded couch with purple hangings, is
compared to "the Adonis for whom
the women wail."

Tarsus in Cilicia and afterwards to Sardes in Lydia. In favour of the former prevalence of the rite in Lydia it may be added that the oldest dynasty of Lydian kings traced their descent, not only from the mythical Assyrian hero Ninus, but also from the Greek hero Hercules,[1] whose legendary death in the fire finds at least a curious echo in the story that Croesus, the last king of Lydia, was laid by his Persian conqueror Cyrus on a great pyre of wood, and was only saved at the last moment from being consumed in the flames.[2] May not this story embody a reminiscence of the manner in which the ancient kings of Lydia, as living embodiments of their god, formerly met their end ? It was thus, as we have seen, that the old Prussian rulers used to burn themselves alive in front of the sacred oak ;[3] and by an odd coincidence, if it is nothing more, the Greek Hercules directed that the pyre on which he was to be consumed should be made of the wood of the oak and the wild olive.[4] Some grounds have also been shewn for thinking that in certain South African tribes the chiefs may formerly have been burnt alive as a religious or magical ceremony.[5] All these facts and indications tend to support the view of Movers that at the Sacaea also the man who played the god for five days was originally burnt at the end of them.[6] Death by hanging or crucifixion may have been a later mitigation of his sufferings, though it is quite possible that

---

[1] Herodotus, i. 7.

[2] Herodotus, i. 86 *sq.*, with J. C. F. Bähr's note. According to another and perhaps more probable tradition the king sought a voluntary death in the flames. See Bacchylides, iii. 24-62 ; *Adonis, Attis, Osiris*, Second Edition, pp. 141 *sqq.*

[3] *The Dying God*, pp. 41 *sq.*

[4] Sophocles, *Trachiniae*, 1195 *sqq.* :

πολλὴν μὲν ὕλην τῆς βαθυρρίζου δρυὸς
κείραντα πολλὸν δ' ἄρσεν ἐκτεμόνθ' ὁμοῦ
ἄγριον ἔλαιον, σῶμα τοὐμὸν ἐμβαλεῖν.

The passage was pointed out to me by my friend the late Dr. A. W. Verrall. The poet's language suggests that of old a sacred fire was kindled by the friction of oak and wild olive wood, and that in accordance with a notion common among rude peoples, one of the pieces

of wood (in this case the wild olive) was regarded as male and the other (the oak) as female. On this hypothesis, the fire was kindled by drilling a hole in a piece of oak with a stick of wild olive. As to the different sorts of wood used by the ancients in making fire by friction, see A. Kuhn, *Die Herabkunft des Feuers und des Göttertranks*[2] (Gütersloh, 1886), pp. 35 *sqq.*; *The Magic Art and the Evolution of Kings*, ii. 249 *sqq.* In South Africa a special fire is procured for sacrifices by the friction of two pieces of the *Uzwati* tree, which are known respectively as husband and wife. See *Spirits of the Corn and of the Wild*, ii. 65.

[5] *Spirits of the Corn and of the Wild*, ii. 68.

[6] F. C. Movers, *Die Phoenizier*, i. (Bonn, 1841) p. 496.

both forms of execution or rather of sacrifice may have been combined by hanging or crucifying the victim first and burning him afterwards,[1] much as our forefathers used to disembowel traitors after suspending them for a few minutes on a gibbet. At Tarsus apparently the custom was still further softened by burning an effigy instead of a man ; but on this point the evidence is not explicit. It is worth observing that as late as Lucian's time the principal festival of the year at Hierapolis—the great seat of the worship of Astarte—fell at the beginning of spring and took its name of the Pyre or the Torch from the tall masts which were burnt in the court of the temple with sheep, goats, and other animals hanging from them.[2] Here the season, the fire, and the gallows-tree all fit our hypothesis ; only the man-god is wanting.

Traces of human sacrifice in the Jewish festival of Purim ; effigies of Haman burnt. If the Jewish festival of Purim was, as I have attempted to shew, directly descended either from the Sacaea or from some other Semitic festival, of which the central feature was the sacrifice of a man in the character of a god, we should expect to find traces of human sacrifice lingering about it in one or other of those mitigated forms to which I have just referred. This expectation is fully borne out by the facts. For from an early time it has been customary with the Jews at the feast of Purim to burn or otherwise destroy effigies of Haman. The practice was well known under the Roman empire, for in the year 408 A.D. the emperors Honorius and Theodosius issued a decree commanding the governors of the provinces to take care that the Jews should not burn effigies of Haman on a cross at one of their festivals.[3] We learn from the decree that the custom gave great offence to the Christians, who regarded it as a blasphemous parody of the central mystery of their own religion, little suspecting that it was

---

[1] This suggestion was made by F. Liebrecht, *Zur Volkskunde* (Heilbronn, 1879), p. 9. It occurred to me independently.

[2] Lucian, *De dea Syria*, 49.

[3] Codex Theodosianus, Lib. XVI. Tit. viii. § 18 : "*Judaeos quodam festivitatis suae solleni Aman ad poenae quondam recordationem incendere, et sanctae crucis adsimulatam speciem in contemptu Christianae fidei sacrilega mente exurere provinciarum rectores prohibeant : ne locis suis fidei nostrae signum immisceant, sed ritus suos infra contemptum Christianae legis retineant : amissuri sine dubio permissa hactenus, nisi ab inlicitis temperaverint.*" The decree is dated at Constantinople, in the consulship of Bassus and Philip. For *locis* we should probably read *jocis* with Mommsen.

nothing but a continuation, in a milder form, of a rite that had probably been celebrated in the East long ages before the birth of Christ. Apparently the custom long survived the publication of the edict, for in a form of abjuration which the Greek church imposed on Jewish converts and which seems to date from the tenth century, the renegade is made to speak as follows: " I curse also those who celebrate the festival of the so-called Mordecai on the first Sabbath (Saturday) of the Christian fast, and who nail Haman forsooth to the tree, attaching to it the symbol of the cross and burning him along with it, while they heap all sorts of imprecations and curses on the Christians."[1] A Jewish account of the custom as it was observed in Babylonia and Persia in the tenth century of our era runs as follows: " It is customary in Babylonia and Elam for boys to make an effigy resembling Haman ; this they suspend on their roofs, four or five days before Purim. On Purim day they erect a bonfire, and cast the effigy into its midst, while the boys stand round about it jesting and singing. And they have a ring suspended in the midst of the fire, which (ring) they hold and wave from one side of the fire to the other."[2] Again, the Arab historian Albîrûnî, who wrote in the year 1000 A.D., informs us that at Purim the Jews of his time rejoiced greatly over the death of Haman, and that they made figures which they beat and burned, " imitating the burning of Haman." Hence one name for the festival was Hâmân-Sûr.[3] Another Arabic writer, Makrîzî, who died in 1442 A.D.,

---

[1] Fr. Cumont, "Une formule grecque de renonciation au judaïsme," *Wiener Studien*, xxiv. (1902) p. 468. The "Christian fast" referred to in the formula is no doubt Lent. The mention of the Jewish Sabbath (the Christian Saturday) raises a difficulty, which has been pointed out by the editor, Franz Cumont, in a note (p. 470): " The festival of Purim was celebrated on the 14th of Adar, that is, in February or March, about the beginning of the Christian Lent, the date of which is fixed in the Jewish calendar, does not always fall on a Saturday. Either the author made a mistake or the civil authority obliged the Jews to transfer their rejoicings to a Sabbath " (Saturday).

[2] Israel Abrahams, *The Book of Delight and other Papers* (Philadelphia, 1912), pp. 266 *sq.* Mr. Abrahams ingeniously suggests (*op. cit.* pp. 267 *sq.*) that the ring waved over the fire was an emblem of the sun, and that the kindling of the Purim fires was originally a ceremony of imitative magic to ensure a supply of solar light and heat.

[3] Albîrûnî, *The Chronology of Ancient Nations*, translated and edited by Dr. C. Edward Sachau (London, 1879), pp. 273 *sq.*

says that at the feast of Purim, which fell on the fifteenth day of the month Adar, some of the Jews used to make effigies of Haman which they first played with and then threw into the fire.[1] During the Middle Ages the Italian Jews celebrated Purim in a lively fashion which has been compared by their own historians to that of the Carnival. The children used to range themselves in rows opposite each other and pelt one another with nuts, while grown-up people rode on horseback through the streets with pine branches in their hands or blew trumpets and made merry round a puppet representing Haman, which was set on a platform or scaffold and then solemnly burnt on a pyre.[2] In the eighteenth century the Jews of Frankfort used at Purim to make pyramids of thin wax candles, which they set on fire; also they fashioned images of Haman and his wife out of candles and burned them on the reading-desk in the synagogue.[3]

Accusations of ritual murder brought against the Jews. Now, when we consider the close correspondence in character as well as in date between the Jewish Purim and the Christian Carnival, and remember further that the effigy of Carnival, which is now destroyed at this merry season, had probably its prototype in a living man who was put to a violent death in the character of Saturn at the Saturnalia, analogy of itself would suggest that in former times the Jews, like the Babylonians, from whom they appear to have derived their Purim, may at one time have burned, hanged, or crucified a real man in the character of Haman. There are some positive grounds for thinking that this was so. The early church historian Socrates informs us that at Inmestar, a town in Syria, the Jews were wont to observe certain sports among themselves, in the course of which they played many foolish pranks. In the year 416 A.D., being heated with wine, they carried these sports further than usual and began deriding Christians and even Christ

---

[1] Quoted by Lagarde, " Purim," p. 13 (*Abhandlungen der königlichen Gesellschaft der Wissenschaften zu Göttingen*, xxxiv. 1887).

[2] M. Güdemann, *Geschichte des Erziehungswesens und der Cultur der abendländischen Juden* (Vienna, 1880–

1888), ii. 211 *sq.* ; I. Abrahams, *Jewish Life in the Middle Ages* (London, 1896), pp. 260 *sq.*

[3] J. J. Schudt, *Jüdische Merkwürdigkeiten* (Frankfort and Leipsic, 1714), ii. Theil, p. *309.

himself, and to give the more zest to their mockery they seized a Christian child, bound him to a cross, and hung him up. At first they only laughed and jeered at him, but soon, their passions getting the better of them, they ill-treated the child so that he died under their hands. The thing got noised abroad, and resulted in a serious brawl between the Jews and their Christian neighbours. The authorities then stepped in, and the Jews had to pay dear for the crime they had perpetrated in sport.[1] The Christian historian does not mention, and perhaps did not know, the name of the drunken and jovial festival which ended so tragically ; but we can hardly doubt that it was Purim, and that the boy who died on the cross represented Haman.[2] In mediæval and modern times many accusations of ritual murders, as they are called, have been brought against the Jews, and the arguments for and against the charge have been discussed on both sides with a heat which, however natural, has tended rather to inflame the passions of the disputants than to elicit the truth.[3] Into this troubled arena I prefer not to enter ; I will only observe that, so far as I have looked into the alleged cases, and these are reported in sufficient detail, the majority of the victims are said to have been children and to have met their fate in spring, often in the week before Easter. This last circumstance points, if there is any truth in the accusations, to a con-nexion of the human sacrifice with the Passover, which falls in this week, rather than with Purim, which falls a month earlier. Indeed it has often been made a part of the accusa-tion that the blood of the youthful victims was intended to

[1] Socrates, *Historia Ecclesiastica*, vii. 16 ; Theophanes, *Chronographia*, ed. J. Classen (Bonn, 1839–1841), vol. i. p. 129. Theophanes places the event in the year 408 A.D. From a note in Migne's edition of Socra-tes, I learn that in the Alexandrian calendar, which Theophanes used, the year 408 corresponded to the year which in our reckoning began on the first of September 415. Hence if the murder was perpetrated in spring at Purim it must have taken place in 416.

[2] This is the view of H. Graetz

(*Geschichte der Juden*,[2] iv. Leipsic, 1866, pp. 393 *sq.*) and Dr. M. R. James (*Life and Miracles of St. William of Norwich* (Cambridge, 1896), by A. Jessopp and M. R. James, pp. lxiii. *sq.*).

[3] For an examination of some of these reported murders, see M. R. James, *op. cit.* pp. lxii. *sqq.* ; H. L. Strack, *Das Blut im Glauben und Aberglauben der Menschheit* (Munich, 1900), pp. 121 *sqq.* Both writers incline to dismiss the charges as groundless.

The
accusations
probably
false.
be used at the Passover.   If all the charges of ritual murder
which have been brought against the Jews in modern times are
not, as seems most probable, mere idle calumnies, the baneful
fruit of bigotry, ignorance, and malice, the extraordinary
tenacity of life exhibited by the lowest forms of superstition
in the minds of ignorant people, whether they are Jews or
Gentiles, would suffice to account for an occasional recrudescence of primitive barbarity among the most degraded part
of the Jewish community.   To make the Jews as a nation
responsible for outrages which, if they occur at all, are
doubtless quite as repugnant to them as they are to every
humane mind, would be a monstrous injustice; it would be
as fair to charge Christians in general with complicity in
the incalculably greater number of massacres and atrocities
of every kind that have been perpetrated by Christians in
the name of Christianity, not merely on Jews and heathen,
but on men and women and children who professed—and
died for—the same faith as their torturers and murderers.
If deeds of the sort alleged have been really done by Jews—
a question on which I must decline to pronounce an opinion
—they would interest the student of custom as isolated
instances of reversion to an old and barbarous ritual which
once flourished commonly enough among the ancestors both
of Jews and Gentiles, but on which, as on a noxious monster,
an enlightened humanity has long set its heel.   Such
customs die hard ; it is not the fault of society as a whole
if sometimes the reptile has strength enough left to lift
its venomous head and sting.

Mitigation
of human
sacrifice
by the
substitu-
tion of a
criminal
for the
victim.
But between the stage when human sacrifice goes on
unabashed in the light of common day, and the stage when
it has been driven out of sight into dark holes and corners,
there intervenes a period during which the custom is slowly
dwindling away under the growing light of knowledge and
philanthropy.   In this middle period many subterfuges are
resorted to for the sake of preserving the old ritual in a
form which will not offend the new morality.   A common
and successful device is to consummate the sacrifice on the
person of a malefactor, whose death at the altar or elsewhere is little likely to excite pity or indignation, since it
partakes of the character of a punishment, and people recog-

nize that if the miscreant had not been dealt with by the priest, it would have been needful in the public interest to hand him over to the executioner. We have seen that in the Rhodian sacrifices to Cronus a condemned criminal was after a time substituted for an innocent victim ;[1] and there can be little doubt that at Babylon the criminals, who perished in the character of gods at the Sacaea, enjoyed an honour which, at an earlier period, had been reserved for more respectable persons. It seems therefore by no means impossible that the Jews, in borrowing the Sacaea from Babylon under the new name of Purim, should have borrowed along with it the custom of putting to death a malefactor who, after masquerading as Mordecai in a crown and royal robe, was hanged or crucified in the character of Haman. There are some grounds for thinking that this or something of this sort was done ; but a consideration of them had better be deferred till we have cleared up some points which still remain obscure in Purim, and in the account which the Jews give of its origin.

In the first place, then, it deserves to be remarked that the joyous festival of Purim on the fourteenth and fifteenth days of the month Adar is invariably preceded by a fast, known as the fast of Esther, on the thirteenth ; indeed, some Jews fast for several days before Purim.[2] In the book of Esther the fast is traditionally explained as a commemoration of the mourning and lamentation excited among the Jews by the decree of King Ahasuerus that they should all be massacred on the thirteenth day of the month Adar ; for " in every province, whithersoever the king's commandment and his decree came, there was great mourning among the Jews, and fasting, and weeping, and wailing ; and many lay in sackcloth and ashes." And Esther, before she went into the presence of the king to plead for the lives of her people, " bade them return answer unto Mordecai, Go, gather together all the Jews that are present in Shushan, and fast ye for me, and neither eat nor drink three days, night or day : I also and my maidens will fast in like manner." Hence fasting

The " fast of Esther ' before Purim.

---

[1] Above, pp. 353 *sq.*
[2] J. Buxtorf, *Synagoga Judaica* (Bâle, 1661), cap. xxix. p. 554 ; J. Chr. G.

Bodenschatz, *Kirchliche Verfassung der heutigen Juden* (Erlangen, 1748), ·ii. 253 *sq.*

and lamentation were ordained as the proper preparation for the happy feast of Purim which commemorated the great deliverance of the Jews from the destruction that had threatened them on the thirteenth day of Adar.[1] Now we have seen that, in the opinion of some eminent modern scholars, the basis of the book of Esther is not history but a Babylonian myth, which celebrated the triumphs and sufferings of deities rather than of men. On this hypothesis, how is the fast that precedes Purim to be explained? The best solution appears to be that of Jensen, that the fasting and mourning were originally for the supposed annual death of a Semitic god or hero of the type of Tammuz or Adonis, whose resurrection on the following day occasioned that outburst of joy and gladness which is characteristic of Purim. The particular god or hero, whose death and resurrection thus touched with sorrow and filled with joy the hearts of his worshippers, may have been, according to Jensen, either the great hero Gilgamesh, or his comrade and friend Eabani.[2] The doughty deeds and adventures of this mighty pair are the theme of the longest Babylonian poem that has been as yet discovered. It is recorded on twelve tablets, and this circumstance has suggested to some scholars the view that the story may be a solar myth, descriptive of the sun's annual course through the twelve months or the twelve signs of the zodiac. However that may be, the scene of the poem is laid chiefly at the very ancient Babylonian city of Erech, the chief seat of the worship of the goddess Ishtar or Astarte, who plays an important part in the story. For the goddess is said to have been smitten with the charms of Gilgamesh, and to have made love to him; but he spurned her proffered favours, and thereafter fell into a sore sickness, probably through the wrath of the offended goddess. His comrade Eabani also

Marginal note: Jensen's theory that the "fast of Esther" was originally a mourning for the annual death of a deity like Tammuz.

---

[1] Esther iv. 3 and 16, ix. 31.

[2] So far as I know, Professor Jensen has not yet published his theory, but he has stated it in letters to correspondents. See W. Nowack, *Lehrbuch der hebräischen Archäologie* (Freiburg i. Baden and Leipsic, 1894), ii. 200; H. Günkel, *Schöpfung und Chaos* (Göttingen, 1895), pp. 311 sqq.; D. G. Wildeboer, in his commentary on Esther, pp. 174 sq. (*Kurzer Hand-*

Commentar zum Alten Testament, herausgegeben von D. K. Marti, Lieferung 6, Freiburg i. B., 1898). In the Babylonian calendar the 13th of Adar was so far a fast day that on it no fish or fowl might be eaten. In one tablet the 13th of Adar is marked "not good," while the 14th and 15th are marked "good." See C. H. W. Johns, *s.v.* "Purim," *Encyclopaedia Biblica,* iii. (London, 1902) col. 3980.

roused the fury of Ishtar, and was wounded to death. For twelve days he lingered on a bed of pain, and, when he died, his friend Gilgamesh mourned and lamented for him, and rested not until he had prevailed on the god of the dead to suffer the spirit of Eabani to return to the upper world. The resurrection of Eabani, recorded on the twelfth tablet, forms the conclusion of the long poem.[1] Jensen's theory is that the death and resurrection of a mythical being, who combined in himself the features of a solar god and an ancient king of Erech, were celebrated at the Babylonian Zakmuk or festival of the New Year, and that the transference of the drama from Erech, its original seat, to Babylon led naturally to the substitution of Marduk, the great god of Babylon, for Gilgamesh or Eabani in the part of the hero. Although Jensen apparently does not identify the Zakmuk with the Sacaea, a little consideration will shew how well his general theory of Zakmuk fits in with those features of the Sacaean festival which have emerged in the course of our enquiry. At the Sacaean festival, if I am right, a man, who personated a god or hero of the type of Tammuz or Adonis, enjoyed the favours of a woman, probably a sacred harlot, who represented the great Semitic goddess Ishtar or Astarte ; and after he had thus done his part towards securing, by means of sympathetic magic, the revival of plant life in spring, he was put to death. We may suppose that the death of this divine man was mourned over by his worshippers, and especially by women, in much the same fashion as the women of

---

[1] M. Jastrow, *The Religion of Babylonia and Assyria* (Boston, U.S.A., 1898), pp. 471 *sq.*, 475 *sq.*, 481-486, 510-512; L. W. King, *Babylonian Religion and Mythology* (London, 1899), pp. 146 *sqq.* ; P. Jensen, *Assyrisch-Babylonische Mythen und Epen* (Berlin, 1900), pp. 116-273; R. F. Harper, *Assyrian and Babylonian Literature* (New York, 1901), pp. 324-368 ; H. Zimmern, in E. Schrader's *Die Keilinschriften und das Alte Testament* [3] (Berlin, 1902), pp. 566-582; *Das Gilgamesch-Epos, neu übersetat von* Arthur Ungnad *und gemeinverständlich erklärt von* Hugo Gressmann (Göttingen, 1911). Professor Jastrow points out that though a relation cannot be traced between each of the tablets of the poem and the corresponding month of the year, such a relation appears undoubtedly to exist between some of the tablets and the months. Thus, for example, the sixth tablet describes the affection of Ishtar for Gilgamesh, and the visit which she paid to Anu, her father in heaven, to complain of the hero's contemptuous rejection of her love. Now the sixth Babylonian month was called the "Mission of Ishtar," and in it was held the festival of Tammuz, the hapless lover of the goddess. Again, the story of the great flood is told in the eleventh tablet, and the eleventh month was called the " month of rain." See M. Jastrow, *op. cit.* pp. 484, 510.

Jerusalem wept for Tammuz at the gate of the temple,[1] and as Syrian damsels mourned the dead Adonis, while the river ran red with his blood. Such rites appear, in fact, to have been common all over Western Asia ; the particular name of the dying god varied in different places, but in substance the ritual was the same. Fundamentally, the custom was a religious or rather magical ceremony intended to ensure the revival and reproduction of life in spring.

The resurrection of the dead god perhaps represented by a living man who afterwards died in earnest in the character of the god.

Now, if this interpretation of the Sacaea is correct, it is obvious that one important feature of the ceremony is wanting in the brief notices of the festival that have come down to us. The death of the man-god at the festival is recorded, but nothing is said of his resurrection. Yet if he really personated a being of the Adonis or Attis type, we may feel pretty sure that his dramatic death was followed at a shorter or longer interval by his dramatic revival, just as at the festivals of Attis and Adonis the resurrection of the dead god quickly succeeded to his mimic death.[2] Here, however, a difficulty presents itself. At the Sacaea the man-god died a real, not a mere mimic death ; and in ordinary life the resurrection even of a man-god is at least not an everyday occurrence. What was to be done ? The man, or rather the god, was undoubtedly dead. How was he to come to life again ? Obviously the best, if not the only way, was to set another and living man to support the character of the reviving god, and we may conjecture that this was done. We may suppose that the insignia of royalty which had adorned the dead man were transferred to his successor, who, arrayed in them, would be presented to his rejoicing worshippers as their god come to life again ; and by his side would probably be displayed a woman in the character of his divine consort,

This would explain the apparent duplication of the principal characters in the book of Esther :

the goddess Ishtar or Astarte. In favour of this hypothesis it may be observed that it at once furnishes a clear and intelligible explanation of a remarkable feature in the book of Esther which has not yet, so far as I am aware, been adequately elucidated ; I mean that apparent duplication of the principal characters to which I have already directed the reader's attention. If I am right, Haman represents

---

[1] Ezekiel viii. 14.

[2] *Adonis, Attis, Osiris*, Second Edition, pp. 183 *sq.*, 227.

the temporary king or mortal god who was put to death at Haman and Vashti would represent the gods dying, while Mordecai and Esther would represent the gods rising from the dead. the Sacaea; and his rival Mordecai represents the other temporary king who, on the death of his predecessor, was invested with his royal insignia, and exhibited to the people as the god come to life again. Similarly Vashti, the deposed queen in the narrative, corresponds to the woman who played the part of queen and goddess to the first mock king, the Haman; and her successful rival, Esther or Ishtar, answers to the woman who figured as the divine consort of the second mock king, the Mordecai or Marduk. A trace of the sexual license accorded to the mock king of the festival seems to be preserved in the statement that King Ahasuerus found Haman fallen on the bed with Esther and asked, "Will he even force the queen before me in the house?"[1] We have seen that the mock king of the Sacaea did actually possess the right of using the real king's concubines, and there is much to be said for the view of Movers that he began his short reign by exercising the right in public.[2] In the parallel ritual of Adonis the marriage of the goddess with her ill-fated lover was publicly celebrated the day before his mimic death.[3] A clear reminiscence of the time when the relation between Esther and Mordecai was conceived as much more intimate than mere cousinship appears to be preserved in some of the Jewish plays acted at Purim, in which Mordecai appears as the lover of Esther; and this significant indication is confirmed by the teaching of the rabbis that King Ahasuerus never really knew Esther, but that a phantom in her likeness lay with him while the real Esther sat on the lap of Mordecai.[4]

The Persian setting, in which the Hebrew author of the The Persian setting of the book of Esther. book of Esther has framed his highly-coloured picture, naturally suggests that the Jews derived their feast of Purim not directly from the old Babylonians, but from their Persian conquerors. Even if this could be demonstrated, it would in no way invalidate the theory that Purim originated

---

[1] Esther vii. 8.

[2] See above, p. 368.

[3] *Adonis, Attis, Osiris,* Second

Edition, p. 183.

[4] J. J. Schudt, *Jüdische Merkwürdigkeiten* (Frankfort and Leipsic, 1714), ii. Theil, p. *316.

in the Babylonian festival of the Sacaea, since we know that the Sacaea was celebrated by the Persians.[1]   Hence it becomes worth while to enquire whether in the Persian religion we can detect any traces of a festival akin to the Sacaea or Purim.   Here Lagarde has shewn the way by directing attention to the old Persian ceremony known as the "Ride of the Beardless One."[2]   This was a rite performed both in Persia and Babylonia at the beginning of spring, on the first day of the first month, which in the most ancient Persian calendar corresponded to March, so that the date of the ceremony agrees with that of the Babylonian New Year festival of Zakmuk.   A beardless and, if possible, one-eyed buffoon was set naked on an ass, a horse, or a mule, and conducted in a sort of mock triumph through the streets of the city.   In one hand he held a crow and in the other a fan, with which he fanned himself, complaining of the heat, while the people pelted him with ice and snow and drenched him with cold water.   He was supposed to drive away the cold, and to aid him perhaps in discharging this useful function he was fed with hot food, and hot stuffs were smeared on his body.   Riding on his ass and attended by all the king's household, if the city happened to be the capital, or, if it was not, by all the retainers of the governor, who were also mounted, he paraded the streets and extorted contributions.   He stopped at the doors of the rich, and if they did not give him what he asked for, he befouled their garments with mud or a mixture of red ochre and water, which he carried in an earthenware pot.   If a shopkeeper hesitated a moment to respond to his demands, the importunate beggar had the right to confiscate all the goods in the shop; so the tradesmen who saw him bearing down on them, not unnaturally hastened to anticipate his wants by contributing of their substance before he could board them.   Everything that he

The Persian ceremony of the "Ride of the Beardless One" in spring.

---

[1] Dio Chrysostom makes Diogenes say to Alexander the Great, οὐκ ἐννενόηκας τὴν τῶν Σακαίων ἑορτήν, ἣν Πέρσαι ἄγουσιν (Or. iv. vol. i. p. 76 ed. L. Dindorf). The festival was mentioned by Ctesias in the second book of his Persian history (Athenaeus, xiv. 44 p. 639 C); and down to the time of Strabo it was associated with the nominal worship of the Persian goddess Anaitis (Strabo, xi. 8. 4 and 5, p. 512).

[2] Lagarde, "Purim," pp. 51 sqq. (Abhandlungen der königl. Gesellschaft der Wissenschaften zu Göttingen, xxxiv. 1887).

thus collected from break of day to the time of morning prayers belonged to the king or governor of the city; but everything that he laid hands on between the first and the second hour of prayer he kept for himself. After the second prayers he disappeared, and if the people caught him later in the day they were free to beat him to their heart's content. "In like manner," proceeds one of the native writers who has described the custom, "people at the present time appoint a New Year Lord and make merry. And this they do because the season, which is the beginning of Azur or March, coincides with the sun's entry into Aries, for on that day they disport themselves and rejoice because the winter is over." [1]

Now in this harlequin, who rode through the streets attended by all the king's men, and levying contributions which went either to the royal treasury or to the pocket of the collector, we recognize the familiar features of the mock or temporary king, who is invested for a short time with the pomp and privileges of royalty for reasons which have been already explained. [2] The abrupt disappearance of the Persian clown at a certain hour of the day, coupled with the leave given to the populace to thrash him if they found him afterwards, points plainly enough to the harder fate that probably awaited him in former days, when he paid with his life for his brief tenure of a kingly crown. The resemblance between his burlesque progress and that of Mordecai through the streets of Susa is obvious; though the Jewish author of Esther has depicted in brighter colours the pomp of his hero "in royal apparel of blue and white, and with a great crown of gold, and with a robe of fine linen and purple," riding the king's own charger, and led through the city by one of the king's most noble princes. [3] The difference between the two scenes is probably not to be explained simply by the desire of the Jewish writer to shed a halo of glory round the personage whom he regarded as the deliverer of his people. So long as the temporary

The "Beardless One" in the Persian ceremony is apparently the degenerate successor of a temporary king.

---

[1] Th. Hyde, *Historia religionis veterum Persarum* (Oxford, 1700), pp. 183, 249-251; Albîrûnî, *The Chronology of Ancient Nations*, translated and edited by Dr. C. Edward Sachau (London, 1879), p. 211.

[2] *The Dying God*, pp. 148 *sqq.*

[3] Esther vi. 8 *sq.*, viii. 15.

king was a real substitute for the reigning monarch, and had
to die sooner ór later in his stead, it was natural that he
should be treated with a greater show of deference, and
should simulate his royal brother more closely than a clown
who had nothing worse than a beating to fear when he laid
down his office.   In short, after the serious meaning of the
custom had been forgotten, and the substitute was allowed
to escape with his life, the high tragedy of the ancient ceremony would rapidly degenerate into farce.

The "Ride
of the
Beardless
One"
seems to be
a magical
ceremony
for the
expulsion
of winter.
But while the "Ride of the Beardless One" is, from
one point of view, a degenerate copy of the original,
regarded from another point of view, it preserves some
features which are almost certainly primitive, though they
do not appear in the kindred Babylonian and Jewish festivals.
The Persian custom bears the stamp of a popular festivity
rather than of a state ceremonial, and everywhere it seems
as if popular festivals, when left to propagate themselves
freely among the folk, reveal their old meaning and intention more transparently than when they have been adopted
into the official religion and enshrined in a ritual.   The
simple thoughts of our simple forefathers are better understood by their unlettered descendants than by the majority
of educated people ; their rude rites are more faithfully preserved and more truly interpreted by a rude peasantry than
by the priest, who wraps up their nakedness in the gorgeous
pall of religious pomp, or by the philosopher, who dissolves
their crudities into the thin air of allegory.   In the present
instance the purpose of the "Ride of the Beardless One"
at the beginning of spring is sufficiently obvious ; it was
meant to hasten the departure of winter and the approach
of summer.   We are expressly told that the clown who
went about fanning himself and complaining of the heat,
while the populace snowballed him, was supposed to dispel
the cold ; and even without any such assurance we should
be justified in inferring as much from his behaviour.   On
the principles of homoeopathic or imitative magic, which is
little more than an elaborate system of make-believe, you
can make the weather warm by pretending that it is so ; or
if you cannot, you may be sure that there is some person
wiser than yourself who can.   Such a wizard, in the estima-

tion of the Persians, was the beardless one-eyed man who went through the performance I have described ; and no doubt his physical defects were believed to contribute in some occult manner to the success of the rite. The ceremony was thus, as Lagarde acutely perceived, the oriental equivalent of those popular European customs which celebrate the advent of spring by representing in a dramatic form the expulsion or defeat of winter by the victorious summer.[1] But whereas in Europe the two rival seasons are often, if not regularly, personated by two actors or two effigies, in Persia a single actor sufficed. Whether he definitely represented winter or summer is not quite clear ; but his pretence of suffering from heat and his final disappearance suggest that, if he personified either of the seasons, it was the departing winter rather than the coming summer.

If there is any truth in the connexion thus traced between Purim and the "Ride of the Beardless One," we are now in a position finally to unmask the leading personages in the book of Esther. I have attempted to shew that Haman and Vashti are little more than doubles of Mordecai and Esther, who in turn conceal under a thin disguise the features of Marduk and Ishtar, the great god and goddess of Babylon. But why, the reader may ask, should the divine pair be thus duplicated and the two pairs set in opposition to each other? The answer is suggested by the popular European celebrations of spring to which I have just adverted. If my interpretation of these customs is right, the contrast between the summer and winter, or between the life and death, which figure in effigy or in the persons of living representatives at the spring ceremonies of our peasantry, is fundamentally a contrast between the dying or dead vegetation of the old and the sprouting vegetation of the new year—a contrast which would lose nothing of its point when, as in ancient Rome and Babylon and Persia, the beginning of spring was also the beginning of the new year. In these and in all the ceremonies we have been examining the antagonism is not between powers of a different order, but between the same power viewed in different aspects as old and young ; it is, in short, nothing

The opposition of Haman and Vashti to Mordecai and Esther seems to be a contrast between the annual death of nature in winter and its revival in spring.

[1] *The Dying God*, pp. 254 *sqq.*

but the eternal and pathetic contrast between youth and age.   And as the power or spirit of vegetation is represented in religious ritual and popular custom by a human pair, whether they be called Ishtar and Tammuz, or Venus and Adonis, or the Queen and King of May, so we may expect to find the old decrepit spirit of the past year personated by one pair, and the fresh young spirit of the new year by another.   This, if my hypothesis is right, is the ultimate explanation of the struggle between Haman and Vashti on the one side, and their doubles Mordecai and Esther on the other.   In the last analysis both pairs stood for the powers that make for the fertility of plants and perhaps also of animals;[1] but the one pair embodied the failing energies of the past, and the other the vigorous and growing energies of the coming year.[2]   Both powers, on my hypothesis, were personified not merely in myth, but in custom; for year by year a human couple undertook to quicken the life of nature by a union in which, as in a microcosm, the loves of tree and plant, of herb and flower, of bird and beast were supposed in some mystic fashion to be summed up.[3]   Originally, we may conjecture, such couples exercised their functions for a whole year, on the conclusion of which the male partner—the divine king—was put to death; but in historical times it seems that, as a rule, the human god—the Saturn, Zoganes, Tammuz, or whatever he was called—enjoyed his divine privileges, and discharged

---

[1] The goddess Ishtar certainly seems to have embodied the principle of fertility in animals as well as in plants; for in the poem which describes her descent into the world of the dead it is said that

"*After the mistress Ishtar had descended to the land of No-Return,*
The bull did not mount the cow, nor did the ass leap upon the she-ass,
The man did not approach the maid in the street,
The man lay down to sleep upon his own couch,
While the maid slept by herself."

See C. F. Harper, *Assyrian and Babylonian Literature* (New York, 1901), pp. 410 *sq.*; P. Jensen, *Assyrisch-*

Babylonische Mythen und Epen (Berlin, 1900), p. 87.

[2] The interpretation here given of the four principal personages in the book of Esther was suggested by me in the second edition of this book (1900). It agrees substantially with the one which has since been adopted by Professor H. Zimmern (in E. Schrader's *Die Keilinschriften und das Alte Testament*,[3] Berlin, 1902, p. 519), and by Professor P. Haupt (*Purim*, Leipsic, 1906, pp. 21 *sq.*).

[3] In this connexion it deserves to be noted that among the ancient Persians marriages are said to have been usually celebrated at the vernal equinox (Strabo, xv. 3. 17, p. 733).

his divine duties only for a short part of the year. This curtailment of his reign on earth was probably introduced at the time when the old hereditary divinities or deified kings contrived to shift the most painful part of their duties to a substitute, whether that substitute was a son or a slave or a malefactor. Having to die as a king, it was necessary that the substitute should also live as a king for a season; but the real monarch would naturally restrict within the narrowest limits both of time and of power a reign which, so long as it lasted, necessarily encroached upon and indeed superseded his own.[1] What became of the divine king's female partner, the human goddess who shared his bed and transmitted his beneficent energies to the rest of nature, we cannot say. So far as I am aware, there is little or no evidence that she like him suffered death when her primary function was discharged.[2] The nature of maternity suggests an obvious reason for sparing her a little longer, till that mysterious law, which links together woman's life with the changing aspects of the nightly sky, had been fulfilled by the birth of an infant god, who should in his turn, reared perhaps by her tender care, grow up to live and die for the world.

§ 6. *Conclusion*

We may now sum up the general results of the enquiry which we have pursued in the present chapter. We have found evidence that festivals of the type of the Saturnalia, characterized by an inversion of social ranks and the sacrifice of a man in the character of a god, were at one time held all over the ancient world from Italy to Babylon. Such festivals seem to date from an early age in the history of

Wide prevalence of festivals like the Saturnalia in antiquity.

---

[1] The five days' duration of the mock king's reign may possibly have been an intercalary period introduced, as in ancient Egypt and Mexico, for the purpose of equalizing a year of 360 days (twelve months of 30 days each) to a solar year reckoned at 365 days. See above, pp. 339 *sqq.*

[2] However, the legend that Semiramis burned herself on a pyre in Babylon for grief at the loss of a favourite horse (Hyginus, *Fab.* 243; compare Pliny, *Nat. Hist.* viii. 155) may perhaps point to an old custom of compelling the human representative of the goddess to perish in the flames. We have seen (above, p. 371) that one of the lovers of Ishtar had the form of a horse. Hence the legend recorded by Hyginus is a fresh link in the chain of evidence which binds Semiramis to Ishtar.

Such
festivals
seem to
have been
held by
agricultural
communi-
ties for the
good of the
crops, and
at them
the king
or his
substitute
appears
to have
personated
the god of
fertility,
and to
have been
put to
death in
that char-
acter in
order to
ensure that
the god
should rise
from the
dead with
renewed
youth and
vigour.

agriculture, when people lived in small communities, each presided over by a sacred or divine king, whose primary duty was to secure the orderly succession of the seasons, the fertility of the earth, and the fecundity both of cattle and of women. Associated with him was his wife or other female consort, with whom he performed some of the necessary ceremonies, and who therefore shared his divine character. Originally his term of office appears to have been limited to a year, on the conclusion of which he was put to death ; but in time he contrived by force or craft to extend his reign and sometimes to procure a substitute, who after a short and more or less nominal tenure of the crown was slain in his stead. At first the substitute for the divine father was probably the divine son, but afterwards this rule was no longer insisted on, and still later the growth of a humane feeling demanded that the victim should always be a condemned criminal. In this advanced stage of degenera-tion it is no wonder if the light of 'divinity suffered eclipse, and many should fail to detect the god in the malefactor. Yet the downward career of fallen deity does not stop here ; even a criminal comes to be thought too good to personate a god on the gallows or in the fire ; and then there is nothing left but to make up a more or less grotesque effigy, and so to hang, burn, or otherwise destroy the god in the person of this sorry representative. By this time the original meaning of the ceremony may be so completely forgotten that the puppet is supposed to represent some historical personage, who earned the hatred and contempt of his fellows in his life, and whose memory has ever since been held up to eternal execration by the annual destruction of his effigy. The figures of Haman, of the Carnival, and of Winter or Death which are or used to be annually destroyed in spring by Jews, Catholics, and the peasants of Central Europe respectively, appear to be all lineal descendants of those human incarnations of the powers of nature whose life and death were deemed essential to the welfare of mankind. But of the three the only one which has preserved a clear trace of its original meaning is the effigy of Winter or Death. In the others the ancient significance of the custom as a magical ceremony designed to direct the course of nature has been almost wholly obscured by a thick aftergrowth of legend and myth. The cause of this distinction is that, whereas the practice of destroying an effigy of Winter or Death has been handed down from time immemorial through generations of simple peasants, the festivals of Purim and the Carnival, as well as their Babylonian and Italian prototypes, the Sacaea and the Saturnalia, were for centuries domesticated in cities, where they were necessarily exposed to those thousand transforming and disintegrating currents of speculation and enquiry, of priestcraft and policy, which roll their turbid waters through the busy haunts of men, but leave undefiled the limpid springs of mythic fancy in the country.

If there is any truth in the analysis of the Saturnalia and kindred festivals which I have now brought to a close, it seems to point to a remarkable homogeneity of civilization throughout Southern Europe and Western Asia in prehistoric times. How far such homogeneity of civilization may be taken as evidence of homogeneity of race is a question for the ethnologist; it does not concern us here. But without discussing it, I may remind the reader that in the far east of Asia we have met with temporary kings whose magical functions and intimate relation to agriculture stand out in the clearest light;[1] while India furnishes examples of kings who have regularly been obliged to sacrifice themselves at the end of a term of years.[2] All these things appear to hang together; all of them may, perhaps, be regarded as the shattered remnants of a uniform zone of religion and society which at a remote era belted the Old World from the Mediterranean to the Pacific. Whether that was so or not, I may at least claim to have made it probable that if the King of the Wood at Aricia lived and died as an incarnation of a sylvan deity, the functions he thus discharged were by no means singular, and that for the nearest parallel to them we need not go beyond the bounds of Italy, where the divine king Saturn—the god of the sown and sprouting seed—was annually slain in the person of a human representative at his ancient festival of the Saturnalia.

It is possible that such sacrifices of deified men, performed for the salvation of the world, may have helped to

The festivals point to a remarkable homogeneity of civilization over a great part of the Old World in antiquity.

[1] *The Dying God*, pp. 148 *sqq.*   [2] *The Dying God*, pp. 46 *sqq.*

The periodical sacrifice of deified men for the sake of maintaining the course of nature perhaps helps to explain traditions which represent the world or parts of it as created out of the bodies of gods.

beget the notion that the universe or some part of it was originally created out of the bodies of gods offered up in sacrifice. Certainly it is curious that notions of this sort meet us precisely in parts of the world where such sacrifices appear to have been regularly accomplished. Thus in ancient Mexico, where the sacrifice of human beings in the character of gods formed a conspicuous feature of the national religion, it is said that in the beginning, when as yet the light of day was not, the gods created the sun to illumine the earth by voluntarily burning themselves in the fire, leaping one after the other into the flames of a great furnace.[1] Again, in the Babylonian Genesis the great god Bel created the world by cleaving the female monster Tiamat in twain and using the severed halves of her body to form the heaven and the earth. Afterwards, perceiving that the earth was waste and void, he obligingly ordered one of the gods to cut off his, the Creator's, head, and with the flowing blood mixed with clay he kneaded a paste out of which he moulded men and animals.[2] Similarly in a hymn of the Rig Veda we read how the gods created the world out of the dismembered body of the great primordial giant Purushu. The sky was made out of his head, the earth out of his feet, the sun out of his eye, and the moon out of his mind; animals and men were also engendered from his dripping fat or his limbs, and the great gods Indra and Agni sprang from his mouth.[3] The crude, nay savage, account of creation thus set forth by the poet was retained by the Brah-

---

[1] B. de Sahagun, *Histoire Générale des Choses de la Nouvelle Espagne*, traduite par D. Jourdanet et R. Simeon (Paris, 1880), pp. 478-480. Compare E. Seler, *Altmexikanische Studien*, ii. (Berlin, 1899) p. 117.

[2] Berosus, quoted by Eusebius, *Chronicorum liber prior*, ed. A. Schoene (Berlin, 1875), coll. 14-18; *id.*, in *Fragmenta Historicorum Graecorum*, ed. C. Muller, ii. 497 *sq.*; P. Jensen, *Assyrisch-Babylonische Mythen und Epen* (Berlin, 1900), pp. 2 *sqq.*; L. W. King, *Babylonian Religion and Mythology* (London, 1899), pp. 54 *sqq.*; M. Jastrow, *The Religion of Babylonia and Assyria* (Boston, U.S.A., 1898), pp. 408 *sqq.*; H. Zimmern, in E.

Schrader's *Die Keilinschriften und das Alte Testament*[3] (Berlin, 1902), pp. 488 *sqq.*; M. J. Lagrange, *Études sur les Religions Sémitiques*[2] (Paris, 1905), pp. 366 *sqq.*; R. W. Rogers, *Cuneiform Parallels to the Old Testament* (Oxford, preface dated 1911), pp. 31 *sq.*, 36. In the Hebrew account of the creation (Genesis i. 2) "the deep" (תְּהוֹם *tĕhom*) is a reminiscence of the Babylonian mythical monster Tiamat.

[3] *Hymns of the Rig Veda*, x. 90 (vol. iv. pp. 289-293 of R. T. H. Griffith's translation, Benares, 1889-1892). Compare A. A. Macdonell, *Vedic Mythology* (Strasburg, 1897), pp. 12 *sq.*

man doctors of a later age and refined by them into a subtle The Brahmanical theory of the perpetual renewal of the creation in the daily sacrifice. theory of sacrifice in general. According to them the world was not only created in the beginning by the sacrifice of the creator Prajapati, the Lord of Creatures ; to this day it is renewed and preserved solely by a repetition of that mystic sacrifice in the daily sacrificial ritual celebrated by the Brahmans. Every day the body of the Creator and Saviour is broken anew, and every day it is pieced together for the restoration and conservation of a universe which otherwise must dissolve and be shattered into fragments. Thus is the world continually created afresh by the self-sacrifice of the deity ; and, wonderful to relate, the priest who offers the sacrifice ·identifies himself with the Creator, and so by the very act of sacrificing renews the universe and keeps up uninterrupted the revolution of time and matter. All things depend on his beneficent, nay divine activity, from the heaven above to the earth beneath, from the greatest god to the meanest worm, from the sun and moon to the humblest blade of grass and the minutest particle of dust. Happily this grandiose theory of sacrifice as a process essential to the salvation of the world does not oblige the priest to imitate his glorious prototype by dismembering his own body and shedding his blood on the altar ; on the contrary a comfortable corollary deduced from it holds out to him the pleasing prospect of living for the unspeakable benefit of society to a good old age, indeed of stretching out the brief span of human existence to a full hundred years.[1] Well is it, not only for the priest but for mankind, when with the slow progress of civilization and humanity the hard facts of a cruel ritual have thus been softened and diluted into the nebulous abstractions of a mystical theology.

---

[1] *The Satapatha Brâhmana*, translated by Julius Eggeling, Part iv. (Oxford, 1897) pp. xiv.-xxiv. (*The Sacred Books of the East*, vol. xliii.).

Compare Sylvain Lévi, *La doctrine du sacrifice dans les Brâhmanas* (Paris, 1898), pp. 13 *sqq.*

NOTE

THE CRUCIFIXION OF CHRIST [1]

The mockery of Christ compared to the mockery of the King of the Saturnalia.

AN eminent scholar has recently pointed out the remarkable resemblance between the treatment of Christ by the Roman soldiers at Jerusalem and the treatment of the mock king of the Saturnalia by the Roman soldiers at Durostorum; and he would explain the similarity by supposing that the soldiers ridiculed the claims of Christ to a divine kingdom by arraying him in the familiar garb of old King Saturn, whose quaint person figured so prominently at the

[1] [The following Note formed part of the text in the Second Edition of *The Golden Bough* (London, 1900), vol. iii. pp. 186-198. The hypothesis which it sets forth has not been confirmed by subsequent research, and is admittedly in a high degree speculative and uncertain. Hence I have removed it from the text but preserved it as an appendix on the chance that, under a pile of conjectures, it contains some grains of truth which may ultimately contribute to a solution of the problem. As my views on this subject appear to have been strangely misunderstood, I desire to point out explicitly that my theory assumes the historical reality of Jesus of Nazareth as a great religious and moral teacher, who founded Christianity and was crucified at Jerusalem under the governorship of Pontius Pilate. The testimony of the Gospels, confirmed by the hostile evidence of Tacitus (*Annals*, xv. 44) and the younger Pliny (*Epist.* x. 96), appears amply sufficient to establish these facts to the satisfaction of all unprejudiced enquirers. It is only the details of the life and death of Christ that remain, and will probably always remain, shrouded in the mists of uncertainty. The doubts which have been cast on the historical reality of Jesus are in my judgment unworthy of serious attention. Quite apart from the positive evidence of history and tradition, the origin of a great religious and moral reform is inexplicable without the personal existence of a great reformer. To dissolve the founder of Christianity into a myth, as some would do, is hardly less absurd than it would be to do the same for Mohammed, Luther, and Calvin. Such dissolving views are for the most part the dreams of students who know the great world chiefly through its pale reflection in books. These extravagances of scepticism have been well exposed by Professor C. F. Lehmann - Haupt in his *Israel, seine Entwicklung im Rahmen der Weltgeschichte* (Tübingen, 1911), pp. 275-285. In reprinting the statement of my theory I have added a few notes, which are distinguished by being enclosed in square brackets.]

winter revels.[1]   Even if the theory should prove to be right, we can hardly suppose that Christ played the part of the regular Saturn of the year, since at the beginning of our era the Saturnalia fell at midwinter, whereas Christ was crucified at the Passover in spring. There is, indeed, as I have pointed out, some reason to think that when the Roman year began in March the Saturnalia was held in spring, and that in remote districts the festival always continued to be celebrated at the ancient date.   If the Roman garrison of Jerusalem conformed to the old fashion in this respect, it seems not quite impossible that their celebration of the Saturnalia may have coincided with the Passover; and that thus Christ, as a condemned criminal, may have been given up to them to make sport with as the Saturn of the year.   But on the other hand it is rather unlikely that the officers, as representatives of the State, would have allowed their men to hold the festival at any but the official date; even in the distant town of Durostorum we saw that the Roman soldiers celebrated the Saturnalia in December.   Thus if the legionaries at Jerusalem really intended to mock Christ by treating him like the burlesque king of the Saturnalia, they probably did so only by way of a jest which was in more senses than one unseasonable.

But closely as the passion of Christ resembles the treatment of the mock king of the Saturnalia, it resembles still more closely the treatment of the mock king of the Sacaea.[2]   The description of the mockery by St. Matthew is the fullest.   It runs thus: "Then released he Barabbas unto them: and when he had scourged Jesus, he delivered him to be crucified.   Then the soldiers of the governor took Jesus into the common hall, and gathered unto him the whole band of soldiers.   And they stripped him, and put on him a scarlet robe.   And when they had platted a crown of thorns, they put it upon his head, and a reed in his right hand: and they bowed the knee before him, and mocked him, saying, Hail, King of the Jews! And they spit upon him, and took the reed, and smote him on the

The mockery of Christ compared to the mockery of the King of the Sacaea.

---

[1] P. Wendland, "Jesus als Saturnalien-König," *Hermes,* xxxiii. (1898) pp. 175-179.

[2] The resemblance had struck me when I wrote this book originally [1889–1890], but as I could not definitely explain it I preferred to leave it unnoticed. [The first in recent years to call attention to the resemblance seems to have been Mr. W. R. Paton, who further conjectured that the crucifixion of Christ between two malefactors was not accidental, but had a ritual significance "as an expiatory sacrifice to a triple god." See F. C. Conybeare, *The*

Apology and Acts of Apollonius and other Monuments of Early Christianity (London, 1894), pp. 257 *sqq.*; W. R. Paton, "Die Kreuzigung Jesu," *Zeitschrift für die neutestamentliche Wissenschaft,* ii. (1901) pp. 339-341.   The grounds for the conjecture are somewhat slender.   It is true that a Persian martyr, S. Hiztibouzit, is said to have been crucified between two malefactors on a hill top, opposite the sun (F. C. Conybeare, *op. cit.* p. 270), but the narrator of the martyrdom gives no hint of any sacred significance attaching to the triple crucifixion.]

head. And after that they had mocked him, they took the robe
off from him, and put his own raiment on him, and led him away
to crucify him."[1]   Compare with this the treatment of the mock
king of the Sacaea, as it is described by Dio Chrysostom: "They
take one of the prisoners condemned to death and seat him upon
the king's throne, and give him the king's raiment, and let him lord
it and drink and run riot and use the king's concubines during
these days, and no man prevents him from doing just what he likes.
But afterwards they strip and scourge and crucify him."[2]   Now it
is quite possible that this remarkable resemblance is after all a mere
coincidence, and that Christ was executed in the ordinary way as a
common malefactor; but on the other hand there are so many
scattered hints and indications of something unusual, so many
broken lines seemingly converging towards the cross on Calvary,
that it is worth while to follow them up and see where they lead us.
In attempting to draw these fragmentary data together, to bridge
the chasms, and to restore the shattered whole, we must beware of
mistaking hypothesis for the facts which it only professes to cement;
yet even if our hypothesis should be thought to bear a somewhat
undue proportion to the facts, the excess may perhaps be overlooked in consideration of the obscurity and the importance of the
enquiry.

At Purim the Jews may have annually put to death a man in the character of Haman, and Christ may have perished in that character.

We have seen reason to think that the Jewish festival of Purim
is a continuation, under a changed name, of the Babylonian Sacaea,
and that in celebrating it by the destruction of an effigy of Haman
the modern Jews have kept up a reminiscence of the ancient
custom of crucifying or hanging a man in the character of a god at
the festival. Is it not possible that at an earlier time they may, like
the Babylonians themselves, have regularly compelled a condemned
criminal to play the tragic part, and that Christ thus perished in
the character of Haman? The resemblance between the hanged
Haman and the crucified Christ struck the early Christians themselves; and whenever the Jews destroyed an effigy of Haman they
were accused by their Christian neighbours of deriding the most
sacred mystery of the new faith.[3]   It is probable that on this
painful subject the Christians were too sensitive; remembering the
manner of their Founder's death it was natural that they should
wince at any pointed allusion to a cross, a gallows, or a public

But the Passover, at which Christ was

execution, even when the shaft was not aimed at them. An objection to supposing that Christ died as the Haman of the year is that
according to the Gospel narrative the crucifixion occurred at the

[1] Matthew xxvii. 26-31. Mark's
description (xv. 15-20) is nearly
identical.
[2] Dio Chrysostom, *Or.* iv. vol. i. p.
76 ed. L. Dindorf. As I have already

mentioned, the Greek word which
describes the execution (ἐκρέμασαν)
leaves it uncertain whether the man
was crucified or hanged.
[3] See above, p. 392.

Passover, on the fourteenth day of the month Nisan, whereas the
feast of Purim, at which the hanging of Haman would naturally
take place, fell exactly a month earlier, namely, on the fourteenth
day of the month Adar. I have no wish to blink or extenuate the
serious nature of the difficulty arising from this discrepancy of dates,
but I would suggest some considerations which may make us
hesitate to decide that the discrepancy is fatal. In the first place,
it is possible, though perhaps not probable, that Christian tradition
shifted the date of the crucifixion by a month in order to make the
great sacrifice of the Lamb of God coincide with that annual sacrifice of the Passover lamb which in the belief of pious hearts had so
long foreshadowed it and was thenceforth to cease.[1] Instances of
gentle pressure brought to bear, for purposes of edification, on
stubborn facts are perhaps not wholly unknown in the annals of religion. But the express testimony of history is never to be lightly
set aside; and in the investigation of its problems a solution which
assumes the veracity and accuracy of the historian is, on an even
balance of probabilities, always to be preferred to one which im-
pugns them both. Now in the present case we have seen reason
to think that the Babylonian New Year festival, of which Purim was
a continuation, did fall in Nisan at or near the time of the Passover,
and that when the Jews borrowed the festival they altered the date
from Nisan to Adar in order to prevent the new feast from clashing
with the old Passover. A reminiscence of the original date of
Purim perhaps survives, as I have already pointed out, in the statement in the book of Esther that Haman caused *pur* or lots to be
cast before him from the month of Nisan onward.[2] It thus seems
not impossible that occasionally, for some special reason, the Jews
should have celebrated the feast of Purim, or at least the death of
Haman, at or about the time of the Passover. But there is another
possibility which, remote and fanciful as it may appear, deserves at
least to be mentioned. The mock king of the Saturnalia, whose
resemblance to the dying Christ was first pointed out by Mr. Wendland, was allowed a period of license of thirty days before he was
put to death. If we could suppose that in like manner the Jews
spared the human representative of Haman for one month from

Margin note: crucified, fell a month after Purim.

Margin note: Perhaps the annual Haman, like the annual Saturn, was allowed a month's license before being put to death.

---

[1] [The extreme improbability in-
volved in the suggested transference of
the date of the Crucifixion is rightly
emphasized by my colleague and friend
Professor C. F. Lehmann-Haupt in
some observations and criticisms with
which he has favoured me. He
writes: "I regard it as out of the
question that 'Christian tradition
shifted the date of the Crucifixion by a
month.' You yourself regard it as

improbable; but in my opinion it is
impossible. All that we hear of the
Passion is only explicable by the Passover festival and by the circumstance
that at that time every believing Jew
had to make a pilgrimage to Jerusalem.
Without the background of the festival
all that we know of the Crucifixion
and of what led up to it is totally unintelligible."]

[2] Esther iii. 7.

Purim, the date of his execution would fall exactly on the Passover. Which, if any, of these conjectural solutions of the difficulty is the true one, I will not undertake to say. I am fully conscious of the doubt and uncertainty that hang round the whole subject; and if in this and what follows I throw out some hints and suggestions, it is more in the hope of stimulating and directing further enquiry than with any expectation of reaching definite conclusions.

The part taken by the soldiers in the mockery of Christ.   It may be objected that the mockery of Christ was done, not by the Jews, but by the Roman soldiers, who knew and cared nothing about Haman; how then can we suppose that the purple or scarlet robe, the sceptre of reed, and the crown of thorns, which the soldiers thrust upon Christ, were the regular insignia of the Haman of the year? To this we may reply, in the first place, that even if the legions stationed in Syria were not recruited in the country, they may have contracted some of the native superstitions and have fallen in with the local customs. This is not an idle conjecture. We know that the third legion during its stay in Syria learned the Syrian custom of saluting the rising sun, and that this formal salute, performed by the whole regiment as one man at a critical moment of the great battle of Bedriacum, actually helped to turn the scale when the fortune of empire hung trembling in the balance.[1] But it is not necessary to suppose that the garrison of Jerusalem really shared the beliefs and prejudices of the mob whom they overawed; soldiers everywhere are ready to go with a crowd bent on sport, without asking any curious questions as to the history or quality of the entertainment, and we should probably do the humanity of Roman soldiers too much honour if we imagined that they would be deterred by any qualm of conscience from joining in the pastime, which is still so popular, of baiting a Jew to death. But in the second place it should be observed that, according to one of the Evangelists, it was not the soldiers of Pilate who mocked Jesus, but the soldiers of Herod,[2] and we may fairly assume that Herod's guards were Jews.

The theory that Christ died, not as a malefactor, but in the character of Haman helps to explain both Pilate's reluctance to put him   The hypothesis that the crucifixion with all its cruel mockery was not a punishment specially devised for Christ, but was merely the fate that annually befell the malefactor who played Haman, appears to go some way towards relieving the Gospel narrative of certain difficulties which otherwise beset it. If, as we read in the Gospels, Pilate was really anxious to save the innocent man whose fine bearing seems to have struck him, what was to hinder him from doing so? He had the power of life and death; why should he not have exercised it on the side of mercy, if his own judgment inclined that way? His reluctant acquiescence in the importunate demand of the rabble becomes easier to understand

---

[1] Tacitus, *Hist.* iii. 24 *sq.*, compared with ii. 74.
[2] Luke xxiii. 11.

if we assume that custom obliged him annually at this season to give up to them a prisoner on whom they might play their cruel pranks. On this assumption Pilate had no power to prevent the sacrifice; the most he could do was to choose the victim.

Again, consider the remarkable statement of the Evangelists that Pilate set up over the cross a superscription stating that the man who hung on it was king of the Jews.[1] Is it likely that in the reign of Tiberius a Roman governor, with the fear of the jealous and suspicious old emperor before his eyes, would have ventured, even in mockery, to blazon forth a seditious claim of this sort unless it were the regular formula employed on such occasions, recognized by custom, and therefore not liable to be misconstrued into treason by the malignity of informers and the fears of a tyrant?

But if the tragedy of the ill-fated aspirant after royal honours was annually enacted at Jerusalem by a prisoner who perished on the cross, it becomes probable that the part of his successful rival was also played by another actor who paraded in the same kingly trappings but did not share the same fate. If Jesus was the Haman of the year, where was the Mordecai? Perhaps we may find him in Barabbas.

We are told by the Evangelists that at the feast which witnessed the crucifixion of Christ it was the custom for the Roman governor to release one prisoner, whomsoever the people desired, and that Pilate, convinced of the innocence of Jesus, attempted to persuade the multitude to choose him as the man who should go free. But, hounded on by the priests and elders who had marked out Jesus for destruction, the rabble would not hear of this, and clamoured for the blood of Jesus, while they demanded the release of a certain miscreant, by name Barabbas, who lay in gaol for murder and sedition. Accordingly Pilate had to give way: Christ was crucified and Barabbas set at liberty.[2] Now what, we may ask, was the reason for setting free a prisoner at this festival? In the absence of positive information, we may conjecture that the gaol-bird whose cage was thrown open at this time had to purchase his freedom by performing some service from which decent people would shrink. Such a service may very well have been that of going about the streets, rigged out in tawdry splendour with a tinsel crown on his head and a sham sceptre in his hand, preceded and followed by all the tag-rag and bobtail of the town hooting, jeering, and breaking coarse jests at his expense, while some pretended to salaam his mock majesty, and others belaboured the donkey on which he rode. It was in this fashion, probably, that in Persia the beardless and one-eyed man made his undignified progress through the town, to

---

[1] Matthew xxvii. 37; Mark xv. 26; Luke xxiii. 38; John xix. 19.

[2] Matthew xxvii. 15-26; Mark xv.

6-15; Luke xxiii. 16-25; John xviii. 38-40.

the delight of ragamuffins and the terror of shopkeepers, whose goods he unceremoniously confiscated if they did not hasten to lay their peace-offerings at his feet.   So, perhaps, the ruffian Barabbas, when his irons were knocked off and the prison door had grated on its hinges to let him forth, tasted the first sweets of liberty in this public manner, even if he was not suffered, like his one-eyed brother, to make raids with impunity on the stalls of the merchants and the tables of the money-changers.   A curious confirmation of this conjecture is supplied by a passage in the writings of Philo the Jew, who lived at Alexandria in the time of Christ.   He tells us that when Agrippa, the grandson of Herod, had received the crown of Judaea from Caligula at Rome, the new king passed through Alexandria on his way to his own country.   The disorderly populace of that great city, animated by a hearty dislike of his nation, seized the opportunity of venting their spite by publicly defaming and ridiculing the Jewish monarch.   Among other things they laid hold of a certain harmless lunatic named Carabas, who used to roam the streets stark naked, the butt and laughing-stock of urchins and idlers.   This poor wretch they set up in a public place, clapped a paper crown on his head, thrust a broken reed into his hand by way of a sceptre, and having huddled a mat instead of a royal robe about his naked body, and surrounded him with a guard of bludgeon-men, they did obeisance to him as to a king and made a show of taking his opinion on questions of law and policy.   To point the jest unmistakably at the Syrian king Agrippa, the bystanders raised cries of "Marin! Marin!" which they understood to be the Syrian word for "lord."[1]   This mockery of the Jewish king closely resembles the mockery of Christ; and the joke, such as it was, would receive a keener edge if we could suppose that the riff-raff of Alexandria were familiar with the Jewish practice of setting up a sham king on certain occasions, and that they meant by implication to ridicule the real King Agrippa by comparing him to his holiday counterfeit.   May we go a step further and conjecture that one at least of the titles of the mock king of the Jews was regularly Barabbas?   The poor imbecile who masqueraded in a paper crown at Alexandria was probably a Jew, otherwise the jest would have lost much of its point; and his name, according to the Greek manuscripts of Philo, was Carabas.   But Carabas is meaningless in Hebrew, whereas Barabbas is a regularly formed Hebrew word

The mock King Carabas in Egypt.

---

[1] Philo Judaeus, *Adversus Flaccum*, vol. ii. pp. 520-523 ed. Th. Mangey (London, 1742).   The first to call attention to this passage was Mr. P. Wendland ("Jesus als Saturnalien-Konig," *Hermes*, xxxiii. (1898) pp. 175 *sq.*).   [Mar·na, "Our Lord," was the title of a Philistine deity worshipped at Gaza and elsewhere.   See C. P. Tiele, *Geschichte der Religion im Altertum* (Gotha, 1896-1903), i. 258.   Compare *Hebrew and English Lexicon*, edited by F. Brown, S. R. Driver, and Ch. A. Briggs (Oxford, 1906), p. 1101.]

meaning "Son of the Father." The palaeographic difference between the two forms is slight, and perhaps we shall hardly be deemed very rash if we conjecture that in the passage in question Philo himself wrote Barabbas, which a Greek copyist, ignorant of Hebrew, afterwards corrupted into Carabas. If this were granted, we should still have to assume that both Philo and the authors of the Gospels fell into the mistake of treating as the name of an individual what in fact was a title of office.

Thus the hypothesis which, with great diffidence, I would put forward for consideration is this. It was customary, we may suppose, with the Jews at Purim, or perhaps occasionally at Passover, to employ two prisoners to act the parts respectively of Haman and Mordecai in the passion-play which formed a central feature of the festival. Both men paraded for a short time in the insignia of royalty, but their fates were different; for while at the end of the performance the one who played Haman was hanged or crucified, the one who personated Mordecai and bore in popular parlance the title of Barabbas was allowed to go free. Pilate, perceiving the trumpery nature of the charges brought against Jesus, tried to persuade the Jews to let him play the part of Barabbas, which would have saved his life; but the merciful attempt failed and Jesus perished on the cross in the character of Haman. The description of his last triumphal ride into Jerusalem reads almost like an echo of that brilliant progress through the streets of Susa which Haman aspired to and Mordecai accomplished; and the account of the raid which he immediately afterwards made upon the stalls of the hucksters and money-changers in the temple, may raise a question whether we have not here a trace of those arbitrary rights over property which it has been customary on such occasions to accord to the temporary king.[1]

If it be asked why one of these temporary kings should bear the remarkable title of Barabbas or "Son of the Father," I can only surmise that the title may perhaps be a relic of the time when the real king, the deified man, used to redeem his own life by deputing his son to reign for a short time and to die in his stead. We have seen that the custom of sacrificing the son for the father was common, if not universal, among Semitic peoples; and if we are right in our interpretation of the Passover, that festival—the traditional date of the crucifixion—was the very season when the dreadful sacrifice of the first-born was consummated.[2] Hence Barabbas or the "Son of the Father" would be a natural enough title for the man or child who reigned and died as a substitute for his royal sire. Even in later times, when the father provided a less

Marginal notes: Hypothesis that every spring at Purim or Passover the Jews paraded two prisoners in the characters of Haman and Mordecai, of whom one was put to death and the other released.

Barabbas ("Son of the Father") may have been the regular title of the prisoner who was released in the character of Mordecai.

---

[1] Matthew xxi. 1-13; Mark xi. 1-17; Luke xix. 28-46; John xii. 12-15. [As to the license accorded to temporary kings, see *The Dying God*, pp. 56 *sq.*, 148 *sqq.*]

[2] [*The Dying God*, pp. 166 *sqq.*]

precious substitute than his own offspring, it would be quite in accordance with the formal conservatism of religion that the old title should be retained after it had ceased to be appropriate; indeed the efficacy of the sacrifice might be thought to require and justify the pious fiction that the substitute was the very son of that divine father who should have died, but who preferred to live, for the good of his people. If in the time of Christ, as I have conjectured, the title of Barabbas or Son of the Father was bestowed on the Mordecai, the mock king who lived, rather than on the Haman, the mock king who died at the festival, this distinction can hardly have been original; for at first, we may suppose, the same man served in both capacities at different times, as the Mordecai of one year and the Haman of the next. The two characters, as I have attempted to shew, are probably nothing but two different aspects of the same deity considered at one time as dead and at another as risen; hence the human being who personated the risen god would in due time, after he had enjoyed his divine honours for a season, act the dead god by dying in good earnest in his own person; for it would be unreasonable to expect of the ordinary man-god that he should play the two parts in the reverse order by dying first and coming to life afterwards. In both parts the substitute would still be, whether in sober fact or in pious fiction, the Barabbas or Son of that divine Father who generously gave his own son to die for the world.[1]

The theory that Christ was put to death, not as a criminal, but as the annual representative of a god, whose counterparts were

To conclude this speculation, into which I have perhaps been led by the interest and importance of the subject somewhat deeper than the evidence warrants, I venture to urge in its favour that it seems to shed fresh light on some of the causes which contributed to the remarkably rapid diffusion of Christianity in Asia Minor. We know from a famous letter of the younger Pliny addressed to the Emperor Trajan in the year 112 A.D. that by the beginning of our era, less than a hundred years after the Founder's death, Christianity had made such strides in Bithynia and Pontus that not only cities but villages and rural districts were affected by it, and

[1] [In favour of the theory in the text, which supposes that in the tragic drama of the crucifixion Jesus and Barabbas played parts which were the complements, if not the duplicates, of each other, it might, as M. Salomon Reinach has pointed out, be alleged that in the Armenian and old Syriac versions of Matthew xxvii. 16 and 17, as well as in some Greek cursive manuscripts, the name of the prisoner whom Pilate proposed to release is given as Jesus Barabbas, a reading which was also known to Origen and was not absolutely rejected by him. See *Encyclopaedia Biblica* (London, 1899–1903), s.v. " Barabbas," vol. i. col. 477 ; *Evangelion da - Mepharreshe*, edited by F. C. Burkitt (Cambridge, 1904), i. 165, ii. 277 *sq*. In the latter passage Prof. Burkitt argues that Jesus Barabbas was probably the original reading in the Greek text, though the name Jesus is omitted in nearly all our existing manuscripts. Compare S. Reinach, " Le roi supplicié," *Cultes, Mythes, et Religions*, i. (Paris, 1905) pp. 339 *sq*.]

that multitudes of both sexes and of every age and every rank professed its tenets; indeed things had gone so far that the temples were almost deserted, the sacred rites of the public religion discontinued, and hardly a purchaser could be found for the sacrificial victims.[1] It is obvious, therefore, that the new faith had elements in it which appealed powerfully to the Asiatic mind. What these elements were, the present investigation has perhaps to some extent disclosed. We have seen that the conception of the dying and risen god was no new one in these regions. All over Western Asia from time immemorial the mournful death and happy resurrection of a divine being appear to have been annually celebrated with alternate rites of bitter lamentation and exultant joy; and through the veil which mythic fancy has woven round this tragic figure we can still detect the features of those great yearly changes in earth and sky which, under all distinctions of race and religion, must always touch the natural human heart with alternate emotions of gladness and regret, because they exhibit on the vastest scale open to our observation the mysterious struggle between life and death. But man has not always been willing to watch passively this momentous conflict; he has felt that he has too great a stake in its issue to stand by with folded hands while it is being fought out; he has taken sides against the forces of death and decay—has flung into the trembling scale all the weight of his puny person, and has exulted in his fancied strength when the great balance has slowly inclined towards the side of life, little knowing that for all his strenuous efforts he can as little stir that balance by a hair's-breadth as can the primrose on a mossy bank in spring or the dead leaf blown by the chilly breath of autumn. Nowhere do these efforts, vain and pitiful, yet pathetic, appear to have been made more persistently and systematically than in

(margin note: well known all over Western Asia, may help to explain his early deification and the rapid spread of his worship.*)*

---

[1] Pliny, *Epist.* x. 96. The province which Pliny governed was known officially as Bithynia and Pontus, and extended from the river Rhyndacos on the west to beyond Amisus on the east. See Professor [Sir] W. M. Ramsay, *The Church in the Roman Empire* (London, 1893), p. 224. Professor Ramsay is of opinion "that the description of the great power acquired by the new religion in the province applies to Eastern Pontus at least." The chief religious centre of this district appears to have been the great sanctuary of Anaitis or Semiramis at Zela, to which I have already had occasion to call the reader's attention. Strabo tells us (xii. 3. 37) that all the people of Pontus took their most solemn oaths at this shrine. In the same district there was another very popular sanctuary of a similar type at Comana, where the worship of a native goddess called Ma was carried on by a host of sacred harlots and by a high priest, who wore a diadem and was second only to the king in rank. At the festivals of the goddess crowds of men and women flocked into Comana from all the region round about, from the country as well as from the cities. The luxury and debauchery of this holy town suggest to Strabo a comparison with the famous or rather infamous Corinth. See Strabo, xii. 3. 32 and 36, compared with xii. 2. 3. Such were some of the hot-beds in which the seeds of Christianity first struck root.

Western Asia. In name they varied from place, to place, but in substance they were all alike. A man, whom the fond imagination of his worshippers invested with the attributes of a god, gave his life for the life of the world; after infusing from his own body a fresh current of vital energy into the stagnant veins of nature, he was cut off from among the living before his failing strength should initiate a universal decay, and his place was taken by another who played, like all his predecessors, the ever-recurring drama of the divine resurrection and death. Such a drama, if our interpretation of it is right, was the original story of Esther and Mordecai or, to give them their older names, of Ishtar and Marduk. It was played in Babylonia, and from Babylonia the returning captives brought it to Judaea, where it was acted, rather as an historical than a mythical piece, by players who, having to die in grim earnest on a cross or gallows, were naturally drawn rather from the gaol than the green-room. A chain of causes which, because we cannot follow them, might in the loose language of daily life be called an accident, determined that the part of the dying god in this annual play should be thrust upon Jesus of Nazareth, whom the enemies he had made in high places by his outspoken strictures were resolved to put out of the way. They succeeded in ridding themselves of the popular and troublesome preacher; but the very step by which they fancied they had simultaneously stamped out his revolutionary doctrines contributed more than anything else they could have done to scatter them broadcast not only over Judaea but over Asia; for it impressed upon what had been hitherto mainly an ethical mission the character of a divine revelation culminating in the passion and death of the incarnate Son of a heavenly Father. In this form the story of the life and death of Jesus exerted an influence which it could never have had if the great teacher had died, as is commonly supposed, the death of a vulgar malefactor. It shed round the cross on Calvary a halo of divinity which multitudes saw and worshipped afar off; the blow struck on Golgotha set a thousand expectant strings vibrating in unison wherever men had heard the old, old story of the dying and risen god. Every year, as another spring bloomed and another autumn faded across the earth, the field had been ploughed and sown and borne fruit of a kind till it received that seed which was destined to spring up and overshadow the world. In the great army of martyrs who in many ages and in many lands, not in Asia only, have died a cruel death in the character of gods, the devout Christian will doubtless discern types and forerunners of the coming Saviour—stars that heralded in the morning sky the advent of the Sun of Righteousness—earthen vessels wherein it pleased the divine wisdom to set before hungering souls the bread of heaven. The sceptic, on the other hand, with equal confidence, will reduce

Jesus of Nazareth to the level of a multitude of other victims of a barbarous superstition, and will see in him no more than a moral teacher, whom the fortunate accident of his execution invested with the crown, not merely of a martyr, but of a god. The divergence between these views is wide and deep. Which of them is the truer and will in the end prevail? Time will decide the question of prevalence, if not of truth. Yet we would fain believe that in this and in all things the old maxim will hold good—*Magna est veritas et praevalebit.*

INDEX

Lightning Source UK Ltd.
Milton Keynes UK
UKHW011844160620
364869UK00001B/26

9 781108 047388